# THE UNDERSIDE OF AMERICAN HISTORY
Other Readings

# THE UNDERSIDE
# OF AMERICAN HISTORY
## Other Readings

**VOLUME I: to 1877**

*Edited by*
**THOMAS R. FRAZIER**
*The Bernard M. Baruch College of The City University of New York*

*Under the General Editorship of*
**JOHN MORTON BLUM**
*Yale University*

**HARCOURT BRACE JOVANOVICH, INC.**
*New York   Chicago   San Francisco   Atlanta*

**To Myles Horton and the Highlander Idea**

ISBN: 0-15-592841-4

Library of Congress Catalog Card Number: 72-155563

PRINTED IN THE UNITED STATES OF AMERICA

# Preface

The United States was forged in the crucible of conflict—conflict of ideas, conflict of economic and political systems, conflict of peoples with different cultural backgrounds, different needs, and different ambitions. Indeed, our history is the story of many peoples and of unsteady progress. Yet traditional history textbooks often trace the development of this country as though it were the gradual, almost natural, growth of a single people into a unified nation. Historians have concentrated on what they considered the dominant themes in American life—themes that almost invariably centered on the dominant groups of Americans. In the process they have sometimes overlooked vital aspects of the American past, neglecting whole groups within the nation. Today, the part of the past that has remained hidden—the "underside" of American history—is forcing itself into the public consciousness, and historians have begun to reexamine the past in order better to understand and to deal with the conflicts and stresses of the present.

*The Underside of American History*, intended to supplement existing textbooks, presents a selection of *un*traditional readings in American history. These readings deal in various ways with a variety of oppressed groups in America. They do not attempt to give an exhaustive catalog of the prejudices and injustices that have plagued American life, but they do offer vivid testimony to the fact that much of today's unrest has its roots deep in the nation's past.

This collection is arranged roughly chronologically: Volume I begins with the colonial period and continues through Reconstruction, and Volume II covers the period from Reconstruction to the present. Each volume contains a general introduction presenting the major themes to be taken up in the readings. In addition, each selection is introduced by a brief headnote placing the selection in the appropriate historical context and explaining its significance. Annotated bibliographies, with books available in paperback marked by an asterisk, close each of the books' major sections.

I gratefully acknowledge the advice and assistance of the following historians: Barton J. Bernstein of Stanford University, Selma Cantor Berrol of the Bernard M. Baruch College of the City University of New York, Dan T. Carter of the University of Maryland, and James M. McPherson of Princeton University. I also want to thank Joanna Freda, who provided valuable assistance in the preparation of the manuscript.

**THOMAS R. FRAZIER**

# Contents

## Colonial**1**America     *9*

# The New Nation                                             *103*

# The Ante-Bellum North and South                   *179*

# Westward Expansion                                         *251*

Contents

# THE UNDERSIDE OF AMERICAN HISTORY
Other Readings

# Introduction

This introduction is intended to provide a broad overview of the often neglected aspects of American history treated in the following selections. In these pages, the traditional emphases have been abandoned. The stress is on the failings of the system; the focus is not on the victors, but on the victims. The result, of course, is not a balanced view of our history, but an attempt to redress the existing imbalance. These notes and these readings, unless they are considered within a larger context, provide a harsher view of American history than might be warranted. They are, however, an essential part of the whole story, and they must be taken into account in any attempt to reach a valid assessment of the American past.

It is natural that the study of the history of the United States should concentrate in the beginning on the English colonization of the North American continent. It was, after all, not the French or Spanish but the English who gained a secure foothold in this part of the New World by the middle of the seventeenth century, and it was their institutions that prevailed in shaping the new society.

When the English began settling the Eastern seaboard of what was to become the United States, they found it virtually free of European colonization from Maine through Georgia, with the exception of the Dutch settlements in New Netherland, around present-day New York. They were thus freed from the necessity of adapting to any established social or religious system. Moreover, chiefly because of the distance that separated the colonies from the mother country, they were very nearly free from English control. Left to their own devices, their first problem was that of surviving in the wilderness—a feat that they were able to accomplish with the help of the Indians who were already well established in the territory. Then, typically, came the problem of turning the vast natural resources of the New World to their profit. As the early colonists concentrated on building up their strength, they began to consider their Indian neighbors a threat to their progress.

The "Indian problem" provided the first major test of English policy in the New World, and the settlers, by all accounts, fell far short of what might be desired. Their way of dealing with these aliens in their new society was simply to displace them by any means at hand. The Indians struggled with all the skill at their disposal—often with French and Spanish support—to preserve their lives, their culture, and their land, but they were no match for the technologically more advanced Europeans, and their civilization ultimately came to an end under the onslaught of Western ideas and ambitions. The Indians who survived the initial confrontations with the colonists were forced to retreat southward and westward, and their sporadic attempts at organization and resistance proved futile.

During the early decades of the nineteenth century, the Indians again mounted a significant opposition to the dominant policy toward them. One group—the Five Civilized Tribes of the southeastern United States—tried to escape alien status by assimilating to the dominant way of life. Their offer was rejected, and they not only remained foreign but were forcibly moved outside the borders of the then existing states. Another group of Indians, in the old Northwest, attempted once again to unify in self-protection, but this too failed. The Indians were continually displaced until there was no more vacant land. They were then removed to reservations on undesirable property, most of them west of the Mississippi River.

A second major threat to the progress of the English in the New World was the chronic shortage of settlers to provide a labor base for economic development in the colonies. Here, two major sources of supply were found. First, poor whites from Europe—primarily from England in the seventeenth century—were brought to the New World as indentured servants. Under the popular "headright" system of land distribution, anyone who paid for a passage to the New World received fifty acres of land. Thus investors could send over settlers, and both would presumably profit from the transaction. The investors, whether or not they also emigrated to the New World, could acquire title to large estates and claim most of the profits from their cultivation. The servants worked for a specified number of years in return for their passage and, sometimes, a percentage of the profits. When their term of service expired, they became freemen with the right to participate in colonial government and to hold land without sharing profits or paying rents to absentee landlords.

During the first hundred and fifty years of settlement, the practice of indentured servitude was a major source of new population for the New World. Moreover, during most of the seventeenth century, indentured servants were the main labor force in the colonies. Many of these servants ultimately prospered in the New World. But others, upon achieving their independence, moved into the yeoman farmer class of the developing society and established small subsistence farms. Though they thus lived in freedom, they never really shared in the nation's wealth, and many of their descendants live in poverty to this day in the foothills of the Appalachian Mountains.

By the end of the seventeenth century, a second and vastly more profitable labor supply had opened up to the colonists—African slavery. The first Africans, involuntary immigrants and, with the Indians, perpetual aliens, were brought to North America in 1619, and Africans arrived in increasing numbers in the two centuries before the trade was officially banned in 1808. By 1790, when the first federal census was taken, black people made up 19.3 percent of the total population of the United States. Over fifty thousand Afro-Americans, scattered throughout the nation, were free, yet even they were not permitted to move into the mainstream of American life. A few blacks in Eastern cities led relatively comfortable lives and attained some measure of economic security, but most lived the lives of unskilled laborers and met racial discrimination on every hand. In the North, white craftsmen protested against the employment of blacks in the skilled trades, giving rise to a pattern of black exclusion from certain crafts that has continued to the present, with ruinous economic results for the black community.

Any consideration of the oppression suffered by blacks in this country, however, must focus first on plantation slavery in the South. From the beginning, the great majority of Afro-Americans were slaves in the South, employed in various occupations ranging from skilled craftsman to common field hand. By 1860 almost half of the four million slaves in North America were engaged in cotton production, an economic fact that seems to have had the deciding voice in the controversy over the continuation of slavery in the South. Relying almost exclusively on imported African labor, nineteenth-century white Southerners developed a thriving plantation economy. In the process, they developed a devastating system of chattel slavery—perhaps the most devastating in the modern world in terms of its long-range impact. Further, by identifying slavery with color, they set into motion a pattern of color discrimination that has had endless reverberations for North American society. Over the years, the African and his descendants, along with the Indians, have been the most oppressed segments of American society.

The life of a Southern slave was almost totally circumscribed by his master. He was deprived of education, was given little opportunity for self-improvement and advancement, and, in some cases, was even denied the security of family life and religion. The slaves fought the system by developing a subculture of their own, reaching back for what they could recover from their African past, borrowing some from the whites, and adding elements drawn from their own unique experience in the Americas. More visibly, they protested their condition by rebelling and conspiring to rebel, by running away, and by refusing in innumerable ways to cooperate with the system.

Nonetheless, the superior power and efficiency of the slave system effectively limited the experiences of most of the black bondsmen. When emancipation came at the conclusion of the Civil War, few of the freedmen were trained in the skills freedom would require, and since racial prejudice persisted among even their liberators, blacks were given little opportunity during Reconstruction to move into positions of economic independence. In 1877, when the Reconstruction period ended and federal troops were removed from the South, most of the freed blacks who remained had been forced back into positions of dependence upon white society. The South's recovery from the war, like her earlier rise to economic stability, was achieved at the expense of the black man, who was relegated by law and custom to a position of agricultural serfdom.

A third initial challenge faced by the English in the New World was basically governmental. How was order to be established and upheld in the vast new territory opened up by colonization? The process was by no means as orderly as some accounts of colonial history suggest. The English system of representative government was adapted for use in some of the colonies, but others were ruled indirectly from England through governors or proprietors. When colonists throughout the country began to demand a high degree of self-government, conflict between governors and settlers became a commonplace, and violence was often the issue. Indeed, violent struggles against the English authorities marked most attempts to establish order within the individual colonies. In addition, in almost every colony serious struggles took place between the settlers in the coastal areas and those of the interior, who vied over the distribution of power and benefits and, not least, the system of taxation.

The issue of colonial self-government ultimately led to the struggle for independence. The leaders in this fight were for the most part members of the political elites of the colonies and descendants of the English settlers. Independence won, it was they who met in Philadelphia in 1787 to shape the American nation.

Although the political genius of a number of the Founding Fathers cannot be questioned, there were grave deficiencies in the outline they drew up for the form of the new nation. Slavery, to take a prime example, was given permanent legal status in the Constitution of 1787, and in the same document Indians were recognized as a people apart from the mass of Americans. A less obvious but perhaps more serious flaw in the legacy of the Founding Fathers was a pattern of thinking not explicitly articulated. That is, many of their ideas seemed to proceed from the assumption that the people of the United States would share the same language, religion, customs, and political and economic institutions. The strain toward homogeneity that can be seen in the thought of the earliest American political theorists has been at the root of many of the nation's difficulties for the past two hundred years. For since the first surges of nationalism in the revolutionary era, American leaders have tended to regard any challenge to the political and economic status quo as an alien threat, as something foreign to and incompatible with the American way of life.

For the first century of the new nation's life, many of the so-called alien ideas came from real aliens—either from immigrants or from domestic aliens who were barred from citizenship, the Indians and the African slaves. Later, even challenges brought by the native-born were frequently considered to be alien-inspired and were suppressed in the name of patriotism. Political power remained largely in the hands of the descendants of the Protestant English settlers, and their traditions continued to set the patterns of political, economic, and cultural life in the United States. Although foreign emigration would continue and would even be promoted, the tacit assumption was that immigrants would conform to the dominant way of life. Those who could not or would not could expect to meet serious opposition.

The first political parties in this country appeared in the 1790's, when Madison and Jefferson sought to organize opposition to Alexander Hamilton, President Washington's strongest advisor. Members of the existing government took the name of Federalists, and their opponents called themselves Republicans. Party organization at state and local levels developed rapidly, and the party system in the United States was institutionalized within a few decades. Naturally, party strife was rampant from the beginning, and one of its first products was the passage of the flagrantly repressive Alien and Sedition Acts in 1798, an expression of early nativist sentiment as well as an attempt to stifle Republican opposition. These acts were hotly protested, and by the time they went out of effect in 1801, they had stirred up the first of many furious debates between nationalists and the advocates of states' rights.

In the nineteenth century, immigration proceeded apace. After the 1840's, a massive influx of Irish and German Catholics began to threaten Protestant hegemony on the Eastern seaboard. Most of the new immigrants were unskilled and penniless, and they came too rapidly to be dispersed and in too great numbers to be assimilated. Public programs to help them get settled in homes and jobs were at first nonexistent. Public systems of education, whatever the good intentions that lay behind them, attempted to drill the newcomers in the dominant way of life, and many immigrant groups, clinging to their traditions, resisted by setting up private school systems. Suspicion of anything foreign, fear that by sheer numbers the immigrants would dilute the dominant Anglo-Saxon strains of the American population, and virulent anti-Catholicism contributed to the rise of a nativist movement that stretched across almost a century before it finally subsided. In many cities of the Northeast, there were violent clashes between Protestants and Irish Catholics, provoked primarily by the refusal of the Catholics to accept Protestant indoctrination.

Along with religious conflicts came bitter competition for jobs in the Northeast. By mid-century the Industrial Revolution had overtaken the United States, and the machinery of production had become so efficient that for the first time in American history there was a surplus of unskilled labor. This provided factory-owners, members of a rising industrialist class, with the opportunity to stretch hours and reduce wages in the search for greater profits. Wage reductions, in turn, often meant that women and children had to go to work in the mills and mines in order to bring family incomes up to survival level. The struggle of the unskilled worker and the urban factory operative, immigrant or native-born, is one of the major motifs of nineteenth- and twentieth-century American life. Workers were able to improve their conditions only when they presented organized resistance to the dominant economic policies through national trade unions, which were slow to evolve.

Up to this point in history, the dominant sector of Americans had been not only white, Protestant, and English, but also male. Indeed, few women in the Western world have had any direct power or influence over the direction of society until quite recently. In America, as elsewhere, women were schooled only in the domestic arts and social graces, were deprived of the right to vote, were denied participation in politics and public life, and were expected to find fulfillment by living in the shadow of a successful male. In the second quarter of the nineteenth century, however, caught up by the general movement for reform, American women began to challenge male dominance. A women's rights movement called attention to the society's prejudices against "the weaker sex," and women, despite stinging denunciations, began to take leading roles in the religious movements and communitarian social experiments of the day. The more radical women joined with radical male reformers in advocating complete reorganization of society and complete restructuring of religious life. Since many theories of male dominance were based on an analogy with the structure of traditional religion, in which God, the father, or Jesus, the male child, was the ruler of the church, many women felt it was especially in their interest to attack the traditional religion. Some became prophets and seers, and some went so far as to found new religious cults.

Even during this first period of awakening to women's rights, most women remained submissive, apparently content in their traditional roles. But as the leisure of the middle-class woman increased and as servants and machines took on many of her customary household duties, masses of women found themselves hard pressed to reconcile the roles society foisted on them with their own feelings and needs. At the same time, a growing factory and commercial system provided a new measure of independence for married and unmarried women alike, and the ranks of working women swelled.

By the 1850's, the size of the American nation had increased dramatically. National interest in geographical expansion soared, and the doctrine of Manifest Destiny emerged to glorify American conquests of new territory. Though one might have expected that the lonely struggle to pacify the wilderness—and the Indians—would lead to strong emphasis on individuality, the westward advance carried with it powerful pressure toward conformity with the Eastern establishment. Perhaps the insecurity of life on the Great Plains and in the Far West lay behind the extravagant attempts to impose on the various Western peoples a homogeneity similar to that which now prevailed in the East. In any case, geographical expansion became synonymous with the expansion of Anglo-Saxon culture and control.

Predictably, those who suffered most from the settlement and development of the West were the aliens. With the conclusion of the Mexican War in 1847, many thousands of persons of Spanish and mixed Spanish-Indian descent suddenly found themselves foreigners living within American territory. "Vigilante" justice all too often held sway in the remote and virtually lawless West, and the Chinese, Mexican-Americans, Indians, and other ethnic minorities were the most frequent victims of the summary justice dealt out by self-appointed citizen groups.

The years between the Mexican War and the Civil War were years of deepening sectional crisis, for with every new state admitted to the union, arguments over slavery grew more pointed and more intense. The westward advance continued as a backdrop to civil war and recovery. By the end of the Reconstruction period, the United States stretched from coast to coast, and Protestant-English influence over the whole area was secured. The dominant Americans would continue to strive vainly to convert all whites to their points of view. More successfully, they would continue to exclude all nonwhites from full participation in American life.

# Colonial
# America

# The Moral and Legal Justifications

# for

# Dispossessing the Indians

## WILCOMB E. WASHBURN

When the Europeans discovered the North American continent at the turn of the sixteenth century, it was inhabited by an estimated 9.8 to 12.5 million people between the Rio Grande and the Arctic. Although it was at first assumed that these people—mistakenly called Indians by Columbus—were members of one cultural group, it was soon clear that they were divided into a large number of separate nations, each with a distinctive cultural tradition.

In the sixteenth century most of the exploration and conquest in the New World was carried out by the Spanish and the Portuguese. These early adventurers were able to justify their activities by citing the authority of the Pope, who had divided the newly discovered hemisphere between Spain and Portugal with the Line of Demarcation of 1493. The Pope had given the Catholic countries a mandate to take possession of the land and to convert the natives to Christianity. And, indeed, the conquistadors were almost always accompanied by missionaries who sought to convince the conquered populations that Catholic Christianity was the one true religion. Much of the Indian population from New Mexico through South America became Christian, at least nominally, during the period of conquest.

The situation was very different in the area colonized by the English, where major settlement was not begun until the seventeenth century. Significantly, the English intended not merely to explore and conquer the land but to settle on it, and the presence of many Indian nations along the Eastern seaboard presented a formidable obstacle to their attempts to secure political control and exclusive ownership of the land. The English were able to exploit existing hostilities among the various Indian groups by allying themselves with one group against another. For many reasons, the English did not devote themselves to converting the Indians to Protestant Christianity. To the contrary, on numerous occasions they used the "heathenism" of the Indians as an excuse for betraying them, arguing that since heathens could not be expected to uphold treaties or agreements, such agreements were invalid from the start.

The English lacked the Pope's sanction for their conquests, since they had not been included in considerations when the Line of Demarcation was drawn. Thus, if they were to operate with the appearance of legality, they had to construct their own rationale for driving the Indians from their homeland. In the following essay, Wilcomb E. Washburn, of the Smithsonian Institution, examines the process by which the colonists developed legal as well as moral justifications for their treatment of the Indians. As Washburn makes clear, law was often created to justify existing conditions in colonial America—a process that did not end with that era in American history.

Many studies tell us what the first explorers were trying to do. Many others tell us why they were trying to do it. But very few have attempted to describe the justice or injustice of the quest. Yet significant moral and legal problems were brought to the fore by the expansion of Europe into the various parts of the world. Kings, judges, soldiers, businessmen, priests, all considered the expansion in terms of right and wrong as well as in terms of personal and national advantage. Some were more explicit than others, but all had a point of view about the moral and legal right of the European to displace the American Indian in the newly discovered lands.

The justifications which governments most frequently brought forward in the period of exploration and settlement—papal or royal grant, discovery, and possession—reflect the fact that the principal ethicolegal concern in the period was about the claims of rival European powers, not about the rights of the American Indian.[1] The bull of Alexander VI in 1493, which divided the world between Spain and Portugal, for example, was principally designed to prevent an unseemly and dangerous scramble among Christian nations for the spoils of the newly discovered areas. Those excluded from its benefits understandably disputed the papal pretensions. When the Spanish ambassador in England complained of Drake's

---

[1] The only principle on which the European nations were in agreement, writes Wheaton, was in "almost entirely disregarding the right of the native inhabitants of these regions." Henry Wheaton, *Elements of International Law*, 1st ed. (1836), The Literal Reproduction of the Edition of 1866 by Richard Henry Dana, Jr., ed. by George Grafton Wilson [The Classics of International Law, No. 19] (Oxford, 1936), Pt. II, nos. 166, 202.

"The Moral and Legal Justifications for Dispossessing the Indians," by Wilcomb E. Washburn. From *Seventeenth-Century America: Essays in Colonial History*, edited by James Morton Smith (Chapel Hill, N.C.: The University of North Carolina Press, 1959), pp. 15–32. Reprinted by permission of The University of North Carolina Press and the Institute of Early American History and Culture.

piratical voyage around the world in 1577–80, he was told that "the queen does not acknowledge that her subjects and those of other nations may be excluded from the Indies on the claim that these have been donated to the king of Spain by the pope, whose authority to invest the Spanish king with the New World as with a fief she does not recognise." "The Spaniards," in Elizabeth's view, had "no claim to property there except that they have established a few settlements and named rivers and capes. . . . Prescription without possession is not valid."[2]

The English sovereigns, denying Rome's prerogatives, issued grants and charters of their own to the new-found lands. Because these concessions proved meaningful in terms of what happened later, modern writers have assumed that they expressed a carefully considered conception of the royal prerogative. It is more accurate to say, however, that because the colonizers were able to assert their paper rights against the Indians and against other Europeans, a literature to justify and explain the kingly attitude arose. Had the charters not proved effectual, there is little doubt that we would now have a literature, as we do in the case of the papal grants, showing that the English sovereigns were not really granting away other peoples' lands but only giving privileges of government conditional upon conversion of the Indians.

A guide to the intent and meaning of the royal grants of land in America is to be found in the previous practices of English sovereigns. In 1109 Henry I granted Gilbert de Clare "all the land of Cardigan, *if he could win it from the Welsh*." One historian has applied the appropriate name "speculative" to this type of grant. It was a form of concession used frequently in later years against the Irish.[3] Similarly, in the letters patent of Henry VII authorizing John Cabot and his sons to seek out and discover "whatsoever isles, countreys, regions or provinces of the heathen and infidels . . . which before this time have bene unknowen to all Christians," the king granted the Cabots the right to "subdue, occupy and possesse all such townes, cities, castles and isles of them found, which they *can* subdue, occupy and possesse. . . ."[4] When Elizabeth I granted Raleigh liberty to "discover, search, finde out, and view such remote, heathen and barbarous lands, countries and territories, not actually possessed of any Christian Prince, nor inhabited by Christian People," and the right to "have, holde, occupie, and enjoy" the same, it was with the assumption that Raleigh would succeed in conquering the regions; otherwise the grant was to be of no force.[5]

[2] Edward P. Cheyney, "International Law Under Queen Elizabeth," *Eng. Hist. Rev.*, 20 (1905), 660, quoting from Camden, *Annales* (1605 ed.), 309, about the reply to Spain, ca. 1580, either in the form of a paper drawn by the Privy Council and afterward lost or suppressed, or in the form of the substance of a verbal statement made to the Spanish ambassador or some later commissioners.

[3] Edmund Curtis, *A History of Medieval Ireland from 1086 to 1513* (London, 1938), 38–39; the statement from Henry I is a direct quotation. My italics.

[4] Letters patent to John Cabot, March 5, 1496, in Henry Steele Commager, ed., *Documents of American History* (New York, 1944), 5. My italics.

[5] Charter to Sir Walter Raleigh, March 25, 1584, *ibid.*, 6.

Most English arguments for title also made use of the Cabots' "discovery" in the Newfoundland area in 1497–98 to strengthen England's right to North America. This was the country's only argument of great priority, for she had slumbered during the hundred years following the Cabot voyages. As in the case of the king's charter, it is doubtful that the argument was accorded much weight even by the English themselves, except as a formal answer to the claims of prior discovery by other nations. Many Oriental regions, unknown in the same sense that many American regions were unknown in the period following Columbus' initial discovery, were "discovered" by Europeans in like fashion but rarely claimed as a result.

"Although many have stated that at the time of the European explorations of the fifteenth through seventeenth centuries discovery was a sufficient basis for a claim to sovereignty," writes William W. Bishop, "it is not clear whether the term 'discovery' meant more than the mere finding of the lands previously unknown to European civilization."[6] Three distinguished students of the question have also concluded that

> throughout this lengthy period, no state appeared to regard mere discovery, in the sense of "physical" discovery or simple "visual apprehension," as being in any way sufficient *per se* to establish a right of sovereignty over, or a valid title to, *terra nullius*. Furthermore, mere disembarkation upon any portion of such regions— or even extended penetration and exploration therein—was not regarded as sufficient itself to establish such a right or title.[7]

The absurdity of gaining possession of a continent by sailing along its coastline was so obvious that some writers facetiously suggested that Europe would have to be conceded to any Indian prince who happened to send a ship to "discover" it.[8] By itself the assertion had little more effect in restraining other countries from colonizing North America than

---

[6] William W. Bishop, Jr., *International Law: Cases and Materials* (New York, 1953), 272.

[7] Arthur S. Keller, Oliver J. Lissitzyn, and Frederick J. Mann, *Creation of Rights of Sovereignty Through Symbolic Acts, 1400–1800* (New York, 1938), 148.

[8] "And to bring in the title of *First-discovery*, to me it seems as little reason, that the sailing of a Spanish Ship upon the coast of *India*, should intitle the King of Spain to that Countrey, as the sayling of an Indian or English Ship upon the coast of *Spain*, should intitle either the *Indians* or *English* unto the Dominion thereof. No question but the just right or title to those Countries appertains to the Natives themselves; who, if they shall willingly and freely invite the *English* to their protection, what title soever they have in them, no doubt but they may legally transferr it or communicate it to others." Thomas Gage, *The English-American his Travail by Sea and Land: Or a New Survey of the West-Indies, containing a Journal of Three thousand and Three hundred Miles within the main Land of America* (London, 1648), Epistle Dedicatory. J. Eric S. Thompson has edited a new edition of Gage's *Travels* (Norman, Okla., 1958).

had the Pope's bulls, which, as Sir Walter Raleigh pointed out, could not gore so well as they could bellow.[9]

It was natural, therefore, to reinforce citations of early discoveries with accounts of actual occupation of the land. Here again the question arose as to how much of the continent passed into the possession of those occupying a portion of it. Did a settlement on the tip of Cape Cod or the Florida peninsula give title to the entire North American continent?

The monarchs were most liberal. Since it cost them nothing to give all, they gave all, with grants usually extending to the South Sea. But with several kings making grants in North America, international conflicts were inevitable. Final settlement depended on the course of events and the power of the claimants. "Why shall they," asked the French, "being at 36 or 37 [degrees], advance to 45, rather than we being, as they admit, at 46, descend as far as 37? What right have they more than we? This is our answer to the English."[10] An early eighteenth-century English chronicler, on the other hand, expressed the English view of the extent of French sovereignty in America (which covered vast expanses on French maps) by asking: "Where then shall we find the Countries of *New-France* and *Louisiana*, unless it be within the reach of the great Guns of their Forts on the Rivers of *St. Lawrence* and *Mississippi* . . . ?"[11]

Unfortunately, international law was not able to resolve the dilemma. This inability is not to be wondered at, since international law has no central coercive power to establish its authority; enforcement must rest on the use of power by the individual sovereign states. Certain conventions, it is true, grew up in this period, but they developed principally because it was more expedient for the individual nations to compromise their exaggerated claims than to fight over them. One of the conventions which appeared at this time was an agreement not to consider acts of violence occurring beyond the papal line of demarcation in the Atlantic as breaking the peace in Europe. Neither Spain nor Portugal was willing at first to concede rights to others within the monopolies fixed by the line, but other European powers were unwilling to recognize that they might be barred. Hence, the area came to be excluded, at first by oral agreement and later by treaty arrangement, from the effect of European peace settlements. The phenomenon of "no peace beyond the line," as it was known, was not allowed to break the peace that might exist on the European side of the line. The special legal and moral character of acts committed in the area thus set aside suggests that the European monarchs realized that their territorial claims in the newly discovered areas had little basis in law or

---

[9] "A Discourse of the Original and Fundamental Cause of Natural, Arbitrary, Necessary, and Unnatural War," in *The Works of Sir Walter Ralegh, Kt.* (Oxford, 1829), VIII, 277.

[10] [Samuel de Champlain?], "Abstract of the Discoveries in New France," 1631, in E. B. O'Callaghan, ed., *Documents Relative to the Colonial History of the State of New York* (Albany, N.Y., 1855), IX, 2.

[11] Thomas Salmon, *Modern History; or, the Present State of All Nations*, XXXI, Being the Fourth Volume of *America* (London, 1738), 557.

morality and could be increased, diminished, or surrendered, as expedient, without seriously threatening the vital interests of the mother country.[12]

Today we visualize English invasion of the North American continent as the establishment of a military beachhead. The assumption is general that the Indian was a hostile occupant of the territory which the English proposed to settle. Although this was true as soon as English intentions to conquer as well as to settle became evident, it is not an accurate description of the initial Indian attitude. Nothing is so frequently recorded in the earliest chronicles as the warmth of the reception accorded the first colonists.

The Indians believed in hospitality. The extent of their hospitality impressed the English; unfortunately, however, they were not impressed with the virtue of the Indians, but only with the power of their own God, who temporarily imbued the Indians with kindness. We read frequently such statements as "God caused the Indians to help us with fish at very cheap rates. . . ."[13] Perhaps such an attitude was natural to a people whose merit was based on salvation through a vicarious atonement. Since earthly success, as well as heavenly salvation, depended on God's will, not on man's effort, God was to be praised, not his terrestrial agents.

Another basis for English suspicion of Indian motives was the inherent fear of the unknown. Indians were strange creatures to the seventeenth-century Englishman, particularly since the sole basis of previous identification was in terms of heathen or infidel opponents of the True Faith. The Indians were expected to react hostilely. Their overt friendliness was often seen as proof of covert antagonism. Captain Christopher Newport, commanding the *Susan Constant, Godspeed,* and *Discovery,* reported after his trip up the James River in 1607 that the Indians "are naturally given to treachery, howbeit we could not finde it in o'r travell up the river, but rather a most kind and loving people."[14] William Symonds, editor of John Smith's *A Map of Virginia* (1612), expressed, with unconscious irony, the often-repeated complaint that the natives were "so malitious, that they seldome forget an injury. . . ."[15]

Nor was the tendency to see evil motives behind good deeds limited to the early colonists. Later writers have assumed that the Indians were secretly hostile to the colonists even when they granted them the most lavish hospitality or supplied food in their periods of want. Alexander Brown in 1898, for example, convinced himself that the Virginia Indians "were really the enemies of the English from the first. . . ." He explained the assistance given the settlers by the Indians in the fall of 1607 as follows:

---

[12] See, for example, Arthur Percival Newton, *The Colonising Activities of the English Puritans* (New Haven, Conn., 1914), 96.

[13] Roger Clap's "Memoirs" (London, 1731), in Alexander Young, ed., *Chronicles of the First Planters of the Colony of Massachusetts, from 1623 to 1636* (Boston, 1846), 350.

[14] "Description of the Now-Discovered River and Country of Virginia," June 21, 1607, in *Va. Mag. of Hist. and Biog.,* 14 (1907), 377.

[15] In Edward Arber and A. G. Bradley, eds., *Travels and Works of Captain John Smith* (Edinburgh, 1910), I, 65.

All accounts agree that for some reason the Indians did daily relieve them for some weeks with corn and flesh. The supplies
brought from England had been nearly exhausted; the colonists
had been too sick to attend to their gardens properly, and this act
of the Indians was regarded as a divine providence at that time.
. . . What was the real motive for the kindly acts of the Indians
may not be certainly known; but it probably boded the little
colony a future harm.[16]

Relations, it is true, did not continue friendly for long; treachery was
being plotted behind the outward benignity. But was it Indian treachery
or white treachery? A detailed examination of the historical record would,
I venture to suggest, show that the treachery was more frequently on the
side of the white.[17]

The Virginia massacre of 1622, however, erased all previous accounts
and provided the English with the "bloody shirt" needed to justify hostilities against the natives whenever convenient. Up until that time it was
necessary to see malice in good will or to cite occasional Indian violence
against small groups of settlers. Now the English could point to a full-
scale war directed against all the settlements and carried out with terrible
effects. Hundreds of English were slaughtered and the colony nearly
wiped out. It would have been appropriate, of course, to determine
whether the Indians were justified in attacking because of previous injuries
and because of the English refusal to respect their unqualified sovereignty
in the area. The importance of such considerations was admitted by
some,[18] but ignored or denied by most. Edward Waterhouse rejoiced that
the massacre had occurred:

Our hands which before were tied with gentlenesse and faire
usage, are now set at liberty by the treacherous violence of the
Sausages [savages]. . . . So that we, who hitherto have had possession of no more ground then their waste, and our purchase at a
valuable consideration to their owne contentment, gained; may
now by right of Warre, and law of Nations, invade the Country,
and destroy them who sought to destroy us. . . . Now their cleared
grounds in all their villages (which are situate in the fruitfullest
places of the land) shall be inhabited by us, whereas heretofore the
grubbing of woods was the greatest labour.[19]

The Virginia Company seized on the massacre to order a war against
the Indians, dispossession of those near the settlements, and, as a gesture

---

[16] Alexander Brown, *The First Republic in America* (Boston, 1898), 41–42.
[17] See the suggestions for such a study in Wilcomb E. Washburn, "A Moral History
of Indian-White Relations: Needs and Opportunities for Study," *Ethnohistory*, 4
(1957), 47–61.
[18] George Thorpe to Sir Edwin Sandys, May 15, 1621, in Susan M. Kingsbury, ed.,
*The Records of the Virginia Company of London* (4 vols.; Washington, D.C.,
1906–35), III, 446.
[19] "A Declaration of the State of the Colony and . . . a Relation of the Barbarous
Massacre . . ." (London, 1622), reprinted, *ibid.*, 556–57.

of mercy, the enslavement rather than slaughter of the younger people of both sexes.[20] The company's instructions were hardly necessary. The governor and council had already initiated a policy of exterminating the neighboring Indians. "Wee have anticipated your desire by settinge uppon the Indyans in all places," they wrote proudly.[21] To aid in the project the natives were lulled into a sense of false security by the conclusion of a treaty, and the council in Virginia even went so far as to boast of this bit of treachery.[22] On one occasion poison was placed in the wine offered to the Indians on the conclusion of a peace treaty.[23] When chided by the company for their "false dealing," the council in Virginia replied that "wee hold nothinge injuste, that may tend to theire ruine, (except breach of faith). Stratagems were ever allowed against all enemies, but with these neither fayre Warr nor good quarter is ever to be held, nor is there any other hope of theire subversione, who ever may informe you to the Contrarie."[24]

Next to treacherousness, "barbarism" was the most convenient accusation to hurl against the Indian in the seventeenth century. Yet, as John Daly Burk, the historian of Virginia, pointed out:

> Notwithstanding the general charge of barbarism and treachery against the Indians of Virginia, and of cruelty and tyranny against Powhatan, with which the early historians abound, not a single fact is brought in support of this accusation; and in several instances, with an inconsistency for which it is difficult to account, the same writers speak with admiration of the exact order, which prevailed among all the tribes of which this empire was composed; and confess at the same time, that this order and security arose from the inviolable observance of customs, which time has consecrated as law and which were equally binding on the King and the people.[25]

Today the character of the American Indian is generally drawn in a derogatory manner. The views of the first explorers and missionaries, who frequently saw heroic qualities in the Indian and whose reports provided the basis for the earlier literary conception of the "noble savage," have

---

[20] Treasurer and Council for Virginia to Governor and Council in Virginia, August 1, 1622, *ibid.*, 672; see also John Martin, "The Manner howe to bringe in the Indians into subjection without makinge an utter exterpation of them together with the reasons," December 15, 1622, *ibid.*, 704–07.

[21] Council in Virginia to Virginia Company of London, January 20, 1622/23, *ibid.*, IV, 9.

[22] See, for example, Council in Virginia to Virginia Company of London, April 3 and 4, 1623, *ibid.*, 99, 102.

[23] Robert Bennett to Edward Bennett, June 9, 1623, *ibid.*, 221–22; also printed in *Amer. Hist. Rev.*, 27 (1922), 505–08.

[24] Virginia Company of London to Governor and Council in Virginia, August 6, 1623, in Kingsbury, ed., *Records of the Virginia Company*, IV, 269–70; Council in Virginia to Virginia Company of London, January 30, 1623/24, *ibid.*, 451.

[25] John Daly Burk, *The History of Virginia from its first Settlement to the Commencement of the Revolution* (Petersburg, Va., 1804–05), I, 308–09.

long since been buried in the shifting sands of more recent intellectual movements. None of the studies of "the myth of the noble savage" considers the possibility that the early favorable observers of Indian character might not have been entirely deceived in their analysis. All such studies assume that any degree of nobility was a myth: so far have white arrogance and Indian abasement proceeded.[26]

Another common charge against the Indians, which became the basis of the most popular eighteenth- and nineteenth-century justification for dispossessing them, was that they were wandering hunters with no settled habitations. This mode of securing their livelihood, it was charged, was too wasteful in a world in which other countries faced (or thought they faced) problems of overpopulation.[27] The argument that hunters might justly be forced to alter their economy by a pastoral or agricultural people was voiced by many, humble and great, in the colonies and in England. John Locke was perhaps its most famous exponent, although, characteristically, he did not develop the argument logically or clearly.[28] The argument was later expressed most succinctly by Theodore Roosevelt, who wrote that "the settler and pioneer have at bottom had justice on their side; this great continent could not have been kept as nothing but a game preserve for squalid savages."[29]

Again, was not the European creating the myth he wished to use? Were the Indians in fact nomadic hunters? It was, of course, possible to find examples of nomadic hunting tribes in North America, and the Indians of the Eastern coast, those referred to by the early theorists, depended upon hunting as an important part of their economy and an integral function of their social and religious life. But agriculture was also a conspicuously essential part of Indian subsistence, and we may regard with suspicion much of the literature of justification which overlooks this aspect of native life. The English knew well enough how important was Indian food: the early accounts are filled with references to the "Indian fields" along the rivers of Virginia, and little else but native produce sustained the whites in the early years of settlement. It was the Indians who taught the settlers techniques of agriculture, as the familiar story of Squanto and the Plymouth Colony relates, and the Virginia colonists also were instructed by the Indians on how to plant crops and how to retrieve

[26] See Washburn, "A Moral History of Indian-White Relations," *Ethnohistory*, 4 (1957), 47–61.

[27] England, in Elizabethan times, had a population of about two and a half to three million persons. J. B. Black, *The Reign of Elizabeth, 1558–1603* (Oxford, 1945), 195.

[28] John Locke, *An Essay Concerning the True Original, Extent and End of Civil Government* (1690), Chap. V, "Of Property." Immanuel Kant in *The Science of Right* (1796), Pt. I, Chap. II, sec. i, no. 15, writing as the representative of a nation which did not participate in the profitable overseas voyages, denounced the doctrine as impious and championed the right of the American Indian to hold his land in whatever way he pleased. Representatives of the expanding maritime nations, however, found no difficulty in justifying their nations' claims.

[29] Theodore Roosevelt, *The Winning of the West* (New York, 1889–96), I, 90.

food from the rivers and bays. The natives were hunters, but they were also, and probably more importantly, agriculturists and fishermen.[30]

The literature of justification similarly tends to overlook the fact that the Indians were, for the most part, town dwellers. The great body of contemporary graphic depictions in French, Spanish, and English sources of the sixteenth and seventeenth centuries shows substantial dwellings, palisaded villages, well-planned streets, garden plots, civic and religious centers. Indeed, throughout most of the seventeenth century in Virginia the only true town dwellers were the Indians; the English lived together compactly only during the fearful early years.

The literature of justification has never come to an easy and final solution. Men have thrashed over the morality of expansion without agreement, and the courts have interpreted the "law" involved without consistency. A few representative individual views and court decisions from the sixteenth to the twentieth century should make this clear.

Sir Thomas More, in his *Utopia* (1516), was one of the first Englishmen to express himself on the justice of expansion. When the Utopians, the inhabitants of More's ideal country, had fully populated their own cities they sent colonists to build "a town . . . in the next land, where the inhabitants have much waste and unoccupied ground." The native inhabitants are invited to dwell with the Utopians—under Utopian laws, of course, which are considered by the Utopians to be greatly superior. If the natives are foolish enough to resist this benevolence, they are driven off the land; if resistance continues, the Utopians have no choice but to make full-scale war against them. More's ideal people considered this the most just cause of war: "when any people holdeth a piece of ground void and vacant to no good or profitable use; keeping others from the use and possession of it, which, notwithstanding, by the law of nature, ought thereof to be nourished and relieved."[31]

Sir Walter Raleigh, a hundred years later, was considerably less positive than More. A people could deceive itself: for example, "a number can do a great wrong and call it right, and not one of that majority blush for it."[32] Raleigh noted sadly and cynically that wars over land ownership were likely to be inevitable because the "great charter whereby God bestowed the whole earth upon Adam and confirmed it unto the sons of Noah, being as brief in words, as large in effect, hath bred much quarrel

[30] See, for example, Harold Underwood Faulkner, *American Economic History*, 5th ed. (New York, 1943), 58–60, and Roy Harvey Pearce, *The Savages of America: A Study of the Indian and the Idea of Civilization* (Baltimore, 1953), 66. An example of the inability to see the Indians as other than hunters is evident in Roger Burlingame's chapter "Mission in Virginia" in *The American Conscience* (New York, 1957). Burlingame quotes the passage of Edward Waterhouse (see p. 17) that "now their cleared lands [*sic*] . . . shall be inhabited by us" and immediately comments that "the policy hitherto observed of keeping hands off the Indian hunting would be ended . . ." (p. 68).

[31] *Utopia*, Robinson trans. of 1551; new ed. by Rev. T. F. Didbin (London, 1808), Bk. II, Chap. V, 191–92.

[32] "A Discourse of the Original and Fundamental Cause of Natural, Arbitrary, Necessary, and Unnatural War," in *Works of Sir Walter Ralegh, Kt.*, VIII, 291.

of interpretation." English occupation of the Bermudas (first "discovered" by the Spanish) was clearly a moral action because the land had been uninhabited when the English landed. But what of inhabited areas? Here Raleigh pondered the question which must continue to be at the heart of all justifications for expansion in a world in which every individual human being is regarded as possessing roughly equivalent rights:

> If the title of occupiers be good in land unpeopled, why should it be bad accounted in a country peopled over thinly? Should one family, or one thousand, hold possession of all the southern undiscovered continent, because they had seated themselves in Nova Guiana, or about the straits of Magellan? Why might not then the like be done in Afric, in Europe, and in Asia? If these were most absurd to imagine, let then any man's wisdom determine, by lessening the territory, and increasing the number of inhabitants, what proportion is requisite to the peopling of a region in such a manner that the land shall neither be too narrow for those whom it feedeth, nor capable of a greater multitude? Until this can be concluded and agreed upon, one main and fundamental cause of the most grievous war that can be imagined is not like to be taken from the earth.[33]

Roger Williams, in the 1630's and 1640's, was one of the few Englishmen who dared to dismiss European claims to American soil as unjustified and illegal if the prior right of the Indian were not recognized. Full title was in the Indian, he asserted, from whom alone a valid title could be derived. The colonists should repent of receiving title by patent from a king who had no right to grant it. Williams, said John Cotton, held it "a National duty to renounce the Patent: which to have done would have subverted the fundamental State and Government of the Country."[34]

The distinction between the "Naturall Right" of the Indians to the land they occupied, now called "original Indian title," and the legal title of the English to sovereignty was thus brought into the open. The distinction has been a basic one throughout American history, but it had to be established as well as asserted. In the seventeenth century the rule was by no means established. It was never made explicit to the Indians, least of all to those who lived in actual independence beyond the frontiers of the various colonies. Nor was it established to the full understanding of those tribes which lived in closer association with the English until their defeat in such conflicts as King Philip's War in New England. The principle of English sovereignty based on the royal grants was, in sum, as "speculative" as the grants themselves and depended for its establishment on the course of events. Fortunately for the English, the fact proved equal to the assertion.

Roger Williams, despite his brave stand against the royal patent, was

---

[33] *Ibid.*, 255.
[34] Mass. Hist. Soc., *Proceedings 1871–1873*, 12 (Boston, 1873), 348, 351.

eventually forced to request a charter from the English parliamentary government in order to prevent the Rhode Island colony from being devoured by her neighboring English colonies.[35]

The question of Indian rights became more and more difficult for jurists and theorists as American settlement advanced and overran not only what European thinkers considered the natural rights of the Indians but those rights guaranteed by solemn treaty. This knowledge pained Thomas Jefferson, who realized that the legal justification for European settlement in territory occupied by another race must necessarily rest on natural injustice.

"Whoever shall attempt to trace the claims of the European Nations to the Countrys in America from the principles of Justice, or reconcile the invasions made on the native Indians to the natural rights of mankind," wrote Jefferson, "will find that he is pursueing a Chimera, which exists only in his own imagination, against the evidence of indisputable facts."[36]

Although he regarded discovery as a fragile support for claims of just settlement, Jefferson, like John Marshall later, accepted its legality. "When America was first discovered by the Europeans," he wrote, "a general notion prevail'd, that the first discoverers of any particular part, had a right to take possession, in the name of that Kingdom or State of which they were Subjects; and that such discovery and formality of taking possession conferred a Title."[37]

As the eighteenth century passed into the nineteenth, the name of John Marshall came to dominate discussions of Indian rights. The great chief justice was in the strategic position of weighing the claims of a vigorous, rising nation and a faltering, declining race. On his decision hinged the title to the real estate of the nation, the independence of numerous Indian nations, the sanctity of treaty rights, and even the very existence of law and order. Marshall had to consider not only law but conscience and expediency as well. The "natural" rights of the Indians had to be seen in terms of the "speculative" rights of the earlier European monarchs, the "juridical" rights of their successor American states, and the "practical" economic demands of the millions who now populated the continent.

Marshall did not hesitate, and his decision has been the basis of all subsequent determinations of Indian right. In the case of *Johnson and Graham's Lessee* v. *McIntosh*, in 1823, Marshall declared that the Indians of the United States did not possess an unqualified sovereignty despite

35 Charles McLean Andrews, *The Colonial Period in American History* (New Haven, Conn., 1934–38), II, 4–5, 24–25.

36 "Vindication of Virginia's Claim Against the Proposed Colony of Vandalia" [ca. 1773–74], attributed to Jefferson by Julian P. Boyd *et al.*, eds., *The Papers of Thomas Jefferson* (Princeton, N.J., 1952), VI, Appendix III, 656.

37 *Ibid.* The "right of discovery" has been more realistically described, in the phrase of A. J. Leibling, as the principle of the "Pre-eminent Right of the First Trespasser." See his "A Reporter at Large: The Lake of the Ciu-ui Eaters—III," *The New Yorker* (January 15, 1955), 36.

the centuries of relations conducted with them in terms of treaties and diplomatic agreements. Their right to "complete sovereignty, as independent nations" was diminished or denied, declared Marshall, by "the original fundamental principle that discovery gave exclusive title to those who made it." "The history of America," the historian-chief justice concluded, "from its discovery to the present day, proves, we think, the universal recognition of these principles." Marshall declared further that the principle of discovery "was a right which all asserted for themselves, and to the assertion of which, by others, all assented." "However extravagant the pretension of converting the discovery of an inhabited country into conquest may appear," wrote Marshall in his decision, "if the principle has been asserted in the first instance, and afterwards sustained; if a country has been acquired and held under it; if the property of the great mass of the community originates in it, it becomes the law of the land and cannot be questioned."[38]

Marshall's decision encouraged the state of Georgia, beginning in 1824, to try to dispossess the Cherokee Indians living within its borders. Hitherto the Cherokee Nation had lived confident in the protection afforded by the many treaties concluded with the English and American governments before and after the Revolution. In all these agreements the Cherokee Nation had been treated as an independent political power possessing proprietary right and political authority in the land it occupied.

The Cherokees had, moreover, in the course of their contact with Europeans, adopted white customs of dress and white modes of cultivation. They had thus, in the words of James Madison, refuted the unfounded claim of the whites that they were nomadic savages, unqualified for formal ownership of land. Yet there was always an answer to Indian claims, and the Cherokees were now opposed on the "strange ground . . . that they had no right to alter their condition and become husbandmen."[39]

In 1828 the Cherokees held a convention to establish a permanent government and write a constitution for their nation. The state, anxious to prevent the creation of further obstacles to Indian removal, replied in 1829 with a series of laws invalidating all statutes and ordinances adopted by the Indians and authorizing the division of their lands. These laws were, of course, in violation of solemn treaties between the United States and the Cherokee Nation. President Jackson, whose frontier upbringing had left him with little sympathy for the Indians, was in complete accord with Georgia. When the Cherokees applied for federal protection against the efforts of Georgia to coerce them in violation of their treaty rights, Jackson replied that "the President of the United States has no power to protect them against the laws of Georgia."[40]

[38] 8 Wheaton 574, 591.
[39] Wirt to Madison, October 5, 1830, quoted in John P. Kennedy, *Memoirs of the Life of William Wirt, Attorney-General of the United States*, rev. ed. (Philadelphia, 1850–54), II, 262.
[40] Quoted in Charles Warren, *The Supreme Court in United States History*, rev. ed. (Boston, 1937), I, 731.

Disappointed by this breach of faith, the Indians initiated legal action before the Supreme Court to prevent Georgia from carrying out its laws in violation of the Cherokee Nation's solemn treaty rights. Two distinguished lawyers agreed to represent the Cherokees: William Wirt, ex-Attorney General of the United States, and John Sergeant, former chief counsel for the Bank of the United States. Before taking the case, Wirt considered the moral and legal issues involved and read extensively on the controversy as it had been argued in Congress. "In making this examination," he said, "I was struck with the manifest determination, both of the President and the States, that the State laws should be extended over . . . [the Cherokees] *at every hazard.* This led me to reflect more seriously on the predicament in which I was about to place myself, and perhaps involve the Supreme Court of the United States."[41]

Chief Justice Marshall, though sympathetic to the plight of the Cherokees, had to consider the incalculable effects a decision in their favor might have on the authority of the Supreme Court: the President's probable refusal to enforce the orders of the court could destroy the authority so painstakingly built up by Marshall.[42] How much effect such considerations had on his decision is uncertain. At any rate, in the action brought by *The Cherokee Nation* v. *The State of Georgia* (1831), Marshall ruled that the Cherokee Nation, though a "State," was not a "foreign State" but a "domestic dependent nation," and that the court had no original jurisdiction of the case.[43] Justice Smith Thompson dissented "in an opinion of immense power" in which Justice Joseph Story concurred.[44]

The decision on the right of the state of Georgia to impose its authority upon the Cherokees, though not met in this case, was faced in the case of *Samuel A. Worcester* v. *The State of Georgia* (1832). Here Georgia's right to force two missionaries with the Cherokees to obtain a license and take an oath of state allegiance was denied. Marshall, in his decision, held the Georgia statute unconstitutional on the ground that the jurisdiction of the federal government over the Cherokees was exclusive. Georgia, the court ruled, had no power to pass laws affecting the Cherokees or their territory.[45]

Having ruled the Cherokees dependent, Marshall now attempted to limit their dependence to the federal government and not to the state of Georgia. But even this ruling was dangerous under the conditions of power which existed. It failed to protect the Indians and it nearly toppled the court's authority. Just what President Jackson's precise feeling in the matter was we do not know; there seems little doubt, however, that he

---

[41] Wirt to Judge Dabney Carr, June 21, 1830, quoted in Kennedy, *Memoirs of Wirt,* II, 255.

[42] Marshall to Judge Carr, n.d., quoted in Kennedy, *Memoirs of Wirt,* II, 258; Warren, *Supreme Court,* I, 751; Albert J. Beveridge, *The Life of John Marshall* (Boston, 1916–19), IV, 546.

[43] 5 Peters 15–18; entire report, 1–80.

[44] Beveridge, *Life of Marshall,* IV, 546.

[45] 6 Peters 515–97.

never intended to enforce the decision of the court against an unwilling Georgia. He wanted the Indians removed, by law or without law, in the name of whatever principle might be applied. And they were removed. The court's impotence threw Marshall into a deep gloom. "I yield slowly and reluctantly to the conviction that our constitution cannot last," he wrote to Justice Story on September 22, 1832.[46]

The success of the state of Georgia in defying the federal government encouraged the state of South Carolina to question the authority of the Supreme Court. But on this question Jackson reacted in a different manner. He rebuked South Carolina with the "Force Bill" and thereby bolstered the authority of the central government and the Supreme Court, even causing Georgia to pardon the missionaries upon the withdrawal of their suit. The crisis involving the court and the federal government passed; the only victim was the Cherokee Nation.

So great were the accumulated injuries suffered by the Indians, so difficult was redress under existing methods, and, most importantly, so sharply did the pricks of conscience begin to disturb the satiated conquerors, that Congress, in 1946, after nearly twenty years of consideration, passed the Indian Claims Commission Act to give belated justice to the Indians. Clause 5 of section 2 of the act provided for "claims based upon fair and honorable dealings that are not recognized by any existing rule of law or equity," an allowance which has introduced a new element into the battle over Indian justice.

The Justice Department has argued consistently that the act did not create any new causes of action, but merely provided a forum where Indian claimants could sue the United States only on those claims upon which the United States had already consented to be sued by non-Indians. It was a political and not a judicial function, it asserted, to recognize liability for claims without a legal or equitable basis under existing law.[47]

The view of the Justice Department, however, has not prevailed in the cases arising under the act of 1946. The Indians have acquired important justiciable rights under the statute as it has been interpreted by the Indian Claims Commission and by the Court of Claims. However, the Indian is still without constitutional support for his rights. In *Tee-Hit-Ton Indians* v. *The United States* (1954–55), a case not arising under the act of 1946, the Indians were held not entitled to compensation under the Fifth Amendment for the taking by the United States of lands long in their possession.[48] In upholding the decision of the Court of Claims, the Supreme Court, with Justice Reed delivering the opinion, noted that the Tee-Hit-Tons occupied the land, prior to the purchase of Alaska by the United States in 1867, by mere possession not specifically recognized as

---

[46] Mass. Hist. Soc., *Proceedings, 1900–1901*, 2d ser., 14 (Boston, 1901), 352.
[47] *Otoe and Missouria Tribe of Indians* v. *United States*, 131 U.S. Court of Claims 598 (1955).
[48] 128 Court of Claims 82.

ownership by Congress or, in the commonly accepted phrase, by "original Indian title." "The line of cases adjudicating Indian rights on American soil," he asserted,

> leads to the conclusion that Indian occupancy, not specifically recognized as ownership by action authorized by Congress, may be extinguished by the Government without compensation. Every American schoolboy knows that the savage tribes of this continent were deprived of their ancestral ranges by force and that, even when the Indian ceded millions of acres by treaty in return for blankets, food and trinkets, it was not a sale but the conquerors' will that deprived them of their land.[49]

The court took notice of certain decisions which had held for compensation under similar circumstances under the Fifth Amendment, but pointed out that they had been altered by later decisions, leaving "unimpaired the rule derived from *Johnson* v. *McIntosh* that the taking by the United States of unrecognized Indian title is not compensable under the Fifth Amendment." Not the least consideration that may have led to this conclusion was the estimate that, if the Fifth Amendment protection were allowed, it might cost the government nine billion dollars to pay for uncompensated aboriginal titles.[50]

Disclaiming any intention of upholding harshness as the most appropriate policy toward the Indians, Justice Reed asserted that the court spoke for the American people, who "have compassion for the descendants of those Indians who were deprived of their homes and hunting grounds by the drive of civilization. . . ." The court spoke approvingly of the "generous provision . . . willingly made to allow tribes to recover for wrongs, as a matter of grace, not of legal liability."[51] The Indian, thus, was to depend on the generosity and the grace of his despoilers. His rights were not to be afforded the protection of "constitutional principle" but satisfied by "gratuities for the termination of Indian occupancy."[52]

The status of Indian claims based on the "unrecognized title" of Indian occupancy, as opposed to "recognized title" deriving from treaties or acts of Congress, was temporarily thrown in doubt by this decision. However, by the *Otoe and Missouria* case (1955), the Court of Claims sustained the decision of the Indian Claims Commission, in an action brought under the Indian Claims Commission Act of 1946, holding the government liable to a claim based on aboriginal Indian title, and the

---

[49] 348 U.S. 289–90. The assumptions of the court as to the savagery of the Indians, their nomadic condition, and their subjection by conquest reflect popular beliefs more than they do historical facts. None of these assumptions can be made so lightly or so generally, particularly in the context of the seventeenth and eighteenth centuries.

[50] 348 U.S. 283n., 284–85.

[51] 348 U.S. 281–82.

[52] 348 U.S. 294. It is noteworthy that three justices, including the Chief Justice, dissented from the opinion of the court.

Supreme Court refused to review the case. The Court of Claims was careful, however, to assert its essential agreement with the reasoning of the high court in the *Tee-Hit-Ton* case. It pointed out that Congress, by passing the Indian Claims Commission Act, had condescended, as a matter of grace, to allow the Indians to sue the United States on moral grounds and on the basis of "Indian title." The legal rights of the sovereign were not to be impaired, but sympathetic justice, not strict legality, was to be the guiding rule. Statutory, but not constitutional, liability, in other words, was to be admitted.[53]

Although cautiously interpreted by the courts, has not the Indian Claims Commission Act perhaps opened the door for broader and more fundamental moral claims? If the cost to honor, dignity, interest, or reason of recognizing the constitutional right of original Indian sovereignty in the New World should not seem too high to future generations, is it not possible that such a right will be conceded as justiciable as well as just?[54] The Indian Claims Commission Act has recognized that law must sometimes concede to morality if justice is not to be a synonym for injustice. Now that morality has a foot in the door, if only by the grace of the present lord of the manor, is it not possible that it will speak more persuasively than ever before? It has been hard for the Indian to accept the good faith of American "justice" based, as it has so often been, on a disregard of moral principle and an exaltation of the fluctuating pronouncements of the white man's law. The legal culture of the American Indian tends to regard the fine distinctions between law and morality so often made in the Western world as the product of a hypocritical mind. Perhaps in the future the Indian and white conceptions of law, justice, and morality will finally blend.

In the meantime the problem of the legality and morality of the expansion of one people into the territory of another will go on. Because the problem is unresolved in the mind of man, it cannot be lost in the mists of history. It is the problem of man attempting to restrain his ungovern-

---

[53] For a full discussion of the question and references to further reading, see Nancy Oestreich Lurie, "The Indian Claims Commission Act," Amer. Acad. of Pol. and Soc. Sci., *Annals*, 311 (1957), 56–70.

[54] For an important example of the growing tendency to concede constitutional protection to those previously excluded, see *U.S.A. ex rel. Gyula Paktorovics v. John L. Murff, District Director, Immigration and Naturalization Service for the District of New York* (U.S. Court of Appeals, Second Circuit), decided November 6, 1958 (Docket No. 24932). By a two-to-one majority the court reversed the decision of a lower tribunal and ruled that refugees from the 1956 Hungarian revolution who came to the United States without visas were nevertheless entitled to the full protection of the due-process clause of the Fifth Amendment to the Constitution. The decision is another indication that "principles" have frequently, in the past, been applied step-by-step, first in behalf of members of the in-group and finally for the benefit of less privileged members of a society. The protection of American constitutional rights has been gradually extended outward from the descendants of the original European immigrants to those with darker skins, different customs, and antagonistic ideologies. It is not inconceivable that the canopy of protection will eventually extend to the American Indian himself.

able passions, man attempting to trust his "sovereign" reason, man attempting to better his economic condition. As we near the era of space travel we hear echoes of those who launched and justified the great age of oceanic discovery. "Space lawyers," noting the successful launching of Russian and American space satellites, advise us that by "international law" the first country able to land a man on the moon—or even to hit it—will be justified in claiming it, and in similar fashion all the other "islands and mainlands" of the celestial "ocean sea." Perhaps the creation of a circular crater resulting from a hydrogen bomb shot will be considered the "symbolic act" or "visible symbol" necessary to claim possession. Shades of Cabot's proprietary cruise down the coast of North America! The possession of worlds in outer space will not be determined fundamentally by priority of national grant, discovery, or occupancy any more than the ownership of the New World was determined by such considerations. Man thinking will continue to tell us what the law ought to be; man acting will tell us what the law is.

# The Beginnings of Slavery

# in

# North America

WINTHROP D. JORDAN

By the end of the seventeenth century the English colonies in southern North America had turned to the African slave and his descendants to solve the problems arising from a chronic shortage of unskilled labor. The English adapted for their own use the Spanish system of African enslavement, which had begun early in the sixteenth century in the Caribbean. Indian slavery, too, had been widely practiced in Latin America, to the point of bringing the native Indian populations close to extinction. But in North American colonies, though Indian captives were frequently enslaved in the early years of colonization, it appears that Indian slavery was never economically profitable. As a result, the African became **the** slave in the English colonies.

Slavery, in the sense of lifetime bondage, is an institution as old as human history. Almost every past civilization has had some system of involuntary service that may with some accuracy be called slavery. Throughout history, military conquest has been the most common means of enslavement. What distinguished North American slavery, however, was its racial character. By the beginning of the eighteenth century, any African in the English colonies was assumed to be a slave unless he could prove otherwise. Except in exceptional circumstances, not only the original African but his descendants forever were confined to slave status.

From the earliest days of settlement in North America, the historical record clearly shows that some blacks were free. What it does not show is the process by which African slavery became the widespread institution that it was by 1700. In fact, historians have argued as to whether slavery produced racial prejudice or racial prejudice produced slavery—a question that could have vital significance for easing racial tensions in America today. If, for instance, slavery, as an absolute form of economic inequality, led to racial prejudice, then the elimination of economic inequality in the United States might contribute immensely to the elimination of racial prejudice. If, on the other hand, prejudice preceded slavery, then equal economic opportunity might not be expected for blacks until the roots of racial prejudice have been identified and removed.

The following selection is drawn from Winthrop D. Jordan's book **White Over Black,** a study of early racial attitudes among the English in the New World. In it, Jordan, of the University of California at Berkeley, argues that neither of the above positions can be demonstrated on the basis of historical evidence, though either is possible. He skillfully contrasts the condition of white semi-slave laborers with that of the blacks and indicates how quickly African slavery took root in the English colonies. Finally, he comes to tentative conclusions about many of the factors leading to the development of a separate and distinctly degrading status for blacks in the New World.

## ENSLAVEMENT: NEW ENGLAND

Negro slavery never really flourished in New England. It never became so important or so rigorous as in the plantation colonies to the southward. There were relatively few Negroes, only a few hundred in 1680 and not more than 3 per cent of the population in the eighteenth century; no one thought that Negroes were about to rise and overwhelm the white community.[1] Treatment of slaves in New England was milder even than the laws allowed: Negroes were not employed in gangs except occasionally in the Narragansett region of Rhode Island, and the established codes of family, congregation, and community mitigated the condition of servitude generally. Negroes were not treated very differently from white servants—except that somehow they and their children served for life.

The question with New England slavery is not why it was weakly rooted, but why it existed at all. No staple crop demanded regiments of raw labor. That there was no compelling economic demand for Negroes is evident in the numbers actually imported: economic exigencies scarcely required establishment of a distinct status for only 3 per cent of the labor force. Indentured servitude was adequate to New England's needs, and in

[1] Lorenzo J. Greene, *The Negro in Colonial New England, 1620–1776* (N.Y., 1942); report by the Massachusetts governor, Box 4, bundle: The Royal African Co. of England, MS. relating to the Company's trade in Negroes (1672–1734/35), 13, Parish Transcripts, N.-Y. Hist. Soc.

"The Beginnings of Slavery in North America." From Winthrop D. Jordan, *White Over Black: American Attitudes Toward the Negro, 1550–1812* (Chapel Hill, N.C.: The University of North Carolina Press, 1968), pp. 66–98. Reprinted by permission of The University of North Carolina Press and the Institute of Early American History and Culture.

fact some Negroes became free servants rather than slaves. Why, then, did New Englanders enslave Negroes, probably as early as 1638? Why was it that the Puritans rather mindlessly (which was not their way) accepted slavery for Negroes and Indians but not for white men?

The early appearance of slavery in New England may in part be explained by the provenance of the first Negroes imported. They were brought by Captain William Peirce of the Salem ship *Desire* in 1638 from the Providence Island colony, where Negroes were already being kept as perpetual servants.[2] A minor traffic in Negroes and other products developed between the two Puritan colonies, though evidently some of the Negroes proved less than satisfactory, for Governor Butler was cautioned by the Providence Company to take special care of "the cannibal negroes brought from New England."[3] After 1640 a brisk trade got under way between New England and the other English islands, and Massachusetts vessels sometimes touched upon the West African coast before heading for the Caribbean. Trade with Barbados was particularly lively, and Massachusetts vessels carried Negroes to that bustling colony from Africa and the Cape Verde Islands. As John Winthrop gratefully described the salvation of New England's economy, "It pleased the Lord to open to us a trade with Barbados and other Islands in the West Indies."[4] These strange Negroes from the West Indies must surely have been accompanied by prevailing notions about their usual status. Ship masters who purchased perpetual service in Barbados would not have been likely to sell service for term in Boston. Then, too, white settlers from the crowded islands migrated to New England, 1,200 from Barbados alone in the years 1643–47.[5]

No amount of contact with the West Indies could have by itself created Negro slavery in New England; settlers there had to be willing to accept the proposition. Because they were Englishmen, they were so prepared—and at the same time they were not. Characteristically, as Puritans, they officially codified this ambivalence in 1641 as follows:

> There shall never be any bond-slavery, villenage or captivitie amongst us; unless it be lawfull captives taken in just warrs, and such strangers as willingly sell themselves, or are solde to us: and such shall have the libertyes and christian usages which the law of God established in Israell concerning such persons doth morally require, provided, this exempts none from servitude who shall be judged thereto by Authoritie.[6]

[2] John Winthrop, *Winthrop's Journal: "History of New England," 1634–1649*, ed. James K. Hosmer, 2 vols. (N.Y., 1908), I, 260.

[3] [Arthur P.] Newton [*The Colonising Activities of the English Puritans: The Last Phase of the Elizabethan Struggle with Spain* (New Haven, 1914)], 260–61.

[4] Winthrop, *Journal*, ed. Hosmer, II, 73–74, 328; [Elizabeth] Donnan, ed. [*Documents Illustrative of the History of the Slave Trade to America*, 4 vols. (Washington, 1930–35)], III, 4–5, 6, 9, 10, 11–14.

[5] [Vincent T.] Harlow [*A History of Barbados, 1625–1685* (Oxford, 1926)], 340.

[6] Max Farrand, ed., *The Laws and Liberties of Massachusetts* (Cambridge, Mass., 1929), 4. See the very good discussion in George H. Moore, *Notes on the History of Slavery in Massachusetts* (N.Y., 1866).

Here were the wishes of the General Court as expressed in the Massachusetts Body of Liberties, which is to say that as early as 1641 the Puritan settlers were seeking to guarantee in writing their own liberty without closing off the opportunity of taking it from others whom they identified with the Biblical term *strangers*. It was under the aegis of this concept that Theophilus Eaton, one of the founders of New Haven, seems to have owned Negroes before 1658 who were "servants forever or during his pleasure, according to Leviticus, 25:45 and 46."[7] ("Of the children of the strangers that do sojourn among you, of them shall ye buy, and of their families . . . : and they shall be your possession. And ye shall take them as an inheritance for your children . . . ; they shall be your bondmen for ever: but over your brethren the children of Israel, ye shall not rule one over another with rigor.") Apart from this implication that bond slavery was reserved to those not partaking of true religion nor possessing proper nationality, the Body of Liberties expressly reserved the colony's right to enslave convicted criminals. For reasons not clear, this endorsement of an existing practice was followed almost immediately by discontinuance of its application to white men. The first instance of penal "slavery" in Massachusetts came in 1636, when an Indian was sentenced to "bee kept as a slave for life to worke, unles wee see further cause." Then in December 1638, ten months after the first Negroes arrived, the Quarter Court for the first time sentenced three white offenders to be "slaves"—a suggestive but perhaps meaningless coincidence. Having by June 1642 sentenced altogether some half dozen white men to "slavery" (and explicitly releasing several after less than a year), the Court stopped.[8] Slavery, as had been announced in the Body of Liberties, was to be only for "strangers."

The Body of Liberties made equally clear that captivity in a just war constituted legitimate grounds for slavery. The practice had begun during the first major conflict with the Indians, the Pequot War of 1637. Some of the Pequot captives had been shipped aboard the *Desire*, to Providence Island; accordingly, the first Negroes in New England arrived in exchange for men taken captive in a just war! That this provenance played an important role in shaping views about Negroes is suggested by the first recorded plea by an Englishman on the North American continent for the establishment of an African slave trade. Emanuel Downing, in a letter to his brother-in-law John Winthrop in 1645, described the advantages:

> If upon a Just warre [with the Narragansett Indians] the Lord should deliver them into our hands, wee might easily have men woemen and children enough to exchange for Moores, which wilbe

[7] Simeon E. Baldwin, "Theophilus Eaton, First Governor of the Colony of New Haven," New Haven Colony Historical Society, *Papers*, 7 (1908), 31.

[8] Nathaniel B. Shurtleff, ed., *Records of the Governor and Company of the Massachusetts Bay in New England*, 5 vols. in 6 (Boston, 1853–54), I, 181, 246; John Noble and John F. Cronin, eds., *Records of the Court of Assistants of the Colony of the Massachusetts Bay, 1630–1692*, 3 vols. (Boston, 1901–28), II, 78–79, 86, 90, 94, 97, 118.

more gaynefull pilladge for us then wee conceive, for I doe not see how wee can thrive untill wee get into a stock of slaves sufficient to doe all our buisiness, for our children's children will hardly see this great Continent filled with people, soe that our servants will still desire freedome to plant for themselves, and not stay but for verie great wages. And I suppose you know verie well how wee shall mayneteyne 20 Moores cheaper than one Englishe servant.[9]

These two facets of justifiable enslavement—punishment for crime and captivity in war—were closely related. Slavery as punishment probably derived from analogy with captivity, since presumably a king or magistrates could mercifully spare and enslave a man whose crime had forfeited his right to life. The analogy had not been worked out by commentators in England, but a fairly clear linkage between crime and captivity seems to have existed in the minds of New Englanders concerning Indian slavery. In 1644 the commissioners of the United Colonies meeting at New Haven decided, in light of the Indians' "proud affronts," "hostile practices," and "protectinge or rescuinge of offenders," that magistrates might "send some convenient strength of English and, . . . seise and bring away" Indians from any "plantation of Indians" which persisted in this practice and, if no satisfaction was forthcoming, could deliver the "Indians seased . . . either to serve or be shipped out and exchanged for Negroes."[10] Captivity and criminal justice seemed to mean the same thing, slavery.

It would be wrong to suppose that all the Puritans' preconceived ideas about freedom and bondage worked in the same direction. While the concepts of difference in religion and of captivity worked against Indians and Negroes, certain Scriptural injunctions and English pride in liberty told in the opposite direction. In Massachusetts the magistrates demonstrated that they were not about to tolerate glaring breaches of "the Law of God established in Israel" even when the victims were Negroes. In 1646 the authorities arrested two mariners, James Smith and Thomas Keyser, who had carried two Negroes directly from Africa and sold them in Massachusetts. What distressed the General Court was that the Negroes had been obtained during a raid on an African village and that this "haynos and crying sinn of man stealing" had transpired on the Lord's Day. The General Court decided to free the unfortunate victims and ship them back to Africa, though the death penalty for the crime (clearly mandatory in Scripture) was not imposed.[11] More quietly than

---

[9] Donnan, ed., *Documents of the Slave Trade*, III, 8.
[10] Nathaniel B. Shurtleff and David Pulsifer, eds., *Records of the Colony of New Plymouth in New England*, 12 vols. (Boston, 1855–61), IX, 70–71. See also Ebenezer Hazard, comp., *Historical Collections; Consisting of State Papers, and Other Authentic Documents* . . . , 2 vols. (Phila., 1792–94), II, 63–64.
[11] Donnan, ed., *Documents of the Slave Trade*, III, 6–9. Exodus 21:16: "And he that stealeth a man, and selleth him, or if he be found in his hand, he shall surely be put to death." Compare with Deuteronomy 24:7: "If a man be found stealing any of his brethren of the children of Israel, and maketh merchandise of him, or selleth him; then that thief shall die; and thou shalt put evil away from among you."

in this dramatic incident, Puritan authorities extended the same protections against maltreatment to Negroes and Indians as to white servants.

Only once before the eighteenth century was New England slavery challenged directly, and in that instance the tone was as much bafflement as indignation. This famous Rhode Island protest perhaps derived from a diffuse Christian equalitarianism which operated to extend the English presumption of liberty to non-Englishmen. The Rhode Island law of 1652 actually forbade enslavement.

> Whereas, there is a common course practised amongst English men to buy negers, to that end they may have them for service or slaves forever; for the preventigge of such practices among us, let it be ordered, that no blacke mankind or white being forced by covenent bond, or otherwise, to serve any man or his assighnes longer than ten yeares, or untill they come to bee twentie four yeares of age, if they bee taken in under fourteen, from the time of thier cominge within the liberties of this Collonie. And at the end or terme of ten yeares to sett them free, as the manner is with the English servants. And that man that will not let them goe free, or shall sell them away elsewhere, to that end that they may bee enslaved to others for a long time, hee or they shall forfeit to the Collonie forty pounds.

Perhaps it was Rhode Island's tolerance of religious diversity and relatively high standard of justice for the Indian which led to this attempt to prevent Englishmen from taking advantage of a different people.[12]

The law remained a dead letter. The need for labor, the example set in the West Indies, the condition of Negroes as "strangers," and their initial connection with captive Indians combined to override any hesitation about introducing Negro bond slavery into New England. Laws regulating the conduct of Negroes specifically did not appear until the 1690's.[13] From the first, however, there were scattered signs that Negroes were regarded as different from English people not merely in their status

---

[12] John R. Bartlett, ed., *Records of the Colony of Rhode Island and Providence Plantations, in New England*, 10 vols. (Providence, 1856–65), I, 243. The act passed during the Coddington secession; only two of the four towns, Providence and Warwick, were represented. Roger Williams was in England, and it seems likely Samuel Gorton pressed passage. The absence of the two southern towns (where trading in Negroes must have centered) suggests a strangely prophetic division of opinion. See Charles M. Andrews, *The Colonial Period of American History*, 4 vols. (New Haven, 1934–38), II, 29–30.

[13] *The Acts and Resolves, Public and Private, of the Province of the Massachusetts Bay* . . . , 21 vols. (Boston, 1869–1922), I, 130, 154, 156, 325, 327; J. Hammond Trumbull and Charles J. Hoadly, eds., *The Public Records of the Colony of Connecticut*, 15 vols. (Hartford, 1850–90), IV, 40. For treatment of servants see Lawrence W. Towner, "'A Fondness for Freedom': Servant Protest in Puritan Society," *Wm. and Mary Qtly.*, 3d ser., 19 (1962), 201–19.

as slaves. In 1639 Samuel Maverick of Noddles Island attempted, apparently rather clumsily, to breed two of his Negroes, or so an English visitor reported:

> *Mr. Maverick* was desirous to have a breed of Negroes, and therefore seeing [that his "Negro woman"] would not yield by persuasions to company with a Negro young man he had in his house; he commanded him will'd she nill'd she to go to bed to her which was no sooner done but she kickt him out again, this she took in high disdain beyond her slavery.

In 1652 the Massachusetts General Court ordered that Scotsmen, Indians, and Negroes should train with the English in the militia, but four years later abruptly excluded Negroes, as did Connecticut in 1660.[14] Evidently Negroes, even free Negroes, were regarded as distinct from the English. They were, in New England, where economic necessities were not sufficiently pressing to determine the decision, treated differently from other men.

## ENSLAVEMENT: VIRGINIA AND MARYLAND

In Virginia and Maryland the development of Negro slavery followed a very different course, for several reasons. Most obviously, geographic conditions and the intentions of the settlers quickly combined to produce a successful agricultural staple. The deep tidal rivers, the long growing season, the fertile soil, and the absence of strong communal spirit among the settlers opened the way. Ten years after settlers first landed at Jamestown they were on the way to proving, in the face of assertions to the contrary, that it was possible "to found an empire upon smoke." More than the miscellaneous productions of New England, tobacco required labor which was cheap but not temporary, mobile but not independent, and tireless rather than skilled. In the Chesapeake area more than anywhere to the northward, the shortage of labor and the abundance of land—the "frontier"—placed a premium on involuntary labor.

This need for labor played more directly upon these settlers' ideas about freedom and bondage than it did either in the West Indies or in New England. Perhaps it would be more accurate to say that settlers in Virginia (and in Maryland after settlement in 1634) made their decisions concerning Negroes while relatively virginal, relatively free from external influences and from firm preconceptions. Of all the important early English settlements, Virginia had the least contact with the Spanish,

---

[14] John Josselyn, *An Account of Two Voyages to New-England* . . . , 2d ed. (London, 1675), reprinted in Massachusetts Historical Society, *Collections*, 3d ser., 3 (1833), 231; Shurtleff, ed., *Records of Massachusetts Bay*, III, 268, 397, IV, Pt. I, 86, 257; *Acts and Resolves Mass.*, I, 130; Trumbull and Hoadly, eds., *Recs. Col. Conn.*, I, 349.

Portuguese, Dutch, and other English colonies. At the same time, the settlers of Virginia did not possess either the legal or Scriptural learning of the New England Puritans, whose conception of the just war had opened the way to the enslavement of Indians. Slavery in the tobacco colonies did not begin as an adjunct of captivity; in marked contrast to the Puritan response to the Pequot War the settlers of Virginia did *not* generally react to the Indian massacre of 1622 with propositions for taking captives and selling them as "slaves." It was perhaps a correct measure of the conceptual atmosphere in Virginia that there was only one such proposition after the 1622 disaster and that that one was defective in precision as to how exactly one treated captive Indians.[15]

In the absence, then, of these influences which obtained in other English colonies, slavery as it developed in Virginia and Maryland assumes a special interest and importance over and above the fact that Negro slavery was to become a vitally important institution there and, later, to the southward. In the tobacco colonies it is possible to watch Negro slavery *develop*, not pop up full-grown overnight, and it is therefore possible to trace, very imperfectly, the development of the shadowy, unexamined rationale which supported it. The concept of Negro slavery there was neither borrowed from foreigners, nor extracted from books, nor invented out of whole cloth, nor extrapolated from servitude, nor generated by English reaction to Negroes as such, nor necessitated by the exigencies of the New World. Not any one of these made the Negro a slave, but all.

In rough outline, slavery's development in the tobacco colonies seems to have undergone three stages. Negroes first arrived in 1619, only a few days late for the meeting of the first representative assembly in America. John Rolfe described the event with the utmost unconcern: "About the last of August came in a dutch man of warre that sold us twenty Negars."[16] Negroes continued to trickle in slowly for the next half century; one report in 1649 estimated that there were three hundred among Virginia's population of fifteen thousand—about 2 per cent.[17] Long before there were more appreciable numbers, the development of slavery had, so far as we can tell, shifted gears. Prior to about 1640, there is very little evidence to show how Negroes were treated—though we will need to return to those first twenty years in a moment. After 1640 there is mounting evidence that some Negroes were in fact being treated as slaves, at least that they were being held in hereditary lifetime service. This is to say that the twin essences of slavery—the two kinds of perpetuity— first become evident during the twenty years prior to the beginning of legal formulation. After 1660 slavery was written into statute law. Negroes began to flood into the two colonies at the end of the seven-

---

[15] [Susan M.] Kingsbury, ed. [*Records of the Virginia Company of London,* 4 vols. (Washington, 1906–35)], III, 672–73, 704–07.

[16] [Edward] Arber, ed. [*Travels and Works of Captain John Smith,* 2 vols. (Edinburgh, 1910)], II, 541.

[17] *A Perfect Description of Virginia* . . . (London, 1649), reprinted in Peter Force, ed., *Tracts* . . . , 4 vols. (N.Y., 1947), II, no. 8.

teenth century. In 1705 Virginia produced a codification of laws applying to slaves.

Concerning the first of these stages, there is only one major historical certainty, and unfortunately it is the sort which historians find hardest to bear. There simply is not enough evidence to indicate with any certainty whether Negroes were treated like white servants or not. At least we can be confident, therefore, that the two most common assertions about the first Negroes—that they were slaves and that they were servants —are *unfounded*, though not necessarily incorrect. And what of the positive evidence?

Some of the first group bore Spanish names and presumably had been baptized, which would mean they were at least nominally Christian, though of the Papist sort. They had been "sold" to the English; so had other Englishmen but not by the Dutch. Certainly these Negroes were not fully free, but many Englishmen were not. It can be said, though, that from the first in Virginia Negroes were set apart from white men by the word *Negroes*. The earliest Virginia census reports plainly distinguished Negroes from white men, often giving Negroes no personal name; in 1629 every commander of the several plantations was ordered to "take a generall muster of all the inhabitants men woemen and Children as well *Englishe* as Negroes."[18] A distinct name is not attached to a group unless it is regarded as distinct. It seems logical to suppose that this perception of the Negro as being distinct from the Englishman must have operated to debase his status rather than to raise it, for in the absence of countervailing social factors, the need for labor in the colonies usually told in the direction of non-freedom. There were few countervailing factors present, surely, in such instances as in 1629 when a group of Negroes were brought to Virginia freshly captured from a Portuguese vessel which had snatched them from Angola a few weeks earlier.[19] Given the context of English thought and experience . . . , it seems probable that the Negro's status was not ever the same as that accorded the white servant. But we do not know for sure.

When the first fragmentary evidence appears about 1640 it becomes clear that *some* Negroes in both Virginia and Maryland were serving for life and some Negro children inheriting the same obligation.[20] Not all Negroes, certainly, for Nathaniel Littleton had released a Negro named Anthony Longoe from all service whatsoever in 1635, and after the mid-1640's the court records show that other Negroes were incontestably free and were accumulating property of their own. At least one Negro freeman, Anthony Johnson, himself owned a Negro. Some Negroes served only terms of usual length, but others were held for terms far longer than

[18] Henry R. McIlwaine, ed., *Minutes of the Council and General Court of Colonial Virginia, 1622–1632, 1670–1676* (Richmond, 1924), 196. Lists and musters of 1624 and 1625 are in John C. Hotten, ed., *The Original Lists of Persons of Quality . . .* (N.Y., 1880), 169–265.

[19] Philip A. Bruce, *Economic History of Virginia in the Seventeenth Century . . .*, 2 vols. (N.Y., 1896), II, 73.

[20] Further details are in Winthrop D. Jordan, "Modern Tensions and the Origins of American Slavery," *Journal of Southern History*, 28 (1962), 18–30.

custom and statute permitted with white servants.[21] The first fairly clear indication that slavery was practiced in the tobacco colonies appears in 1639, when a Maryland statute declared that "all the Inhabitants of this Province being Christians (Slaves excepted) Shall have and enjoy all such rights liberties immunities priviledges and free customs within this Province as any naturall born subject of England." Another Maryland law passed the same year provided that "all persons being Christians (Slaves excepted)" over eighteen who were imported without indentures would serve for four years.[22] These laws make very little sense unless the term *slaves* meant Negroes and perhaps Indians.

The next year, 1640, the first definite indication of outright enslavement appears in Virginia. The General Court pronounced sentence on three servants who had been retaken after absconding to Maryland. Two of them, a Dutchman and a Scot, were ordered to serve their masters for one additional year and then the colony for three more, but "the third being a negro named John Punch shall serve his said master or his assigns for the time of his natural life here or else where." No white servant in any English colony, so far as is known, ever received a like sentence. Later the same month a Negro (possibly the same enterprising fellow) was again singled out from a group of recaptured runaways; six of the seven culprits were assigned additional time while the Negro was given none, presumably because he was already serving for life.[23]

After 1640, when surviving Virginia county court records began to mention Negroes, sales for life, often including any future progeny, were recorded in unmistakable language. In 1646 Francis Pott sold a Negro woman and boy to Stephen Charlton "to the use of him . . . forever." Similarly, six years later William Whittington sold to John Pott "one Negro girle named Jowan; aged about Ten yeares and with her Issue and produce duringe her (or either of them) for their Life tyme. And their Successors forever"; and a Maryland man in 1649 deeded two Negro men and a woman "and all their issue both male and Female." The executors of a York County estate in 1647 disposed of eight Negroes—four men, two women, and two children—to Captain John Chisman "to have hold occupy posesse and injoy and every one of the afforementioned Negroes forever."[24] The will of Rowland Burnham of "Rapahanocke," made in 1657, dispensed his considerable number of Negroes and white servants in language which clearly differentiated between the two by specifying that the whites were to serve for their "full terme of tyme"

---

[21] Susie M. Ames, *Studies of the Virginia Eastern Shore in the Seventeenth Century* (Richmond, 1940), 99; John H. Russell, *The Free Negro in Virginia, 1619–1865* (Baltimore, 1913), 23–39; and his "Colored Freemen as Slave Owners in Virginia," *Journal of Negro History*, 1 (1916), 234–37.

[22] *Archives Md.*, I, 41, 80, also 409, 453–54.

[23] "Decisions of the General Court," *Virginia Magazine of History and Biography*, 5 (1898), 236–37.

[24] For these four cases, Northampton County Deeds, Wills, etc., no. 4 (1651–54), 28 (misnumbered 29), 124, Virginia State Library, Richmond; *Archives Md.*, XLI, 261–62; York County Records, no. 2 (transcribed Wills and Deeds, 1645–49), 256–57, Va. State Lib.

and the Negroes "for ever."[25] Nothing in the will indicated that this distinction was exceptional or novel.

Further evidence that some Negroes were serving for life in this period lies in the prices paid for them. In many instances the valuations placed on Negroes (in estate inventories and bills of sale) were far higher than for white servants, even those servants with full terms yet to serve. Higher prices must have meant that Negroes were more highly valued because of their greater length of service. Negro women may have been especially prized, moreover, because their progeny could also be held perpetually. In 1643, for example, William Burdett's inventory listed eight servants, with the time each had still to serve, at valuations ranging from 400 to 1,100 pounds of tobacco, while a "very anntient" Negro was valued at 3,000 and an eight-year-old Negro girl at 2,000 pounds, with no time remaining indicated for either. In the late 1650's an inventory of Thomas Ludlow's estate evaluated a white servant with six years to serve at less than an elderly Negro man and only one half of a Negro woman.[26] Similarly, the labor owned by James Stone in 1648 was evaluated as follows:

|                                   | lb tobo |
|-----------------------------------|---------|
| Thomas Groves, 4 yeares to serve  | 1300    |
| Francis Bomley for 6 yeares       | 1500    |
| John Thackstone for 3 yeares      | 1300    |
| Susan Davis for 3 yeares          | 1000    |
| Emaniell a Negro man              | 2000    |
| Roger Stone 3 yeares              | 1300    |
| Mingo a Negro man                 | 2000[27] |

The 1655 inventory of Argoll Yeardley's estate provides clear evidence of a distinction between perpetual and limited service for Negroes. Under the heading "Servants" were listed "Towe Negro men, towe Negro women (their wifes) one Negro girle aged 15 yeares, Item One Negro girle aged about teen yeares and one Negro child aged about sixe moneths," valued at 12,000 pounds, and under the heading "Corne" were "Servants, towe men their tyme three months," valued at 300 pounds, and "one Negro boye ["about three yeares old"] (which by witness of his godfather) is to bee free att twenty foure yeares of age and then to have towe cowes given him," valued at 600 pounds.[28] Besides setting a higher value on Negroes, these inventories failed to indicate the number

[25] Lancaster County Loose Papers, Box of Wills, 1650–1719, Folder 1656–1659, Va. State Lib.

[26] Northampton County Orders, Deeds, Wills, etc., no. 2 (1640–45), 224; York County Deeds, Orders, Wills, etc. (1657–62), 108–09; in 1645 two Negro women and a boy sold for 5,500 lbs. of tobacco, York County Records, no. 2, 63; all Va. State Lib.

[27] York County Records, no. 2, 390, Va. State Lib.

[28] Nora Miller Turman and Mark C. Lewis, eds., "Inventory of the Estate of Argoll Yeardley of Northampton County, Virginia, in 1655," *Va. Mag. of Hist. and Biog.*, 70 (1962), 410–19.

of years they had still to serve, presumably because their service was for an unlimited time.

Where Negro women were involved, higher valuations probably reflected the facts that their issue were valuable and that they could be used for field work while white women generally were not. This latter discrimination between Negro and white women did not necessarily involve perpetual service, but it meant that Negroes were set apart in a way clearly not to their advantage. This was not the only instance in which Negroes were subjected to degrading distinctions not immediately and necessarily attached to the concept of slavery. Negroes were singled out for special treatment in several ways which suggest a generalized debasement of Negroes as a group. Significantly, the first indications of this debasement appeared at about the same time as the first indications of actual enslavement.

The distinction concerning field work is a case in point. It first appears on the written record in 1643, when Virginia almost pointedly endorsed it in a tax law. Previously, in 1629, tithable persons had been defined as "all those that worke in the ground of what qualitie or condition soever." The new law provided that *all* adult men were tithable and, in addition, *Negro* women. The same distinction was made twice again before 1660. Maryland adopted a similar policy beginning in 1654.[29] This official discrimination between Negro and other women was made by men who were accustomed to thinking of field work as being ordinarily the work of men rather than women. As John Hammond wrote in a 1656 tract defending the tobacco colonies, servant women were not put to work in the fields but in domestic employments, "yet som wenches that are nasty, and beastly and not fit to be so employed are put into the ground."[30] The essentially racial character of this discrimination stood out clearly in a law passed in 1668 at the time slavery was taking shape in the statute books:

> Whereas some doubts, have arisen whether negro women set free were still to be accompted tithable according to a former act, *It is declared by this grand assembly* that negro women, though permitted to enjoy their Freedome yet ought not in all respects to be admitted to a full fruition of the exemptions and impunities of the English, and are still lyable to payment of taxes.[31]

Virginia law set Negroes apart from all other groups in a second way by denying them the important right and obligation to bear arms. Few restraints could indicate more clearly the denial to Negroes of member-

[29] [William Waller] Hening, ed. [*The Statutes at Large Being a Collection of All the Laws of Virginia*, 13 vols. (Richmond, N.Y., and Phila., 1809–23)], I, 144, 242, 292, 454; *Archives Md.*, I, 342, II, 136, 399, 538–39, XIII, 538–39.
[30] John Hammond, *Leah and Rachel, or, the Two Fruitfull Sisters Virginia, and Mary-land: Their Present Condition, Impartially Stated and Related* . . . (London, 1656), 9.
[31] Hening, ed., *Statutes Va.*, II, 267.

ship in the white community. This first foreshadowing of the slave codes came in 1640, at just the time when other indications first appeared that Negroes were subject to special treatment.³²

Finally, an even more compelling sense of the separateness of Negroes was revealed in early reactions to sexual union between the races. Prior to 1660 the evidence concerning these reactions is equivocal, and it is not possible to tell whether repugnance for intermixture preceded legislative enactment of slavery. In 1630 an angry Virginia court sentenced "Hugh Davis to be soundly whipped, before an assembly of Negroes and others for abusing himself to the dishonor of God and shame of Christians, by defiling his body in lying with a negro," but it is possible that the "negro" may not have been female. With other instances of punishment for inter-racial union in the ensuing years, fornication rather than miscegenation may well have been the primary offense, though in 1651 a Maryland man sued someone who he claimed had said "that he had a black bastard in Virginia." (The court recognized the legitimacy of his complaint, but thought his claim for £20,000 sterling somewhat overvalued his reputation and awarded him 1500 pounds "of Tobacco and Cask.")³³ There may have been no racial feeling involved when in 1640 Robert Sweet, a gentleman, was compelled "to do penance in church according to laws of England, for getting a negroe woman with child and the woman whipt."³⁴ About 1650 a white man and a Negro woman were required to stand clad in white sheets before a congregation in lower Norfolk County for having had relations, but this punishment was sometimes used in cases of fornication between two whites.³⁵ A quarter century later in 1676, however, the

³² *Ibid.*, I, 226; for the same act in more detail, "Acts of General Assembly, Jan. 6, 1639–40," *Wm. and Mary Qtly.*, 2d ser., 4 (1924), 147. In Bermuda, always closely connected with Virginia, the first prohibition of weapons to Negroes came in 1623, only seven years after the first Negro landed. The 1623 law was the first law anywhere in English specifically dealing with Negroes. After stressing the inso-lence of Negroes secretly carrying "cudgells and other weapons and working tools, very dangerous and not meete to be suffered to be carried by such vassalls," it prohibited (in addition to arms) Negroes going abroad at night, trespassing on other people's lands, and trading in tobacco without permission of their masters. Unfortunately the evidence concerning lifetime service for Negroes is much less definite in the scanty Bermuda sources than in those for Maryland and Virginia; the first known incident suggestive of the practice might reasonably be placed anywhere from 1631 to 1656. Later evidence shows Bermuda's slavery and propor-tion of Negroes similar to Virginia's, and it seems unlikely that the two colonies' early experience was radically different. Henry C. Wilkinson, *The Adventures of Bermuda; A History of the Island from Its Discovery Until the Dissolution of the Somers Island Company in 1684* (London, 1933), 114; J. H. Lefroy, comp., *Memorials of the Discovery and Early Settlement of the Bermudas or Somers Islands, 1515–1685* . . . , 2 vols. (London, 1877–79), I, 308–09, 505, 526–27, 633, 645, II, 34–35, 70. But Negroes were to be armed at times of alarm (*ibid.*, II, 242, 366, 380 [1666–73]): Bermuda was exposed to foreign attack.

³³ Hening, ed., *Statutes Va.*, I, 146. (The term "negro woman" was in very common use.) *Archives Md.*, X, 114–15.

³⁴ Hening, ed., *Statutes Va.*, I, 552; McIlwaine, ed., *Minutes Council Va.*, 477.

³⁵ Bruce, *Economic History of Va.*, II, 110.

emergence of distaste for racial intermixture was unmistakable. A contemporary account of Bacon's Rebellion caustically described one of the ringleaders, Richard Lawrence, as a person who had eclipsed his learning and abilities "in the darke imbraces of a Blackamoore, his slave: And that in so fond a Maner, . . . to the noe meane Scandale and affrunt of all the Vottrisses in or about towne."[36]

Such condemnation was not confined to polemics. In the early 1660's when slavery was gaining statutory recognition, the assemblies acted with full-throated indignation against miscegenation. These acts aimed at more than merely avoiding confusion of status. In 1662 Virginia declared that "if any christian shall committ Fornication with a negro man or woman, hee or shee soe offending" should pay double the usual fine. (The next year Bermuda prohibited all sexual relations between whites and Negroes.) Two years later Maryland banned interracial marriages: "forasmuch as divers freeborne English women forgettfull of their free Condicion and to the disgrace of our Nation doe intermarry with Negro Slaves by which alsoe divers suites may arise touching the Issue of such woemen and a great damage doth befall the Masters of such Negros for prevention whereof for deterring such freeborne women from such shamefull Matches," strong language indeed if "divers suites" had been the only problem. A Maryland act of 1681 described marriages of white women with Negroes as, among other things, "always to the Satisfaccion of theire Lascivious and Lustfull desires, and to the disgrace not only of the English butt allso of many other Christian Nations." When Virginia finally prohibited all interracial liaisons in 1691, the Assembly vigorously denounced miscegenation and its fruits as "that abominable mixture and spurious issue."[37]

From the surviving evidence, it appears that outright enslavement and these other forms of debasement appeared at about the same time in Maryland and Virginia. Indications of perpetual service, the very nub of slavery, coincided with indications that English settlers discriminated against Negro women, withheld arms from Negroes, and—though the timing is far less certain—reacted unfavorably to interracial sexual union. The coincidence suggests a mutual relationship between slavery and unfavorable assessment of Negroes. Rather than slavery causing "prejudice," or vice versa, they seem rather to have generated each other. Both were, after all, twin aspects of a general debasement of the Negro. Slavery and "prejudice" may have been equally cause and effect, continuously reacting upon each other, dynamically joining hands to hustle the Negro down the road to complete degradation. Much more than with the other English

[36] "The History of Bacon's and Ingram's Rebellion, 1676," in Charles M. Andrews, ed., *Narratives of the Insurrections, 1675–1690* (N.Y., 1915), 96. Cf. the will of John Fenwick (1683), *Documents Relating to the Colonial, Revolutionary and Post-Revolutionary History of the State of New Jersey* . . . [New Jersey Archives], 1st ser. (Newark, etc., 1880–1949), XXIII, 162.

[37] Hening, ed., *Statutes Va.*, II, 170, III, 86–87; *Archives Md.*, I, 533–34, VII, 204; Lefroy, comp., *Memorials Bermudas*, II, 190 (a resolution, not a statute). Some evidence suggests miscegenation was not taken as seriously in seventeenth-century Bermuda as on the mainland: *ibid.*, I, 550, II, 30, 103, 141, 161, 228, 314.

colonies, where the enslavement of Negroes was to some extent a borrowed practice, the available evidence for Maryland and Virginia points to less borrowing and to this kind of process: a mutually interactive growth of slavery and unfavorable assessment, with no cause for either which did not cause the other as well. If slavery caused prejudice, then invidious distinctions concerning working in the fields, bearing arms, and sexual union should have appeared *after* slavery's firm establishment. If prejudice caused slavery, then one would expect to find these lesser discriminations preceding the greater discrimination of outright enslavement. Taken as a whole, the evidence reveals a process of debasement of which hereditary lifetime service was an important but not the only part.

White servants did not suffer this debasement. Rather, their position improved, partly for the reason that they were not Negroes. By the early 1660's white men were loudly protesting against being made "slaves" in terms which strongly suggest that they considered slavery not as wrong but as inapplicable to themselves. The father of a Maryland apprentice petitioned in 1663 that "he Craves that his daughter may not be made a Slave a tearme soe Scandalous that if admitted to be the Condicon or tytle of the Apprentices in this Province will be soe distructive as noe free borne Christians will ever be induced to come over servants."[38] An Irish youth complained to a Maryland court in 1661 that he had been kidnapped and forced to sign for fifteen years, that he had already served six and a half years and was now twenty-one, and that eight and a half more years of service was "contrary to the lawes of God and man that a Christian Subject should be made a Slave." (The jury blandly compromised the dispute by deciding that he should serve only until age twenty-one, but that he was now only nineteen.) Free Negro servants were generally increasingly less able to defend themselves against this insidious kind of encroachment.[39] Increasingly, white men were more clearly free because Negroes had become so clearly slave.

Certainly it was the case in Maryland and Virginia that the legal enactment of Negro slavery followed social practice, rather than vice versa, and also that the assemblies were slower than in other English colonies to declare how Negroes could or should be treated. These two patterns in themselves suggest that slavery was less a matter of previous conception or external example in Maryland and Virginia than elsewhere.

The Virginia Assembly first showed itself incontrovertibly aware that Negroes were not serving in the same manner as English servants in 1660 when it declared "that for the future no servant comeing into the country without indentures, of what christian nation soever, shall serve longer then those of our own country, of the like age." In 1661 the Assembly indirectly provided statutory recognition that some Negroes served for life: "That in case any English servant shall run away in company with any negroes who are incapable of making satisfaction by addition of

[38] *Archives Md.*, I, 464.
[39] *Ibid.*, XLI, 476–78, XLIX, 123–24. Compare the contemporary difficulties of a Negro servant: William P. Palmer *et al.*, eds., *Calendar of Virginia State Papers* . . . , 11 vols. (Richmond, 1875–93), I, 9–10.

time," he must serve for the Negroes' lost time as well as his own. Maryland enacted a closely similar law in 1663 (possibly modeled on Virginia's) and in the following year, on the initiative of the lower house, came out with the categorical declaration that Negroes were to serve "Durante Vita."[40] During the next twenty-odd years a succession of acts in both colonies defined with increasing precision what sorts of persons might be treated as slaves.[41] Other acts dealt with the growing problem of slave control, and especially after 1690 slavery began to assume its now familiar character as a complete deprivation of all rights.[42] As early as 1669 the Virginia Assembly unabashedly enacted a brutal law which showed where the logic of perpetual servitude was inevitably tending. Unruly servants could be chastened by sentences to additional terms, but "WHEREAS the only law in force for the punishment of refractory servants resisting their master, mistris or overseer cannot be inflicted upon negroes, nor the obstinacy of many of them by other then violent meanes supprest," if a slave "by the extremity of the correction should chance to die" his master was not to be adjudged guilty of felony "since it cannot be presumed that prepensed malice (which alone makes murther Felony) should induce any man to destroy his owne estate."[43] Virginia planters felt they acted out of mounting necessity: there were disturbances among slaves in several areas in the early 1670's.[44]

By about 1700 the slave ships began spilling forth their black cargoes in greater and greater numbers. By that time, racial slavery and the necessary police powers had been written into law. By that time, too, slavery had lost all resemblance to a perpetual and hereditary version of English servitude, though service for life still seemed to contemporaries its most essential feature.[45] In the last quarter of the seventeenth century the trend was to treat Negroes more like property and less like men, to send them to the fields at younger ages, to deny them automatic existence as inherent members of the community, to tighten the bonds on their personal and civil freedom, and correspondingly to loosen the traditional restraints on the master's freedom to deal with his human property as he saw fit.[46] In

---

[40] Hening, ed., *Statutes Va.*, I, 539, II, 26; *Archives Md.*, I, 449, 489, 526, 533–34. The "any negroes who are incapable" suggests explicit recognition that some were free, but in several sources the law as re-enacted the next year included a comma between "negroes" and "who," as did the Maryland act of 1663. See *The Lawes of Virginia Now in Force: Collected out of the Assembly Records . . .* (London, 1662), 59.

[41] Hening, ed., *Statutes Va.*, II, 170, 270, 283, 490–91, III, 137–40, 447–48; *Archives Md.*, VII, 203–05, XIII, 546–49, XXII, 551–52.

[42] Especially Hening, ed., *Statutes Va.*, II, 270–71, 481–82, 493, III, 86, 102–03; *Archives Md.*, XIII, 451–53, XIX, 167, 193, XXII, 546–48, XXVI, 254–56.

[43] Hening, ed., *Statutes Va.*, II, 270; compare law for servants, I, 538, II, 118.

[44] *Ibid.*, II, 299.

[45] Robert Beverley, *The History and Present State of Virginia*, ed. Louis B. Wright (Chapel Hill, 1947), 271–72.

[46] For illustration, Hening, ed., *Statutes Va.*, II, 288, 479–80 (Negro *children* taxed from age 12, white *boys* from 14), III, 102–03; *Archives Md.*, VII, 76 (county courts required to register births, marriages, burials of all "Except Negroes Indians and Molottos").

1705 Virginia gathered up the random statutes of a whole generation and baled them into a "slave code" which would not have been out of place in the nineteenth century.[47]

## ENSLAVEMENT: NEW YORK AND THE CAROLINAS

While the development of Negro slavery followed a different pattern in the tobacco colonies than in New England, and while, indeed, there were distinctive patterns of development in each of the English colonies, there were also factors which made for an underlying similarity in the slavery which emerged. The universal need for labor, the common cultural background and acceptance of English law, and the increasing contacts among the various colonies all worked eventually to make Negro slavery a roughly similar institution from one colony to the next, especially where economic and demographic conditions did not differ markedly. In each of the colonies which England acquired after the Restoration of Charles II, slavery developed in a distinctive fashion, yet by 1700 New York's slavery was much like New England's and Carolina's much like Virginia's.

In 1664, at about the time slavery was being written into law in the tobacco colonies, the English took over a Dutch colony which had been in existence for over forty years. New York was already a hodgepodge of nationalities—Dutch, English, Walloons, French, Negroes, and others. The status of Negroes under Dutch rule lies enshrouded in the same sort of fog which envelops the English colonies. It is clear, however, that the early and extensive Dutch experience in the international slave trade must have had some influence on the treatment of Negroes in New Amsterdam. There were Negroes in the colony as early as 1628. In that year (perhaps by coincidence) came the colony's first minister, the Reverend Jonas Michaëlius, who had previously been on the West African coast. Yet the first clearly indicated status of any Negroes was freedom, in the 1640's; indeed it remains possible that Negroes were not slaves in New Netherland until the 1650's.[48] In 1650 two sparring pamphleteers disagreed as to whether some Negroes were actually slaves.[49] Within a very few years, though, the records show indisputably that certain colonists were actively interested in the African slave trade. Possibly this interest may have been stimulated by Jacob Steendam, a poet who had resided at a Dutch fort in Guinea before coming to New Amsterdam about 1652.[50]

So far as their response to Negroes is concerned, the cultural background of Dutchmen was not very different from Englishmen. They shared a similar commercial orientation and large portions of religious and intellectual heritage. One of Steendam's poems, addressed to his legitimate mulatto son in Africa, lamented (in translation):

---

[47] Hening, ed., *Statutes Va.*, III, 447–62.

[48] Ellis Lawrence Raesly, *Portrait of New Netherland* (N.Y., 1945), 161–62, 201–02.

[49] J. Franklin Jameson, ed., *Narratives of New Netherland, 1609–1664* (N.Y., 1909), 329–30, 364.

[50] Raesly, *New Netherland*, 160–62, 269–84.

Since two bloods course within your veins,
Both Ham's and Japhet's intermingling;
One race forever doomed to serve,
The other bearing freedom's likeness.[51]

Certainly there is no evidence of friction concerning slave-owning when Englishmen took over the Dutch colony in 1664. The first English code (the "Duke's Laws"), adopted in 1665 by an assemblage composed largely of New Englanders who had migrated to Long Island and presided over by the newly appointed English governor, specifically recognized the practice of service for life in a proviso patterned after the Massachusetts Bay law of 1641.[52] During the remaining years of the century Negro slavery flourished, and New York eventually came to have a higher proportion of Negroes than any other colony north of Delaware. In New York more than anywhere else, Negro slavery seems to have grown Topsy fashion.

By contrast, in the Carolinas Negro slavery was deliberately planted and cultivated. In the 1660's a group of enterprising gentlemen in Barbados, well acquainted with perpetual slavery, proposed removal with some Negroes to the new mainland colony; their agreement with the proprietors in England clearly distinguished between white servants and Negro slaves. Barbadian influence remained strong in South Carolina throughout the seventeenth century. The establishment of slavery in the Carolinas was the more easily accomplished because after 1660 traditional controls over master-servant relations were breaking down rapidly in England itself. Since the state in England was abdicating some of its traditional responsibilities for overseeing the relationship between landlords and tenants at home, it felt little solicitude for the relations between planters and Negroes in far-off plantations. Besides, a good supply of sugar was enough to bury any questions about its production. It was a telling measure of how far this process had advanced in the English-speaking world that the famous Fundamental Constitutions of Carolina (1669) should have granted each freeman of the colony "absolute power and authority over his negro slaves, of what opinion or religion soever." English civil authorities offered little or no resistance to the growth of this new idea of uncontrolled personal dominion in the colonies; they knew perfectly well what was going on and were inclined to welcome it, for, as the Council for Foreign Plantations exclaimed happily in 1664, "Blacks [are] the most useful appurtenances of a Plantation and perpetual servants."[53] For their part, the planters demanded that their legislative assemblies regulate Negro slavery, but what they wanted and got was unfettering of their personal power over their slaves and the force of the

---

[51] *Ibid.*, 276. Quoted by permission of the Columbia University Press.
[52] Colonial Office Papers, 5/1142, f. 33v., Public Record Office, London.
[53] William L. Saunders, ed., *The Colonial Records of North Carolina*, 10 vols. (Raleigh, 1886–90), I, 41, 86–89, 204; William Noël Sainsbury, ed., "Virginia in 1662–1665," *Va. Mag. of Hist. and Biog.*, 18 (1910), 420.

state to back it up. In the 1690's the South Carolina Assembly borrowed from the already mature slave code of Barbados in an effort to maintain control over the growing masses of slaves.[54] Negroes were given virtually none of the protections accorded white servants, protections which were in fact designed to encourage immigration of white men to counterbalance the influx of Negroes. A requirement that "all slaves shall have convenient clothes, once every year," the only right accorded slaves by an act of 1690, was dropped in 1696. Perhaps it would have comforted slaves had they known that anyone killing a slave "cruelly or willfully" (death or dismemberment during punishment specifically excepted) was liable to a fine of five hundred pounds.[55] By the end of the seventeenth century the development of rice plantations and the Barbadian example had combined to yield in South Carolina the most rigorous deprivation of freedom to exist in institutionalized form anywhere in the English continental colonies.

## THE UN-ENGLISH: SCOTS, IRISH, AND INDIANS

In the minds of overseas Englishmen, slavery, the new tyranny, did not apply to any Europeans. Something about Negroes, and to lesser extent Indians, set them apart for drastic exploitation, oppression, and degradation. In order to discover why, it is useful to turn the problem inside out, to inquire why Englishmen in America did not treat any other peoples like Negroes. It is especially revealing to see how English settlers looked upon the Scotch (as they frequently called them) and the Irish, whom they often had opportunity and "reason" to enslave, and upon the Indians, whom they enslaved, though only, as it were, casually.

In the early years Englishmen treated the increasingly numerous settlers from other European countries, especially Scottish and Irish servants, with condescension and frequently with exploitive brutality. Englishmen seemed to regard their colonies as exclusively *English* preserves and to wish to protect English persons especially from the exploitation which inevitably accompanied settlement in the New World. In Barbados, for example, the assembly in 1661 denounced the kidnapping of youngsters for service in the colony in a law which applied only to "Children of the *English* Nation."[56] In 1650 Connecticut provided that debtors were not to "bee sould to any but of the English Nation."[57]

While Englishmen distinguished themselves from other peoples, they

---

[54] Conclusive evidence of Barbadian influence is in M. Eugene Sirmans, "The Legal Status of the Slave in South Carolina, 1670–1740," *Jour. Southern Hist.*, 28 (1962), 462–66.

[55] Thomas Cooper and David J. McCord, eds., *Statutes at Large of South Carolina*, 10 vols. (Columbia, 1836–41), VII, 343, 393 (1696 code misdated 1712).

[56] Hening, ed., *Statutes Va.*, I, 161; *Acts of Assembly, Passed in the Island of Barbadoes, from 1648, to 1718* (London, 1721), 22.

[57] Trumbull and Hoadly, eds., *Recs. Col. Conn.*, I, 510.

also distinguished *among* those different peoples who failed to be English. It seems almost as if Englishmen possessed a view of other peoples which placed the English nation at the center of widening concentric circles each of which contained a people more alien than the one inside it. On occasion these social distances felt by Englishmen may be gauged with considerable precision, as in the sequence employed by the Committee for Trade and Foreign Plantations in a query to the governor of Connecticut in 1680: "What number of English, Scotch, Irish or Forreigners have . . . come yearly to . . . your Corporation. And also, what Blacks and Slaves have been brought in." Sometimes the English sense of distance seems to have been based upon a scale of values which would be thought of today in terms of nationality. When the Leeward Islands encouraged immigration of foreign Protestants the Assembly stipulated that the number of such aliens "shall not exceed the One Fourth of *English, Scotch, Irish,* and *Cariole* [Creole] Subjects." Jamaica achieved a finer discrimination: the colony offered a bounty of £18 in time of war, £14 in peace, for importing English, Welsh, Scots, or residents of "*Jersey, Gernsey,* or *Man,*" and lower bounties of £15 and £12 for Irish. Maryland placed a discriminatory duty on Irish servants while Virginia did the same with all servants not born in England or Wales.[58]

At other times, though, the sense of foreignness seems to have been explicitly religious, as instanced by Lord William Willoughby's letter from Barbados in 1667: "We have more than a good many Irish amongst us, therefore I am for the down right Scott, who I am certain will fight without a crucifix about his neck."[59] It is scarcely surprising that hostility toward the numerous Irish servants should have been especially strong, for they were doubly damned as foreign and Papist. Already, for Englishmen in the seventeenth century, the Irish were a special case, and it required more than an ocean voyage to alter this perception. In the 1650's, while Cromwell was wielding the sword of Protestantism in Ireland and while Puritan factions held sway in Virginia, Maryland, and Bermuda, the Virginia Assembly assigned Irish servants arriving without indentures somewhat longer terms than other Europeans (the previous blanket act "being only [for] the benefitt of our own nation") and then extended this discrimination to "all aliens." With re-establishment of royal control in 1660 the assembly repealed these laws, terming them full of "rigour and inconvenience" and a discouragement to immigration of servants, and

---

58 *Ibid.*, III, 293 (an inquiry also sent other governors); *Acts of Assembly, Passed in the Charibbee Leeward Islands, from 1690, to 1730* (London, 1734), 127; *Acts of Assembly, Passed in the Island of Jamaica; From 1681, to 1737, Inclusive* (London, 1738), 100; also *Montserrat Code of Laws: from 1668, to 1788* (London, 1790), 19; Hening, ed., *Statutes Va.*, III, 193; Thomas Bacon, ed., *Laws of Maryland at Large, 1637–1763* (Annapolis, 1765), 1715, chap. xxxvi, 1717, chap. x, 1732, chap. xxii. The Maryland laws aimed at Irish Papists.

59 Willoughby, quoted in C. S. S. Higham, *The Development of the Leeward Islands Under the Restoration, 1660–1688; A Study of the Foundations of the Old Colonial System* (Cambridge, Eng., 1921), 170n.

declared with finality "that for the future no servant comeing into the country without indentures, of what christian nation soever, shall serve longer then those of our own country, of the like age."[60]

As time went on Englishmen began to absorb the idea that their settlements in America were not going to remain exclusively English preserves. In 1671 Virginia began encouraging naturalization of legal aliens, so that they might enjoy "all such liberties, priviledges, immunities whatsoever, as a naturall borne Englishman is capable of," and Maryland accomplished the same end with private naturalization acts that frequently included a potpourri of French, Dutch, Swiss, Swedes, and so forth.[61]

The necessity of peopling the colonies transformed the long-standing urge to discriminate among non-English peoples into a necessity. Which of the non-English were sufficiently different and foreign to warrant treating as "perpetual servants"? The need to answer this question did not mean, of course, that upon arrival in America the colonists immediately jettisoned their sense of distance from those persons they did not actually enslave. They discriminated against Welshmen and Scotsmen who, while admittedly "the best servants," were typically the servants of Englishmen. There was a considerably stronger tendency to discriminate against Papist Irishmen, those "worst" servants, but never to make slaves of them.[62] And here lay the crucial difference. Even the Scottish prisoners taken by Cromwell at Worcester and Dunbar—captives in a just war!—were never treated as slaves in England or the colonies. Certainly the lot of those sent to Barbados was miserable, but it was a different lot from the African slave's. In New England they were quickly accommodated to the prevailing labor system, which was servitude. As the Reverend Mr. Cotton of the Massachusetts Bay described the situation to Oliver Cromwell in 1651,

> The Scots, whom God delivered into you hand at Dunbarre, and whereof sundry were sent hither, we have been desirous (as we could) to make their yoke easy. Such as were sick of the scurvy or other diseases have not wanted physick and chyrurgery. They have not been sold for slaves to perpetuall servitude, but for 6 or 7 or 8 yeares, as we do our owne; and he that bought the most of them (I heare) buildeth houses for them, for every 4 an house, layeth some acres of ground thereto, which he giveth them as their owne, re-

[60] Hening, ed., *Statutes Va.*, I, 257, 411, 471, 538–39. In Barbados ca. 1660 there was apprehension concerning the "turbulent and dangerous" Irish. William Noël Sainsbury *et al.*, eds., *Calendar of State Papers, Colonial Series* (London, 1860–  ), *America and West Indies, 1574–1600*, 481, 483, 487.

[61] Hening, ed., *Statutes Va.*, II, 289–90, 464–65; for one of many in Maryland, *Archives Md.*, II, 205–06.

[62] The designations are a prominent planter's, quoted in Higham, *Development of the Leeward Islands*, 169, also 170n.

quiring 3 dayes in the weeke to worke for him (by turnes) and 4
dayes for themselves, and promisteth, as soone as they can repay
him the money he layed out for them, he will set them at liberty.[63]

Here was the nub: captive Scots were men "as our owne." Negroes were
not. They were almost hopelessly far from being of the English nation.
As the Bermuda legislature proclaimed in 1663, even such Negroes "as
count themselves Free because no p.ticler masters claymeth their services,
in our judgments are not Free to all nationall priviledges."[64]

    Indians too seemed radically different from Englishmen, far more so
than any Europeans. They were enslaved, like Negroes, and so fell on the
losing side of a crucial dividing line. It is easy to see why: whether considered in terms of complexion, religion, nationality, savagery, bestiality,
or geographical location, Indians were more like Negroes than like
Englishmen. Given this resemblance the essential problem becomes why
Indian slavery never became an important institution in the colonies. Why
did Indian slavery remain numerically insignificant and typically incidental in character? Why were Indian slaves valued at much lower prices
than Negroes? Why were Indians, as a kind of people, treated like
Negroes and yet at the same time very differently?
    Certain obvious factors made for important differentiations in the
minds of the English colonists. As was the case with first confrontations
in America and Africa, the different contexts of confrontation made
Englishmen more interested in converting and civilizing Indians than
Negroes. That this campaign in America too frequently degenerated into
military campaigns of extermination did nothing to eradicate the initial
distinction. Entirely apart from English intentions, the culture of the
American Indians probably meant that they were less readily enslavable
than Africans. By comparison, they were less used to settled agriculture,
and their own variety of slavery was probably even less similar to the
chattel slavery which Englishmen practiced in America than was the
domestic and political slavery of the West African cultures. But it was
the transformation of English intentions in the wilderness which counted
most heavily in the long run. The Bible and the treaty so often gave way
to the clash of flintlock and tomahawk. The colonists' perceptions of the
Indians came to be organized not only in pulpits and printshops but at
the bloody cutting edge of the English thrust into the Indians' lands.
Thus the most pressing and mundane circumstances worked to make
Indians seem very different from Negroes. In the early years especially,
Indians were in a position to mount murderous reprisals upon the English
settlers, while the few scattered Negroes were not. When English-Indian

---

[63] Boston, July 28, 1651, W. H. Whitmore and W. S. Appleton, eds., *Hutchinson
    Papers*, 2 vols. (Prince Society, *Publications* [Albany, 1865]), I, 264–65. For prison-
    ers to Barbados see [Abbot Emerson] Smith [*Colonists in Bondage: White Ser-
    vitude and Convict Labor in America, 1607–1776* (Chapel Hill, 1947)], 152–59.
[64] Lefroy, comp., *Memorials Bermudas*, II, 190–91.

relations did not turn upon sheer power they rested on diplomacy. In many instances the colonists took assiduous precautions to prevent abuse of Indians belonging to friendly tribes. Most of the Indians enslaved by the English had their own tribal enemies to thank. It became a common practice to ship Indian slaves to the West Indies, where they could be exchanged for slaves who had no compatriots lurking on the outskirts of English settlements.[65] In contrast, Negroes presented much less of a threat —at first.

Equally important, Negroes had to be dealt with as individuals— with supremely impartial anonymity, to be sure—rather than as nations. Englishmen wanted and had to live with their Negroes, as it were, side by side. Accordingly their impressions of Negroes were forged in the heat of continual, inescapable personal contacts. There were few pressures urging Englishmen to treat Indians as integral constituents in their society, which Negroes were whether Englishmen liked or not. At a distance the Indian could be viewed with greater detachment and his characteristics acknowledged and approached more coolly and more rationally. At a distance, too, Indians could retain the quality of nationality, a quality which Englishmen admired in themselves and expected in other peoples. Under contrasting circumstances in America, the Negro nations tended to become Negro people.

Here lay the rudiments of certain shadowy but persistent themes in what turned out to be a multi-racial nation. Americans came to impute to the braves of the Indian "nations" an ungovernable individuality (which was perhaps not merited in such exaggerated degree) and at the same time to impart to Negroes all the qualities of an eminently governable sub-nation, in which African tribal distinctions were assumed to be of no consequence and individuality unaspired to. More immediately, the two more primitive peoples rapidly came to serve as two fixed points from which English settlers could triangulate their own position in America; the separate meanings of *Indian* and *Negro* helped define the meaning of living in America. The Indian became for Americans a symbol of their American experience; it was no mere luck of the toss that placed the profile of an American Indian rather than an American Negro on the famous old five-cent piece. Confronting the Indian in America was a testing experience, common to all the colonies. Conquering the Indian symbolized and personified the conquest of the American difficulties, the surmounting of the wilderness. To push back the Indian was to prove the worth of one's own mission, to make straight in the desert a highway for civilization. With the Negro it was utterly different.

[65] Hening, ed., *Statutes Va.,* II, 299. A good study of Indian slavery is needed, but see Almon Wheeler Lauber, *Indian Slavery in Colonial Times Within the Present Limits of the United States* (N.Y., 1913). In 1627 some imported Carib Indians proved unsalable in Virginia and were turned over to the colony; the General Court decided that, since the Caribs had stolen goods, attempted murder, tried to run away to the Virginia Indians, and might prove the downfall of the whole colony, the best way to dispose of the problem was to hang them: McIlwaine, ed., *Minutes Council Va.,* 155.

## RACIAL SLAVERY: FROM REASONS TO RATIONALE

And *difference*, surely, was the indispensable key to the degradation of Negroes in English America. In scanning the problem of *why* Negroes were enslaved in America, certain constant elements in a complex situation can be readily, if roughly, identified. It may be taken as given that there would have been no enslavement without economic need, that is, without persistent demand for labor in underpopulated colonies. Of crucial importance, too, was the fact that for cultural reasons Negroes were relatively helpless in the face of European aggressiveness and technology. In themselves, however, these two elements will not explain the enslavement of Indians and Negroes. The pressing exigency in America was labor, and Irish and English servants were available. Most of them would have been helpless to ward off outright enslavement if their masters had thought themselves privileged and able to enslave them. As a group, though, masters did not think themselves so empowered. Only with Indians and Negroes did Englishmen attempt so radical a deprivation of liberty— which brings the matter abruptly to the most difficult and imponderable question of all: what was it about Indians and Negroes which set them apart, which rendered them *different* from Englishmen, which made them special candidates for degradation?

To ask such questions is to inquire into the *content* of English attitudes, and unfortunately there is little evidence with which to build an answer. It may be said, however, that the heathen condition of the Negroes seemed of considerable importance to English settlers in America —more so than to English voyagers upon the coasts of Africa—and that heathenism was associated in some settlers' minds with the condition of slavery.[66] This is not to say that the colonists enslaved Negroes because they were heathens. The most clear-cut positive trace of such reasoning was probably unique and certainly far from being a forceful statement: in 1660 John Hathorne declared, before a Massachusetts court in partial

[66] See . . . John C. Hurd, *The Law of Freedom and Bondage in the United States*, 2 vols. (Boston, 1858–62), I, 159–60; [Andrew] Horne, *The Mirror of Justices*, ed. [William C.] Robinson [Washington, 1903], 124; Marcus W. Jernegan, *Laboring and Dependent Classes in Colonial America, 1607–1783; Studies of the Economic, Educational, and Social Significance of Slaves, Servants, Apprentices, and Poor Folk* (Chicago, 1931), 24–26; Helen T. Catterall, ed., *Judicial Cases Concerning American Slavery and the Negro*, 5 vols. (Washington, 1926–37), I, 55n. Data in the following pages suggest this. The implication that slavery could last only during the heathen state is in Providence Company to Gov. Philip Bell, London, Apr. 20, 1635, Box 9, bundle: List no. 7, 2d portion, MS. relating to the Royal African Co. and Slavery matters, 43, Parish Transcripts, N.-Y. Hist. Soc.: ". . . a Groundless opinion that Christians may not lawfully keepe such persons in a state of Servitude during their strangeness from Christianity." In 1695 Gov. John Archdale of South Carolina prohibited sale of some Indians, captured by his own Indian allies, as slaves to the West Indies and freed them because they were Christians: John Archdale, *A New Description of That Fertile and Pleasant Province of Carolina* . . . (London, 1707), in Alexander S. Salley, Jr., ed., *Narratives of Early Carolina, 1650–1708* (N.Y., 1911), 300.

support of his contention that an Indian girl should not be compelled to return to her master, that "first the law is undeniable that the indian may have the same distribusion of Justice with our selves: ther is as I humbly conceive not the same argument as amongst the negroes[,] for the light of the gospell is begineing to appear amongst them—that is the indians."[67]

The importance and persistence of the tradition which attached slavery to heathenism did not become evident in any positive assertions that heathens might be enslaved. It was not until the period of legal establishment of slavery after 1660 that the tradition became manifest at all, and even then there was no effort to place heathenism and slavery on a one-for-one relationship. Virginia's second statutory definition of a slave (1682), for example, awkwardly attempted to rest enslavement on religious difference while excluding from possible enslavement all heathens who were not Indian or Negro.[68] Despite such logical difficulties, the old European equation of slavery and religious difference did not rapidly vanish in America, for it cropped up repeatedly after 1660 in assertions that slaves by becoming Christian did not automatically become free. By about the end of the seventeenth century, Maryland, New York, Virginia, North and South Carolina, and New Jersey had all passed laws reassuring masters that conversion of their slaves did not necessitate manumission.[69] These acts were passed in response to occasional pleas that Christianity created a claim to freedom and to much more frequent assertions by men interested in converting Negroes that nothing could be accomplished if masters thought their slaves were about to be snatched from them by meddling missionaries.[70] This decision that the slave's religious condition had no relevance to his status as a slave (the only one possible if an already valuable economic institution was to be retained) strongly suggests that heathenism was an important component in the colonists' initial reaction to Negroes early in the century.

---

[67] *Records and Files of the Quarterly Courts of Essex County Massachusetts, 1636–1683*, 8 vols. (Salem, 1911–21), II, 240–42.

[68] Hening, ed., *Statutes Va.*, II, 490–92.

[69] *Archives Md.*, I, 526, 533 (1664), II, 272; "Duke's Laws," C. O. 5/1142, f. 33v., P. R. O., a portion of the section of "Bondslavery" omitted from the standard New York printed sources which reads "And also provided that This Law shall not extend to sett at Liberty Any Negroe or Indian Servant who shall turne Christian after he shall have been bought by Any Person." (This unpublished Crown Copyright material is reproduced by permission of the Controller of H. M. Stationery Office.) *The Colonial Laws of New York from the Year 1664 to the Revolution . . .*, 5 vols. (Albany, 1894–96), I, 597–98 (1706); Hening, ed., *Statutes Va.*, II, 260 (1667); Saunders, ed., *Col. Recs. N.C.*, I, 204 (1670), II, 857; Cooper and McCord, eds., *Statutes S.C.*, VII, 343 (1691), 364–65; *Anno Regni Reginae Annae . . . Tertio; [The Acts Passed by the Second Assembly of New Jersey in December, 1704]* ([N.Y., 1704]), 20, an act which was disallowed for other reasons.

[70] For example, in 1652 a mulatto girl pleaded Christianity as the reason why she should not be "a perpetuall slave" (Lefroy, comp., *Memorials Bermudas*, II, 34–35, also 293–94), and in 1694 some Massachusetts ministers asked the governor and legislature to remove that "wel-knowne Discouragement" to conversion of slaves with a law denying that baptism necessitated freedom (*Acts and Resolves Mass.*, VII, 537).

Yet its importance can easily be overstressed. For one thing, some of the first Negroes in Virginia had been baptized before arrival. In the early years others were baptized in various colonies and became more than nominally Christian; a Negro woman joined the church in Dorchester, Massachusetts, as a full member in 1641.[71] With some Negroes becoming Christian and others not, there might have developed a caste differentiation along religious lines, yet there is no evidence to suggest that the colonists distinguished consistently between the Negroes they converted and those they did not. It was racial, not religious, slavery which developed in America.

Still, in the early years, the English settlers most frequently contrasted themselves with Negroes by the term *Christian*, though they also sometimes described themselves as *English;*[72] here the explicit religious distinction would seem to have lain at the core of English reaction. Yet the concept embodied by the term *Christian* embraced so much more meaning than was contained in specific doctrinal affirmations that it is scarcely possible to assume on the basis of this linguistic contrast that the colonists set Negroes apart because they were heathen. The historical experience of the English people in the sixteenth century had made for fusion of religion and nationality; the qualities of being English and Christian had become so inseparably blended that it seemed perfectly consistent to the Virginia Assembly in 1670 to declare that "noe negroe or Indian though baptised and enjoyned their owne Freedome shall be capable of any such purchase of christians, but yet not debarred from buying any of their owne nation." Similarly, an order of the Virginia Assembly in 1662 revealed a well-knit sense of self-identity of which Englishness and Christianity were interrelated parts: "METAPPEN a Powhatan Indian being sold for life time to one Elizabeth Short by the king of Wainoake Indians who had no power to sell him being of another nation, *it is ordered* that the said Indian be free, he speaking perfectly the English tongue and desiring baptism."[73]

From the first, then, vis-à-vis the Negro the concept embedded in the term *Christian* seems to have conveyed much of the idea and feeling of *we* as against *they:* to be Christian was to be civilized rather than barbarous, English rather than African, white rather than black. The term *Christian* itself proved to have remarkable elasticity, for by the end of the seventeenth century it was being used to define a species of slavery which had altogether lost any connection with explicit religious difference. In the Virginia code of 1705, for example, the term sounded much more like a definition of race than of religion:

> And for a further christian care and usage of all christian servants, *Be it also enacted, by the authority aforesaid, and it is hereby enacted,* That no negroes, mulattos, or Indians, although christians,

---

[71] Winthrop, *Journal*, ed. Hosmer, II, 26.

[72] These statements on prevailing word usage are based on a wide variety of sources, many of them cited in this chapter; some passages already quoted may serve to amplify the illustrations in the following paragraphs.

[73] Hening, ed., *Statutes Va.,* II, 281 (1670), 155 (1662).

> or Jews, Moors, Mahometans, or other infidels, shall, at any time, purchase any christian servant, nor any other, except of their own complexion, or such as are declared slaves by this act.

By this time "Christianity" had somehow become intimately and explicitly linked with "complexion." The 1705 statute declared

> that all servants imported and brought into this country, by sea or land, who were not christians in their native country (except Turks and Moors in amity with her majesty, and others that can make due proof of their being free in England, or any other christian country, before they were shipped, in order to transportation hither) shall be accounted and be slaves, and as such be here bought and sold notwithstanding a conversion to christianity afterwards.[74]

As late as 1753 the Virginia slave code anachronistically defined slavery in terms of religion when everyone knew that slavery had for generations been based on the racial and not the religious difference.[75]

It is worth making still closer scrutiny of the terminology which Englishmen employed when referring both to themselves and to the two peoples they enslaved, for this terminology affords the best single means of probing the content of their sense of difference. The terms *Indian* and *Negro* were both borrowed from the Hispanic languages, the one originally deriving from (mistaken) geographical locality and the other from human complexion. When referring to the Indians the English colonists either used that proper name or called them *savages*, a term which reflected primarily their view of Indians as uncivilized, or occasionally (in Maryland especially) *pagans*, which gave more explicit expression to the missionary urge. When they had reference to Indians the colonists occasionally spoke of themselves as *Christians* but after the early years almost always as *English*.

In significant contrast, the colonists referred to *Negroes* and by the eighteenth century to *blacks* and to *Africans*, but almost never to *Negro heathens* or *pagans* or *savages*. Most suggestive of all, there seems to have been something of a shift during the seventeenth century in the terminology which Englishmen in the colonies applied to themselves. From the initially most common term *Christian*, at mid-century there was a marked drift toward *English* and *free*. After about 1680, taking the colonies as a whole, a new term appeared—*white*.

So far as the weight of analysis may be imposed upon such terms, diminishing reliance upon *Christian* suggests a gradual muting of the specifically religious element in the Christian-Negro disjunction in favor

---

[74] *Ibid.*, III, 447–48 (1705), also 283, V, 547–48, VI, 356–57. Lingering aftereffects of the old concept cropped up as late as 1791, when *Negro* was still contradistinguished by *Christian*: Certificate of character of Negro Phill, Feb. 20, 1791, Character Certificates of Negroes, Papers of the Pennsylvania Abolition Society, Historical Society of Pennsylvania, Philadelphia.

[75] Hening, ed., *Statutes Va.*, I, 356–57.

of secular nationality: Negroes were, in 1667, "not in all respects to be admitted to a full fruition of the exemptions and impunities of the English."[76] As time went on, as some Negroes became assimilated to the English colonial culture, as more "raw Africans" arrived, and as increasing numbers of non-English Europeans were attracted to the colonies, the colonists turned increasingly to the striking physiognomic difference. By 1676 it was possible in Virginia to assail a man for "eclipsing" himself in the "darke imbraces of a Blackamoore" as if "Buty consisted all together in the Antiphety of Complections." In Maryland a revised law prohibiting miscegenation (1692) retained *white* and *English* but dropped the term *Christian*—a symptomatic modification. As early as 1664 a Bermuda statute (aimed, ironically, at protecting Negroes from brutal abandonment) required that the "last Master" of senile Negroes "provide for them such accommodations as shall be convenient for Creatures of that hue and colour untill their death." By the end of the seventeenth century dark complexion had become an independent rationale for enslavement: in 1709 Samuel Sewall noted in his diary that a "Spaniard" had petitioned the Massachusetts Council for freedom but that "Capt. Teat alledg'd that all of that Color were Slaves."[77] Here was a barrier between *we* and *they* which was visible and permanent: the Negro could not become a white man. Not, at least, as yet.

What had occurred was not a change in the justification of slavery from religion to race. No such justifications were made. There seems to have been, within the unarticulated concept of the Negro as a different sort of person, a subtle but highly significant shift in emphasis. Consciousness of the Negro's heathenism remained through the eighteenth and into the nineteenth and even the twentieth century, and an awareness, at very least, of his different appearance was present from the beginning. The shift was an alteration in emphasis within a single concept of difference rather than a development of a novel conceptualization. The amorphousness and subtlety of such a change is evident, for instance, in the famous tract, *The Negro's and Indians Advocate*, published in 1680 by the Rever-

[76] *Ibid.*, II, 267.
[77] "History of Bacon's and Ingram's Rebellion," Andrews, ed., *Narratives of the Insurrections*, 96; *Archives Md.*, XIII, 546–49; Lefroy, comp., *Memorials Bermudas*, II, 216; *Diary of Samuel Sewall, 1674–1729* (Mass. Hist. Soc., *Collections*, 5th ser. 5–7 [1878–82]), II, 248. In 1698 Gov. Francis Nicholson informed the Board of Trade that the "major part" of Negroes in Maryland spoke English: *Archives Md.*, XXIII, 499. For first use of "white" in statutes of various colonies, Bartlett, ed., *Recs. Col. R.I.*, I, 243 (1652); *Archives Md.*, VII, 204–05 (1681); Aaron Leaming and Jacob Spicer, eds., *The Grants, Concessions, and Original Constitutions of the Province of New Jersey . . .* , 2d ed. (Somerville, N.J., 1881), 236 (1683); *Col. Laws N.Y.*, I, 148 (1684); Cooper and McCord, eds., *Statutes S.C.*, VII, 343 (1691); Hening, ed., *Statutes Va.*, III, 86–87 (1691); *Acts of Assembly, Made and Enacted in the Bermuda or Summer-Islands, from 1690, to 1713–14* (London, 1719), 12–13 (1690 or 1691). West Indian assemblies used the term in the 1680's and 1690's, possibly earlier. Officials in England were using "whites" and "blacks" as early as 1670 in questionnaires to colonial governors: Hening, ed., *Statutes Va.*, II, 515; Trumbull and Hoadly, eds., *Recs. Col. Conn.*, III, 293.

end Morgan Godwyn. Baffled and frustrated by the disinterest of planters in converting their slaves, Godwyn declared at one point that "their *Complexion,* which being most obvious to the sight, by which the *Notion* of things doth seem to be most certainly conveyed to the Understanding, is apt to make no *slight* impressions upon rude Minds, already prepared to admit of any thing for *Truth* which shall make for Interest." Altering his emphasis a few pages later, Godwyn complained that "these two words, *Negro* and *Slave,*" are "by custom grown Homogeneous and Convertible; even as *Negro* and *Christian, Englishman* and *Heathen,* are by the like corrupt Custom and Partiality made Opposites."[78] Most arresting of all, throughout the colonies the terms *Christian, free, English,* and *white* were for many years employed indiscriminately as metonyms. A Maryland law of 1681 used all four terms in one short paragraph![79]

Whatever the limitations of terminology. as an index to thought and feeling, it seems likely that the colonists' initial sense of difference from the Negro was founded not on a single characteristic but on a congeries of qualities which, taken as a whole, seemed to set the Negro apart. Virtually every quality in the Negro invited pejorative feelings. What may have been his two most striking characteristics, his heathenism and his appearance, were probably prerequisite to his complete debasement. His heathenism alone could never have led to permanent enslavement since conversion easily wiped out that failing. If his appearance, his racial characteristics, meant nothing to the English settlers, it is difficult to see how slavery based on race ever emerged, how the concept of complexion as the mark of slavery ever entered the colonists' minds. Even if the colonists were most unfavorably struck by the Negro's color, though, blackness itself did not urge the complete debasement of slavery. Other qualities— the utter strangeness of his language, gestures, eating habits, and so on— certainly must have contributed to the colonists' sense that he was very different, perhaps disturbingly so. In Africa these qualities had for Englishmen added up to *savagery;* they were major components in that sense of *difference* which provided the mental margin absolutely requisite for placing the European on the deck of the slave ship and the Negro in the hold.

The available evidence (what little there is) suggests that for Englishmen settling in America, the specific religious difference was initially of greater importance than color, certainly of much greater relative importance than for the Englishmen who confronted Negroes in their African homeland. Perhaps Englishmen in Virginia, living uncomfortably close to nature under a hot sun and in almost daily contact with tawny Indians, found the Negro's color less arresting than they might have in other circumstances. Perhaps, too, these first Virginians sensed how inadequately they had reconstructed the institutions and practices of Christian piety in the wilderness; they would perhaps appear less as failures to themselves in this respect if compared to persons who as Christians were *totally* defective. In this connection they may be compared to their brethren in

---

[78] Godwyn, *The Negro's and Indians Advocate,* 20, 36.
[79] *Archives Md.,* VII, 204.

New England, where godliness appeared (at first) triumphantly to hold full sway; in New England there was distinctly less contrasting of Negroes on the basis of the religious disjunction and much more militant discussion of just wars. Perhaps, though, the Jamestown settlers were told in 1619 by the Dutch shipmaster that these "negars" were heathens and could be treated as such. We do not know. The available data will not bear all the weight that the really crucial questions impose.

Of course once the cycle of degradation was fully under way, once slavery and racial discrimination were completely linked together, once the engine of oppression was in full operation, then there is no need to plead *ignoramus*. By the end of the seventeenth century in all the colonies of the English empire there was chattel racial slavery of a kind which would have seemed familiar to men living in the nineteenth century. No Elizabethan Englishman would have found it familiar, though certain strands of thought and feeling in Elizabethan England had intertwined with reports about the Spanish and Portuguese to engender a willingness on the part of English settlers in the New World to treat some men as suitable for private exploitation. During the seventeenth century New World conditions had exploited this predisposition and vastly enlarged it, so much so that English colonials of the eighteenth century were faced with full-blown slavery—something they thought of not as an institution but as a host of ever present problems, dangers, and opportunities.

# The Economic and Social Influence

# of the

# Indentured Servant

## MARCUS W. JERNEGAN

Though African slavery was to become the most important form of unfree labor in North America in the eighteenth and nineteenth centuries, during the first hundred years of English colonization the labor force was made up primarily of indentured servants from England— men, women, and children who sold themselves into temporary bondage in return for passage to the New World. It has been recently estimated that from one-half to three-fourths of the immigrants to the English colonies in the seventeenth century fit into this category.

In view of the many hazards faced by New World settlers, the reluctance of prosperous English tradesmen or craftsmen to journey to North America is understandable. The three thousand miles that separated it from England, the strangeness of the land, and the danger of conflict with the Indians made the attraction of the New World slight for those with any degree of comfort in the old. Apart from a few daring speculators, most of the prosperous immigrants were men seeking the freedom to practice Puritan or other non-Anglican religions. Most of these immigrants settled in New England and in Pennsylvania.

There was, however, a great demand for new population in the New World. Laborers were needed to grow food for the colonists and thus to allow the development of ordinary commerce. Moreover, additional manpower was needed to defend the settlements against increasingly hostile Indians as well as against the French and the Spanish.

Fortunately for the development of the colonies, several sources of labor were available. First, there was a growing surplus of population in England. Farmland, which had hitherto been divided into individually owned strips and farmed communally, was increasingly consolidated into large tracts of land, thereby forcing the peasants either to become tenant farmers or to look for new means of livelihood. Industrialization, which might have absorbed these landless peasants, was more than a century away, and city life held little promise for them. Many turned to indentured servitude as a solution to their problems, to the relief of both England and the colonies.

Other servants came to the colonies as the result of the civil wars in the British Isles during the seventeenth century. James I, Oliver Cromwell, and the later Stuart kings sent Scottish and Irish prisoners to the colonies—chiefly to the West Indies but also to the North American mainland.

In the following essay, Marcus W. Jernegan, late professor of history at the University of Chicago and a pioneer in the study of colonial labor, describes still other sources of the dependent labor class that grew up in the New World. In addition, he offers a comparison of the living conditions of the immigrants before they left England with those that awaited them in the New World.

Except during brief periods of recession, the shortage of labor in the colonies and then in the United States continued until the enormous mid-nineteenth-century influx of poor Irish and German immigrants. Skilled labor was always in short supply, and despite various attempts by legislative bodies to set maximum wages, craftsmen were always among the most favored of immigrants.

---

Could we draw the curtain which conceals the life of prehistoric people, we should see that the servant problem is as old as the human race. Indeed, if it were possible for extremes to meet, cave-dwellers and denizens of twentieth-century skyscrapers would doubtless converse sympathetically on this never-ending problem. Its existence is due to the universal desire of man to use the strength of others for his own profit and pleasure—an unchangeable trait of human nature.

During the colonial period of our history, service was performed in the main by two classes—the Negro slave and the indentured white servant.[1] The white servant, a semi-slave, was more important in the seven-

[1] . . . The more important studies of the indentured servant system are those by James C. Ballagh, "White Servitude in the Colony of Virginia," in *Johns Hopkins Studies*, etc. (Ser. X); E. I. McCormac, "White Servitude in Maryland," in *J. H. Studies* (Ser. XXII); J. S. Bassett, "Slavery and Servitude in North Carolina," in *J. H. Studies* (Ser. XIV); E. McCrady, "Slavery in South Carolina," in *Report Amer. Hist. Assoc., 1895*; K. F. Geiser, *Redemptioners and Indentured Servants in the Colony and Commonwealth of Pennsylvania* (New Haven, 1901); Frank R. Diffenderfer, *German Immigration into Pennsylvania* (Lancaster, 1900); and C. A. Herrick, *White Servitude in Pennsylvania* (Philadelphia, 1926). A short account is in P. A. Bruce, *Econ. Hist. of Va. in the Seventeenth Cent.*, Vol. I, chap. ix; Vol. II, chap. x.

"The Economic and Social Influence of the Indentured Servant." From Marcus W. Jernegan, *Laboring and Dependent Classes in Colonial America, 1607–1783* (Chicago: The University of Chicago Press, 1931), pp. 45–56. First published in *Harper's Monthly Magazine* (October 1913) under the title "A Forgotten Slavery of Colonial Days." Reprinted by permission.

teenth century than even the Negro slave, in respect to both numbers and economic significance. Perhaps the most pressing of the early needs of the colonists was for a certain and adequate supply of labor. It was the white servants who supplied this demand and made possible a rapid economic development, particularly of the middle and southern colonies. In 1683 there were twelve thousand of these semi-slaves in Virginia, composing about one-sixth of the population, while nearly two-thirds of the immigrants to Pennsylvania during the eighteenth century were white servants. Every other colony made greater or less use of them, and it is likely that more than a quarter of a million persons were of this class during the colonial period.[2]

Such a widespread and important institution has great significance for the social and economic history of Europe and America in the seventeenth and eighteenth centuries. Moreover, the story is full of human interest because of methods used to supply the demand, similar to methods in the slave-trade: the classes of people from which some servants were drawn—convicts, paupers, and dissolute persons of every type; the stormy life of many servants and the troublesome moral and social problems which their presence engendered, such as intermarriage with Negro slaves; the runaway criminal servants, and their influence on moral standards and on other phases of life in the colonies.

White servitude developed rapidly because of favorable conditions— a large demand for servants coupled with a large supply. The economic theory of European states in the seventeenth century called for a large population in their colonies, in order that trade and commerce might develop rapidly. The colonists were to supply food and raw materials, and the home country was to develop manufactures. Means, therefore, must be devised, first, to attract settlers who would develop the economic resources of the colonies, and, second, to provide them with an adequate supply of labor. There were vast areas of rich virgin lands, which, in the southern and middle colonies, were usually granted in a manner to promote rapid increase of population and extension of cultivated tracts. This method was known as the "head-right" system. Anyone emigrating was rewarded with a gift of land—about a hundred and fifty acres. Since labor was needed to clear and work this land, anyone importing a servant was entitled to an additional allotment, a "head right." To induce laborers to emigrate, a similar allotment was promised to them after each had served a term of years as a servant. Thus free land solved the two most pressing problems mentioned above.

Fortunately, the enormous demand for white servants came when economic conditions had created a large supply. In the sixteenth century, English agriculture was giving way to sheep-raising, so that a few herders often took the place of many farm laborers. As a result, the unemployed, the poor, and the criminal classes increased rapidly. Justices, who were landowners, had the power to fix the maximum wages of farm laborers. Sometimes they made them very low, hardly a shilling a day; for the lower the wage the greater the profits of the tenant farmer, and, therefore,

[2] For numbers see estimates in books listed above, especially Bruce, *op. cit.*, I, 610, and Geiser, *op. cit.*, p. 41, for estimate of 60,000 servants in Pennsylvania in 1754.

the greater his ability to pay higher rents demanded by the landowner. Thus, while wages remained practically stationary, wheat multiplied in price nearly four times in this period, 1500–1600. In other words, a man worked forty weeks in 1600 for as much food as he received in 1500 by working ten weeks. To prevent scarcity of farm laborers, the statute of apprentices (1562) forbade anyone below the rank of a yeoman to withdraw from agricultural pursuits to be apprenticed to a trade. Moreover, the poor laws passed in this period compelled each parish to support its poor, and provided penalties for vagrancy. Thus the farm laborer had no chance to better himself. Conditions were almost beyond description, and in dear years people perished from famine. Sheffield in 1615, with a population of 2,207, had 725 relying on charity, 37.8 per cent of the population. As a result, the colonies were regarded as a convenient dumping ground for undesirable citizens. Velasco, the Spanish minister in England, wrote his sovereign, 1611, "Their principal reason for colonizing these parts is to give an outlet to so many idle, wretched people as they have in England, and thus prevent the dangers that might be feared of them."

It is evident that if this surplus population could be transferred to the American colonies, both the mother country and the colonists would profit. One of the earliest proposals was made by Sir George Peckham, 1582. He declared that there were such great numbers living in penury and want that they might be willing to "hazard their lives and serve one year for meat, drinke, and apparell only without wages, in hope thereby to amend their estates."[3] It was natural for men and women, in order to secure free transportation to America, to bind themselves by written contract, called an indenture, to serve some individual for a term of years.

There were three main classes of servants.[4] One who entered into such a contract with an agent, often the shipmaster, was called an indentured servant. The shipmaster reimbursed himself, on arrival in America, by selling the time of the servant to the highest bidder. The second class included the "redemptioners," or "free-willers." They signed no contract beforehand, but were given transportation by the shipmaster with the understanding that on arrival they were to have a few days to indenture themselves to someone to pay for their passage. Failing this, the shipmaster could sell them himself. The free-willer then was at a great disadvantage. He had to bargain in competition with many others, and was so much at the mercy of the buyer or shipmaster that laws were passed by several colonies limiting his time of service and defining his rights.

The third class consisted of those forced into servitude, such as convicts,[5] felons, vagrants, and dissolute persons, and those kidnaped or "spirited" away by the so-called "spirits" or "crimps." Convicts were often granted royal pardon on condition of being transported. For ex-

[3] Richard Hakluyt, *Voyages, Navigations,* etc., III (London, 1599), 167–81.
[4] See references, n. 1, and Hugh Jones, *Present State of Virginia* (Sabin reprint, 1865), pp. 53–54.
[5] J. D. Butler, "British Convicts Shipped to American Colonies" in *Amer. Hist. Rev.,* II, 12–34, and references.

ample, Charles I, in 1635, gave orders to the sheriff of London to deliver to Captain Thomas Hill or Captain Richard Carleton nine female convicts for removal to Virginia, to be sold as servants. At an early date judges imposed penalties of transportation on convicted criminals and others. Thus Narcissus Luttrell notes in his diary, November 17, 1692, that the magistrates had ordered on board a ship lying at Leith, bound for Virginia, fifty lewd women out of the house of correction and thirty others who walked the streets at night. An act of Parliament in 1717[6] gave judges still greater power by allowing them to order the transportation of convicts for seven years, known as "His Majesty's seven-year passengers," and, in case the penalty for the crime was death, for fourteen years. Those agreeing to transport convicts could sell them as servants. From London prisons, especially Newgate and the Old Bailey, large numbers were sent forth, the latter alone supplying not far from 10,000 between 1717 and 1775. Scharf, the historian of Maryland, declares that 20,000 felons were imported into that colony before the Revolution. At least nine of the colonies are known to have received felons as servants, so that the total number sent was not far from 50,000.[7] Lists of felons ordered transported were often printed in the *Gentleman's Magazine;*[8] one of May, 1747, numbering 887. Remembering this, perhaps, Dr. Johnson said in 1769, "Sir, they are a race of convicts, and ought to be content with anything we may allow them short of hanging."[9]

The colonists became alarmed as early as 1670.[10] At that date Virginia passed an act prohibiting the importation of convicts. The preamble speaks "of the great nombers of felons and other desperate villaines sent hither from the several prisons of England." Later, communications which ap-

---

[6] For regulation of traffic by King and Parliament see E. D. Collins, "Studies in the Colonial Policy of England, 1672–1680," in *Rpt. Amer. Hist. Assoc., 1900,* I, 146–48. See also *Acts of the Privy Council, Colonial,* I, 10–12, 56, 370–71; *Statutes of the Realm,* V (1662), 402, 405; (1679) p. 937; VII (1696), 274; Danby Pickering, *Statutes at Large,* XIII (1717), 471–75; XIV (1719), 292–95. See nn. 10 and 14.

[7] Butler, *op. cit.,* 29, and J. T. Scharf, *Hist. of Md.,* I, 371. See references in n. 1, especially McCormac, chap. viii, "Convicts." See nn. 10–18.

[8] *Gentleman's Magazine,* XVII, 246. In 1731 "upwards of 100 convicts remained to be transported to America" (*ibid.,* I, 224). See also *ibid.,* XXXII (1762), 92. In 1732, 68 men and 50 women, "felons convict," were carried from Newgate to Black Fryars to be shipped for transportation to Virginia (*London Magazine,* I, 368).

[9] *Life of Samuel Johnson* by Boswell (ed. by Hill), II, 302.

[10] W. W. Hening, *Statutes of Virginia,* II (1670), 509–10. H. R. McIlwaine, *Minutes of the Council of the General Court of Virginia,* 209–10: "We apparently lose our reputation, whilest we are believed to be a place only fitt to receive such base and lewd persons." For action on a case involving the importation of ten "jailbirds" see Bruce, *op. cit.,* I, 605–06. For a letter from Virginia to the Privy Council complaining of the grave dangers of importing felons, see *Acts of the Privy Council, Colo.,* I, 553. An order in Council provided that after January 20, 1671, no more felons should be sent to Virginia, but the order was disregarded (*Acts of the Privy Council, Colo.,* I, 553; H. R. McIlwaine, *op. cit.,* 252). In *Acts of the Privy Council,* I (1678), 788, is an order for 52 Scotch convicts to be transported to Virginia. See also *Pa. Colo. Recs.,* II (1728), 342. See nn. 6 and 14.

peared in the newspapers show great indignation. One writer speaks of the practice as a "vile importation" and comments particularly on the bad moral effects of such persons.[11] Even at an earlier date Lord Bacon had commented on the injustice and fallacy of this policy as follows: "It is a shameful and unblessed thing to take the scum of people and wicked, condemned men to be the people with whom you plant."[12] And Benjamin Franklin, in reply to the arguments of British authorities that it was necessary to get rid of convicts, asked whether Americans for the same reason would be justified in sending their rattlesnakes to England![13] For a brief period Great Britain listened to the complaints of the colonists, confirmed the Virginia Act of 1670, and made it apply to other colonies. But in 1717 Parliament in effect repealed it by the act of that date mentioned above,[14] and, throughout the eighteenth century, convicts were a never-failing source of supply for white servants. In this connection it has been suggested that American genealogists in search of missing data to complete their family tree would find a rich mine of unexplored material in the

[11] *Md. Gaz.*, July 30, 1767. *American Weekly Mercury* (Pa.), October 29, 1720, and February 7, 1721. Compare the lament in *ibid.*, February 14, 1721, that these "promising" plantations in America "cannot be ordered to be better populated than by such absolute villains and loose women, as these proved to be by their wretched lives and criminal actions, and if they settle anywhere in these parts can only by a natural consequence leave bad seeds amongst us." Compare also the *Va. Gaz.*, May 24, 1751, "When we see our papers filled continually with accounts of the most audacious Robberies, the most cruel Murders, and infinite other Villanies perpetuated by Convicts transported from Europe, what melancholy and what terrible Reflections must it occasion. . . . These are some of the Favours Britain, Thou art called Mother Country; but what good Mother ever sent thieves and villains to accompany her children; to corrupt with their infectious vices and to murder the rest."

[12] Alexander Brown, *The Genesis of the U.S.*, I, 456.

[13] This is found in the communication signed "Americus" attributed to Franklin, *Pa. Gaz.*, May 24, 1751, in Smyth, *Writings of Franklin*, III, 45–48. See letter of Franklin to Peter Colinson, May 9, 1753. He charges that shipmasters were taking felons from German jails for the sake of profits. Franklin, *Works* (Bigelow ed.), II, 299. Franklin wrote the *London Chronicle* (1769), "Their emptying their jails into our settlements, is an insult and a contempt, the cruelest that ever one people offered to another" (*ibid.*, IV, 255). In another letter to the same magazine he lists the acts for sending criminals to America as one of the causes of discontent (*ibid.*, IV [1768], 108).

[14] See nn. 6 and 10. Many acts were passed by the colonial assemblies levying heavy duties on convicts imported, but these were disallowed. See J. C. Hurd, *Law of Slavery and Bondage*, Vol. I. Compare *Archives of Md.*, II (1676), 540–41; *Pa. Statutes at Large*, III (1722), 264; XXII, 560. See *Cal. St. Pa., Colo.*, XV, 666; XVII, 347. Proprietors vetoed acts of this sort because [they were] against English law. Calvert's "Letter to the Maryland Assembly" is in *Archives of Md.*, XXXV (1724), 212. See also *ibid*, XXXI (1756), 118. For a case of disallowance see *Acts of the Privy Council, Colo.*, V, 163, and *Pa. Colo. Recs.*, V, 499. The Virginia act of 1670 (Hening, *op. cit.*, II, 509) was confirmed by the Privy Council (*Acts*, etc., I [1671] 553) but violated nevertheless and, finally, the act of Parliament in 1717 made legal again the transportation of convicts to the colonies (see n. 6).

archives of Newgate and Old Bailey, the latter filling 110 manuscript volumes![15]

The reasons for sending so many convicts were several. It is obvious why Great Britain was particularly anxious to rid herself of this class of her population. Criminals were not only unproductive but entailed a great expense on the country. Economists urged their transportation, while others argued that in a new country many criminals would forsake their old habits and become good citizens.[16] Some of the colonists were certainly not averse to convicts as servants, since their term of service was longer. The committee of trade for New York even petitioned the authorities, 1693, to send them all the prisoners who were to be transported from Newgate.[17] It should be remembered, too, that the word "felon" in the seventeenth and eighteenth centuries conveyed a different meaning from that at present. The penal code of England in 1600 provided a death penalty for hundreds of offenses, many of which were of a trivial nature,[18] and even just before the American Revolution Blackstone states that there were some one hundred and fifty capital crimes. Thus many persons called "felons" were less objectionable as servants than might be supposed, and there was good reason to expect that a number would become respectable when transported.[19]

One of the most interesting sources of supply was kidnaping.[20] The profits gained by such practices were so great that this developed as a regular business in London and seaport towns like Bristol. "Spirits" would pounce on all classes of persons and entice them on board ships bound for the colonies, and even children were induced to go by offers of sweetmeats. The county court records of Middlesex[21] give evidence of this practice. A record for November 7, 1655, states that Dorothy Perkins accuses Christian Chacrett, alias Sacrett, "for a Spirit, one that taketh upp men and women and children and sells them on a shipp to bee conveyed beyond the sea, having entised and inveagled one Edward Furnifull and Anne his wife with her infant to the waterside and put them aboard the shipp called *The Planter* to be conveyed to Virginia." Parliament passed an act in 1671 providing a death penalty for this crime.[22]

Analogous to the spirits were the "newlanders," or "soul-sellers." The great German immigration to America in the eighteenth century de-

---

[15] Butler, *op. cit.*
[16] Hugh Jones, *op. cit.*, pp. 53–54.
[17] *Doc. Rel. Colo. Hist.*, *N.Y.*, IV, 31. Convicts were wanted for military service. See also *Cal. St. Pa.*, *Colo.*, XV, 559; *Archives of Md.*, XXXV, 212; William Eddis, *Letters from America*, etc. (London, 1792), pp. 69–70.
[18] A man was convicted of stealing a horse and sentenced to be transported to Virginia or Bermuda (*Acts of the Privy Council, Colo.*, I [1662] 56).
[19] Political prisoners were also called criminals. Compare Bruce, *op. cit.*, I, 608.
[20] On "spiriting" and kidnaping see Butler, *op. cit.*, pp. 17–19. Verney papers in *Camden Society*, LVI, 160–62; Eddis, *Letters from America*, p. 68. *Va. Mag. of Hist.*, VI, 231 (Children); *Middlesex County Recs.* (J. C. Jeafferson ed.), III, 337.
[21] *Ibid.*, III, 337.
[22] The evils are stated in a Bristol report (*Cal. St. Pa.*, *Colo.*, 1661–68, p. 220).

veloped this class of agents, who traveled up and down the Rhine Valley, persuading peasants to sell their belongings and migrate to the colonies. They pretended that they were rich merchants from Philadelphia, dressed in costly clothes, and wore wigs and ruffles. They would seek acquaintance with a merchant in Holland and agree with him upon a sum for every person persuaded to remove. They described Pennsylvania as a land of Elysian fields flowing with milk and honey, where gold and silver could be picked up on the hills, and servants could become independent and live like noblemen. The simple German peasant would often sell his belongings and trust himself to the mercy of the soul-seller. Many were forced to become servants by indenture, because the excessive charges imposed for transportation from the Rhine Valley to the port of departure used up their small capital.[23]

The voyage over often repeated the horrors of the famous "middle passage" of slavery fame. An average cargo was three hundred, but the shipmaster, for greater profit, would sometimes crowd as many as six hundred into a small vessel. Picture to yourself several hundred people of all ages with only six feet by two feet allotted between decks for one adult person, with no privacy whatever, wearing the same clothing for the whole voyage—from four weeks to four months or even more—and often lying flat for whole days at a time when the ship was tossed by terrific storms. Imagine the vile atmosphere in an unventilated space containing hundreds of people, many ill with all manner of contagious diseases, living and dead side by side, without medical attendance, moaning and shrieking, praying and crying, and perhaps crazed by famine and thirst.[24] John Harrower, an indentured servant, describing in his diary a scene between decks during a storm, says, "There was some sleeping, some daming, some blasting their leggs and thighs, some their liver, lungs, lights, and eyes, and for to make the scene the odder, some curs'd Father, Mother, Sister, Brother." When food ran short it was doled out at the rate of three ounces of bread a day.[25] Mittelberger, an eyewitness, says that spoiled biscuit were given the passengers, "dirty and full of red worms and spiders' nests." When such vile stuff called food was lacking, rats and mice were eaten.[26]

The mortality under such circumstances was tremendous, sometimes more than half of the passengers dying of hunger and privation. Children from one to seven rarely survived. Mittelberger says he saw thirty-two little children thrown into the ocean during one voyage.[27] It must be remembered, of course, that a safe, short passage of thirty days was not un-

---

[23] Gottlieb Mittelberger, *Journey to Pa. in 1750,* pp. 16, 38. Diffenderfer, *op. cit.,* pp. 188, 190. John Harrower, "Diary" (of Indentured Servant) in *Amer. Hist. Rev.,* VI, 77.

[24] Descriptions are found in *Pa. Mag. of Hist.,* X, 167; XXVI, 112; XXXVII, 94; XXXVIII, 65.

[25] Harrower's "Diary," pp. 74–76.

[26] Mittelberger, *op. cit.,* pp. 48–49.

[27] *Ibid.*

common. Still, conditions were so terrible that several colonies passed laws regulating food, the number of passengers to be carried, and care of the sick.[28] Philadelphia and other ports were exposed to constant dangers from contagious diseases. Sickness continued after landing, so that much legislation was necessary respecting quarantine, inspection of vessels, and the building of pesthouses.[29]

When the vessel finally made her port,[30] no one was permitted to leave unless the passage had been paid for. The sick and old always fared worst, the very ones whose misery ought to have been relieved first. Parents were forced to sell their children to service, perhaps never to see them again. Husband and wife were often separated. Children under five were sometimes given away to serve until they were twenty-one. "Soul-drivers" would purchase fifty or more servants from the captain of one of these ships, and drive them through the country like a drove of cattle, offering them for sale to the highest bidder.[31] They were protected, in part, however, first by their indenture, which specified the term of service, lodging, food, and apparel; and, second, by "freedom dues," which were provided for by law, and included such things as clothing, corn, a gun, and sometimes a fifty-acre tract of land.[32]

Most of the servants were unskilled laborers, though many artisans and some in the professions bound themselves to service. The following advertisement in the *Virginia Gazette* for March 28, 1771, will give one an idea of their occupation.[33]

> Just arrived at Leeds Town, the Ship *Justitia*, with about one Hundred Healthy Servants.
>
> Men, Women and Boys, among which are many Tradesmen—viz. Blacksmiths, Shoemakers, Tailors, House Carpenters and Joiners, a Cooper, a Bricklayer and Plaisterer, a Painter, a Watchmaker and Glaizer, several Silversmiths, Weavers, a Jeweler, and many others. The Sale will Commence on Tuesday, the 2d of April, at Leeds Town on Rappahannock River. A Reasonable Credit will be allowed, giving Bond with Approved Security to
>
> THOMAS HODGE.

---

[28] *Pa. Statutes at Large*, V (1749–50), 94–97, and *ibid.*, VIII (1774), 369. A law of 1766 was disallowed. *Acts of Privy Council, Colo.*, IV, 763. See also *Mass. Acts and Resolves*, III (1750), 536. T. Cooper, *South Carolina Statutes at Large*, IV (1759), 78.

[29] Mittelberger, *op. cit.*, pp. 20–22.

[30] *Ibid.*, pp. 25–29.

[31] Geiser, *op. cit.*, p. 54. Letter of Phineas Bond (1788), in *Rpt. Amer. Hist. Assoc.*, *1896*, I, 583, "They [passengers] are 'frequently hurried in droves, under the custody of severe brutal drivers (for these are the terms) into the Back Country to be disposed of as servants.'" For an indenture see *Md. Archives*, IV (1647), 327.

[32] See records of indentures, 1771–73, *Pa. German Society Proc.*, Vol. XVI.

[33] *Va. Gaz.* (Purdie and Dixon), March 28, 1771.

The advertisements for runaway servants are numerous,[34] give descriptions of their appearance and dress, mention little peculiarities, and bring before us vividly the personality of these servants. Richard Kinnersley, an English servant-man, had "a pretty long visage of a lightish complexion, and thin-flaxen hair; his eye tooth sticks out over his lower teeth in a very remarkable manner." James Murphy, an Irish servant-schoolmaster, was "somewhat long visaged, with sharp nose, much pitted with the small pox, flaxen hair, reddish beard, sometimes ties his hair behind with a string, a very proud fellow, loves drink and when drunk is very impudent and talkative, pretends much, and knows little, was sometime in the French service and can talk French." Then there was the fat pock-broken tailor with a "hard look," the carpenter who wore his own black hair, the convict servant-woman who could knit and spin, the shoemaker and fiddler who "loves to be at frolicks and taverns and is apt to get in liquor and when so is subject to fits."

The variety of dress was astonishing. We read of cinnamon-colored vests, blue, green, and yellow coats with brass buttons, and breeches with silk puffs. Shoes were of all styles, square-toed and peeked-toed, with buckles and without. An Irish runaway servant-man, Daniel Macdonald, had "a double-breasted cape-coat, with white metal buttons, a little flowered on the top, an ozenbrigs shirt, tow-linen trousers, and an old jacket of a bluish color, good shoes, and large white buckles, had no stockings except he stole them."[35]

The general character of the servants varied in different colonies according to the class from which they came.[36] Of course, not much could be expected of the criminal classes. On the other hand, there were honest artisans and German peasants, seeking a new home for wife and children. The runaway servants represented the worst element, and frequently had stolen horses, clothing, or silver. One was described as "so prodigious a lyer that if observed he may easily be discovered." A tract published in London, in 1708, entitled "The Sot Weed Factor or a Voyage to Maryland,"[37] is a poem by a tobacco agent, Ebenezer Cook, describing the manners and customs of the ruder elements of Maryland society at this date. In picturing a coarse group of female servants who had gathered about the fireside to play games, he says:

> To fire-side I did repair;
> Near which a jolly Female Crew,
> Were deep engag'd at *Lanctre-Love;*
> In Night-rails white, with dirty Mein,
> Such Sights are scarce in *England* seen;

[34] *New Jersey Archives* (newspaper extracts), XIX, 351, 353, 399, 499, etc. In the *Va. Gaz.,* 1736–39, there are 110 advertisements of runaway servants, 24.5 per cent being listed as convicts.

[35] U. B. Phillips, *Plantation and Frontier Documents,* I, 346, 352, 355, 357.

[36] See nn. 34 and 35 and *New Jersey Archives,* XI, 237.

[37] "Md. Hist. Soc. Fund Publications," No. 36.

I thought them first some Witches bent,
On Black Designs in dire Convent.

.    .    .    .    .    .

We scarce had play'd a Round about,
But that these *Indian* Foes fell out.
D—m you, says one, tho' now so brave,
I knew you late a Four-Years Slave;
What if for Planter's Wife you go,
Nature designed you for the Hoe.

The main work[38] of the servant was to clear the land and cultivate the crop, though artisans, of course, worked at their trades. Boucher asserts[39] that two-thirds of the persons employed as schoolmasters in Maryland just before the Revolution were either indentured servants or convicts. A letter[40] from Washington's overseer complains of the fact that his servants were difficult to manage because of a liking for liquor. "The Sot Weed Factor" makes one of the female servants "who passed for a chambermaid" speak thus:

In better Times, e'er to this Land
I was unhappily Trapann'd;
Perchance as well I did appear,
As any Lord or Lady here,
Not then a Slave for twice two Year.
My cloaths were fashonably new,
Nor were my Shifts of Linnen Blue;
But things are changed, now at the Hoe,
I daily work, and Barefoot go,
In weeding Corn or feeding Swine,
I spend my melancholy Time.
Kidnap'd and Fool'd, I thither fled,
To Shun a hated Nuptial Bed,
And to my cost already find,
Worse Plagues than those I left behind.

---

[38] Mittelberger, *op. cit.*, p. 29. Eddis, *op. cit.*, etc., pp. 69–70.

[39] J. Boucher, *A View of the Causes and Consequences of the Amer. Revolution, etc.* (London, 1797), pp. 183–84. "What is still less credible is, that at least two-thirds of the little education we receive are derived from instructors, who are either *indented servants*, or *transported felons*. Not a ship arrives either with redemptioners or convicts, in which schoolmasters are not as regularly advertised for sale, as weavers, tailors, or any other trade; with little other difference, that I can hear of, excepting perhaps that the former do not usually fetch so good a price as the latter."

[40] Crawford to Washington, June 8, 1774, in J. M. Hamilton's *Letters to Washington*, V, 12–14.

Interesting phases of the institution of white servitude appear in the laws regulating their status.[41] Unlike the slave, the white servant could bring suit for justice. The court could order his freedom or lessen his term of service. It could require the master to provide the servant with medical attendance, see that freedom dues were paid and that he had sufficient food and clothing. On the other hand, his time belonged to his master, and severe work could be exacted. His privileges and freedom of movement were restricted. He could not absent himself from his master without permission. He could be whipped for disobedience. He was not allowed to buy or sell anything without leave. Tavern-keepers could not entertain him or sell him liquor. He could neither marry without his master's consent, nor could he vote or hold office, but he could be sold or seized to satisfy an outstanding debt.

The treatment and condition of servants varied widely in different colonies and at different periods, depending on the nature of the work and the character of the servant and the master.[42] In general, their treatment was better in New England and the middle colonies than in the southern. Harrowing tales of cruelty and abuse of white servants are common, but the same kind of treatment was meted out to servants in England during this period. In the court records of Middlesex County, England, 1673, we find that Thomas Tooner was cited to answer to the charge of inhumanly beating his female servant with knotted whip-cords, so that "the poor servant is a lamentable spectacle to behold." The lash was likewise the usual mode of correction in the colonies. Eddis, writing in 1769–77, declares that servants in Maryland groaned beneath a worse than Egyptian bondage. Runaway servants were severely punished, and elaborate laws were passed to secure their arrest and punish all who aided them to freedom.[43]

Some perplexing moral problems[44] were caused by white servants. The question of intermarriage between servant and slave arose, as well as that of restraining looser relations between these classes. Nearly all the colonies were forced to pass laws to prevent such relations between servants, between free men and servants, and between Negro slaves and servants. A great increase of illegitimate mulatto children in the eighteenth century is one evidence of low moral standards. In Virginia, the parish vestry books record large sums expended for the support of such children. Laws were passed to prevent intermarriage of black and white. For example, the preamble of the Virginia Act of 1691 states that it was enacted "for the prevention of that abominable and spurious mixture which hereafter may increase in this dominion as well by negroes inter-

---

[41] See n. 37. A digest of the laws governing the indentured servant for all the colonies is in J. C. Hurd, *The Law of Slavery and Bondage*, I.

[42] See elaborate acts in T. Cooper, *Statutes at Large* (South Carolina), III (1717, 1744), 15, 621; W. W. Hening, *op. cit.* (1662–1705), II, 65; III, 449.

[43] See n. 37 and Eddis, *op. cit.*, pp. 69–70. Harrower's "Diary" in *op. cit.*, Vol. VI; George Alsop, *The Character of the Province of Maryland*, 1666, in "Md. Hist. Soc. Fund Publications," No. 15, p. 94.

[44] For Franklin's letter of 1751 see n. 13. See also Eddis, *op. cit.*, p. 66. . . .

marrying with English or other white women as by their unlawful intercourse with one another." A Maryland act provided that the children of a servant-woman resulting from intermarriage with a Negro slave should be slaves to her master for life. But since unprincipled masters urged the marriage of their servant-women to slaves, the law was repealed. Nevertheless, miscegenation continued.[45]

It is obvious that the economic significance of the white servant was very important. Benjamin Franklin said in 1759, "The labor of the plantations is performed chiefly by indentured servants brought from Great Britain, Ireland, and Germany, because the high price it bears cannot be performed in any other way." Free labor on a wage system was impossible because of both high wages and scarcity of labor. Few would work for hire when land could be had for almost nothing. The certainty of supply, the power of control, its economy, and the large profits resulting made the system superior to other forms until the Negro slave was imported on a large scale.[46] John Pory, of Virginia, wrote in 1619 that "one man by the means of six servants hath cleared at one crop [tobacco] a thousand pounds English. . . . Our principal wealth consisteth of servants."[47]

Socially, the white servant was an important factor in helping to build up a landed aristocracy in the South, because he made possible the cultivation of extensive areas of land.[48] But in the course of a few years he became a free citizen and owner of a small estate. Thus was developed a yeoman class, a much-needed democratic element in the southern colonies, while at the same time settlers were secured for the back lands, where they were needed to protect the frontier. Nevertheless, they did not form a distinct class after becoming freedmen. Some were doubtless the progenitors of the "poor white trash" of the South, but it is likely that environment rather than birth was the main factor in producing this class. While comparatively few rose to prominence, yet there are some notable examples to the contrary. Two signers of the Declaration of Independence—George Taylor and Mathew Thornton—and Charles Thompson, the Secretary of the Continental Congress, had all been white servants. It is certain also that many became successful planters, and perhaps the majority, respectable and desirable citizens.

[45] Hening, *op. cit.*, III, 87. Maryland act of 1664 is in *Md. Archives*, I, 533.

[46] Geiser, *op. cit.*, p. 24.

[47] John Pory, Secretary of Virginia, Letter to Sir Dudley Carlton, 1619. "All our riches for the present doe consiste in Tobacco, wherein one man by his owne labour hath in one yeare raised to himselfe to the value of 200 £ sterling; and another by the meanes of six servants hath cleared at one crop a thousand pound English. These be true, yet indeed rare examples, yet possible to be done by others. Our principall wealth (I should have said) consisteth in servants: but they are chardgeable to be furnished with armes, apparell and bedding, and for their transportation, and casuall both at sea, and for their first yeare commonly at lande also: but if they escape, they prove very hardy, and sound able men (*Collecs. Mass. Hist. Soc.* [4th ser.] IX, 9–10).

[48] See n. 37; William Eddis, *op. cit.* (London, 1792), p. 66.

On the whole, the effects of the institution were beneficial. Great Britain was relieved of her undesirable citizens; many German peasants were given the opportunity to better their condition; the colonies were supplied with laborers for the rougher work, and servant-artisans supplied wants impossible to meet in any other way.[49] That the white servant was useful, even after the Revolution, is seen by the fact that large numbers continued to come to Pennsylvania, where the institution existed until 1831. By that time various causes were leading to its abolition. Opposition developed in Europe because of the drain of the labor supply to America. In the South the Negro slave had tended to supplant the white servant, while in the North labor-saving machinery was doing so much of his work that he was no longer needed.

[49] Geiser, *op. cit.*, pp. 102, 109.

# Popular Uprisings and Civil Authority

# in

# Eighteenth-Century America

PAULINE MAIER

From the Stamp Act revolts of 1765 to today's ghetto uprisings, mob violence has been a powerful influence in American history. Although the specific intent of the mobs has varied greatly, the process by which they formed has tended to be much the same, and the uprisings have generally had certain characteristics in common.

First, mobs rarely see the purpose of their action as illegal, although on occasion they see it as supralegal—that is, as carrying the enforcement of the law beyond its stated limits. A lynch mob, for example, may be unwilling to wait for or to trust the court system to reach what they consider a just verdict; thus the mob may see itself as the executor of proper justice. Similarly, the vigilante groups that administered dubious justice in the old West joined together in posses presumably to enforce the law.

Generally, mobs tend to rally around some real or imagined grievance that they have reason to believe the recognized authorities will not deal with properly. This is especially apt to be the situation when the ultimate authorities are far away or unsympathetic to local conditions, as in colonial America, the old West, or the pre–Civil War South; when authorities are nearby and repressive, as in urban ghettoes; or when local authorities side with citizen groups in opposition to higher authorities, as in colonial America or the South during the school desegregation crisis of the late 1950's and early 1960's.

It is important to note that mob action is rarely directed against the **idea** of authority or order, but rather against some particular condition that the authority has either caused or allowed to exist. Studies of mob action in Europe in the eighteenth and nineteenth centuries as well as studies of more recent riots in the United States have shown that the targets of mob violence are limited and quite selective. This has been the case in the twentieth-century ghetto revolts in Northern cities, for instance, in which attacks have been primarily on property and very few deaths have occurred at the hands of the rioters.

In the following essay, Pauline Maier, a member of the history department at the University of Massachusetts in Boston, describes
what she calls popular uprisings in eighteenth-century America. She
indicates some of the problems that arise in trying to evaluate this
kind of violence in historical perspective, shows how the authorities
at various levels tried to deal with it, and concludes with some suggestions as to how and why the United States government changed
its views on violence after the founding of the American nation.

It is only natural that the riots and civil turbulence of the past decade
and a half have awakened a new interest in the history of American mobs.
It should be emphasized, however, that scholarly attention to the subject
has roots independent of contemporary events and founded in long-
developing historiographical trends. George Rudé's studies of pre-indus-
trial crowds in France and England, E. J. Hobsbawm's discussion of
"archaic" social movements, and recent works linking eighteenth-century
American thought with English revolutionary tradition have all, in different ways, inspired a new concern among historians with colonial uprisings.[1] This discovery of the early American mob promises to have a
significant effect upon historical interpretation. Particularly affected are the
Revolutionary struggle and the early decades of the new nation, when
events often turned upon well-known popular insurrections.

Eighteenth-century uprisings were in some important ways different
than those of today—different in themselves, but even more in the political

[1] See the following by George Rudé: *The Crowd in the French Revolution* (Oxford,
1959); "The London 'Mob' of the Eighteenth Century," *The Historical Journal*, II
(1959), 1–18; *Wilkes and Liberty: A Social Study of 1763 to 1774* (Oxford, 1962);
*The Crowd in History: A Study of Popular Disturbances in France and England,
1730–1848* (New York, 1964). See also E. J. Hobsbawm, *Primitive Rebels: Studies
in Archaic Forms of Social Movement in the Nineteenth and Twentieth Centuries*
(New York, 1959), esp. "The City Mob," 108–25. For recent discussions of the
colonial mob see Bernard Bailyn, *Pamphlets of the American Revolution* (Cambridge, Mass., 1965), I, 581–84; Jesse Lemisch, "Jack Tar in the Street: Merchant
Seamen in the Politics of Revolutionary America," *William and Mary Quarterly*,
3d ser., XXV (1968), 371–407; Gordon S. Wood, "A Note on Mobs in the American Revolution," *Wm. and Mary Qtly.*, 3d ser., XXIII (1966), 635–42, and more
recently Wood's *Creation of the American Republic, 1776–1787* (Chapel Hill, 1969),
*passim*, but esp. 319–28. Wood offers an excellent analysis of the place of mobs
and extralegal assemblies in the development of American constitutionalism. Hugh
D. Graham and Ted R. Gurr, *Violence in America: Historical and Comparative
Perspectives* (New York, 1969), primarily discusses uprisings of the nineteenth and
twentieth centuries, but see the chapters by Richard M. Brown, "Historical Patterns
of Violence in America," 45–84, and "The American Vigilante Tradition," 154–226.

"Popular Uprisings and Civil Authority in Eighteenth-Century America," by Pauline
Maier. From *William and Mary Quarterly*, XXVII, Series 3 (January 1970), 3–35.
Reprinted by permission of *William and Mary Quarterly* and Pauline Maier.

context within which they occurred. As a result they carried different con-
notations for the American Revolutionaries than they do today. Not all
eighteenth-century mobs simply defied the law: some used extralegal
means to implement official demands or to enforce laws not otherwise
enforceable; others in effect extended the law in urgent situations beyond
its technical limits. Since leading eighteenth-century Americans had
known many occasions on which mobs took on the defense of the public
welfare, which was, after all, the stated purpose of government, they were
less likely to deny popular upheavals all legitimacy than are modern
leaders. While not advocating popular uprisings, they could still grant
such incidents an established and necessary role in free societies, one that
made them an integral and even respected element of the political order.
These attitudes, and the tradition of colonial insurrections on which they
drew, not only shaped political events of the Revolutionary era but also lay
behind many laws and civil procedures that were framed during the 1780's
and 1790's, some of which still have a place in the American legal system.

Not all colonial uprisings were identical in character or significance.
Some involved no more than disorderly vandalism or traditional brawls
such as those that annually marked Pope's Day on November 5, particularly in New England. Occasional insurrections defied established laws and
authorities in the name of isolated private interests alone—a set of Hartford
County, Connecticut, landowners arose in 1722, for example, after a court
decision imperiled their particular land titles. Still others—which are of
interest here—took on a broader purpose, and defended the interests of
their community in general where established authorities failed to act.[2]
This common characteristic linked otherwise diverse rural uprisings in
New Jersey and the Carolinas. The insurrectionists' punishment of outlaws,
their interposition to secure land titles or prevent abuses at the hands of
legal officials, followed a frustration with established institutions and a
belief that justice and even security had to be imposed by the people
directly.[3] The earlier Virginia tobacco insurrection also illustrates this

[2] Carl Bridenbaugh, *Cities in the Wilderness: The First Century of Urban Life in
America, 1625–1742* (New York, 1964), 70–71, 223–24, 382–84; and Carl Bridenbaugh, *Cities in Revolt: Urban Life in America, 1743–1776* (New York, 1964),
113–18; Charles J. Hoadly, ed., *The Public Records of the Colony of Connecticut
. . .* (Hartford, 1872), VI, 332–33, 341–48.

[3] See particularly Richard M. Brown, *The South Carolina Regulators* (Cambridge,
Mass., 1963). There is no published study of the New Jersey land riots, which
lasted over a decade and were due above all to the protracted inability of the
royal government to settle land disputes stemming from conflicting proprietary
grants made in the late seventeenth century. See, however, "A State of Facts Concerning the Riots and Insurrections in New Jersey, and the Remedies Attempted to
Restore the Peace of the Province," William A. Whitehead *et al.*, eds., *Archives of
the State of New Jersey* (Newark, 1883), VII, 207–26. On other rural insurrections see Irving Mark, *Agrarian Conflicts in Colonial New York, 1711–
1775* (New York, 1940), Chaps. IV, V; Staughton Lynd, "The Tenant Rising at
Livingston Manor," *New-York Historical Society Quarterly*, XLVIII (1964), 163–
77; Matt Bushnell Jones, *Vermont in the Making, 1750–1777* (Cambridge, Mass.,
1939), Chaps. XII, XIII; John R. Dunbar, ed., *The Paxton Papers* (The Hague,
1957), esp. 3–51.

common pattern well: Virginians began tearing up young tobacco plants in 1682 only after Governor Thomas Culpeper forced the quick adjournment of their assembly, which had been called to curtail tobacco planting during an economic crisis. The insurrections in Massachusetts a little over a century later represent a variation on this theme. The insurgents in Worcester, Berkshire, Hampshire, Middlesex, and Bristol counties—often linked together as members of "Shays's Rebellion"—forced the closing of civil courts, which threatened to send a major portion of the local population to debtors' prison, only until a new legislature could remedy their pressing needs.[4]

This role of the mob as extralegal arm of the community's interest emerged, too, in repeated uprisings that occurred within the more densely settled coastal areas. The history of Boston, where by the mid-eighteenth century "public order . . . prevailed to a greater degree than anywhere else in England or America," is full of such incidents. During the food shortage of 1710, after the governor rejected a petition from the Boston selectmen calling for a temporary embargo on the exportation of foodstuffs, one heavily laden ship found its rudder cut away, and fifty men sought to haul another outward-bound vessel back to shore. Under similar circumstances Boston mobs again intervened to keep foodstuffs in the colony in 1713 and 1729. When there was some doubt a few years later whether or not the selectmen had the authority to seize a barn lying in the path of a proposed street, a group of townsmen, their faces blackened, leveled the structure and the road went through. Houses of ill fame were attacked by Boston mobs in 1734, 1737, and 1771; and in the late 1760's the *New York Gazette* claimed that mobs in Providence and Newport had taken on responsibility for "disciplining" unfaithful husbands. Meanwhile in New London, Connecticut, another mob prevented a radical religious sect, the Rogerenes, from disturbing normal Sunday services, "a practice they . . . [had] followed more or less for many years past; and which all the laws made in that government, and executed in the most judicious manner could not put a stop to."[5]

Threats of epidemic inspired particularly dramatic instances of this community oriented role of the mob. One revealing episode occurred in Massachusetts in 1773–1774. A smallpox hospital had been built on Essex Island near Marblehead "much against the will of the multitude" according

---

[4] Richard L. Morton, *Colonial Virginia* (Chapel Hill, 1960), I, 303–04; Jonathan Smith, "The Depression of 1785 and Daniel Shays' Rebellion," *Wm. and Mary Qtly.*, 3d ser., V (1948), 86–87, 91.

[5] Bridenbaugh, *Cities in Revolt*, 114; Bridenbaugh, *Cities in the Wilderness*, 196, 383, 388–89; Edmund S. and Helen M. Morgan, *The Stamp Act Crisis*, rev. ed. (New York, 1963), 159; Anne Rowe Cunningham, ed., *Letters and Diary of John Rowe, Boston Merchant, 1759–1762, 1764–1779* (Boston, 1903), 218. On the marriage riots, see *New York Gazette* (New York City), July 11, 1765—and note that when the reporter speaks of persons "concern'd in such unlawful Enterprises" he clearly is referring to the husbands, not their "Disciplinarians." On the Rogerenes, see item in *Connecticut Gazette* (New Haven), Apr. 5, 1766, reprinted in Lawrence H. Gipson, *Jared Ingersoll* (New Haven, 1920), 195, n. 1.

to John Adams. "The patients were careless, some of them wantonly so; and others were suspected of designing to spread the smallpox in the town, which was full of people who had not passed through the distemper." In January 1774 patients from the hospital who tried to enter the town from unauthorized landing places were forcefully prevented from doing so; a hospital boat was burned; and four men suspected of stealing infected clothes from the hospital were tarred and feathered, then carted from Marblehead to Salem in a long cortege. The Marblehead town meeting finally won the proprietors' agreement to shut down the hospital; but after some twenty-two new cases of smallpox broke out in the town within a few days "apprehension became general," and some "Ruffians" in disguise hastened the hospital's demise by burning the nearly evacuated building. A military watch of forty men was needed for several nights to keep the peace in Marblehead.[6]

A similar episode occurred in Norfolk, Virginia, when a group of wealthy residents decided to have their families inoculated for smallpox. Fears arose that the lesser disease brought on by the inoculations would spread and necessitate a general inoculation, which would cost "more money than is circulating in Norfolk" and ruin trade and commerce such that "the whole colony would feel the effects." Local magistrates said they could not interfere because "the law was silent in the matter." Public and private meetings then sought to negotiate the issue. Despite a hard-won agreement, however, the pro-inoculation faction persisted in its original plan. Then finally a mob drove the newly inoculated women and children on a five-mile forced march in darkness and rain to the common Pest House, a three-year-old institution designed to isolate seamen and others, particularly Negroes, infected with smallpox.[7]

These local incidents indicate a willingness among many Americans to act outside the bounds of law, but they cannot be described as anti-authoritarian in any general sense. Sometimes in fact—as in the Boston bawdy house riot of 1734, or the Norfolk smallpox incident—local magistrates openly countenanced or participated in the mob's activities. Far from opposing established institutions, many supporters of Shays's Rebellion honored their leaders "by no less decisive marks of popular favor than elections to local offices of trust and authority."[8] It was above all the

---

[6] John Adams, "Novanglus," in Charles F. Adams, ed., *The Works of John Adams* (Boston, 1850-1856), IV, 76–77; Salem news of Jan. 25 and Feb. 1, 1774, in *Providence Gazette* (Rhode Island), Feb. 5 and Feb. 12, 1774.

[7] Letter from "Friends to the borough and county of Norfolk," in Purdie and Dixon's *Virginia Gazette Postscript* (Williamsburg), Sept. 8, 1768, which gives the fullest account. This letter answered an earlier letter from Norfolk, Aug. 6, 1768, available in Rind's *Va. Gaz. Supplement* (Wmsbg.), Aug. 25, 1768. See also letter of Cornelius Calvert in Purdie and Dixon's *Va. Gaz.* (Wmsbg.), Jan. 9, 1772. Divisions over the inoculation seemed to follow more general political lines. See Patrick Henderson, "Smallpox and Patriotism, The Norfolk Riots, 1768–1769," *Virginia Magazine of History and Biography*, LXXIII (1965), 413–24.

[8] James Madison to Thomas Jefferson, Mar. 19, 1787, in Julian P. Boyd, ed., *The Papers of Thomas Jefferson* (Princeton, 1950– ), XI, 223.

existence of such elections that forced local magistrates to reflect community feelings and so prevented their becoming the targets of insurrections. Certainly in New England, where the town meeting ruled, and to some extent in New York, where aldermen and councilmen were annually elected, this was true; yet even in Philadelphia, with its lethargic closed corporation, or Charleston, which lacked municipal institutions, authority was normally exerted by residents who had an immediate sense of local sentiment. Provincial governments were also for the most part kept alert to local feelings by their elected assemblies. Sometimes, of course, uprisings turned against domestic American institutions—as in Pennsylvania in 1764, when the "Paxton Boys" complained that the colony's Quaker assembly had failed to provide adequately for their defense against the Indians. But uprisings over local issues proved *extra-institutional* in character more often than they were anti-institutional; they served the community where no law existed, or intervened beyond what magistrates thought they could do officially to cope with a local problem.

The case was different when imperial authority was involved. There legal authority emanated from a capital an ocean away, where the colonists had no integral voice in the formation of policy, where governmental decisions were based largely upon the reports of "king's men" and sought above all to promote the king's interests. When London's legal authority and local interest conflicted, efforts to implement the edicts of royal officials were often answered by uprisings, and it was not unusual in these cases for local magistrates to participate or openly sympathize with the insurgents. The colonial response to the White Pines Acts of 1722 and 1729 is one example. Enforcement of the acts was difficult in general because "the various elements of colonial society . . . seemed inclined to violate the pine laws—legislatures, lumbermen, and merchants were against them, and even the royal governors were divided." At Exeter, New Hampshire, in 1734 about thirty men prevented royal officials from putting the king's broad arrow on some seized boards; efforts to enforce the acts in Connecticut during the 1750's ended after a deputy of the surveyor general was thrown in a pond and nearly drowned; five years later logs seized in Massachusetts and New Hampshire were either "rescued" or destroyed.[9] Two other imperial issues that provoked local American uprisings long before 1765 and continued to do so during the Revolutionary period were impressment and customs enforcement.

As early as 1743 the colonists' violent opposition to impressment was said to indicate a "Contempt of Government." Some captains had been mobbed, the Admiralty complained, "others emprisoned, and afterwards held to exorbitant Bail, and are now under Prosecutions carried on by Combination, and by joint Subscription towards the expense." Colonial governors, despite their offers, furnished captains with little real aid

[9] Bernhard Knollenberg, *Origin of the American Revolution: 1759–1766* (New York, 1965), 126, 129. See also Robert G. Albion, *Forests and Sea Power* (Cambridge, Mass., 1926), 262–63, 265. Joseph J. Malone, *Pine Trees and Politics* (Seattle, 1964), includes less detail on the forceful resistance to the acts.

either to procure seamen or "even to protect them from the Rage and Insults of the People." Two days of severe rioting answered Commodore Charles Knowles's efforts to sweep Boston harbor for able-bodied men in November 1747. Again in 1764 when Rear Admiral Lord Alexander Colville sent out orders to "procure" men in principal harbors between Casco Bay and Cape Henlopen, mobs met the ships at every turn. When the *St. John* sent out a boat to seize a recently impressed deserter from a Newport wharf, a mob protected him, captured the boat's officer, and hurled stones at the crew; later fifty Newporters joined the colony's gunner at Fort George in opening fire on the king's ship itself. Under threat to her master the *Chaleur* was forced to release four fishermen seized off Long Island, and when that ship's captain went ashore at New York a mob seized his boat and burned it in the Fields. In the spring of 1765 after the *Maidstone* capped a six-month siege of Newport harbor by seizing "all the Men" out of a brigantine from Africa, a mob of about five hundred men similarly seized a ship's officer and burned one of her boats on the Common. Impressment also met mass resistance at Norfolk in 1767 and was a major cause of the famous *Liberty* riot at Boston in 1768.[10]

Like the impressment uprisings, which in most instances sought to protect or rescue men from the "press," customs incidents were aimed at impeding the customs service in enforcing British laws. Tactics varied, and although incidents occurred long before 1764—in 1719, for example, Caleb Heathcote reported a "riotous and tumultuous" rescue of seized claret by Newporters—their frequency, like those of the impressment "riots," apparently increased after the Sugar Act was passed and customs enforcement efforts were tightened. The 1764 rescue of the *Rhoda* in Rhode Island preceded a theft in Dighton, Massachusetts, of the cargo from a newly seized vessel, the *Polly*, by a mob of some forty men with blackened faces. In 1766 again a mob stoned a customs official's home in

[10] Admiralty to Gov. George Thomas, Sept. 26, 1743, in Samuel Hazard *et al.*, eds., *Pennsylvania Archives* (Philadelphia, 1852–1949), I, 639. For accounts of the Knowles riot, see Gov. William Shirley to Josiah Willard, Nov. 19, 1747, Shirley's Proclamation of Nov. 21, 1747, and his letter to the Board of Trade, Dec. 1, 1747, in Charles H. Lincoln, ed., *The Correspondence of William Shirley . . . 1731–1760* (New York, 1912), I, 406–19; see also Thomas Hutchinson, *History of the Province of Massachusetts Bay*, ed. Lawrence S. Mayo (Cambridge, Mass., 1936), II, 330–33; and *Reports of the Record Commissioners of Boston* (Boston, 1885), XIV, 127–30. David Lovejoy, *Rhode Island Politics and the American Revolution, 1760–1776* (Providence, 1958), 36–39, and on the *Maidstone* in particular see "O. G." in *Newport Mercury* (Rhode Island), June 10, 1765. Bridenbaugh, *Cities in Revolt*, 309–11; documents on the *St. John* episode in *Records of the Colony of Rhode Island and Providence Plantations* (Providence, 1856–1865), VI, 427–30. George G. Wolkins, "The Seizure of John Hancock's Sloop *Liberty*," Massachusetts Historical Society, *Proceedings* (1921–1923), LV, 239–84. See also Lemisch, "Jack Tar," *Wm. and Mary Qtly.*, 3d ser., XXV (1968), 391–93; and Neil R. Stout, "Manning the Royal Navy in North America, 1763–1775," *American Neptune*, XXIII (1963), 179–81.

Falmouth (Portland), Maine, while "Persons unknown and disguised" stole sugar and rum that had been impounded that morning. The intimidation of customs officials and of the particularly despised customs informers also enjoyed a long history. In 1701 the South Carolina attorney general publicly attacked an informer "and struck him several times, crying out, this is the Informer, this is he that will ruin the country." Similar assaults occurred decades later, in New Haven in 1766 and 1769, and New London in 1769, and were then often distinguished by their brutality. In 1771 a Providence tidesman, Jesse Saville, was seized, stripped, bound hand and foot, tarred and feathered, had dirt thrown in his face, then was beaten and "almost strangled." Even more thorough assaults upon two other Rhode Island tidesmen followed in July 1770 and upon Collector Charles Dudley in April 1771. Finally, customs vessels came under attack: the *St. John* was shelled at Newport in 1764 where the customs ship *Liberty* was sunk in 1769—both episodes that served as prelude to the destruction of the *Gaspée* outside Providence in 1772.[11]

Such incidents were not confined to New England. Philadelphia witnessed some of the most savage attacks, and even the surveyor of Sassafras and Bohemia in Maryland—an office long a sinecure, since no ships entered or cleared in Sassafras or Bohemia—met with violence when he tried to execute his office in March 1775. After seizing two wagons of goods being carried overland from Maryland toward Duck Creek, Delaware, the officer was overpowered by a "licentious mob" that kept shouting "Liberty and Duck Creek forever" as it went through the hours-long rituals of tarring and feathering him and threatening his life. And at Norfolk, Virginia, in the spring of 1766 an accused customs informer was

---

[11] Heathcote letter from Newport, Sept. 7, 1719, *Records of the Colony of Rhode Island*, IV, 259–60; Lovejoy, *Rhode Island Politics*, 35–39. There is an excellent summary of the *Polly* incident in Morgan, *Stamp Act Crisis*, 59, 64–67; and see also *Providence Gaz.* (R.I.), Apr. 27, 1765. On the Falmouth incident see the letter from the collector and comptroller of Falmouth, Aug. 19, 1766, Treasury Group 1, Class 453, Piece 182, Public Records Office. Hereafter cited as T. 1/453, 182. See also the account in Appendix I of Josiah Quincy, Jr., *Reports of the Cases Argued and Adjudged in the Superior Court of Judicature of the Province of Massachusetts Bay, Between 1761 and 1772* (Boston, 1865), 446–47. W. Noël Sainsbury *et al.*, ed., *Calendar of State Papers, Colonial Series, America and the West Indies, 1701* (London, 1910), no. 1042, xi, a. A summary of one of the New Haven informer attacks is in Willard M. Wallace, *Traitorous Hero: The Life and Fortunes of Benedict Arnold* (New York, 1954), 20–23. Arnold's statement on the affair which he led is in Malcolm Decker, *Benedict Arnold, Son of the Havens* (Tarrytown, N.Y., 1932), 27–29. Gipson, in *Jared Ingersoll*, 277–78, relates the later incidents. For the New London informer attacks, see documents of July 1769 in T. 1/471. On the Saville affair see Saville to collector and comptroller of customs in Newport, May 18, 1769, T. 1/471, and *New York Journal* (New York), July 6, 1769. On later Rhode Island incidents see Dudley and John Nicoll to governor of Rhode Island, Aug. 1, 1770, T. 1/471. Dudley to commissioners of customs at Boston, Newport, Apr. 11, 1771, T. 1/482. On the destruction of the *Liberty* see documents in T. 1/471, esp. comptroller and collector to the governor, July 21, 1769.

tarred and feathered, pelted with stones and rotten eggs, and finally thrown in the sea where he nearly drowned. Even Georgia saw customs violence before independence, and one of the rare deaths resulting from a colonial riot occurred there in 1775[12]

White Pines, impressment, and customs uprisings have attracted historians' attention because they opposed British authority and so seemed to presage the Revolution. In fact, however, they had much in common with many exclusively local uprisings. In each of the incidents violence was directed not so much against the "rich and powerful"[13] as against men who—as it was said after the Norfolk smallpox incident—"in every part of their conduct . . . acted very inconsistently as good neighbors or citizens." The effort remained one of safeguarding not the interests of isolated groups alone, but the community's safety and welfare. The White Pines Acts need not have provoked this opposition had they applied only to trees of potential use to the Navy, and had they been framed and executed with concern for colonial rights. But instead the acts reserved to the crown all white pine trees, including those "utterly unfit for masts, yards, or bowsprits," and prevented colonists from using them for building materials or lumber exportation even in regions where white pine constituted the principal forest growth. As a result the acts "operated so much against the convenience and even necessities of the inhabitants," Surveyor John Wentworth explained, that "it became almost a general interest of the country" to frustrate the acts' execution. Impressment offered a more immediate effect, since the "press" could quickly cripple

[12] On Philadelphia violence see William Sheppard to commissioners of customs, Apr. 21, 1769, T. 1/471; Deputy Collector at Philadelphia John Swift to commissioners of customs at Boston, Oct. 13, 1769, *ibid.*; and on a particularly brutal attack on the son of customsman John Hatton, see Deputy Collector John Swift to Boston customs commissioners, Nov. 15, 1770, and related documents in T. 1/476. See also Alfred S. Martin, "The King's Customs: Philadelphia, 1763–1774," *Wm. and Mary Qtly.*, 3d ser., V (1948), 201–16. Documents on the Maryland episode are in T. 1/513, including the following: Richard Reeve to Grey Cooper, Apr. 19, 1775; extracts from a council meeting, Mar. 16, 1775; deposition of Robert Stratford Byrne, surveyor of His Majesty's Customs at Sassafras and Bohemia; and Byrne to customs commissioners, Mar. 17, 1775. On the Virginia incident see William Smith to Jeremiah Morgan, Apr. 3, 1766, Colonial Office Group, Class 5, Piece 1331, 80, Public Records Office. Hereafter cited as C. O. 5/1331, 80. W. W. Abbot, *The Royal Governors of Georgia, 1754–1775* (Chapel Hill, 1959), 174–75. These customs riots remained generally separate from the more central intercolonial opposition to Britain that emerged in 1765. Isolated individuals like John Brown of Providence and Maximilian Calvert of Norfolk were involved both in the organized intercolonial Sons of Liberty and in leading mobs against customs functionaries or informers. These roles, however, for the most part were unconnected, that is, there was no radical program of customs obstruction *per se*. Outbreaks were above all local responses to random provocations and, at least before the Townshend duties, usually devoid of explicit ideological justifications.

[13] Hobsbawm, *Primitive Rebels*, 111. For a different effort to see class division as relevant in eighteenth-century uprisings, see Lemisch, "Jack Tar," *Wm. and Mary Qtly.*, 3d ser., XXV (1968), 387.

whole towns. Merchants and masters were affected as immediately as seamen: the targeted port, as Massachusetts' Governor William Shirley explained in 1747, was drained of mariners by both impressment itself and the flight of navigation to safer provinces, driving the wages for any remaining seamen upward. When the press was of long duration, moreover, or when it took place during a normally busy season, it could mean serious shortages of food or firewood for winter and a general attrition of the commercial life that sustained all strata of society in trading towns. Commerce seemed even more directly attacked by British trade regulations, particularly by the proliferation of customs procedures in the mid-1760's that seemed to be in no American's interest, and by the Sugar Act with its virtual prohibition of the trade with the foreign West Indies that sustained the economies of colonies like Rhode Island. As a result even when only a limited contingent of sailors participated in a customs incident, officials could suspect—as did the deputy collector at Philadelphia in 1770—that the mass of citizens "in their Hearts" approved of it.[14]

Because the various uprisings discussed here grew out of concerns essential to wide sections of the community, the "rioters" were not necessarily confined to the seamen, servants, Negroes, and boys generally described as the staple components of the colonial mob. The uprising of Exeter, New Hampshire, townsmen against the king's surveyor of the woods in 1754 was organized by a member of the prominent Gillman family who was a mill owner and a militia officer. Members of the upper classes participated in Norfolk's smallpox uprising, and Cornelius Calvert, who was later attacked in a related incident, protested that leading members of the community, doctors and magistrates, had posted securities for the good behavior of the "Villains" convicted of mobbing him. Captain Jeremiah Morgan complained about the virtually universal participation of Norfolkers in an impressment incident of 1767, and "all the principal Gentlemen in Town" were supposedly present when a customs informer was tarred and feathered there in 1766. Merchant Benedict Arnold admitted leading a New Haven mob against an informer in 1766; New London merchants Joseph Packwood and Nathaniel Shaw commanded the mob that first accosted Captain William Reid the night the *Liberty* was destroyed at Newport in 1769, just as John Brown, a leading Providence merchant, led that against the *Gaspée*. Charles Dudley reported in April 1771 that the men who beat him in Newport "did not come from the . . . lowest class of Men" but were "stiled Merchants and the Masters of their Vessels"; and again in 1775 Robert Stratford Byrne said many of his Maryland and Pennsylvania attackers were "from Appear-

---

[14] "Friends to the borough and county of Norfolk," Purdie and Dixon's *Va. Gaz. Postscrpt.* (Wmsbg.), Sept. 8, 1768. Wentworth quoted in Knollenberg, *Origin of American Revolution,* 124–25. Lemisch, "Jack Tar," *Wm. and Mary Qtly.,* 3d ser., XXV (1968), 383–85. Shirley to Duke of Newcastle, Dec. 31, 1747, in Lincoln, ed., *Shirley Correspondence,* I, 420–23. Dora Mae Clark, "The Impressment of Seamen in the American Colonies," *Essays in Colonial History Presented to Charles McLean Andrews* (New Haven, 1931), 199–200; John Swift to Boston customs commissioners, Nov. 15, 1770, T. 1/476.

ance . . . Men of Property." It is interesting, too, that during Shays's Rebellion—so often considered a class uprising—"men who were of good property and owed not a shilling" were said to be "involved in the train of desperados to suppress the courts."[15]

Opposition to impressment and customs enforcement in itself was not, moreover, the only cause of the so-called impressment or customs "riots." The complete narratives of these incidents indicate again not only that the crowd acted to support local interests but that it sometimes enforced the will of local magistrates by extralegal means. Although British officials blamed the *St. John* incident upon that ship's customs and impressment activities, colonists insisted that the confrontation began when some sailors stole a few pigs and chickens from a local miller and the ship's crew refused to surrender the thieves to Newport officials. Two members of the Rhode Island council then ordered the gunner of Fort George to detain the schooner until the accused seamen were delivered to the sheriff, and "many People went over the Fort to assist the Gunner in the Discharge of his Duty." Only after this uprising did the ship's officers surrender the accused men.[16] Similarly, the 1747 Knowles impressment riot in Boston and the 1765 *Maidstone* impressment riot in Newport broke out after governors' requests for the release of impressed seamen had gone unanswered, and only after the outbreaks of violence were the governors' requests honored. The crowd that first assembled on the night the *Liberty* was destroyed in Newport also began by demanding the allegedly drunken sailors who that afternoon had abused and shot at a

---

[15] Malone, *White Pines*, 112. "Friends to the borough and county of Norfolk," Purdie and Dixon's *Va. Gaz. Postscrpt.* (Wmsbg.), Sept. 8, 1768; Calvert letter, *ibid.*, Jan. 9, 1772. Capt. Jeremiah Morgan, quoted in Lemisch, "Jack Tar," *Wm. and Mary Qtly.*, 3d ser., XXV (1968), 391; and William Smith to Morgan, Apr. 3, 1766, C. O. 5/1331, 80. Decker, *Benedict Arnold*, 27–29; deposition of Capt. William Reid on the *Liberty* affair, July 21, 1769, T. 1/471; Ephraim Bowen's narrative on the *Gaspée* affair, *Records of the Colony of Rhode Island*, VII, 68–73; Charles Dudley to Boston customs commissioners, Apr. 11, 1771, T. 1/482, and deposition by Byrne, T. 1/513. Edward Carrington to Jefferson, June 9, 1787, Boyd, ed., *Jefferson Papers*, XI, 408; and see also Smith, "Depression of 1785," *Wm. and Mary Qtly.*, 3d ser., V (1948), 88—of the twenty-one men indicted for treason in Worcester during the court's April term 1787, fifteen were "gentlemen" and only six "yeomen."

[16] Gov. Samuel Ward's report to the Treasury lords, Oct. 23, 1765, Ward Manuscripts, Box 1, fol. 58, Rhode Island Historical Society, Providence. See also deposition of Daniel Vaughn of Newport—Vaughn was the gunner at Fort George—July 8, 1764, Chalmers Papers, Rhode Island, fol. 41, New York Public Library, New York City. For British official accounts of the affair, see Lieut. Hill's version in James Munro, ed., *Acts of the Privy Council of England, Colonial Series* (London, 1912), VI, 374–76, and the report of John Robinson and John Nicoll to the customs commissioners, Aug. 30, 1765, Privy Council Group, Class I, Piece 51, Bundle 1 (53a), Public Records Office. Hill, whose report was drawn up soon after the incident, does not contradict Ward's narrative, but seems oblivious of any warrant-granting process on shore; Robinson and Nicoll—whose report was drawn up over a year later, and in the midst of the Stamp Act turmoil—claimed that a recent customs seizure had precipitated the attack upon the *St. John*.

colonial captain, Joseph Packwood, so they could be bound over to local magistrates for prosecution.[17]

In circumstances such as these, the "mob" often appeared only after the legal channels of redress had proven inadequate. The main thrust of the colonists' resistance to the White Pines Acts had always been made in their courts and legislatures. Violence broke out only in local situations where no alternative was available. Even the burning of the *Gaspée* in June 1772 was a last resort. Three months before the incident a group of prominent Providence citizens complained about the ship's wanton severity with all vessels along the coast, and the colony's governor pressed their case with the fleet's admiral. The admiral, however, supported the *Gaspée*'s commander, Lieutenant William Dudingston; and thereafter, the *Providence Gazette* reported, Dudingston became "more haughty, insolent and intolerable, . . . personally ill treating every master and merchant of the vessels he boarded, stealing sheep, hogs, poultry, etc. from farmers round the bay, and cutting down their fruit and other trees for firewood." Redress from London was possible but time-consuming, and in the meantime Rhode Island was approaching what its governor called "the deepest calamity" as supplies of food and fuel were curtailed and prices, especially in Newport, rose steeply. It was significant that merchant John Brown finally led the Providence "mob" that seized the moment in June when the *Gaspée* ran aground near Warwick, for it was he who had spearheaded the effort in March 1772 to win redress through the normal channels of government.[18]

There was little that was distinctively American about the colonial insurrections. The uprisings over grain exportations during times of dearth, the attacks on brothels, press gangs, royal forest officials, and customsmen, all had their counterparts in seventeenth- and eighteenth-century England. Even the Americans' hatred of the customs establishment mirrored the Englishman's traditional loathing of excisemen. Like the customsmen in the colonies, they seemed to descend into localities armed with extraordinary prerogative powers. Often, too, English excisemen were "thugs and brutes who beat up their victims without compunction or stole or wrecked their property" and against whose extravagances little redress was possible through the law.[19] Charges of an identical

---

[17] On the Knowles and *Maidstone* incidents see above, n. 10. On the *Liberty* affair see documents in T. 1/471, esp. the deposition of Capt. William Reid, July 21, 1769, and that of John Carr, the second mate, who indicates that the mob soon forgot its scheme of delivering the crew members to the magistrates.

[18] Malone, *White Pines*, 8–9, and *passim*. *Records of the Colony of Rhode Island*, VII, 60, 62–63, 174–75, including the deposition of Dep. Gov. Darius Sessions, June 12, 1772, and Adm. Montagu to Gov. Wanton, Apr. 8, 1772. Also, Wanton to Hillsborough, June 16, 1772, and Ephraim Bowen's narrative, *ibid.*, 63–73, 90–92. *Providence Gaz.* (R.I.), Jan. 9, 1773.

[19] Max Beloff, *Public Order and Popular Disturbances, 1660–1714* (London, 1938), *passim*; Albion, *Forests and Sea Power*, 263; J. H. Plumb, *England in the Eighteenth Century* (Baltimore, 1961 [orig. publ., Oxford, 1950]), 66.

character were made in the colonies against customsmen and naval officials as well, particularly after 1763 when officers of the Royal Navy were commissioned as deputy members of the customs service,[20] and a history of such accusations lay behind many of the best-known waterfront insurrections. The Americans' complaints took on particular significance only because in the colonies those officials embodied the authority of a "foreign" power. Their arrogance and arbitrariness helped effect "an estrangement of the Affections of the People from the Authority under which they act," and eventually added an emotional element of anger against the crown to a revolutionary conflict otherwise carried on in the language of law and right.[21]

The focused character of colonial uprisings also resembled those in England and even France where, Rudé has pointed out, crowds were remarkably single-minded and discriminating.[22] Targets were characteristically related to grievances: the Knowles rioters sought only the release of the impressed men; they set free a captured officer when assured he had nothing to do with the press, and refrained from burning a boat near Province House for fear the fire would spread. The Norfolk rioters, driven by fear of smallpox, forcefully isolated the inoculated persons where they would be least dangerous. Even the customs rioters vented their brutality on customs officers and informers alone, and the Shaysite "mobs" dispersed after closing the courts which promised most immediately to effect their ruin. So domesticated and controlled was the Boston mob that it refused to riot on Saturday and Sunday nights, which were considered holy by New Englanders.[23]

When colonists compared their mobs with those in the mother country they were struck only with the greater degree of restraint among Americans. "These People bear no Resemblance to an English Mob," John Jay wrote of the Shaysites in December 1786; "they are more tem-

---

[20] See, for example, "A Pumkin" in the *New London Gazette* (Connecticut), May 14, 18, 1773; "O. G." in *Newport Merc.* (R.I.), June 10, 1765; *New London Gaz.* (Conn.), Sept. 22, 1769; complaints of Marylander David Bevan, reprinted in Rind's *Va. Gaz.* (Wmsbg.), July 27, 1769, and *New London Gaz.* (Conn.), July 21, 1769. Stout, "Manning the Royal Navy," *American Neptune*, XXIII (1963), 174. For a similar accusation against a surveyor general of the king's woods, see Albion, *Forests and Sea Power*, 262.

[21] Joseph Reed to the president of Congress, Oct. 21, 1779, in Hazard *et al.*, eds., *Pennsylvania Archives*, VII, 762. Five years earlier Reed had tried to impress upon Lord Dartmouth the importance of constraining crown agents in the colonies if any reconciliation were to be made between Britain and the colonies. See his letter to Earl of Dartmouth, Apr. 4, 1774, in William B. Reed, *Life and Correspondence of Joseph Reed* (Philadelphia, 1847), I, 56–57. For a similar plea, again from a man close to the American Revolutionary leadership, see Stephen Sayre to Lord Dartmouth, Dec. 13, 1766, Dartmouth Papers, D. 1778/2/258, William Salt Library, Stafford, England.

[22] Rudé, *Crowd in History*, 60, 253–54. The restraint exercised by eighteenth-century mobs has often been commented upon. See, for example, Wood, "A Note on Mobs," *Wm. and Mary Qtly.*, 3d ser., XXIII (1966), 636–37.

[23] Joseph Harrison's testimony in Wolkins, "Seizure of Hancock's Sloop *Liberty*," Mass. Hist. Soc., *Proceedings*, LV, 254.

perate, cool and regular in their Conduct—they have hitherto abstained
from Plunder, nor have they that I know of committed any outrages but
such as the accomplishment of their Purpose made necessary." Similar
comparisons were often repeated during the Revolutionary conflict, and
were at least partially grounded in fact. When Londoners set out to "pull
down" houses of ill fame in 1688, for example, the affair spread, prisons
were opened, and disorder ended only when troops were called out. But
when eighteenth-century Bostonians set out on the same task, there is no
record that their destruction extended beyond the bordellos themselves.
Even the violence of the customs riots—which contrast in that regard
from other American incidents—can sometimes be explained by the presence of volatile foreign seamen. The attack on the son of customsman
John Hatton, who was nearly killed in a Philadelphia riot, occurred, for
example, when the city was crowded by over a thousand seamen. His
attackers were apparently Irish crew members of a vessel he and his
father had tried to seize off Cape May, and they were "set on," the
Philadelphia collector speculated, by an Irish merchant in Philadelphia
to whom the vessel was consigned. One of the most lethal riots in the
history of colonial America, in which rioters killed five people, occurred
in a small town near Norfolk, Virginia, and was significantly perpetrated
entirely by British seamen who resisted the local inhabitants' efforts to
reinstitute peace.[24] During and immediately after the Revolutionary War
some incidents occurred in which deaths are recorded; but contemporaries
felt these were historical aberrations, caused by the "brutalizing" effect
of the war itself. "Our citizens, from a habit of putting . . . [the British]
to death, have reconciled their minds to the killing of each other," South
Carolina Judge Aedanus Burke explained.[25]

To a large extent the pervasive restraint and virtual absence of blood-
shed in American incidents can best be understood in terms of social and
military circumstance. There was no large amorphous city in America
comparable to London, where England's worst incidents occurred. More
important, the casualties even in eighteenth-century British riots were

[24] Jay to Jefferson, Dec. 14, 1786, Boyd, ed., *Jefferson Papers*, X, 597. Beloff, *Public
Order*, 30. John Swift to Boston customs commissioners, Nov. 15, 1770, Gov.
William Franklin's Proclamation, Nov. 17, 1770, and John Hatton to Boston customs commissioners, Nov. 20, 1770, T. 1/476. The last mentioned riot occurred in
November 1762. A cartel ship from Havana had stopped for repairs in October.
On November 21 a rumor spread that the Spaniards were murdering the inhabitants, which drew seamen from His Majesty's Ship *Arundel*, also in the harbor, into
town, where the seamen drove the Spaniards into a house, set fire to it, and
apparently intended to blow it up. A dignitary of the Spanish colonial service,
who had been a passenger on the cartel ship, was beaten and some money and
valuables were stolen from him. Local men tried to quell the riot without success.
It was eventually put down by militiamen from Norfolk. See "A Narrative of a
Riot in Virginia in November 1762," T. 1/476.
[25] Burke and others to the same effect, quoted in Jerome J. Nadelhaft, The Revolutionary Era in South Carolina, 1775–1788 (unpubl. Ph.D. diss., University of Wisconsin, 1965), 151–52. See also account of the "Fort Wilson" riot of October 1779
in J. Thomas Scharf and Thompson Westcott, *History of Philadelphia, 1609–1884*
(Philadelphia, 1884), I, 401–03.

rarely the work of rioters. No deaths were inflicted by the Wilkes, anti-Irish, or "No Popery" mobs, and only single fatalities resulted from other upheavals such as the Porteous riots of 1736. "It was authority rather than the crowd that was conspicuous for its violence to life and limb": all 285 casualties of the Gordon riots, for example, were rioters.[26] Since a regular army was less at the ready for use against colonial mobs, casualty figures for American uprisings were naturally much reduced.

To some extent the general tendency toward a discriminating purposefulness was shared by mobs throughout western Europe, but within the British Empire the focused character of popular uprisings and also their persistence can be explained in part by the character of law enforcement procedures. There were no professional police forces in the eighteenth century. Instead the power of government depended traditionally upon institutions like the "hue and cry," by which the community in general rose to apprehend felons. In its original medieval form the "hue and cry" was a form of summary justice that resembled modern lynch law. More commonly by the eighteenth century magistrates turned to the *posse commitatus*, literally the "power of the country," and in practice all able-bodied men a sheriff might call upon to assist him. Where greater and more organized support was needed, magistrates could call out the militia.[27] Both the *posse* and the militia drew upon local men, including many of the same persons who made up the mob. This was particularly clear where these traditional mechanisms failed to function effectively. At Boston in September 1766 when customsmen contemplated breaking into the house of merchant Daniel Malcom to search for contraband goods, Sheriff Stephen Greenleaf threatened to call for support from members of the very crowd suspected of an intent to riot; and when someone suggested during the Stamp Act riots that the militia be raised he was told it had already risen. This situation meant that mobs could naturally assume the manner of a lawful institution, acting by habit with relative restraint and responsibility. On the other hand, the militia institutionalized the practice of forcible popular coercion and so made the formation of extra-legal mobs more natural that J. R. Western has called the militia "a relic of the bad old days" and hailed its passing as "a step towards . . . bringing civilization and humanity into our [English] political life."[28]

These law-enforcement mechanisms left magistrates virtually helpless whenever a large segment of the population was immediately involved in the disorder, or when the community had a strong sympathy for the rioters. The Boston militia's failure to act in the Stamp Act riots, which

[26] Rudé, *Crowd in History*, 255–57.

[27] On the "hue and cry" see Frederick Pollock and Frederic W. Maitland, *The History of English Law Before the Time of Edward I* (Cambridge, Eng., 1968 [orig. publ., Cambridge, Eng., 1895]), II, 578–80, and William Blackstone, *Commentaries on the Laws of England* (Philadelphia, 1771), IV, 290–91. John Shy, *Toward Lexington: The Role of the British Army in the Coming of the American Revolution* (Princeton, 1965), 40. The English militia underwent a period of decay after 1670 but was revived in 1757. See J. R. Western, *The English Militia in the Eighteenth Century* (London, 1965).

[28] Greenleaf's deposition, T. 1/446; *Providence Gaz.* (R.I.), Aug. 24, 1765. Western, *English Militia*, 74.

was repeated in nearly all the North American colonies, recapitulated a
similar refusal during the Knowles riot of 1747.[29] If the mob's sym-
pathizers were confined to a single locality, the governor could try to call
out the militias of surrounding areas, as Massachusetts Governor William
Shirley began to do in 1747, and as, to some extent, Governor Francis
Bernard attempted after the rescue of the *Polly* in 1765.[30] In the case of
sudden uprisings, however, these peace-keeping mechanisms were at best
partially effective since they required time to assemble strength, which
often made the effort wholly pointless.

When the disorder continued and the militia either failed to appear
or proved insufficient, there was, of course, the army, which was used
periodically in the eighteenth century against rioters in England and
Scotland. Even in America peacetime garrisons tended to be placed where
they might serve to maintain law and order. But since all Englishmen
shared a fear of standing armies the deployment of troops had always to
be a sensitive and carefully limited recourse. Military and civil spheres
of authority were rigidly separated, as was clear to Lord Jeffery Amherst,
who refused to use soldiers against antimilitary rioters during the Seven
Years' War because that function was "entirely foreign to their command
and belongs of right to none but the civil power." In fact troops could
be used against British subjects, as in the suppression of civil disorder, only
upon the request of local magistrates. This institutional inhibition carried,
if anything, more weight in the colonies. There royal governors had
quickly lost their right to declare martial law without the consent of the
provincial councils that were, again, usually filled with local men.[31]

For all practical purposes, then, when a large political unit such as an
entire town or colony condoned an act of mass force, problems were
raised "almost insoluble without rending the whole fabric of English
law." Nor was the situation confined to the colonies. After describing
England's institutions for keeping the peace under the later Stuarts, Max
Beloff suggested that no technique for maintaining order was found until
nineteenth-century reformers took on the task of reshaping urban government. Certainly by the 1770's no acceptable solution had been found—
neither by any colonists nor "anyone in London, Paris, or Rome, either,"
as Carl Bridenbaugh has put it. To even farsighted contemporaries like
John Adams the weakness of authority was a fact of the social order that

[29] Governor William Shirley explained the militia's failure to appear during the
opening stages of the Knowles riot by citing the militiamen's opposition to impressment and consequent sympathy for the rioters. See his letter to the Lords of
Trade, Dec. 1, 1747, in Lincoln, ed., *Shirley Correspondence*, I, 417–18. The English militia was also unreliable. It worked well against invasions and unpopular
rebellions, but was less likely to support the government when official orders
"clashed with the desires of the citizens" or when ordered to protect unpopular
minorities. Sir Robert Walpole believed "that if called on to suppress smuggling,
protect the turnpikes, or enforce the gin act, the militia would take the wrong
side." Western, *English Militia*, 72–73.

[30] Shirley to Josiah Willard, Nov. 19, 1747, Lincoln, ed., *Shirley Correspondence*, I,
407; Bernard's orders in *Providence Gaz.* (R.I.), Apr. 27, 1765.

[31] Shy, *Toward Lexington*, 39–40, 44, 47, 74. Amherst, quoted in J. C. Long, *Lord
Jeffery Amherst* (New York, 1933), 124.

necessarily conditioned the way rulers could act. "It is vain to expect or hope to carry on government against the universal bent and genius of the people," he wrote; "we may whimper and whine as much as we will, but nature made it impossible when she made man."[32]

The mechanisms of enforcing public order were rendered even more fragile since the difference between legal and illegal applications of mass force was distinct in theory, but sometimes indistinguishable in practice. The English common law prohibited riot, defined as an uprising of three or more persons who performed what Blackstone called an "unlawful act of violence" for a private purpose. If the act was never carried out or attempted the offense became unlawful assembly; if some effort was made toward its execution, rout; and if the purpose of the uprising was public rather than private—tearing down whore houses, for example, or destroying all enclosures rather than just those personally affecting the insurgents —the offense became treason since it constituted a usurpation of the king's function, a "levying war against the King." The precise legal offense lay not so much in the purpose of the uprising as in its use of force and violence "wherein the Law does not allow the Use of such Force." Such unlawful assumptions of force were carefully distinguished by commentators upon the common law from other occasions on which the law authorized a use of force. It was, for example, legal for force to be used by a sheriff, constable, "or perhaps even . . . a private Person" who assembled "a competent Number of People, in Order with Force to suppress Rebels, or Enemies, or Rioters"; for a justice of the peace to raise the *posse* when opposed in detaining lands, or for crown officers to raise "a Power as may effectually enable them to over-power any . . . Resistance" in the execution of the king's writs.[33]

In certain situations these distinctions offered at best a very uncertain guide as to who did or did not exert force lawfully. Should a *posse* employ more force than was necessary to overcome overt resistance, for example, its members acted illegally and were indictable for riot. And where established officials supported both sides in a confrontation, or where the legality of an act that officials were attempting to enforce was itself disputed, the decision as to who were or were not rioters seemed to depend upon the observer's point of view. Impressment is a good example. The colonists claimed that impressment was unlawful in North America under an act of 1708, while British authorities and some— but not all—spokesmen for the government held that the law had lapsed in 1713. The question was settled only in 1775, when Parliament finally repealed the "Sixth of Anne." Moreover, supposing impressment could indeed be carried on, were press warrants from provincial authorities still necessary? Royal instructions of 1697 had given royal governors the "sole power of impressing seamen in any of our plantations in America or in

---

[32] Shy, *Toward Lexington*, 44; Beloff, *Public Order*, 157–58; Bridenbaugh, *Cities in Revolt*, 297; C. F. Adams, ed., *Works of Adams*, IV, 74–75, V, 209.

[33] The definition of the common law of riot most commonly cited—for example, by John Adams in the Massacre trials—was from William Hawkins, *A Treatise of the Pleas of the Crown* (London, 1716), I, 155–59. See also Blackstone, *Commentaries*, IV, 146–47, and Edward Coke, *The Third Part of the Institutes of the Laws of England* (London, 1797), 176.

sight of them." Admittedly that clause was dropped in 1708, and a subsequent parliamentary act of 1746, which required the full consent of the governor and council before impressment could be carried on within their province, applied only to the West Indies. Nonetheless it seems that in 1764 the Lords of the Admiralty thought the requirement held throughout North America.[34] With the legality of impressment efforts so uncertain, especially when opposed by local authorities, it was possible to see the press gangs as "rioters" for trying *en masse* to perpetrate an unlawful act of violence. In that case the local townsmen who opposed them might be considered lawful defenders of the public welfare, acting much as they would in a *posse*. In 1770 John Adams cited opposition to press gangs who acted without warrants as an example of the lawful use of force; and when the sloop of war *Hornet* swept into Norfolk, Virginia, in September 1767 with a "bloody riotous plan . . . to impress seamen, without consulting the Mayor, or any other magistrate," the offense was charged to the pressmen. Roused by the watchman, who called out *"a riot by man of war's men,"* the inhabitants rose to back the magistrates, and not only secured the release of the impressed men but also imprisoned ten members of the press gang. The ship's captain, on the other hand, condemned the townsmen as "Rioters." Ambiguity was present, too, in Newport's *St. John* clash, which involved both impressment and criminal action on the part of royal seamen and culminated with Newporters firing on the king's ship. The Privy Council in England promptly classified the incident as a riot, but the Rhode Island governor's report boldly maintained that "the people meant nothing but to assist [the magistrates] in apprehending the Offenders" on the vessel, and even suggested that "their Conduct be honored with his Majesty's royal Approbation."[35]

The enforcement of the White Pines Acts was similarly open to legal dispute. The acts seemed to violate both the Massachusetts and Connecticut charters; the meaning of provisions exempting trees growing within townships (act of 1722) and those which were "the property of private persons" (act of 1729) was contested, and royal officials tended to work on the basis of interpretations of the laws that Bernhard Knollenberg has called farfetched and, in one case, "utterly untenable." The Exeter, New Hampshire, "riot" of 1734, for example, answered an attempt of the surveyor to seize boards on the argument that the authorization to seize logs from allegedly illegally felled white pine trees in the act of 1722 included an authorization to seize processed lumber. As a result, Knollenberg concluded, although the surveyors' reports "give the impression that the New Englanders were an utterly lawless lot, . . . in many if not most cases

[34] Clark, "Impressment of Seamen," *Essays in Honor of Andrews*, 198–224; Stout, "Manning the Royal Navy," *American Neptune*, XXIII (1963), 178–79; and Leonard W. Labaree, ed., *Royal Instructions to British Colonial Governors, 1670–1776* (New York, 1935), I, 442–43.

[35] L. Kinvin Wroth and Hiller B. Zobel, eds., *Legal Papers of John Adams* (Cambridge, Mass., 1965), III, 253. Account of the Norfolk incident by George Abyvon, Sept. 5, 1767, in Purdie and Dixon's *Va. Gaz.* (Wmsbg.), Oct. 1, 1767. Capt. Morgan quoted in Lemisch, "Jack Tar," *Wm. and Mary Qtly.*, 3d ser., XXV (1968), 391. Munro, ed., *Acts of the Privy Council, Colonial Series*, VI, 374; Gov. Samuel Ward to Treasury lords, Oct. 23, 1765, Ward MSS, Box 1, fol. 58.

they were standing for what they believed, with reason, were their legal and equitable rights in trees growing on their own lands."[36]

Occasions open to such conflicting interpretations were rare. Most often even those who sympathized with the mobs' motives condemned its use of force as illegal and unjustifiable. That ambiguous cases did arise, however, indicates that legitimacy and illegitimacy, *posses* and rioters, represented but poles of the same spectrum. And where a mob took upon itself the defense of the community, it benefited from a certain popular legitimacy even when the strict legality of its action was in doubt, particularly among a people taught that the legitimacy of law itself depended upon its defense of the public welfare.

Whatever quasi-legal status mobs were accorded by local communities was reinforced, moreover, by formal political thought. "Riots and rebellions" were often calmly accepted as a constant and even necessary element of free government. This acceptance depended, however, upon certain essential assumptions about popular uprisings. With words that could be drawn almost verbatim from John Locke or any other English author of similar convictions, colonial writers posited a continuing moderation and purposefulness on the part of the mob. "Tho' innocent Persons may sometimes suffer in popular Tumults," observed a 1768 writer in the *New York Journal*, "yet the general Resentment of the People is principally directed according to Justice, and the greatest Delinquent feels it most." Moreover, upheavals constituted only occasional interruptions in well-governed societies. "Good Laws and good Rulers will always be obey'd and respected"; "the Experience of all Ages proves, that Mankind are much more likely to submit to bad Laws and wicked Rulers, than to resist good ones." "Mobs and Tumults," it was often said, "never happen but thro' Oppression and a scandalous Abuse of Power."[37]

In the hands of Locke such remarks constituted relatively inert statements of fact. Colonial writers, however, often turned these pronouncements on their heads such that observed instances of popular disorder became *prima facie* indictments of authority. In 1747, for example, New Jersey land rioters argued that "from their Numbers, Violences, and unlawful Actions" it was to be "inferred that . . . they are wronged and oppressed, or else they would never *rebell agt. the Laws*." Always, a New

---

[36] Knollenberg, *Origin of the Revolution*, 122–30; Albion, *Forests and Sea Power*, 255–58.

[37] *N.Y. Jour.* (N.Y.C.), Aug. 18, 1768 (the writer was allegedly drawing together arguments that had recently appeared in the British press); and *N.Y. Jour. Supp.* (N.Y.C.), Jan. 4, 1770. Note also that Jefferson accepted Shays's Rebellion as a sign of health in American institutions only after he had been assured by men like Jay that the insurgents had acted purposely and moderately, and after he had concluded that the uprising represented no continuous threat to established government. "An insurrection in one of the 13. states in the course of 11. years that they have subsisted amounts to one in any particular state in 143 years, say a century and a half," he calculated. "This would not be near as many as has happened in every other government that has ever existed," and clearly posed no threat to the constitutional order as a whole. To David Hartley, July 2, 1787, Boyd, ed., *Jefferson Papers*, XI, 526.

York writer said in 1770, when "the People of any Government" become "turbulent and uneasy," it was above all "a certain Sign of Maladministration." Even when disorders were not directly leveled against government they provided "strong proofs that something is much amiss in the state" as William Samuel Johnson put it; that—in Samuel Adams's words—the "wheels of good government" were "somewhat clogged." Americans who used this argument against Britain in the 1760's continued to depend upon it two decades later when they reacted to Shays's Rebellion by seeking out the public "Disease" in their own independent governments that was indicated by the "Spirit of Licentiousness" in Massachusetts.[38]

Popular turbulence seemed to follow so naturally from inadequacies of government that uprisings were often described with similes from the physical world. In 1770 John Adams said that there were "Church-quakes and state-quakes in the moral and political world, as well as earthquakes, storms and tempests in the physical." Two years earlier a writer in the *New York Journal* likened popular tumults to "Thunder Gusts" which "commonly do more Good than Harm." Thomas Jefferson continued the imagery in the 1780's, particularly with his famous statement that he liked "a little rebellion now and then" for it was "like a storm in the atmosphere." It was, moreover, because of the "imperfection of all things in this world," including government, that Adams found it "vain to seek a government in all points free from a possibility of civil wars, tumults and seditions." That was "a blessing denied to this life and preserved to complete the felicity of the next."[39]

If popular uprisings occurred "in all governments at all times," they were nonetheless most able to break out in free governments. Tyrants imposed order and submission upon their subjects by force, thus dividing society, as Jefferson said, into wolves and sheep. Only under free governments were the people "nervous," spirited, jealous of their rights, ready to react against unjust provocations; and this being the case, popular disorders could be interpreted as "Symptoms of a strong and healthy Constitution" even while they indicated some lesser shortcoming in administration. It would be futile, Josiah Quincy, Jr., said in 1770, to expect "that pacific, timid, obsequious, and servile temper, so predominant in more despotic governments" from those who lived under free British institutions. From "our happy constitution," he claimed, there resulted as "very natural Effects" an "impatience of injuries, and a strong resentment of insults."[40]

[38] John Locke, *The Second Treatise of Government*, paragraphs 223–25. "A State of Facts Concerning the Riots . . . in New Jersey," *New Jersey Archives*, VII, 217. *N.Y. Jour. Supp.* (N.Y.C.), Jan. 4, 1770. Johnson to Wm. Pitkin, Apr. 29, 1768, Massachusetts Historical Society, *Collections*, 5th ser., IX (1885), 275. Adams as "Determinus" in *Boston Gazette*, Aug. 8, 1768; and Harry A. Cushing, ed., *The Writings of Samuel Adams* (New York, 1904–1908), I, 237. Jay to Jefferson, Oct. 27, 1786, Boyd, ed., *Jefferson Papers*, X, 488.

[39] Wroth and Zobel, ed., *Adams' Legal Papers*, III, 249–50; *N.Y. Jour. Supp.* (N.Y.C.), Aug. 18, 1768; Jefferson to Abigail Adams, Feb. 22, 1787, Boyd, ed., *Jefferson Papers*, XI, 174. C. F. Adams, ed., *Works of Adams*, IV, 77, 80 (quoting Algernon Sydney).

[40] Jefferson to Edward Carrington, Jan. 16, 1787, Boyd, ed., *Jefferson Papers*, XI, 49, and Rev. James Madison to Jefferson, Mar. 28, 1787, *ibid.*, 252. Wroth

This popular impatience constituted an essential force in the maintenance of free institutions. "What country can preserve it's [*sic*] liberties
if their rulers are not warned from time to time that their people preserve
the spirit of resistance?" Jefferson asked in 1787. Occasional insurrections
were thus "an evil . . . productive of good": even those founded on
popular error tended to hold rulers "to the true principles of their institution" and generally provided "a medicine necessary for the sound health
of government." This meant that an aroused people had a role not only in
extreme situations, where revolution was requisite, but in the normal
course of free government. For that reason members of the House of
Lords could seriously argue—as A. J. P. Taylor has pointed out—that
"rioting is an essential part of our constitution"; and for that reason, too,
even Massachusetts' conservative Lieutenant Governor Thomas Hutchinson could remark in 1768 that "mobs a sort of them at least are
constitutional."[41]

It was, finally, the interaction of this constitutional role of the mob
with the written law that makes the story of eighteenth-century popular
uprisings complexity itself.[42] If mobs were appreciated because they provided a check on power, it was always understood that, insofar as upheavals threatened "running to such excesses, as will overturn the whole
system of government," "strong discouragements" had to be provided
against them. For eighteenth-century Americans, like the English writers

---

and Zobel, eds., *Adams' Legal Papers*, III, 250. Quincy's address to the jury
in the soldiers' trial after the Boston Massacre in Josiah Quincy, *Memoir of the
Life of Josiah Quincy, Junior, of Massachusetts Bay, 1744–1775*, ed. Eliza Susan
Quincy, 3d ed. (Boston, 1875), 46. See also Massachusetts Assembly's similar statement in its address to Gov. Hutchinson, Apr. 24, 1770, Hutchinson, *History of
Massachusetts Bay*, ed. Mayo, III, 365–66. This eighteenth-century devotion to
political "jealousy" resembles the doctrine of "vigilance" that was defended by
nineteenth-century vigilante groups. See Graham and Gurr, *Violence in America*,
179–83.

[41] Jefferson to William Stephen Smith, Nov. 13, 1787, Boyd, ed., *Jefferson Papers*,
XII, 356; Jefferson to Carrington, Jan. 16, 1787, *ibid*., XI, 49; Jefferson to James
Madison, Jan. 30, 1787, *ibid*., 92–93. Taylor's remarks in "History of Violence,"
*The Listener*, CXXIX (1968), 701. ("Members of the House of Lords . . . said
. . . if the people really don't like something, then they work our carriages and
tear off our wigs and throw stones through the windows of our town-houses. And
this is an essential thing to have if you are going to have a free country.") Hutchinson to [John or Robert] Grant, July 27, 1768, Massachusetts Archives, XXVI,
317, State House, Boston. See also the related story about John Selden, the famous
seventeenth-century lawyer, told to the House of Commons in January 1775 by
Lord Camden and recorded by Josiah Quincy, Jr., in the "Journal of Josiah
Quincy, Jun., During His Voyage and Residence in England from September 28th,
1774, to March 3d, 1775," Massachusetts Historical Society, *Proceedings*, L (1916–
1917), 462–63. Selden was asked what lawbook contained the laws for resisting
tyranny. He replied he did not know, "but I'll tell [you] what is most certain, that
it has always been the custom of England—and the Custom of England is the
*Law* of the *Land*."

[42] On the developing distinction Americans drew between what was legal and constitutional, see Wood, *Creation of the American Republic*, 261–68.

they admired, liberty demanded the rule of law. In extreme situations where the rulers had clearly chosen arbitrary power over the limits of law, men like John Adams could prefer the risk of anarchy to continued submission because "anarchy can never last long, and tyranny may be perpetual," but only when "there was any hope that the fair order of liberty and a free constitution would arise out of it." This desire to maintain the orderly rule of law led legislatures in England and the colonies to pass antiriot statutes and to make strong efforts—in the words of a 1753 Massachusetts law—to discountenance "a mobbish temper and spirit in . . . the inhabitants" that would oppose "all government and order."[43]

The problem of limiting mass violence was dealt with most intensely over a sustained period by the American Revolutionary leadership, which has perhaps suffered most from historians' earlier inattention to the history of colonial uprisings. So long as it could be maintained—as it was only fifteen years ago—that political mobs were "rare or unknown in America" before the 1760's, the Revolutionaries were implicitly credited with their creation. American patriots, Charles McLean Andrews wrote, were often "lawless men who were nothing more than agitators and demagogues" and who attracted a following from the riffraff of colonial society. It now seems clear that the mob drew on all elements of the population. More important, the Revolutionary leaders had no need to create mob support. Instead they were forced to work with a "permanent entity," a traditional crowd that exerted itself before, after, and even during the Revolutionary struggle over issues unrelated to the conflict with Britain, and that, as Hobsbawm has noted, characteristically aided the Revolutionary cause in the opening phases of conflict but was hard to discipline thereafter.[44]

In focusing popular exuberance the American leaders could work with long-established tendencies in the mob toward purposefulness and responsibility. In doing so they could, moreover, draw heavily upon the

[43] *N.Y. Jour. Supp.* (N.Y.C.), Jan. 4, 1770; Wroth and Zobel, eds., *Adams' Legal Papers*, III, 250; and C. F. Adams, ed., *Works of Adams*, VI, 151. Adams's views were altered in 1815, *ibid.*, X, 181. It is noteworthy that the Boston town meeting condemned the Knowles rioters not simply for their method of opposing impressment but because they insulted the governor and the legislature, and the Massachusetts Assembly acted against the uprising only after Governor Shirley had left Boston and events seemed to be "tending to the destruction of all government and order." Hutchinson, *History of Massachusetts Bay*, ed. Mayo, II, 332–33. *Acts and Resolves of the Province of Massachusetts Bay*, III, 647. (Chap. 18 of the Province laws, 1752–1753, "An Act for Further Preventing all Riotous, Tumultuous and Disorderly Assemblies or Companies or Persons. . . .") This act, which was inspired particularly by Pope's Day violence, was renewed after the Boston Massacre in 1770 even though the legislature refused to renew its main Riot Act of 1751. *Ibid.*, IV, 87.

[44] Arthur M. Schlesinger, "Political Mobs and the American Revolution, 1765–1776," *Proceedings of the American Philosophical Society*, XCIX (1955), 246; Charles M. Andrews, *The Colonial Background of the American Revolution*, rev. ed. (New Haven, 1939), 176; Charles M. Andrews, "The Boston Merchants and the Non-Importation Movement," Colonial Society of Massachusetts, *Transactions*, XIX (1916–1917), 241; Hobsbawm, *Primitive Rebels*, 111, 123–24.

guidelines for direct action that had been defined by English radical writers since the seventeenth century. Extralegal action was justified only when all established avenues to redress had failed. It could not answer casual errors or private failings on the part of the magistrates, but had to await fundamental public abuses so egregious that the "whole people" turned against their rulers. Even then, it was held, opposition had to be measured so that no more force was exerted than was necessary for the public good. Following these principles colonial leaders sought by careful organization to avoid the excesses that first greeted the Stamp Act. Hutchinson's query after a crowd in Connecticut had forced the resignation of stampman Jared Ingersoll—whether "such a public regular assembly can be called a mob"—could with equal appropriateness have been repeated during the tea resistance, or in 1774 when Massachusetts *mandamus* councillors were forced to resign.[45]

From the first appearance of an organized resistance movement in 1765, moreover, efforts were made to support the legal magistrates such that, as John Adams said in 1774, government would have "as much vigor then as ever" except where its authority was specifically under dispute. This concern for the maintenance of order and the general framework of law explains why the American Revolution was largely free from the "universal tumults and all the irregularities and violence of mobbish factions [that] naturally arise when legal authority ceases." It explains, too, why old revolutionaries like Samuel Adams or Christopher Gadsden disapproved of those popular conventions and committees that persisted after regular independent state governments were established in the 1770's. "Decency and Respect [are] due to Constitutional Authority," Samuel Adams said in 1784, "and those Men, who under any Pretence or by any Means whatever, would lessen the Weight of Government lawfully exercised must be Enemies to our happy Revolution and the Common Liberty."[46]

In normal circumstances the "strong discouragements" to dangerous disorder were provided by established legislatures. The measures enacted by them to deal with insurrections were shaped by the eighteenth-century understanding of civil uprisings. Since turbulence indicated above all some shortcoming in government, it was never to be met by increasing the authorities' power of suppression. The "weakness of authority" that was a function of its dependence upon popular support appeared to contemporary Americans as a continuing virtue of British institutions, as one reason why rulers could not simply dictate to their subjects and why Britain had for so long been hailed as one of the freest nations in Europe. It was "far less dangerous to the Freedom of a State" to allow "the laws

---

[45] Hutchinson to Thomas Pownall, [Sept. or Oct. 1765], Mass. Archives, XXVI, 157. Pauline Maier, From Resistance to Revolution: American Radicals and the Development of Intercolonial Opposition to Britain, 1765–1776 (unpubl. Ph.D. diss., Harvard University, 1968), I, 37–45, 72–215.

[46] C. F. Adams, ed., *Works of Adams*, IV, 51; Rev. Samuel Langdon's election sermon to third Massachusetts Provincial Congress, May 31, 1775, quoted in Richard Frothingham, *Life and Times of Joseph Warren* (Boston, 1865), 499; Samuel Adams to Noah Webster, Apr. 30, 1784, Cushing, ed., *Writings of Samuel Adams*, IV, 305–06. On Gadsden see Richard Walsh, *Charleston's Sons of Liberty* (Columbia, 1959), 87.

to be trampled upon, by the licence among the rabble . . . than to dispence with their force by an act of power." Insurrections were to be answered by reform, by attacking the "Disease"—to use John Jay's term of 1786—that lay behind them rather than by suppressing its "Symptoms." And ultimately, as William Samuel Johnson observed in 1768, "the only effectual way to prevent them is to govern with wisdom, justice, and moderation."[47]

In immediate crises, however, legislatures in both England and America resorted to special legislation that supplemented the common law prohibition of riot. The English Riot Act of 1714 was passed when disorder threatened to disrupt the accession of George I; a Connecticut act of 1722 followed a rash of incidents over land title in Hartford County; the Massachusetts act of 1751 answered "several tumultuous assemblies" over the currency issue and another of 1786 was enacted at the time of Shays's Rebellion. The New Jersey legislature passed an act in 1747 during that colony's protracted land riots; Pennsylvania's Riot Act of 1764 was inspired by the Paxton Boys; North Carolina's of 1771 by the Regulators; New York's of 1774 by the "land wars" in Charlotte and Albany counties.[48] Always the acts specified that the magistrates were to depend upon the *posse* in enforcing their provisions, and in North Carolina on the militia as well. They differed over the number of people who had to remain "unlawfully, riotously, and tumultuously assembled together, to the Disturbance of the Publick Peace" for one hour after the reading of a prescribed riot proclamation before becoming judicable under the act. Some colonies specified lesser punishments than the death penalty provided for in the English act, but the American statutes were not in general more "liberal" than the British. Two of them so violated elementary judicial rights that they were subsequently condemned—North Carolina's by Britain, and New York's act of 1774 by a later, Revolutionary state legislature.[49]

In one important respect, however, the English Riot Act was reformed. Each colonial riot law, except that of Connecticut, was enacted for only one to three years, whereas the British law was perpetual. By this provision colonial legislators avoided the shortcoming which, it was said,

---

[47] *N.Y. Jour. Supp.* (N.Y.C.), Jan. 4, 1770; Jay to Jefferson, Oct. 27, 1786, Boyd, ed., *Jefferson Papers*, X, 488; Johnson to William Pitkin, July 23, 1768, Massachusetts Historical Society, *Collections*, 5th ser., IX, 294–95.

[48] *The Statutes at Large* [of Great Britain] (London, 1786), V, 4–6; Hoadly, ed., *Public Records of Connecticut*, VI, 346–48, for the law, and see also 332–33, 341–48; *Acts and Resolves of Massachusetts Bay*, III, 544–46, for the Riot Act of 1751, and see also Hutchinson, *History of Massachusetts Bay*, ed. Mayo, III, 6–7; and *Acts and Laws of the Commonwealth of Massachusetts* (Boston, 1893), 87–88, for Act of 1786; "A State of Facts Concerning the Riots . . . in New Jersey," *N.J. Archives*, VII, 211–12, 221–22; *The Statutes at Large of Pennsylvania . . .* (n.p., 1899), VI, 325–28; William A. Saunders, ed., *The Colonial Records of North Carolina* (Raleigh, 1890), VIII, 481–86; *Laws of the Colony of New York in the Years 1774 and 1775* (Albany, 1888), 38–43.

[49] See additional instruction to Gov. Josiah Martin, Saunders, ed., *Colonial Records of North Carolina*, VIII, 515–16; and *Laws of the State of New York* (Albany, 1886), I, 20.

was "more likely to introduce *arbitrary Power* than even an *Army* itself," because a perpetual riot act meant that "in all future time" by "reading a Proclamation" the crown had the power "of hanging up their Subjects wholesale, or of picking out Those, to whom they have the greatest Dislike." If the death penalty was removed, the danger was less. When, therefore, riot acts without limit of time were finally enacted—as Connecticut had done in 1722, Massachusetts in 1786, New Jersey in 1797—the punishments were considerably milder, providing, for example, for imprisonment not exceeding six months in Connecticut, one year in Massachusetts, and three years in New Jersey.[50]

Riot legislation, it is true, was not the only recourse against insurgents, who throughout the eighteenth century could also be prosecuted for treason. The colonial and state riot acts suggest, nonetheless, that American legislators recognized the participants in civil insurrections as guilty of a crime peculiarly complicated because it had social benefits as well as damages. To some degree, it appears, they shared the idea expressed well by Jefferson in 1787: that "honest republican governors" should be "so mild in their punishments of rebellions, as not to discourage them too much."[51] Even in countering riots the legislators seemed as intent upon preventing any perversion of the forces of law and order by established authorities as with chastising the insurgents. Reform of the English Riot Act thus paralleled the abolition of constituent treasons—a traditional recourse against enemies of the crown—in American state treason acts of the Revolutionary period and finally in Article III of the federal Constitution.[52] From the same preoccupation, too, sprang the limitations placed upon the regular army provided for in the Constitution in part to assure the continuation of republican government guaranteed to the states by Article IV, Section iv. Just as the riot acts were for so long limited in duration, appropriations for the army were never to extend beyond two years (Article I, Section viii, 12); and the army could be used within a state against domestic violence only after application by the legislature or governor, if the legislature could not be convened (Article IV, Section iv).

A continuing desire to control authority through popular action also underlay the declaration in the Second Amendment that "a well regulated Militia being necessary to the security of a free State," citizens were assured the "right . . . to keep and bear Arms." The militia was meant above all "to prevent the establishment of a standing army, the bane of liberty"; and the right to bear arms—taken in part from the English Bill of Rights of 1689—was considered a standing threat to would-be tyrants. It embodied "a public allowance, under due restrictions, of the *natural right of resistance and self-preservation*, when the sanctions of society and laws are found *insufficient* to restrain the *violence of oppression*." And on the basis of their eighteenth-century experience, Americans could con-

---

[50] *The Craftsman* (London, 1731), VI, 263–64. Connecticut and Massachusetts laws cited in n. 45; and *Laws of the State of New Jersey* (Trenton, 1821), 279–81.

[51] Jefferson to Madison, Jan. 30, 1787, Boyd, ed., *Jefferson Papers*, XI, 93.

[52] See Bradley Chapin, "Colonial and Revolutionary Origins of the American Law of Treason," *Wm. and Mary Qtly.*, 3d ser., XVII (1960), 3–21.

sider that right to be "perfectly harmless. . . . If the government be equitable; if it be reasonable in its exactions; if proper attention be paid to the education of children in knowledge, and religion," Timothy Dwight declared, "few men will be disposed to use arms, unless for their amusement, and for the defence of themselves and their country."[53]

The need felt to continue the eighteenth-century militia as a counterweight to government along with the efforts to outlaw rioting and to provide for the use of a standing army against domestic insurrections under carefully defined circumstances together illustrate the complex attitude toward peacekeeping that prevailed among the nation's founders. The rule of law had to be maintained, yet complete order was neither expected nor even desired when it could be purchased, it seemed, only at the cost of forcefully suppressing the spirit of a free people. The constant possibility of insurrection—as institutionalized in the militia—was to remain an element of the United States Constitution, just as it had played an essential role in Great Britain's.

This readiness to accept some degree of tumultuousness depended to a large degree upon the lawmakers' own experience with insurrections in the eighteenth century, when "disorder" was seldom anarchic and "rioters" often acted to defend law and justice rather than to oppose them. In the years after independence this toleration declined, in part because mass action took on new dimensions. Nineteenth-century mobs often resembled in outward form those of the previous century, but a new violence was added. Moreover, the literal assumption of popular rule in the years after Lexington taught many thoughtful Revolutionary partisans what was for them an unexpected lesson—that the people were "as capable of despotism as any prince," that "public liberty was no guarantee after all of private liberty."[54] With home rule secured, attention focused more exclusively upon minority rights, which mob action had always to some extent imperiled. And the danger that uprisings carried for individual freedom became ever more egregious as mobs shed their former restraint and burned Catholic convents, attacked nativist speakers, lynched Mormons, or destroyed the presses and threatened the lives of abolitionists.

Ultimately, however, changing attitudes toward popular uprisings turned upon fundamental transformations in the political perspective of Americans after 1776. Throughout the eighteenth century political institutions had been viewed as in a constant evolution: the colonies' relationship with Britain and with each other, even the balance of power within the governments of various colonies, remained unsettled. Under such circumstances the imputations of governmental shortcoming that uprisings carried could easily be accepted and absorbed. But after Independence, when the form and conduct of the Americans' governments were under their exclusive control, and when those governments represented, more-

[53] Elbridge Gerry in Congressional debates, quoted in Irving Brant, *The Bill of Rights, Its Origin and Meaning* (Indianapolis, 1965), 486; Samuel Adams, quoting Blackstone, as "E. A." in *Boston Gaz.*, Feb. 27, 1769, and Cushing, ed., *Writings of Samuel Adams*, I, 317. Timothy Dwight, quoted in Daniel J. Boorstin, *The Americans: The Colonial Experience* (New York, 1958), 353.

[54] Wood, *Creation of the American Republic*, 410.

over, an experiment in republicanism on which depended their own happiness and "that of generations unborn," Americans became less ready to endure domestic turbulence or accept its disturbing implications. Some continued to argue that "distrust and dissatisfaction" on the part of the multitude were "always the consequence of tyranny or corruption." Others, however, began to see domestic turbulence not as indictments but as insults to government that were likely to discredit American republicanism in the eyes of European observers. "Mobs are a reproach to Free Governments," where all grievances could be legally redressed through the courts or the ballot box, it was argued in 1783. They originated there "not in Oppression, but in Licentiousness," an "ungovernable spirit" among the people. Under republican governments even that distrust of power colonists had found so necessary for liberty, and which uprisings seemed to manifest, could appear outmoded. "There is some consistency in being jealous of power in the hands of those who assume it by birth . . . and over whom we have no controul . . . as was the case with the Crown of England over America," another writer suggested. "But to be jealous of those whom we chuse, the instant we have chosen them" was absurd: perhaps in the transition from monarchy to republic Americans had "bastardized" their ideas by placing jealousy where confidence was more appropriate.[55] In short, the assumptions behind the Americans' earlier toleration of the mob were corroded in republican America. Old and new attitudes coexisted in the 1780's and even later. But the appropriateness of popular uprisings in the United States became increasingly in doubt after the federal Constitution came to be seen as the final product of long-term institutional experimentation, "a momentous contribution to the history of politics" that rendered even that most glorious exertion of popular force, revolution itself, an obsolete resort for Americans.[56]

Yet this change must not be viewed exclusively as a product of America's distinctive Revolutionary achievement. J. H. Plumb has pointed out that a century earlier, when England passed beyond her revolutionary era and progressed toward political "stability," radical ideology with its talk of resistance and revolution was gradually left behind. A commitment to peace and permanence emerged from decades of fundamental change. In America as in England this stability demanded that operative sovereignty, including the right finally to decide what was and was not in the community's interest, and which laws were and were not constitutional, be entrusted to established governmental institutions. The result was to minimize the role of the people at large, who had been the ultimate arbiters of those questions in English and American Revolutionary thought. Even law enforcement was to become the task primarily of professional agencies. As a result in time all popular upheavals alike became menacing efforts to "pluck up law and justice by the roots,"

---

[55] Judge Aedanus Burke's Charge to the Grand Jury at Charleston, June 9, 1783, in *South-Carolina Gazette and General Advertiser* (Charleston), June 10, 1783; "A Patriot," *ibid.*, July 15, 1783; and "Another Patriot," *ibid.*, July 29, 1783; and on the relevance of jealousy of power, see a letter to Virginia in *ibid.*, Aug. 9, 1783. "Democratic Gentle-Touch," *Gazette of the State of South Carolina* (Charleston), May 13, 1784.

[56] Wood, *Creation of the American Republic*, 612–14.

and riot itself gradually became defined as a purposeless act of anarchy, "a blind and misguided outburst of popular fury," of "undirected violence with no articulated goals."[57]

[57] J. H. Plumb, *The Origins of Political Stability, England 1675–1725* (Boston, 1967), XV, 187; John Adams on the leaders of Shays's Rebellion in a letter to Benjamin Hitchborn, Jan. 27, 1787, in C. F. Adams, ed., *Works of Adams*, IX, 551; modern definitions of riot in "Riot Control and the Use of Federal Troops," *Harvard Law Review*, LXXXI (1968), 643.

# Suggestions for Further Reading

Two good general introductions to American Indian life are Alvin M. Josephy, Jr., *The Indian Heritage of America** (Knopf, 1968), and Peter Farb, *Man's Rise to Civilization as Shown by the Indians of North America from Primeval Times to the Coming of the Industrial State** (Dutton, 1968). Relations between Indians and whites throughout American history are treated in William T. Hagan, *American Indians** (University of Chicago Press, 1961); Roy Harvey Pearce, *The Savages of America: A Study of the Indian and the Idea of Civilization** (Johns Hopkins Press, 1953); and a collection of documents edited by Wilcomb E. Washburn, *The Indian and the White Man** (Doubleday, 1964). Indian wars of the colonial period are dealt with in Alden Vaughan, *New England Frontier: Puritans and Indians, 1620–1675** (Little, Brown, 1965), and Douglas Leach, *Flintlock and Tomahawk: New England in King Philip's War** (Norton, 1958). Nancy Oestreich Lurie considers the cultural impact of the colonists on the Indians in "Indian Cultural Adjustment to European Civilization," in James Morton Smith (ed.), *Seventeenth-Century America: Essays on Colonial History** (University of North Carolina Press, 1959).

An excellent study of American slavery in the context of world history is David B. Davis, *The Problem of Slavery in Western Culture** (Cornell University Press, 1966). On the question of whether slavery led to prejudice or prejudice led to slavery, see Oscar and Mary Handlin, "Origins of the Southern Labor System," *William and Mary Quarterly*, 3d Ser., Vol. 7 (April, 1950), 199–222, reprinted as Chapter 1 of Oscar Handlin, *Race and Nationality in American Life** (Little, Brown, 1957); Carl Degler, "Slavery and the Genesis of American Race Prejudice," *Comparative Studies in Society and History*, Vol. 2 (October, 1959), 49–66, enlarged, revised, and reprinted in Degler's *Out of Our Past** (Harper and Row, 1959), pp. 26–39; and Winthrop D. Jordan, "Modern Tensions and the Origins of American Slavery," *Journal of Southern History*, Vol. 28 (February, 1962), 18–30. Two excellent collections of essays on the development of slavery in the New World are Allen Weinstein and Frank O. Gatell (eds.), *American Negro Slavery: A Modern Reader** (Oxford University Press, 1968), and Laura Foner and Eugene Genovese (eds.), *Slavery in the New World: A Reader in Comparative History** (Prentice-Hall, 1969). The basic primary source on the slave trade is Elizabeth Donnan (ed.), *Documents Illustrative of the Slave Trade in America* (4 vols.; Carnegie Institution, 1930–35). A good secondary treatment of the trade is Daniel P. Mannix and Malcolm Cowley, *Black Cargoes: The*

* Available in paperback edition.

*Story of the Atlantic Slave Trade, 1518–1865\** (Viking, 1962). Little
has been written on slavery in the colonies, but two pertinent studies
are Lorenzo Greene, *The Negro in Colonial New England\** (Columbia University Press, 1942), and Thaddeus Tate, Jr., *The Negro
in Eighteenth-Century Williamsburg\** (University of Virginia
Press, 1965).

The standard works on white servants and laborers in the col-
onies are Abbot E. Smith, *Colonists in Bondage: White Servitude
and Convict Labor in America, 1607–1776* (University of North
Carolina Press, 1947), and Richard B. Morris, *Government and
Labor in Early America\** (Columbia University Press, 1946).
Warren B. Smith examines the situation in a particular state in
*White Servitude in Colonial South Carolina* (University of South
Carolina Press, 1961). John Barth's novel *The Sot-Weed Factor\**
(Doubleday, 1960) gives a hilarious, bawdy, and authentic picture
of life in colonial Maryland, in the process conveying a good deal
of information about white servitude.

A number of studies of violence in American history have appeared in recent years, but most have been superficial and lacking
in perspective. A rather good collection of essays, prepared for the
President's Commission on the Causes and Prevention of Violence,
is Hugh Davis Graham and Ted Robert Gurr (eds.), *Violence in
America: Historical and Comparative Perspectives\** (2 vols.; U.S.
Government Printing Office, 1969), also available in one-volume
paperbound editions from New American Library and Bantam. A
useful collection of primary sources is Richard Hofstadter and
Michael Wallace (eds.), *American Violence: A Documentary His-
tory\** (Knopf, 1970), which includes a long introductory essay by
Hofstadter. With regard to violence in colonial and revolutionary
America, see also Richard M. Brown, *The South Carolina Regulators* (Harvard University Press, 1963), and two essays by Jesse
Lemisch, "Jack Tar in the Streets: Merchant Seamen in the Politics
of Revolutionary America," *William and Mary Quarterly*, 3d Ser.,
Vol. 21 (July, 1968), 371–407, and "The American Revolution
Seen from the Bottom Up," in Barton J. Bernstein (ed.), *Toward
a New Past: Dissenting Essays in American History\** (Pantheon,
(1967), pp. 3–45.

# The New
# Nation

# Enforcement of the Alien

# and

# Sedition Acts

## JAMES MORTON SMITH

Nativism, or anti-foreign sentiment, has been a persistent theme in American history. Between the 1840's and the 1920's this feeling reached a peak of virulence, but intimations of it were present much earlier. The Alien and Sedition Acts, for instance, passed in 1798 by the Federalist-dominated Congress, provide an example of nativism as well as of early attempts to suppress political dissent. This group of four laws included the Naturalization Act, which increased the residency requirement for naturalization from five to fourteen years; the Act Concerning Aliens (the Alien Friends Act), which allowed the President to imprison or deport any alien who threatened the national welfare; the Act Respecting Alien Enemies, which empowered the President to imprison or deport enemy aliens in time of war; and the Act for the Punishment of Certain Crimes (the Sedition Act), which forbade, among other things, that anyone should "write, print, utter, or publish, or shall cause or procure to be written, printed, uttered, or published . . . any false, scandalous, and malicious writing or writings against the government of the United States, or either House of Congress of the United States, or the President of the United States, with intent to defame . . . or to bring them into contempt or disrepute."

Although the suppression of the growing Republican opposition to the Federalist party was the general aim of these laws, the occasion for their passage was a great influx of refugees from two abortive republican revolutions in Europe—the French Revolution, which began in 1789 and ended with the start of the Napoleonic era in 1799, and the uprising of the United Irishmen in 1798. Large groups of French and Irish fled to American shores when their cause was lost. They were natural recruits for the Republican party, and the Federalists sought to limit their potential political power by the Naturalization Act.

The Alien Acts were partially a response to the growing hostility between France and the United States that erupted in 1798 into a two-year quasi-war. Anti-French feeling reached a peak after the XYZ affair, when official agents of the French government known only as X, Y, and Z demanded a bribe and a "loan" before they were willing to begin negotiations with American envoys to avoid impending hostilities. The envoys left France in a huff, and citizens at home raised the cry "Millions for defense but not one cent for tribute." From that time on, the Federalists tended to regard all Frenchmen as enemies of the American state.

The Sedition Act, which dealt less with sedition than with political dissent, was clearly intended to destroy the Republican press. It drew an angry response from many quarters, most notably in the Kentucky and Virginia resolves, written by Jefferson and Madison respectively, which declared the Alien and Sedition Acts unconstitutional and laid the groundwork for the increasingly important and complex doctrine of states' rights.

Had the Federalists won the election of 1800, it is not unlikely that these repressive laws would have seriously divided the country and led to internal hostilities. Jefferson and the Republicans won, however, and the Alien and Sedition Acts that had not expired were repealed.

In subsequent years, domestic crisis frequently brought forth fears of foreign intrigue and attempts at domestic repression. The Espionage Act of 1917, for example, was a much more severe sedition act than the one of 1798, and the Cold War years of our own time have increased fears of both foreign and domestic intrigue.

The following study, by James Morton Smith of the Wisconsin Historical Society, describes the enforcement of two of the acts of 1798, the Alien Friends Act and the Sedition Act, and indicates the excesses of the latter.

---

*Would to God the immigrants could be collected and retransported to the climes from whence they came.*

GAZETTE OF THE UNITED STATES, 1798

The test of the effectiveness of an act presumably lies in the extent to which it was invoked and enforced. Thirteen years after the expiration

"Enforcement of the Alien and Sedition Acts." Reprinted from James Morton Smith, *Freedom's Fetters: The Alien and Sedition Laws and American Civil Liberties*, pp. 159–87. Copyright © 1956 by Cornell University. Used by permission of Cornell University Press. The first part of this chapter was originally published in *The Mississippi Valley Historical Review*, XLI (1954), 85–104.

of the Alien Friends Act, former President Adams wrote that he had not applied it in a single instance.[1] Although the arbitrary measure was never officially invoked, it was not without effect. Adams' statement left out of consideration two important things: first, the effect which the discussion and passage of the law had in bringing about the departure of numerous foreigners who might otherwise have run afoul of its provisions; and second, the persistent efforts of some of the officials in the Adams administration to obtain action against other foreigners who had not departed and whose activities made them especially objectionable to the Federalists.

## DANGEROUS ALIENS: THE ENFORCEMENT OF THE ALIEN FRIENDS ACT

Shortly after the introduction of the alien bills in Congress, apprehensive Frenchmen began scheduling passage from the United States. In May, 1798, nearly two months before the law was passed, Jefferson wrote that

the threatening appearances from the Alien bills have so alarmed the French who are among us, that they are going off. A ship, chartered by themselves for this purpose, will sail within a fortnight for France, with as many as she can carry. Among these I believe will be Volney, who has in truth been the principal object aimed at by the law.[2]

This reference to the Federalist attitude toward Constantin François Chasseboeuf, Comte de Volney, French scientist and author, was strikingly confirmed when, on June 22, *Porcupine's Gazette*, edited by the English expatriate William Cobbett, published a letter which charged that the country had become the resort "of abominably seditious foreigners of every distinction." Using the pseudonym "An American," this correspondent singled out Volney as an especially dangerous "French democrat," an atheist, and a disciple of French revolutionary thought.

It is a fact not to be controverted at this day [the letter continued], that the French have done more toward the destruction of the government of Europe, by their political emissaries, preaching the vile doctrine of infidelity and atheism, and by their spies sent to creat[e] divisions among the people, and distinction between them and their government; they have done more by this means of intrigue, than by the combined strength of their armies or the bravery of their military force.—With this truth we cannot be too

---

[1] Adams to Jefferson, Quincy, June 14, 1813, *Adams' Works*, X, 42.
[2] Jefferson to Madison, May 3, 1798, *Jefferson's Writings* (Ford ed.), VII, 248. Also see Jefferson to Monroe, May 21, 1798, *ibid.*, 257.

strongly impressed. Americans! Beware—at this moment beware
of the diplomatic skill of the French republic.[3]

Shifting his attack to Jefferson, the writer suggested that since the vice-
president did not seem to consider an infidel and an atheist as dangerous
to society, the continued presence of Volney was even more dangerous
to the people of the United States.

To avoid expulsion, however, Volney had sailed for France aboard
the *Benjamin Franklin* on June 7, nearly three weeks before the alien bill
became law, and Jefferson, who had feared that those Frenchmen leaving
to avoid the law would go "under irritations calculated to fan the flame,"
was relieved to find that Volney, at least, harbored no such animosity.
"He is most thoroughly impressed with the importance of preventing
war," he reported, "whether considered with reference to the interests of
the two countries, of the cause of republicanism, or of man on the broad
scale."[4]

Also sailing on the *Franklin* was Victor Marie DuPont, the newly
appointed consul general of the French Republic to the United States,
who had arrived in May and, on finding that the government refused to
accept his credentials, had decided to return to France with Volney and
the other fleeing Frenchmen.[5] These departures met with administrative
approval, and Secretary Pickering promptly requested free and un-
molested passage for their ship en route to France. A similar permit was
issued a month later to guarantee safe passage for a shipload of Frenchmen bound for Bordeaux; and in July and August, directly after the
adoption of the Alien Friends Act, more than a dozen additional shiploads
of anxious Frenchmen sailed for France or Santo Domingo.[6] The departure of Volney was hailed as "good riddance" by at least one New York
newspaper, and so strong did the anti-alien feeling run in June that the
*Aurora* soberly reported that "Cremona fiddles are to be ordered out of
the kingdom under the *Alien Bill*," on the ground that their tones were
"calculated to bring the *constitutional* music of *organs* and *kettle-drums*
into contempt."[7] Although violins were not ousted, anti-French sentiment

[3] *Porcupine's Gazette*, June 22, 1798, as quoted in Gilbert Chinard, *Volney et
l'Amérique d'après des documents inédits et sa correspondance avec Jefferson* (Baltimore, 1923), 97–99.

[4] Jefferson to Madison, May 31 and June 7, 1798, *Jefferson's Writings* (Ford ed.),
VII, 262, 267.

[5] Samuel E. Morison, "DuPont, Talleyrand, and the French Spoliations," Mass. Hist.
Soc., *Proceedings*, 49 (1915), 64–65, citing a letter from Volney to Louis Marie de
la Révellière-Lépeaux.

[6] Fifteen ships sailed in two months. Although most of the passengers were French
merchants forced to leave because of the suspension of commercial intercourse between France and America, many of them left because of the passage of the Alien
Act. For the official correspondence see Domestic Letters, XI (1798–99), 11–35,
General Records of the Department of State, RG 59 (National Archives). Also see
Frances S. Childs, *French Refugee Life in the United States, 1790–1800* (Baltimore,
1940), 190–91.

[7] New York *Daily Advertiser*, July 4, 1798; *Aurora*, June 23, 1798.

reached such heights in July that the first lady predicted that if a new French minister were to arrive he would not find the United States a resting place for twenty-four hours.[8] The nativist pressure became so pervasive that the rhymed review of the year's political events by one of the "Hartford Wits" included the observation that

> Each factious alien shrinks with dread
> And hides his hemp-devoted head.[9]

The Federalist press made every attempt to uncover the hidden heads of factious aliens and clamored for the enforcement of the Alien Law. The *Gazette of the United States* claimed that the source of all political evils and misfortunes in the nation was "the facility with which foreigners acquire the full and perfect right of citizenship." This was the fountain from which defamation, falsehood, and sedition "so plenteously flowed."[10] A New York paper asked how a sound American could read with cold indifference

> the vile incendiary publications of foreign hirelings among us. . . . Such abominable miscreants deserve no place on the American soil. When the state is in danger and strong remedies are necessary . . . none but an ENEMY can resist their use. Such remedies have been provided by the late Session of Congress; and however long the partisans of France may declaim against them, every good citizen rejoices in the provision, and will aid in giving it efficacy.[11]

In a letter to the New York *Commercial Advertiser* on Christmas Eve, "Marcus Brutus" questioned the value of immigration in general. He confessed that many foreigners had quickly imbibed American principles, but denounced many others as "turbulent and disaffected zealots . . . the commodious instrument of the agents of France." Another New York correspondent had earlier opposed the "false sentiment" that America was an asylum for the oppressed. He called for the blanket enforcement of the Alien Law in a classic statement of an oft-repeated nativist sentiment: "Would to God the immigrants could be collected and retransported to the climes from whence they came."[12]

Although President John Adams did not go this far, he traveled a long way down the same road in his answer to a New York address. It was exceedingly regrettable, he wrote, that any marks of disaffection had appeared in New York. If this was due to "the influx of foreigners, of discontented characters, it ought to be a warning. If we glory in making our country an asylum for virtue in distress and for innocent industry, it

[8] Abigail Adams to Mary Cranch, July 17, 1798, Mitchell, *New Letters*, 205–06.
[9] Richard Alsop, *The Political Green-House for the Year 1798* (Hartford, 1799).
[10] *Gazette of the United States*, reprinted in the *Albany Centinel*, Aug. 3, 1798.
[11] *Albany Centinel*, Aug. 7, 1798. This story bears a New York dateline of Aug. 2, 1798.
[12] *Commercial Advertiser*, Dec. 24, 1798; *Daily Advertiser*, Sept. 2, 1798.

behoves us to beware, that under this pretext it is not made a receptacle of malevolence and turbulence, for the outcasts of the universe."[13]

Despite Adams' claim of nonexecution, then, his administration did not refrain on principle from enforcing the Alien Law. As a matter of fact, Secretary Pickering early complained that the law was so weak that the administration might be embarrassed in its enforcement efforts. Two omissions aroused his apprehensions: the law did not require aliens to post sureties pending their departure, and the president was not authorized to seize and confine them while waiting for their departure or deportation.[14]

These drawbacks, however, did not prevent the secretary from proposing a vigorous enforcement policy. Since President Adams was spending the time between sessions of Congress at his home in Massachusetts, Pickering hoped to expedite action by having the chief executive delegate his power over aliens to the Cabinet. The heads of the departments could then confer and decide by majority vote which aliens to expel; the president would have only to sign blank arrest warrants which would be filled in by the Cabinet.[15]

On October 11, therefore, Pickering mailed some blank deportation orders to the president.[16] On the same day, however, the secretary sent a second letter proposing an alternative method of handling cases against undesirable aliens. Lest Adams should have any doubt about the legality or expediency of delegating his powers under the Alien Act to the decision of the Cabinet, Pickering suggested three aliens whom he was sure that the president would agree were dangerous and asked him to sign the blank warrants for use against this trio.[17] Although the president did not question the legality of delegating his powers, he was convinced that the law's broad powers ought to receive "a strict construction." Adams therefore wrote his secretary that he preferred to make the decisions himself.[18]

Nonetheless, it was Pickering who became the chief enforcement officer. As the leading official in the Cabinet, he carried on an extensive correspondence with important Federalists in the Middle states, traditionally the most liberal in their immigration policies. Philadelphia and New York, the nation's leading ports of debarkation, received most of his attention, and the United Irishmen were most often mentioned as a dangerous group. On August 23, 1798, the United States district attorney for Pennsylvania, William Rawle, wrote Pickering about some unidentified "secret projects" of the United Irishmen. On the next day Richard Peters, United States district judge, notified the secretary that Philadelphia and

[13] To the Grand Jury of the County of Dutchess, N.Y., Sept. 22, 1798, *Adams' Works*, IX, 223.

[14] Pickering to the President of the United States, Trenton, Aug. 28, 1798, Pickering Papers, XXXVII, 325 (Mass. Hist. Soc.).

[15] Pickering to the President, Oct. 4, 1798, *ibid.*, IX, 426.

[16] Pickering to the President, Oct. 11, 1798, *Adams' Works*, VIII, 607n.

[17] Pickering to the President, Oct. 11, 1798, Pickering Papers, IX, 453 (Mass. Hist. Soc.).

[18] Adams to Pickering, Quincy, Oct. 17, 1798, *ibid.*, XXIII, 241. This letter is printed in *Adams' Works*, VIII, 606–07, under the date of Oct. 16.

vicinity contained "some Rascals . . . both Aliens and infamous Citizens" whom he wanted to handle if he could do it legally. He promised to send a full account of the "Alien Scoundrels" to Pickering if he could obtain one.[19]

Since both men were concerned about "the same discontented characters which infest our country," Pickering suggested that the judge talk with the district attorney about the steps necessary to cope with the dangerous aliens. He promised Rawle that he would "do anything to aid the measures you think proper respecting them," and "cheerfully" engaged to reimburse any expenses incurred in detecting the Irish "villains . . . who you have reason to apprehend are plotting mischief against your country." Later in the year John Jay, former chief justice of the United States Supreme Court and then governor of New York, sent Pickering an extract from an original letter which he claimed proved the existence of American societies of United Irishmen and of a design to increase their number.[20]

As early as August 18, less than two months after Adams signed the Alien Law and nearly two months before he decided not to delegate his authority to the Cabinet, Pickering informed the president that he was considering the use of the law. Ten days later he mentioned persons who "were objects of the alien law and ought to be sent out of the country." It was not until October, however, that Pickering launched his most concerted effort at enforcement. On October 4 he suggested that the French general, Victor Collot, and "some other foreigners ought to be ordered to depart from the United States."[21]

Like Volney, and perhaps for better reasons, Collot had been one of the targets of the Federalists in the passage of the Alien Act; but unlike Volney he did not leave the country because of its threats. While serving as the French governor of Guadeloupe he had surrendered that island to the British in 1794 with the understanding that he would be permitted to return to France. In order to avoid involvement in the Reign of Terror, however, he later persuaded the British officials to let him come

[19] Pickering to Rawle, Aug. 28, 1798, Pickering Papers, XXXVII, 326 (Mass. Hist. Soc.), acknowledges Rawle's letter of Aug. 23; Peters to Pickering, Belmont, Pa., Aug. 24, 1798, *ibid.*, XXIII, 71.

[20] Pickering to Peters, Aug. 28, 1798, Peters Manuscripts, X (1792–1807) (Hist. Soc. Pa.); Pickering to Rawle, Aug. 28, 1798, Pickering Papers, XXXVII, 326 (Mass. Hist. Soc.); and Jay to Pickering, Albany, Dec. 21, 1798, *ibid.*, XXIII, 372. That Rawle kept close tab on foreigners in Philadelphia is shown by this extract from a letter to Pickering: "I am also told there is in Philadelphia a Madame D'Autrement the mother of the present confidential secretary to Talleyrand which as foreign letters sometimes pass through your office it may be well to remember— She lately received a very large basket from Paris—." See his letter of Oct. 31, 1798, *ibid.*, XXIII, 275.

[21] Pickering to the President, Aug. 28 and Oct. 4, 1798, *ibid.*, XXXVII, 325, and IX, 426. In August, Adams had sent Pickering a copy of a letter from a Mr. Barnes who referred to these persons. Barnes' letter has not been located, and Pickering does not identify the aliens.

to the United States on parole as a prisoner of war. Acting under a commission from the French minister to the United States, he made a trip in 1796 along the Ohio and Lower Mississippi, from Pittsburgh by way of St. Louis to New Orleans, and aroused the suspicions of both the Federalists and the Spanish authorities because of the thoroughness of his examination of the topography, the resources, and the military establishments in the American West and in Spanish Louisiana.[22] In the course of his journey he was arrested and temporarily detained by the American commander at Fort Massac on the Ohio and by the Spanish governor in New Orleans. Following his return to Philadelphia early in 1797, administration agents kept close track of his activities. In November of that year Secretary Pickering received a report that Collot was connected with a French project for the seizure of Louisiana and the western part of the United States, and in February, 1798, Secretary of War James McHenry was given similar information, which he turned over to Pickering after the passage of the Alien Act.[23]

It was apparently on the basis of these reports that Pickering now decided to act. On October 11, a week after he had first suggested that Collot and other foreigners be ordered to depart, he submitted several blank orders and requested Adams to sign three of them for use against Collot, one of his associates named Sweitzer, and the French scientist, Pierre Samuel DuPont de Nemours, if he should arrive in the United States. At the same time he communicated the recommendation of Secretary of the Treasury Wolcott that the secretary of state should be designated as the proper officer to take evidence from aliens living in the vicinity of the nation's capital who wished to prove their innocence in order to obtain a license to remain in the United States. In cases such as Collot's, Pickering added, allowing an alien permission to offer these proofs would be a mere formality "in compliance with the *letter* of the law: for it is impossible for him to offer a good reason for staying here,

---

[22] For an excellent account of this mission, see George W. Kyte, "A Spy on the Western Waters: The Military Intelligence Mission of General Collot in 1796," *Mississippi Valley Historical Review*, 34 (1947), 427–42. Collot's own detailed notes on the expedition were published after his death as *Voyage dans l'Amérique septentrionale* (2 vols. and Atlas; Paris, 1826). For a statement from the French minister to his home government, see Pierre Auguste Adet to Minister of Foreign Affairs, June 21, 1796, Frederick J. Turner, ed., "Correspondence of the French Ministers to the United States, 1791–1797," Amer. Hist. Assoc., *Annual Report for 1903*, II, 928–29; and for the official American attempt to hamper Collot's mission, see James McHenry, secretary of war, to Arthur St. Clair, May, 1796, William H. Smith, ed., *The St. Clair Papers: The Life and Public Services of Arthur St. Clair* (Cincinnati, 1882), II, 395–96.

[23] J. J. Ulrich to Pickering, Nov. 29, 1797, Pickering Papers, XXI, 368 (Mass. Hist. Soc.); McHenry to Pickering, Sept. 10, 1798, quoting a report from Colonel Francis Mentges to McHenry, Feb. 13, 1798, *ibid.*, XXIII, 137. Mentges had received his information from Joseph Anthony Mercier, a French brick mason, who had conversed with Collot at his lodgings on the Schuylkill, near Philadelphia. Also see Durand Echeverria, "General Collot's Plan for a Reconnaissance of the Ohio and Mississippi Valleys, 1796," *William and Mary Quarterly*, 3d ser., 9 (1952), 512–20.

or any facts to prove that he is not a French intriguer and bitter enemy to this country." Even though Adams favored a strict interpretation of the law, he not only signed blank warrants to be filled out for the arrest of Collot and Sweitzer, and for DuPont de Nemours, "if he is to be found," but he also authorized Pickering to issue licenses to aliens "within a reasonable distance from the seat of government."[24]

Instead of moving against Collot and Sweitzer immediately, Pickering engaged Colonel Francis Mentges, Secretary McHenry's informant of the preceding February, to keep check on Collot and to get information on Sweitzer. When the colonel informed Pickering that General Jean M. P. Serurier was in the United States in disguise, the secretary launched a search for him and other Frenchmen, postponing the arrest of Collot and Sweitzer so as not to tip off the new suspects.[25]

While Pickering was trying to implicate additional aliens, General Collot decided to take advantage of the 1794 Articles of Capitulation. A change in the administration in France and an intensification of the anti-French mood in the United States led the general to apply to Robert Liston, British minister to the United States, for a passport to protect him on his return to France. When Liston informed Pickering of Collot's desire to depart, the secretary, who had earlier favored the general's immediate expulsion, now opposed his departure.[26] The British minister therefore refused to issue the passport, and the agents of the secretary of state continued to check on Collot in the hope that he would reveal the whereabouts of General Serurier and other suspects. After months of suspense, Pickering concluded that Serurier was not in the United States. By that time, he confessed to the president, "so many months had elapsed, and the session of Congress commenced, when other business pressed, the pursuit of these aliens was overlooked."[27]

On June 21, 1799, a Federalist paper reported that Collot was preparing to leave the United States.[28] A little later Colonel Mentges advised Pickering that Sweitzer was ready to depart for Hamburg. On August 1,

---

[24] Pickering to the President, Oct. 11, 1798, Pickering Papers, IX, 453 (Mass. Hist. Soc.); Adams to Pickering, Oct. 17, 1798, *ibid.*, XXIII, 241. The letter is endorsed on the back by Pickering: "received 26th with three Orders relative to Aliens."

[25] Pickering to the President, Aug. 1, 1799, *ibid.*, XI, 525. See also *Adams' Works*, IX, 6.

[26] See George W. Kyte, "The Detention of General Collot: A Sidelight on Anglo-American Relations, 1798–1800," *William and Mary Quarterly*, 3d ser., 6 (1949), 628–30. Liston wrote that Pickering opposed Collot's removal because he feared that the general would turn over to the French government the valuable military information which he had obtained concerning the West and would seek French authorization for an attack on the United States from that quarter with himself in command. While these reasons are plausible, they were as applicable at the time Pickering favored Collot's removal as when he opposed it. It seems more probable that Pickering opposed the removal of Collot because he considered him as the key man who would lead government agents to a round-up of many other suspects.

[27] Pickering to the President, Aug. 1, 1799, Pickering Papers, XI, 525 (Mass. Hist. Soc.).

[28] *Gazette of the United States,* June 21, 1799.

1799, nearly a year after Adams had authorized the expulsion of these aliens, Pickering relayed this information to the president but claimed that Collot, contrary to the press reports, remained in the country. Moreover, he added, the general was as much disposed as ever to do all the mischief in his power. Because of the reiterated observations that the Alien Law was a dead letter, the secretary of state suggested a new method of handling Collot as an alternative to deportation. Inasmuch as he was still a British prisoner of war, the United States might compel him to place himself under British jurisdiction, "where he can do no harm."[29]

President Adams, however, preferred to try the Alien Law against Collot. Although he feared it would prove "inadequate to the object intended," he asserted that he had always been ready and willing to execute it against the French general. The fact that the United States was about to enter a second negotiation with France did not alter the situation; the president was satisfied that Collot was "a pernicious and malicious intriguer." It was therefore more necessary than ever "to remove such an instrument of mischief from among our people, for his whole time will be employed in exciting corrupt divisions, whether he can succeed or not."[30]

Again Collot was not arrested immediately, although a close watch was kept on his activities. Elisha Boudinot, one of the justices of the New Jersey Supreme Court, notified Pickering on August 7, 1799, that the general was residing at Newark incognito. "He cannot be here for any good," the vigilant judge wrote, "and if sufficient cause could be obtained to send him off, I suppose it would be but doing what the public voice says ought to have been done long ago—hither to the *Alien bill* as to any good it has done is a meer [*sic*] dead letter—."

To buttress his suggestion that Collot should be deported, the New Jersey Federalist reported several bits of derogatory information, which he thought worthy of communication even though they might be "of no moment." For one thing, the general subscribed to the leading Republican journal, the Philadelphia *Aurora*, thus proving that he was a dangerous democrat. Moreover, Collot took the opposition paper under an assumed name. And, wrote the judge, this was not all. One of his informants had mentioned Collot's "intriguing spirit," and another had heard him criticize the government. Finally, he reported, he knew a Frenchman who knew a lady who lodged where Collot was staying, and this lady, the judge assured Pickering, thought that the general was "very inquisitive of the character of every frenchman in . . . the neighborhood—and also of the principal inhabitants. . . ."[31]

A week later Boudinot again pressed Pickering to authorize the arrest of Collot, assuring the secretary that "the business would be effectually

29 Pickering to the President, Aug. 1, 1799, Pickering Papers, XI, 525 (Mass. Hist. Soc.).

30 Adams to Pickering, Aug. 13, 1799, *Adams' Works*, IX, 13–14.

31 Elisha Boudinot to Pickering, Aug. 7, 1799, Pickering Papers, XXV, 84–85 (Mass. Hist. Soc.).

done." If the law would justify the seizure of papers, the judge was certain that some of importance could be obtained by a prudently managed raid.

In his effort to have Collot expelled, Boudinot sought information from a Mr. Boisobier, who had already testified to having heard Collot criticize General Washington and the American government "in a very virulent manner." Boisobier now declared that Collot was "a very dangerous character in this country"; the general, he declared, had once said "that if there was Warr between france and this Country, he would be one of the first to step forward and plunder the property of certain Individuals."[32]

Even as he relayed his new findings, however, the judge was apprehensive that his investigation might be futile. Boisobier was reluctant to appear as an informer against Collot, fearing that the general might exert influence in such a way as to cause trouble for his family in Guadeloupe. But this refusal to testify against Collot was not the only source of discouragement for Boudinot. He complained to Pickering that the reopening of negotiations with France might make the general's removal unnecessary. To the disgruntled New Jersey justice, these developments were regrettable: peace with France might mean that "this Spy may appear triumphant and in a capacity to take vengeance on his enemies."[33]

Despite the persistent attempts of top Federalists to deport Collot, the French general was never arrested, nor was he sent away under the Alien Law. Although there is no further reference to Collot in Pickering's papers after 1799, he remained in the United States, still a British prisoner of war, until about August, 1800. When Liston refused to give him a passport of safe conduct to France, the general applied to the French government. It turned his case over to the French agent in England in charge of the exchange of prisoners, who eventually obtained an order authorizing Collot's return to France. Upon receiving this order, Liston granted a passport to Collot, who sailed about August, 1800. By that time, however, the Alien Friends Law had expired.[34]

Less fortunate than Volney in anticipating the adoption of the Alien Act and less resourceful than Collot in evading its enforcement was Médéric Louis Elie Moreau de St. Méry, a French scholar and a former member of the French Assembly, who had fled the Reign of Terror and had established a bookstore in Philadelphia in 1794. Here he enjoyed the friendship and patronage of the officials of the Washington administration, and Vice-President Adams, a frequent customer, even exchanged copies

[32] Boudinot to Pickering, Aug. 15 and 26, 1799, with enclosures, *ibid.*, 102, 115–16. Collot was reported to have remarked in 1795 that in case of a disturbance in America, "he would make himself Chief of Walloons, and that the first house he would plunder or strip would be of his friend Mr. FitzSimmons." See the deputation of J. A. Mercier to Boudinot, Aug. 8, 1799, *ibid.*, 86.

[33] Boudinot to Pickering, Aug. 26, 1799, *ibid.*, 115.

[34] Kyte, "Detention of General Collot," *William and Mary Quarterly*, 3d ser., 6 (1949), 630.

of his own writings for books written by Moreau de St. Méry.[35] Not until 1798 did this French bookseller become an object of Federalist suspicion, when, as he confided to his diary, "everybody was suspicious of everybody else: everywhere one saw murderous glances."[36] Realizing the seriousness of the swelling wave of anti-French sentiment, he had already decided to leave the United States when he received a warning from the French consul in New York that "all those who have no love for Robespierism had better get out and get out quick."[37] But he did not act quickly enough to avoid having his name included in the president's list of Frenchmen to be deported under the Alien Act. Curious as to why he was listed with Volney and Collot, Moreau de St. Méry asked Senator John Langdon of New Hampshire to question the president about the nature of the charge against him. "Nothing in particular," was Adams' laconic reply, "but he's too French."[38]

As the tension grew, some of Moreau's friends gave him keys to two shelters where he and his family could take refuge should their home be attacked. On the same day, July 14, he obtained passports for himself and his family, but it was to be more than a month before he could get out of the country. On August 3, three weeks after issuing the passports, Secretary Pickering gave him a letter of safe conveyance requesting all American ships of war or private armed vessels to allow him and his family to make their trip to France "without any hindrance or molestation whatsoever" and to furnish any assistance or protection that he might need during the voyage. After receiving similar guarantees from the British and Spanish ministers, Moreau de St. Méry sailed for France on August 23, 1798.[39]

Not always as helpful as in the Moreau case, Pickering requested the use of the Alien Law in three other types of cases—against incoming aliens, against diplomatic personnel, and against alien writers who criticized the administration too vigorously. When he first recommended proceedings against Collot and Sweitzer, Pickering also mentioned DuPont de Nemours.[40] In July, 1798, the American minister to England, Rufus King, wrote Pickering that DuPont and a delegation of French philosophers from the National Institute had applied for passports from the English government after the Directory had given them passports to go to the United States to improve and extend the sciences. King understood that the group planned to settle on the Upper Mississippi out of the limits of

[35] Moreau de St. Méry's Diary, entry of July 18, 1798, Kenneth and Anna M. Roberts, eds., *Moreau de St. Méry's American Journey, 1793–1798* (New York, 1947), 253.

[36] Diary entry of June 27, 1798, *ibid.*, 252.

[37] Jean-Antoine B. Rozier to Moreau, June 27, 1798, *ibid.*

[38] Diary entry of July 14, 1798, *ibid.*, 253.

[39] See Diary entries of July 14, 18, and Aug. 1, 3, 18, 23, 1798, *ibid.*, 253–255, 364. A copy of Pickering's letter of safe conveyance is in Pickering Papers, IX, 139 (Mass. Hist. Soc.), and Dept. of State *Domestic Letters*, XI (1798–1799), 35, RG 59 (National Archives).

[40] Pickering to the President, Oct. 11, 1798, Pickering Papers, IX, 453 (Mass. Hist. Soc.).

the United States and within the boundaries of Spain, but he expressed doubt that either the American or English government would "give any encouragement to this mission of the Directory."[41]

When Pickering relayed this information to the president, Adams replied that King had judged correctly of the American government; he hoped that he had conjectured equally well of the English. The president was not willing to grant passports to DuPont or any other French philosopher "in the present situation of our country. We have had too many French philosophers already," Adams continued, "and I really begin to think, or rather to suspect, that learned academies, not under the immediate inspection and control of government, have disorganized the world, and are incompatible with social order."[42]

It was a foregone conclusion, then, that the president would agree with Pickering that if DuPont "should arrive in the United States and be discovered, he ought if possible, not to be allowed even to breathe the air of the United States." Exactly one month after he vowed not to grant passports to DuPont's group, Adams signed a blank arrest warrant to be used against the French scientist, "if he is to be found."[43] This warrant was never executed because DuPont did not arrive in the United States until after the expiration of the Alien Law.

President Adams did not always approve Pickering's proposals. When the secretary suggested that the Alien Law might be utilized against French diplomatic personnel in the United States, the president forbade it. Before the passage of the act, the United States had refused exequaturs to French consuls in America in retaliation for France's rejection of the American negotiators. The government also refused to accept Victor Marie DuPont in May as a replacement for Letombe as consul at Philadelphia. Nevertheless, the French consuls who were already resident in the United States were allowed to remain.

In October, 1798, Pickering called the president's attention to the arrival of a new consul at Boston and suggested that he and any other new ministers ought to be ordered away as soon as they arrived. "Perhaps," he added, "the old French consuls should not much longer be permitted: nothing but the actual charge of numerous French people who need their pecuniary assistance can countenance their remaining among us."[44] There is no indication, however, that Adams took any action against

---

[41] Rufus King to the Secretary of State, July 14, 1798, *King's Correspondence*, II, 368.

[42] Adams to Pickering, Sept. 16, 1798, *Adams' Works*, VIII, 596. Even after the expiration of the Alien Act in June, 1800, President Adams refused to grant passports to aliens whom he considered undesirable. Writing in August, 1800, to Pickering's successor as secretary of state, he said: "The German letter proposing to introduce into this country a company of schoolmasters, painters, poets, &c., all of them disciples of Mr. Thomas Paine, will require no answer. I had rather countenance the introduction of Ariel and Caliban, with a troop of spirits the most mischievous from fairy land." Adams to John Marshall, Aug. 11, 1800, *ibid.*, IX, 73.

[43] Adams to Pickering, Oct. 16, 1798, *ibid.*, VIII, 606–07.

[44] Pickering to the President, Oct. 11, 1798, Pickering Papers, IX, 453 (Mass. Hist. Soc.).

either new or old French consuls, except in the case of Victor Marie DuPont.

Nearly a year later Pickering was still trying to obtain the removal of Letombe. He wrote the president that the French consul not only exercised his usual functions but also that he used the title of Consul General of the French Republic, even though his exequatur had been withdrawn. Moreover, Pickering charged, Letombe "held the pursestrings of the republic in this country, and paid the bribes ordered by the French Minister Adet; the minister being gone, he is probably vested with powers adequate to the object. With much softness of manners, he is capable of submitting to, and doing, anything corruptly which his government directs."[45]

Remembering the French minister's exertions against him in the election of 1796, Adams replied that if Pickering could prove that Letombe had paid the bribes ordered by Adet, or anything like it, the consul ought to be sent away. Even in that case, however, the president thought it would be better to inform him that he was expected to go rather than to order him out at first by proclamation under the Alien Act. "There is a respect due to public commissions," wrote the president, who had spent several years in the diplomatic service, "which I should wish to preserve as far as may be consistent with safety."[46]

A final type of case in which the administration contemplated using the Alien Law was that of alien writers who were critical of the Federalists. Less than two weeks after Congress passed the Alien Act and a week before Adams signed the Sedition Law, John D. Burk, co-editor of the New York *Time Piece*, was arrested for seditious statements against the president and the government of the United States. Burk had fled Ireland in 1796 in order to avoid arrest for sedition. In New York he headed the local lodge of United Irishmen. This made him doubly offensive to Pickering, who wrote the New York district attorney: "If Burk is an alien no man is a fitter object for the operation of the alien law. Even if Burk should prove to be an alien it may be expedient to punish him for his libels before he is sent away."[47]

Eventually the Adams administration decided to expel Burk rather than to prosecute him for sedition; it made a deal with him, offering to waive legal proceedings if he should promise to leave the country. Although Burk agreed to this bargain, he violated it by going into hiding in Virginia until the Alien and Sedition Laws expired.

In an effort to suppress the Philadelphia *Aurora*, the Federalists attempted to utilize both the Alien and Sedition Acts. William Duane, the paper's editor, was indicted several times for his continued invective against the administration, but Pickering thought that the best way to deal with the offensive editor was to deport him. In 1799 he wrote Adams that

[45] Pickering to the President, Aug. 1, 1799, *Adams' Works*, IX, 6–7.

[46] Adams to Pickering, Aug. 13, 1799, *ibid.*, 13–14.

[47] For the arrest, see the New York *Time Piece*, July 9, 1798; *Aurora*, July 10, 1798. Pickering's instructions of July 7, 1798, to Richard Harison are in Pickering Papers, XXXVII, 315 (Mass. Hist. Soc.).

Duane pretended "that he is an *American citizen*, saying that he was born in Vermont." But the secretary thought that Duane had left America before the Revolution and had returned only recently; he therefore concluded that the editor was really a British subject who might be banished from the United States under the Alien Law. President Adams agreed with this analysis and authorized the execution of that statute. This permission was never used, however, either because the editor claimed to be a native-born citizen or because Pickering thought it would be easier to prosecute the sedition case against him rather than try to prove that he was an alien.

In only one instance did the president overrule the secretary of state in a decision to use the Alien Law against an alien writer. Pickering suggested that it might be used against Dr. Joseph Priestley for his part in circulating an anti-administration article written by Thomas Cooper, the Republican publicist who was later tried for sedition.[48] The president had known Priestley in England as an eminent scientist and a liberal theologian. When the latter fled the repression of liberal groups in Great Britain in 1794, he settled in Pennsylvania. In 1796 he preached a series of sermons in Philadelphia which Vice-President Adams attended faithfully. When these lectures were published, the Unitarian minister dedicated them to Adams.[49]

After Adams became president, Priestley wrote him in August, 1797, recommending Cooper, a fellow immigrant, for a political appointment. Adams failed to answer because of his practice of never replying to letters of solicitation, and by the spring of 1798 a coolness had developed between the two men politically.[50] When Pickering reported that Priestley was involved in the circulation of Cooper's anti-administration view, therefore, he must have been confident that the president would agree that Priestley ought to be removed from the United States as a measure "of maintaining our internal tranquility." But this was too much for Adams. In the same letter in which he authorized the use of the Alien Law against Collot and the Sedition Law against Cooper, he notified Pickering that he did not think it wise to execute the Alien Law "against poor Priestley at present. He is as weak as water, as unstable as Reuben, or the wind. His influence is not an atom in the world." Although this view was hardly flattering to one of the most influential scientists of that

[48] Pickering to the President, Aug. 1, 1799, Pickering Papers, XI, 524 (Mass. Hist. Soc.). The secretary of state observed that Priestley's dangerous political prejudices were indicated by the fact that he "was at the *democratic* assembly on the 4th of July at Northumberland [Pa.]."

[49] For Adams' association with Priestley in England, see *Adams' Works*, III, 396–97, 420. The dedication of the sermons is in Priestley, *Discourses Relating to the Evidences of Revealed Religion* (Philadelphia, 1796), iii–vii.

[50] The letter is in *An Account of the Trial of Thomas Cooper* (Philadelphia, 1800), 5–7. Adams' reason for not answering this letter is in Adams to Pickering, Aug. 13, 1799, *Adams' Works*, IX, 13. Priestley mentions the growing political split with Adams in his letter to the Reverend T. Belsham, Jan. 11, 1798, in Joseph Torvill Rutt, *Life and Correspondence of Joseph Priestly* (London, 1831), II, 391.

day, it was enough to forestall his deportation by the zealous secretary of state.[51]

Adams contemplated the use of the Alien Law against one other alien writer. The vehement "Porcupine" broke with the administration in February, 1799, after the president decided to send a second peace commission to France. Charging that Adams had sold out to the French-loving Republicans, Cobbett's denunciations of the president reflected the extreme Federalist point of view and were as bitter as any writings which the Republican papers leveled at Adams when he signed the Alien and Sedition Laws. Indeed, Adams confided to his wife that Cobbett merited the Alien Law, and one Federalist journal erroneously reported Porcupine's expulsion, but the president never followed up this threat.[52] Instead, Cobbett lost a libel suit to Dr. Benjamin Rush in Philadelphia, retreated to New York to edit the *Rush Light*, a paper which concentrated on his controversy with Dr. Rush about the practice of bloodletting, and finally returned to his native England in June, 1800, the same month in which the Alien Law expired.

Despite repeated demands by the Federalist press, there was not a single deportation under the arbitrary statute which Congress had justified as a measure of national defense against dangerous aliens.[53] The chief reason for the record of nonenforcement was the determination of John Adams to give the law a much stricter interpretation than the Federalist extremists desired. Refusing to become a rubber stamp to the zealots in his Cabinet, two of whom he subsequently dismissed, he preferred to retain the power of final decision rather than to sign blank warrants which Pickering and his colleagues might use as they pleased. Yet he was always willing to enforce the law against aliens whom he deemed dangerous and gladly signed warrants for the seizure of Collot, Sweitzer, and DuPont.

Another explanation of the administration's failure to deport any aliens was, of course, the mass exodus of frightened foreigners even before the passage of the law. Moreover, both Adams and Pickering were convinced that even the arbitrary Alien Act was too weak to be effective; both bemoaned the fact that the law would not allow the confinement of an alien until his departure or deportation.

Paradoxically enough, the administration's most persistent enforcement effort failed because of the zeal of Timothy Pickering. His anxiety to implicate and track down additional suspects allowed Collot to remain in the United States until the expiration of the Alien Law. When the

[51] Pickering to the President, Aug. 1, 1799, Pickering Papers, XI, 524 (Mass. Hist. Soc.); Adams to Pickering, Aug. 13, 1799, *Adams' Works*, IX, 13–14. For Priestley's defense of his action, see his *Letters to the Inhabitants of Northumberland and Its Neighborhood, on Subjects Interesting to the Author and to Them* (2d ed.; Philadelphia, 1801), 11–16, 44–49, and 68–71.

[52] Adams to Abigail Adams, Feb. 22, 1799, quoted by C. F. Adams, *Life and Works of John Adams*, I, 545. See the *Massachusetts Mercury* (Boston), March 5 and 8, 1799, for reports of Cobbett's arrest under both the Alien Friends and the Sedition Laws.

[53] For a demand that the Alien Act should be used against immigrants from France, Ireland, and the West Indies, see the *Columbian Centinel*, May 8, 1799.

French general departed, therefore, he left at his leisure rather than under duress. In the only instance where the administration made a deal to avoid using the law, moreover, the offender did not leave the United States but went into hiding.

Inaction by President Adams, overzealousness by Secretary Pickering, and evasion of the law by John D. Burk combined to thwart the most strenuous efforts to enforce the Alien Friends Law, making it a dead letter from enactment to expiration. Only the *Columbian Centinel* in Boston noted the death of the law with regret. Its short epitaph observed that "not one of the numerous alien incendiaries which have infested, and now infest, the *United States*, have suffered any of the penalties of it,— and as they will attribute the forbearance of government to scar[e], not clemency, we cannot but add, more's the pity."[54]

## THE PRESS AND FREEDOM OF POLITICAL OPINION: A SURVEY OF THE ENFORCEMENT OF THE SEDITION LAW

*It is patriotism to write in favor of our government—it is sedition to write against it.*

BOSTON COLUMBIAN CENTINEL, OCTOBER 5, 1798

Although the Alien Law became something of a dead letter, the Sedition Act was not neglected by the administration. In the famous XYZ papers which President Adams communicated to Congress during the diplomatic difficulties with France in 1798, the French negotiators boasted of their ability to separate the American people from their government. Although the American envoys bluntly replied that this was mere braggadocio,[55] the Federalists in Congress accepted the French assertion as a statement of fact and concluded that it could be refuted only by presenting to the world a united front free from dissent. When the Democratic-Republicans, long their opponents on political and economic programs, refused to co-operate in the new "unanimity"—especially if it meant unqualified support of the Federalist war program—the Federalists enacted the Sedition Law to intimidate or silence their domestic critics and thus to force a united front.[56]

Although some historians have asserted that the law was passed in a moment of panic and was little enforced during its lifetime,[57] most agree that the Federalists executed it in a vigorous and systematic manner,

---

[54] *Columbian Centinel*, July 2, 1800.

[55] Envoys to the French Minister of Exterior Affairs, *Annals*, 5C, 3355.

[56] A typical toast of the Federalists was given by the New York Society of the Cincinnati: "The Congress: Unanimity and vigor to their councils." *Gazette of the United States*, July 7, 1798.

[57] Channing, *History of the United States*, IV, 222, says that although its passage was regrettable, "there were a few prosecutions under the Sedition Act, but not many." He deemed the law and its enforcement so unimportant that he did not discuss a single one of the trials, although he defended the sedition statute. *Ibid.*, 231–32.

directing it exclusively against their Jeffersonian opponents. During the debates on the law, the Federalists openly avowed their intentions of repressing "licentious" Republican criticism.

The same animus which marked the congressional debates characterized the Federalist enforcement policy. By identifying their administration with the government and the government with the Constitution, the Federalists construed criticism of the administration as opposition to the government and an attempt to subvert the Constitution.[58] The most insistent pressure for execution of the law came from the Federalist newspapers, which constantly clamored for action against their Republican competitors. The stronger the Federalist control of an area, the stronger was the demand for strict enforcement of the law. In Pennsylvania the *Gazette of the United States* led the chorus; in New York it was the *New York Gazette,* the New York *Commercial Advertiser,* and the *Albany Centinel;* and in New England it was the *Columbian Centinel* and *J. Russell's Gazette* in Boston and the *Connecticut Courant* in Hartford. All agreed with the Fourth of July toast offered by the Federalists of Dedham, Massachusetts: "Freedom of speech—let the revilers of our government have *rope* enough. For honest men of all parties the cord of friendship; for traitors and foreign spies the hangman's cord."[59]

Even before the XYZ affair, there were complaints against the pressures for conformity of political opinion. "Anything opposed to the ideas of the Administration," one writer complained, was branded as "Jacobinism," a scare word intended to denote the anarchy in France in 1793–1794. "To be true Federalists," he lamented, "we must be at once deaf, dumb and blind; we must hear nothing—say nothing—see nothing." Yet the editor who allowed the insertion of these remarks in 1797 announced after the passage of the Sedition Law that "his Paper now is, and henceforth shall be, completely, positively, and absolutely Federal." Since the crisis with France called for "decided and unequivocal support of Government, order and Laws," he resolved that his paper would no longer accept any writing "whose direct or covert tendency, is to vilify your own administration, and to justify the conduct of foreign and internal foes."[60]

Less than three weeks after the XYZ papers were given to Congress, the *Gazette of the United States,* edited by the printer to the United States Senate, called for more drastic steps than the exclusion of anti-administration views in Federalist newspapers; it urged the repression of Republican presses. On the Fourth of July the Boston *Independent Chronicle,* the leading Republican paper in New England, was burned at a Federalist celebration in Newburyport, Massachusetts. After the passage of the Sedition Law, an upstate New York printer urged that a

---

[58] Marshall Smelser, "The Jacobin Phrenzy: Federalism and the Menace of Liberty, Equality and Fraternity," *Review of Politics,* 13 (1951), 457–82.

[59] *Columbian Centinel,* July 11, 1798.

[60] For the earlier comments, see the *Oracle of the Day* (Portsmouth, N.H.), Oct. 7, 1797, quoted in William Robinson, *Jeffersonian Democracy in New England* (New Haven, 1916), 23. The editor's later views are expressed in the issue of July 28, 1798, reprinted in the *Albany Centinel,* Aug. 7, 1798.

conflagration be made of such "seditious papers" as the Philadelphia *Aurora* and the New York *Argus*. A New Hampshire writer declared that "certain gazettes are industriously disseminated, each paragraph a scandalous libel, each line a malicious lie. To 'fat headed' fools, to flagitious . . . and desperate disappointments and to scooling envy, the trumpet of sedition 'discourses sweet music.' " In charging the Republicans with being seditious, the *Albany Centinel* defined sedition as an attempt "to weaken the arm of Government, by undermining the confidence of the community in its measures."[61]

The Boston *Centinel* flatly stated that "whatever American is a friend of the present administration of the American Government is undoubtedly a true republican, a true Patriot. . . . Whatever American opposes the Administration is an Anarchist, a Jacobin and a Traitor." The administration represented the majority of the people and all honest men should support it, "exercising only the constitutional mode of changing men and of course measures." Since the constitutional mode of changing men was by electing different ones, this assertion limited political participation to voting and eliminated oral or written opposition to men and measures. Nor did the *Centinel* deny this limitation. "It is patriotism to write in favor of our government," it said tersely; "it is sedition to write against it."[62]

As decisive evidence that the nation contained "internal enemies and foreign mercenaries," the *New York Gazette* cited newspapers which defamed the national administration and the Federalist-dominated Congress. Although it agreed that opposition to bad government was justifiable, the paper declared that all resistance and opposition to a "really legitimate government is treason against the People, and deserves the severest punishment." Yet the Republican papers were "indiscriminately defaming the Legislature and Administration—of course openly vilifying that very PEOPLE for whom they profess so deep a respect." Although it did not think every opposition journal was supported by French money, the Federalist paper nevertheless accused the leading Republican papers of deriving assistance from sources other than their subscription lists.

Whether they were supported by foreign money or not, however, the Republican papers were real evils. "They are the greatest curse to which free governments are liable," the New York paper charged. They circulated falsehoods about men chosen by the people, thus promoting the anarchical and despotic principles of France, America's deadliest enemy. "Whoever does this is a foe—whoever countenances it is a traitor, —the PEOPLE should watch him with a jealous eye, and consider him ripe for *'treason stratagems* and *spoils.'* . . . They should be ferreted out of their lurking places, and condemned to the punishment merited by every patricide from the days of Adam to our own."[63] With the Federalists in

---

[61] *Gazette of the United States*, April 24, 1798; *Albany Centinel*, Aug. 3, 10, 1798; "The Lay Preacher," *Farmers Weekly Museum* (Walpole, N.H.), reprinted in the *Albany Centinel*, Aug. 21, 1798.

[62] *Columbian Centinel*, Oct. 5, 1798, quoted in the *Albany Centinel*, Oct. 12, 1798.

[63] *Gazette and General Advertiser*, Nov. 13, 1798.

this state of mind, the wonder is not the number of Republicans prosecuted, but that more were not seized.

Not only was it seditious and treasonable to write against the administration; Republican papers were suspect even if they remained quiet. The *Connecticut Courant* warned that when the Jacobins were silent it was "ominous of evil. The murderer listens to see if all is quiet, then he begins. So it is with the Jacobins."[64] Warning against these "incorrect" papers, the correct *Courant* suggested that the least they deserved was contempt.

> And lo! in meretricious dress,
> Forth comes a strumpet called "The Press,"
> Whose haggard, unrequested charms
> Rush into every blackguard's arms,
> Ye weak, deluded minds, beware!
> Nought but the outside, here is fair!
> Then spurn the offers of her sway
> And kick the loathsome hag away.[65]

In a plea for the enforcement of the Sedition Law, the *New York Gazette* ran a series of articles on "The Crisis" and called for vigilante groups to prosecute not only newspaper editors but other enemies of the country. "Your country was never more in jeopardy than at the present moment," "Plain Truth" asserted. The danger, however, was no longer from a foreign foe. "The long knives of Kentucky, the whiskey boys of the woods of Pennsylvania, the United Irishmen of Virginia are all cock a top . . . for insurrection and confusion."

To Americans he propounded this question: "Why do you not form associations to prosecute the enemies of your country, until that country is rid of them, and they are safe in the arms of their *beloved* France?"[66] The way to deal with the domestic danger facing them was for Americans "in deed, as well as in words, to rally round our government, and swear to bring every man to punishment, who vilifies the men of your choice, or strives to weaken the barrier of your country's independence." Americans ought to make one last struggle to destroy its internal enemies, and "Plain Truth" thought the time had come. The number of internal enemies were "as the opposition of a knat [*sic*] to an Elephant." The

---

[64] *Connecticut Courant* (Hartford), Aug. 13, 1798, quoted in Robinson, *Jeffersonian Democracy in New England*, 24.

[65] New Year's Address of 1801, *Connecticut Courant*.

[66] *Gazette and General Advertiser*, Dec. 15, 1798. This policy had been followed in England, where, after the French Revolution, extralegal bodies formed associations for the purpose of suppressing political reform and prosecuting "seditious utterances." The parent group was called the "Society for the Protection of Liberty and Property against Republicans and Levellers." See Sir Thomas Erskine May, *The Constitutional History of England* (New York, 1889), II, 144, who says that "such associations were repugnant to the policy of our law."

pointed moral of this series of articles was—strike at the Republicans while they are weak.[67]

In denouncing the Democratic-Republicans as factious sedition-mongers, *J. Russell's Gazette* singled out several Republican congressmen as likely victims of the Sedition Law. If the American people wished to build up the kingdom of Satan, the *Gazette* announced, "let them chuse [*sic*] democrats to Congress." But if they wanted to purify Congress and perpetuate purity in elections, they would have to "set their faces against the French pharisees, who would have delivered up our widows, houses and our country too, to the Directory to be devoured." Gallatin, Findley, and Lyon were fitter subjects for the execution of the Sedition Law than for the framing of statutes.[68] The New York *Commercial Advertiser*, another administration defender, evolved a rule of thumb whereby to judge the seditious: "When a man is heard to inveigh against the Sedition Law, set him down as one who would submit to no restraint which is calculated for the peace of society. He deserves to be suspected."[69]

> *Most High God . . . withhold us from unreasonable discontent, from disunion, faction, sedition, and insurrection.*
>
> PRESIDENT ADAMS, PROCLAMATION OF DAY OF FASTING, MARCH 6, 1799

These papers need not have clamored so much, because John Adams' administration had every intention of enforcing the Sedition Law. Indeed, the most powerful of all the Republican editors, Benjamin Franklin Bache of the Philadelphia *Aurora*, was indicted even before the law was passed. His arrest under the common law for seditious libels against the president and the government was a forerunner of the trials that followed. A common law indictment was also returned against the New York *Time Piece* while the sedition bill was before Congress.

Once the law was on the books, leaders of the administration, from the president to the district attorneys, took an active interest in its enforcement. Although President Adams did not initiate any legal proceedings against his critics, his correspondence shows that he personally approved of two of the major trials against Republican editors in 1799–1800. Whereas he gave the provisions of the Alien Friends Law a strict interpretation, the vague language of the Sedition Law was enforced against the most trivial writings and oral statements. In no instance did he veto any prosecution under the act, nor did he take any action on petitions for pardon which he received from offenders against the Sedition Law.[70]

---

[67] *Gazette and General Advertiser*, Dec. 19, 1798.

[68] *J. Russell's Gazette* (Boston), reprinted in the *Commercial Advertiser*, Sept. 3, 1798.

[69] *Commercial Advertiser*, Dec. 29, 1798.

[70] Although Adams pardoned one offender, he did so not on the prisoner's petition but on the recommendation of the government attorney who had prosecuted the case. . . .

As in the proceedings under the Alien Friends Law, the chief enforcement officer was Secretary of State Timothy Pickering. More than any other official, he "typified extreme Federalism of the purest and most rigid kind." One of his biographers has described him as one who believed so firmly that he was right that he denied there could be any honest difference of opinion. "To him the maxim that there are two sides to every question seemed an insult to the understanding. There was right and wrong, and the eternal battle between them; there could be nothing else."[71]

Pickering scanned Republican newspapers systematically. Even before the passage of the Sedition Law he wrote letters directing the New York district attorney to institute common law proceedings against the Mount Pleasant, New York, *Register*, and the New York *Time Piece*. After the passage of the law he not only continued his attentive reading of the opposition press, but, according to an *Aurora* report, he assigned a special State Department clerk "to search the *obnoxious papers* for suitable matter to cut them up at law."[72] He also received volunteer reports from faithful Federalists calling his attention to items that he or his agents might have overlooked.[73]

Before any case had been tried under the law, Pickering received an address to President Adams from Prince Edward County, Virginia, which urged the repeal of the Alien and Sedition Acts. Not only did the secretary refuse to forward the petition to the president, but he also issued a public letter severely censuring the Virginians and strongly supporting the constitutionality and necessity of the laws. The Sedition Act, he said, prescribed punishment only for "pests of society, and disturbers of order and tranquillity," and could not be considered as an attack on freedom of speech and of the press.

The president thought this answer "concinnate and consummate" and Mrs. Adams was delighted with it. She thought it worth all the answers that had ever been written in response to impudent petitions. The reply was so excellent, Adams assured Pickering, that he wished the secretary had to answer all the "saucy addresses" which he received.[74] The Federalist press also praised Pickering's comments as just but feared that "with determined oppositionists, and rancourous Jacobins, not any thing will have a good effect." It was fortunate, therefore, that the Sedition Law existed, because the Jacobins would "pursue the beaten path of

---

[71] Lodge, "Timothy Pickering," *Studies in History*, 183, 200–01.

[72] *Aurora*, Nov. 9, 1798.

[73] Parker Campbell sent a "highly inflammatory and prejudicial" Kentucky newspaper to William Rawle, district attorney for Pennsylvania, who forwarded it to Pickering. See Campbell to Rawle, Washington [Pa.], July 12, 1798, Pickering Papers, XXV, 22 (Mass. Hist. Soc.), and Rawle to Pickering, July 21, 1798, *ibid.*, 45. . . .

[74] Pickering to P. Johnson, Sept. 22, 1798, *Albany Centinel*, Oct. 16, 1798; and Adams to Pickering, Oct. 15, 1798, *Adams' Works*, VIII, 605–06. C. F. Adams observes that Adams' "praise appears to savor too much of partisan feeling. The sharp reply to the address placed Mr. Adams . . . in the attitude of combat with the opposition." See *ibid.*, 606n.

clamor, and their railings against wholesome restraint, till their villainies successively come within the cognizance of the law."[75]

Pickering saw no reason to restrict the Sedition Law to public utterances. When his vigilant eye noted a statement in a Richmond paper that Congressman John Clopton wrote not only circular letters to his constituents but also *"private* ones 'too violent to be made circular,'" the secretary immediately ordered the examination of the Republican representative's private letter with a view to prosecuting him for sedition. Clopton, who was then running for Congress against John Marshall, was reported to have written that the president was a traitor, grasping at absolute power by bribing a majority of the House. Since the original was in the possession of a Federalist, William Pollard, "a very worthy man of Hanover," Pickering suggested that the letter be authenticated by him so that Clopton's infamous and mischievous lies would not pass unnoticed.[76]

Federalist district attorneys and federal marshals, of course, cooperated closely with Pickering. Nor were the justices of the United States Supreme Court remiss in their attention to the enforcement of the Sedition Law. Although Judge Samuel Chase was the leading judicial advocate of prosecutions against the seditious, it was the uniform practice of federal judges, and especially Supreme Court justices on circuit, to charge grand juries with the duty of inquiring into all offenses against the Sedition Law.[77]

Over a year before the law was passed, a federal grand jury, after receiving a charge from Judge James Iredell, brought in a presentment against Congressman Samuel J. Cabell for his circular letters to his constituents. In turn, the representative claimed that it had been

> a regular practice of the federal judges to make political discourses to the grand jurors throughout the United States. They have become a band of political preachers, instead of a sage body to administer the law:—They seem to be making use of their power and influence both personally and politically to control the freedom of opinion, and these things excite a suspicion that the time will come when men of different political and religious sentiments from the judges will not find that easy access to justice which different opinions may expect.[78]

The most striking example of judicial prosecution was that which

[75] *Albany Centinel,* Oct. 16, 1798.

[76] Pickering to Edward Carrington, Oct. 23, 1798, Pickering Papers, IX, 512. No action was taken in this case. Clopton was defeated by Marshall for Congress. For a report on the campaign, in which Marshall opposed the Alien and Sedition Laws, see Beveridge, *Marshall,* II, 375 ff.

[77] Answer and Pleas of Judge Samuel Chase, *Report of the Trial of Hon. Samuel Chase . . . Before the High Court of Impeachment* (Baltimore, 1805), 36.

[78] *Aurora,* May 31, 1797. For one of Iredell's charges under the Sedition Law, see his instructions to the Philadelphia grand jury, Griffith J. McRee, ed., *Life and Correspondence of James Iredell* (New York, 1857), II, 551, 570.

Chase conducted against James T. Callender, correspondent of the Richmond *Examiner* and a pamphleteer whose talent for vituperation was a match for the most vindictive Federalist writer. The judge not only charged the jury to bring an indictment, but furnished them with a copy of the writing in which the offensive passages had been marked. On his return trip to Philadelphia after presiding at this trial, Judge Chase held court in New Castle, Delaware, where he detained the grand jury an extra day in his attempt to secure an indictment against a "seditious printer" in Wilmington. District Judge Gunning Bedford, who sat with Chase at this session, later testified that the Supreme Court justice had observed "in a public and in a jocular way" "that it was hard he could not get a single man indicted in Delaware, while he could in every other place."[79]

During the Federalist "reign of witches,"[80] newspapers reported a number of arrests under the Sedition Law which I have been unable to track down beyond the mere mention of arrest. During the Pennsylvania gubernatorial contest in 1799, a German-language newspaper in Reading printed an attack on the Federalist candidate, Senator James Ross, who had voted for the Sedition Act. Branding that law as "a dreadful, shameless, and destroying attempt" against the Constitution, Editor Schneider urged the defeat of Ross, one of the "political murderers of our liberty"; he should not be "rewarded for having tied our tongues, and gagged us." This attack upon a prominent Federalist and the laws of the land led Pickering to instruct the district attorney to prosecute Schneider, but there is no indication that a sedition charge was brought.[81] The co-editors of the *Harrisburger Morgenrothe*, however, were charged with publishing seditious statements against the laws and government of the United States. Benjamin Mayer and Conrad Fahnestock were arrested in August, 1799, and posted bail for their appearance before the federal circuit court in Philadelphia.[82]

Judah P. Spooner, a printer in Fairhaven, Vermont, was reported under arrest both in 1798 and 1799. There seems to be no evidence that he was indicted in 1798, but a charge apparently was filed the next year, although Spooner was discharged without being tried.[83] Another Vermont case on which there is little evidence should be mentioned. News-

---

[79] See the *Report of the Trial of Hon. Samuel Chase*, 22, 4, 63–64, 219, 223.

[80] This is Jefferson's phrase; see his letter to John Taylor, Phila., June 1, 1798, *Jefferson's Writings* (Ford ed.), VII, 265.

[81] *Aurora*, July 30, 1799; Pickering to Rawle, July 5, 1799, Pickering Papers, XI, 390 (Mass. Hist. Soc.).

[82] *Bee* (New London, Conn.), Sept. 18, 1799; *Palladium* (Frankfort, Ky.), Oct. 3, 1799. There is no indication that the editors were tried.

[83] For the report of the alleged indictment of Spooner and James Lyon at the time of Congressman Lyon's arrest, see the *Vermont Gazette* (Bennington), Oct. 12, 1798, and the *Independent Chronicle*, Oct. 22, 1798. In 1799 Spooner was reported under arrest in the New York *Spectator*, Oct. 19, 26, 1799; *Aurora*, Oct. 24, 1799; *Gazette of the United States*, Nov. 6, 1799. The *Spectator*, Oct. 26, 1799, reports his release.

paper reports listed Dr. Shaw of Castleton as being arrested in 1799, tried in 1800, and acquitted.[84] If these reports are true, the doctor was the only victim of the law who was not fined or imprisoned.[85]

Federalist enforcement machinery ground out at least seventeen verifiable indictments. Fourteen were found under the Sedition Act, and three were returned under the common law, two before and one after the passage of the statute. Although most of the prosecutions were initiated in 1798 and 1799, the majority of the cases did not come to trial until April, May, and June, 1800. Indeed, the chief enforcement effort was tied directly to the presidential campaign of 1800. As the contest between Adams and Jefferson approached, Pickering laid systematic plans for action against the leading Jeffersonian journals in the United States. The opposition press was led by five papers—the Philadelphia *Aurora*, the Boston *Independent Chronicle*, the New York *Argus*, the Richmond *Examiner*, and the Baltimore *American*. Because of their strategic geographical location and their able editorial direction, these gazettes circulated widely. Nor was their influence confined to their subscription lists. In those days before the communications revolution, the smaller newspapers consisted largely of material reprinted from the important journals. Thus, a blow at any of the "big five" Republican presses would be a severe setback to the Democratic-Republican party in 1800.

In the summer of 1799 Pickering launched a campaign to prosecute every one of the leading Republican papers which either had not been prosecuted under the Sedition Law or which had no cases pending against it. He took personal charge of the proceedings against William Duane, editor of the *Aurora*, and received the approval of President Adams. The secretary wrote identical directives to the district attorneys in New York, Richmond, and Baltimore instructing them to scrutinize the Republican papers issued in their cities and to prosecute them for any seditious libels against the president or any federal official.[86] Since the *Chronicle* had been chastised, Pickering did not send a directive to Boston.

The timing of these communiqués is important. They were written early in August, 1799, so that the district attorneys would have time to bring indictments at the September or October term of circuit court. Even if the trials had to be postponed until the April or May term in 1800,

---

[84] Shaw's arrest is mentioned in the *Spectator*, Oct. 19, 26, 1799. His trial and acquittal is reported briefly in *Spooner's Vermont Journal* (Windsor), May 13, 1800; the *Connecticut Gazette and Commercial Intelligencer* (New London), May 21, 1800; and the *Connecticut Courant*, May 26, 1800.

[85] For references to other arrests and attempted prosecutions, see the *Independent Chronicle*, July 30, 1798, which reports the arrest of James Bell in Carlisle, Pa., for "treasonable expressions"; Charles P. Polk to James Madison, Fredericktown, Md., June 20, 1800, Madison Papers, XXI, 89 (Lib. Cong.), for the attempted prosecution of Dr. John Tyler; and Dr. John Vaughn to Jefferson, Wilmington [Del.], Jan. 10, 1801, Jefferson Papers, CVIII, 18605 (Lib. Cong.), for the attempted prosecution of the doctor "under the *ignoble* Sedition law."

[86] For Pickering's instructions to the district attorneys, see his letters to Zebulon Hollingsworth, Aug. 12, 1799; to Richard Harison; and to Thomas Nelson, Aug. 14, 1799, Pickering Papers, XI, 602–03, 599, 611 (Mass. Hist. Soc.).

as was the case against the New York *Argus*, they would still come in time to silence the papers or their editors during the campaign of 1800. As a result of Pickering's efforts, suits were brought against every one of the "big five" Republican journals except the Baltimore *American*. Moreover, the editors of four other Democratic newspapers of lesser importance were indicted, and two of these gazettes ceased publication. In New York, the *Time Piece* and the Mount Pleasant *Register* folded as a result of sedition proceedings. In New England, the New London, Connecticut, *Bee* suspended operation from April until August, 1800, while editor Charles Holt served his sedition sentence. Only the Bennington *Vermont Gazette* continued to appear regularly while its editor was in federal prison for criticizing the authorities.

The fact that the most prominent Republican papers were assailed through prosecutions of their proprietors, editors, chief writers, or foremen, combined with the attacks on less important journals, affirmed the Federalist assertions and the Republican fears that the Sedition Law was passed to silence or intimidate the opposition press. In addition to the proceedings against major and minor Republican newspapermen, there were prosecutions launched against individual Republicans, some of state and national stature and others of local, or indeed little, political significance. The first group was headed by the initial victim of the act, Congressman Matthew Lyon, who criticized President Adams in a letter to the editor of a Federalist newspaper. This group also included Republican publicist Dr. Thomas Cooper and New York State Assemblyman Jedidiah Peck. In the latter category were the victims of panicky localities. One of these prosecuted a man in his cups for expressing a desire that the shot from a cannon had lodged in the president's posterior. "That there should have been any such cases," Professor Anderson concludes, ". . . illustrates the possibilities of oppression which lay in the sedition law."[87]

Strictest enforcement of the law came in areas that were either thoroughly Federalist, as in New England, or in states where Federalist supremacy was threatened by the rising Republicans, as in New York and Pennsylvania. All the indictments in 1798–1799 were returned in the New England or Middle states—three in Massachusetts, three in New Jersey, and one each in Vermont, New York, and Pennsylvania. All the proceedings in 1800, except the one against Callender in Virginia, also were instituted in New England and the Middle states—three in New York, two in Pennsylvania, and one each in Vermont and Connecticut. Thus sixteen of the seventeen federal proceedings against sedition were concentrated in the Federalist-dominated New England and Middle states. The only Republican state in which a sedition trial occurred was Virginia, and Callender's case there was the final one to go to a jury. Symbolically enough, his sentence was to end on March 3, 1801, the same day on which the Sedition Law was to expire.

---

[87] Anderson, "The Alien and Sedition Laws," Amer. Hist. Assoc., *Annual Report for 1912*, 122. Once again I have relied heavily on Professor Anderson's work for this summary.

# Tecumseh,

# the

# Greatest Indian

ALVIN M. JOSEPHY, JR.

The Indians met the advance of white settlers in various ways. During the colonial period and in the early years of the American nation, some Indians must have hoped to halt the white man through military action. However, the peace treaties that followed military skirmishes were regularly ignored by whites, and endless armed conflict was obviously out of the question. Some Indians must have considered the possibility of seeking admission to the union as separate Indian states. Though in retrospect this may seem a vain hope, it did not appear to be so at the time. Article VI of the Delaware Treaty of September 17, 1778, for example, contained the following statement:

> The United States do engage to guarantee to the aforesaid nation of Delawares, and their heirs, all their territorial rights in the fullest and most ample manner as it hath been bound by former treaties, as long as they the said Delaware nation shall abide by and hold fast the chain of friendship now entered into. And it is further agreed on between the contracting parties should it for the future be found conducive for the mutual interest of both parties to invite any other tribes who have been friends to the interest of the United States, to join the present confederation, and to form a state whereof the Delaware nation shall be the head, and have a representation in Congress: Provided, nothing contained in this article to be considered as conclusive until it meets with the approbation of Congress.

Indian unity must also have seemed to hold out genuine possibilities. However, the history of the Indian nations in America is anything but the story of increasing cooperation. Although there were some confederations among Indian groups, such as those of the Creek and the Iroquois, not even the presence of a common enemy led to the formation of permanent alliances. Pan-Indianism met the fate of similar movements the world over—Pan-Slavism, Pan-Arabism, Pan-Africanism, all have demonstrated a low degree of cohesiveness and effectiveness.

Early in the nineteenth century, a movement led by Tecumseh and his brother the Shawnee Prophet came closer than any other to uniting the various Indian nations on the western frontier of the United States. Using the twin poles of nationalism—political leadership and religious vision—these two Indian leaders were well on the way to developing a broad-based alliance of Indian nations stretching from Canada to the Gulf Coast. Had they had more time to develop the administrative machinery that would have strengthened the alliance and led, perhaps, to a permanent confederation, they might indeed have presented a formidable obstacle to westward expansion. As it was, the disaster at Tippecanoe led Tecumseh to split with his brother, and the onset of the War of 1812 precipitated the Indians into conflict. Tecumseh and many of his followers fought for the British, hoping thus to gain British support in negotiating a peace that would recognize three nations in North America—the British, the American, and the Indian. In the end, however, the British betrayed their Indian allies and left them defenseless against the Americans. Tecumseh himself was killed in battle, and the weakened remnants of his alliance were pushed west of the Mississippi to await again the inexorable tide of white settlers.

The story of Tecumseh's attempt to unify the Indians is told by Alvin M. Josephy, Jr., in the following chapter from his book **The Patriot Chiefs,** a study of the leaders of Indian resistance.

---

In its issue of December 2, 1820, the *Indiana Centinel* of Vincennes, Indiana, published a letter praising a late and much-hated enemy. "Every schoolboy in the Union now knows that Tecumseh was a great man," it read. "He was truly great—and his greatness was his own, unassisted by science or the aids of education. As a statesman, a warrior and a patriot, take him all in all, we shall not look upon his like again."

Seven years earlier, frontier communities throughout the territory of the old Northwest had exulted over the death of the "yaller devil" who had tried to bar white men from the rich lands north of the Ohio River.

"Tecumseh, the Greatest Indian." From *The Patriot Chiefs: A Chronicle of American Indian Resistance* by Alvin M. Josephy, Jr., pp. 131–73, 351–52. Copyright © 1958, 1961 by Alvin M. Josephy, Jr. All rights reserved. Reprinted by permission of The Viking Press, Inc., and International Famous Agency, Inc.

But with the disappearance of danger thoughtful citizens, such as the *Centinel*'s correspondent, had at last begun to realize that a native of soaring greatness had been in their midst. Along the waterways and dirt roads of Ohio and Indiana, settlers who still shuddered with memories of the warfare that had wrested the region from the Indians talked of Tecumseh with admiration and agreed with the verdict of their own hero, General William Henry Harrison, who had led them against the war chief. Tecumseh, Harrison had reported to Washington, was "one of those uncommon geniuses, which spring up occasionally to produce revolutions and overturn the established order of things. If it were not for the vicinity of the United States, he would perhaps be the founder of an Empire that would rival in glory that of Mexico or Peru."

Tecumseh had no opportunity to demonstrate his leadership of Indians in peacetime. He was a product of one of the most critical periods in the history of American Indians, and from birth to death was involved in conflict and war. But by 1846 an American historian, Henry Trumbull, stamped him as "the most extraordinary Indian that has appeared in history," and today, a century and a half after his death, as made clear by Glenn Tucker, his most recent and ablest biographer, he still looms as the greatest native leader in the long and tragic resistance of the Indians of the United States. He was a brilliant orator and warrior and a brave and distinguished patriot of his people. He was learned and wise, and was noted, even among his white enemies, for his integrity and humanity. But his unique greatness lay in the fact that, unlike all previous native leaders, he looked beyond the mere resistance by a tribe or group of tribes to white encroachments. He was a Shawnee, but he considered himself first an Indian, and fought to give all Indians a national rather than a tribal consciousness, and to unite them in defense of a common homeland where they might all continue to dwell under their own laws and leaders. In modern days, world opinion which endorses the right of self-determination of peoples might have supported before the United Nations his dream of a country of, by, and for Indians. But the crisis he faced came too early in history, and he failed. His failure meant considerably more than that the main theater of his struggle, Indiana, originally "the country of Indians," became a white rather than an Indian state. It threw all the tribes back upon their separate resources, as they had been since the beginning of their conflict with white men, and reestablished a pattern in which individual tribes or regional confederacies sought hopelessly to cope alone with the invaders. More important, it ended for all time the possibility that an Indian free state or nation might be created within territory won or purchased by the United States from white governments.

The establishment of such a state in Tecumseh's day was not implausible. The United States, which had just won its own independence, had received from Great Britain sovereignty over the vast wilderness of the Northwest Territory. But definition of that sovereignty was in question. France, the first European power to claim possession of the area, had built a few forts and trading posts, but had not otherwise disturbed the Indians' freedom or ownership of the land. The British had followed the French lead, and in 1763, while defending their western forts during the

Pontiac uprising, had tried to reassure the Indians by proclaiming native rights to all territory west of the Appalachians. Royal officials had attempted to halt purchases of land west of the mountains and void purchases already made, and until the Revolution they issued numerous edicts designed to stop westward expansion. In 1772 General Thomas Gage, commander-in-chief of British forces in North America, ordered all settlers beyond the Appalachians to "quit those countries instantly and without delay," and the following year Governor John Penn of Pennsylvania announced, "I do hereby prohibit and forbid all His Majesty's Subjects of this, or any other Province or Colony, on any pretence whatsoever, to intrude upon, Settle, or Possess any of the aforesaid unpurchased Lands (beyond the last Pennsylvania purchase), as they will answer the contrary at their Peril."

Many colonial settlers and land speculators, including George Washington, had ignored such proclamations, and despite the efforts of British officials a stream of frontier families had moved into Kentucky and down the Ohio after the collapse of Pontiac. But by the end of the Revolution their inroads had been negligible, and, save for a few small edges where settlers had established themselves, the country north of the Ohio River was still firmly in Indian hands. Furthermore, though the United States assumed possession of the region, it acknowledged that it did not own title to the land. What it owned was simply the exclusive right to treat with the Indians for the land. On June 15, 1789, Secretary of War Henry Knox confirmed this understanding in a letter to President Washington. "The Indians, being the prior occupants, possess the right of soil," he wrote. "It cannot be taken from them unless by their free consent, or by right of conquest in case of a just war. To dispossess them on any other principle would be a gross violation of the fundamental laws of nature, and of that distributive justice which is the glory of a nation."

This policy, soon ratified by Congress, was later affirmed by the Supreme Court, which held, in addition, that Indian tribes were "distinct, independent, political communities" with which the United States must deal, as it did with all foreign nations, by treaties subject to ratification by the Senate. Thus from the early days of the American Republic it was established that the Indian tribes were separate nations existing on their own lands over which, strangely, the United States government simultaneously exercised sovereignty. For almost a century, as Americans expanded westward, the confusing policy dictated relations between the government and Indian tribes, and until an exasperated Congress finally ended the legal fiction in 1871 it caused endless difficulties and conflicts between the two races. But from the beginning it also offered an obvious opportunity to a determined Indian nationalist: if a tribe possessed the right of soil and, as later acknowledged, an independent status, why did it not also have the right to establish itself as a free nation? In the days immediately after the Revolution time was advantageous for the forcing of the question. The new states had only loose ties to the Indian country of the interior, where there were still few settlers and only a minimum of government. Moreover, the colonists' own struggle for independence and their ideals of liberty and self-government had set burning examples for the natives. The United States had taken the Northwest Territory from Great Britain without either country's having consulted the wishes of the Indian inhabitants. Hailing the fresh words of the Declaration of Independence, public opinion would not have been able to argue with conviction that the idea of a free Indian nation within that region was untenable.

For a number of years after the Revolution, however, the realities of white expansion and the primitive level of native society precluded such a development. Under the leadership of Joseph Brant, who had been educated by the whites, the Iroquois of New York, politically more sophisticated than any other tribe in contact with the Americans, managed to win certain concessions that established United States acknowledgment of Indian rights of possession of soil. But most of the Iroquois had sided with the British during the Revolution and had suffered disastrous defeat in the war, and as beaten enemies they were in no position to proclaim an independent nation in territory claimed by New York.

Elsewhere the possibilities were equally elusive. Even before Yorktown, settlers in the middle Atlantic and southern colonies, guided by Daniel Boone and other frontiersmen, had quickened their move into Indian country, pouring through passes such as the Cumberland Gap that led across the Appalachians, and in 1782 North Carolina had even given western Indian lands to its veterans before bothering to negotiate with the natives for the property. The interior tribes fought hard, alone or in alliance, to drive the invaders from their hunting grounds, but their resistance only brought down upon them the superior fire-power of organized bodies of militia and, eventually, of American troops whose punitive expeditions inevitably became armies of conquest that forced the beaten natives to withdraw from the lands they had been contesting. The Indians had neither the time nor the understanding to set up a free state, and if they had tried to do so they would have lacked a unified force with which to defend their country, as well as the historical setting in which to appeal to world opinion for support. At the same time many chiefs undermined the native position by selling parts of the Indian domain to the invaders. The end of the prosperous days of the fur trade in the trans-mountain region had impoverished them, and in return for trade goods and promises of annuities they signed away lands, whether the areas belonged to them or not, and moved westward toward the Mississippi, allowing a flood of whites to pour across the abandoned regions and engulf tribes that were still trying to resist. As the white tide moved steadily into Kentucky and Tennessee and down the Ohio River, the demand for land increased, and at length in the early years of the nineteenth century the government in Washington embarked on a determined attempt to extinguish Indian title to all territory east of the Mississippi.

For dozens of tribes, numbering thousands of Indians, the moment of both crisis and opportunity had arrived. Defeat would now sweep them all away and unleash an even greater westward surge that no combination of Indians would ever again be able to halt. At the same time the traditional form of resistance, in which individual tribes fought merely to retain their lands, had no better chance of success than in the past. If the Indians were to hold, not for the moment but forever, powerful new ideas were needed, and they had to be political as well as military in nature.

It was the genius of Tecumseh that he, alone among all the natives, saw what was now required. The action of the increasing pressure by whites had finally produced the need for revolutionary reaction. As the greatest Indian nationalist, Tecumseh countered American expansionism with Indian unity, preaching for the first time that Indian land belonged to all the tribes in common, and that no chief could sell any part of it. By rallying natives of every tribe to that policy he would effectively block the American government's attempt to acquire the land by purchase. If the whites tried to seize it by conquest, violating treaties already signed, he would lead an army of every tribe in defense of their common country. The story of how he failed was a tragedy, for in the end it was a white man's war between the United States and Great Britain that obscured his nationalist cause and made the Americans feel that they were fighting merely a military auxiliary of their enemies. The true nature of his struggle was apparent only after his death, but before that day his courage and energy brought the Indians startlingly close to victory.

Tecumseh's real name was Tecumtha, which in the Shawnee language and allegory could be interpreted as "panther lying in wait." White men pronounced it Tecumseh, however, and understood that it meant "shooting star." He was born in March 1768 in one of the villages that formed a large, straggling settlement of Indian wigwams and bark cabins called Old Piqua on the bluffs above Ohio's Mad River northeast of present-day Dayton. His father, a Shawnee war chief named Puckeshinwa, was a proud, intelligent man who had been born in Florida, and his mother, Methoataske, probably a Creek Indian, was from eastern Alabama. Their birthplace, far from Ohio, reflected the long, nomadic history of the Shawnees, an Algonquian-speaking people, whose restless migrations, tribal divisions, and simultaneous occupancy of areas in widely separated parts of the frontier made it difficult for white contemporaries to conceive of them as a single nation.

The original homeland, it is believed, had been in the Ohio River Valley, but French explorers had first found Shawnees living along the Cumberland River in Tennessee and Kentucky; their name meant "southerners." They were a hardy, warlike people, whose hunting bands were already used to ranging long distances along the rivers and forest trails in the hilly Appalachian country, looking for enemies as well as game. In their wanderings the belligerent bands met distant tribes and joined them in warfare, and the attachments led some of them to break away from their own people and establish permanent settlements in their allies' countries. Shortly after 1674 one group of Shawnees migrated to South Carolina, where white men called them Savannahs and gave their name to a river and a colonial settlement. Another band of Shawnees went in the opposite direction, into Pennsylvania, where they settled among the Delaware and other eastern tribes on the Susquehanna, Delaware, Lehigh, and Schuylkill Rivers. Still other Shawnees remained on the Cumberland, concentrated in the vicinity of present-day Nashville, Tennessee, but hunting in Kentucky and the western country of Virginia and North Carolina. In time the South Carolina group divided, some moving west to settle among the Creeks in Georgia and Alabama, and the rest trekking slowly all the way north to Pennsylvania, where they joined their relatives who were beginning to be pushed west by the colonists. The Shawnees who had stayed on the Cumberland, meanwhile, also began to move. Under pressure from Cherokee and Chickasaw enemies, they migrated in a long, circuitous route through Kentucky, and eventually halted in eastern Ohio. Soon most of the Pennsylvania Shawnees, waging rear-guard border warfare against the advancing settlers, joined them, though one band, possibly Puckeshinwa's, migrated at that time all the way from Pennsylvania to Florida. After a while its members again headed north, pausing among friendly Creeks in eastern Alabama, and finally rejoining the main body of their own people, who by then had united in large villages along the Mad River and other streams in western Ohio.

The long, confused wanderings, marked by numerous alliances with other tribes and constant guerrilla warfare against advancing whites, had made the Shawnees more conscious than most natives of the similarity and urgency of the racial struggles being waged against the settlers on many different fronts. To them, the major enemy of all Indians was the English colonist, and from the time of the French and Indian War, when they sided with the French, they were in constant conflict with frontier settlers and with punitive English and colonial expeditions that were sent against them. During the Pontiac War they fought fiercely under Corn-stalk and other Shawnee leaders for their lands in western Pennsylvania, and after the defeat of Pontiac they continued to raid and skirmish against the settlers everywhere from Ohio to the mountains of western North Carolina. In Kentucky and Tennessee, where the wooded hills and valleys still provided the Shawnees with their best hunting grounds, the frontiers-men feared and hated them above all the other tribes, and after the American Revolution their great numbers and continued resistance made them one of the leading native forces in the Ohio Valley and a prime target of the settlers.

Tecumseh's father, like most Shawnee men, was a forest hunter and fighter, constantly involved in violence. Nevertheless, he was at home enough to sire an unusually large Indian family. In eastern Alabama, before he and his wife started north, they had a son. During the long migration to the Mad River, Methoataske, whose name to the Shawnees meant, appropriately, "a turtle laying eggs in the sand," gave birth to two daughters and another son. Tecumseh, born soon after they reached the Mad River, was the fifth child. Later a third daughter and two more sons, including one who was to be known as the Shawnee Prophet, were added to the family.

The Pontiac War had only recently ended when Tecumseh was born, but the defeat of the Indians had encouraged settlers to start mov-ing west of the mountains, and soon the Shawnees were engaged in trying to hold their hunting grounds in Kentucky as well as their village sites in Ohio. Border warfare raged steadily in both regions, and in 1774, when Tecumseh was six years old, the skirmishing erupted in a formal conflict,

known as Lord Dunmore's War, between the Shawnees and the colonists
of Virginia. Some two thousand of the latter, led by Dunmore, their
aristocratic and overbearing governor, marched into Kentucky and Ohio.
In a fierce battle at the site of Point Pleasant, West Virginia, both sides
lost heavily, but the Shawnee commander, Cornstalk, a brave and dignified man, eventually agreed to peace and, to save his people's villages in
Ohio, surrendered the Shawnee claim to lands south of the Ohio River
and allowed the Virginians to open Kentucky to settlement.

   Both Puckeshinwa and Tecumseh's oldest brother, a youth named
Cheeseekau, had fought courageously under Cornstalk, and both had survived the war and returned to the family home at Old Piqua. Soon, however, the young Tecumseh experienced two examples of the value of a
treaty with white men. Despite the fact that Dunmore had acknowledged
Indian right to the country north of the Ohio, frontiersmen continued
to invade it, and one day a band of them accosted Puckeshinwa in the
woods near Old Piqua and shot him in the breast. That night, when the
father failed to return to his family, Methoataske and Tecumseh went in
search of him. They found him dying, and learned what had happened.
The brutal episode filled Tecumseh with horror and hate, and as his
mourning mother urged him to remember the scene he resolved to become a warrior like his father and be "a fire spreading over the hill and
valley, consuming the race of dark souls." A few years later white men
also treacherously murdered Cornstalk, who had become Tecumseh's idol.
The Shawnee war leader had remained at peace under the terms of the
Dunmore Treaty, and in friendship had visited an American fort at Point
Pleasant. While he was there a mob of soldiers, inflamed by the death of
a white man on the Ohio River, had marched on the chief's cabin and
shot him down. His death shocked the youthful Tecumseh and again
filled him with hatred for white men.

   After the death of Puckeshinwa a chief named Blackfish, who ruled
the Indian town of Old Chillicothe a few miles from Old Piqua, adopted
Tecumseh into his family, and the boy traveled back and forth between
the two villages, receiving at both places education in personal conduct,
oratory, and tribal lore. The murder of Cornstalk enraged Blackfish, and
under his leadership the Shawnees commenced a new war of revenge. In
1778 Blackfish invaded Kentucky, struck at some of the settlements, and
captured Daniel Boone and twenty-six other whites. He brought the
frontiersman back to Old Chillicothe, where Tecumseh saw him. Later
Boone escaped, but the youthful Tecumseh witnessed many other dramatic events at the Indian headquarters, and the fierce border war that
raged through Kentucky and Ohio heightened his instincts against the
whites. The fighting, a peripheral part of the Revolution, involved the
British, who bought American scalps and prisoners from the Indians and
at times sent expeditions from the north to help the Indians against the
colonists. In the turmoil the natives experienced defeat as well as victory,
and at one time a large group of Shawnees, fearful of their future in that
part of the country, abandoned the area and the rest of the tribe, and
headed westward across Indiana, Illinois, and the Mississippi River and
established new homes in what is now the state of Missouri. With them, it

is believed, went Tecumseh's mother, who left the youth in Ohio in the care of his older brother, Cheeseekau.

In 1780 an American army under George Rogers Clark drove the natives from both Old Chillicothe and Old Piqua. The two cities were burned, and farther west on the Miami River the defeated Shawnees, Tecumseh with them, built another city, also called Piqua, which meant "town that rises from the ashes." Conflict continued, and two years later Tecumseh, as a youthful observer rather than a warrior, accompanied a group of British and Indians in another invasion of Kentucky. Without taking part in the fighting, he watched the Indians try in vain to capture one of the settlements and then saw them administer a severe drubbing to an army of Kentuckians on the Licking River. Soon afterward, just before the end of the Revolution, he got into his first battle, fighting by the side of Cheeseekau in a small skirmish in Ohio. Cheeseekau was wounded, and Tecumseh was unnerved and fled from the battlefield. That night he upbraided himself for his cowardice. He had finally been tested by fire, and had been found wanting, but it would be the last time anywhere that he would show fear.

With the end of the Revolution, the British withdrew offensive forces from along the Ohio River, and the Indians at last accepted as permanent the loss of their hunting grounds south of the river in Kentucky. But there was still little peace for them. The flood of westward-moving settlers was increasing, and the newcomers now had their eyes on the rich Indian lands that lay north of the river. In the East, many Americans did not agree that sovereignty over the Northwest Territory did not also mean possession of its soil, and land-grabbing syndicates, backed by state laws, made speculative purchases of huge tracts of the Indian country and drummed up profitable sales among innocent settlers and colonizers. The Indians soon felt the pressure of the new arrivals, and once more border warfare blazed.

Tecumseh, still in his middle teens, joined a band of Shawnees that tried to halt the invasion by intercepting settlers' flatboats that came down the Ohio from Pennsylvania. For a while the Indians made the route so hazardous that river traffic almost ceased. With Tecumseh's band at the time was a white youth who had been captured years before and had been adopted into the Shawnee tribe. Though he was almost an Indian, he later returned to civilization and related a significant story concerning this period in Tecumseh's life. After a certain battle on the river the Indians captured a settler and burned him at the stake. Tecumseh, then about fifteen years old, watched the spectacle with horror. Suddenly he leaped to his feet and made an eloquent appeal that shamed the Indians for their inhumanity. Somewhere, despite his deep hostility for the whites, he had gained compassion, and the indignity of the torture revolted him. This revulsion at vengeful cruelty was to be a notable part of his personality throughout his life, and the admiration which white men eventually acquired for him stemmed, in the beginning, from their gratitude for incidents in which he demonstrated his own humane conduct or halted with furious condemnation the excesses of other natives.

In time, as the tide of settlers increased, Tecumseh became the leader of his own band of warriors and waged guerrilla warfare against the whites. In the late 1780's he traveled with his brother, Cheeseekau, to visit his mother in Missouri, pausing for a while with the Miami Indians in Indiana and with Shawnees who were living in southern Illinois. At the latter place, during a buffalo hunt, he suffered a broken thigh when his pony threw him, and spent a year letting the injury heal. In the meanwhile Cheeseekau either took their mother back to her own people among the Creeks or followed her to the South and decided to remain there among Shawnees who were still living in that part of the country.

The border conflict in the Northwest Territory had by now become critical for the settlers, and in 1790 General Josiah Harmar of the United States Army was ordered to give protection to the whites. At the head of fourteen hundred men, he marched into the Ohio and Indiana countries of the Shawnees and Miamis, determined to teach the natives a lesson. At the site of present-day Fort Wayne, a Miami war chief named Little Turtle issued an appeal for all Indians to join him, and Tecumseh, whose injury had now healed, hurried there to participate in the defense of the Indian country. In a series of sharp encounters the natives defeated Harmar and forced him to withdraw, but in the following months other expeditions of regulars and militia continued to harass the natives, and in 1791 General Arthur St. Clair, a hero of the Revolution, led a new and powerful army of more than two thousand men up the Miami River. This time Tecumseh, now a twenty-three-year-old veteran leader of warriors, hung on the Americans' flanks as a scout and raider. In the wilderness Little Turtle, aided by a Shawnee chief named Blue Jacket and a Delaware named Buckongahelos, again waited for the invaders, and at dawn on November 4, 1791, near the headwaters of the Wabash River, they fell on St. Clair and completely destroyed his army. In the disastrous battle, during which Tecumseh stood out as a brave and daring fighter, the Indians killed more than six hundred soldiers and sent the shattered survivors flying back to the Ohio River. It was one of the worst routs ever suffered by an American army, and for a while it spread terror among the whites in the Northwest Territory and halted the flow of new settlers.

Tecumseh followed the victory by leading raids against white frontiersmen in both Ohio and Kentucky. In 1792 he received a request from Cheeseekau to bring a band of Shawnees south to help the Cherokees in their war against the Tennessee settlers. He responded at once, and at the head of twenty or thirty warriors joined Cheeseekau's Shawnees and a large body of Cherokees and Creeks in attacks on settlements near Nashville. In one of the encounters Cheeseekau was killed. Tecumseh buried the body of the brother he had adored, and was then chosen to succeed him as leader of all the Shawnee warriors in the South. For several months he led them in a series of fierce skirmishes and raids against settlers, traveling through large sections of the present states of Tennessee, Mississippi, Alabama, Georgia, and Florida, and winning friendships and renown among the southern tribes. In 1793 he broke off his forays to hurry his followers back north to help defend the Ohio country against an invasion

by a new American army, this one commanded by Major General
Anthony Wayne.

The native chiefs in the Northwest Territory had deposed Little
Turtle, who had begun to preach peace with the whites, and the Shawnee,
Blue Jacket, was now in command of the Indian forces. Once more
Tecumseh and his followers were assigned as scouts to follow the American army as it moved north. Wayne advanced from Cincinnati in October
1793 with more than thirty-six hundred regulars, marching slowly and
building forts at key points in the wilderness. Eighty miles north of
Cincinnati he erected a fort at Greenville, Ohio, and paused for the
winter. He stayed there during the spring, and in June Tecumseh and a
number of Indians routed one of his convoy trains and attacked the
fort. They were driven off, and soon afterward Wayne started forward
again toward the Maumee River in northwestern Ohio. He had three
thousand men with him, but Blue Jacket with fourteen hundred warriors
decided to engage him. On August 20, 1794, the two forces met in a
large clearing along the Maumee River where a tornado had blown
down many big trees. Tecumseh's scouts began the fight by firing on
Wayne's advance guard, and in the battle that followed Tecumseh added
to his reputation among the Indians by his boldness and courage.
Throughout the fight among the fallen trees, he was seen wherever the
action was most desperate, and even after his rifle jammed and became
unusable he continued to lead and inspire his companions. At the height
of the battle another of his brothers was killed, but there was no time
for grief. Wayne's sharpshooters kept the Indians pinned down behind
the trees, his cavalry thrashed at them, and at length the infantry launched
a frenzied bayonet charge across the timbers. It scattered the natives and
ended the battle that became known as Fallen Timbers. Leaving their
dead behind them, the Indians fled to a British fort lower down on the
Maumee, and after being refused admittance retreated toward the site of
the present city of Toledo. Wayne destroyed every Indian village he
could find, built Fort Wayne at the head of the Maumee in Indiana, and
retired for the winter to Greenville.

In the spring he invited the vanquished warriors to a peace meeting.
Nearly a thousand of them responded, representing twelve different tribes
of the Northwest Territory, and after two months of pressure their chiefs
reluctantly signed the Greenville Treaty, which ceded to the United
States for sale to settlers almost two-thirds of Ohio, including the Shawnee centers of Old Piqua and Old Chillicothe on the Mad River; a
triangular tract in southeastern Indiana; and sixteen strategically located
areas in the Northwest, among them the sites of Detroit, Toledo, Peoria,
and Chicago. In return the Indians divided among themselves about
$20,000 in goods and received the promise of $9,500 in annuities.

Tecumseh had refused to attend the council, and after the treaty
provisions became known he split with Blue Jacket and announced that
he would not accept what the chiefs had done. Nevertheless, as settlers
moved into the ceded territory, he recognized the hopelessness of resistance, and withdrew westward with his followers into Indiana. His

anger and opposition to the treaty furthered his reputation among both Indians and whites, and as large numbers of disgruntled warriors began to give him their loyalty and call him *their* chief, he became the dominant native leader in the Northwest. He was twenty-seven now, five feet, ten inches tall, a powerful and handsome man with a proud, aggressive bearing. Though there is no definitely established contemporary portrait of him, white men who knew him describe him as hard and fiery, a man who with great authority would announce sternly, "I am Tecumseh," and if challenged would menacingly touch the stem of his tomahawk. At the same time he had a complex personality in which many forces were apparently in conflict, for he could also be tender and sentimental, thoughtful and kind, or even playful and good-humored.

In 1796 he married a half-breed named Manete, who is described as an "old woman." She bore Tecumseh a son, but soon afterward he quarreled with her, and they parted. Toward the end of the century, during a visit to an older sister, Tecumapease, who had remained living near Old Chillicothe in Ohio, he met a sensitive, young white girl named Rebecca Galloway, the daughter of an intelligent pioneer farmer who had once been a hunter for George Rogers Clark. She was blond and beautiful, and he was magnetic and interesting, and a strange, romantic attachment developed between them. In time, as Tecumseh continued to call on her, she taught him to speak better English and read to him from the Bible, Shakespeare, and history. In their conversations she talked earnestly to him about humaneness and love of fellow men, and found him surprisingly tender and understanding. Tecumseh broadened in dramatic fashion under Rebecca's sympathetic teaching. He absorbed the history of Alexander the Great and other leaders of white civilization, pondered over new philosophy from the Bible, and thirsted for even more knowledge that would make him better equipped to understand and deal with the Americans. His regard for the blond, blue-eyed girl also increased, and eventually he asked her father if he might marry her. Mr. Galloway respected Tecumseh and advised him to ask Rebecca. Tecumseh did so, and the girl said that she would be willing if he would agree to give up his Indian ways and live with her as a white man. The decision was painful for Tecumseh, and he took a month to make up his mind. Finally, in sadness, he returned to Rebecca, and told her that he could not abandon his people. He said good-by to her and never saw her again. But the memory of her loveliness and guidance stayed with him, and he never took another wife.

The peace envisioned for the Northwest Territory by Wayne's treaty lasted little more than a decade, and was never more than a truce. As Tecumseh had foreseen, the line established at Greenville between the races could not halt conflict. Though the Indians acknowledged white possession of southern Ohio, many of them continued to live and hunt on their former lands, and they were in constant friction with frontier settlers. Moreover, as whites continued to come down the Ohio River, they began to press for the opening of new Indian lands, and in 1800, as if preparing to slice another large piece from the natives' domain, the government established administrative machinery for a Territory of Indiana, west of Ohio.

During this period another tragedy struck the Indians. Traders and settlers brought liquor into the region in huge quantities, and native bands in close contact with the whites could not resist it. They traded land, possessions, and their services for the alcohol, and almost overnight large segments of once proud and dignified tribes became demoralized in drunkenness and disease. As poverty and death claimed the natives, whole bands disappeared, and the weakened survivors clung together in ragged misery. The Miamis, who in 1791 had helped to destroy St. Clair's army, became, in the view of William Henry Harrison, "a poor, miserable drunken set, diminishing every year." The Piankashaws and Weas, almost extinct, were "the most depraved wretches on earth," and the Chippewas, who had fought nobly under Pontiac, were described as "frightful drunkards." Almost every tribe in the Northwest, including the Potawatomis, Kickapoos, Ottawas, Peorias, Kaskaskias, and Winnebagos, felt the effects of the firewater, and as their bands were reduced to poverty they were forced to steal from the whites to stay alive.

Tribes that remained farthest from contact with the traders, such as the Shawnees, retained their independence and strength. Tecumseh himself refused to drink whisky, and preached angrily against its use by his followers. Nevertheless, the liquor trade continued to threaten his people in Indiana. Despite his opposition, as well as government attempts to stop whisky sales to natives, unscrupulous traders managed to sneak more than six thousand gallons up the Wabash River annually for a trade of no more than six hundred warriors. One of the Shawnees who became most noted among his own people as a depraved drunk was Tecumseh's younger brother, Laulewasika. A loud-mouthed idler and loafer, he had lost an eye in an accident and wore a handkerchief over the empty socket. For years he drank heavily and lived in laziness. Then, suddenly, in 1805, he was influenced by the great religious revival taking place among white settlers on the frontier, and particularly by itinerant Shaker preachers, whose jerking, dancing, and excessive physical activity stirred mystic forces within him.

During a frightening epidemic of sickness among the Shawnees, Laulewasika was overcome by a "deep and awful sense" of his own wickedness, and fell into the first of many trances, during which he thought he met the Indian Master of Life. The latter showed him the horrible torments and sufferings of persons doomed by drink, and then pointed out another path, "beautiful, sweet, and pleasant," reserved for abstainers. Laulewasika's regeneration was instantaneous. He began to preach against the use of liquor, and the intensity of his words drew followers to him. As he continued to have trances and commune with the Master of Life, he changed his name to Tenskwatawa, "the open door," which he took from the saying of Jesus, "I am the door." He allied himself to Tecumseh, and gradually under the war chief's influence broadened his doctrine of abstinence into an anti-white code that urged Indians to return to the ways of their fathers and end intertribal wars.

Like other native prophets who had arisen among the Indians in earlier days of crisis, Tenskwatawa soon became a dynamic force for opposition to the whites, but many of his sermons were the words of Tecumseh, who now saw, more than ever before, that the Indians must maintain their self-respect and dignity if they were to have the strength to halt another westward advance by the whites. The two brothers joined forces and moved to Greenville, Ohio, at the very place where the chiefs had signed their treaty with Wayne in 1795; there they built a large frame meeting house and fifty or sixty cabins for their converts.

The Prophet's emotional appeals traveled quickly across the Northwest Territory, and he soon gained followers from almost every tribe. His growing influence and the dangerous concentration of natives around him disturbed General Harrison at his territorial headquarters in Vincennes, and he began to scoff publicly at the Shawnee, hoping that ridicule would undermine the natives' belief in him. He made little progress, however, and in April 1806 he challenged Tenskwatawa to perform a miracle. "If he is really a prophet," he wrote to one group of Indians, "ask him to cause the sun to stand still, the moon to alter its course, the rivers to cease to flow, or the dead to rise from their graves. If he does these things, you may then believe he has been sent from God."

Harrison's challenge was disastrous. From some white source, perhaps from a British agent in the North, the Prophet learned that a total eclipse of the sun would occur on June 16. In a bold and boastful response to Harrison, he proclaimed to the Indians that he would make the sun darken, and on the designated day a huge crowd of natives assembled at Greenville. Moving into their center, Tenskwatawa pointed commandingly at the sun, and at 11:32 in the morning, the moon began to darken the sun's face. The Indians were stricken with awe. As night descended over the gathering the Prophet called to the Master of Life to bring back the sun. In a moment light began to reappear. With the return of full daylight the Prophet's reputation and power were assured. Word of the miracle electrified the tribes of the Northwest, and as far away as Minnesota entire bands gave their loyalty to the Shawnee's code. But it was only the beginning.

Miracle begat miracle, and as agents of the Prophet traveled from tribe to tribe, carrying sacred strings of beans to peoples as remote as the Arikaras, Sioux, Mandans, and Blackfeet on the upper Missouri and the plains of central Canada, the Indians accepted any new wonder that was credited to the mystic Shawnee. In the Northwest Territory particularly, the Prophet's preachings inspired the natives with new pride and purpose, and, as Tecumseh hoped, helped to strengthen the feeling of unity among them. Moreover, as Tenskwatawa's personal power increased, he began to stir his followers with demagogic appeals against Christianized Indians and others who weakened the native cause by their friendship for the whites. Violence flared at first against Christian Delawares in Indiana, and soon spread to the Wyandots, Kickapoos, and other tribes, where the Prophet's followers slew natives who were considered bewitched or under the influence of white men. Several hundred Indians were killed before Tecumseh personally stopped the purge. But an idea had been launched, and Tecumseh now continued it by peaceful methods, encouraging and aiding the transfer of power within tribes from weak and venal chiefs who were too friendly to the Americans to young warriors who had promised loyalty to himself and his brother.

Harrison became alarmed as his agents sent reports of the tribes that had deposed their old chiefs and gone over to the Prophet. Tension between Great Britain and the United States, ever-present since the end of the Revolution, had reached a critical point again, and Harrison and most western settlers were certain that the British in Canada were the real troublemakers behind Tenskwatawa. "I really fear that this said Prophet is an engine set to work by the British for some bad purpose," Harrison wrote the Secretary of War on July 11, 1807. As the clouds of international conflict continued to travel across the Appalachians from Washington, the settlers' dread of a new frontier war with the English and Indians heightened, and they looked on the Prophet's successes with increasing suspicion and hostility. Gradually Tecumseh felt the growing animosity toward the natives, and recognized its ultimate consequences. In their fear of the British, the Americans would again attack the Indians, and try to drive them out of more of their lands. He saw only one hope— a dream which had been influenced by his knowledge of both the Iroquois League and the formation of the United States, and which he had long nourished for the Indians during his many travels and frontier fights. The unity among the Indians which he and his brothers were beginning to achieve must be broadened and strengthened. All the tribes must be brought together to be ready to fight as a single people in defense of their common lands. To avoid premature conflict he ordered Tenskwatawa to evacuate Greenville, which was too close to settlers in Ohio, and move his center westward to a tract of land that the Potawatomi and Kickapoo Indians had offered him in Indiana. The site lay along the west bank of the Tippecanoe River; its name was an English corruption of a Potawatomi word that meant "great clearing." In May 1808, at the stream's confluence with the Wabash River, Tenskwatawa and the families of eighty of his followers raised the mission house and bark dwellings of a new Prophet's Town. As soon as it was established, Tecumseh and his brother, accompanied by several companions and attendants, set out on horseback to unite the tribes for defense.

Forty-five years before, Pontiac had sent deputies to urge the chiefs and their warriors to war against the English. Now Tecumseh himself, already a war chief of great prestige, appeared at village after village, exciting the people with the presence of the Prophet and himself, and appealing for their support with thrilling patriotic oratory. At many places, chiefs who had signed the Treaty of Greenville and wanted no more war with the Americans opposed him, and he suffered many rebuffs. Elsewhere, whole tribes responded with enthusiasm to his speeches or divided their loyalties between their old chiefs and eager, young warriors who agreed with Tecumseh's appeals. In Illinois he won the Potawatomis to him, and rode away with a new and influential companion, a young Ottawa chief named Shabbona, who had married into the Potawatomi nation. In Wisconsin the civil chiefs of the Sauk and Foxes opposed the mission, but Tecumseh gained another resolute convert in a war leader named Black Hawk, who would one day fight his own war against the Americans. Most of the Menominees and Winnebagos near Green Bay pledged support, and back in Indiana the Kickapoos and Ottawas also agreed to join if war came. The Mississinewa and Miami Indians, who still looked to Little Turtle for leadership, had by now degenerated into weak and dissolute peoples, and Tecumseh made no impression on them. But almost the whole tribe of Wyandots and many villages of Delawares, Weas, Chippewas, Illinois, and Piankashaws, smarting under the frustrations of debauchery and idleness, found new pride in the Shawnee's patriotic appeals and promised to take up arms again in defense of their lands.

After covering the Northwest country, Tecumseh turned south and west, and in 1809, accompanied by a small band of followers, visited dozens of tribes, from the Seminoles in Florida to the Osages in Missouri. He received attention and sympathy and made many friends, and among most of the peoples he visited he managed to sow the seeds of future action against the Americans. Before the end of the year he was back in the North and heading into New York State, where he tried in vain to enlist the Iroquois tribes in his alliance. After being rebuffed by the Senecas and Onondagas he returned to Indiana and rejoined the Prophet on the Tippecanoe River. Despite his tireless journeys, he still had much work to do to achieve the unity he envisioned. He had to revisit many of the tribes he had met, make new appeals to those who had turned him down, and secure more binding agreements with his allies. But he had already made remarkable progress. From Lake Superior to the Gulf of Mexico he had laid the groundwork for the common defense of the Indians' country by the greatest military alliance in native history.

While he had been away the situation had worsened in Indiana. The war scare had abated, but additional pressures were threatening the natives. There were now more than twenty thousand Americans in southern Indiana, and if they were to receive statehood, for which they were clamoring, they would have to secure more Indian land on which to support a larger white population. The politically ambitious Governor Harrison was as aggressive as any of the settlers, and during the summer of 1809 he decided to force the Indians into a new cession. He sent his agents to Little Turtle and a host of the older and weaker chiefs and, armed with maps of central Indiana, met them at Fort Wayne in September. Harrison's letters reveal that he had little conscience in his dealings with the Indians, and that he was not above deceit. He "mellowed" the chiefs with alcohol, and after he had placed considerable pressure on them, they proved obliging. For $7,000 in cash and an annuity of $1,750, they ceded three million acres of land in Indiana, much of it owned by tribes that were not even present.

The new cession enraged Tecumseh, who heard about it while he was returning from New York. Included in the ceded territory were some of the Shawnees' best hunting grounds. Moreover, while he had been trying to unite the Indians in defense of the country they still owned, Indians behind his back had sold more of it, demonstrating once more that as long as individual tribes and chiefs were allowed to sell land as their own the Americans would find weak and greedy traitors to the native cause. More determined than ever, Tecumseh circulated word that Indian country was the common property of all the tribes, and that he and his allies would refuse to recognize the latest piece of treachery. Angry Indians who agreed with him flocked to the Tippecanoe, and in the spring of 1810 Tecumseh had a force of a thousand warriors at the Prophet's Town, training to repel, if necessary, any attempt by Americans to settle the newly ceded lands.

The hostile preparations disturbed Harrison, and he was further concerned by reports that the Wyandots, Creeks, and Choctaws were in sympathy with the Shawnees, and that a force of eleven hundred Sauk, Foxes, and Winnebagos was marching to the Prophet's Town. Harrison still thought that Tenskwatawa was the main agitator of the native opposition, and in an attempt to calm him he sent a messenger to the Tippecanoe settlement, inviting the Prophet to visit the President of the United States in Washington. Early in August he was surprised to learn from his agent that the Prophet's brother Tecumseh was the real leader of the Indians, and that the two men were coming to see him at Vincennes.

On August 11, 1810, the Shawnee brothers, accompanied by several hundred armed and painted warriors, swept down the Wabash River in a fleet of eighty canoes. At Fort Knox, three miles north of Vincennes, an Army captain observed them and reported that, true enough, "they were headed by the brother of the Prophet—Tecumseh—who, perhaps, is one of the finest-looking men I ever saw." Preliminaries and rain delayed the council for several days, but when it began it was tense and dramatic. In a grove near the governor's mansion Tecumseh and Harrison faced one another, both strong, willful leaders of national forces that had met in head-on collision. The two men were proud and suspicious, and as their followers stood nervously in the background, eyeing each other for sign of treachery, the air bristled with hostility. Tecumseh spoke first, beginning slowly, but soon pouring out his words in such swift and passionate flights of oratory that the interpreter had difficulty following him.

The Shawnee first reviewed the history of Indian-white relations in the Ohio Valley, and reminded Harrison of every wrong suffered by the natives at the hands of the Americans. Now, he told the governor, he was trying to unite the Indians, but the American leader was fomenting enmities among them. Tecumseh's words were lofty and eloquent, but we have only the interpreter's stilted translation of his ideas. "You endeavor to make distinctions," the translation of the speech reads.

> You endeavor to prevent the Indians from doing what we, their leaders, wish them to do—unite and consider their land the common property. . . . I am a Shawnee. My forefathers were warriors. Their son is a warrior. From them I take only my existence. From my tribe I take nothing. I have made myself what I am. And I would that I could make the red people as great as the conceptions of my mind, when I think of the Great Spirit that rules over all. I

would not then come to Governor Harrison to ask him to tear the
treaty. But I would say to him, Brother, you have liberty to return
to your own country.

Several times Tecumseh turned to his dream of uniting the tribes in
order to halt the whites. "The way, the only way to stop this evil," he
told Harrison,

> is for all the red men to unite in claiming a common and equal
> right in the land, as it was at first, and should be now—for it never
> was divided, but belongs to all. No tribe has a right to sell, even to
> each other, much less to strangers, who demand all, and will take
> no less. . . . Sell a country! Why not sell the air, the clouds and
> the great sea, as well as the earth? Did not the Great Spirit make
> them all for the use of his children?

Toward the end of his speech, he apparently tried to nettle Harrison.
"How can we have confidence in the white people?" he asked him.
"When Jesus Christ came upon the earth, you killed Him, and nailed
Him to a cross. You thought He was dead, but you were mistaken. You
have Shakers among you, and you laugh and make light of their worship."
Finally he pointed to the United States as a model for the natives. "The
states," he said, "have set the example of forming a union among all the
fires [states]—why should they censure the Indians for following it?" He
ended brusquely. "I shall now be glad to know immediately what is your
determination about the land."

Harrison began his reply by insisting that Tecumseh had no right to
contest the sale of land in Indiana, because the Shawnee homeland had
been in Georgia. The Indian chief stirred angrily, recognizing the deliberate evasion of his thesis that Indian land everywhere belonged to all
natives. As Harrison went on he became more impatient, and tension
among the onlookers began to mount. Suddenly Harrison asserted that
the United States had always been fair in its dealings with Indians. Tecumseh leaped to his feet and shouted, "It is false! He lies!" As he poured his
wrath on Harrison, the governor unsheathed his sword and started forward. Several whites aimed their guns, and the Indians behind Tecumseh
drew their tomahawks. For an instant a fight seemed imminent. Then
Harrison coolly declared the council adjourned and strode to his house.
As the other whites followed him, Tecumseh motioned his warriors back
to their camp.

The next morning Tecumseh's temper had subsided, and he sent his
apologies to Harrison. The governer accepted them, and visited the chief's
camp. Tecumseh was in a good mood, and the two men sat down together
on a bench. Gradually the Indian kept pushing against Harrison, forcing
the American to move closer to one end. Finally, as Harrison was about
to be shoved off, he objected, and Tecumseh laughed, pointing out that
that was what the American settlers were doing to the Indians.

The council reconvened the same day, but accomplished nothing,
and Tecumseh and his party soon left Vincennes and returned to the

Prophet's Town. Harrison had made no concessions to the natives. He sent the War Department the Indians' complaint that "the Americans had driven them from the seacoast, and would shortly, if not stopped, push them into the lakes," and though he added, "they were determined to make a stand where they were," the prospect that such a stand might be made did not seem to worry him. Six weeks later, alluding to Northwest Territory lands that the Indians still held, he asked the members of the Indiana legislature, "Is one of the fairest portions of the globe to remain in a state of nature, the haunt of a few wretched savages, when it seems destined, by the Creator, to give support to a large population, and to be the sea of civilization, of science, and true religion?"

The issue was joined. Harrison's attitude served notice that he intended to keep pressing for more Indian land, and Tecumseh knew that to stop him he had to hurry his alliances and strengthen the natives' will to resist. Once more the Shawnee leader made rapid visits to the tribes of Ohio, Indiana, and Michigan, delivering passionate pleas for his confederation. On November 15, 1810, he even crossed to the Canadian side of the Detroit River and at the British post of Fort Malden addressed a council of Potawatomis, Ottawas, Sauk, Foxes, and Winnebagos. Harrison and most of the settlers were confident now that the British were instigating Tecumseh, though this time the reverse was actually the case. Documentary evidence, found in later days, showed clearly that before the War of 1812 the British Government definitely opposed any Indian action that would imperil English relations with the United States or disrupt the lucrative Great Lakes fur trade, and that from Downing Street to Fort Malden British officials were irritated by Tecumseh's activities and tried to discourage his agitation against the Americans. Nevertheless, appearances convinced the settlers that unless something was soon done, the Indians with British assistance would again threaten the entire Ohio Valley. To Harrison the best defense was vigorous offense, and in 1811, he decided that the time had come to smash the Prophet's Town and scatter the leaders of Indian opposition.

All he needed was an overt act by the natives to justify his invasion of the Indians' country, and in July 1811 he gained his excuse when Potawatomis killed some white men in Illinois. Harrison claimed at once that they were followers of the Prophet, and demanded that the Shawnees on the Tippecanoe surrender them to him for justice. In reply, Tecumseh and the Prophet again visited Vincennes for a personal meeting with the American leader. They refused to deliver the Potawatomis, and once more the council ended in an impasse. The Prophet returned to his center on the Tippecanoe, and Tecumseh, accompanied by twenty-four warriors, set off down the Wabash River, bound on a second attempt to unite the southern tribes behind him. As soon as the Indian leader had disappeared, Harrison began preparations for his expedition to the Tippecanoe. "I hope," he wrote the Secretary of War regarding the departed Tecumseh, "before his return that that part of the fabrick which he considered complete will be demolished and even its foundations rooted up."

Tecumseh's second southern journey was an heroic and memorable effort; in six months it took him down the Ohio and Mississippi Rivers to the present site of Memphis, through Tennessee to Mississippi, Alabama, Georgia, and Florida, back north again across Georgia to the Carolinas, through the full length of Tennessee to the Ozark Mountains of Arkansas and Missouri, north into Iowa, and eventually back home. Once more he hurried from village to village, visiting strong interior tribes such as the Choctaws, Chickasaws, Cherokees, Creeks, Osages, and Iowas, and pleading with them for a united war against the Americans. Generally he met with opposition, and was disappointed. Great councils, sometimes numbering more than five thousand natives, gathered to listen to him, and white traders and Indian agents who also managed to be present reported the fervor and eloquence with which the Shawnee spoke.

His words "fell in avalanches from his lips," General Sam Dale said. "His eyes burned with supernatural lustre, and his whole frame trembled with emotion. His voice resounded over the multitude—now sinking in low and musical whispers, now rising to the highest key, hurling out his words like a succession of thunderbolts. . . . I have heard many great orators, but I never saw one with the vocal powers of Tecumseh." Wearing only a breechclout and moccasins, with lines of red war paint beneath his eyes, the Shawnee stood alone with his followers amid the throngs and cried to the Indians to stop their intertribal wars, to unite in a single nation as the states had done, and to fight together for all their land before it was too late. Old chiefs listened to him uneasily, and argued back. They would not unite with old, hereditary enemies. They would not give up their autonomy in a federation that would make them subordinate to strangers. The kind of union that Tecumseh talked about was for white men, not Indians. And besides, it was already too late.

In historic debates with the greatest chiefs of the South, Tecumseh continued to plead his cause, and on several occasions white agents who were present were able to record some of his thoughts, but again in the flowery language of awkward translations:

> Where today are the Pequot? Where the Narrangansett, the Mohican, the Pokanoket and many other once powerful tribes of our people? They have vanished before the avarice and oppression of the white man, as snow before a summer sun. . . . Will we let ourselves be destroyed in our turn without making an effort worthy of our race? Shall we, without a struggle, give up our homes, our country bequeathed to us by the Great Spirit, the graves of our dead and everything that is dear and sacred to us? I know you will cry with me, Never! Never!

The white observer, writing down the speech, had difficulty translating the Indian's expressions, but as the Shawnee continued the meaning of his words was not lost. "That people," he warned his listeners, "will continue longest in the enjoyment of peace who timely prepare to vindicate themselves and manifest a determination to protect themselves whenever they are wronged."

Again and again young warriors shouted their approval, and small groups promised to strike the Americans when Tecumseh gave them the signal. But the older leaders were wary and afraid. Some of them were receiving annuities and gifts from the Americans, some saw only ruin in Tecumseh's plans, and some thought that their people could do well enough by themselves. Only the Creeks and Seminoles, already smoldering with hatred for the Americans, provided the Shawnee with hope. To them he gave bundles of red-painted sticks. When they received word from him they were to start throwing one stick away each day, and when all were gone it would be the day on which all the tribes in every part of the frontier would commence a simultaneous attack on the whites.

Disappointed by his failures in the South, Tecumseh returned to the Tippecanoe River early in 1812, only to be met by news of a more stunning setback at home. During the Shawnee leader's absence, Harrison had finally struck at the Prophet's Town. At the head of an army of almost a thousand men the American governor had marched up the Wabash River, and on the night of November 6, 1811, had camped near the Indian settlement at the mouth of the Tippecanoe. The ominous arrival of the hostile force alarmed the Indians; at first, without Tecumseh to direct them, they were undecided what to do. A band of Winnebagos, bolder than the others, argued for an immediate attack on the invading whites, and finally won Tenskwatawa's approval. In the early hours of morning, some 450 natives crawled through the darkness toward the Americans. Harrison had placed his men in an unbroken line around the three sides of his triangular-shaped camp, and shortly before four o'clock a sentry on the northern perimeter saw an Indian moving in the gloom and shot him. In an instant the whooping natives were on their feet, charging toward the whites. The Americans met them with blazing musketry, and only a few of the Indians were able to crash into the camp, where Harrison's men battled them in hand-to-hand struggles. The rest were chased back, and though they launched a series of rushes at other sides of the camp they failed to break through. As the sky lightened they finally withdrew among the trees, and kept up a desultory fire from cover during the day. By the second day they had all disappeared, and Harrison moved his men, unopposed, into the abandoned Prophet's Town. He fired the buildings and destroyed all the natives' possessions, including their stores of food.

The number of Indian dead in the battle was never known, though it was estimated to be between 25 and 40. Harrison lost 61 killed and 127 wounded, but on his return to the settlements he announced that he had won a great victory and wrote to the Secretary of War that "the Indians have never sustained so severe a defeat since their acquaintance with the white people." The importance of the battle was soon exaggerated beyond reality, and in the flush of excitement many of the western settlers began to think that Harrison had beaten Tecumseh himself. The facts of what had been little more than an inconclusive swipe at a small segment of Tecumseh's followers never fully caught up with the legend of a dramatic triumph, and in 1840 the magic of Tippecanoe's memory still worked well enough to help elect Harrison to the Presidency.

The Americans' aggression, meanwhile, had caused serious repercussions among the natives. By the time Tecumseh returned home the Prophet had moved back into the ruins of the settlement and was sending messengers to all the Northwest tribes, telling them what had happened. Tecumseh reached the Tippecanoe in late February or early March 1812, and seethed with rage as he viewed what had happened behind his back. "I stood upon the ashes of my own home," he said later, "where my own wigwam had sent up its fire to the Great Spirit, and there I summoned the spirits of the braves who had fallen in their vain attempt to protect their homes from the grasping invader, and as I snuffed up the smell of their blood from the ground I swore once more eternal hatred—the hatred of an avenger."

The Shawnee's first anger was directed against his brother for not having prevented the battle. The southern trip had shown Tecumseh that his confederation was far from ready for the united movement he had planned to lead, and the clash on the Tippecanoe would now set off just the kind of a border war he had striven to avoid. Individual tribes would rise by themselves, and once more the Americans would deal with them piecemeal. The Prophet tried lamely to blame the Winnebagos, but Tecumseh shook him by the hair, threatened to kill him for his mismanagement, and finally drove him from the town. The Prophet became a wanderer, still preaching his doctrine, but eventually lost influence and followers and ended his life in obscurity among Indians farther west.

The isolated uprisings Tecumseh feared had meanwhile already begun. Irate bands, crying for revenge, fell on settlers in Indiana and Illinois. They raided independently of one another and without plan, but the panic they aroused united the Americans against all the natives and strengthened the settlers' conviction that the British and Tecumseh were directing the new attacks. Frontier feelings flamed against both the English and the Indians, and as frightened settlers abandoned their homes and fled south to safety, angry militia units built forts and blockhouses north of the Ohio River. In Ohio a large American army under Brigadier General William Hull began to march north to Detroit, and in Vincennes Harrison prepared for the full-scale war of decision for which Tecumseh was not yet ready.

During the spring the tension on the frontier spread to Washington, where it became one of the precipitating factors of the War of 1812. On June 18 the United States, under the pressure of Henry Clay and other "War Hawk" legislators from Kentucky and the West, began the war against Great Britain. Almost immediately both the British and the Americans sent agents among the tribes, appealing for their help in the struggle. Several of the older chiefs, who had opposed Tecumseh and maintained their loyalty to the United States, argued the American case before their tribesmen. But in a large council called by the Americans at Fort Wayne Tecumseh defied them. "Here is a chance . . . ," he cried scornfully,

> yes, a chance such as will never occur again—for us Indians of North America to form ourselves into one great combination and cast our lot with the British in this war. And should they conquer and again get the mastery of all North America, our rights to at least a portion of the land of our fathers would be respected by the King. If they should not win and the whole country should pass

into the hands of the Long Knives—we see this plainly—it will not be many years before our last place of abode and our last hunting ground will be taken from us, and the remnants of the different tribes between the Mississippi, the Lakes, and the Ohio River will all be driven toward the setting sun.

His words fired his listeners, and twice he dramatically broke in two the peace pipes which an American envoy handed him. Then, with a large party of Shawnees, Delawares, Kickapoos, and Potawatomis, he marched off to Fort Malden and announced his allegiance to the British. Other bands, remembering his visits and ardent appeals of the past, soon began to join him. Wyandots, Chippewas, and Sioux came from Canada, Michigan, and Minnesota, while his old acquaintance Black Hawk moved across the northern wilderness from Illinois and Wisconsin and arrived with a war party of Sauk, Foxes, and Winnebagos. Elsewhere, Indian runners and British agents carried word that Tecumseh had finally declared war on the Americans, and the response of many tribes showed that the Shawnee's travels had not been entirely in vain. Though they fought without Tecumseh's guiding direction, and not as the united Indian people he had envisioned, bands rose against the Americans on every front, driving United States settlers, traders, and armed forces into retreat in the Northwest, the upper Mississippi, and the deep South. Before the war ended the Americans had stopped them, but the costly months of their hostility were scarred by massacres, the disruption of commerce, and the desolation of settlements from the outskirts of St. Louis to the Creek country of Alabama and Georgia.

On the Detroit River, where Tecumseh soon had a native army that fluctuated between 1,000 and 3,000 warriors, the American General William Hull established his headquarters at the town of Detroit, and on July 12 launched an invasion of Canada. He crossed the river with 3,000 men and prepared to attack the 300-man British garrison at Fort Malden. Hull was an elderly hero of the Revolution, who had become weak and timid with age. His advance guard won a preliminary skirmish with a small, mixed body of Indians and British, but soon afterward Tecumseh and 150 warriors ambushed another of his scouting parties, and Hull pulled up in alarm. While the Americans paused, worried over the size of the Shawnee's Indian force. Tecumseh learned of a United States supply convoy, protected by 230 militiamen under Captain Henry Brush, that was nearing Detroit from Ohio. He slipped a party of Indians across the river and prepared to intercept the column. Brush had already sent a messenger to Hull to ask for troops to help guard the convoy on the final, dangerous portion of its journey, and on August 4 Hull sent 200 men to meet the convoy. Tecumseh trapped the relief column a short distance south of Detroit, killed a large number of soldiers, and sent the rest retreating to Hull. During the battle he also came into possession of the American general's dispatches, which Hull was sending home, and he forwarded them to the British commander at Malden.

The battle forced Brush to withdraw his convoy to the south and wait behind the River Raisin for help. The news that Tecumseh was behind him and had cut his supply line panicked Hull, and when he further learned that Chippewa allies of Tecumseh had assisted in the British capture of Michilimackinac in northern Michigan and were probably canoeing south to attack Detroit, he hastily abandoned his invasion of Canada and recrossed the river to the American shore. His officers and men were appalled by his cowardice, but the threat of Indian strength now hung heavy over them all. On August 8, Hull sent a new force of 600 men to try to rescue Brush's trapped convoy. By this time some British troops had also crossed the river, and at Monguaga, a few miles south of Detroit, they joined Tecumseh's Indians and helped to intercept the new American relief column. There was a furious battle, during which Tecumseh fought bravely and received a wound in the leg, but the British and Indians were eventually forced to abandon the field and withdraw to the Canadian side of the river. Still, the mauled American troops dared move no farther south, and Brush's supply convoy remained dug in defensively south of the River Raisin.

On August 13 Major General Isaac Brock arrived at Malden with 300 British reinforcements from the east. Brock, the lieutenant governor of Canada, was an able and resolute military leader, well over six feet tall, with a powerful physique and a gentle and considerate nature. He had heard great praise of Tecumseh, and had already formed a high opinion of the Indian chief. On the night he reached Malden he read Hull's dispatches which Tecumseh had captured, and realized from them the extent of the American commander's fears and weaknesses. When Tecumseh came in to be introduced to him, Brock asked the Shawnee leader for his opinion of what they ought to do next. Tecumseh pleased him by urging an immediate attack on Detroit. Only one British officer supported the Indian's view, but at four o'clock in the morning Brock decided to follow Tecumseh's advice, and sent a message across the river, calling on Hull to surrender. The American refused, and as British guns opened fire on Detroit Tecumseh's Indians embarked for the American shore.

At the same time Brock allowed one of his couriers to be captured by the Americans. The courier shattered Hull's nerves by reporting that 5,000 Indians were arriving from the upper lakes to join Tecumseh. Hull had still been occupied in trying to rescue Brush's convoy, and had just dispatched a third force of 350 men to bring it in. Tecumseh's men landed between Detroit and the new expedition, and once more the American relief column was brought to a halt when its leaders realized what had happened. As the men wheeled about to march against the Indians in their rear, Tecumseh ranged his warriors around the fort and tried a ruse. He moved them in single file three times out of the woods and across a clearing in full view of the fort's defenders, so that it looked as if the expected Chippewa reinforcements had arrived from the north. The stratagem worked. Brock had just crossed the river with 700 English and Canadian troops and was inspecting the siege lines with Tecumseh, preparing to launch an assault on the fort, when Hull gave up. Without consulting his officers he raised a white flag and surrendered Detroit.

The American commander's ignominious action shocked the United

States. His capitulation included even Brush's beleaguered column, but those men, learning what had happened, turned around in fright and raced safely back to the Ohio settlements. The fall of Detroit spread new panic across the frontier, but in the fallen city the helpless members of the garrison soon found themselves turning from contempt for Hull to appreciation for Tecumseh. Though he had fought as an Indian, stripped to leggings and breechclout, the Shawnee chief dressed proudly in white men's clothes for his entrance into Detroit, and like an English staff officer occupied a bedroom and sitting room in the same house with Brock. Many of the Americans had expected to be massacred by the natives, but Tecumseh's absolute control over them and his friendly and dignified conduct gradually won the admiration of the prisoners; later, when they were paroled back to the settlements, they talked of him as a gallant and honorable enemy, and spread a new conception of him as a humane Indian who had treated the captives and inhabitants of the city with consideration.

The dramatic victory, meanwhile, had given the Shawnee leader new hope that he might, after all, achieve his dream of an Indian nation. Additional tribes were entering the war and were striking at other American strongholds. Potawatomis had captured Fort Dearborn and, aided even by a band of Miamis, who had long opposed Tecumseh's appeal for unity, were laying siege to Fort Wayne. If victories continued, the Americans might well be forced to recognize an Indian country. In the fall of 1812 Tecumseh made another tour to the South, principally to see the Creeks, who had promised to support his cause. No white man was present to record his speeches this time, but soon after the Shawnee returned north the powerful Creek Confederation commenced a war across the South that cost the Americans thousands of lives and millions of dollars.

By April 1813 Tecumseh was once again back at Malden. On his way home he picked up 600 recruits from among the Illinois tribes, and now had 3,000 natives under his command, one of the largest Indian armies ever assembled. During the Shawnee's absence, General Brock had been killed in action on the Niagara border, and Colonel Henry Procter, a petulant, small-minded officer, had taken command at Malden. He was a fat, haughty man who was disdainful of Indians, and Tecumseh let him know quickly that he considered him a poor substitute for the bold, imaginative Brock. In January, Procter and a force of Indians had gained a notable victory at the River Raisin over an army of 850 Kentuckians, killing or capturing the entire American force. Procter had assured the Americans that he would not allow the Indians to harm the prisoners, but when some of the natives got drunk he looked the other way and did nothing to halt their butchery of all the wounded and defenseless captives. When Tecumseh learned about it he criticized the British commander for weakness in not having controlled the natives. If the Indians were ever to gain recognition of their own state, he told both the British and tribal leaders, they must gain the respect of white men for their humanity and civilized conduct.

The grisly massacre had also aroused the American West to a spirit of no-quarter revenge, and by the time Tecumseh returned from the South his old adversary, General William Henry Harrison, was marching toward Detroit with a new army to avenge the savagery at the River Raisin. On the Maumee River, near the site of Wayne's victory of Fallen Timbers, Harrison paused to build a new post called Fort Meigs, and suddenly on April 25, 1813, found himself besieged by an army of British and Indians, which had come south from Malden under Procter and Tecumseh. A brigade of 1,100 Kentuckians made its way through the wilderness to reinforce Harrison's army, and arrived at the river a little more than a week after the siege had begun. In an effort to break through the British lines and get into the fort, the Kentuckians divided their forces and moved down both banks of the river, attempting a complicated plan that included a diversionary fight on the shore opposite the fort. The Americans' scheme miscarried, and the battle that followed engulfed the Kentuckians in another bloody catastrophe. Before they could reach the fort, some 800 troops were surrounded and hacked to pieces by Tecumseh's Indians. Almost 500 Americans were killed and 150 captured.

While Tecumseh remained at the siege lines some of the English and Indians marched the prisoners down-river to Procter's headquarters at the British Fort Miami. Once more the Indians began to murder the captives as they had at the River Raisin, and again Procter did nothing to halt them. This time, however, a native carried word to Tecumseh of what was happening. The Shawnee leader galloped to the British camp and hurled himself into the scene of massacre. The Indians had already killed more than twenty captives, and were tomahawking and scalping others. Tecumseh knocked down one Indian with his sword, grabbed another by the throat, and lunged at the rest. As the natives drew back he shouted at them, "Are there no men here?" The carnage stopped abruptly, and the Shawnee chief hastened to see Procter. When he demanded to know why the natives had again been allowed to kill prisoners, Procter answered lamely, "Your Indians cannot be controlled. They cannot be commanded." His reply filled the Shawnee with contempt. "You are unfit to command," he said to the British leader. "Go and put on petticoats." Then he added, "I conquer to save, and you to murder."

A couple of days later, over Tecumseh's objection, Procter lifted the siege of Fort Meigs. The Indian leader was disgusted, and two months later forced the British commander to surround the post once more. But Procter was weak and indecisive, and soon afterward he again abandoned the attempt to take the American fort. As opportunities continued to slip away from him, the Indians lost faith in his leadership. Finally, on September 13, disaster struck them all in a naval battle on Lake Erie. At Put-in Bay an American fleet under Commodore Oliver Hazard Perry swept the British from the lake and cut Procter's army in the west from its supply bases in the east. The British commander, aware of his isolation, and fearing Harrison, who was now beginning to move against him with a heavily reinforced army, decided to abandon the Detroit region and withdraw along the northern shore of Lake Erie to join other English troops on the Niagara frontier. For a while he concealed his plans from Tecumseh, but the Shawnee observed his preparations and realized that the British leader was about to withdraw from the country and leave the Indians to shift for themselves.

Procter's duplicity inflamed Tecumseh. He called his Indians together on the Fort Malden parade ground and humiliated the British commander in front of the other white officers, telling the natives that the English were flying from the enemy. "Listen, Father!" he roared at Procter.

> You have the arms and ammunition which our great father sent for his red children. If you have an idea of going away, give them to us, and you may go and welcome. Our lives are in the hands of the Great Spirit. He gave to our ancestors the lands which we possess. We are determined to defend them, and if it is His will, our bones shall whiten on them, but we will never give them up.

His speech failed to move Procter, and Tecumseh finally called him "a miserable old squaw."

That same day Procter began his withdrawal, and in time Tecumseh and his Indians were forced to follow him. The Shawnee was crushed. He had managed to wring from the British general a promise to retreat only as far as the Thames River, about fifty miles away, but as the natives trooped off, leaving behind them the country Tecumseh had worked so hard and for so long to save for his people, the chief's spirits flagged, and he was overcome with gloom. "We are now going to follow the British," he told one of his warriors, "and I feel certain that we shall never return."

On September 27 Harrison's army crossed Lake Erie to Canada, and commenced its pursuit of the British. Procter led the retreating army; Tecumseh and the Indians, including a band of Sioux from far-off Minnesota, brought up the rear, holding off advance units of the Americans, and denouncing Procter for refusing to stand and fight. In one sharp skirmish Tecumseh was wounded in the arm. He had decided to try to turn back the Americans without aid from Procter, but after thirteen of his men had been killed and many others wounded, he ordered the natives to continue the withdrawal. On the night of October 4 he went into camp with the British near the present town of Thamesville, a short distance up the Thames River. They had now reached the line which Procter had promised to hold. But that night, as if he had accepted the final defeat of everything he had lived and fought for, Tecumseh had a premonition of death. As he sat by his fire with his closest Indian lieutenants, men who had followed him loyally for years, he said to them calmly, "Brother warriors, we are about to enter an engagement from which I shall not return. My body will remain on the field of battle."

The next morning Procter again wanted to retreat, and Tecumseh had another bitter quarrel with him, this time threatening to shoot him with a rifle. Finally the British commander agreed to honor his promise and make a stand at their present location. But it was Tecumseh, the Indian, who suddenly became the leader of the entire army. While Procter issued fainthearted orders to his British and Canadian units, Tecumseh selected a defensive position where the main highway ran between the

Thames River and a wooded swamp. Organizing the field of combat, the Shawnee placed the British in a line across the highway, with the river and swamp protecting the left and right flanks respectively. On the other side of the swamp he divided the Indians into two groups, putting one of them under his own command as an extension of the British line and placing the other in a larger swamp which paralleled the highway, and from which the warriors could sweep the road with flanking fire.

As the British and Indians took their positions Tecumseh hunted up Procter and, in a forgiving mood, tried to reassure him. "Father," he said, "have a big heart! Tell your young men to be firm and all will be well." Then the Indian moved along the British line, inspecting the positions of the men and pausing to raise their spirits with friendly words. "He pressed the hand of each officer as he passed," a British major related after the battle. "[He] made some remark in Shawnee, which was sufficiently understood by the expressive signs accompanying, and then passed away forever from our view."

At four in the afternoon the Americans appeared down the road. Harrison's force of 3,500 troops included 1,500 mounted Kentuckians under Colonel Richard Johnson, and two infantry divisions. Against him were 700 British troops and slightly more than 1,000 Indians. Harrison had scouted the English positions, and decided to attack with his cavalry-men, sending the infantry after them in close support. As a bugle sounded the charge, Johnson's Kentuckians galloped forward, shouting "Remember the River Raisin." Johnson himself led one battalion against Tecumseh's Indians, and sent the rest of his men toward the British lines which were barring the road. Those horsemen smashed headlong into the English units, and the terrified British gave way at once. Procter, who had been waiting in the rear, jumped in his carriage and fled from the battlefield, abandoning the army and racing for safety in eastern Ontario. His troops, cut to pieces by the Kentuckians and by Harrison's infantrymen, who were now also descending on them, threw up their hands and surrendered in a body.

On the British right flank, meanwhile, Tecumseh's Indians met Johnson's charge with a blaze of musketry that threw the Americans back, and forced the horsemen to dismount and fight from behind trees. At the same time a division of infantry advanced on the run to support the cavalry. They spotted the Indians in the swamp that flanked the road and veered off to attack them. As the Americans pressed into the woods and through the miry underbrush, the battle mounted. Over the din, many men could hear Tecumseh's huge voice, shouting at the Indians to turn back the Americans. "He yelled like a tiger, and urged his braves to the attack," one of the Kentuckians later said. Other men caught glimpses of the Shawnee leader, running among the Indians with a bandage still tied around his injured arm. In the closeness of the combat, the Americans hit him again and again. Blood poured from his mouth and ran down his body but the great warrior staggered desperately among the trees, still crying to his Indians to hold. The dream of an Indian nation was slipping fast, and as twilight came it disappeared entirely. Suddenly the Americans realized that they no longer heard Tecumseh's voice, or saw his reckless figure. As darkness halted the battle the Indians slipped away through the swamp, and the Americans established defensive positions along the road.

In the morning Harrison's men hunted in vain for Tecumseh's body. Somehow, during the night it had vanished, and though several of the Shawnee chieftain's closest followers said later that they had taken it away during the night and buried it secretly, some white men wondered for years whether Tecumseh was still alive. The Americans captured no Indians during the battle, but the struggle on the Thames scattered the warriors and ended further serious resistance in the Northwest. Tecumseh's dream, unrecognized by his enemies, disappeared with his body. No new native leader arose to unite the tribes, and in a few years the advancing tide of civilization completed the demoralization and decay of the proud peoples who had once called the country of the Northwest Territory their home. In time the pitiful survivors, reduced to poverty and sickness, were forcibly dispossessed of what little land remained to them, and were removed to reservations on the west side of the Mississippi River. Many of them, as Tecumseh had foreseen, were moved again and again to make way for new advances of the whites. Today, across the state of Oklahoma, the dispersed descendants of the Shawnee chief's warriors live among other and more numerous tribes, ignored and forgotten by most Americans. To them, however, belongs the pride of knowing that one of their people was the greatest of all the American Indian leaders, a majestic human who might have given all the Indians a nation of their own.

## BIBLIOGRAPHY

Arnow, Harriette S. *Seedtime on the Cumberland.* New York, 1960.

Bakeless, John. *Daniel Boone.* New York, 1938.

Beard, Reed. *The Battle of Tippecanoe.* Chicago, 1889.

Blumenthal, Walter Hart. *American Indians Dispossessed.* Philadelphia, 1955.

Bodley, Temple. *History of Kentucky.* Chicago, 1928.

Brady, Cyrus T. *Border Fights and Fighters.* New York, 1902.

Britt, Albert. *Great Indian Chiefs.* New York, 1938.

Carter, Clarence E. *The Territorial Papers of the United States,* VII, VIII (Indiana, 1800–1810 and 1810–1816). Washington, 1939.

Catlin, George. *Manners, Customs and Condition of the North American Indians.* New York, 1842.

Cleaves, Freeman. *Old Tippecanoe: William Henry Harrison and His Time.* New York, 1939.

Drake, Benjamin. *The Life of Tecumseh and His Brother the Prophet.* Cincinnati, 1841.

Eggleston, Edward, and Seelye, Lillie Eggleston. *Tecumseh and the Shawnee Prophet.* New York, 1878.

Esarey, Logan, ed. *Messages and Letters of William Henry Harrison.* Indianapolis, 1922.

Fey, Harold E., and McNickle, D'Arcy. *Indians and Other Americans.* New York, 1959.

Gray, Elma E. *Wilderness Christians.* Ithaca, N.Y., 1956.

Gurd, Norman S. *The Story of Tecumseh.* Toronto, 1912.

Hodge, Frederick W. *Handbook of American Indians North of Mexico.* Washington, 1907.

Lossing, Benson J. *The Pictorial Field Book of the War of 1812.* New York, 1869.

MacLean, J. P. "The Shaker Mission to the Shawnee Indians." *Ohio Archeological and Historical Society Proceedings,* XI, 1903.

McKenney, Thomas L., and Hall, James. *The Indian Tribes of North America,* ed. by Frederick W. Hodge. Edinburgh, 1933.

Mooney, James. *The Ghost Dance Religion.* Washington, D.C., 1896.

Oskinson, John M. *Tecumseh and His Times.* New York, 1938.

Royce, Charles C. *Indian Land Cessions in the United States.* Washington, D.C., 1899.

Swanton, John R. *The Indian Tribes of North America.* Washington, D.C., 1952.

Trumbull, Henry. *History of Indian Wars.* Boston, 1846.

Tucker, Glenn. *Tecumseh, Vision of Glory.* Indianapolis, 1956.

Underhill, Ruth M. *Red Man's America.* Chicago, 1953.

Witherell, B. F. H. "Reminiscences of the Northwest." *Wisconsin State Historical Collections,* III, 1857.

Wood, Norman B. *Lives of Famous Indian Chiefs.* Chicago, 1906.

Wood, William. *Select British Documents on the War of 1812.* Toronto, 1928.

# Indian Removal and Land Allotment: The Civilized Tribes and Jacksonian Justice

MARY E. YOUNG

Much has been written about the removal of the Cherokee Indian nation from Georgia, partly because this episode furnishes a dramatic illustration of conflict between the executive and judicial branches of the government, in the persons of President Andrew Jackson and Chief Justice John Marshall. But the removal of the Creeks, Choctaws, and Chickasaws from the South has been less widely noted, although it offers valuable insights into conflicts between red and white culture in the United States as well as into the government's method of handling Indian affairs.

Unlike the Indians of the old Northwest who joined together to fight under Tecumseh, the Five Civilized Tribes of the South—the Cherokee, Choctaw, Creek, Chickasaw, and Seminole nations—adopted the goal of assimilation. By tradition these Indians were village agriculturalists rather than nomads, so it was relatively easy for them to adjust to white ways. Many of them embraced white culture completely, drawing up constitutions, accepting the white man's religion and style of dress, and even owning Negro slaves. Only the Seminoles maintained a warrior tradition; the other nations settled down to farm their rich lands, feeling secure under the eighteenth-century treaties. By denying their own cultural traditions, the Indians eliminated much of the basis for white antipathy. Yet they stood in the way of the advancing white frontier, and methods of removing them were found. Ironically, they were ultimately dispossessed as a result of a cultural difference that remained between them and the colonists—a difference in the idea of land ownership.

When the English colonists first arrived in the New World, they brought with them the recently developed Anglo-Saxon notion of private ownership. In fact, many of the white settlers had themselves been driven off land in the Old World during the eighteenth century as a result of the consolidation of communally held lands into large, single-owner estates. Thus the colonists believed that land could be permanently and exclusively owned by individuals. In contrast, the Indians understood possession of the land as a matter of use rather than ownership. Since the New World seemed to contain plenty of land for all, the Indians originally greeted the white man hospitably.

As white settlers occupied more and more land and barred the Indians from their claims, the implications of exclusive ownership became clear. Even then, however, the Indians rarely grasped the notion of individual land ownership. Rather, they considered their land the property of the community, and they left all decisions about its use to community councils.

In the following study, Mary E. Young, a member of the history department of Ohio State University, describes the process by which federal and state governments in the nineteenth century cooperated to divide community-owned lands among individual Indians, who were then persuaded, sometimes fraudulently, to sell their property to speculators. The growth of large-scale cotton culture in the Deep South was a major factor in the ultimate removal of the Indians from their home ground.

In the twentieth century, the federal government has used the same method of individualizing land ownership in pursuit of its policy of "terminating" Indian reservations. Again, the result has been the reduction of the amount of land under Indian ownership.

---

By the year 1830, the vanguard of the southern frontier had crossed the Mississippi and was pressing through Louisiana, Arkansas, and Missouri. But the line of settlement was by no means as solid as frontier lines were classically supposed to be. East of the Mississippi, white occupancy was limited by Indian tenure of northeastern Georgia, enclaves in western North Carolina and southern Tennessee, eastern Alabama, and the northern two thirds of Mississippi. In this twenty-five-million-acre domain lived nearly 60,000 Cherokees, Creeks, Choctaws, and Chickasaws.[1]

The Jackson administration sought to correct this anomaly by removing the tribes beyond the reach of white settlements, west of the Mississippi. As the President demanded of Congress in December, 1830: "What good man would prefer a country covered with forests and ranged by a few thousand savages to our extensive Republic, studded with cities, towns, and prosperous farms, embellished with all the improvements which art can devise or industry execute, occupied by more than

---

[1] Ellen C. Semple, *American History and Its Geographic Conditions* (Boston, Mass., 1933), p. 160; Charles C. Royce, "Indian Land Cessions in the United States," Bureau of American Ethnology, *Eighteenth Annual Report, 1896–1897* (2 vols., Washington, D.C., 1899), II, Plates 1, 2, 15, 48, 54–56.

"Indian Removal and Land Allotment: The Civilized Tribes and Jacksonian Justice," by Mary E. Young. From *The American Historical Review*, LXIV (October 1958), 31–45. This article, in slightly different form, was delivered as a paper at the joint meeting of the Southern Historical Association and the American Historical Association in New York City, December 29, 1957. Reprinted by permission of the author.

12,000,000 happy people, and filled with all the blessings of liberty, civilization, and religion?"[2]

The President's justification of Indian removal was the one usually applied to the displacement of the Indians by newer Americans—the superiority of a farming to a hunting culture, and of Anglo-American "liberty, civilization, and religion" to the strange and barbarous way of the red man. The superior capacity of the farmer to exploit the gifts of nature and of nature's God was one of the principal warranties of the triumph of westward-moving "civilization."[3]

Such a rationalization had one serious weakness as an instrument of policy. The farmer's right of eminent domain over the lands of the savage could be asserted consistently only so long as the tribes involved were "savage." The southeastern tribes, however, were agriculturists as well as hunters. For two or three generations prior to 1830, farmers among them fenced their plantations and "mixed their labor with the soil," making it their private property according to accepted definitions of natural law. White traders who settled among the Indians in the mid-eighteenth century gave original impetus to this imitation of Anglo-American agricultural methods. Later, agents of the United States encouraged the traders and mechanics, their half-breed descendants, and their fullblood imitators, who settled out from the tribal villages, fenced their farms, used the plow, and cultivated cotton and corn for the market. In the decade following the War of 1812, missionaries of various Protestant denominations worked among the Cherokees, Choctaws, and Chickasaws, training hundreds of Indian children in the agricultural, mechanical, and household arts and introducing both children and parents to the further blessings of literacy and Christianity.[4]

---

[2] James Richardson, *A Compilation of the Messages and Papers of the Presidents of the United States* (New York, 1897), III, 1084.

[3] Roy H. Pearce, *The Savages of America: A Study of the Indian and the Idea of Civilization* (Baltimore, Md., 1953), p. 70; *House Report 227*, 21 Cong., 1 sess., pp. 4–5.

[4] Moravian missionaries were in contact with the Cherokees as early as the 1750's. Henry T. Malone, *Cherokees of the Old South: A People in Transition* (Athens, Ga., 1956), p. 92. There is a voluminous literature on the "civilization" of the civilized tribes. Among secondary sources, the following contain especially useful information: Malone, *Cherokees;* Marion Starkey, *The Cherokee Nation* (New York, 1946); Angie Debo, *The Rise and Fall of the Choctaw Republic* (Norman, Okla., 1934) and *The Road to Disappearance* (Norman, Okla., 1941); Grant Foreman, *Indian Removal: The Emigration of the Five Civilized Tribes of Indians* (2d ed., Norman, Okla., 1953); Robert S. Cotterill, *The Southern Indians: The Story of the Civilized Tribes Before Removal* (Norman, Okla., 1954); Merrit B. Pound, *Benjamin Hawkins, Indian Agent* (Athens, Ga., 1951). Among the richest source material for tracing the agricultural development of the tribes are the published writings of the Creek agent, Benjamin Hawkins: *Letters of Benjamin Hawkins, 1796–1806* in Georgia Historical Society *Collections,* IX (Savannah, 1916), and *Sketch of the Creek Country in the Years 1798 and 1799* in Georgia Historical Society *Publications,* III (Americus, 1938). For the Choctaws and Cherokees, there is much information in the incoming correspondence of the American Board of Commissioners for Foreign Missions, Houghton Library, Harvard University. On the Chickasaws, see James Hull, "A Brief History of the Mississippi Territory," Mississippi Historical Society *Publications,* IX (Jackson, 1906).

The "civilization" of a portion of these tribes embarrassed United States policy in more ways than one. Long-term contact between the southeastern tribes and white traders, missionaries, and government officials created and trained numerous half-breeds. The half-breed men acted as intermediaries between the less sophisticated Indians and the white Americans. Acquiring direct or indirect control of tribal politics, they often determined the outcome of treaty negotiations. Since they proved to be skillful bargainers, it became common practice to win their assistance by thinly veiled bribery. The rise of the half-breeds to power, the rewards they received, and their efforts on behalf of tribal reform gave rise to bitter opposition. By the mid-1820's, this opposition made it dangerous for them to sell tribal lands. Furthermore, many of the new leaders had valuable plantations, mills, and trading establishments on these lands. Particularly among the Cherokees and Choctaws, they took pride in their achievements and those of their people in assimilating the trappings of civilization. As "founding Fathers," they prized the political and territorial integrity of the newly organized Indian "nations." These interests and convictions gave birth to a fixed determination, embodied in tribal laws and intertribal agreements, that no more cessions of land should be made. The tribes must be permitted to develop their new way of life in what was left of their ancient domain.[5]

Today it is a commonplace of studies in culture contact that the assimilation of alien habits affects different individuals and social strata in different ways and that their levels of acculturation vary considerably. Among the American Indian tribes, it is most often the families with white or half-breed models who most readily adopt the Anglo-American way of life. It is not surprising that half-breeds and whites living among the Indians should use their position as go-betweens to improve their status and power among the natives. Their access to influence and their efforts toward reform combine with pressures from outside to disturb old life ways, old securities, and established prerogatives. Resistance to their leadership and to the cultural alternatives they espouse is a fertile source of intratribal factions.[6]

To Jacksonian officials, however, the tactics of the half-breeds and the struggles among tribal factions seemed to reflect a diabolical plot.

[5] Paul W. Gates, "Introduction," *The John Tipton Papers* (3 vols., Indianapolis, Ind., 1942), I, 3–53; A. L. Kroeber, *Cultural and Natural Areas of Native North America* (Berkeley, Calif., 1939), pp. 62–63; John Terrell to General John Coffee, Sept. 15, 1829, Coffee Papers, Alabama Dept. of Archives and History; Campbell and Merriwether to Creek Chiefs, Dec. 9, 1824, *American State Papers: Indian Affairs*, II, 570; Clark, Hinds, and Coffee to James Barbour, Nov. 19, 1826, *ibid.*, p. 709.

[6] See, for example, Edward M. Bruner, "Primary Group Experience and the Processes of Acculturation," *American Anthropologist*, LVIII (Aug., 1956), 605–23; SSRC Summer Seminar on Acculturation, "Acculturation: An Exploratory Formulation," *American Anthropologist*, LVI (Dec., 1954), esp. pp. 980–86; Alexander Spoehr, "Changing Kinship Systems: A Study in the Acculturation of the Creeks, Cherokee, and Choctaw," Field Museum of Natural History, *Anthropological Series*, XXXIII, no. 4, esp. pp. 216–26.

Treaty negotiators saw the poverty and "depravity" of the common Indian, who suffered from the scarcity of game, the missionary attacks on his accustomed habits and ceremonies, and the ravages of "demon rum" and who failed to find solace in the values of Christian and commercial civilization. Not unreasonably, they concluded that it was to the interest of the tribesman to remove west of the Mississippi. There, sheltered from the intruder and the whisky merchant, he could lose his savagery while improving his nobility. Since this seemed so obviously to the Indian's interest, the negotiators conveniently concluded that it was also his desire. What, then, deterred emigration? Only the rapacity of the half-breeds, who were unwilling to give up their extensive properties and their exalted position.[7]

These observers recognized that the government's difficulties were in part of its own making. The United States had pursued an essentially contradictory policy toward the Indians, encouraging both segregation and assimilation. Since Jefferson's administration, the government had tried periodically to secure the emigration of the eastern tribes across the Mississippi. At the same time, it had paid agents and subsidized missionaries who encouraged the Indian to follow the white man's way. Thus it had helped create the class of tribesmen skilled in agriculture, pecuniary accumulation, and political leadership. Furthermore, by encouraging the southeastern Indians to become cultivators and Christians, the government had undermined its own moral claim to eminent domain over tribal lands. The people it now hoped to displace could by no stretch of dialectic be classed as mere wandering savages.[8]

By the time Jackson became President, then, the situation of the United States vis-à-vis the southeastern tribes was superficially that of irresistible force and immovable object. But the President, together with such close advisers as Secretary of War John H. Eaton and General John Coffee, viewed the problem in a more encouraging perspective. They believed that the government faced not the intent of whole tribes to remain near the bones of their ancestors but the selfish determination of a few quasi-Indian leaders to retain their riches and their ill-used power. Besides, the moral right of the civilized tribes to their lands was a claim not on their whole domain but rather on the part cultivated by individuals. Both the Indian's natural right to his land and his political capacity for keeping it were products of his imitation of white "civilization." Both might be eliminated by a rigorous application of the principle that to treat an Indian fairly was to treat him like a white man. Treaty negotiations by the

[7] Wilson Lumpkin, *The Removal of the Cherokee Indians from Georgia* (2 vols., New York, 1907), I, 61–77; Thomas L. McKenney to James Barbour, Dec. 27, 1826, *House Doc. 28*, 19 Cong., 2 sess., pp. 5–13; Andrew Jackson to Colonel Robert Butler, June 21, 1817, *Correspondence of Andrew Jackson*, ed. John Spencer Bassett (6 vols., Washington, D.C., 1926–28), II, 299.

[8] For brief analyses of government policy, see Annie H. Abel, "The History of Events Resulting in Indian Consolidation West of the Mississippi," *Annual Report of the American Historical Association for the Year 1907* (2 vols., Washington, D.C., 1908), I, 233–450; George D. Harmon, *Sixty Years of Indian Affairs, 1789–1850* (Chapel Hill, N.C., 1941).

tried methods of purchase and selective bribery had failed. The use of naked force without the form of voluntary agreement was forbidden by custom, by conscience, and by fear that the administration's opponents would exploit religious sentiment which cherished the rights of the red man. But within the confines of legality and the formulas of voluntarism it was still possible to acquire the much coveted domain of the civilized tribes.

The technique used to effect this object was simple: the entire population of the tribes was forced to deal with white men on terms familiar only to the most acculturated portion of them. If the Indian is civilized, he can behave like a white man. Then let him take for his own as much land as he can cultivate, become a citizen of the state where he lives, and accept the burdens which citizenship entails. If he is not capable of living like this, he should be liberated from the tyranny of his chiefs and allowed to follow his own best interest by emigrating beyond the farthest frontiers of white settlement. By the restriction of the civilized to the lands they cutivate and by the emigration of the savages millions of acres will be opened to white settlement.

The first step dictated by this line of reasoning was the extension of state laws over the Indian tribes. Beginning soon after Jackson's election, Georgia, Alabama, Mississippi, and Tennessee gradually brought the Indians inside their borders under their jurisdiction. Thus an Indian could be sued for trespass or debt, though only in Mississippi and Tennessee was his testimony invariably acceptable in a court of law. In Mississippi, the tribesmen were further harassed by subjection—or the threat of subjection—to such duties as mustering with the militia, working on roads, and paying taxes. State laws establishing county governments within the tribal domains and, in some cases, giving legal protection to purchasers of Indian improvements encouraged the intrusion of white settlers on Indian lands. The laws nullified the legal force of Indian customs, except those relating to marriage. They provided heavy penalties for anyone who might enact or enforce tribal law. Finally, they threatened punishment to any person who might attempt to deter another from signing a removal treaty or enrolling for emigration. The object of these laws was to destroy the tribal governments and to thrust upon individual Indians the uncongenial alternative of adjusting to the burdens of citizenship or removing beyond state jurisdiction.[9]

The alternative was not offered on the unenlightened supposition that the Indians generally were capable of managing their affairs unaided in a white man's world. Governor Gayle of Alabama, addressing the "former chiefs and headmen of the Creek Indians" in June of 1834, urged them to remove from the state on the grounds that

[9] Georgia, *Acts,* Dec. 12, 1828; Dec. 19, 1829; Alabama, *Acts,* Jan. 27, 1829; Dec. 31, 1831; Jan. 16, 1832; Dec. 18, 1832; Mississippi, *Acts,* Feb. 4, 1829; Jan. 19, 1830; Feb. 12, 1830; Dec. 9, 1831; Oct. 26, 1832; Tennessee, *Acts,* Nov. 8, 1833; George R. Gilmer to Augustus S. Clayton, June 7, 1830, Governor's Letterbook, 1829–31, p. 36, Georgia Dept. of Archives and History.

you speak a different language from ours. You do not understand our laws and from your habits, cannot be brought to understand them. You are ignorant of the arts of civilized life. You have not like your white neighbors been raised in habits of industry and economy, the only means by which anyone can live, in settled countries, in even tolerable comfort. You know nothing of the skill of the white man in trading and making bargains, and cannot be guarded against the artful contrivances which dishonest men will resort to, to obtain your property under forms of contracts. In all these respects you are unequal to the white men, and if your people remain where they are, you will soon behold them in a miserable, degraded, and destitute condition.[10]

The intentions of federal officials who favored the extension of state laws are revealed in a letter written to Jackson by General Coffee. Referring to the Cherokees, Coffee remarked:

Deprive the chiefs of the power they now possess, take from them their own code of laws, and reduce them to plain citizenship . . . and they will soon determine to move, and then there will be no difficulty in getting the poor Indians to give their consent. All this will be done by the State of Georgia if the U. States do not interfere with her law. . . . This will of course silence those in our country who constantly seek for causes to complain—It may indeed turn them loose upon Georgia, but that matters not, it is Georgia who clamors for the Indian lands, and she alone is entitled to the blame if any there be.[11]

Even before the laws were extended, the threat of state jurisdiction was used in confidential "talks" to the chiefs. After the states had acted, the secretary of war instructed each Indian agent to explain to his charges the meaning of state jurisdiction and to inform them that the President could not protect them against the enforcement of the laws.[12] Although the Supreme Court, in *Worcester* vs. *Georgia*, decided that the state had no right to extend its laws over the Cherokee nation, the Indian tribes being "domestic dependent nations" with limits defined by treaty, the President refused to enforce this decision.[13] There was only one means by

[10] Governor John Gayle to former chiefs and headmen of the Creek Indians, June 16, 1834, Miscellaneous Letters to and from Governor Gayle, Alabama Dept. of Archives and History.

[11] Feb. 3, 1830, Jackson Papers, Library of Congress.

[12] John H. Eaton to John Crowell, Mar. 27, 1829, Office of Indian Affairs, Letters Sent, V, 372–73, Records of the Bureau of Indian Affairs, National Archives; Middleton Mackey to John H. Eaton, Nov. 27, 1829, Choctaw Emigration File 111, *ibid.*; Andrew Jackson to Major David Haley, Oct. 10, 1829, Jackson Papers.

[13] 6 *Peters*, 515–97.

which the government might have made "John Marshall's decision" effective—directing federal troops to exclude state officials and other intruders from the Indian domain. In January, 1832, the President informed an Alabama congressman that the United States government no longer assumed the right to remove citizens of Alabama from the Indian country. By this time, the soldiers who had protected the territory of the southeastern tribes against intruders had been withdrawn. In their unwearying efforts to pressure the Indians into ceding their lands, federal negotiators emphasized the terrors of state jurisdiction.[14]

Congress in May, 1830, complemented the efforts of the states by appropriating $500,000 and authorizing the President to negotiate removal treaties with all the tribes east of the Mississippi.[15] The vote on this bill was close in both houses. By skillful use of pamphlets, petitions, and lobbyists, missionary organizations had enlisted leading congressmen in their campaign against the administration's attempt to force the tribes to emigrate.[16] In the congressional debates, opponents of the bill agreed that savage tribes were duty-bound to relinquish their hunting grounds to the agriculturist, but they argued that the southeastern tribes were no longer savage. In any case, such relinquishment must be made in a freely contracted treaty. The extension of state laws over the Indian country was coercion; this made the negotiation of a free contract impossible. Both supporters and opponents of the bill agreed on one cardinal point—the Indian's moral right to keep his land depended on his actual cultivation of it.[17]

A logical corollary of vesting rights in land in proportion to cultivation was the reservation to individuals of as much land as they had improved at the time a treaty was signed. In 1816, Secretary of War William H. Crawford had proposed such reservations, or allotments, as a means of accommodating the removal policy to the program of assimilation. According to Crawford's plan, individual Indians who had demonstrated their capacity for civilization by establishing farms and who were willing to become citizens should be given the option of keeping their cultivated lands, by fee simple title, rather than emigrating. This offer was expected to reconcile the property-loving half-breeds to the policy of emigration.

[14] Wiley Thompson to Messrs. Drew and Reese, Jan. 18, 1832, Indian Letters, 1782–1839, pp. 173–74, Georgia Dept. of Archives and History; John H. Eaton to Jackson, Feb. 21, 1831, Sen. Doc. 65, 21 Cong., 2 sess., p. 6; Cyrus Kingsbury to Jeremiah Evarts, Aug. 11, 1830, American Board of Commissioners for Foreign Missions Manuscripts; Tuskeneha to the President, May 21, 1831, Creek File 176, Records of the Bureau of Indian Affairs; Journal of the Commissioners for the Treaty of Dancing Rabbit Creek, Sen. Doc. 512, 23 Cong., 1 sess., p. 257.

[15] 4 Statutes-at-Large, 411–12.

[16] J. Orin Oliphant, ed., Through the South and West with Jeremiah Evarts in 1826 (Lewisburg, Pa., 1956), pp. 47–61; Jeremiah Evarts to Rev. William Weisner, Nov. 27, 1829, American Board of Commissioners for Foreign Missions Manuscripts; Sen. Docs. 56, 59, 66, 73, 74, 76, 77, 92, 96, 21 Cong., 1 sess.

[17] Gales and Seaton, Register of Debates in Congress, VI, 311, 312, 320, 357, 361, 1022, 1024, 1039, 1061, 1110, 1135.

It also recognized their superior claim, as cultivators, on the regard and generosity of the government. The proposal was based on the assumption that few of the Indians were sufficiently civilized to want to become full-time farmers or state citizens.[18]

The Crawford policy was applied in the Cherokee treaties of 1817 and 1819 and the Choctaw treaty of 1820. These agreements offered fee simple allotments to heads of Indian families having improved lands within the areas ceded to the government. Only 311 Cherokees and eight Choctaws took advantage of the offer. This seemed to bear out the assumption that only a minority of the tribesmen would care to take allotments. Actually, these experiments were not reliable. In both cases, the tribes ceded only a fraction of their holdings. Comparatively few took allotments; but on the other hand, few emigrated. The majority simply remained within the diminished tribal territories east of the Mississippi.[19]

The offer of fee simple allotments was an important feature of the negotiations with the tribes in the 1820's. When the extension of state laws made removal of the tribes imperative, it was to be expected that allotments would comprise part of the consideration offered for the ceded lands. Both the ideology which rationalized the removal policy and the conclusions erroneously drawn from experience with the earlier allotment treaties led government negotiators to assume that a few hundred allotments at most would be required.

The Choctaws were the first to cede their eastern lands. The treaty of Dancing Rabbit Creek, signed in September, 1830, provided for several types of allotment. Special reservations were given to the chiefs and their numerous family connections; a possible 1,600 allotments of 80 to 480 acres, in proportion to the size of the beneficiary's farm, were offered others who intended to emigrate. These were intended for sale to private persons or to the government, so that the Indian might get the maximum price for his improvements. The fourteenth article of the treaty offered any head of an Indian family who did not plan to emigrate the right to take up a quantity of land proportional to the number of his dependents. At the end of five years' residence those who received these allotments were to have fee simple title to their lands and become citizens. It was expected that approximately two hundred persons would take land under this article.[20]

The Creeks refused to sign any agreements promising to emigrate, but their chiefs were persuaded that the only way to put an end to intrusions

---

[18] *American State Papers: Indian Affairs*, II, 27. A general history of the allotment policy is Jay P. Kinney, *A Continent Lost—A Civilization Won: Indian Land Tenure in America* (Baltimore, Md., 1937).

[19] 7 *Statutes-at-Large*, 156–60, 195–200, 210–14; Cherokee Reservation Book, Records of the Bureau of Indian Affairs; Special Reserve Book A, *ibid.*; James Barbour to the Speaker of the House, Jan. 23, 1828, *American State Papers: Public Lands*, V, 396–97.

[20] 7 *Statutes-at-Large*, 334–41; manuscript records of negotiations are in Choctaw File 112, Records of the Bureau of Indian Affairs.

on their lands was to sign an allotment treaty.[21] In March, 1832, a Creek delegation in Washington signed a treaty calling for the allotment of 320 acres to each head of a family, the granting of certain supplementary lands to the chiefs and to orphans, and the cession of the remaining territory to the United States. If the Indian owners remained on their allotments for five years, they were to receive fee simple titles and become citizens.[22] Returning to Alabama, the chiefs informed their people that they had not actually sold the tribal lands but "had only made each individual their own guardian, that they might take care of their own possessions, and act as agents for themselves."[23]

Unlike the Creeks, the Chickasaws were willing to admit the inevitability of removal. But they needed land east of the Mississippi on which they might live until they acquired a home in the west. The Chickasaw treaty of May, 1832, therefore, provided generous allotments for heads of families, ranging from 640 to 3,200 acres, depending on the size of the family and the number of its slaves. These allotments were to be auctioned publicly when the tribe emigrated and the owners compensated for their improvements out of the proceeds.[24] Although the fullblood Chickasaws apparently approved of the plan for a collective sale of the allotments, the half-breeds, abetted by white traders and planters, persuaded the government to allow those who held allotments to sell them individually.[25] An amended treaty of 1834 complied with the half-breeds' proposals. It further stipulated that leading half-breeds and the old chiefs of the tribe comprise a committee to determine the competence of individual Chickasaws to manage their property. Since the committee itself disposed of the lands of the "incompetents," this gave both protection to the unsophisticated and additional advantage to the half-breeds.[26]

Widespread intrusion on Indian lands began with the extension of state laws over the tribal domains. In the treaties of cession, the government promised to remove intruders, but its policy in this respect was vacillating and ineffective. Indians whose allotments covered valuable plantations proved anxious to promote the sale of their property by allowing buyers to enter the ceded territory as soon as possible. Once this group of whites was admitted, it became difficult to discriminate against others.

---

[21] John Crowell to Lewis Cass, Jan. 25, 1832, Creek File 178, Records of the Bureau of Indian Affairs.

[22] 7 *Statutes-at-Large*, 366–68.

[23] John Scott to Lewis Cass, Nov. 12, 1835, Creek File 193, Records of the Bureau of Indian Affairs.

[24] 7 *Statutes-at-Large*, 381–89.

[25] John Terrell to Henry Cook, Oct. 29, 1832 (copy), John D. Terrell Papers, Alabama Dept. of Archives and History; Benjamin Reynolds to John Coffee, Dec. 12, 1832, Chickasaw File 83, Records of the Bureau of Indian Affairs; Terrell to John Tyler, Feb. 26, 1841 (draft), Terrell Papers; G. W. Long to John Coffee, Dec. 15, 1832, Coffee Papers; Rev. T. C. Stuart to Daniel Green, Oct. 14, 1833, American Board of Commissioners for Foreign Missions Manuscripts.

[26] 7 *Statutes-at-Large*, 450–57.

Thus a large number of intruders settled among the Indians with the passive connivance of the War Department and the tribal leaders. The task of removing them was so formidable that after making a few gestures the government generally evaded its obligation. The misery of the common Indians, surrounded by intruders and confused by the disruption of tribal authority, was so acute that any method for securing their removal seemed worth trying. Furthermore, their emigration would serve the interest of white settlers, land speculators, and their representatives in Washington. The government therefore chose to facilitate the sale of allotments even before the Indians received fee simple title to them.[27]

The right to sell his allotment was useful to the sophisticated tribesman with a large plantation. Such men were accustomed to selling their crops and hiring labor. Through their experience in treaty negotiations, they had learned to bargain over the price of lands. Many of them received handsome payment for their allotments. Some kept part of their holdings and remained in Alabama and Mississippi as planters—like other planters, practicing as land speculators on the side.[28] Nearly all the Indians had some experience in trade, but to most of them the conception of land as a salable commodity was foreign. They had little notion of the exact meaning of an "acre" or the probable value of their allotments.[29] The government confused them still further by parceling out the lands according to Anglo-American rather than aboriginal notions of family structure and land ownership. Officials insisted, for example, that the "father"

---

[27] William Ward to Secretary of War, Oct. 22, 1831, Choctaw Reserve File 133; Mushulatubbee to Lewis Cass, Feb. 9, 1832, Choctaw File 113; W. S. Colquhoun to General George S. Gibson, Apr. 20, 1832, Choctaw Emigration File 121; A. Campbell to Secretary of War, Aug. 5, 1832, Choctaw File 113; John Kurtz to Benjamin Reynolds, Aug. 9, 1833, Office of Indian Affairs, Letters Sent, XI, 74; S. C. Barton to Elbert Herring, Nov. 11, 1833, Choctaw File 113; William M. Gwin to Lewis Cass, Apr. 8, 1834, Choctaw File 84, Records of the Bureau of Indian Affairs; Mary E. Young, "The Creek Frauds: A Study in Conscience and Corruption," *Mississippi Valley Historical Review*, XLVII (Dec., 1955), 415–19.

[28] Benjamin Reynolds to Lewis Cass, Dec. 9, 1832, Apr. 29, 1835, Chickasaw File 83, 85, Records of the Bureau of Indian Affairs; David Haley to Jackson, Apr. 15, 1831, *Sen. Doc.* 512, 23 Cong., 1 sess., p. 426; Elbert Herring to George W. Elliott, Jan. 23, 1833, Office of Indian Affairs, Letters Sent, IX, 516, Records of the Bureau of Indian Affairs; J. J. Abert to J. R. Poinsett, July 19, 1839, Creek File 220, *ibid*. See Special Reserve Books and Special Reserve Files A and C, and William Carroll's list of Certified Contracts for the Sale of Chickasaw Reservations, Special File, Chickasaw, Records of the Bureau of Indian Affairs, and compare Chickasaw Location Book, Records of the Bureau of Land Management, National Archives.

[29] George S. Snyderman, "Concepts of Land Ownership Among the Iroquois and their Neighbors," in *Symposium on Local Variations in Iroquois Culture*, ed. William N. Fenton, Bureau of American Ethnology *Bulletin 149* (Washington, D.C., 1951), pp. 16–26; Petition of Choctaw Chiefs and Headmen, Mar. 2, 1832, Choctaw Reserve File 133; James Colbert to Lewis Cass, June 5, 1835, Chickasaw File 84; Benjamin Reynolds to Elbert Herring, Mar. 11, 1835, Chickasaw File 85, Records of the Bureau of Indian Affairs.

rather than the "mother" must be defined as head of the family and righteously refused to take cognizance of the fact that many of the "fathers" had "a plurality of wives."[30]

Under these conditions, it is not surprising that the common Indian's legal freedom of contract in selling his allotment did not necessarily lead him to make the best bargain possible in terms of his pecuniary interests. Nor did the proceeds of the sales transform each seller into an emigrant of large independent means. A right of property and freedom to contract for its sale did not automatically invest the Indian owner with the habits, values, and skills of a sober land speculator. His acquisition of property and freedom actually increased his dependence on those who traditionally mediated for him in contractual relations with white Americans.

Prominent among these mediators were white men with Indian wives who made their living as planters and traders in the Indian nations, men from nearby settlements who traded with the leading Indians or performed legal services for them, and interpreters. In the past, such individuals had been appropriately compensated for using their influence in favor of land cessions. It is likely that their speculative foresight was in part responsible for the allotment features in the treaties of the 1830's. When the process of allotting lands to individuals began, these speculative gentlemen made loans of whisky, muslin, horses, slaves, and other useful commodities to the new property-owner. They received in return the Indian's written promise to sell his allotment to them as soon as its boundaries were defined. Generally they were on hand to help him locate it on "desirable" lands. They, in turn, sold their "interest" in the lands to men of capital. Government agents encouraged the enterprising investor, since it was in the Indian's interest and the government's policy that the lands be sold and the tribes emigrate.[31] Unfortunately, the community of interest among the government, the speculator, and the Indian proved largely fictitious. The speculator's interest in Indian lands led to frauds which

---

[30] Memorial of Chickasaw Chiefs to the President, Nov. 25, 1835, Chickasaw File 84; Thomas J. Abbott and E. Parsons, Sept. 7, 1832, *Sen. Doc.* 512, 23 Cong., 1 sess., pp. 443–44; Elbert Herring to E. Parsons, B. S. Parsons, and John Crowell, Oct. 10, 1832, *ibid.*, p. 524; Leonard Tarrant to E. Herring, May 15, 1833, Creek File 202, Records of the Bureau of Indian Affairs; Alexander Spoehr, "Kinship Systems," pp. 201–31; John R. Swanton, *Indians of the Southeastern United States*, Bureau of American Ethnology *Bulletin 137* (Washington, D.C., 1946).

[31] John Coffee to Andrew Jackson, July 10, 1830, Creek File 192, Records of the Bureau of Indian Affairs; John Crowell to John H. Eaton, Aug. 8, 1830, Creek File 175, *ibid.*; John H. Brodnax to Lewis Cass, Mar. 12, 1832, *Sen. Doc.* 512, 23 Cong., 1 sess., III, 258–59; John Terrell to General John Coffee, Sept. 15, 1829, Coffee Papers; J. J. Abert to [Lewis Cass], June 13, 1833, Creek File 202, Records of the Bureau of Indian Affairs; contract between Daniel Wright and Mingo Mushulatubbee, Oct. 7, 1830, *American State Papers: Public Lands*, VII, 19; W. S. Colquhoun to Lewis Cass, Sept. 20, 1833, *ibid.*, p. 13; Chapman Levy to Joel R. Poinsett, June 19, 1837, Choctaw Reserve File 139, Records of the Bureau of Indian Affairs; James Colbert to Lewis Cass, June 5, 1835, Chickasaw File 84, *ibid.*; Chancery Court, Northern District of Mississippi, Final Record A, 111, M, 235–37, Courthouse, Holly Springs, Mississippi.

impoverished the Indians, soiled the reputation of the government, and retarded the emigration of the tribes.

An important factor in this series of complications was the government's fallacious assumption that most of the "real Indians" were anxious to emigrate. Under the Choctaw treaty, for example, registration for fee simple allotments was optional, the government expecting no more than two hundred registrants. When several hundred fullbloods applied for lands, the Choctaw agent assumed that they were being led astray by "designing men" and told them they must emigrate. Attorneys took up the Choctaw claims, located thousands of allotments in hopes that Congress would confirm them, and supported their clients in Mississippi for twelve to fifteen years while the government debated and acted on the validity of the claims. There was good reason for this delay. Settlers and rival speculators, opposing confirmation of the claims, advanced numerous depositions asserting that the attorneys, in their enterprising search for clients, had materially increased the number of claimants.[32] Among the Creeks, the Upper Towns, traditionally the conservative faction of the tribe, refused to sell their allotments. Since the Lower Towns proved more compliant, speculators hired willing Indians from the Lower Towns to impersonate the unwilling owners. They then bought the land from the impersonators. The government judiciously conducted several investigations of these frauds, but in the end the speculators outmaneuvered the investigators. Meanwhile, the speculators kept the Indians from emigrating until their contracts were approved. Only the outbreak of fighting between starving Creeks and their settler neighbors enabled the government, under pretext of a pacification, to remove the tribe.[33]

Besides embarrassing the government, the speculators contributed to the demoralization of the Indians. Universal complaint held that after paying the tribesman for his land they often borrowed back the money without serious intent of repaying it, or recovered it in return for overpriced goods, of which a popular article was whisky. Apprised of this situation, Secretary of War Lewis Cass replied that once the Indian had been paid for his land, the War Department had no authority to circumscribe his freedom to do what he wished with the proceeds.[34]

Nevertheless, within their conception of the proper role of government, officials who dealt with the tribes tried to be helpful. Although the Indian must be left free to contract for the sale of his lands, the United States sent agents to determine the validity of the contracts. These agents sometimes refused to approve a contract that did not specify a fair price for the land in question. They also refused official sanction when it could not be shown that the Indian owner had at some time been in possession

[32] Mary E. Young, "Indian Land Allotments in Alabama and Mississippi, 1830–1860" (manuscript doctoral dissertation, Cornell University, 1955), pp. 70–82; Franklin L. Riley, "The Choctaw Land Claims," Mississippi Historical Society *Publications*, VIII (1904), 370–82; Harmon, *Indian Affairs*, pp. 226–59.

[33] Young, "Creek Frauds," pp. 411–37.

[34] Lewis Cass to Return J. Meigs, Oct. 31, 1834, *Sen. Doc.* 428, 24 Cong., 1 sess., p. 23.

of the sum stipulated.[35] This protective action on the part of the government, together with its several investigations into frauds in the sale of Indian lands, apparently did secure the payment of more money than the tribesmen might otherwise have had. But the effort was seriously hampered by the near impossibility of obtaining disinterested testimony.

In dealing with the Chickasaws, the government managed to avoid most of the vexing problems which had arisen in executing the allotment program among their southeastern neighbors. This was due in part to the improvement of administrative procedures, in part to the methods adopted by speculators in Chickasaw allotments, and probably most of all to the inflated value of cotton lands during the period in which the Chickasaw territory was sold. Both the government and the Chickasaws recognized that the lands granted individuals under the treaty were generally to be sold, not settled. They therefore concentrated on provisions for supervising sales and safeguarding the proceeds.[36] Speculators in Chickasaw lands, having abundant resources, paid an average price of $1.70 per acre. The Chickasaws thereby received a better return than the government did at its own auctions. The buyers' generosity may be attributed to their belief that the Chickasaw lands represented the last first-rate cotton country within what were then the boundaries of the public domain. In their pursuit of a secure title, untainted by fraud, the capitalists operating in the Chickasaw cession established a speculators' claim association which settled disputes among rival purchasers. Thus they avoided the plots, counterplots, and mutual recriminations which had hampered both speculators and government in their dealings with the Creeks and Choctaws.[37]

A superficially ironic consequence of the allotment policy as a method of acquiring land for white settlers was the fact that it facilitated the engrossment of land by speculators. With their superior command of capital and the influence it would buy, speculators acquired 80 to 90 per cent of the lands allotted to the southeastern tribesmen.[38]

For most of the Indian beneficiaries of the policy, its most important consequence was to leave them landless. After selling their allotment, or a

---

[35] Lewis Cass, "Regulations," for certifying Creek contracts, Nov. 28, 1833, *Sen. Doc.* 276, 24 Cong., 1 sess., pp. 88–89; *id.*, "Regulations," Feb. 8, 1836, Chickasaw Letterbook A, 76–78, Records of the Bureau of Indian Affairs; Secretary of War to the President, June 27, 1836, Choctaw Reserve File 136, *ibid.* For adjudications based on the above regulations, see Special Reserve Files A and C and Choctaw, Creek, and Chickasaw Reserve Files, Records of the Bureau of Indian Affairs, *passim.*

[36] "Memorial of the Creek Nation . . . ," Jan. 29, 1883, *House Misc. Doc.* 18, 47 Cong., 2 sess.

[37] Average price paid for Chickasaw lands computed from William Carroll's List of Certified Contracts, Special Reserve File, Chickasaw, Records of the Bureau of Indian Affairs; Young, "Indian Allotments," pp. 154–67.

[38] See calculations in Young, "Indian Allotments," pp. 141–42, 163–64. No system of estimating percentages of land purchased for speculation from figures of sales is foolproof. The assumption used in this estimate was that all those who bought 2,000 acres or more might be defined as speculators. Compare James W. Silver, "Land Speculation Profits in the Chickasaw Cession," *Journal of Southern History,* X (Feb., 1944), 84–92.

claim to it, they might take to the swamp, live for a while on the bounty of a still hopeful speculator, or scavenge on their settler neighbors. But ultimately most of them faced the alternative of emigration or destitution, and chose to emigrate. The machinations of the speculators and the hopes they nurtured that the Indians might somehow be able to keep a part of their allotted lands made the timing of removals less predictable than it might otherwise have been. This unpredictability compounded the evils inherent in a mass migration managed by a government committed to economy and unversed in the arts of economic planning. The result was the "Trail of Tears."[39]

The spectacular frauds committed among the Choctaws and Creeks, the administrative complications they created, and the impression they gave that certain self-styled champions of the people were consorting with the avaricious speculator gave the allotment policy a bad reputation. The administration rejected it in dealing with the Cherokees,[40] and the policy was not revived on any considerable scale until 1854, when it was applied, with similar consequences, to the Indians of Kansas.[41] In the 1880's, when allotment in severalty became a basic feature of American Indian policy, the "civilized tribes," then in Oklahoma, strenuously resisted its application to them. They cited their memories of the 1830's as an important reason for their intransigence.[42]

The allotment treaties of the 1830's represent an attempt to apply Anglo-American notions of justice, which enshrined private property in land and freedom of contract as virtually absolute values, to Indian tribes whose tastes and traditions were otherwise. Their history illustrates the limitations of intercultural application of the Golden Rule. In a more practical sense, the treaties typified an effort to force on the Indians the alternative of complete assimilation or complete segregation by placing individuals of varying levels of sophistication in situations where they must use the skills of businessmen or lose their means of livelihood. This policy secured tribal lands while preserving the forms of respect for property rights and freedom of contract, but it proved costly to both the government and the Indians.

How lightly that cost was reckoned, and how enduring the motives

[39] For the story of emigration, see Foreman, *Indian Removal;* Debo, *Road to Disappearance*, pp. 103–07, and *Choctaw Republic*, pp. 55–57. Relations between speculation and emigration can be traced in the Creek, Choctaw, and Chickasaw Emigration and Reserve Files, Records of the Bureau of Indian Affairs.

[40] Hon. R. Chapman to Lewis Cass, Jan. 25, 1835, Cherokee File 7, Records of the Bureau of Indian Affairs; Lewis Cass to Commissioners Carroll and Schermerhorn, Apr. 2, 1835, Office of Indian Affairs, Letters Sent, XV, 261, *ibid.;* "Journal of the Proceedings at the Council held at New Echota . . . ," Cherokee File 7, *ibid.;* Joint Memorial of the Legislature of the State of Alabama . . . , Jan. 9, 1836, *ibid.;* William Gilmer to Andrew Jackson, Feb. 9, 1835, Jackson Papers; 7 *Statutes-at-Large*, 483–84, 488–89.

[41] Paul W. Gates, *Fifty Million Acres: Conflicts over Kansas Land Policy, 1854–1890* (Ithaca, N.Y., 1954), pp. 11–48.

[42] Memorial of the Creek Nation on the Subject of Lands in Severalty Among the Several Indian Tribes," Jan. 29, 1883, *House Misc. Doc.* 18, 47 Cong., 2 sess.

and rationalizations that gave rise to it, may be gathered from the subsequent experience of the southeastern tribes in Oklahoma. There, early in the twentieth century, the allotment policy was again enforced, with safeguards hardly more helpful to the unsophisticated than those of the 1830's. Once more, tribal land changed owners for the greater glory of liberty, civilization, and profit.[43]

[43] Compare Angie Debo, *The Five Civilized Tribes of Oklahoma: Report on Social and Economic Conditions* (Philadelphia, Pa., 1951), and Kinney, *Indian Land Tenure*, pp. 243–44.

# Suggestions for Further Reading

For a well-rounded introduction to the United States in its first years, see Gordon S. Wood, *The Creation of the American Republic, 1776–1787* (University of North Carolina Press, 1969). Several of the essays in Staughton Lynd, *Class Conflict, Slavery, and the United States Constitution* (Bobbs-Merrill, 1967), deal with the role of class conflict in shaping the new nation.

In *Crisis in Freedom: The Alien and Sedition Acts\** (Little, Brown, 1951), John C. Miller provides a brief introduction to the issues raised by the repressive Federalist legislation of 1798. Zechariah Chafee treats the problem of freedom of speech in *Free Speech in the United States\** (Harvard University Press, 1948). Three works by Leonard W. Levy deal with various aspects of freedom of expression: *Legacy of Suppression* (Harvard University Press, 1960), a discussion of freedom of the press in colonial times; *Freedom of the Press from Zenger to Jefferson: Early American Libertarian Theories\** (Bobbs-Merrill, 1966), a collection; and *Jefferson and Civil Liberties: The Darker Side* (Harvard University Press, 1963), on suppression under the Republicans.

For the Indian policy of the federal government in the early years of the new nation, see Reginald Horsman, *Expansion and American Indian Policy, 1783–1812* (Michigan State University Press, 1967), and F. P. Prucha, *American Indian Policy in the Formative Years\** (Harvard University Press, 1962). An excellent study of the impact of white settlement on a specific Indian nation is Anthony F. C. Wallace, *The Death and Rebirth of the Seneca* (Knopf, 1970). The best available biography of Tecumseh is Glenn Tucker, *Tecumseh, Vision of Glory* (Bobbs-Merrill, 1956).

The literature on Indian removal from the Southeast is voluminous. Good starting points are Dale Van Every's *Disinherited: The Lost Birthright of the American Indian\** (Morrow, 1966) and the collection of documents edited by Louis Filler and Allan Guttman, *Removal of the Cherokee Nation: Manifest Destiny or National Dishonor\** (Heath, 1962). Robert S. Cotterill discusses the life of the Indians before their dispossession in *The Southern Indians: The Story of the Civilized Tribes Before Removal* (University of Oklahoma Press, 1954); and Grant Foreman tells the sad tale of removal in *Indian Removal: The Emigration of the Five Civilized Tribes of Indians* (2d ed.; University of Oklahoma Press, 1953). Angie Debo takes a close look at two of the Five Civilized Tribes in *The Road to Disappearance: A History of the Creek Indians* (University of Oklahoma Press, 1941) and *The Rise and Fall of the Choctaw Republic* (University of Oklahoma Press, 1961).

---

\* Available in paperback edition.

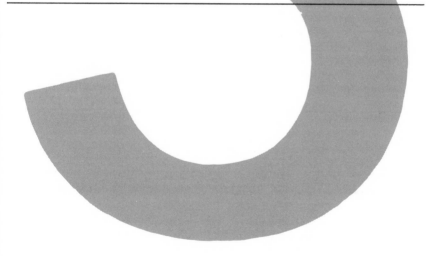

# The Ante-Bellum
# North and South

# Religious Conflict

# in

# Ante-Bellum Boston

## OSCAR HANDLIN

Religious conflict in early American history involved not merely discrimination against the non-Christian Indians and Africans but also hostility among competing Christian sects. Puritan intolerance in New England and Anglican establishment in the Southern colonies worked against the unification of the several Christian denominations. Although the Bill of Rights established a legal basis for religious toleration—at least at the federal level—as early as 1789, religious discrimination has been a persistent problem in American society.

One of the most virulent outbreaks of religious prejudice in American history occurred in the 1840's and 1850's, when tens of thousands of Irish Catholic immigrants arrived on the Eastern seaboard. Fleeing the horrors of famine in Ireland, many came to America destitute and deeply antagonistic toward all things English, including the Protestant religion. There had been Irish immigrants to America before—those deported in the civil wars of the seventeenth century and the United Irishmen refugees from the attempted republican rebellion of 1798. But never before had the Irish come in such numbers, and never had America been so ill prepared to receive them.

Many German Catholics also emigrated to America in these years, but the majority of the Germans avoided religious conflict by moving to the West, where they formed homogeneous farming communities and settled in cities such as St. Louis and Milwaukee. The Irish, in contrast, tended to gather in the older cities and in the new factory towns of the East, where they competed with the established residents for unskilled and industrial labor, thus intensifying negative feelings toward them. The United States economy had just begun to recover from the depression of 1837, which had closed thousands of businesses and manufacturing plants and caused widespread unemployment. Now, suddenly, there was a great flood of cheap labor, creating the first real labor surplus in American history. Industrialists responded by cutting wages drastically in the mills and other Eastern manufacturing enterprises. The laboring classes tended to blame the Irish for the worsening economic conditions. Religious bigotry and nativism added to the discontent, and violence of major proportions erupted in several Eastern cities. In Philadelphia, for example, a request that Catholic children be allowed to use the Catholic version of the Bible in public schools and that they be excused from Protestant religious exercises led to riots in which houses and churches were burned and at least thirty people were killed and over a hundred wounded.

The following selection is reprinted from a chapter in **Boston's Immigrants,** a study of Irish immigrants to Boston by Oscar Handlin, of Harvard University. In it, Handlin examines the rise of nativism and anti-Catholicism in Boston toward the middle of the nineteenth century.

---

*We still drive out of Society the Ishmaels and Esaus. This we do not so much from ill-will as want of thought, but thereby we lose the strength of these outcasts. So much water runs over the dam— wasted and wasting![1]*

Consciousness of identity particularized groups; but mere pluralism evoked no conflict in Boston society. Those coherently welded by circumstances of origin, economic status, cultural variations, or color differences often moved in distinct orbits, but were part of a harmonious system. In some instances, native Bostonians adopted newcomers; in others, they adapted themselves to the existence of aliens in their community. But whatever friction arose out of the necessity for making adjustments produced no conflict, until the old social order and the values upon which it rested were endangered.

Thus, while prejudice against color and servile economic origin confined the Negroes to restricted residential areas, distinct churches, special jobs, separate schools, and undesirable places in theaters until the 1850's, the relationships between Negroes and other Bostonians were stable and

[1] Theodore Parker, *A Sermon of the Dangerous Classes in Society* . . . (Boston, 1847), 12.

"Religious Conflict in Ante-Bellum Boston." Reprinted by permission of the publishers. From Oscar Handlin, *Boston's Immigrants*, Cambridge, Mass.: The Belknap Press of Harvard University Press, pp. 178–206. Copyright, 1941, 1959, by the President and Fellows of Harvard College.

peaceful.[2] Social and legal discriminations still limited Negro privileges in the Park Street Church in 1830, and incited protests when Alcott included a Negro child in his infant school.[3] But the stigmata and penalties for being different were slowly vanishing. Those who urged equality for the South were perforce obliged to apply their convictions at home. An attempt in 1822 to restrict the immigration of Negro paupers failed and repeated petitions after 1839 finally secured the repeal of laws against intermarriage, thus legalizing a process already in existence.[4] In 1855 separate schools were abolished and colored children unconditionally admitted to the public schools, so that by 1866 some 150 Negroes attended the primary, 103 the grammar, and five the high schools of Boston—in all, a high percentage of the Negro children of the city.[5] The state actively defended and protected Negroes' rights, even establishing missions for that purpose in Charleston and New Orleans where Boston colored seamen were often seized as fugitive slaves.[6] Public pressure forced the Eastern and New Bedford Railroads to admit colored people to their cars in the forties; and former slaves began to move to the same streets as whites.[7] In 1863, they were permitted to fight in the Union Army when Governor Andrew, with the aid of Lewis Hayden, recruited the Fifty-fourth Massachusetts Regiment, which included 300 fugitive slaves. In the same year, the militia was opened to them, and a colored company in Ward Six received a grant from the city. Negro regiments were segregated, but many prominent Bostonians "taking life and honor in their hands cast in their lot with" them.[8] By 1865, the Negroes, though still a separate part of Boston society, participated in its advantages without conflict. And most Bostonians agreed that "the theory of a natural antagonism and in-

[2] Cf., e.g., the sober editorial on Negro problems in *Daily Evening Transcript*, September 28, 1830; cf. also Mary Caroline Crawford, *Romantic Days in Old Boston* . . . (Boston, 1910), 249; Helen T. Catterall, *Judicial Cases Concerning American Slavery and the Negro* . . . (Washington, 1936), IV, 524.

[3] Cf. E. S. Abdy, *Journal of a Residence and Tour in the United States* . . . (London, 1835), I, 133 ff.; Odell Shepard, *Journals of Bronson Alcott* (Boston, 1938), 110.

[4] Cf. [Theodore Lyman, Jr.], *Free Negroes and Mulattoes, House of Representatives, January 16, 1822 . . . Report* . . . (Boston, n.d.); Henry Wilson, *History of the Rise and Fall of the Slave Power in America* (Boston, 1872), I, 489–92.

[5] 316 between the ages of 10 and 15 ("Report of the School Committee, 1866," *Boston City Documents, 1866*, no. 137, p. 188). Cf. also *Boston Pilot*, September 15, October 6, 1855.

[6] Cf. the letters of Edward Everett to John P. Bigelow, dated July 23, 1839, September 30, 1839 (Bigelow Papers [MSS., H. C. L.], Box V, VI); Arthur B. Darling, *Political Changes in Massachusetts* . . . (New Haven, 1925), 320; Catterall, *op. cit.*, IV, 511, 524; Edward Channing, *History of the United States* (New York, 1925), VI, 93 ff.

[7] Cf. Wilson, *op. cit.*, I, 492–95; Lady Emmeline S. Wortley, *Travels in the United States* . . . (New York, 1851), 60; Edward Dicey, *Six Months in the Federal States* (London, 1863), II, 215.

[8] *Exercises at the Dedication of the Monument to Colonel Robert Gould Shaw* . . . *May 31, 1897* . . . (Boston, 1897), 10; Henry Greenleaf Pearson, *Life of John A. Andrew* . . . (Boston, 1904), II, 70 ff.; William S. Robinson, *"Warrington" Pen-Portraits* . . . (Boston, 1877), 107, 274, 406; A. B. Hart, *Commonwealth History of Massachusetts* . . . (New York, 1930), IV, 535; *Boston City Documents, 1863*, no. 100, pp. 11, 18.

superable prejudice on the part of the white man against the black is a pure fiction. Ignorant men are always full of prejudices and antagonisms; and color has nothing to do with it."[9]

Group consciousness based upon religious differences was likewise not conducive to conflict. The Puritan dislike of Catholics had subsided during the eighteenth century,[10] and had disappeared in the early nineteenth as a result of the good feelings produced by revolutionary collaboration with the French and the growth of the latitudinarian belief that "inside of Christianity reason was free."[11] Governor Hancock had early abolished Pope's Day, and the Constitution of 1780 had eliminated the legal restrictions against Catholics. Catholics established a church in the city in 1789 "without the smallest opposition, for persecution in Boston had wholly ceased," and "all violent prejudices against the good bishop of Rome and the Church . . . he governs" had vanished, along with hostility towards hierarchical institutions in general.[12] Bishop Carroll, visit-

[9] Robinson, *op. cit.*, 298; cf. also Dicey, *op. cit.*, I, 70, 74; *Massachusetts Senate Documents, 1841*, no. 51; *Massachusetts House Documents, 1841*, no. 17.

[10] Thus with few exceptions there was a "general absence of anti-Catholic references" in eighteenth-century textbooks, and the Dudleian lectures were founded to counteract "the rapid rise of liberalism" (Rev. Arthur J. Riley, *Catholicism in New England* . . . [Washington, 1936], 307, 23, 31, 225). The only exception was the hostility, primarily political, to Jesuit activities in Maine (*ibid.*, 6, 193 ff.; Channing, *op. cit.*, II, 131 ff., 531, 545 ff.). Puritan intolerance sprang from the desire to found a "bible commonwealth" and was therefore directed against Baptists, Quakers, and Arminians as well (cf. Channing, *op. cit.*, II, 68; Ray Allen Billington, *Protestant Crusade, 1800–1860, A Study of the Origins of American Nativism* [New York, 1938], 7, 15, 18; Riley, *op. cit.*, 45 ff., 217 ff.). When priests visited Boston under circumstances that did not endanger the "Standing Order" they "received a cordial welcome befitting the social amenities exchanged between educated persons" (Riley, *op. cit.*, 190, 184 ff., 206, 207).

[11] Octavius B. Frothingham, *Boston Unitarianism, 1820–1850* . . . (New York, 1890), 23; Archibald H. Grimké, *Life of Charles Sumner* . . . (New York, 1892), 38. For the popularity of the French in Boston, cf. H. M. Jones, *America and French Culture* . . . (Chapel Hill, 1927), 126; for the effect of the Revolution, cf. John G. Shea, "Catholic Church in American History," *American Catholic Quarterly Review*, January, 1876, I, 155; Billington, *op. cit.*, 19.

Those who regard anti-Catholicism as inherent in the nature of Protestant society and define "the Protestant milieu" as "nothing else than opposition to Catholicism" (Riley, *op. cit.*, vii, 1; "Anti-Catholic Movements in the United States," *Catholic World*, XXII [1876], 810; Billington, *op. cit.*, 1) have been hard put to explain the tolerance of the early nineteenth century. The simplest escape has been to mark it a period of subsidence arising from absorption in other problems (cf. Billington, *op. cit.*, 32; Humphrey J. Desmond, *Know-Nothing Party* [Washington, 1904], 12), with the anti-Catholicism of the forties and fifties simply a recrudescence of forces always present, thus missing completely the significance of the special factors that produced it in those two decades.

[12] Samuel Breck, "Catholic Recollections," *American Catholic Historical Researches*, XII (1895), 146, 148; E. Percival Merritt, "Sketches of the Three Earliest Roman Catholic Priests in Boston," *Publications of the Colonial Society of Massachusetts*, XXV, 218 ff.; William Wilson Manross, *Episcopal Church in the United States, 1800–1840, A Study in Church Life* (New York, 1938), 59; Samuel Eliot Morison, *History of the Constitution of Massachusetts* . . . (Boston, 1917), 24.

ing Boston in 1791, preached before the Governor, pronounced the blessing at the annual election of the Ancient and Honorables, and was amazed
at the good treatment accorded him. Bishop Cheverus commanded the
respect and affection of all Protestants.

Thereafter the government was no longer hostile. The City Council
frequently gave Catholics special privileges to insure freedom of worship,
closing the streets near Holy Cross Church to exclude the noise of passing
trucks.[13] It never took advantage of the laws that permitted it to tax all
residents for sectarian purposes; on the contrary, Boston Protestants often
contributed to Catholic churches and institutions. After 1799 no tithes
were collected, by 1820 religious tests were abolished, and in 1833 Church
and State completely separated.[14] The anti-Catholic activities of the *New
York Protestant* and of the New York Protestant Association in the early
thirties had no counterpart in Boston where an attempt to found an anti-
Catholic paper (*Anti-Jesuit*) in 1829 failed.[15] Accepted as loyal members
of the community, Catholics could easily partake of its opportunities.[16]
Their right to be different was consistently defended by natives who
urged that the particular sect each person chose was a private matter.

> In individual instances where our friends and acquaintances join
> the Romish Church, there may be reason either to be glad of it or
> to grieve. If they join the Church . . . because they need its peculiar
> influence for their own good, if never having found peace in Christ
> elsewhere they do find it there, ought we not to rejoice in such a
> result? Why should we doubt that some minds are better fitted
> to find a personal union with God by the methods of the Catholic
> Church than by any other?[17]

There were of course differences between the sects, expressed in
theological disputations. As early as 1791 Thayer offered to debate any

---

[13] Cf. Merritt, *loc. cit.*, 205–07; Billington, *op. cit.*, 20; Josiah Quincy, *Figures of the
Past from the Leaves of Old Journals* (Boston, 1883), 311, 312; *Minutes of the
Selectmen's Meetings, 1811 to 1817* . . . (*Volume of Records Relating to the
Early History of Boston*, XXXVIII), *Boston City Documents, 1908*, no. 60, p. 69;
James Bernard Cullen, *Story of the Irish in Boston* . . . (Boston, 1890), 125; Leo
F. Ruskowski, *French Emigré Priests in the United States* . . . (Washington,
1940), 85.

[14] Cf. Morison, *op. cit.*, 24, 32; *Boston Catholic Observer*, April 17, 1847; Rev. James
Fitton, *Sketches of the Establishment of the Church in New England* (Boston,
1872), 141; Darling, *op. cit.*, 23; Hart, *op. cit.*, IV, 12.

[15] Cf. Billington, *op. cit.*, 53 ff., 76. The Boston Irish Protestant Association which
Billington claimed was anti-Catholic (*ibid.*, 78, n. 48) specifically disavowed such
activities (cf. the correspondence in *Boston Pilot*, June 25, July 2, 1842; also *Boston
Catholic Observer*, August 2, 1848).

[16] Cf., e.g., *Jesuit or Catholic Sentinel*, July 23, 1831; Marcus Lee Hansen, *Immigrant
in American History* . . . (Cambridge, 1940), 107.

[17] James Freeman Clarke, *The Church . . . as It Was, as It Is, as It Ought to Be, a
Discourse at the . . . Chapel . . . Church of the Disciples . . . 1848* (Boston,
1848), 13; Arthur M. Schlesinger, Jr., *Orestes A. Brownson* . . . (Boston, 1939),
175.

Protestant in a "controversial lecture."[18] Beecher and Bishop Fenwick, assisted by Father O'Flaherty, engaged in a series of debates in 1830–34, the most prominent of the period. And the religious press and sermons occasionally attacked Catholicism, sometimes violently, in the spirit of all contemporary disputes, while Protestant denominations urged their ministers to resist the spread of "Popery."[19]

But the expression of theological differences did not imply intolerance. Thus the Congregationalists urged their ministers to labor "in the spirit of prayer and Christian love . . . ," and even the *Christian Alliance and Family Visitor,* founded "to promote the union of Christians against Popery," failed to print "a single article or paragraph of any description against . . . Catholics."[20] Arguments were aimed against Catholicism, not against Catholics, just as they were against Methodism, or by the Orthodox against Unitarianism and by "Christians" against transcendentalists.[21] When Beecher became too violent, the *Boston Courier* and the Boston Debating Society, both non-Catholic, denounced him. For though some preferred one sect to another, the predominant feeling among Bostonians of this period was that "wherever holiness reigns, whether in the Protestant or Catholic communion . . . wherever there is a pious heart . . . there is a member of the true church."[22] Indeed, such men as Channing cared little for the particular sect in which they ministered. Their "whole concern was with religion, not even with Christianity otherwise than as it was, in . . . [their] estimation, the highest form of religion. . . ."[23]

Those who recognized distinctions between the sects generally felt that more important were

> the grand facts of Christianity, which *Calvinists* and *Arminians, Trinitarians* and *Unitarians, Papists* and *Protestants, Churchmen* and *Dissenters* all equally believe. . . . We all equally hold that he came . . . to save us from sin and death, and to publish a covenant of grace, by which all sincere penitents and good men are assured of favour and complete happiness in his future everlasting kingdom.[24]

In that vein, Holmes' "Cheerful Parson" affirmed,

[18] Cf. *Columbian Centinel* (Boston), January 26, 1791; *ibid.,* February 2, 1791; *American Catholic Historical Researches,* V (1888), 51.

[19] Cf. Dissertation Copy, 347, 348; Billington, *op. cit.,* 43 ff., 69 ff., 79. For the religious press in general, cf. Frank Luther Mott, *History of American Magazines* . . . (Cambridge, 1938), II, 60.

[20] Cf. the complaints on this score in *Boston Catholic Observer,* March 1, 1848; also Billington, *op. cit.,* 177, 86.

[21] Cf., e.g., Darling, *op. cit.,* 29; Clarence Hotson, "Christian Critics and Mr. Emerson," *New England Quarterly,* March, 1938, XI, 29 ff.

[22] R. C. Waterston, *"The Keys of the Kingdom of Heaven,"* a *Sermon* . . . (Boston, 1844), 13; cf. also Frothingham, *op. cit.,* 48; *Jesuit or Catholic Sentinel,* December 29, 1830; *ibid.,* February 26, 1831.

[23] Frothingham, *op. cit.,* 6.

[24] Richard Price, *Sermons on the Christian Doctrine as Received by the Different Denominations of Christians* . . . (Boston, 1815), 8.

> Not damning a man for a different opinion,
> I'd mix with the Calvinist, Baptist, Arminian,
> Greet each like a man, like a Christian and brother,
> Preach love to our Maker, ourselves and each other.[25]

And even the more conservative Baptists granted that "the various erring sects which constitute the body of Antichrist, have among them those who are beloved of God. . . ." "Wherein we think others err, they claim our pity; wherein they are right, our affection and concurrence."[26] In this roseate scheme of salvation there was room even for Jews, and from Bunker Hill, a poet proclaimed:

> Christian and Jew, they carry out one plan,
> For though of different faith, each in heart a man.[27]

Government action reflected the community's attitude towards immigrants. They were still welcome. The state had no desire to exclude foreigners or to limit their civic rights; on the contrary, during this period it relaxed some surviving restrictions.[28] Since the care of aliens was charged to the Commonwealth, the problem of poor relief aroused less hostility within Boston than outside it.[29] Yet nowhere was pauperism transmuted into a pretext for discrimination against the Irish. Legislation aimed only at barring the dependent, the insane, and the unfit, and shifted to newcomers part of the cost of those who could not support themselves. The function of the municipal Superintendent of Alien Passengers, under the act of 1837, was merely to prevent the landing of persons incompetent to maintain themselves, unless a bond be given that no such individual become a public charge within ten years, and to collect the sum of two dollars each from all other alien passengers as a commutation for such a bond.[30] All the subsequent changes in the law only modified it to conform with a decision of the Supreme Court.[31] Attempts to extend these

---

[25] Cf. M. A. DeWolfe Howe, *Holmes of the Breakfast Table* . . . (New York, 1939), 17.

[26] *Minutes of the Boston Baptist Association . . . 1812* (Boston, n.d.), 13.

[27] Cf. Morris A. Gutstein, *Aaron Lopez and Judah Touro* . . . (New York, 1939), 98.

[28] Cf. Massachusetts Commissioners of Alien Passengers and Foreign Paupers, *Report . . . 1851* (Boston, 1852), 14; also Edith Abbott, *Historical Aspects of the Immigration Problem* . . . (Chicago, 1926), 622, 739 ff.; *Cork Examiner*, July 6, 1853; *Massachusetts House Documents, 1828–29*, no. 25; *ibid., 1829–30,* no. 8; *Massachusetts Senate Documents, 1852*, no. 11.

[29] Cf. the source of petitions for repeal of the state pauper laws, *Massachusetts Senate Documents, 1847*, no. 109.

[30] *Ordinances of the City of Boston Passed Since the Year 1834* . . . (Boston, 1843), 3, 4; Hart, *op. cit.,* IV, 143 ff.; Edith Abbott, *Immigration, Select Documents* . . . (Chicago, 1924), 105 ff., 148.

[31] Cf. Norris v. City of Boston (7 *Howard's U.S. Reports,* 283, XVII, 139 ff.); *Massachusetts Senate Documents, 1847,* no. 109; *ibid., 1848,* no. 46; Peleg W. Chandler, *Charter and Ordinances of the City of Boston Together with Acts of the Legislature Relating to the City* . . . (Boston, 1850), 25 ff.; *Charter and Ordinances of the City of Boston Together with the Acts of the Legislature* . . . (Boston, 1856), 34 ff.

restrictive provisions failed, partly because of the pressure of shipping firms which profited by the immigrant traffic, but primarily because successive administrations recognized that, "The evils of foreign pauperism we cannot avoid," and it is "wise to avail ourselves of the advantages of direct emigration which increases the business of the State."[32]

In the two decades after 1830, however, the differences so tolerantly accepted impinged ever more prominently upon the Bostonians' consciousness. The economic, physical, and intellectual development of the town accentuated the division between the Irish and the rest of the population and engendered fear of a foreign group whose appalling slums had already destroyed the beauty of a fine city and whose appalling ideas threatened the fondest conceptions of universal progress, of grand reform, and a regenerated mankind. The vague discomforts and the latent distrusts produced by the problems of these strangers festered in the unconscious mind of the community for many years. Though its overt manifestations were comparatively rare, the social uneasiness was none the less real.

Thus pauperism aroused some resentment among those who saw Massachusetts overwhelmed by a rising tax bill;[33] and indigent artisans continually complained that Irishmen displaced "the honest and respectable laborers of the State; and . . . from their manner of living . . . work for much less per day . . . being satisfied with food to support the animal existence alone . . . while the latter not only labor for the body but for the mind, the soul, and the State."[34] Above all, as the newcomers developed consciousness of group identity and sponsored institutions that were its concrete expression, they drove home upon other Bostonians a mounting awareness of their differences, and provoked complaints that

> instead of assimilating at once with the customs of the country of their adoption, our foreign population are too much in the habit of retaining their own national usages, of *associating too exclusively with each other*, and living in groups together. These practices serve no good purpose, and tend merely to alienate those among whom they have chosen to reside. *It would be the part of wisdom, to* ABANDON AT ONCE ALL USAGES AND ASSOCIATIONS WHICH MARK THEM AS FOREIGNERS, *and to become in feeling and custom, as well as in privileges and rights, citizens of the United States.*[35]

The inability of the native-born to understand the ideas of their new neighbors perpetuated this gap between them, rousing the vivid fear that

---

[32] *Massachusetts Senate Documents, 1852*, no. 7, p. 7. For the influence of shipping firms, cf. *Massachusetts Senate Documents, 1847*, no. 109, p. 5; Boston Board of Trade, *Second Annual Report of the Government . . . 1856* (Boston, 1856), 3.

[33] For evidence of this complaint, cf. *American Traveller* (Boston), August 5, 1834; *American*, October 21, 1837; Abbott, *Immigration*, 112 ff.; Edith Abbott, *Historical Aspects of the Immigration Problem . . .* (Chicago, 1926), 572 ff., 758 ff.; *Massachusetts House Documents, 1836*, no. 30, pp. 9 ff.

[34] Cf. *Massachusetts Senate Documents, 1847*, no. 109, p. 4.

[35] *American* (Boston), October 21, 1837.

the Irish were "a race that will never be infused into our own, but on the contrary will always remain distinct and hostile."[36]

That fear was the more pronounced because the Catholic Church in these years was a church militant, conscious of its mission in the United States, vigorous and active in proselytization and the search for converts. In the strategy of the hierarchy, and in their own minds, immigrants played a clear role in this process of redemption: they had been carried across the waters by a Divine Providence to present an irrefutable example of fortitude and faith to their unbelieving neighbors, to leaven the dull mass of Protestant America and ultimately to bring the United States into the ranks of Catholic powers.[37] No figure was more insistently, clearly, and admiringly drawn in immigrant literature than that of the humble Irishman in every walk of life who succeeded in converting his employer, friend, or patron.[38] Though Bostonians could not do without the Irish servant girl, distrust of her mounted steadily; natives began to regard her as a spy of the Pope who revealed their secrets regularly to priests at confession.[39] The growth of Catholicism in England warned them that a staunchly Protestant country might be subverted. Meanwhile, close at home, the mounting power of the Oxford movement in the Episcopal Church, reflected in the estrangement of Bishop Eastburn and the Church of the Advent (1844 ff.), and a growing list of widely publicized conversions lent reality to the warning of Beecher and Morse that Catholics plotted to assume control of the West.[40]

Before 1850, the potential friction inherent in these fears broke out only infrequently and sporadically. Incepted by irresponsible elements, these spontaneous brawls were always severely criticized by the community. Indeed, they were only occasionally directed against aliens, more often involving neighborhoods or fire companies. The rowdies singled out no special group. In 1814 West Enders rioted against Spanish sailors, in 1829 against Negroes and Irishmen, and in 1846 against some drunken Irishmen in Roxbury; but these were no more significant than the count-

[36] Mayor Lyman (*Inaugural Addresses of the Mayors of Boston* . . . [Boston, 1894], I, 195).

[37] Cf., e.g., *Boston Catholic Observer*, February 16, 1848; Thomas D'Arcy McGee, *History of the Irish Settlers in North America* . . . (Boston, 1852), 71; Billington, *op. cit.*, 291.

[38] Cf. e.g., Ellie in Agnes E. St. John, "Ellie Moore or the Pilgrim's Crown," *Boston Pilot*, June 30–September 1, 1860.

[39] Cf. James O'Connor, "Anti-Catholic Prejudice," *American Catholic Quarterly Review*, I (1876), 13.

[40] Cf. Billington, *op. cit.*, 118 ff., 263; William Wilson Manross, *History of the American Episcopal Church* (New York, 1935), 283 ff.; *Boston Catholic Observer*, July 24, 1847; S. F. B. Morse, *Foreign Conspiracy Against the United States* (s.l., n.d. [186–], 26, 3, 29; S. F. B. Morse, *Imminent Dangers to the Free Institutions of the United States* . . . (New York, 1854), *passim;* Louis Dow Scisco, *Political Nativism in New York State* (New York, 1901), 21.

less feuds between North Enders and South Enders, or between truckmen and sailors, details of which enlivened many a police dossier.[41]

The Broad Street riot was exceptional only in size. On June 11, 1837, a collision between a volunteer fire company and an Irish funeral procession led to an outbreak, quelled after an hour or so by the militia. Caused by hotheaded, unruly firemen, proverbially a disruptive factor, it in no way reflected the feeling of the community. The firemen were immediately repudiated, and partly as a result of the affair, Mayor Lyman took the first steps towards replacing the volunteer system with a paid fire department.[42] A less permanent result was the establishment by the disbanded firemen of the *American*, the first anti-Catholic paper in Boston which for somewhat less than a year attacked alternately the Irish and the *"paid patriots"* who replaced them.[43]

Because it served for many years as an argument throughout the country in the propaganda for and against Catholics, the Charlestown Convent fire received a greater degree of notoriety than any other riot.[44] This disturbance grew primarily out of the failure of the school and the rural community in which it was located to adjust themselves to each other. To the laborers who lived nearby, the convent was a strange and unfamiliar institution, with which it was difficult to be neighborly or to follow the customary social forms. In addition, Catholicism meant Irishmen and for non-Irish laborers the convent was a symbol of the new competition they daily encountered. Rebecca Reed's lurid stories of life in the convent and the bickering of the Bishop and the Charlestown Selectman over a cemetery on Bunker Hill provoked a sense of irritation that came to a head with the appearance and disappearance of Elizabeth Harrison, a demented nun.[45] The refusal of the Mother Superior to admit the Charlestown Selectmen to investigate the purported existence of dungeons and torture chambers until the very day of the fire inflamed

[41] Cf. "Boston as It Appeared to a Foreigner at the Beginning of the Nineteenth Century," *Bostonian Society Publications*, Series I, IV, 117, 118; Joseph E. Chamberlin, *Boston Transcript* . . . (Boston, 1930), 37 ff.; *Minutes of the Selectmen's Meetings, 1811 to 1817* . . . (*Volume of Records* . . . , XXXVIII), *Boston City Documents, 1908*, no. 60, p. 113; *Boston Pilot*, September 12, 1846; Arthur Wellington Brayley, *Complete History of the Boston Fire Department* . . . (Boston, 1889), 185, 186; Edward H. Savage, *Police Records and Recollections* . . . (Boston, 1873), 65, 66, 110, 257.

[42] Chamberlin, *op. cit.*, 48 ff.; Brayley, *Complete History*, 197 ff.; State Street Trust Company, *Mayors of Boston* . . . (Boston, [1914]), 15.

[43] Cf. *American*, October 21, 1837, March 17, 1838.

[44] There are numerous short accounts of this affair; but the best, though differing in interpretation from that offered here, is in Billington, *op. cit.*, 68 ff.

[45] Billington, *op. cit.*, 71 ff.; Shea, *op. cit.*, III, 462, 463; Charles Greely Loring, *Report of the Committee Relating to the Destruction of the Ursuline Convent* . . . (Boston, 1834), 8. Miss Harrison's disappearance was probably not important. In 1830 a rumor spread by the *New England Herald* (Vol. I, no. 28) that "a young lady, an orphan, has lately been inveigled into the Ursuline Convent . . . after having been cajoled to transfer a large fortune to the Popish massmen" was ridiculed and had no repercussions (cf. *United States Catholic Intelligencer*, April 24, 1830).

the forty or fifty Charlestown truckmen and New Hampshire Scotch-Irish brickmakers who led the curious mob; and her threat that, unless they withdrew, she would call upon the Bishop for a defense contingent of 20,000 Irishmen precipitated the holocaust.[46]

After the initial excitement, every section of public opinion in Boston greeted the fire with horror and surprise. Bostonians had not disliked the school; many had actually sent their children there. There is no evidence that the residents of the city had any connection with the plot; not a voice was raised in its support. The press condemned the absence of adequate protection, and deplored the "high-handed outrage." Bostonians asserted that "The Catholics . . . are as . . . loyal citizens as their brethren of any other denomination." A mass meeting at Faneuil Hall expressed sympathy with the unfortunate victims of mob action and, resolving "to unite with our Catholic brethren in protecting their persons, their property, and their civil and religious rights," recommended a reward for the capture of the criminals and compensation to the convent, as did similar meetings under John Cotton in Ward Eight, under Everett at Charlestown, and under Story at Cambridge.[47] A reward of $500 offered by Governor Davis resulted in the arrest of thirteen men, the trial of eight, and the conviction of one. The life imprisonment sentence for the one of whose guilt there seemed to be no doubt was far more significant than failure to convict those who might have been innocent.[48]

The convent, reestablished in Roxbury, failed "because of lack of harmony among the Sisters."[49] But the legislature was petitioned for compensation repeatedly in the next twenty years. Despite persistent reluctance to grant public funds for religious purposes, $10,000 was voted in 1846, but rejected by the Ursulines.[50] The rise of Know-Nothing sentiments thwarted further overtures, while anti-Catholic activities of city rowdies and the circulation of *Six Months in a Convent* somewhat balanced expressions of sympathy. But these antagonisms were more marked outside than within the city. None of the anti-Catholic papers founded after the publication of that scurrilous book were published in Boston.[51]

Occasional manifestations of hostility in the next few years were restricted in scope. The Montgomery Guards, the first Irish military

---

[46] Billington, *op. cit.*, 81, n. 85; Benj. F. Butler, *Autobiography and Personal Reminiscences* . . . (Boston, 1892), 111; Darling, *op. cit.*, 165, n. 79.

[47] Cf. Billington, *op. cit.*, 69, 81–85, 86, 108; Loring, *op. cit.*, 2, 6, 16; *American Traveller*, August 15, 19, 1834; [H. Ware, Jr.], *An Account of the Conflagration of the Ursuline Convent . . . by a Friend of Religious Toleration* (Boston, 1834), 3; Chamberlin, *op. cit.*, 44 ff.; *Jesuit or Catholic Sentinel*, August 16, 1834; *ibid.*, August 23, 1834; Crawford, *Romantic Days*, 22.

[48] Cf. Ware, *op. cit.*, 10; *Jesuit or Catholic Sentinel*, August 23, 1834; Billington, *op. cit.*, 86, 87; Loring, *op. cit.*, 4.

[49] Robert H. Lord, "Organizer of the Church in New England," *Catholic Historical Review*, XXII (1936), 182.

[50] Cf. Billington, *op. cit.*, 89, 110, n. 27; *Documents Relating to the Ursuline Convent in Charlestown* (Boston, 1842), 21, 22, 31; "Anti-Catholic Movements in the United States," *Catholic World*, XXII (1876), 814; *Boston Pilot*, February 18, 1854.

[51] Cf. *Boston Pilot*, April 16, 1853; Billington, *op. cit.*, 92 ff.

company, were attacked in 1837 by the rank and file of the Boston City
Guards who refused to parade with an Irish company to uphold "the
broad principle . . . that *in all institutions springing from our own laws,
we all mingle in the same undisguised mass, whether native or naturalized.*" Although the native militiamen complained that "the press . . .
condemned our conduct with . . . openmouthed language of wholesale
reprehension . . . ," the very next year the same newspapers severely
criticized the Irish soldiers who were finally disbanded in 1839.[52] In 1844
the reaction to the school quarrels in New York, to the riots in Philadelphia,
and to the defeat of the national Whig ticket by the Irish vote produced a
short-lived nativist branch of the Whig Party. Although the American
Republicans under T. A. Davis gained the mayoralty in 1845, it was only
on the eighth ballot, in an election fought primarily on the issue of the
local water supply.[53] Nativism declined steadily thereafter. An attempt to
revive it in 1847 failed so disastrously, that the *Boston Catholic Observer*
could triumphantly proclaim nativism dying.[54]

Nativist fears failed to develop more significantly because the Irish
before 1845 presented no danger to the stability of the old society. They
were in a distinct minority and, above all, were politically impotent. In
1843 the Irish claimed no more than 200 voters in all Suffolk County,
and in 1839, no more than 500, while in 1845 less than one-sixth of the
adult male foreigners in Boston were citizens.[55] Only a few had secured the
right to vote, or took an interest in politics; their opinions were still a
matter of private judgment, with no influence upon the policies of the
community. The old inhabitants, as individuals, might look down upon
their new neighbors as unabsorbable incubi, but the still powerful tradition of tolerance stifled their accumulated resentments. The dominant
group took no step to limit social and political rights or privileges until
the ideals of the newcomers threatened to replace those of the old society.
At that moment the tradition of tolerance was breached and long re-
pressed hostilities found highly inflammable expression.

The crisis came when, after a decade of efforts in that direction, the
Irish acquired a position of political importance. After 1840 their press
insisted upon the duty "to themselves as well as to their families" of
naturalization and a role in the government. Politicians sponsored societies
which aided the unknowing and stimulated the indifferent to become
citizens, and professional agents drew up papers, filled out forms, and
rapidly turned out new voters for the sake of fees and political power.[56]
Between 1841 and 1845, the number of qualified voters increased by 50

[52] Cf. *American*, October 21, 1837; *Boston Pilot*, February 3, 17, 1838, October 12,
1839.

[53] Cf. State Street Trust Company, *Mayors of Boston*, 17; Darling, *op. cit.*, 327–29;
William G. Bean, Party Transformation in Massachusetts . . . (MS. H. C. L.),
228 ff.

[54] *Boston Catholic Observer*, August 28, June 19, July 24, 1847; Bean, *op. cit.*, 232 ff.

[55] Cf. *Jesuit or Catholic Sentinel*, January 18, 1834; *Boston Pilot*, November 9, 1839;
George H. Haynes, "Causes of Know-Nothing Success in Massachusetts," *American Historical Review*, III (1897), 74, n. 1.

[56] Cf. *Boston Pilot*, February 19, 1853; Dissertation Copy, 367.

per cent, then remained stable until 1852, when it grew by almost 15 per cent in two years, while in the five years after 1850, the number of naturalized voters increased from 1,549 to 4,564. In the same period, the number of native voters grew only 14 per cent.[57] Perennial political organizations flourished with every campaign and further mobilized the Irish vote.[58]

The coherence and isolation of Irish ideas facilitated political organization. And Irish leaders, consciously or unconsciously, encouraged group solidarity and the maintenance of a virtual Irish party. Though the Irish vote was not yet used to serve corrupt personal interest,[59] both those who aspired to gain public office in America through the support of a large bloc of voters and those who hoped to return as liberators to the Emerald Isle directed their energies towards activizing their countrymen. These efforts were so widespread that one of the most far-sighted Irish leaders complained that Irish political influence was being "fatally misused" and warned that "keeping up an Irish party in America is a fatal mistake, and . . . I will seek to induce them rather to blend and fuse their interests with American parties, than cause jealousy and distrust by acting as an exclusive and independent faction . . . a man has no right to interfere in American politics unless he thinks as an American. . . ."[60] But such views were rare.

With the political mobilization of the Irish in Boston, tolerance finally disappeared. The possibilities of Irish domination were the more startling because the political situation in Massachusetts, 1845–55, permitted a coherent, independent group to exercise inordinate influence. The unity of the old parties was crumbling as dissatisfied elements demanded new policies to meet the problems of reform, particularly those posed by slavery.[61] Although all, including the most conservative Abbott Lawrence, agreed on the ultimate desirability of reform, they were divided as to the methods of attaining it. Within each political party a restless group contended that the forces of good must prevail immediately, even at the expense of failure in national politics. Their insistence upon immediate, unequivocal action destroyed the coherence of the old alignments and yielded to the unified Irish the balance of power. For four years the reformers found these foreigners square in their path, defeating their most valued measures. In the critical year of 1854 this opposition drove them into a violent xenophobic movement that embodied all the hatreds stored up in the previous two decades.

Rantoul and Morton had blasted the stability of the Democrats, but

[57] Cf. Josiah Curtis, *Report of the Joint Special Committee . . . 1855 . . .* (Boston, 1856), 11; "Report and Tabular Statement of the Censors," *Boston City Documents, 1850,* no. 42, p. 12; Billington, *op. cit.,* 325, 326.

[58] Cf., e.g., *Boston Pilot,* July 8, 1860.

[59] The only instance of devious Irish politics in this period came in the election of John C. Tucker to the legislature in 1860 (cf. E. P. Loring and C. T. Russell, Jr., *Reports of Controverted Elections . . . 1853 to 1885 . . .* [Boston, 1886], 89 ff.).

[60] Richard O'Gorman to W. S. O'Brien, May 24, 1849, W. S. O'Brien Papers and Letters, 1819–1854 (MSS., N. L. I.), XVIII, no. 2, 547.

[61] Cf. Darling, *op. cit.,* 312 ff.

the Whig party was the first torn asunder by the anti-slavery men. In the early forties, some members had already deserted to the Liberty party, but until 1846 most anti-slavery Whigs continued to believe in "reform within the Party." Even in that year the magic personality of Webster nullified the damage done by Southern aggressions and the turbulent Texas and Mexico questions, and held in rein such conscientious rebels as Stephen C. Phillips, Charles Allen, and Sumner. But the Whig nomination of a slaveholder to the presidency and the rejection of the Wilmot Proviso by their National Convention in 1848 opened an unbridgeable gap between the two factions, though the Whigs remained strong enough to win the gubernatorial election that year and again in 1849.[62]

A similar development among the Democrats led a few to support Van Buren, the Free-Soil nominee in 1848, but the party quickly united to profit from the more serious division of its rivals. In addition, hoping for a coalition, it offered the Whig dissidents an anti-slavery plank in 1849. But these overtures failed; Free-Soilers still preferred cooperation with the Whigs to alliance with the Democrats who, nationally, were the most prominent supporters of the South's peculiar institution. But while Webster squinted at the federal scene and dreamed of the White House, the Whigs would have no meddling with reform. Though controlling the legislature of 1849, they failed to pass a single Free-Soil measure. Finally, their support of the Fugitive Slave Law, and particularly Webster's role in its enactment, completed the cleavage and consolidated the Free-Soil party in Massachusetts.[63]

When the gubernatorial election of 1850 gave no candidate a majority, Democratic ambitions, after seven years of famine, approached fulfillment. The constitution provided for the choice of a governor by an absolute majority, in the absence of which the election was thrown into the legislature—a situation susceptible to a great deal of political maneuvering. In this election the Democratic state platform had endorsed the Free-Soil program, though without a formal coalition. A trade between the two parties, which together had a majority in the legislature that convened in January, 1851, was inevitable. The Free-Soilers, anxious to be heard in Washington, were impatient with the Whig demand that the designation of a senator wait eleven months for a new legislature, and threw their votes for a Democratic governor. In return, the Democrats supported a radical policy and handed the United States senatorship and the organization of the legislature to the Free-Soilers. Banks became speaker of the House, and Henry Wilson, president of the Senate; although the former was nominally a Democrat, both were actually Free-Soilers. The reformers got the better of the bargain, passing a series of radical measures,

[62] Cf. Robinson, *op. cit.*, 28–38, 416, 513; Bean, *op. cit.*, 8–38; Darling, *op. cit.*, 245 ff., 317, 334, 290, n. 67, 326; Wilson, *op. cit.*, I, 545 ff., II, 145 ff.; George S. Merriam, *Life and Times of Samuel Bowles* (New York, 1885), I, 45 ff.; *Reunion of the Free-Soilers of 1848–1852 . . . June 28, 1888* (Cambridge, 1888), 15, 17; Hart, *op. cit.*, IV, 97; Grimké, *op. cit.*, 182 ff., 190 ff.

[63] Bean, *op. cit.*, 17, 28, 35 ff., 53 ff.; Darling, *op. cit.*, 340, 349–54; Grimké, *op. cit.*, 205; Haynes, *loc. cit.*, 80; Wilson, *op. cit.*, II, 247 ff.

including a general incorporation law to break the power of monopolies, a law for more democratic control of Harvard College, a homestead and mechanics' lien law, and measures ensuring the secret ballot and plurality voting in national elections.[64]

The coalition held through the election of 1851. But though the Free-Soilers managed to push through the Maine Law over Governor Boutwell's veto, they were dissatisfied. They disliked the governor, who had obstructed many reform measures, and they distrusted their Democratic allies, who had bolted in considerable numbers on Sumner's election to the United States Senate and had contrived to defeat a personal liberty law, acts to liberalize divorce, to protect the property rights of women, and to extend the powers of juries. Whittier voiced the apprehension of the Free-Soilers when he wrote, after seeing the governor's first message, "It is . . . monstrous and insulting. May God forgive us for permitting his election."[65]

The Free-Soilers now recognized the need of a reform in government to gain complete control of the state—a reform impossible under the existing conditions of amending the constitution, which called for a two-thirds vote in the House of Representatives of two successive legislatures on each clause.[66] With parties divided as they were, a simple majority was difficult enough, two-thirds almost impossible, and two-thirds in two successive legislatures out of the question. One solution was to change the basis of representation to reduce the influence of the conservative elements opposing them in Boston. But an attempt to do so in 1851 failed, leaving the reformers no alternative but a complete revamping of the constitution by a convention.[67]

In 1851 the Free-Soilers forced through the legislature a resolution for a constitutional convention. But when the question was presented to the voters, Democratic support was weak. The Irish, theretofore consistently Democrats, failed to follow their representatives who had indorsed revision. In the election several thousand who had voted for coalition candidates turned against the constitutional convention.[68] Of

---

[64] Cf. Bean, *op. cit.*, 54, 57, 64–87; Wilson, *op. cit.*, II, 347 ff.; *Address to the People of Massachusetts* (s.l., n.d., [Boston, 1852]), 3, 6, 7, 10 ff.; Robinson, *op. cit.*, 47, 433; Hart, *op. cit.*, IV, 99, 475.

[65] Alfred S. Roe, "Governors of Massachusetts . . . ," *New England Magazine*, XXV (1902), 547; Bean, *op. cit.*, 90–92, 113–20; Robinson, *op. cit.*, 433; *Address*, 5 ff.; Grimké, *op. cit.*, 209.

[66] A simple majority sufficed in the Senate (Bean, *op. cit.*, 116; Morison, *op. cit.*, 38).

[67] Bean, *op. cit.*, 88, 89. Legislators from Boston were elected on a general ticket which usually denied representation to minorities and gave the whole delegation to the Whigs (cf. Morison, *op. cit.*, 41).

[68] The election of 1851:

| | GOVERNOR | | | CONVENTION | |
|---|---|---|---|---|---|
| | State | Boston | | State | Boston |
| Winthrop (W) | 64,611 | 7,388 | no | 65,846 | 7,135 |
| Boutwell (D) | 43,992 | 3,632 | | | |
| Palfrey (FS) | 28,599 | 1,294 | yes | 60,972 | 3,813 |

(*Boston Semi-Weekly Advertiser*, November 12, 1851; Bean, *op. cit.*, 109, 111.) Cf. also Morison, *op. cit.*, 42.

these, more than 1,100 were in Boston, and they were predominantly Irish Democrats bolting the party.[69]

When the Democratic State Convention again supported coalition and revision the following year, the Irish, under J. W. James, the Repeal leader, finally seceded from the party. Though opposing the Democrats in the state election of 1852, they supported the national Democratic party, which had repudiated Rantoul and coalition and whose presidential candidate, Pierce, was most acceptable as a conservative. Following the advice of Brownson and the *Pilot*, the Boston Irish became national Democrats and state Whigs. As a result of the confusion, the coalition ticket lost, but the project for a convention won.[70]

Impressed with the opportunity the convention presented for strengthening the party and consolidating its position, the Free-Soilers made special exertions in the March election and gained control. Their imprint upon the constitution that resulted was unmistakable. Single-unit senatorial districts and plurality elections by secret ballots were proposed. To decrease the power of the executive, many appointive offices, including the Council, became elective; the judiciary was controlled by limiting the term of office and extending the powers of jurors; and the use of public funds for religious education was prohibited. While these measures would render government more responsive to the voice of the people, the proposed constitution was undemocratic in its most important provision. By changing the system of representation to favor country towns at the expense of large cities, bailiwicks of conservatism, the reformers unquestionably compromised their principles.[71]

With one important exception party lines held in the vote on the adoption of the constitution. The opposition of the few conscientious Free-Soilers who would not support the unfair system of representation was trivial compared with the force of conservative Irish Catholic opinion clamoring for defeat.[72] At the Democratic Convention which indorsed the constitution, James again led a seceding group of Boston Irishmen who formed a party of their own. Pressure for recruitment and organization of voters increased. In September the Calvert Naturalization Society in the South End joined the Ward Three Association of the North End. The *Pilot* repeatedly warned that "no Catholic . . . can possibly vote for this . . . Constitution without giving up rights for which he has been all along contending," and Brownson pointed out its revolutionary implications.[73]

---

[69] Bean's claim that the Free-Soilers bolted (*op. cit.*, 111) is wholly illogical since they wanted the convention and the Irish did not (for the Free-Soilers' attitude on constitutional change, cf. Robinson, *op. cit.*, 401 ff.).

[70] Cf. in general, Bean, *op. cit.*, 127 ff., 217–20. For the new attempt to revise the constitution, cf. *Massachusetts Senate Documents, 1852*, no. 36, pp. 6 ff.

[71] Cf. J. B. Mann, *Life of Henry Wilson* . . . (Boston, 1872), 36 ff.; Hon. Charles Allen, *Speech . . . at Worcester, Nov. 5, 1853* (s.l., n.d.), 1–3; Bean, *op. cit.*, 147–66; Morison, *op. cit.*, 49–60; Henry F. Brownson, *Orestes A. Brownson's Middle Life* . . . (Detroit, 1899), II, 465, 466; Mann, *op. cit.*, 43.

[72] For Free-Soil opposition, cf. Bean, *op. cit.*, 168, 177.

[73] Cf. Brownson, *Brownson's Middle Life*, II, 455 ff.; Dissertation Copy, 377–78; Bean, *op. cit.*, 221.

In their campaign, the Irish joined the die-hard Whigs under Abbott Lawrence, who led "hundreds of honest men gulled by their sophistry" in opposing a constitution which seriously curtailed the influences of State Street in politics. Lawrence conferred with Bishop Fitzpatrick on the problem, and Whig newspapers appealed particularly to the Irish. Against this alliance the reformers' contention that the *Boston Pilot* was "trying to lead Irishmen into the jaws of a Boston aristocracy as remorseless as the one they had left Ireland to get rid of" counted little. The combination of Irish votes and cotton money in Boston defeated the constitution and elected a Whig ticket.[74]

In this crisis the reformers inveighed against the lords of the counting house and bemoaned the slowness of rank-and-file Whigs to recognize their true interests, but concluded that while the former could never be redeemed, and the latter would have to be educated, the main obstacle to reform was Catholic opposition. And by this time they had learned that differences with the Irish were too deep to be easily eradicated; they could only be fought. Butler, sensitive to every shift in popular opinion, realized that the "performance, which struck down the Constitution, invoked a bitterness among the people against the Catholic religion, such as had never before been, to any considerable degree, either felt or foreshadowed in the State of Massachusetts."[75]

Through the early months of 1854 a series of unconnected events heightened resentment against Catholics and evoked many antipathies developed since 1830. In December, 1853, Father Gavazzi, a rebellious priest, lectured in Boston on the reactionary role of the Church.[76] A few months later, the visit of the papal nuncio Bedini, who had been connected with the massacre of revolutionaries in Bologna, though not provoking the expected riot, did refresh memories of Irish opposition to liberalism.[77] Meanwhile, events at home confirmed that impression. Failure of the enforcement of the prohibition laws was laid at the door of the Irish, and the State Temperance Committee announced it would fight Catholicism as part of its struggle for human freedom.[78] The Burns case

[74] Robinson, *op. cit.*, 204; Bean, *op. cit.*, 162, 166, 174–79; Butler, *op. cit.*, 119. The analysis of the vote from which Morison concludes that "the wards where most of the Irish-born population then lived did not poll so heavy a negative vote as the fashionable residential districts" (*op. cit.*, 63) is not valid because the wards were gerrymandered in the redistricting of 1850 to split the Irish vote (cf. Dissertation Copy, 383). Even in 1854 votes against the Know-Nothings showed no special concentration in any area (cf. *Boston Atlas*, November 14, 1854). Bean has shown that votes to defeat the constitution came from Boston: the 5,915 negative balance of Suffolk County more than offset the 997 positive balance elsewhere in the state (*op. cit.*, 173).

[75] Butler, *op. cit.*, 120.

[76] Cf. *Boston Semi-Weekly Advertiser*, November 30, December 3, 1853; Billington, *op. cit.*, 301.

[77] *Boston Pilot*, October 8, 1853, February 11, 1854; Billington, *op. cit.*, 300–02; Desmond, *op. cit.*, 72; Shea, *op. cit.*, IV, 360 ff.

[78] *Massachusetts Life Boat*, September 19, 1854; cf. also *Address of the State Temperance Committee to the Citizens of Massachusetts on the Operation of the Anti-Liquor Law* (Boston, 1853), 2; Billington, *op. cit.*, 323.

clearly linked the immigrants to pro-slavery forces and man-hunters. The *Pilot* supported the rendition of the fugitive slave; and the selection of the Columbian Artillery and Sarsfield Guards to protect him against indignant mobs seeking his freedom incited an inflammatory handbill:

AMERICANS TO THE RESCUE!
AMERICANS! SONS OF THE REVOLUTION!!
A body of seventy-five Irishmen, known as the
*"Columbian Artillery"*
have volunteered their services to shoot down the
citizens of Boston! and are now under arms to defend
Virginia in kidnapping a Citizen of Massachusetts!
Americans! These Irishmen have called us
"Cowards and Sons of Cowards"!
Shall we submit to have our Citizens shot
down by a set of Vagabond Irishmen?

that turned many reformers against the Irish.[79] Finally, their defense of the Kansas-Nebraska Act connected them with the slave power, and drew criticism from such respectable sources as the *Commonwealth*, the *Worcester Spy*, and Theodore Parker.[80]

Distrust of the Irish at once encouraged and was stimulated by attacks upon Catholics. Hatred and violence marched arm in arm, sustaining and strengthening each other. Early in 1853, the purported kidnapping of Hannah Corcoran, a Baptist convert, almost led to a riot. In the same year the city government entered into a long-drawn-out controversy with the Catholics over their right to build a church on the "Jail lands." In May, 1854, John S. Orr, the Angel Gabriel, led a mob that carried away a cross from the Catholic Church in Chelsea, and in July a church was blown up in Dorchester. *The Wide Awake: and the Spirit of Washington*, a vituperative sheet, appeared in October, 1854, to combat the "swarms of lazaroni from abroad"; and a venomous stream of anti-Papist literature reached Boston, particularly in the form of Frothingham's convent novels (1854).[81]

Meanwhile, as slavery absorbed the attention of Congress and the country, excited Free-Soilers found "every indication that the people are awakening from their unaccountable stupor on the . . . question."[82] The Kansas-Nebraska Bill infuriated even Everett and the conservative

[79] Cf. *Boston Pilot*, June 3, 1854; *Irish-American*, September 23, 1854; Billington, *op. cit.*, 435, n. 81; Bean, *op. cit.*, 187, 239, 241.
[80] Cf. Bean, *loc. cit.*, 239 ff.; Carl Wittke, *We Who Built America* . . . (New York, 1939), 168.
[81] *Boston Pilot*, April 9, December 10, 1853, May 13, 1854, January 20, 1855; *Wide Awake: and the Spirit of Washington* (Boston), October 7, 1854; Billington, *op. cit.*, 305–13, 348 ff., 368; Bean, *op. cit.*, 207, 209; Shea, *op. cit.*, IV, 509; Charles W. Frothingham, *Six Hours in a Convent:—or—The Stolen Nuns!* . . . (Boston, 1855).
[82] Albert G. Browne to Sumner, July 28, 1854, Sumner Correspondence (MSS., H. C. L.), XXV, no. 109.

Webster Whigs. Sumner's correspondents informed him that "all parties seem to be approaching that happy state of . . . dissolution, for which we have sighed so long."[83] A Freedom party tentatively formed in Boston, a "Republican" convention adopted a radical program, and a host of excited energies eagerly sought an outlet. Precisely where the immense anti-slavery impulse would be exerted was uncertain, however.[84]

But the Boston municipal elections of December, 1853, had already revealed the ultimate outlet. Only one month after their decisive defeat on the constitution, the reformers rallied to resist the reelection of Nathaniel Seaver, a Whig supported by the liquor interests. As the "Citizens Union party," they appealed to nativist feelings and drew 2,000 Whig votes, the entire Free-Soil vote, and 500 voters who had not troubled to go to the polls a month earlier.[85] These 500 voters came from a tremendous fund of non-voting citizens, many of them Whigs disgusted with their party's vacillation.[86] The lesson to the reformers was obvious and was confirmed by simultaneous elections in Charlestown and Roxbury:[87] the Irish stood in the way of reform; reform forces could best be augmented and galvanized on an anti-Irish basis; the dormant voters must be awakened by an anti-alien alarm.

By 1853 the Order of the Star-Spangled Banner, a nativist secret organization popularly known as the Know-Nothings, had emerged in New York State.[88] Early in 1854 it spread into Massachusetts, swiftly, though quietly and unobtrusively, drawing "into its lodges tens of thousand of . . . anti-Nebraska men, ripe for Republicanism. . . ."[89] These recruits, inwardly ashamed of adopting means incompatible with the principles they professed, wrapped themselves in mantles of secrecy which served as a "spiritual fist-law" for gaining ascendancy without the use of force, and pursued their "purposes with the same disregard of the purposes of the structure external to . . . [themselves] which in the case of the individual is called egoism."[90]

In July, Henry Wilson, already a member, began to harness Know-

[83] Seth Webb, Jr., July 14, 1854, *ibid.*, XXV, no. 72; also Bean, *op. cit.*, 188 ff.

[84] Cf. Amasa Walker to Sumner, Sumner Correspondence, July 2, 1854, XXV, no. 15; Bean, *op. cit.*, 193; Merriam, *op. cit.*, I, 122.

[85] Cf. *Boston Semi-Weekly Advertiser*, December 10, 1853.

BOSTON ELECTIONS, 1853

| GOVERNOR | (Nov.) | MAYOR | (Dec.) |
|---|---|---|---|
| Whig | 7,730 | Whig | 5,651 |
| Free-Soil | 1,403 | Citizens Union | 4,691 |
| Coalition Democrat | 2,455 | Young Men's League | 2,010 |
| Hunker Democrat | 821 | Democrat | 596 |
| Total | 12,409 | Total | 12,948 |

(*Boston Semi-Weekly Advertiser*, November 16, December 14, 1853.)

[86] Cf. Darling, *op. cit.*, 290. . . .

[87] Cf. Bean, *op. cit.*, 246.

[88] Cf. Billington, *op. cit.*, 380; Bean, *op. cit.*, 226; Desmond, *op. cit.*, 66; Scisco, *op. cit.*, 63 ff., 71 ff.

[89] Pearson, *op. cit.*, I, 65.

[90] Cf. Georg Simmel, "Sociology of Secrecy and of Secret Societies," *American Journal of Sociology*, XI (1906), 446 ff., 489.

Nothingism to the anti-slavery cause, and Seth Webb, Jr., decided, "Know-Nothingism is to be an important, perhaps the controlling, element in our state election; it will probably take us out of the hands of the Whigs. Into whose hands it will put us, nobody can tell."[91] The Know-Nothings presented the clearest platform in the next election. Without the support of the intellectual fronts of reform—Adams, Phillips, and Sumner—who felt no ends justified nativist methods, they elected Henry J. Gardner, formerly president of the Boston Common Council, to the governorship by the unprecedented majority of 33,000, and gained complete control of the legislature in November. Until 1857, they ruled the state.[92]

Everywhere the success of the party rested upon thousands of new men drawn into politics by nativism.[93] The complexion of the new legislators reflected the ranks from which they rose. Among them were no politicians, and few lawyers. They were true representatives of those for whom they spoke. They included a few rascals and self-seekers; but by and large they were honest men, convinced that they were acting in the best interests of the community. Even the Democratic editor of the *Post* had to admit later that "the moral tone of the party was unquestioned. . . ."[94] Many did not even feel a personal antagonism to the Irish; J. V. C. Smith, an amateur sculptor, and Know-Nothing mayor in 1854, associated with them in business and executed a fine bust of Bishop Fitzpatrick.[95]

Although the Know-Nothings made numerous mistakes, their administration was progressive and fruitful. They relaid the basis for the school system, abolished imprisonment for debt, established the first insurance commission, took the first steps to eliminate danger from railroad

[91] Webb to Sumner, July 14, 1854, Sumner Correspondence, XXV, no. 72; cf. also Wilson to Sumner, July 2, 1854, *ibid.*, XXV, no. 12; Bean, *op. cit.*, 192; Harry J. Carman and R. H. Luthin, "Some Aspects of the Know-Nothing Movement Reconsidered," *South Atlantic Quarterly*, XXXIX (1940), 221.

[92] Roe, *loc. cit.*, 653; Haynes, *loc. cit.*, 68; Bean, *op. cit.*, 259 ff.; George H. Haynes, "Know-Nothing Legislature," *New England Magazine*, XVI (1897), 21, 22.

[93] Robinson, *op. cit.*, 219. In Boston, 1,101 voters who had not gone to the polls in 1853 cast their ballots for the Know-Nothings together with the whole coalition reform vote, and almost half the Whig vote.

GUBERNATORIAL VOTES IN BOSTON

|  | 1853 | 1854 |
|---|---|---|
| Whig | 7,730 | 4,196 |
| Know-Nothing | ... | 7,661 |
| Free-Soil | 1,403 | 401 |
| Democrat | 2,455 | 1,252 |
| Hunker Democrat | 821 | ... |
|  | 12,409 | 13,510 |

(*Boston Atlas*, November 14, 1854; *Boston Semi-Weekly Advertiser*, November 16, 1853.)

[94] Benjamin P. Shillaber, "Experiences During Many Years," *New England Magazine*, VIII (1893), 722; George H. Haynes, "Know-Nothing Legislature," *Annual Report of the American Historical Association . . . 1896* (Washington, 1897), I, 178 ff.; Roe, *loc. cit.*, 654.

[95] State Street Trust Company, *Mayors of Boston*, 23.

crossings, extended the power of juries, strengthened the temperance, homestead and women's rights laws, made vaccination compulsory, and assumed a firm anti-slavery position by passing a personal liberty law and petitioning for the removal of Judge Loring, who had presided at the fugitive slave cases. In general, they embodied in their legislation the program of the party of reform. By 1855, they had sent Wilson to the United States Senate, amended the constitution so that a plurality sufficed in the gubernatorial election, and introduced many other innovations vetoed by the more conservative governor.[96]

The party's anti-foreign accomplishments were quite insignificant. To begin with, they disclaimed any intention of excluding immigrants, but stressed the necessity of making them "be as we are."[97] The most prominent achievement was the disbanding of the Irish military companies which annoyed natives particularly because they carried off prizes at drills. They served no useful purpose and in 1853 the *Boston Pilot* had itself suggested their dissolution. A breach of military discipline provided the pretext for the abolition of the Bay State Artillery in September, followed early the next year by the elimination of the remaining companies. Foreigners on the police force and in state agencies were discharged, and a number of cruel deportations displayed an ugly animus against helpless aliens. Finally, the misdeeds of individual members, notably of the Hiss Nunnery Commitee, were exploited by the opposition and did much to discredit the party and obscure its constructive achievements.[98]

Ostensibly the party had acquired power to restrict the influence of immigrants in politics. Yet, though it had absolute control of the government, it failed to pass a single measure to that effect. In 1854, a bill to exclude paupers was not considered until the end of the session, and then referred to committee where it died. A literacy amendment to the constitution was rejected, and an amendment requiring a twenty-one-year residence for citizenship, which passed, was defeated at the second vote by the next Know-Nothing legislature.[99] Once reform, the essential feature of Know-Nothingism in Massachusetts, was assured, the party

[96] Cf. Billington, *op. cit.*, 425; Robinson, *op. cit.*, 62, 209, 210; Bean, *op. cit.*, 166, 268, 272–77, 284, 286–88; Merriam, *op. cit.*, I, 126, 132 ff., 164; Haynes, "Know-Nothing Legislature," *Annual Report of the American Historical Association . . . 1896,* I, 180–84; Bean, *loc. cit.*, 322.

[97] Bean, *op. cit.*, 261.

[98] Cf. Dissertation Copy, 389; Desmond, *op. cit.*, 77; *Boston Pilot,* May 13, 1854, April 7, May 12, 1855; Abbott, *Immigration,* 160, 161; Billington, *op. cit.*, 414 ff.; Bean, *op. cit.*, 291 ff.; Shea, *op. cit.*, IV, 510.

[99] Cf. *Debates and Proceedings in the Massachusetts Legislature . . . 1856, Reported for the Boston Daily Advertiser* (Boston, 1856), 141, 343, 348; Bean, *loc. cit.*, 322; Billington, *op. cit.*, 413. Most of these measures were sponsored by the purely nativist branch of the party, which declined in importance after 1854 and left the reformers in complete control (cf. Bean, *op. cit.*, 248). To those overlooking the concrete accomplishments of the 1854 legislature, the Free-Soilers under Wilson seemed to have "captured" the Know-Nothing organization in 1855 (cf., e.g., Haynes, "Causes of Know-Nothing Success," *loc. cit.*, III, 81). In fact, true nativists like Morse had so little sympathy for Massachusetts Know-Nothingism that they charged it was "a Jesuitical ruse, gotten up for the purpose of creating a sympathy in favor of the church" (Morse, *Foreign Conspiracy,* 31).

leaders attempted to jettison the anti-Catholic program. But the intolerance they had evoked could not readily be dispelled. Its influence persisted long after the death of the party it had served.

The Know-Nothings dissolved over the question of slavery, for the national party drew its strength from incompatible sources. In Massachusetts it was anti-slavery; elsewhere in the North it was unionist; in Virginia and throughout the South, it was pro-slavery.[100] Lack of a unified program inevitably split the party. Despite their strategic position in Congress, they could unite on few measures. Finally, when the national convention adopted a pro-slavery plank in June, 1855, the Northerners under Henry Wilson bolted and the Massachusetts Council on August 7 adopted an uncompromising liberal position. At the same time a section of the party broke away and met at Worcester in June, called itself the Know-Somethings or American Freemen, and advocated an abolition platform and an end to secrecy.

The nomination of Fillmore, a pro-slavery man, in 1856, completed the break between the state and national parties and a *de facto* coalition with the rising Republican party spontaneously formed. The latter nominated no candidate to oppose Gardner for the governorship, and most Know-Nothings voted for Frémont.[101] Thereafter the Know-Nothings in the state were absorbed in the tremendous growth of the new party, and Banks led the remnants to the Republicans in 1857–58 on his election to the governorship.[102]

---

[100] Cf. Bean, *loc. cit.*, 324 ff.; E. Merton Coulter, *William Brownlow* . . . (Chapel Hill, 1937), 124 ff.; Scisco, *op. cit.*, 137; Carman and Luthin, *loc. cit.*, 223.

[101] Cf. Billington, *op. cit.*, 407 ff., 426; James Ford Rhodes, *History of the United States* . . . (New York, 1893), II, 89 ff.; Bean, *op. cit.*, 295–322, 339 ff.; Mann, *op. cit.*, 50; Scisco, *op. cit.*, 146 ff.; Wilson, *op. cit.*, II, 423 ff.; Merriam, *op. cit.*, I, 165, 173 ff.; cf. also Fred H. Harrington, "Frémont and the North Americans," *American Historical Review*, XLIV (1939), 842 ff.

VOTE IN BOSTON, 1856

| PRESIDENTIAL | | GUBERNATORIAL | |
|---|---|---|---|
| Frémont (R) | 7,646 | Gardner (KN) | 7,513 |
| Fillmore (KN) | 4,320 | Gordon (Fillmore KN) | 7,511 |
| Buchanan (D) | 5,458 | Bell (Whig) | 1,449 |
| | 17,424 | Beach (D) | 5,392 |
| | | | 16,865 |

(*Boston Semi-Weekly Advertiser*, November 5, 1856.)

[102] Cf. Fred H. Harrington, "Nathaniel Prentiss Banks . . . ," *New England Quarterly*, IX (1936), 645 ff. The "straight" American party nominated candidates in 1857 and 1858 but received a meager vote and then expired (Bean, *op. cit.*, 362–65). Gardner's personal popularity helped them in the former year but in the latter they received less than 2,000 votes.

VOTES FOR GOVERNOR IN BOSTON

|  | 1857 | 1858 |
|---|---|---|
| Republicans | 4,224 | 6,298 |
| Know-Nothings | 4,130 | 1,899 |
| Democrats | 5,171 | 6,369 |
| | 13,525 | 14,566 |

(*Boston Semi-Weekly Advertiser*, November 4, 1857; *Boston Daily Courier*, November 3, 1858.)

Produced by the same reform impulse that fathered Know-Nothing-ism, the Republican party continued to express animosity towards the Irish, "their declared and uncompromising foe." The defeat of Frémont in 1856 was laid at the door of the Irish Catholics, and confirmed the party's hostility to them. In retaliation, it helped pass an amendment in 1857 making ability to read the state constitution in English and to write prerequisites to the right to vote; and in 1859, another, preventing for-eigners from voting for two years after naturalization.[103]

Though the restrictive legislation affected all foreigners, the venom of intolerance was directed primarily against the Irish. Waning group consciousness among the non-Irish gave promise of quick acculturation, and similarities in economic condition, physical settlement, and intellectual outlook had left little room for disagreement. In fact, the Irish found all others united with the natives against them. A Negro was as reluctant to have an Irishman move into his street as any Yankee,[104] and though the Germans distrusted the Know-Nothings and resented the two-year amendment, liberal principles led them into the Republican party.[105]

Indirectly, the Know-Nothing movement revived Irish nationalism. In Boston, nationalist activities first assumed the guise of the Irish Emi-grant Aid Society, whose innocuous title concealed a secret revolutionary club, ostensibly aimed at organizing a liberating invasion of Ireland. Though some hotheads spoke of chartering ships to transport an army of Irish-Americans across the Atlantic, most recognized the obvious futility of such efforts. By and large, they hoped to organize politically, to sup-port anti-English parties in America, to prepare for the Anglo-American war that would free Ireland, and to mobilize support against Know-Nothingism.[106] That the last motive, presumably incidental, was in fact primary, was clear from the movement's exclusively American character: it had no counterpart in Ireland. While expanding rapidly throughout 1855, the organization had little ultimate success. The clergy opposed it, cautious prosecution of would-be liberators in Cincinnati checked its growth, and internal quarrels finally dissipated its strength.[107]

But failure did not end the quest for a fatherland. So long as the Irish were unaccepted in Boston, they looked back across the ocean. There was "always . . . some . . . machination to draw money from the pockets of the deluded lower order of Irish. . . ."[108] The Fenian

---

[103] Cf. Bean, *op. cit.*, 367–72; Bean, *loc. cit.*, 323; Charles Theo. Russell, *Disfranchise-ment of Paupers* . . . (Boston, 1878), 8; *Massachusetts House Documents, 1857*, no. 114; *ibid., 1859*, no. 34.

[104] Cf., e.g., the petition of the residents of Elm Street (Bean, *op. cit.*, 206).

[105] Cf. Ernest Bruncken, *German Political Refugees in the United States* . . . (s.l., 1904), 45 ff.

[106] Cf. the illuminating report of Consul Grattan to Crampton, Boston, November 23, 1855, British Embassy Archives, F.O. 115/160; also Rowcroft to Crampton, November 12, 1855, *ibid.*, F.O. 115/160.

[107] Cf. Grattan to Crampton, January 21, 1856, *ibid.*, F.O. 115/172; Grattan to Crampton, March 4, 1856, *ibid.*, F.O. 115/172; Abbott, *Historical Aspects*, 475, 476; *Citizen* (New York), August 25, 1855, February 9, 1856.

[108] Lousada to Russell, September 8, 1864, British Consular Correspondence, F.O. 5/973.

Brotherhood emerged after 1859 and despite ecclesiastical disapproval grew in secret until it held its first national convention in Chicago in 1863. Its "centres" in Boston were numerous and active.[109]

Moreover, the Irish persisted in their opposition to reform. With Brownson, they believed Know-Nothingism "an imported combination of Irish Orangism, German radicalism, French Socialism and Italian . . . hate" and regarded Republicanism as its pernicious successor.[110] After 1856 they consistently supported the conservative Democratic party, voting for Buchanan and Douglas.[111] Although the violent phase had passed, the bitterness of conflict and antagonism remained. Out of it had grown a confirmed definition of racial particularism: the Irish were a different group, Celtic by origin, as distinguished from the "true" Americans, who were Anglo-Saxon, of course.[112] Once aroused, hatred could not be turned off at the will of those who had provoked it. The *Springfield Republican* sanely pointed out that "the American party, starting upon a basis of truth . . . has gone on, until [it] . . . denies to an Irishman . . . any position but that of a nuisance. . . ."[113] Group conflict left a permanent scar that disfigured the complexion of Boston social life even after the malignant growth producing it had disappeared.

[109] Cf. Jeremiah O'Donovan-Rossa, *Rossa's Recollections* . . . (Mariner's Harbor, N.Y., 1898), 271, 272, 381; "Proceedings . . . ," British Consular Correspondence, F.O. 5/973; E. Wells to Lousada, *ibid.*, F.O. 5/973; *Boston Pilot*, November 21, 1863.

[110] Cf. Bean, *op. cit.*, 257.

[111] Cf. references to *Irish-American* and *Boston Pilot*, 1856–1860, Dissertation Copy, 397, ns. 301–03; *Boston Pilot*, November 3, 1860; *Boston Post*, November 7, 1860.

[112] Cf., e.g., "The Anglo-Saxon Race," *North American Review*, LXXIII (1851), 53, 34 ff.

[113] *Springfield Daily Republican*, July 10, 1857.

# The Cult of True Womanhood: 1820-1860

## BARBARA WELTER

The decades before the Civil War resounded with the cry of reform. Hardly any institution in American life escaped the scrutiny of some group determined to change it. There were campaigns for the abolition of slavery, for penal reform, for better care of the insane, for temperance, for communal living, for industrial socialism, and for many other schemes to improve the status quo. Not the least of these was a campaign for women's rights led by such impressive figures as Elizabeth Cady Stanton, Frances Wright, and the Grimke sisters.

Women had always been a valuable commodity in colonial America. In seventeenth-century Virginia, wives were actually sold by the Virginia Company, which transported young women from England and exchanged them for one hundred and fifty pounds of good tobacco. The rigors of frontier life and the dangers of continuous child-bearing without proper hygienic or medical care made the female mortality rate—along with that of infants—extremely high. Indeed, it was not unusual for a hardy male settler to go through three or four wives in his lifetime.

As long as American society was primarily agricultural, there was a fairly clear-cut distinction between the functions of men and women. Most of the woman's time was taken up with housework and child-rearing. When she had time, she joined the men in the fields, where there was always plenty of labor for both sexes.

With urban society, however, came challenges to the traditional division of labor between the sexes. As industrialization proceeded and the income of factory workers dropped, it became necessary for some women to leave the home to take factory jobs alongside their husbands. Thus, instead of finding themselves with more free time as a result of increasing mechanization, they found themselves working at two full-time jobs—as factory operative and housewife. "Woman's work" of caring for the home had by this time acquired a taboo for most men, and a double standard of behavior that bore no relation to the actual circumstances of society or the differences between the sexes was fast taking root.

For the growing ranks of middle-class women, however, the Industrial Revolution brought an increase in leisure time. These women did not have to work outside the home, and the multiplication of labor-saving household devices, coupled with the availability of household servants as a result of recent immigration, freed them considerably for new interests and activities. It was this newly leisured class of women that produced most of the members of the ante-bellum women's rights movement. In fact, many of the leaders of this campaign were women who had become interested in the anti-slavery movement but found themselves excluded from active participation in it merely on the basis of their sex.

In the following study, Barbara Welter, of Hunter College, describes the ideal of "True Womanhood" that was exalted in the popular literature of the day—partly as a reaction against the rising ambitions of many middle-class women. This literature, which stressed the desirability of such "feminine" traits as submissiveness and domesticity, ran decidedly counter to the movement for women's rights. Apparently, the literature enjoyed a wider and more influential audience than did the feminists.

---

The nineteenth-century American man was a busy builder of bridges and railroads, at work long hours in a materialistic society. The religious values of his forebears were neglected in practice if not in intent, and he occasionally felt some guilt that he had turned this new land, this temple of the chosen people, into one vast countinghouse. But he could salve his conscience by reflecting that he had left behind a hostage, not only to fortune, but to all the values which he held so dear and treated so lightly. Woman, in the cult of True Womanhood[1] presented by the women's

---

[1] Authors who addressed themselves to the subject of women in the mid-nineteenth century used this phrase as frequently as writers on religion mentioned God. Neither group felt it necessary to define their favorite terms; they simply assumed—with some justification—that readers would intuitively understand exactly what they meant. Frequently what people of one era take for granted is most striking and revealing to the student from another. In a sense this analysis of the ideal woman of the mid-nineteenth century is an examination of what writers of that period actually meant when they used so confidently the vague phrase True Womanhood.

"The Cult of True Womanhood: 1820–1860," by Barbara Welter. From *American Quarterly*, XVIII (Summer 1966), 151–74. Copyright, 1966, Trustees of the University of Pennsylvania. Reprinted by permission of the University of Pennsylvania and the author.

magazines, gift annuals and religious literature of the nineteenth century, was the hostage in the home.[2] In a society where values changed frequently, where fortunes rose and fell with frightening rapidity, where social and economic mobility provided instability as well as hope, one thing at least remained the same—a true woman was a true woman, wherever she was found. If anyone, male or female, dared to tamper with the complex of virtues which made up True Womanhood, he was damned immediately as an enemy of God, of civilization, and of the Republic. It was a fearful obligation, a solemn responsibility, which the nineteenth-century American woman had—to uphold the pillars of the temple with her frail white hand.

The attributes of True Womanhood, by which a woman judged herself and was judged by her husband, her neighbors and society, could be divided into four cardinal virtues—piety, purity, submissiveness and domesticity. Put them all together and they spelled mother, daughter, sister, wife—woman. Without them, no matter whether there was fame, achievement or wealth, all was ashes. With them she was promised happiness and power.

Religion or piety was the core of woman's virtue, the source of her strength. Young men looking for a mate were cautioned to search first for piety, for if that were there, all else would follow.[3] Religion belonged to woman by divine right, a gift of God and nature. This "peculiar susceptibility" to religion was given her for a reason: "the vestal flame of piety, lighted up by Heaven in the breast of woman" would throw its beams into the naughty world of men.[4] So far would its candle power reach that the "Universe might be Enlightened, Improved, and Harmo-

---

[2] The conclusions reached in this article are based on a survey of almost all of the women's magazines published for more than three years during the period 1820–60 and a sampling of those published for less than three years; all the gift books cited in Ralph Thompson, *American Literary Annuals and Gift Books, 1825–1865* (New York, 1936), deposited in the Library of Congress, the New York Public Library, the New-York Historical Society, Columbia University Special Collections, Library of the City College of the University of New York, Pennsylvania Historical Society, Massachusetts Historical Society, Boston Public Library, Fruitlands Museum Library, the Smithsonian Institution and the Wisconsin Historical Society; hundreds of religious tracts and sermons in the American Unitarian Society and the Galatea Collection of the Boston Public Library; and the large collection of nineteenth-century cookbooks in the New York Public Library and the Academy of Medicine of New York. Corroborative evidence not cited in this article was found in women's diaries, memoirs, autobiographies and personal papers, as well as in all the novels by women which sold over 75,000 copies during this period, as cited in Frank Luther Mott, *Golden Multitudes: The Story of Best Sellers in the United States* (New York, 1947), and H. R. Brown, *The Sentimental Novel in America, 1789–1860* (Durham, N.C., 1940). This latter information also indicated the effect of the cult of True Womanhood on those most directly concerned.

[3] As in "The Bachelor's Dream," in *The Lady's Gift: Souvenir for All Seasons* (Nashua, N.H., 1849), p. 37.

[4] *The Young Ladies' Class Book: A Selection of Lessons for Reading in Prose and Verse*, ed. Ebenezer Bailey, Principal of Young Ladies' High School, Boston (Boston, 1831), p. 168.

nized by WOMAN!!"[5] She would be another, better Eve, working in cooperation with the Redeemer, bringing the world back "from its revolt and
sin."[6] The world would be reclaimed for God through her suffering, for
"God increased the cares and sorrows of woman, that she might be sooner
constrained to accept the terms of salvation."[7] A popular poem by Mrs.
Frances Osgood, "The Triumph of the Spiritual over the Sensual," expressed just this sentiment, woman's purifying passionless love bringing
an erring man back to Christ.[8]

   Dr. Charles Meigs, explaining to a graduating class of medical students why women were naturally religious, said that "hers is a pious mind.
Her confiding nature leads her more readily than men to accept the prof-
fered grace of the Gospel."[9] Caleb Atwater, Esq., writing in *The Ladies'
Repository*, saw the hand of the Lord in female piety: "Religion is exactly
what a woman needs, for it gives her that dignity that best suits her dependence."[10] And Mrs. John Sandford, who had no very high opinion of
her sex, agreed thoroughly: "Religion is just what woman needs. Without
it she is ever restless or unhappy. . . ."[11] Mrs. Sandford and the others did
not speak only of that restlessness of the human heart, which St. Augustine notes, that can only find its peace in God. They spoke rather of religion as a kind of tranquilizer for the many undefined longings which
swept even the most pious young girl, and about which it was better to
pray than to think.

   One reason religion was valued was that it did not take a woman
away from her "proper sphere," her home. Unlike participation in other
societies or movements, church work would not make her less domestic or
submissive, less a True Woman. In religious vineyards, said the *Young
Ladies' Literary and Missionary Report*, "you may labor without the apprehension of detracting from the charms of feminine delicacy." Mrs.
S. L. Dagg, writing from her chapter of the Society in Tuscaloosa, Alabama, was equally reassuring: "As no sensible woman will suffer her intellectual pursuits to clash with her domestic duties" she should concentrate on religious work "which promotes these very duties."[12]

[5] A Lady of Philadelphia, *The World Enlightened, Improved, and Harmonized by
WOMAN!!* A lecture, delivered in the City of New York, before the Young
Ladies' Society for Mutual Improvement, on the following question, proposed by
the society, with the offer of $100 for the best lecture that should be read before
them on the subject proposed:—What is the power and influence of woman in
moulding the manners, morals and habits of civil society? (Philadelphia, 1840), p. 1.

[6] *The Young Lady's Book: A Manual of Elegant Recreations, Exercises, and Pursuits* (Boston, 1830), p. 29.

[7] *Woman as She Was, Is, and Should Be* (New York, 1849), p. 206.

[8] "The Triumph of the Spiritual over the Sensual: An Allegory," in *Ladies' Companion: A Monthly Magazine Embracing Every Department of Literature, Embellished with Original Engravings and Music* (New York), XVII (1842), 67.

[9] *Lecture on Some of the Distinctive Characteristics of the Female*, delivered before
the class of the Jefferson Medical College, Jan. 1847 (Philadelphia, 1847), p. 13.

[10] "Female Education," *Ladies' Repository and Gatherings of the West: A Monthly
Periodical Devoted to Literature and Religion*, I (Cincinnati), 12.

[11] *Woman, in Her Social and Domestic Character* (Boston, 1842), pp. 41–42.

[12] *Second Annual Report of the Young Ladies' Literary and Missionary Association
of the Philadelphia Collegiate Institution* (Philadelphia, 1840), pp. 20, 26.

The women's seminaries aimed at aiding women to be religious, as well as accomplished. Mt. Holyoke's catalogue promised to make female education "a handmaid to the Gospel and an efficient auxiliary in the great task of renovating the world."[13] The Young Ladies' Seminary at Bordentown, New Jersey, declared its most important function to be "the forming of a sound and virtuous character."[14] In Keene, New Hampshire, the Seminary tried to instill a "consistent and useful character" in its students, to enable them in this life to be "a good friend, wife and mother," but more important, to qualify them for "the enjoyment of Celestial Happiness in the life to come."[15] And Joseph M'D. Mathews, Principal of Oakland Female Seminary in Hillsborough, Ohio, believed that "female education should be preeminently religious."[16]

If religion was so vital to a woman, irreligion was almost too awful to contemplate. Women were warned not to let their literary or intellectual pursuits take them away from God. Sarah Josepha Hale spoke darkly of those who, like Margaret Fuller, threw away the "One True Book" for others, open to error. Mrs. Hale used the unfortunate Miss Fuller as fateful proof that "the greater the intellectual force, the greater and more fatal the errors into which women fall who wander from the Rock of Salvation, Christ the Saviour. . . ."[17]

One gentleman, writing on "Female Irreligion," reminded his readers that "man may make himself a brute, and does so very often, but can woman brutify herself to his level—the lowest level of human nature—without exerting special wonder?" Fanny Wright, because she was godless, "was no woman, mother though she be." A few years ago, he recalls, such women would have been whipped. In any case, "woman never looks lovelier than in her reverence for religion" and, conversely, "female irreligion is the most revolting feature in human character."[18]

Purity was as essential as piety to a young woman, its absence as unnatural and unfeminine. Without it she was, in fact, no woman at all, but a member of some lower order. A "fallen woman" was a "fallen angel," unworthy of the celestial company of her sex. To contemplate the loss of purity brought tears; to be guilty of such a crime, in the women's magazines at least, brought madness or death. Even the language of the flowers had bitter words for it: a dried white rose symbolized "Death Preferable to Loss of Innocence."[19] The marriage night was the single

---

[13] *Mt. Holyoke Female Seminary: Female Education. Tendencies of the Principles Embraced, and the System Adopted in the Mt. Holyoke Female Seminary* (Boston, 1839), p. 3.

[14] *Prospectus of the Young Ladies' Seminary at Bordentown, New Jersey* (Bordentown, 1836), p. 7.

[15] *Catalogue of the Young Ladies' Seminary in Keene, New Hampshire* (n.p., 1832), p. 20.

[16] "Report to the College of Teachers, Cincinnati, October, 1840" in *Ladies' Repository*, I (1841), 50.

[17] *Woman's Record: or Sketches of All Distinguished Women from "The Beginning" Till A.D. 1850* (New York, 1853), pp. 665, 669.

[18] "Female Irreligion," *Ladies' Companion*, XIII (May–Oct. 1840), 111.

[19] *The Lady's Book of Flowers and Poetry*, ed. Lucy Hooper (New York, 1842), has a "Floral Dictionary" giving the symbolic meaning of floral tributes.

great event of a woman's life, when she bestowed her greatest treasure upon her husband, and from that time on was completely dependent upon him, an empty vessel,[20] without legal or emotional existence of her own.[21]

Therefore all True Women were urged, in the strongest possible terms, to maintain their virtue, although men, being by nature more sensual than they, would try to assault it. Thomas Branagan admitted in *The Excellency of the Female Character Vindicated* that his sex would sin and sin again, they could not help it, but woman, stronger and purer, must not give in and let man "take liberties incompatible with her delicacy." "If you do," Branagan addressed his gentle reader, "you will be left in silent sadness to bewail your credulity, imbecility, duplicity, and premature prostitution."[22]

Mrs. Eliza Farrar, in *The Young Lady's Friend*, gave practical logistics to avoid trouble: "Sit not with another in a place that is too narrow; read not out of the same book; let not your eagerness to see anything induce you to place your head close to another person's."[23]

If such good advice was ignored the consequences were terrible and inexorable. In *Girlhood and Womanhood: or, Sketches of My Schoolmates*, by Mrs. A. J. Graves (a kind of mid-nineteenth-century *The Group*), the bad ends of a boarding school class of girls are scrupulously recorded. The worst end of all is reserved for "Amelia Dorrington: The Lost One." Amelia died in the almshouse "the wretched victim of depravity and intemperance" and all because her mother had let her be "high-spirited not prudent." These girlish high spirits had been misinterpreted by a young man, with disastrous results. Amelia's "thoughtless levity" was "followed by a total loss of virtuous principle" and Mrs. Graves editorializes that "the coldest reserve is more admirable in a woman a man wishes to make his wife, than the least approach to undue familiarity."[24]

A popular and often reprinted story by Fanny Forester told the sad tale of "Lucy Dutton." Lucy "with the seal of innocence upon her heart, and a rose-leaf on her cheek" came out of her vine-covered cottage and ran into a city slicker. "And Lucy was beautiful and trusting, and thoughtless: and he was gay, selfish and profligate. Needs the story to be

[20] See, for example, Nathaniel Hawthorne, *The Blithedale Romance* (Boston, 1852), p. 71, in which Zenobia says: "How can she be happy, after discovering that fate has assigned her but one single event, which she must contrive to make the substance of her whole life? A man has his choice of innumerable events."

[21] Mary R. Beard, *Woman as Force in History* (New York, 1946), makes this point at some length. According to common law, a woman had no legal existence once she was married and therefore could not manage property, sue in court, etc. In the 1840's and 1850's laws were passed in several states to remedy this condition.

[22] *Excellency of the Female Character Vindicated: Being an Investigation Relative to the Cause and Effects on the Encroachments of Men upon the Rights of Women, and the Too Frequent Degradation and Consequent Misfortunes of the Fair Sex* (New York, 1807), pp. 277, 278.

[23] By a Lady (Eliza Ware Rotch Farrar), *The Young Lady's Friend* (Boston, 1837), p. 293.

[24] *Girlhood and Womanhood: or, Sketches of My Schoolmates* (Boston, 1844), p. 140.

told? . . . Nay, censor, Lucy was a child—consider how young, how very untaught—oh! her innocence was no match for the sophistry of a gay, city youth! Spring came and shame was stamped upon the cottage at the foot of the hill." The baby died; Lucy went mad at the funeral and finally died herself. "Poor, poor Lucy Dutton! The grave is a blessed couch and pillow to the wretched. Rest thee there, poor Lucy!"[25] The frequency with which derangement follows loss of virtue suggests the exquisite sensibility of woman, and the possibility that, in the women's magazines at least, her intellect was geared to her hymen, not her brain.

If, however, a woman managed to withstand man's assaults on her virtue, she demonstrated her superiority and her power over him. Eliza Farnham, trying to prove this female superiority, concluded smugly that "the purity of women is the everlasting barrier against which the tides of man's sensual nature surge."[26]

A story in *The Lady's Amaranth* illustrates this dominance. It is set, improbably, in Sicily, where two lovers, Bianca and Tebaldo, have been separated because her family insisted she marry a rich old man. By some strange circumstance the two are in a shipwreck and cast on a desert island, the only survivors. Even here, however, the rigid standards of True Womanhood prevail. Tebaldo unfortunately forgets himself slightly, so that Bianca must warn him: "We may not indeed gratify our fondness by caresses, but it is still something to bestow our kindest language, and looks and prayers, and all lawful and honest attentions on each other." Something, perhaps, but not enough, and Bianca must further remonstrate: "It is true that another man is my husband, but you are my guardian angel." When even that does not work she says in a voice of sweet reason, passive and proper to the end, that she wishes he wouldn't but "still, if you insist, I will become what you wish; but I beseech you to consider, ere that decision, that debasement which I must suffer in your esteem." This appeal to his own double standards holds the beast in him at bay. They are rescued, discover that the old husband is dead, and after "mourning a decent season" Bianca finally gives in, legally.[27]

Men could be counted on to be grateful when women thus saved them from themselves. William Alcott, guiding young men in their relations with the opposite sex, told them that "nothing is better calculated to preserve a young man from contamination of low pleasures and pursuits than frequent intercourse with the more refined and virtuous of the other sex." And he added, one assumes in equal innocence, that youths should "observe and learn to admire, that purity and ignorance of evil which is the characteristic of well-educated young ladies, and which, when we are near them, raises us above those sordid and sensual considerations which hold such sway over men in their intercourse with each other."[28]

[25] Emily Chubbuck, *Alderbook* (2nd. ed.; Boston, 1847), II, 121, 127.

[26] *Woman and Her Era* (New York, 1864), p. 95.

[27] "The Two Lovers of Sicily," *The Lady's Amaranth: A Journal of Tales, Essays, Excerpts—Historical and Biographical Sketches, Poetry and Literature in General* (Philadelphia), II (Jan. 1839), 17.

[28] *The Young Man's Guide* (Boston, 1833), pp. 229, 231.

The Rev. Jonathan F. Stearns was also impressed by female chastity in the face of male passion, and warned woman never to compromise the source of her power: "Let her lay aside delicacy, and her influence over our sex is gone."[29]

Women themselves accepted, with pride but suitable modesty, this priceless virtue. *The Ladies' Wreath*, in "Woman the Creature of God and the Manufacturer of Society," saw purity as her greatest gift and chief means of discharging her duty to save the world: "Purity is the highest beauty—the true pole-star which is to guide humanity aright in its long, varied, and perilous voyage."[30]

Sometimes, however, a woman did not see the dangers to her treasure. In that case, they must be pointed out to her, usually by a male. In the nineteenth century any form of social change was tantamount to an attack on woman's virtue, if only it was correctly understood. For example, dress reform seemed innocuous enough and the bloomers worn by the lady of that name and her followers were certainly modest attire. Such was the reasoning only of the ignorant. In another issue of *The Ladies' Wreath* a young lady is represented in dialogue with her "Professor." The girl expresses admiration for the bloomer costume—it gives freedom of motion, is healthful and attractive. The "Professor" sets her straight. Trousers, he explains, are "only one of the many manifestations of that wild spirit of socialism and agrarian radicalism which is at present so rife in our land." The young lady recants immediately: "If this dress has any connexion with Fourierism or socialism, or fanaticism in any shape whatever, I have no disposition to wear it at all . . . no true woman would so far compromise her delicacy as to espouse, however unwittingly, such a cause."[31]

America could boast that her daughters were particularly innocent. In a poem on "The American Girl" the author wrote proudly:

> Her eye of light is the diamond bright,
> Her innocence the pearl,
> And these are ever the bridal gems
> That are worn by the American girl.[32]

Lydia Maria Child, giving advice to mothers, aimed at preserving that spirit of innocence. She regretted that "want of confidence between mothers and daughters on delicate subjects" and suggested a woman tell her daughter a few facts when she reached the age of twelve to "set her

[29] *Female Influence: and the True Christian Mode of Its Exercise; a Discourse Delivered in the First Presbyterian Church in Newburyport, July 30, 1837* (Newburyport, 1837), p. 18.

[30] W. Tolles, "Woman the Creature of God and the Manufacturer of Society," *Ladies' Wreath* (New York), III (1852), 205.

[31] Prof. William M. Heim, "The Bloomer Dress," *Ladies' Wreath*, III (1852), 247.

[32] *The Young Lady's Offering: or Gems of Prose and Poetry* (Boston, 1853), p. 283. The American girl, whose innocence was often connected with ignorance, was the spiritual ancestress of the Henry James heroine. Daisy Miller, like Lucy Dutton, saw innocence lead to tragedy.

mind at rest." Then Mrs. Child confidently hoped that a young lady's "instinctive modesty" would "prevent her from dwelling on the information until she was called upon to use it."[33] In the same vein, a book of advice to the newly married was titled *Whisper to a Bride*.[34] As far as intimate information was concerned, there was no need to whisper, since the book contained none at all.

A masculine summary of this virtue was expressed in a poem, "Female Charms":

> I would have her as pure as the snow on the mount—
> As true as the smile that to infamy's given—
> As pure as the wave of the crystalline fount,
> Yet as warm in the heart as the sunlight of heaven.
> With a mind cultivated, not boastingly wise,
> I could gaze on such beauty, with exquisite bliss;
> With her heart on her lips and her soul in her eyes—
> What more could I wish in dear woman than this.[35]

Man might, in fact, ask no more than this in woman, but she was beginning to ask more of herself, and in the asking was threatening the third powerful and necessary virtue, submission. Purity, considered as a moral imperative, set up a dilemma which was hard to resolve. Woman must preserve her virtue until marriage and marriage was necessary for her happiness. Yet marriage was, literally, an end to innocence. She was told not to question this dilemma, but simply to accept it.

Submission was perhaps the most feminine virtue expected of women. Men were supposed to be religious, although they rarely had time for it, and supposed to be pure, although it came awfully hard to them, but men were the movers, the doers, the actors. Women were the passive, submissive responders. The order of dialogue was, of course, fixed in Heaven. Man was "woman's superior by God's appointment, if not in intellectual dowry, at least by official decree." Therefore, as Charles Elliott argued in *The Ladies' Repository*, she should submit to him "for the sake of good order at least."[36] In *The Ladies' Companion* a young wife was quoted approvingly as saying that she did not think woman should "feel and act for herself" because "when, next to God, her husband is not the tribunal to which her heart and intellect appeals—the golden bowl of affection is broken."[37] Women were warned that if they tampered with this quality they tampered with the order of the Universe.

*The Young Lady's Book* summarized the necessity of the passive vir-

---

[33] *The Mother's Book* (Boston, 1831), pp. 151, 152.

[34] Mrs. L. H. Sigourney, *Whisper to a Bride* (Hartford, 1851), in which Mrs. Sigourney's approach is summed up in this quotation: "Home! Blessed bride, thou art about to enter this sanctuary, and to become a priestess at its altar!," p. 44.

[35] S. R. R., "Female Charms," *Godey's Magazine and Lady's Book* (Philadelphia), XXXIII (1846), 52.

[36] Charles Elliott, "Arguing with Females," *Ladies' Repository*, I (1841), 25.

[37] *Ladies' Companion*, VIII (Jan. 1838), 147.

tues in its readers' lives: "It is, however, certain, that in whatever situation of life a woman is placed from her cradle to her grave, a spirit of obedience and submission, pliability of temper, and humility of mind, are required from her."[38]

Woman understood her position if she was the right kind of woman, a true woman. "She feels herself weak and timid. She needs a protector," declared George Burnap, in his lectures on *The Sphere and Duties of Woman*. "She is in a measure dependent. She asks for wisdom, constancy, firmness, perseverance, and she is willing to repay it all by the surrender of the full treasure of her affections. Woman despises in man every thing like herself except a tender heart. It is enough that she is effeminate and weak; she does not want another like herself."[39] Or put even more strongly by Mrs. Sandford: "A really sensible woman feels her dependence. She does what she can, but she is conscious of inferiority, and therefore grateful for support."[40]

Mrs. Sigourney, however, assured young ladies that although they were separate, they were equal. This difference of the sexes did not imply inferiority, for it was part of that same order of Nature established by Him "who bids the oak brave the fury of the tempest, and the alpine flower lean its cheek on the bosom of eternal snows."[41] Dr. Meigs had a different analogy to make the same point, contrasting the anatomy of the Apollo of the Belvedere (illustrating the male principle) with the Venus de Medici (illustrating the female principle). "Woman," said the physician, with a kind of clinical gallantry, "has a head almost too small for intellect but just big enough for love."[42]

This love itself was to be passive and responsive. "Love, in the heart of a woman," wrote Mrs. Farrar, "should partake largely of the nature of gratitude. She should love, because she is already loved by one deserving her regard."[43]

Woman was to work in silence, unseen, like Wordsworth's Lucy. Yet, "working like nature, in secret" her love goes forth to the world "to regulate its pulsation, and send forth from its heart, in pure and temperate flow, the life-giving current."[44] She was to work only for pure affection, without thought of money or ambition. A poem, "Woman and Fame," by Felicia Hemans, widely quoted in many of the gift books, concludes with a spirited renunciation of the gift of fame:

> Away! to me, a woman, bring
> Sweet flowers from affection's spring.[45]

[38] *The Young Lady's Book* (New York, 1830), American edition, p. 28. (This is a different book than the one of the same title and date of publication cited in note 6.)

[39] *Sphere and Duties of Woman* (5th ed.; Baltimore, 1854), p. 47.

[40] *Woman*, p. 15.

[41] *Letters to Young Ladies* (Hartford, 1835), p. 179.

[42] *Lecture*, p. 17.

[43] *The Young Lady's Friend*, p. 313.

[44] Maria J. McIntosh, *Woman in America: Her Work and Her Reward* (New York, 1850), p. 25.

[45] *Poems and a Memoir of the Life of Mrs. Felicia Hemans* (London, 1860), p. 16.

"True feminine genius," said Grace Greenwood (Sara Jane Clarke), "is ever timid, doubtful, and clingingly dependent; a perpetual childhood." And she advised literary ladies in an essay on "The Intellectual Woman"—"Don't trample on the flowers while longing for the stars."[46] A wife who submerged her own talents to work for her husband was extolled as an example of a true woman. In *Women of Worth: A Book for Girls*, Mrs. Ann Flaxman, an artist of promise herself, was praised because she "devoted herself to sustain her husband's genius and aid him in his arduous career."[47]

Caroline Gilman's advice to the bride aimed at establishing this proper order from the beginning of a marriage: "Oh, young and lovely bride, watch well the first moments when your will conflicts with his to whom God and society have given the control. Reverence his *wishes* even when you do not his *opinions*."[48]

Mrs. Gilman's perfect wife in *Recollections of a Southern Matron* realizes that "the three golden threads with which domestic happiness is woven" are "to repress a harsh answer, to confess a fault, and to stop (right or wrong) in the midst of self-defense, in gentle submission." Woman could do this, hard though it was, because in her heart she knew she was right and so could afford to be forgiving, even a trifle condescending. "Men are not unreasonable," averred Mrs. Gilman. "Their difficulties lie in not understanding the moral and physical nature of our sex. They often wound through ignorance, and are surprised at having offended." Wives were advised to do their best to reform men, but if they couldn't, to give up gracefully. "If any habit of his annoyed me, I spoke of it once or twice, calmly, then bore it quietly."[49]

A wife should occupy herself "only with domestic affairs—wait till your husband confides to you those of a high importance—and do not give your advice until he asks for it," advised *The Lady's Token*. At all times she should behave in a manner becoming a woman, who had "no arms other than gentleness." Thus "if he is abusive, never retort."[50] *A Young Lady's Guide to the Harmonious Development of a Christian Character* suggested that females should "become as little children" and "avoid a controversial spirit."[51] *The Mother's Assistant and Young Lady's Friend* listed "Always Conciliate" as its first commandment in "Rules for Conjugal and Domestic Happiness." Small wonder that these same rules ended with the succinct maxim: "Do not expect too much."[52]

---

[46] Letter "To an Unrecognized Poetess, June, 1846" (Sara Jane Clarke), *Greenwood Leaves* (2nd ed.; Boston, 1850), p. 311.

[47] "The Sculptor's Assistant: Ann Flaxman," in *Women of Worth: A Book for Girls* (New York, 1860), p. 263.

[48] Mrs. Clarissa Packard (Mrs. Caroline Howard Gilman), *Recollections of a Housekeeper* (New York, 1834), p. 122.

[49] *Recollections of a Southern Matron* (New York, 1838), pp. 256, 257.

[50] *The Lady's Token: or Gift of Friendship*, ed. Colesworth Pinckney (Nashua, N.H., 1848), p. 119.

[51] Harvey Newcomb, *Young Lady's Guide to the Harmonious Development of Christian Character* (Boston, 1846), p. 10.

[52] "Rules for Conjugal and Domestic Happiness," *Mother's Assistant and Young Lady's Friend* (Boston, III (April 1843), 115.

As mother, as well as wife, woman was required to submit to fortune. In *Letters to Mothers* Mrs. Sigourney sighed: "To bear the evils and sorrows which may be appointed us, with a patient mind, should be the continual effort of our sex. . . . It seems, indeed, to be expected of us; since the passive and enduring virtues are more immediately within our province." Of these trials "the hardest was to bear the loss of children with submission" but the indomitable Mrs. Sigourney found strength to murmur to the bereaved mother: "The Lord loveth a cheerful giver."[53] *The Ladies' Parlor Companion* agreed thoroughly in "A Submissive Mother," in which a mother who had already buried two children and was nursing a dying baby saw her sole remaining child "probably scalded to death. Handing over the infant to die in the arms of a friend, she bowed in sweet submission to the double stroke." But the child "through the goodness of God survived, and the mother learned to say 'Thy will be done.' "[54]

Woman then, in all her roles, accepted submission as her lot. It was a lot she had not chosen or deserved. As *Godey's* said, "The lesson of submission is forced upon woman." Without comment or criticism the writer affirms that "to suffer and to be silent under suffering seems the great command she has to obey."[55] George Burnap referred to a woman's life as "a series of suppressed emotions."[56] She was, as Emerson said, "more vulnerable, more infirm, more mortal than man."[57] The death of a beautiful woman, cherished in fiction, represented woman as the innocent victim, suffering without sin, too pure and good for this world but too weak and passive to resist its evil forces.[58] The best refuge for such a delicate creature was the warmth and safety of her home.

The true woman's place was unquestionably by her own fireside—as daughter, sister, but most of all as wife and mother. Therefore domesticity was among the virtues most prized by the women's magazines. "As society is constituted," wrote Mrs. S. E. Farley, in the "Domestic and Social Claims on Woman," "the true dignity and beauty of the female character seem to consist in a right understanding and faithful and cheerful performance of social and family duties."[59] Sacred Scripture reenforced social pressure: "St. Paul knew what was best for women when he

---

[53] *Letters to Mothers* (Hartford, 1838), p. 199. In the diaries and letters of women who lived during this period the death of a child seemed consistently to be the hardest thing for them to bear and to occasion more anguish and rebellion, as well as eventual submission, than any other event in their lives.

[54] "A Submissive Mother," *The Ladies' Parlor Companion: A Collection of Scattered Fragments and Literary Gems* (New York, 1852), p. 358.

[55] "Woman," *Godey's Lady's Book*, II (Aug. 1831), 110.

[56] *Sphere and Duties of Woman*, p. 172.

[57] Ralph Waldo Emerson, "Woman," *Complete Writings of Ralph Waldo Emerson* (New York, 1875), p. 1180.

[58] As in Donald Fraser, *The Mental Flower Garden* (New York, 1857). Perhaps the most famous exponent of this theory is Edgar Allan Poe, who affirms in "The Philosophy of Composition" that "the death of a beautiful woman is unquestionably the most poetical topic in the world. . . ."

[59] "Domestic and Social Claims on Woman," *Mother's Magazine*, VI (1846), 21.

advised them to be domestic," said Mrs. Sandford. "There is composure at home; there is something sedative in the duties which home involves. It affords security not only from the world, but from delusions and errors of every kind."[60]

From her home woman performed her great task of bringing men back to God. *The Young Ladies' Class Book* was sure that "the domestic fireside is the great guardian of society against the excesses of human passions."[61] *The Lady at Home* expressed its convictions in its very title and concluded that "even if we cannot reform the world in a moment, we can begin the work by reforming ourselves and our households—It is woman's mission. Let her not look away from our own little family circle for the means of producing moral and social reforms, but begin at home."[62]

Home was supposed to be a cheerful place, so that brothers, husbands and sons would not go elsewhere in search of a good time. Woman was expected to dispense comfort and cheer. In writing the biography of Margaret Mercer (every inch a true woman) her biographer (male) notes: "She never forgot that it is the peculiar province of woman to minister to the comfort, and promote the happiness, first, of those most nearly allied to her, and then of those, who by the Providence of God are placed in a state of dependence upon her."[63] Many other essays in the women's journals showed woman as comforter: "Woman, Man's Best Friend," "Woman, the Greatest Social Benefit," "Woman, a Being to Come Home To," "The Wife: Source of Comfort and the Spring of Joy."[64]

One of the most important functions of woman as comforter was her role as nurse. Her own health was probably, although regrettably, delicate.[65] Many homes had "little sufferers," those pale children who wasted

---

[60] *Woman,* p. 173.

[61] *The Young Ladies' Class Book,* p. 166.

[62] T. S. Arthur, *The Lady at Home: or, Leaves from the Every-Day Book of an American Woman* (Philadelphia, 1847), pp. 177, 178.

[63] Caspar Morris, *Margaret Mercer* (Boston, 1840), quoted in *Woman's Record,* p. 425.

[64] These particular titles come from: *The Young Ladies' Oasis: or Gems of Prose and Poetry,* ed. N. L. Ferguson (Lowell, 1851), pp. 14, 16; *The Genteel School Reader* (Philadelphia, 1849), p. 271; and *Magnolia,* I (1842), 4. A popular poem in book form, published in England, expressed very fully this concept of woman as comforter: Coventry Patmore, *The Angel in the Home* (Boston, 1856 and 1857). Patmore expressed his devotion to True Womanhood in such lines as:

> The gentle wife, who decks his board
> And makes his day to have no night,
> Whose wishes wait upon her Lord,
> Who finds her own in his delight. (p. 94)

[65] The women's magazines carried on a crusade against tight lacing and regretted, rather than encouraged, the prevalent ill health of the American woman. See, for example, *An American Mother, Hints and Sketches* (New York, 1839), pp. 28 ff., for an essay on the need for a healthy mind in a healthy body in order to better be a good example for children.

away to saintly deaths. And there were enough other illnesses of youth and age, major and minor, to give the nineteenth-century American woman nursing experience. The sickroom called for the exercise of her higher qualities of patience, mercy and gentleness as well as for her house-wifely arts. She could thus fulfill her dual feminine function—beauty and usefulness.

The cookbooks of the period offer formulas for gout cordials, oint-ment for sore nipples, hiccough and cough remedies, opening pills and re-freshing drinks for fever, along with recipes for pound cake, jumbles, stewed calf's head and currant wine.[66] *The Ladies' New Book of Cookery* believed that "food prepared by the kind hand of a wife, mother, sister, friend" tasted better and had a "restorative power which money cannot purchase."[67]

A chapter of *The Young Lady's Friend* was devoted to woman's privilege as "ministering spirit at the couch of the sick." Mrs. Farrar ad-vised a soft voice, gentle and clean hands, and a cheerful smile. She also cautioned against an excess of female delicacy. That was all right for a young lady in the parlor, but not for bedside manners. Leeches, for ex-ample, were to be regarded as "a curious piece of mechanism . . . their ornamental stripes should recommend them even to the eye, and their val-uable services to our feelings." And she went on calmly to discuss their use. Nor were women to shrink from medical terminology, since "if you cultivate right views of the wonderful structure of the body, you will be as willing to speak to a physician of the bowels as the brains of your patient."[68]

Nursing the sick, particularly sick males, not only made a woman feel useful and accomplished, but increased her influence. In a piece of heavy-handed humor in *Godey's* a man confessed that some women were only happy when their husbands were ailing that they might have the joy of nursing him to recovery, "thus gratifying their medical vanity and their love of power by making him more dependent upon them."[69] In a similar vein a husband sometimes suspected his wife "almost wishes me dead—for the pleasure of being utterly inconsolable."[70]

In the home women were not only the highest adornment of civiliza-tion, but they were supposed to keep busy at morally uplifting tasks.

---

[66] The best single collection of nineteenth-century cookbooks is in the Academy of Medicine of New York Library, although some of the most interesting cures were in handwritten cookbooks found among the papers of women who lived during the period.

[67] Sarah Josepha Hale, *The Ladies' New Book of Cookery: A Practical System for Private Families in Town and Country* (5th ed.; New York, 1852), p. 409. Similar evidence on the importance of nursing skills to every female is found in such books of advice as William A. Alcott, *The Young Housekeeper* (Boston, 1838), in which, along with a plea for apples and cold baths, Alcott says, "Every female should be trained to the angelic art of managing properly the sick," p. 47.

[68] *The Young Lady's Friend*, pp. 75–77, 79.

[69] "A Tender Wife," *Godey's*, II (July 1831), 28.

[70] "MY WIFE! A Whisper," *Godey's*, II (Oct. 1831), 231.

Fortunately most of housework, if looked at in true womanly fashion, could be regarded as uplifting. Mrs. Sigourney extolled its virtues: "The science of housekeeping affords exercise for the judgment and energy, ready recollection, and patient self-possession, that are the characteristics of a superior mind."[71] According to Mrs. Farrar, making beds was good exercise, the repetitiveness of routine tasks inculcated patience and perseverance, and proper management of the home was a surprisingly complex art: "There is more to be learned about pouring out tea and coffee, than most young ladies are willing to believe."[72] *Godey's* went so far as to suggest coyly, in "Learning vs. Housewifery," that the two were complementary, not opposed: chemistry could be utilized in cooking, geometry in dividing cloth, and phrenology in discovering talent in children.[73]

Women were to master every variety of needlework, for, as Mrs. Sigourney pointed out, "needle-work, in all its forms of use, elegance, and ornament, has ever been the appropriate occupation of woman."[74] Embroidery improved taste; knitting promoted serenity and economy.[75] Other forms of artsy-craftsy activity for her leisure moments included painting on glass or velvet, Poonah work, tussy-mussy frames for her own needlepoint or water colors, stands for hyacinths, hair bracelets or baskets of feathers.[76]

She was expected to have a special affinity for flowers. To the editors of *The Lady's Token*, "A Woman never appears more truly in her sphere, than when she divides her time between her domestic avocations and the culture of flowers."[77] She could write letters, an activity particularly feminine since it had to do with the outpourings of the heart,[78] or practice her drawingroom skills of singing and playing an instrument. She might even read.

Here she faced a bewildering array of advice. The female was dangerously addicted to novels, according to the literature of the period. She should avoid them, since they interfered with "serious piety." If she simply couldn't help herself and read them anyway, she should choose

---

[71] *Letters to Young Ladies*, p. 27. The greatest exponent of the mental and moral joys of housekeeping was the *Lady's Annual Register and Housewife's Memorandum Book* (Boston, 1838), which gave practical advice on ironing, hair curling, budgeting and marketing, and turning cuffs—all activities which contributed to the "beauty of usefulness" and "joy of accomplishment" which a woman desired (I, 23).

[72] *The Young Lady's Friend*, p. 230.

[73] "Learning vs. Housewifery," *Godey's*, X (Aug. 1839), 95.

[74] *Letters to Young Ladies*, p. 25. W. Thayer, *Life at the Fireside* (Boston, 1857), has an idyllic picture of the woman of the house mending her children's garments, the grandmother knitting and the little girl taking her first stitches, all in the light of the domestic hearth.

[75] "The Mirror's Advice," *Young Maiden's Mirror* (Boston, 1858), p. 263.

[76] Mrs. L. Maria Child, *The Girl's Own Book* (New York, 1833).

[77] P. 44.

[78] T. S. Arthur, *Advice to Young Ladies* (Boston, 1850), p. 45.

edifying ones from lists of morally acceptable authors. She should study history since it "showed the depravity of the human heart and the evil nature of sin." On the whole, "religious biography was best."[79]

The women's magazines themselves could be read without any loss of concern for the home. *Godey's* promised the husband that he would find his wife "no less assiduous for his reception, or less sincere in welcoming his return" as a result of reading their magazine.[80] *The Lily of the Valley* won its right to be admitted to the boudoir by confessing that it was "like its namesake humble and unostentatious, but it is yet pure, and, we trust, free from moral imperfections."[81]

No matter what later authorities claimed, the nineteenth century knew that girls *could* be ruined by a book. The seduction stories regard "exciting and dangerous books" as contributory causes of disaster. The man without honorable intentions always provides the innocent maiden with such books as a prelude to his assault on her virtue.[82] Books which attacked or seemed to attack woman's accepted place in society were regarded as equally dangerous. A reviewer of Harriet Martineau's *Society in America* wanted it kept out of the hands of American women. They were so susceptible to persuasion, with their "gentle yielding natures" that they might listen to "the bold ravings of the hard-featured of their own sex." The frightening result: "Such reading will unsettle them for their true station and pursuits, and they will throw the world back again into confusion."[83]

The debate over women's education posed the question of whether a "finished" education detracted from the practice of housewifely arts. Again it proved to be a case of semantics, for a true woman's education was never "finished" until she was instructed in the gentle science of homemaking.[84] Helen Irving, writing on "Literary Women," made it very clear that if women invoked the muse, it was as a genie of the household lamp. "If the necessities of her position require these duties at her hands, she will perform them nonetheless cheerfully, that she knows herself capable of higher things." The literary woman must conform to the same standards as any other woman: "That her home shall be made a loving place of rest and joy and comfort for those who are dear to her, will be the first wish of every true woman's heart."[85] Mrs. Ann Stephens told women who wrote to make sure they did not sacrifice one domestic duty.

---

[79] R. C. Waterston, *Thoughts on Moral and Spiritual Culture* (Boston, 1842), p. 101. Newcomb's *Young Lady's Guide* also advised religious biography as the best reading for women (p. 111).

[80] *Godey's*, I (1828), 1. (Repeated often in *Godey's* editorials.)

[81] *The Lily of the Valley*, n. v. (1851), p. 2.

[82] For example, "The Fatalist," *Godey's*, IV (Jan. 1834), 10, in which Somers Dudley has Catherine reading these dangerous books until life becomes "a bewildered dream. . . . O passion, what a shocking perverter of reason thou art!"

[83] Review of *Society in America* (New York, 1837) in *American Quarterly Review* (Philadelphia), XXII (Sept. 1837), 38.

[84] "A Finished Education," *Ladies' Museum* (Providence), I (1825), 42.

[85] Helen Irving, "Literary Women," *Ladies' Wreath*, III (1850), 93.

"As for genius, make it a domestic plant. Let its roots strike deep in your house. . . ."[86]

The fear of "blue stockings" (the eighteenth-century male's term of derision for educated or literary women) need not persist for nineteenth-century American men. The magazines presented spurious dialogues in which bachelors were convinced of their fallacy in fearing educated wives. One such dialogue took place between a young man and his female cousin. Ernest deprecates learned ladies ("A *Woman* is far more lovable than a *philosopher*") but Alice refutes him with the beautiful example of their Aunt Barbara, who "although she *has* perpetrated the heinous crime of writing some half dozen folios" is still a model of "the spirit of feminine gentleness." His memory prodded, Ernest concedes that, by George, there was a woman: "When I last had a cold she not only made me a bottle of cough syrup, but when I complained of nothing new to read, set to work and wrote some twenty stanzas on consumption."[87]

The magazines were filled with domestic tragedies in which spoiled young girls learned that when there was a hungry man to feed French and china painting were not helpful. According to these stories many a marriage is jeopardized because the wife has not learned to keep house. Harriet Beecher Stowe wrote a sprightly piece of personal experience for *Godey's,* ridiculing her own bad housekeeping as a bride. She used the same theme in a story, "The Only Daughter," in which the pampered beauty learns the facts of domestic life from a rather difficult source, her mother-in-law. Mrs. Hamilton tells Caroline in the sweetest way possible to shape up in the kitchen, reserving her rebuke for her son: "You are her husband—her guide—her protector—now see what you can do," she admonishes him. "Give her credit for every effort: treat her faults with tenderness; encourage and praise whenever you can, and depend upon it, you will see another woman in her." He is properly masterful, she properly domestic, and in a few months Caroline is making lumpless gravy and keeping up with the darning. Domestic tranquility has been restored and the young wife moralizes: "Bring up a girl to feel that she has a responsible part to bear in promoting the happiness of the family, and you make a reflecting being of her at once, and remove that lightness and frivolity of character which makes her shrink from graver studies."[88] These stories end with the heroine drying her hands on her apron and vowing that *her* daughter will be properly educated, in piecrust as well as Poonah work.

The female seminaries were quick to defend themselves against any suspicion of interfering with the role which nature's God had assigned to women. They hoped to enlarge and deepen that role, but not to change its setting. At the Young Ladies' Seminary and Collegiate Institute in Monroe City, Michigan, the catalogue admitted few of its graduates would be likely "to fill the learned professions." Still, they were called to "other scenes of usefulness and honor." The average woman is to be "the

[86] "Women of Genius," *Ladies' Companion,* XI (1839), 89.
[87] "Intellect vs. Affection in Woman," *Godey's,* XVI (1846), 86.
[88] "The Only Daughter," *Godey's,* X (Mar. 1839), 122.

presiding genius of love" in the home, where she is to "give a correct and elevated literary taste to her children, and to assume that influential station that she ought to possess as the companion of an educated man."[89]

At Miss Pierce's famous school in Litchfield, the students were taught that they had "attained the perfection of their characters when they could combine their elegant accomplishments with a turn for solid domestic virtues."[90] Mt. Holyoke paid pious tribute to domestic skills: "Let a young lady despise this branch of the duties of woman, and she despises the appointments of her existence." God, nature and the Bible "enjoin these duties on the sex, and she cannot violate them with impunity." Thus warned, the young lady would have to seek knowledge of these duties elsewhere, since it was not in the curriculum at Mt. Holyoke. "We would not take this privilege from the mother."[91]

One reason for knowing her way around a kitchen was that America was "a land of precarious fortunes," as Lydia Maria Child pointed out in her book *The Frugal Housewife: Dedicated to Those Who Are Not Ashamed of Economy.* Mrs. Child's chapter "How to Endure Poverty" prescribed a combination of piety and knowledge—the kind of knowledge found in a true woman's education, "a thorough religious *useful* education."[92] The woman who had servants today might tomorrow, because of a depression or panic, be forced to do her own work. If that happened she knew how to act, for she was to be the same cheerful consoler of her husband in their cottage as in their mansion.

An essay by Washington Irving, much quoted in the gift annuals, discussed the value of a wife in case of business reverses: "I have observed that a married man falling into misfortune is more apt to achieve his situation in the world than a single one . . . it is beautifully ordained by Providence that woman, who is the ornament of man in his happier hours, should be his stay and solace when smitten with sudden calamity."[93]

A story titled simply but eloquently "The Wife" dealt with the quiet heroism of Ellen Graham during her husband's plunge from fortune to poverty. Ned Graham said of her: "Words are too poor to tell you what I owe to that noble woman. In our darkest seasons of adversity, she has been an angel of consolation—utterly forgetful of self and anxious only to comfort and sustain me." Of course she had a little help from "faithful Dinah who absolutely refused to leave her beloved mistress," but even so Ellen did no more than would be expected of any true woman.[94]

[89] *The Annual Catalogue of the Officers and Pupils of the Young Ladies' Seminary and Collegiate Institute* (Monroe City, 1855), pp. 18, 19.

[90] *Chronicles of a Pioneer School* from 1792 to 1833: Being the History of Miss Sarah Pierce and Her Litchfield School, Compiled by Emily Noyes Vanderpoel; ed. Elizabeth C. Barney Buel (Cambridge, 1903), p. 74.

[91] *Mt. Holyoke Female Seminary*, p. 13.

[92] *The Frugal Housewife* (New York, 1838), p. 111.

[93] "Female Influence," in *The Ladies' Pearl and Literary Gleaner: A Collection of Tales, Sketches, Essays, Anecdotes, and Historical Incidents* (Lowell), I (1841), 10.

[94] Mrs. S. T. Martyn, "The Wife," *Ladies' Wreath*, II (1848–49), 171.

Most of this advice was directed to woman as wife. Marriage was the proper state for the exercise of the domestic virtues. "True Love and a Happy Home," an essay in *The Young Ladies' Oasis*, might have been carved on every girl's hope chest.[95] But although marriage was best, it was not absolutely necessary. The women's magazines tried to remove the stigma from being an "Old Maid." They advised no marriage at all rather than an unhappy one contracted out of selfish motives.[96] Their stories showed maiden ladies as unselfish ministers to the sick, teachers of the young, or moral preceptors with their pens, beloved of the entire village. Usually the life of single blessedness resulted from the premature death of a fiancé, or was chosen through fidelity to some high mission. For example, in "Two Sisters," Mary devotes herself to Ellen and her abandoned children, giving up her own chance for marriage. "Her devotion to her sister's happiness has met its reward in the consciousness of having fulfilled a sacred duty."[97] Very rarely, a "woman of genius" was absolved from the necessity of marriage, being so extraordinary that she did not need the security or status of being a wife.[98] Most often, however, if girls

---

[95] *The Young Ladies' Oasis*, p. 26.

[96] "On Marriage," *Ladies' Repository*, I (1841), 133; "Old Maids," *Ladies' Literary Cabinet* (Newburyport), II (1822) (microfilm), 141; "Matrimony," *Godey's*, II (Sept. 1831), 174; and "Married or Single," *Peterson's Magazine* (Philadelphia), IX (1859), 36, all express the belief that while marriage is desirable for a woman it is not essential. This attempt to reclaim the status of the unmarried woman is an example of the kind of mild crusade which the women's magazines sometimes carried on. Other examples were their strictures against an overly genteel education and against the affectation and aggravation of ill health. In this sense the magazines were truly conservative, for they did not oppose all change but only that which did violence to some cherished tradition. The reforms they advocated would, if put into effect, make woman even more the perfect female, and enhance the ideal of True Womanhood.

[97] *Girlhood and Womanhood*, p. 100. Mrs. Graves tells the stories in the book in the person of an "Old Maid" and her conclusions are that "single life has its happiness too," for the single woman "can enjoy all the pleasures of maternity without its pains and trials" (p. 140). In another one of her books, *Woman in America* (New York, 1843), Mrs. Graves speaks out even more strongly in favor of "single blessedness" rather than "a loveless or unhappy marriage" (p. 130).

[98] A very unusual story is Lela Linwood, "A Chapter in the History of a Free Heart," *Ladies' Wreath*, III (1853), 349. The heroine, Grace Arland, is "sublime" and dwells "in perfect light while we others struggle yet with the shadows." She refuses marriage and her friends regret this but are told her heart "is rejoicing in its *freedom.*" The story ends with the plaintive refrain:

> But is it not a happy thing,
>   All fetterless and free,
> Like any wild bird, on the wing,
>   To carol merrily?

But even in this tale the unusual, almost unearthly rarity of Grace's genius is stressed; she is not offered as an example to more mortal beings.

proved "difficult," marriage and a family were regarded as a cure.[99] The "sedative quality" of a home could be counted on to subdue even the most restless spirits.

George Burnap saw marriage as "that sphere for which woman was originally intended, and to which she is so exactly fitted to adorn and bless, as the wife, the mistress of a home, the solace, the aid, and the counsellor of that ONE, for whose sake alone the world is of any consequence to her."[100] Samuel Miller preached a sermon on women:

> How interesting and important are the duties devolved on females as WIVES . . . the counsellor and friend of the husband; who makes it her daily study to lighten his cares, to soothe his sorrows, and to augment his joys; who, like a guardian angel, watches over his interests, warns him against dangers, comforts him under trials; and by her pious, assiduous, and attractive deportment, constantly endeavors to render him more virtuous, more useful, more honourable, and more happy.[101]

A woman's whole interest should be focused on her husband, paying him "those numberless attentions to which the French give the title of *petits soins* and which the woman who loves knows so well how to pay . . . she should consider nothing as trivial which could win a smile of approbation from him."[102]

Marriage was seen not only in terms of service but as an increase in authority for woman. Burnap concluded that marriage improves the female character "not only because it puts her under the best possible tuition, that of the affections, and affords scope to her active energies, but because it gives her higher aims, and a more dignified position."[103] *The Lady's Amaranth* saw it as a balance of power: "The man bears rule over his wife's person and conduct. She bears rule over his inclinations: he governs by law; she by persuasion. . . . The empire of the woman is an empire of softness . . . her commands are caresses, her menaces are tears."[104]

[99] Horace Greeley even went so far as to apply this remedy to the "dissatisfactions" of Margaret Fuller. In his autobiography, *Recollections of a Busy Life* (New York, 1868), he says that "noble and great as she was, a good husband and two or three bouncing babies would have emancipated her from a deal of cant and nonsense" (p. 178).

[100] *Sphere and Duties of Woman*, p. 64.

[101] *A Sermon: Preached March 13, 1808, for the Benefit of the Society Instituted in the City of New-York, for the Relief of Poor Widows with Small Children* (New York, 1808), pp. 13, 14.

[102] *Lady's Magazine and Museum: A Family Journal* (London), IV (Jan. 1831), 6. This magazine is included partly because its editorials proclaimed it "of interest to the English-speaking lady at home and abroad" and partly because it shows that the preoccupation with True Womanhood was by no means confined to the United States.

[103] *Sphere and Duties of Woman*, p. 102.

[104] "Matrimony," *Lady's Amaranth*, II (Dec. 1839), 271.

Woman should marry, but not for money. She should choose only the high road of true love and not truckle to the values of a materialistic society. A story, "Marrying for Money" (subtlety was not the strong point of the ladies' magazines), depicts Gertrude, the heroine, ruing the day she made her crass choice: "It is a terrible thing to live without love. . . . A woman who dares marry for aught but the purest affection, calls down the just judgments of heaven upon her head."[105]

The corollary to marriage, with or without true love, was motherhood, which added another dimension to her usefulness and her prestige. It also anchored her even more firmly to the home. "My Friend," wrote Mrs. Sigourney, "if in becoming a mother, you have reached the climax of your happiness, you have also taken a higher place in the scale of being . . . you have gained an increase of power."[106] The Rev. J. N. Danforth pleaded in *The Ladies' Casket*, "Oh, mother, acquit thyself well in thy humble sphere, for thou mayest affect the world."[107] A true woman naturally loved her children; to suggest otherwise was monstrous.[108]

America depended upon her mothers to raise up a whole generation of Christian statesmen who could say "all that I am I owe to my angel mother."[109] The mothers must do the inculcating of virtue since the fathers, alas, were too busy chasing the dollar. Or as *The Ladies' Companion* put it more effusively, the father "weary with the heat and burden of life's summer day, or trampling with unwilling foot the decaying leaves of life's autumn, has forgotten the sympathies of life's joyous springtime. . . . The acquisition of wealth, the advancement of his children in worldly honor—these are his self-imposed tasks." It was his wife who formed "the infant mind as yet untainted by contact with evil . . . like wax beneath the plastic hand of the mother."[110]

[105] Elizabeth Doten, "Marrying for Money," *The Lily of the Valley*, n. v. (1857), p. 112.

[106] *Letters to Mothers*, p. 9.

[107] "Maternal Relation," *Ladies' Casket* (New York, 1850?), p. 85. The importance of the mother's role was emphasized abroad as well as in America. *Godey's* recommended the book by the French author Aimée-Martin on the education of mothers to "be read five times," in the original if possible (XIII, Dec. 1842, 201). In this book the highest ideals of True Womanhood are upheld. For example: "Jeunes filles, jeunes épouses, tendres mères, c'est dans votre âme bien plus que dans les lois du législateur que reposent aujourd'hui l'avenir de l'Europe et les destinées du genre humain," L. Aimée-Martin, *De l'Education des mères de famille ou de la civilisation du genre humain par les femmes* (Bruxelles, 1857), II, 527.

[108] *Maternal Association of the Amity Baptist Church:* Annual Report (New York, 1847), p. 2: "Suffer the little children to come unto me and forbid them not, is and must ever be a sacred commandment to the Christian woman."

[109] For example, Daniel Webster, "The Influence of Woman," in *The Young Ladies' Reader* (Philadelphia, 1851), p. 310.

[110] Mrs. Emma C. Embury, "Female Education," *Ladies' Companion*, VIII (Jan. 1838), 18. Mrs. Embury stressed the fact that the American woman was not the "mere plaything of passion" but was in strict training to be "the mother of statesmen."

*The Ladies' Wreath* offered a fifty-dollar prize to the woman who submitted the most convincing essay on "How May an American Woman Best Show Her Patriotism." The winner was Miss Elizabeth Wetherell, who provided herself with a husband in her answer. The wife in the essay of course asked her husband's opinion. He tried a few jokes first—"Call her eldest son George Washington," "Don't speak French, speak American"—but then got down to telling her in sober prize-winning truth what women could do for their country. Voting was no asset, since that would result only in "a vast increase of confusion and expense without in the smallest degree affecting the result." Besides, continued this oracle, "looking down at their child," if "we were to go a step further and let the children vote, their first act would be to vote their mothers at home." There is no comment on this devastating male logic and he continues: "Most women would follow the lead of their fathers and husbands, and the few who would fly off on a tangent from the circle of home influence would cancel each other out."

The wife responds dutifully: "I see all that. I never understood so well before." Encouraged by her quick womanly perception, the master of the house resolves the question—an American woman best shows her patriotism by staying at home, where she brings her influence to bear "upon the right side for the country's weal." That woman will instinctively choose the side of right he has no doubt. Besides her "natural refinement and closeness to God" she has the "blessed advantage of a quiet life," while man is exposed to conflict and evil. She stays home with "her Bible and a well-balanced mind" and raises her sons to be good Americans. The judges rejoiced in this conclusion and paid the prize money cheerfully, remarking "they deemed it cheap at the price."[111]

If any woman asked for greater scope for her gifts the magazines were sharply critical. Such women were tampering with society, undermining civilization. Mary Wollstonecraft, Frances Wright and Harriet Martineau were condemned in the strongest possible language—they were read out of the sex. "They are only semi-women, mental hermaphrodites." The Rev. Harrington knew the women of America could not possibly approve of such perversions and went to some wives and mothers to ask if they did want a "wider sphere of interest" as these nonwomen claimed. The answer was reassuring. " 'NO!' they cried simultaneously. 'Let the men take care of politics, *we will take care of the children!* " Again female discontent resulted only from a lack of understanding: women were not subservient, they were rather "chosen vessels." Looked at in this light the conclusion was inescapable: "Noble, sublime is the task of the American mother."[112]

111 "How May an American Woman Best Show Her Patriotism?" *Ladies' Wreath*, III (1851), 313. Elizabeth Wetherell was the pen name of Susan Warner, author of *The Wide Wide World* and *Queechy*.

112 Henry F. Harrington, "Female Education," *Ladies' Companion*, IX (1838), 293, and "Influence of Woman—Past and Present," *Ladies' Companion*, XIII (1840), 245.

"Women's Rights" meant one thing to reformers, but quite another to the True Woman. She knew her rights,

> The right to love whom others scorn,
> The right to comfort and to mourn,
> The right to shed new joy on earth,
> The right to feel the soul's high worth,
>
> .     .     .     .     .     .
>
> Such women's rights, and God will bless
> And crown their champions with success.[113]

The American woman had her choice—she could define her rights in the way of the women's magazines and insure them by the practice of the requisite virtues, or she could go outside the home, seeking other rewards than love. It was a decision on which, she was told, everything in her world depended. "Yours it is to determine," the Rev. Mr. Stearns solemnly warned from the pulpit, "whether the beautiful order of society . . . shall continue as it has been" or whether "society shall break up and become a chaos of disjointed and unsightly elements."[114] If she chose to listen to other voices than those of her proper mentors, sought other rooms than those of her home, she lost both her happiness and her power —"that almost magic power, which, in her proper sphere, she now wields over the destinies of the world."[115]

But even while the women's magazines and related literature encouraged this ideal of the perfect woman, forces were at work in the nineteenth century which impelled woman herself to change, to play a more creative role in society. The movements for social reform, westward migration, missionary activity, utopian communities, industrialism, the Civil War—all called forth responses from woman which differed from those she was trained to believe were hers by nature and divine decree. The very perfection of True Womanhood, moreover, carried within itself the seeds of its own destruction. For if woman was so very little less than the angels, she should surely take a more active part in running the world, especially since men were making such a hash of things.

Real women often felt they did not live up to the ideal of True Womanhood: some of them blamed themselves, some challenged the standard, some tried to keep the virtues and enlarge the scope of womanhood.[116] Somehow through this mixture of challenge and acceptance, of change and continuity, the True Woman evolved into the New Woman— a transformation as startling in its way as the abolition of slavery or the coming of the machine age. And yet the stereotype, the "mystique" if

---

[113] Mrs. E. Little, "What Are the Rights of Women?" *Ladies' Wreath*, II (1848–49), 133.

[114] *Female Influence*, p. 18.

[115] *Ibid.*, p. 23.

[116] Even the women reformers were prone to use domestic images, i.e. "sweep Uncle Sam's kitchen clean" and "tidy up our country's house."

you will, of what woman was and ought to be persisted, bringing guilt and confusion in the midst of opportunity.[117]

The women's magazines and related literature had feared this very dislocation of values and blurring of roles. By careful manipulation and interpretation they sought to convince woman that she had the best of both worlds—power and virtue—and that a stable order of society depended upon her maintaining her traditional place in it. To that end she was identified with everything that was beautiful and holy.

"Who Can Find a Valiant Woman?" was asked frequently from the pulpit and the editorial pages. There was only one place to look for her —at home. Clearly and confidently these authorities proclaimed the True Woman of the nineteenth century to be the Valiant Woman of the Bible, in whom the heart of her husband rejoiced and whose price was above rubies.

---

[117] The "Animus and Anima" of Jung amounts almost to a catalogue of the nineteenth-century masculine and female traits, and the female hysterics whom Freud saw had much of the same training as the nineteenth-century American woman. Betty Friedan, *The Feminine Mystique* (New York, 1963), challenges the whole concept of True Womanhood as it hampers the "fulfillment" of the twentieth-century woman.

# Through the Prism
# of Folklore:
# The Black Ethos in Slavery

## STERLING STUCKEY

When African slaves were first brought to the New World, the circumstances of their new life worked powerfully to destroy their cultural heritage. Members of the same political groups were separated, use of an African language was forbidden, and blacks were discouraged from continuing their religious practices. Since most African religions were linked with a specific land area where the ancestors of the people were buried, these religions would not have traveled well in any case. Unlike blacks in the Caribbean and in Brazil, who were able to preserve certain aspects of African culture because of the enormous concentrations of slaves from the same African regions, blacks in the United States were effectively cut off from most of their past.

It does not necessarily follow, however, that American blacks were left with no cultural and intellectual resources with which to form a new culture. Nor does the fact that they left few written records of their past imply that their inner lives suffered from lack of substance. In recent years, historians and anthropologists have vehemently disagreed over the extent to which Africanisms survived among American blacks and over the impact of African culture on the United States, especially the South. In addition, the emphasis of some historians on the passivity and the childlike qualities often attributed to the slaves has given rise to an impassioned controversy over the slave personality. These and other debates centering on the experience of slavery have aroused a greater interest than ever before in exploring the cultural and intellectual life of the slaves, and historians are now probing into a substantial body of source material that until quite recently was almost exclusively utilized by anthropologists. Apart from the descriptions of slave life provided by white observers, both sympathetic and hostile, the slaves themselves left a mass of illuminating material, including several hundred narratives composed by fugitive slaves, the religious and secular slave songs (primarily spirituals and work songs), and a large body of folktales.

The spirituals, particularly, provide significant insights into the developing intellectual life of the American bondsmen. After the

beginning of the Second Great Awakening at the turn of the nineteenth century, revivalist churches, chiefly Baptist and Methodist,
began to seek actively the conversion of the slaves. In this they
sometimes had the support of slaveowners who were genuinely concerned for the spiritual welfare of their slaves or who were convinced
that Christianity would increase the slaves' passivity. Other, perhaps
more perceptive masters recognized the revolutionary potential of a
religion that proclaimed all men equal before God, and they prohibited their slaves from participating in religious services of any
kind. During the nineteenth century, what has been called the "in-
visible church" grew up among the slaves, who were taking the ideas
of Christianity but altering them in subtle ways to make them their
own. It was this church that produced many of the spirituals and that
inspired such rebels as Nat Turner, who drew his imagery of wrath
and judgment from the Bible.

In the essay that follows, Sterling Stuckey, a historian associated
with the Institute of the Black World in Atlanta, provides a sensitive
introduction to the "ethos" of the slaves, basing his analysis on the
oral tradition, both songs and tales, that grew up among American
blacks. In the process, he gives a clear indication of the richness of
the life to be uncovered through the use of this kind of source
material.

---

It is not excessive to advance the view that some historians, because they
have been so preoccupied with demonstrating the absence of significant
slave revolts, conspiracies, and "day to day" resistance among slaves, have
presented information on slave behavior and thought which is incomplete
indeed. They have, in short, devoted very little attention to trying to get
"inside" slaves to discover what bondsmen thought about their condition.
Small wonder we have been saddled with so many stereotypical treatments
of slave thought and behavior.[1]

Though we do not know enough about the institution of slavery or
the slave experience to state with great precision how slaves felt about

[1] Historians who have provided stereotypical treatments of slave thought and personality are Ulrich B. Phillips, *American Negro Slavery* (New York, 1918); Samuel
Eliot Morison, and Henry Steele Commager, *The Growth of the American Republic* (New York, 1950); and Stanley Elkins, *Slavery: A Problem in American
Institutional and Intellectual Life* (Chicago, 1959).

their condition, it is reasonably clear that slavery, however draconic and well supervised, was not the hermetically sealed monolith—destructive to the majority of slave personalities—that some historians would have us believe. The works of Herbert Aptheker, Kenneth Stampp, Richard Wade, and the Bauers, allowing for differences in approach and purpose, indicate that slavery, despite its brutality, was not so "closed" that it robbed most of the slaves of their humanity.[2]

It should, nevertheless, be asserted at the outset that blacks could not have survived the grim experience of slavery unscathed. Those historians who, for example, point to the dependency complex which slavery engendered in many Afro-Americans, offer us an important insight into one of the most harmful effects of that institution upon its victims. That slavery caused not a few bondsmen to question their worth as human beings—this much, I believe, we can posit with certitude. We can also safely assume that such self-doubt would rend one's sense of humanity, establishing an uneasy balance between affirming and negating aspects of one's being. What is at issue is not whether American slavery was harmful to slaves but whether, in their struggle to control self-lacerating tendencies, the scales were tipped toward a despair so consuming that most slaves, in time, became reduced to the level of "Sambos."[3]

My thesis, which rests on an examination of folk songs and tales, is that slaves were able to fashion a life style and set of values—an ethos—which prevented them from being imprisoned altogether by the definitions which the larger society sought to impose. This ethos was an amalgam of Africanisms and NewWorld elements which helped slaves, in Guy Johnson's words, "feel their way along the course of American slavery, enabling them to endure. . . ."[4] As Sterling Brown, that wise student of Afro-American culture, has remarked, the values expressed in folklore acted as a "wellspring to which slaves" trapped in the wasteland of American slavery "could return in times of doubt to be refreshed."[5] In short, I shall contend that the process of dehumanization was not nearly as pervasive as Stanley Elkins would have us believe; that a very large number

[2] See Herbert Aptheker, *American Negro Slave Revolts;* Kenneth M. Stampp, *The Peculiar Institution* (New York, 1956); Richard Wade, *Slavery in the Cities* (New York, 1964); and Alice and Raymond Bauer, "Day to Day Resistance to Slavery," *Journal of Negro History,* XXVII, No. 4 (October, 1942).

[3] I am here concerned with the Stanley Elkins version of "Sambo," that is, the inference that the overwhelming majority of slaves, as a result of their struggle to survive under the brutal system of American slavery, became so callous and indifferent to their status that they gave survival primacy over all other considerations. See Chapters III through VI of *Slavery* for a discussion of the process by which blacks allegedly were reduced to the "good humor of everlasting childhood" (p. 132).

[4] I am indebted to Guy Johnson of the University of North Carolina for suggesting the use of the term "ethos" in this piece, and for helpful commentary on the original paper which was read before the Association for the Study of Negro Life and History at Greensboro, North Carolina, on October 13, 1967.

[5] Professor Brown made this remark in a paper delivered before The Amistad Society in Chicago, Spring, 1964. Distinguished poet, literary critic, folklorist, and teacher, Brown has long contended that an awareness of Negro folklore is essential to an understanding of slave personality and thought.

of slaves, guided by this ethos, were able to maintain their essential humanity. I make this contention because folklore, in its natural setting, is of, by, and for those who create and respond to it, depending for its survival upon the accuracy with which it speaks to needs and reflects sentiments. I therefore consider it safe to assume that the attitudes of a very large number of slaves are represented by the themes of folklore.[6]

Frederick Douglass, commenting on slave songs, remarked his utter astonishment, on coming to the North, "to find persons who could speak of the singing among slaves as evidence of their contentment and happiness."[7] The young DuBois, among the first knowledgeable critics of the spirituals, found white Americans as late as 1903 still telling Afro-Americans that "life was joyous to the black slave, careless and happy." "I can easily believe this of some," he wrote, "of many. But not all the past South, though it rose from the dead, can gainsay the heart-touching witness of these songs."

> They are the music of an unhappy people, of the children of disappointment; they tell of death and suffering and unvoiced longing toward a truer world, of misty wanderings and hidden ways.[8]

Though few historians have been interested in such wanderings and ways, Frederick Douglass, probably referring to the spirituals, said the songs of slaves represented the sorrows of the slave's heart, serving to relieve the slave "only as an aching heart is relieved by its tears." "I have often sung," he continued, "to drown my sorrow, but seldom to express my happiness. Crying for joy, and singing for joy, were alike uncommon to me while in the jaws of slavery."[9]

[6] I subscribe to Alan Lomax's observation that folk songs "can be taken as the signposts of persistent patterns of community feeling and can throw light into many dark corners of our past and our present." His view that Afro-American music, despite its regional peculiarities, "expresses the same feelings and speaks the same basic language everywhere" is also accepted as a working principle in this paper. For an extended treatment of these points of view, see Alan Lomax, *Folk Songs of North America* (New York, 1960), Introduction, p. xx. [*Folk Songs of North America* by Alan Lomax, copyright © 1960 by Alan Lomax. © 1960 by Cassell & Co. Ltd. These and subsequent quotations reprinted by permission of Doubleday & Company, Inc., and Cassell & Co. Ltd.]

[7] Frederick Douglass, *Narrative of the Life of Frederick Douglass* (Cambridge, Massachusetts: The Belknap Press, 1960), p. 38. Originally published in 1845.

[8] John Hope Franklin (ed.), *Souls of Black Folk*, in *Three Negro Classics* (New York, 1965), p. 380. Originally published in 1903.

[9] Douglass, *Narrative*, p. 38. Douglass' view adumbrated John and Alan Lomax's theory that the songs of the folk singer are deeply rooted "in his life and have functioned there as enzymes to assist in the digestion of hardship, solitude, violence [and] hunger." John A. and Alan Lomax, *Our Singing Country* (New York: The Macmillan Co., 1941), Preface, p. xiii.

Sterling Brown, who has much to tell us about the poetry and meaning of these songs, has observed: "As the best expression of the slave's deepest thoughts and yearnings, they [the spirituals] speak with convincing finality against the legend of contented slavery."[10] Rejecting the formulation that the spirituals are mainly otherworldly, Brown states that though the creators of the spirituals looked toward heaven and "found their triumphs there, they did not blink their eyes to trouble here." The spirituals, in his view, "never tell of joy in the 'good old days.' . . . The only joy in the spirituals is in dreams of escape."[11]

Rather than being essentially otherworldly, these songs, in Brown's opinion, "tell of this life, or 'rollin' through an unfriendly world!" To substantiate this view, he points to numerous lines from spirituals: "Oh, bye and bye, bye and bye, I'm going to lay down this heavy load"; "My way is cloudy"; "Oh, stand the storm, it won't be long, we'll anchor by and by"; "Lord help me from sinking down"; and "Don't know what my mother wants to stay here fuh, Dis ole world ain't been no friend to huh."[12] To those scholars who "would have us believe that when the Negro sang of freedom, he meant only what the whites meant, namely freedom from sin," Brown rejoins:

> Free individualistic whites on the make in a prospering civilization, nursing the American dream, could well have felt their only bondage to be that of sin, and freedom to be religious salvation. But with the drudgery, the hardships, the auction block, the slave-mart, the shackles, and the lash so literally present in the Negro's experience, it is hard to imagine why for the Negro they would remain figurative. The scholars certainly did not make this clear, but rather take refuge in such dicta as "the slave never contemplated his low condition."[13]

"Are we to believe," asks Brown, "that the slave singing 'I been rebuked, I been scorned, done had a hard time sho's you bawn,' referred to his being outside the true religion?" A reading of additional spirituals indicates that they contained distinctions in meaning which placed them outside the confines of the "true religion." Sometimes, in these songs, we hear slaves relating to divinities on terms more West African than American. The easy intimacy and argumentation, which come out of a West African frame of reference, can be heard in "Hold the Wind."[14]

[10] Sterling Brown, "Negro Folk Expression," *Phylon* (October, 1953), p. 47. [This and subsequent quotations reprinted by permission.]

[11] Brown, "Folk Expression," p. 48.

[12] *Ibid.*, p. 407.

[13] *Ibid.*, p. 48.

[14] Addressing himself to the slave's posture toward God, and the attitudes toward the gods which the slave's African ancestors had, Lomax has written: "The West African lives with his gods on terms of intimacy. He appeals to them, reviles them, tricks them, laughs at their follies. In this spirit the Negro slave humanized the stern religion of his masters by adopting the figures of the Bible as his intimates." Lomax, *Folk Songs of North America*, p. 463.

When I get to heaven, gwine be at ease,
Me and my God *gonna do as we please.*

Gonna chatter with the Father, argue with the Son,
*Tell um 'bout the world I just come from.*[15] (Italics added.)

If there is a tie with heaven in those lines from "Hold the Wind," there is also a clear indication of dislike for the restrictions imposed by slavery. And at least one high heavenly authority might have a few questions to answer. *Tell um 'bout the world I just come from* makes it abundantly clear that some slaves—even when released from the burdens of the world—would keep alive painful memories of their oppression.

If slaves could argue with the son of God, then surely, when on their knees in prayer, they would not hesitate to speak to God of the treatment being received at the hands of their oppressors.

Talk about me much as you please, (2)
Chillun, talk about me much as you please,
Gonna talk about you when I get on my knees.[16]

That slaves could spend time complaining about treatment received from other slaves is conceivable, but that this was their only complaint, or even the principal one, is hardly conceivable. To be sure, there is a certain ambiguity in the use of the word "chillun" in this context. The reference appears to apply to slaveholders.

The spiritual, "Samson," as Vincent Harding has pointed out, probably contained much more (for some slaves) than mere biblical implications. Some who sang these lines from "Samson," Harding suggests, might well have meant tearing down the edifice of slavery. If so, it was the antebellum equivalent of today's "burn baby burn."

He said, "An' if I had-'n my way,"
He said, "An' if I had-'n my way,"
He said, "An' if I had-'n my way,
I'd tear the buildin' down!"

He said, "And now I got my way, (3)
And I'll tear this buildin' down."[17]

Both Harriet Tubman and Frederick Douglass have reported that some of the spirituals carried double meanings. Whether most of the

[15] Quoted from Lomax, *Folk Songs of North America*, p. 475.
[16] Quoted from Brown, Sterling A., Davis, Arthur P., and Lee, Ulysses, *The Negro Caravan* (New York: The Dryden Press, 1941), p. 436. [Brown, Lee and Davis, *The Negro Caravan*, Arno Press Edition 1969. This and subsequent quotations reprinted by permission.]
[17] Vincent Harding, *Black Radicalism in America*. An unpublished work which Dr. Harding recently completed.

slaves who sang those spirituals could decode them is another matter. Harold Courlander has made a persuasive case against widespread understanding of any given "loaded" song,[18] but it seems to me that he fails to recognize sufficiently a further aspect of the subject: slaves, as their folktales make eminently clear, used irony repeatedly, especially with animal stories. Their symbolic world was rich. Indeed, the various masks which many put on were not unrelated to this symbolic process. It seems logical to infer that it would occur to more than a few to seize upon some songs, even though created originally for religious purposes, assign another meaning to certain words, and use these songs for a variety of purposes and situations.

At times slave bards created great poetry as well as great music. One genius among the slaves couched his (and their) desire for freedom in a magnificent line of verse. After God's powerful voice had "Rung through Heaven and down in Hell," he sang, "My dungeon shook and my chains, they fell."[19]

In some spirituals, Alan Lomax has written, Afro-Americans turned sharp irony and "healing laughter" toward heaven, again like their West African ancestors, relating on terms of intimacy with God. In one, the slaves have God engaged in a dialogue with Adam:

> "Stole my apples, I believe."
> "No, marse Lord, I spec it was Eve."
> Of this tale there is no mo'
> Eve et the apple and Adam de co'.[20]

Douglass informs us that slaves also sang ironic seculars about the institution of slavery. He reports having heard them sing: "We raise de wheat, dey gib us de corn; We sift de meal, dey gib us de huss; We peel de meat, dey gib us de skin; An dat's de way dey take us in."[21] Slaves would often stand back and see the tragicomic aspects of their situation, sometimes admiring the swiftness of blacks:

> Run, nigger, run, de patrollers will ketch you,
> Run, nigger, run, it's almost day.

[18] See Harold Courlander, *Negro Folk Music, U.S.A.* (New York: Columbia University Press, 1963), pp. 42, 43. If a great many slaves did not consider Harriet Tubman the "Moses" of her people, it is unlikely that most failed to grasp the relationship between themselves and the Israelites, Egypt and the South, and Pharaoh and slavemasters in such lines as: "Didn't my Lord deliver Daniel / And why not every man"; "Oh Mary don't you weep, don't you moan / Pharaoh's army got drowned / Oh Mary don't you weep"; and "Go down Moses / Way down in Egypt-land / Tell old Pharaoh / To let my people go."

[19] Quoted from Lomax, *Folk Songs of North America*, p. 471.

[20] *Ibid.*, p. 476.

[21] Frederick Douglass, *The Life and Times of Frederick Douglass* (New York: Collier Books, 1962), p. 146. [Copyright © The Crowell-Collier Publishing Company, 1962. Reprinted by permission.]

> Dat nigger run, dat nigger flew; 
> Dat nigger tore his shirt in two.[22]

And there is:

> My ole mistiss promise me 
> W'en she died, she'd set me free, 
> She lived so long dat 'er head got bal' 
> An' she give out'n de notion a-dyin' at all.[23]

In the ante-bellum days, work songs were of crucial import to slaves. As they cleared and cultivated land, piled levees along rivers, piled loads on steamboats, screwed cotton bales into the holds of ships, and cut roads and railroads through forest, mountain, and flat, slaves sang while the white man, armed and standing in the shade, shouted his orders.[24] Through the sense of timing and coordination which characterized work songs well sung, especially by the leaders, slaves sometimes quite literally created works of art. These songs not only militated against injuries but enabled the bondsmen to get difficult jobs done more easily by not having to concentrate on the dead level of their work. "In a very real sense the chants of Negro labor," writes Alan Lomax, "may be considered the most profoundly American of all our folk songs, for they were created by our people as they tore at American rock and earth and reshaped it with their bare hands, while rivers of sweat ran down and darkened the dust."

> Long summer day makes a white man lazy, 
> Long summer day. 
> Long summer day makes a nigger run away, sir, 
> Long summer day.[25]

Other slaves sang lines indicating their distaste for slave labor:

> Ol' massa an' ol' missis, 
> Sittin' in the parlour, 
> Jus' fig'in' an' a-plannin' 
> How to work a nigger harder.[26]

And there are these bitter lines, the meaning of which is clear:

> Missus in the big house, 
> Mammy in the yard,

---

[22] Brown, "Folk Expression," p. 51. 
[23] Brown, *Caravan*, p. 447. 
[24] Lomax, *Folk Songs of North America*, p. 514. 
[25] *Ibid.*, p. 515. 
[26] *Ibid.*, p. 527.

> Missus holdin' her white hands,
> Mammy workin' hard, (3)
> Missus holdin' her white hands,
> Mammy workin' hard.

> Old Marse ridin' all time,
> Niggers workin' round,
> Marse sleepin' day time,
> Niggers diggin' in the ground, (3)
> Marse sleepin' day time,
> Niggers diggin' in the ground.[27]

Courlander tells us that the substance of the work songs "ranges from the humorous to the sad, from the gentle to the biting, and from the tolerant to the unforgiving." The statement in a given song can be metaphoric, tangent or direct, the meaning personal or impersonal. "As throughout Negro singing generally, there is an incidence of social criticism, ridicule, gossip, and protest."[28] Pride in their strength rang with the downward thrust of axe—

> When I was young and in my prime, (hah!)
> Sunk my axe deep every time, (hah!)

Blacks later found their greatest symbol of manhood in John Henry, descendant of Trickster John of slave folk tales:

> A man ain't nothing but a man,
> But before I'll let that steam driver beat me down
> I'll die with my hammer in my hand.[29]

---

[27] Courlander, *Negro Folk Music*, p. 117. [This and subsequent quotations reprinted by permission.]

[28] *Ibid.*, p. 89.

[29] Brown, "Folk Expression," p. 54. Steel-driving John Henry is obviously in the tradition of the axe-wielding blacks of the ante-bellum period. The ballad of John Henry helped spawn John Henry work songs:

> Dis ole hammer—hunh
> Ring like silver—hunh (3)
> Shine like gold, baby—hunh
> Shine like gold—hunh.

> Dis ole hammer—hunh
> Killt John Henry—hunh (3)
> Twon't kill me, baby, hunh
> Twon't kill me.

(Quoted from Brown, "Folk Expression," p. 57.)

Though Frances Kemble, an appreciative and sensitive listener to work songs, felt that "one or two barbaric chants would make the fortune of an opera," she was on one occasion "displeased not a little" by a self-deprecating song, one which "embodied the opinion that 'twenty-six black girls not make mulatto yellow girl,' and as I told them I did not like it, they have since omitted it."[30] What is pivotal here is not the presence of self-laceration in folklore, but its extent and meaning. While folklore contained some self-hatred, on balance it gives no indication whatever that blacks, as a group, liked or were indifferent to slavery, which is the issue.[31]

To be sure, only the most fugitive of songs sung by slaves contained direct attacks upon the system. Two of these were associated with slave rebellions. The first, possibly written by ex-slave Denmark Vesey himself, was sung by slaves on at least one island off the coast of Charleston, S.C., and at meetings convened by Vesey in Charleston. Though obviously not a folk song, it was sung by the folk.

> Hail! all hail! ye Afric clan,
> Hail! ye oppressed, ye Afric band,
> Who toil and sweat in slavery bound
> And when your health and strength are gone
> Are left to hunger and to mourn,
> Let independence be your aim,
> Ever mindful what 'tis worth.
> Pledge your bodies for the prize,
> Pile them even to the skies![32]

The second, a popular song derived from a concrete reality, bears the marks of a conscious authority:

30 Frances Anne Kemble, *Journal of a Residence on a Georgia Plantation, 1838–1839* (New York: Alfred Knopf [1863]), pp. 260–61. Miss Kemble heard slaves use the epithet "nigger": "And I assure you no contemptuous intonation ever equalled the prepotenza [arrogance] of the despotic insolence of this address of these poor wretches to each other." Kemble, *Journal*, p. 281. Here she is on solid ground, but the slaves also used the word with glowing affection, as seen in the "Run, Nigger, Run" secular. At other times they leaned toward self-laceration but refused to go the whole route: "My name's Ran, I wuks in de sand, I'd rather be a nigger dan a po' white man." Brown, "Folk Expression," p. 51. Some blacks also sang, "It takes a long, lean, black-skinned gal, to make a preacher lay his Bible down." Newman I. White, *American Negro Folk Songs* (Cambridge, 1928), p. 411.
31 Elkins, who believes Southern white lore on slavery should be taken seriously, does not subject it to serious scrutiny. For a penetrating—and devastating—analysis of "the richest layers of Southern lore," which, according to Elkins, resulted from "an exquisitely rounded collective creativity," see Sterling A. Brown, "A Century of Negro Portraiture in American Literature," *The Massachusetts Review* (Winter, 1966).
32 Quoted from Archie Epps, "A Negro Separatist Movement," *The Harvard Review*, IV, No. I (Summer–Fall, 1956), p. 75.

> You mought be rich as cream
> And drive you coach and four-horse team,
> But you can't keep de world from moverin' round
> Nor Nat Turner from gainin' ground.
>
> And your name it mought be Caesar sure,
> And got you cannon can shoot a mile or more,
> But you can't keep de world from moverin' round
> Nor Nat Turner from gainin' ground.[33]

The introduction of Denmark Vesey, class leader in the A.M.E. [African Methodist Episcopal] Church, and Nat Turner, slave preacher, serves to remind us that some slaves and ex-slaves were violent as well as humble, impatient as well as patient.

It is also well to recall that the religious David Walker, who had lived close to slavery in North Carolina, and Henry Highland Garnet, ex-slave and Presbyterian minister, produced two of the most inflammatory, vitriolic and doom-bespeaking polemics America has yet seen.[34] There was theological tension here, loudly proclaimed, a tension which emanated from and was perpetuated by American slavery and race prejudice. This dimension of ambiguity must be kept in mind, if for no other reason than to place in bolder relief the possibility that a great many slaves and free Afro-Americans could have interpreted Christianity in a way quite different from white Christians.

Even those songs which seemed most otherworldly, those which expressed profound weariness of spirit and even faith in death, through their unmistakable sadness, were accusatory, and God was not their object. If one accepts as a given that some of these appear to be almost wholly escapist, the indictment is no less real. Thomas Wentworth Higginson came across one—". . . a flower of poetry in that dark soil," he called it.[35]

> I'll walk in de graveyard, I'll walk through de graveyard,
>     To lay dis body down.
> I'll lie in de grave and stretch out my arms,
>     Lay dis body down.

Reflecting on "I'll lie in de grave and stretch out my arms," Higginson said that "never, it seems to me, since man first lived and suffered, was

---

[33] Quoted in William Styron, "This Quiet Dust," *Harper's* (April, 1965), p. 135.

[34] For excerpts from David Walker's *Appeal* and Henry H. Garnet's *Call to Rebellion*, see Herbert Aptheker (ed.), *A Documentary History of the Negro People in the United States*, 2 vols. (New York: Citadel Press, 1965). Originally published in 1951.

[35] Thomas Wentworth Higginson, *Army Life in a Black Regiment* (New York: Collier, 1962), p. 199.

his infinite longing for peace uttered more plaintively than in that line."[36]

There seems to be small doubt that Christianity contributed in large measure to a spirit of patience which militated against open rebellion among the bondsmen. Yet to overemphasize this point leads one to obscure a no less important reality: Christianity, after being reinterpreted and recast by slave bards, also contributed to that spirit of endurance which powered generations of bondsmen, bringing them to that decisive moment when for the first time a real choice was available to scores of thousands of them.

When that moment came, some slaves who were in a position to decide for themselves did so. W. E. B. DuBois re-created their mood and the atmosphere in which they lived.

> There came the slow looming of emancipation. Crowds and armies of the unknown, inscrutable, unfathomable Yankees; cruelty behind and before; rumors of a new slave trade, but slowly, continuously, the wild truth, the bitter truth, the magic truth, came surging through. There was to be a new freedom! And a black nation went tramping after the armies no matter what it suffered; no matter how it was treated, no matter how it died.[37]

The gifted bards, by creating songs with an unmistakable freedom ring, songs which would have been met with swift, brutal repression in the ante-bellum days, probably voiced the sentiments of all but the most degraded and dehumanized. Perhaps not even the incredulous slavemaster could deny the intent of the new lyrics. "In the wake of the Union Army and in the contraband camps," remarked Sterling Brown, "spirituals of freedom sprang up suddenly. . . . Some celebrated the days of Jubilo: 'O Freedom; O Freedom!' and 'Before I'll be a slave, I'll be buried in my grave!' and 'Go home to my lord and be free.'" And there was: " 'No more driver's lash for me. . . . Many thousand go.' "[38]

DuBois brought together the insights of the poet and historian to get inside the slaves:

> There was joy in the South. It rose like perfume—like a prayer. Men stood quivering. Slim dark girls, wild and beautiful with wrinkled hair, wept silently; young women, black, tawny, white and golden, lifted shivering hands, and old and broken mothers, black and gray, raised great voices and shouted to God across the fields, and up to the rocks and the mountains.[39]

Some sang:

> Slavery chain done broke at last, broke at last, broke at last,
> Slavery chain done broke at last,
> Going to praise God till I die.

[36] Ibid.
[37] W. E. B. DuBois, Black Reconstruction (Philadelphia: Albert Saifer [1943]), p. 122. Originally published in 1935 by Harcourt, Brace and Company.
[38] Brown, "Folk Expression," p. 49.
[39] DuBois, Reconstruction, p. 124.

I did tell him how I suffer,
In de dungeon and de chain,
*And de days I went with head bowed down,*
And my broken flesh and pain,
Slavery chain done broke at last, broke at last, broke at last.[40]

Whatever the nature of the shocks generated by the war, among those vibrations felt were some that had come from Afro-American singing ever since the first Africans were forcibly brought to these shores. DuBois was correct when he said that the new freedom song had not come from Africa, but that "the dark throb and beat of that Ancient of Days was in and through it."[41] Thus, the psyches of those who gave rise to and provided widespread support for folk songs had not been reduced to *tabula rasas* on which a slave-holding society could at pleasure sketch out its wish fulfillment fantasies.

We have already seen the acute degree to which some slaves realized they were being exploited. Their sense of the injustice of slavery made it so much easier for them to act out their aggression against whites (by engaging in various forms of "day to day" resistance) without being overcome by a sense of guilt, or a feeling of being ill-mannered. To call this nihilistic thrashing about would be as erroneous as to refer to their use of folklore as esthetic thrashing about.[42] For if they did not regard them-

---

[40] Quoted in Brown, *Caravan*, pp. 440–41. One of the most tragic scenes of the Civil War period occurred when a group of Sea Island freedmen, told by a brigadier-general that they would not receive land from the government, sang, "Nobody knows the trouble I've seen." DuBois, *Souls*, p. 381.

[41] DuBois, *Reconstruction*, p. 124.

[42] If some slavemasters encouraged slaves to steal or simply winked at thefts, then slaves who obliged them were most assuredly *not acting against their own interests,* whatever the motivation of the masters. Had more fruitful options been available to them, then and only then could we say that slaves were playing into the hands of their masters. Whatever the masters thought of slaves who stole from them—and there is little reason to doubt that most slaves considered it almost obligatory to steal from white people—the slaves, it is reasonable to assume, were aware of the unparalleled looting in which masters themselves were engaged. To speak therefore of slaves undermining their sense of self-respect as a result of stealing from whites—and this argument has been advanced by Eugene Genovese—is wide of the mark. Indeed, it appears more likely that those who engaged in stealing were, in the context of an oppressor-oppressed situation, on the way to realizing a larger measure of self-respect. Moreover, Genovese, in charging that certain forms of "day to day" resistance, in the absence of general conditions of rebellion, "amounted to individual and essentially nihilistic thrashing about," fails to recognize that that which was possible, that which conditions permitted, was pursued by slaves in preference to the path which led to passivity or annihilation. Those engaging in "day to day" resistance were moving along meaningful rather than nihilistic lines, for their activities were designed to frustrate the demands of the authority-system. For a very suggestive discussion of the dependency complex engendered by slavery and highly provocative views on the significance of "day to day" resistance among slaves, see Eugene Genovese, "The Legacy of Slavery and the Roots of Black Nationalism," *Studies on the Left,* VI, No. 6 (Nov.–Dec., 1966), especially **p. 8.**

selves as the equals of whites in many ways, their folklore indicates that the generality of slaves must have at least felt superior to whites morally. And that, in the context of oppression, could make the difference between a viable human spirit and one crippled by the belief that the interests of the master are those of the slave.

When it is borne in mind that slaves created a large number of extraordinary songs and greatly improved a considerable proportion of the songs of others, it is not at all difficult to believe that they were conscious of the fact that they were leaders in the vital area of art—giving protagonists rather than receiving pawns. And there is some evidence that slaves were aware of the special talent which they brought to music. Higginson has described how reluctantly they sang from hymnals—"even on Sunday"—and how "gladly" they yielded "to the more potent excitement of their own 'spirituals.' "[43] It is highly unlikely that the slaves' preference for their own music went unremarked among them, or that this preference did not affect their estimate of themselves. "They soon found," commented Alan Lomax, "that when they sang, the whites recognized their superiority as singers, and listened with respect."[44] He might have added that those ante-bellum whites who listened probably seldom understood.

What is of pivotal import, however, is that the esthetic realm was the one area in which slaves knew they were not inferior to whites. Small wonder that they borrowed many songs from the larger community, then quickly invested them with their own economy of statement and power of imagery rather than yield to the temptation of merely repeating what they had heard. Since they were essentially group rather than solo performances, the values inherent in and given affirmation by the music served to strengthen bondsmen in a way that solo music could not have done.[45] In a word, slave singing often provided a form

[43] Higginson, *Black Regiment*, p. 212. Alan Lomax reminds us that the slaves sang "in leader-chorus style, with a more relaxed throat than the whites and in deeper-pitched, mellower voices, which blended richly." "A strong, surging beat underlay most of their American creations . . . words and tunes were intimately and playfully united, and 'sense' was often subordinated to the demands of rhythm and melody." Lomax, *Folk Songs of North America*, Introduction, p. xx.

[44] Lomax, *Folk Songs*, p. 460.

[45] Commenting on the group nature of much of slave singing, Alan Lomax points out that the majority of the bondsmen "came from West Africa, where music-making was largely a group activity, the creation of a many-voiced, dancing throng. . . . Community songs of labour and worship [in America] and dance songs far outnumbered narrative pieces, and the emotion of the songs was, on the whole, joyfully erotic, deeply tragic, allusive, playful, or ironic rather than nostalgic, withdrawn, factual, or aggressively comic—as among white folk singers." Lomax, *Folk Songs*, pp. xix and xx of Introduction. For treatments of the more technical aspects of Afro-American music, see Courlander, *Negro Folk Music*, especially Chapter II; and Richard A. Waterman, "African Influences on the Music of the Americas," in *Acculturation in the Americas*, edited by Sol Tax.

of group therapy, a way in which a slave, in concert with others, could fend off some of the debilitating effects of slavery.

The field of inquiry would hardly be complete without some mention of slave tales. Rich in quantity and often subtle in conception, these tales further illumine the inner world of the bondsmen, disclosing moods and interests almost as various as those found in folk songs. That folk tales, like the songs, indicate an African presence, should not astonish; for the telling of tales, closely related to the African griot's vocation of providing oral histories of families and dynasties, was deeply rooted in West African tradition. Hughes and Bontemps have written that the slaves brought to America the "habit of storytelling as pastime, together with a rich bestiary." Moreover, they point out that the folk tales of slaves "were actually projections of personal experiences and hopes and defeats, in terms of symbols," and that this important dimension of the tales "appears to have gone unnoticed."[46]

Possessing a repertoire which ranged over a great many areas, perhaps the most memorable tales are those of Brer Rabbit and John.[47] Brer Rabbit, now trickster, ladies' man, and braggart, now wit, joker, and glutton, possessed the resourcefulness, despite his size and lack of strength, to outsmart stronger, larger animals. "To the slave in his condition," according to Hughes and Bontemps, "the theme of weakness overcoming strength through cunning proved endlessly fascinating."[48] John, characterized by a spiritual resilience born of an ironic sense of life, was a secular high priest of mischief and guile who delighted in matching wits with Ole Marster, the "patterollers," Ole Missy, and the devil himself. He was clever enough to sense the absurdity of his predicament and that of white people, smart enough to know the limits of his powers and the boundaries of those of the master class. While not always victorious, even on the spacious plane of the imagination, he could hardly be described as a slave with an inferiority complex. And

---

[46] Arna Bontemps and Langston Hughes (eds.), *The Book of Negro Folklore* (New York: Dodd, Mead & Company, 1965), Introduction, p. viii. Of course if one regards each humorous thrust of the bondsmen as so much comic nonsense, then there is no basis for understanding, to use Sterling Brown's phrase, the slave's "laughter out of hell." Without understanding what humor meant to slaves themselves, one is not likely to rise above the superficiality of a Stephen Foster or a Joel Chandler Harris. But once an effort has been made to see the world from the slave's point of view, then perhaps one can understand Ralph Ellison's reference to Afro-Americans, in their folklore, "backing away from the chaos of experience and from ourselves," in order to "depict the humor as well as the horror of our living." Ralph Ellison, "A Very Stern Discipline," *Harper's* (March, 1967), p. 80.

[47] For additional discussions of folk tales, see Zora Neale Hurston, *Mules and Men* (Philadelphia: J. B. Lippincott, 1935); Richard Dorson, *American Negro Folktales* (Greenwich, Connecticut: Fawcett, 1967); and B. A. Botkin, *Lay My Burden Down* (Chicago: University of Chicago Press, 1945).

[48] Bontemps and Hughes, *Negro Folklore*, Introduction, p. ix.

in this regard it is important to note that his varieties of triumphs, though they sometimes included winning freedom, often realistically cluster about ways of coping with everyday negatives of the system.[49]

Slaves were adept in the art of storytelling, as at home in this area as they were in the field of music. But further discussion of the scope of folklore would be uneconomical, for we have already seen a depth and variety of thought among bondsmen which embarrasses stereotypical theories of slave personality. Moreover, it should be clear by now that there are no secure grounds on which to erect the old, painfully constricted "Sambo" structure.[50] For the personalities which lay beneath the plastic exteriors which slaves turned on and off for white people were too manifold to be contained by cheerful, childlike images. When it is argued, then, that "too much of the Negro's own lore" has gone into the making of the Sambo picture "to entitle one in good conscience to condemn it as 'conspiracy,' "[51] one must rejoin: Only if you strip the masks from black faces while refusing to read the irony and ambiguity and cunning which called the masks into existence. Slave folklore, on balance, decisively repudiates the thesis that Negroes *as a group* had internalized "Sambo" traits, committing them, as it were, to psychological marriage.

It is one of the curiosities of American historiography that a people who were as productive esthetically as American slaves could be studied as if they had moved in a cultural cyclotron, continually bombarded by devastating, atomizing forces which denuded them of meaningful African-isms while destroying any and all impulses toward creativity. One his-torian, for example, has been tempted to wonder how it was ever possible that "*all* this [West African] native resourcefulness and vitality have

[49] The fact that slaveowners sometimes took pleasure in being outwitted by slaves in no way diminishes from the importance of the trickster tales, for what is essential here is how these tales affected the slave's attitude toward himself, not whether his thinking or behavior would impress a society which considered black people little better than animals. DuBois' words in this regard should never be forgotten: "Everything Negroes did was wrong. If they fought for freedom, they were beasts; if they did not fight, they were born slaves. If they cowered on the planta-tion, they loved slavery; if they ran away, they were lazy loafers. If they sang, they were silly; if they scowled, they were impudent. . . . And they were funny, funny—ridiculous baboons, aping men." DuBois, *Reconstruction*, p. 125.

[50] Ralph Ellison offers illuminating insight into the group experience of the slave: "Any people who could endure all of that brutalization and keep together, who could undergo such dismemberment and resuscitate itself, and endure until it could take the initiative in achieving its own freedom is obviously more than the sum of its brutalization. Seen in this perspective, theirs has been one of the great human experiences and one of the great triumphs of the human spirit in modern times, in fact, in the history of the world." Ellison, "A Very Stern Discipline," p. 84.

[51] Elkins sets forth this argument in *Slavery*, p. 84.

been brought to such a point of *utter* stultification in America."[52] (Italics added.) This sadly misguided view is, of course, not grounded in any recognition or understanding of the Afro-American dimension of American culture. In any event, there is a great need for students of American slavery to attempt what Gilberto Freyre tried to do for Brazilian civilization—an effort at discovering the contributions of slaves toward the shaping of the Brazilian national character.[53] When such a study has been made of the American slave we shall probably discover that, though he did not rival his Brazilian brother in staging bloody revolutions, the quality and place of art in his life compared favorably. Now this suggests that the humanity of people can be asserted through means other than open and widespread rebellion, a consideration that has not been appreciated in violence-prone America. We would do well to recall the words of F. S. C. Northrop, who has observed:

> During the pre–Civil War period shipowners and southern landowners brought to the United States a considerable body of people with a color of skin and cultural values different from those of its other inhabitants. . . . Their values are more emotive, esthetic and intuitive. . . . [These] characteristics can become an asset for our culture. For these are values with respect to which Anglo-American culture is weak.[54]

These values were expressed on the highest level in the folklore of slaves. Through their folklore black slaves affirmed their humanity and left a lasting imprint on American culture. No study of the institutional aspects of American slavery can be complete, nor can the larger dimensions of slave personality and style be adequately explored, as long as historians continue to avoid that realm in which, as DuBois has said, "the soul of the black slave spoke to man."[55]

In its nearly two and one-half centuries of existence, the grim system of American slavery doubtless broke the spirits of uncounted numbers of slaves. Nevertheless, if we look through the prism of folklore, we can see others transcending their plight, appreciating the tragic irony of their condition, then seizing upon and putting to use those aspects of their experience which sustain in the present and renew in the future. We can see them opposing their own angle of vision to that of their oppressor,

[52] *Ibid.*, p. 93.

[53] Gilberto Freyre, *The Masters and the Slaves* (New York: Alfred A. Knopf, 1956). Originally published by Jose Olympio, Rio de Janeiro, Brazil.

[54] F. S. C. Northrop, *The Meeting of East and West* (New York: The Macmillan Co., 1952), pp. 159–60.

[55] DuBois, *Souls*, p. 378. Kenneth M. Stampp, in his *The Peculiar Institution* (New York: Alfred A. Knopf, 1956), employs to a limited extent some of the materials of slave folklore. Willie Lee Rose, in *Rehearsal for Reconstruction* (New York: The Bobbs-Merrill Company, 1964), makes brief but highly informed use of folk material.

fashioning their own techniques of defense and aggression in accordance with their own reading of reality and doing those things well enough to avoid having their sense of humanity destroyed.

Slave folklore, then, affirms the existence of a large number of vital, tough-minded human beings who, though severely limited and abused by slavery, had found a way both to endure and preserve their humanity in the face of insuperable odds. What they learned about handling misfortune was not only a major factor in their survival as a people, but many of the lessons learned and esthetic standards established would be used by future generations of Afro-Americans in coping with a hostile world. What a splendid affirmation of the hopes and dreams of their slave ancestors that some of the songs being sung in ante-bellum days are the ones Afro-Americans are singing in the freedom movement today: "Michael, row the boat ashore"; "Just like a tree planted by the water, I shall not be moved."

# Suggestions for Further Reading

An excellent introduction to the experiments in social reform that swept America in the first half of the nineteenth century is Alice Felt Tyler, *Freedom's Ferment: Phases of American Social History from the Colonial Period to the Outbreak of the Civil War*\* (University of Minnesota Press, 1944). The religious revivals that flourished in New York State during the same period are treated in W. R. Cross, *The Burned-Over District*\* (Cornell University Press, 1950). Early experiments in communal living are described in A. E. Bestor, Jr., *Backwoods Utopias: The Sectarian and Owenite Phases of Communitarian Socialism in America, 1663–1829* (University of Pennsylvania Press, 1950).

A growing awareness of poverty in ante-bellum America is described in the first part of R. H. Bremmer's *From the Depths: The Discovery of Poverty in the United States*\* (New York University Press, 1956). Norman J. Ware considers the changing condition of the laborer in the years just before the Civil War in *The Industrial Worker, 1840–1860*\* (Houghton-Mifflin, 1924). The problems of blacks in the free states before the war are described in Leon F. Litwack, *North of Slavery: The Negro in the Free States, 1790–1860*\* (University of Chicago Press, 1961). The reputation of the much maligned abolitionists is defended in Martin Duberman (ed.), *The Anti-Slavery Vanguard*\* (Princeton University Press, 1965).

A general introduction to the history of immigration in the United States is M. A. Jones, *American Immigration*\* (University of Chicago Press, 1960). On ante-bellum immigration in particular, the standard work is Marcus L. Hansen, *The Atlantic Migration, 1607–1860*\* (Harvard University Press, 1940). The conflict between established settlers and Irish immigrants in Boston is discussed in Barbara Miller Solomon, *Ancestors and Immigrants*\* (Harvard University Press, 1956). Ray A. Billington, in *The Protestant Crusade, 1800–1860*\* (Macmillan, 1938), deals more generally with religious conflict in the first half of the nineteenth century. The story of the Irish community in the United States is told by Carl Wittke in *The Irish in America*\* (Louisiana State University Press, 1956). John Higham's *Strangers in the Land: Patterns of American Nativism, 1860–1925*\* (Rutgers University Press, 1955) provides useful insights into nativist sentiment during the ante-bellum years, although it is primarily concerned with a later period.

The current interest in women's liberation will undoubtedly bring forth many books dealing with the condition of women in the period before the Civil War. In the meantime, there is useful

---

\* Available in paperback edition.

information in the relevant portions of several general studies of American women. See, for example, Andrew Sinclair, *The Emancipation of the American Woman** (Harper and Row, 1965), first published under the title *The Better Half;* Eleanor Flexner, *Century of Struggle: The Women's Rights Movement in the United States** (Harvard University Press, 1959); and Robert E. Riegel, *American Feminists** (University of Kansas Press, 1963). A useful collection of documents is Aileen S. Kraditor (ed.), *Up from the Pedestal: Selected Writings in the History of American Feminism** (Quadrangle, 1968). Hannah Josephson examines the plight of women textile workers in *The Golden Threads: New England's Mill Girls and Magnates* (Duell, Sloan and Pearce, 1949). Impressive biographies of leading feminists in the ante-bellum period are Gerda Lerner, *The Grimke Sisters from South Carolina: Rebels Against Slavery* (Houghton-Mifflin, 1967), and *Created Equal: A Biography of Elizabeth Cady Stanton* (Day, 1940) and *Susan B. Anthony: Rebel, Crusader, Humanitarian* (Beacon, 1959), both by Alma Lutz. A study related to the role of women in American society is Bernard Wishy, *The Child and the Republic: The Dawn of Modern American Child Nurture* (University of Pennsylvania Press, 1967). Of special interest to the specialist is E. Leonard, S. Drinker, and M. Holden, *The American Woman in Colonial and Revolutionary Times, 1565–1800: A Syllabus with Bibliography* (University of Pennsylvania Press, 1962).

The history of the ante-bellum South as a distinct region with a distinct subculture is considered thoroughly in three works by Clement Eaton: *A History of the Old South* (2d ed.; Macmillan, 1966); *The Growth of Southern Civilization** (Harper and Row, 1961); and *The Mind of the Old South** (Louisiana State University Press, 1964). A valuable primary source for the ante-bellum South is Frederick Law Olmstead, *The Cotton Kingdom* (2 vols.; Mason, 1861), reissued in abridged form under the title *Slave States Before the Civil War**. The militarism of Southern culture is presented in John Hope Franklin, *The Militant South, 1800–1861** (Harvard University Press, 1956). Important aspects of Reconstruction in the South are explored in the following: Willie Lee Rose, *Rehearsal for Reconstruction: The Port Royal Experiment** (Bobbs-Merrill, 1964); Lerone Bennett, Jr., *Black Power U.S.A.: The Human Side of Reconstruction** (Johnson, 1967); and Robert Cruden, *The Negro in Reconstruction** (Prentice-Hall, 1969).

A number of good books have appeared on slavery in the United States. Some of these are noted in the suggestions for further reading at the close of Section 1 (see p. 101). Of particular interest here are works pertaining to the slaves' formulations of their own experience—the folktales, songs, and narratives that make up the distinctive oral tradition of black America. A brief presentation of the variety of primary source materials available to historians is William F. Cheek (ed.), *Black Resistance Before the Civil War** (Glencoe, 1970). Spirituals are collected in James

Weldon Johnson and J. Rosamond Johnson (eds.), *The Books of American Negro Spirituals** (Viking, 1925, 1926). See also Harold Courlander, *Negro Folk Music U.S.A.* (Columbia University Press, 1963). On the relationship between African and New World religion, see Melville J. Herskovits, *The Myth of the Negro Past** (Harper and Row, 1941). Folktales are collected in Langston Hughes and Arna Bontemps (eds.), *The Book of Negro Folklore** (Dodd, Mead, 1958); Richard Dorson (ed.), *American Negro Folklore** (Fawcett, 1967); and J. Mason Brewer (ed.), *American Negro Folklore* (Quadrangle, 1968). Charles H. Nichols has surveyed and analyzed narratives composed by fugitive slaves in *Many Thousand Gone: The Ex-Slaves' Account of Their Bondage and Freedom** (Brill, 1963). Perhaps the most important of these narratives is the *Narrative of the Life of Frederick Douglass, an American Slave, Written by Himself** (Anti-Slavery Office, 1845). Readily available collections of narratives by former slaves are Gilbert Osofsky (ed.), *Puttin' On Ole Massa: The Slave Narratives of Henry Bibb, William Wells Brown, and Solomon Northrup** (Harper and Row, 1969), and Arna Bontemps (ed.), *Great Slave Narratives** (Beacon, 1969), which presents the narratives of Olaudah Equiano, W. C. Pennington, and William and Ellen Craft. B. A. Botkin (ed.), *Lay My Burden Down: A Folk History of Slavery** (University of Chicago Press, 1945), and Norman R. Yetman (ed.), *Life Under the Peculiar Institution: Selections from the Slave Narrative Collection** (Holt, Rinehart and Winston, 1970), are samplings of narratives collected from former slaves under the auspices of the Federal Writers' Project in the 1930's. Two novels that expertly explore slave attitudes are Arna Bontemps' *Black Thunder** (Macmillan, 1936), the story of Gabriel's rebellion in 1800, and Harold Courlander's *The African** (Crown, 1967), the tale of an African boy who is captured and sold into slavery in the Caribbean and the United States South.

The impact of the Civil War on Southern agriculture is described in Paul W. Gates, *Agriculture and the Civil War* (Knopf, 1965), and in Ralph Andreano (ed.), *The Economic Impact of the American Civil War** (Schenkman, 1962). The South's agricultural problems are placed in perspective in Fred A. Shannon, *The Farmer's Last Frontier: Agriculture, 1860–1897** (Holt, Rinehart and Winston, 1945). Studies of the Afro-American's position in specific states during Reconstruction are Vernon L. Wharton, *The Negro in Mississippi, 1860–1890** (University of North Carolina Press, 1947), and Joel R. Williamson, *After Freedom: The Negro in South Carolina During Reconstruction, 1861–1877** (University of North Carolina Press, 1965).

# Westward
# Expansion

# The Mormon Struggle

# for

# Autonomy

## NORMAN F. FURNISS

Upper New York State was known as the "burned-over district" in the decade before the Civil War because of the large number of religious revivals and new cults that swept across the area. The movement that made the greatest impact on American history was that of the Mormons, members of the Church of Jesus Christ of the Latter-day Saints. This was a sect founded by Joseph Smith, who claimed that an angel appeared to him and showed him where he could find buried tablets of gold bearing miraculous revelations, which Smith was permitted to read by means of special eyeglasses. These revelations, the Book of Mormon, were first printed in 1830, establishing the mission of the Latter-day Saints and granting them exclusive salvation.

In keeping with the communitarian religious ideals of the period, Smith organized his church as a cooperative theocracy with himself at the head, bearing the title of "First Elder." Thus the Mormons were able to avoid what seems to be the central problem in communitarianism—that of authority. The First Elder and his successors claimed divine authority and ruled autocratically in a direct line from God. In a further departure from strict communitarianism, Brigham Young, Smith's immediate successor, devised a judicious mix of private and communal ownership of property. Undoubtedly, this system helped to ensure the subsequent economic development of the Mormon state of Deseret, later incorporated into Utah. In any case, by the time the Civil War broke out, most of the communal religious groups that had flourished in New York and the old Northwest had died or were declining. The Mormons alone gathered size and strength.

As they developed their unique religious system, the Mormons met continued opposition from their non-Mormon neighbors, whom they called gentiles. Harassment of various sorts forced them to move from New York to Ohio, then to Missouri, then to Illinois, and finally to the basin of the Great Salt Lake, an area so isolated and so forbidding that it at least offered them the freedom to live as they chose. After their long migration, they somehow managed to transform the Salt Lake area into a beautiful and rich agricultural center —a feat that ranks among the economic miracles of modern history.

Much of the opposition to the Mormons resulted from three aspects of Mormon belief and practice. First was the select nature of the faith: believers were saved, nonbelievers doomed. Men have never taken lightly revelations of their own damnation, and the gentiles who came in contact with the Mormons resented their claims to exclusive salvation. Second was the authoritarian political organization of the Mormons, which seemed suspiciously un-American in an age of growing democratic sentiment. Third was the practice of polygamy, a clear violation of a taboo observed in American society at large. This was a practical measure for the Mormons because there was a surplus of women in their membership. If men could have more than one wife, all the women could be married and their children could increase the ranks of the church.

In his book on the conflicts between the Mormons and the federal government, the first chapter of which is reprinted here, the late Norman Furniss of Colorado State University points out that opposition to the Mormons contained a strong nativist strain. Clearly, the most important factor in this opposition was the Mormons' decision to maintain themselves apart from the rest of America and to maintain a high degree of autonomy over their affairs.

---

In the summer of 1838 many Missourians found the presence of a large Mormon community in the northwestern corner of their state no longer tolerable. Wholeheartedly sympathetic with this opinion, Governor Lilburn Boggs had informed his militia commander that "the Mormons must be treated as enemies and must be exterminated or driven from the state, if necessary, for the public good." Already the two parties had fought a number of brief skirmishes, among them the Battle of Crooked River, and the outnumbered Latter-day Saints had hastily assembled in their city of Far West to prepare measures of self-defense.

Jacob Haun, an industrious Church member proud of his new flour mill a few miles from the town, refused to retreat, and enough of his brethren joined him to make his position appear secure. Yet on the eve-

"The Mormon Struggle for Autonomy." From Norman F. Furniss, *The Mormon Conflict, 1850–1859* (New Haven, Conn.: Yale University Press, 1960), pp. 1–20. Copyright © 1960 by Yale University Press. Reprinted by permission.

ning of October 30 two hundred militiamen descended upon Haun's mill, drove the Mormons into a nearby blacksmith shop, and there enthusiastically shot many of them through the unchinked walls of the makeshift fortress. When the attackers finally stormed into the building, they spared no one who showed a sign of life. Even nine-year-old Sardius Smith was dispatched with a bullet through the head because one trooper feared that "nits will make lice." At daybreak, of the thirty-eight men and boys who had sought refuge on Jacob Haun's property, seventeen were dead and fifteen wounded.

Although the massacre at Haun's mill was the bloodiest engagement between Mormon and Gentile in the eight years following the establishment of the Church in 1830, it was not the first evidence that the sect would continue to have trouble with hostile neighbors. A few months earlier the young founder of the new faith, Joseph Smith, had led many of his followers to Missouri from Kirtland, Ohio, where the doctrines of his Church and the failure of his "Kirtland Safety Society Bank" had enraged nonbelievers. But if he had expected to erect a New Zion in this frontier state without molestation, he was disappointed. From the days of the earliest Mormon colony in Missouri in 1831 the Gentiles had resented the Saints' claim to a superior religion, feared the political power of their united communities, suspected them of tampering with the Indians, and anticipated their free-soil sympathies. To escape this animosity the Mormons had moved from county to county, seeking freedom in isolation, but the inevitable approach of Gentile settlers had always reawakened hostilities. In retaliation some of the Saints had formed a group to protect the Church against attack both from without and from within. Although the actions, and even the existence, of this fellowship—the mysterious Sons of Dan, or Danites—were concealed in secrecy, Gentiles were sure that it was a terroristic band of murderers dedicated to the destruction of any person who incurred the wrath of the Hierarchy. As the opposition of the Missourians to the Mormons rose in intensity, Joseph Smith finally permitted his people to use their weapons in defense of their homes; but the episode at Haun's mill revealed their hopeless military inferiority.

As overpowering numbers of the militia surrounded Far West, the Prophet, Smith, saw that further resistance would surely destroy many of his followers and might even endanger the very existence of his Church. With other Mormon dignitaries he accordingly surrendered himself to his enemies and promised that his people would leave the state. While the prisoners awaited an uncertain future in jail, the Mormons straggled across the Mississippi River to Illinois, sustained only by their faith and the organizational abilities of Brigham Young, the one important member of the Hierarchy to escape the dragnet in Missouri.

For a few years after their grim experiences with Lilburn Boggs' men, the Latter-day Saints enjoyed a period of peace rare in their early history. Joseph Smith and his fellow prisoners were permitted to escape after the officials of Missouri failed to devise a practicable punishment for them. On a bend in the Mississippi the Church began construction of a new city, Nauvoo, which soon outshone Kirtland, Far West, and the other way-stations on the road to denominational permanence. Both Whigs and Democrats wooed their votes with political favors, principally a city charter granting Nauvoo an impressive measure of self-government in Illinois. With a bodyguard of hardy fighters, among them William Hickman, Porter Rockwell, Hosea Stout, and John D. Lee, Smith feared neither the wrath of unreconciled Missourians nor the depredations of nearer opponents.

Yet by 1844 opinion in Illinois had hardened into the anti-Mormon sentiments so familiar in the past. Rumors that members of the priesthood were indulging in polygamous marriages offended some Gentile sensibilities. Of more importance, neither political party in the state found that it could depend upon Mormon promises of support, a situation which became dramatically apparent in 1844, when Smith announced his own candidacy in the presidential campaign. Furthermore, the occupants of Nauvoo, no longer satisfied with their position of autonomy, had established courts that recognized no superior review, an army of formidable size called the Nauvoo Legion, a powder factory, and other trappings of an independent community. People in nearby Carthage and Warsaw began to frown upon their neighbors and restlessly awaited an excuse to strike at them.

A plausible pretext for attack at last arrived. Early in June 1844 a few apostates established the Nauvoo *Expositor* to broadcast their dissatisfaction with Church leaders, and published an issue condemning the Hierarchy for despotic control and the introduction of polygamy. Believing that his people no longer were compelled to accept criticism meekly, as they had in past crises, Joseph Smith moved with haste to crush this adversary. On the advice of the city officials and such counselors as Almon W. Babbitt and George P. Stiles, he ordered the *Expositor* destroyed as a public nuisance, a judgment his followers promptly executed. Irate Gentiles needed no further incentive to action. On the threat of reducing Nauvoo to ashes they forced Joseph and his brother Hyrum to surrender themselves for imprisonment and trial. Three days later, on June 27, a mob assaulted the Carthage jail where the captives were held. When it disbanded, the body of Joseph, riddled with bullets, lay beneath the window from which he had jumped; Hyrum was dead on the floor of his cell.

Although the lynching of the two men quieted the anger of many rancorous Gentiles, the Mormons' further residence in Illinois was now patently impossible. An uneasy peace prevailed during the next year, but by September 1845 the Church could forestall an onslaught upon Nauvoo only by a public promise to leave the state within a reasonable time. During February 1846 the first Mormons crossed the frozen Mississippi to camp on the Iowa shore in subzero temperatures. Later in the year more than twelve thousand Church members followed them across the river and on over the Iowa hills to temporary settlements near the Missouri. Throughout the exodus, inflamed Gentiles, impatient with the slowness of the evacuation, clashed with remaining Mormons embittered by this new enforced emigration. The final days of the Saints' occupation of Nauvoo were marked by organized warfare, during which the Mormons discovered an effective commander in Daniel Hanmer Wells, a recent convert to the faith. Wells would recall these scenes when, eleven years later, he led the Mormons' resistance to a federal army approaching Utah.

The Church was not blameless in the difficulties that brought about its removal from Ohio, Missouri, and Illinois. Although Governor Boggs had had no valid occasion for his "extermination order," as the Mormons called it, a few months before the issuance of that unfortunate command Sidney Rigdon, close to Joseph Smith in the councils of the sect, had also spoken publicly of a war of annihilation against the Missourians. If Smith received no justice from the Carthage mob, his "trial" of the Nauvoo *Expositor* had likewise been conducted without a jury and in the absence of the defendant. But the Mormons had experienced shameful persecution in their long search for a home, and as they huddled in their quarters on the banks of the Missouri they realized that they would find peace only in an area remote from Gentile neighbors. Texas, California, and Oregon, all sparsely settled in 1846, were nevertheless attractive enough to invite the migration of many American pioneers in this period of Manifest Destiny; but between the Rockies and the Sierra Nevadas, the Mormon leaders knew, lay the basin of the Great Salt Lake, which trappers and explorers had reported inhabitable. If the Zion of the Church could not be built on the green plains of Missouri or the fertile banks of the Mississippi River, the empty reaches of the Far West might provide sanctuary.

Having resolved upon the region of the Great Salt Lake for its next effort at colonization, the Church early in 1847 sent an advance party to make the initial explorations and settlements there. In this trek from the Missouri River the carefully selected vanguard encountered fewer difficulties than the Mormons had faced as they crossed the roadless, rolling hills of Iowa in cold and mud during their flight from the turbulent scenes surrounding Nauvoo. Fur trappers and Oregon-bound farmers had made the route along the shallow Platte River and across the South Pass of the Continental Divide a much-traveled one. It remained for the Mormons only to find their way from Jim Bridger's Fort in what is now southwestern Wyoming to the Salt Lake Valley, and even here they had the benefit of the hapless Donner Party's experiences the year before. The pioneer band, numbering 148 men, women, and children under the capable leadership of Brigham Young, accomplished the journey in a little over three months. During the latter part of July they reached the shores of the Great Salt Lake, where they were joined in subsequent months by the remainder of their brethren.

In addition to the use of a familiar overland road at a favorable season, the Mormons had assistance in their undertaking from the federal government, never quick in other emergencies of the Church to extend comfort. The Polk Administration, then at war with Mexico, saw that in its plan to acquire California it could make use of a people already determined upon a migration to the West. An agent of the sect in Washington had indeed pressed this consideration upon the President. Accordingly the Mormons received a call for volunteers during their march across Iowa in 1846, and Brigham Young hastily accepted. In this way the Church obtained two fortuitous blessings from the Mexican War: some 300 members were transported to the West Coast at public expense, and the pay these men earned for their services helped to stabilize the group's shaky finances at a critical time. Only in later years, when the Church endeavored to increase the devotion of its members by reminding them of their past martyrdoms, did Young and his colleagues refer to the raising of the Mormon Battalion as another attempt by evil men to dragoon the Saints.

Safely arrived in Salt Lake Valley, the Mormons had no difficulty establishing a framework of government. The organization of the Church provided for authoritarian leadership from the First Presidency, composed of Young as president and his two counselors, the flamboyant Heber Chase Kimball and the quiet, erudite physician Willard Richards, who had miraculously escaped death in Carthage jail. Only a little inferior to this body was the Council or Quorum of the Twelve Apostles. During the early months of the colony's existence, these officers functioned as executive, legislative, and judiciary. When the system was altered at the end of 1847, the identification of church and state persisted, the Hierarchy retaining general supervision of all affairs but delegating the direct government of the people to officials of the "stake," a name given large territorial units of the Church. Soon the stake was subdivided into wards, each presided over by a bishop, who now exercised secular as well as religious jurisdiction. In this manner the Mormons quietly and effectively constructed a political arrangement from the materials of their own denominational system.[1]

Although the Church had deliberately built its new home in a region far removed from other settlements, its leaders in 1849 realized that Salt Lake Valley would need a more temporal government, in form at least, than the one they had first devised. Already a few Gentiles had passed through the community on their way to California, and more would arrive when news of the West Coast's opportunities became widely known. In early March, therefore, a convention of Church members drew up a constitution for the proposed State of Deseret, and immediately upon ratification of this document the people elected men to fill the offices. But the change in governmental organization did not in the least bring about a relaxation of ecclesiastical supervision; the new officials were for the most part the same members of the Hierarchy who had previously held political power. Brigham Young became governor and his two counselors assumed the next most important positions, secretary and chief justice. In like fashion trusted Mormons filled the other subordinate posts.[2]

Accustomed as they were to complete dependence upon their denominational directors in their previous travails, the Saints would naturally place these same dignitaries of the Church in the provisional state regime.

[1] Andrew L. Neff, *History of Utah, 1848 to 1869* (Salt Lake City, Deseret News Press, 1940), p. 108. Thomas C. Romney, *The Story of Deseret* (Independence, Zion's Printing and Publishing Co., 1948), p. 61.

[2] Neff, pp. 114 ff. John H. Evans, *One Hundred Years of Mormonism: A History of the Church of Jesus Christ of Latter-day Saints from 1805 to 1905* (Salt Lake City, Deseret Sunday School Union, 1909), p. 485. Andrew Jenson, *Encyclopedic History of the Church of Jesus Christ of Latter-day Saints* (Salt Lake City, Deseret News Press, 1941), p. 181.

But to make certain that no doctrinally unreliable figure slipped into political office, Young and his closest advisors composed a ticket only eight days before the election and made sure the voters approved it.[3] This authoritarian disposition was to produce strife when individualistic Gentiles moved in among the regimented members of the Church.

When the United States acquired possession of the Salt Lake Basin as a result of its war with Mexico, the Mormons found themselves once more encamped upon American territory. Now under the jurisdiction of the federal Congress, they needed its acknowledgment of their new state if it was to have any pretense to legality. Accordingly, the General Assembly in July 1849 delegated Almon W. Babbitt to secure this recognition from the Government. The choice of emissary was an unhappy one, for Babbitt, whose eccentric conduct later earned him the perilous disfavor of Young, succeeded only in drawing upon himself the dislike and ridicule of Whigs and Democrats in the Capitol.[4] As a counterweight to this agent the Mormons had two other advocates, men of greater ability than Babbitt. Dr. John Bernhisel, who had in May brought the formal petition for statehood to Washington, soon proved that his quiet lobbying was more effective than Babbitt's brash conviviality. The other spokesman for the Mormons was young Thomas Leiper Kane, a self-chosen champion of the oppressed who, though not a member of the Church, used his considerable political influence throughout the 1850's to advance its interests.

To the extent that his frail health would permit, Kane had devoted much of his early life to supporting humanitarian causes with missionary earnestness. When the struggle over slavery burst out after the Mexican War, he joined the Free Soil party in 1848 and later took part in the Underground Railroad. In the Civil War he was wounded and captured but later fought at Gettysburg, despite a debilitating attack of pneumonia; his heroism on this occasion earned him the rank of brevet major general. Except in Utah his modest accomplishments were overshadowed by the greater reputations of his father, John K. Kane, judge of the United States district court in Pennsylvania, and his brother, Elisha Kent Kane, whose arctic explorations had made him a national hero in the 1850's. Yet this short, dark-complexioned man, only thirty-five years old when the Mormon War occupied the attention of the country, was a valuable ally to those whom he championed, for he had many friends in Washington, even though he had opposed his acquaintance Lewis Cass in the campaign of 1848.

Kane first became aware of the Latter-day Saints in the spring of 1846, when he heard Jesse A. Little describe the piteous fall of Nauvoo to a sectarian meeting in Philadelphia. He invited Little to his home, where he learned that the elder was bound for Washington to seek help for his brethren. After giving him an introduction to Vice President George M. Dallas, Kane sped to the Mormons' temporary settlements in Iowa, hoping

---

[3] Neff, pp. 114 ff.

[4] Jay D. Ridd, "Almon Whiting Babbitt, Mormon Emissary" (M.A. thesis, University of Utah, 1953), pp. 58–59. Evans, *One Hundred Years of Mormonism*, p. 487. Hubert H. Bancroft, *History of Utah* (San Francisco, The History Co., 1889), pp. 451–55.

to ease their distress. Instead of helping them, he became deathly ill and almost died on their hands. Later, his health partially restored and now more devoted to the Mormons than ever because of their solicitous nursing, he began his long career as public defender of the faith. In a short pamphlet entitled *Account of the Inhuman Behavior of the Anti-Mormons in Illinois* he described the experiences of a Baptist who, having joined the Church, was driven by angry Gentiles to Nauvoo and later, a bed-ridden invalid, was carried across the Mississippi River to die on the Iowa shore. To Horace Greeley he wrote of the Mormons' encounters with persecutions and of their courageous endurance of hardships. Upon his return to the East he persuaded the Government to let the Mormons occupy the lands of the Omaha Indians until they found a new home; at the same time he advised Secretary of War William Marcy that the Church merited other forms of federal assistance in its desperate struggle for survival. This restless young man also organized public meetings in Philadelphia, New York, and other cities to raise money for the relief of the Saints as they straggled from Illinois to the uncharted region of the Great Salt Lake.

In the summer of 1850 Kane, given to hypochondria, felt that he was dying and wrote a letter to the leaders of the sect. He had fought for them, he said, because "the personal assaults upon myself made your cause become so identified with my own that your vindication became my own defense. . . . We stand or fall together." He had altered his will, he said, in order to leave his estate "to some who need it at home" rather than to the Church, but he would assign his heart to the Mormons, "to be deposited in the Temple of your Salt Lake City, that, after death, it may repose, where in metaphor at least, it oftener was when living." The clumsily expressed sentiment was sincere, but Kane's premonition of his own demise proved unfounded on this occasion, as on many others until 1883, and he was soon strong enough to resume his role as the Mormons' champion in the East. To reduce the popular prejudice against the Saints he delivered a number of lectures, one of which he printed at his own expense and presented to newspapers, the Library of Congress, the Smithsonian Institution, and many congressmen.[5]

Despite Kane's and Bernhisel's enterprising work, the Saints failed to secure the desired position of statehood, receiving only territorial status. Their request encountered several obstacles. In the first place the congressmen, now deeply embroiled in debate over the extension of slavery

[5] [*Dictionary of American Biography* (hereafter cited as *DAB*).] Wendell J. Ashton, *Theirs Is the Kingdom* (Springville, Utah, Art City Publishing Co., 1945), pp. 208 ff. Oscar O. Winther, ed., *The Private Papers of Thomas Leiper Kane, a Friend of the Mormons* (San Francisco, Gelber-Lilienthal, 1937), pp. vi, 1, 21–22. Bernard De Voto, *The Year of Decision* (Boston, Little, Brown, 1943), p. 242. "Journal History," Church Archives, Salt Lake City (hereafter cited as JH), July 11, Sept. 24, 1850. Kane to Black, Dec. 21, 1857, in Jeremiah Black MSS, Library of Congress. Kane to Marcy, April 30, 1847; Medill to Kane, Jan. 1848: Kane MSS, Library of Congress. "Notes for an Address on the Mormons Introducing Elders Benson and Little" and "Report to the Commissioner of Indian Affairs on the Status of the Mormons": Yale Collection of Western Americana.

into the area won from Mexico, were not in a mood to view the Mormons' arguments with dispassion. Indeed, the irrelevant issue of slavery was to have deleterious effects upon the Church's relations with the Government during the entire decade. Furthermore, a number of congressional leaders in 1850 revealed the same uncritical animus toward the Church that had generated dispute in Missouri and Illinois.

Shortly after the Mormons' memorial reached Washington, Representative Warner Underwood of Kentucky read to the House a long indictment of the sect written by William Smith, the erratic, unprincipled younger brother of the Prophet Joseph and now among the Church's most dedicated enemies. Several years earlier Smith had accused the Mormon priesthood of plotting to establish an independent nation in the West and of oppressing its followers with a "sacerdotal tyranny." Now, to the great excitement of the legislators, he and his thirteen supporters presented the sensational charge that the Mormons practiced polygamy, maintaining also that during the last days of Nauvoo the Saints had sworn a dreadful oath to avenge the lynching of their martyred leaders and to "carry out hostility against this nation." Other animadversions further shocked the congressmen. In March the unfriendly Underwood presented a second accusatory memorial, this time from Gentiles in Council Bluffs; and later Representative John Wentworth of Illinois introduced a petition from his constituents requesting for travelers in the Far West federal protection against the murderous designs of the Mormons.[6]

William Smith's philippic was characteristic of attacks upon the Church. In this as in many similar cases the indictment came from an embittered apostate. These attacks played upon a fear uppermost in Gentiles' minds when they meditated upon the "Mormon problem," namely that the Saints were leagued together in an infamous conspiracy to destroy or dismember the nation. Furthermore, the sect's peculiar system of plural marriage served to antagonize congressmen as well as the general public.

Bernhisel labored industriously to overcome these unfavorable opinions of his brethren. Senator Truman Smith of Connecticut introduced him to Millard Fillmore, newly elevated to the Presidency by Zachary Taylor's death, and he found the chief executive most sympathetic toward his people, in great contrast to Taylor's antagonism. The quiet doctor's conversation with Secretary of State Daniel Webster and Secretary of the Treasury Thomas Corwin helped to win from these men some expression of support for the Mormons. In the course of his perambulations through Washington he had interviews with Clay, Benton, Calhoun, Cass, Seward, Foote, Chase, Cobb, Douglas, Wilmot, and other influential men. Senator Thomas J. Rusk of Texas offered to help him in any way possible, and Mrs. John McLean, wife of an associate justice of the Supreme Court, even asked him to preach to her. With Truman Smith's permission, Bernhisel had inserted in the *Congressional Globe* a letter to the senator

---

[6] Leland H. Creer, *Utah and the Nation* (Seattle, University of Washington, 1929), p. 77. William A. Linn, *The Story of the Mormons* (New York, Macmillan, 1902), p. 431. Romney, *Story of Deseret*, p. 96. *Congressional Globe*, Dec. 31, 1849. JH, March 21, 1850.

from a recent visitor to Salt Lake Valley enthusiastically praising the Mormons' accomplishments there.[7]

These activities failed to secure legislative acceptance of the State of Deseret. Instead, Congress voted early in September 1850 to establish the Territory of Utah, and Fillmore signed the bill on September 9. Too late, the Church leaders tried to forestall this event by instructing Bernhisel to withdraw their petition, since they realized that they would suffer less from Gentile interference as an unsupervised provisional state than as a territory under congressional regulation, an opinion shared by Senator Stephen A. Douglas. The law, however, had already been enacted. Bernhisel watched this development unhappily: "I feel entirely unwilling," he wrote, "to run the risk of having a set of whippersnappers or brokendown politicians to tyrannize over us . . . for I have every reason to apprehend that we should be constantly brought into collision with the Central Government."[8]

Upon learning of the President's territorial appointees, however, the Mormons in Salt Lake Valley felt no great concern for the future. Of primary satisfaction to them was Brigham Young's continuance as governor under the new dispensation. In this selection Fillmore had depended upon the counsel of Thomas L. Kane, a member of the opposition Democratic party, and Kane had convinced the President that Young possessed two eminent qualifications for the position, an upright character and the undivided allegiance of his people.[9] The Mormons, as one contemporary Gentile observer noted, would have received the appointment of any other man "as in some sort a renewal, on the part of the General Government, of that series of persecutions to which they have already been subjected."[10] Three other churchmen also found places in the territorial offices. True, the secretary and two of the three federal judges were now Gentiles, but there was at first no reason to believe that they would use their powers in inimical fashion. This estimate proved far from accurate.

Even at this point in the chronicle of the Mormons' early history, when the Saints were enjoying an amicable relation with the Government, it is possible to observe causes of future difficulties. True enough, in 1850 there seemed to be little reason to anticipate a recurrence of the old troubles left behind in Missouri and Illinois. A thousand miles of prairie to the east and five hundred miles of sand and mountains to the west separated the Church from that close association with Gentiles that had previously been so unharmonious. With little dispute the Mormons had been accepted into the American nation and a friendly president had selected their ecclesiastical ruler as their governor. Yet within fifteen months this

[7] JH, March 21, April 4, Aug. 9, 1850. *Cong. Globe*, July 8, 18, Sept. 7, 1850.

[8] For the debates in Congress concerning the creation of the Territory of Utah see *Cong. Globe*, Dec. 27, 1849, Jan. 22, 1850. See also JH, March 5, 27, 1850.

[9] JH, July 4, 1851.

[10] Howard Stansbury, *Exploration and Survey of the Valley of the Great Salt Lake of Utah* (Philadelphia, Lippincott, Grambo, 1852), p. 147.

benign situation had disappeared, replaced by a period of stormy accusation and bombast, with many eastern Gentiles speaking loudly of settling the Mormon question by force. A number of factors, both new and old, combined to produce this and subsequent crises.

One basic cause of the difficulties throughout this decade, and indeed in later years, was the existence of a public opinion extremely hostile to the Mormons and prepared to seize upon any pretext, whether valid or not, to renew the attack upon the Church. Many of the reasons for the eviction of the Saints from the eastern states were still operative in the 1850's, and the distances temporarily separating Mormon from Gentile did not greatly obscure them. Polygamy, an open secret at best until it was officially announced as a doctrine of the Church in 1852, was not compatible with the "domestic manners of the Americans" (as Mrs. Trollope called them). And the conviction that the Saints, despite their denials, were only awaiting an opportune moment to announce the political independence of their settlement aroused the anger of patriots. In a land priding itself on its democratic customs, the hierarchical religious and political practices of the Mormons appeared tyrannous. Furthermore, a large portion of the Gentiles took at face value the charges of William Smith and others that the Mormons had formed a secret, armed band, known as Danites (above, p. 255), sworn to shed the blood of nonbelievers. Finally, a great many Americans found unbearable the Saints' serene assumption that their sect, the only one on earth possessing God's endorsement, would speedily spread until all peoples and denominations had acknowledged Joseph Smith as Prophet, Seer, and Revelator. Holding these beliefs, Easterners were disposed to believe any unfavorable report concerning the Latter-day Saints.

Hostile American opinion not only accounted the Mormons guilty of murderous plotting, subversive desire, and other criminal inclinations; it also considered the Church in great part composed of recent immigrants drawn from the lowest classes of other lands. In the 1850's the United States was experiencing in the Know-Nothing movement a wave of nativism later to find expression in the American Protective Association, the Ku Klux Klan, and periodic immigration acts. As the people watched a host of new Mormon converts from abroad arrive on their shores, many were easily convinced that the Church was as dangerous to their institutions as they supposed the Roman Catholics, the swollen Irish minority, or any other alien group to be.

At the present time it is difficult to estimate the number of aliens in Utah during the late 1850's, or even to fix with certainty the actual population of the Territory.[11] Yet in 1857 Stephen A. Douglas, his early friendliness toward the Church now grown cold, stated that possibly seven

---

[11] Some say 40,000 in the late 1850's; others, 60,000 or more: Neff, *History of Utah*, p. 165; Ephraim E. Ericksen, *The Psychological and Ethical Aspects of Mormon Group Life* (Chicago, University of Chicago Press, 1922), p. 44. The census of 1860 set the foreign segment at 12,000, but Ericksen states that between 1849 and 1858 at least 22,000 Mormon immigrants arrived. It would seem safe to say that approximately a third of the Mormons during the years under consideration were of foreign origin.

out of ten Mormons in Utah had emigrated there from other countries, and many commentators of his day agreed in general with his conclusions. The popular view further held these newcomers to be for the most part indigent, illiterate men and women menacing the economic and social standards of the United States. Reports to the contrary did not greatly weaken the judgment that the Mormons were undesirable candidates for American citizenship, since it was based less on dispassionate investigation than on prejudice drawn from the spirit of the decade.[12] In the words of one historian, "These individuals, so long as they remained members of orthodox denominations of the day, were regarded as worthy members of society. Only when they affiliated with the despised sect, known as Mormons, did they become objects of execration."[13]

A second cause of trouble between the Mormons in Utah and the Government was the selection of inferior men to fill the Territory's offices. Although good appointees did on occasion make their toilsome way to Utah, Bernhisel's prediction of an infestation of "whippersnappers and brokendown politicians" frequently came true. To Easterners, Utah was a remote and desolate region; political jobs there brought a remuneration inadequate to pay expenses; and the problem of living with the Mormons and governing them was known to be exacting. It was accordingly not strange that few men of ability regarded appointment to office in the Territory politically or financially rewarding. As a result, administrations in Washington could often find only inept or, on occasion, morally reprehensible men to fill the positions. The common practice of using the Territory's posts as payment for political debts reduced even further the possibility of selecting suitable men for public service. The wisdom of Solon would have been severely taxed to keep peace in the relations between Utah and the rest of the Union, given the many factors productive of friction, but the presence of men like Perry Brocchus and W. W. Drummond, too often typical of federal place-seekers, could only exacerbate the difficulties.

Another irritant, of lesser importance than some mentioned here, was the question of land ownership. When Brigham Young embarked upon the trek to the Salt Lake Basin in early 1847, his pioneer band journeyed to a region that was part of Mexico; but by the time the Church had built its permanent settlements, the place had come into the possession of the United States. Before the Saints could claim the land as their own, therefore, certain procedures established by Congress had to be followed, among them disposal of Indian rights and a survey of the area. Only after they had met these requirements could the Mormons acquire the land lawfully, and even then they were compelled to obtain legal title by purchase or other means. The Government was slow in negotiating

[12] M. R. Werner, *Brigham Young* (New York, Harcourt, Brace, 1925), pp. 271–72. Bancroft, *History of Utah*, pp. 414–15, 449. *Annals of Cleveland, 1818–1935* (WPA, 1935), *43*, 516. *National Intelligencer*, May 8, 1857. New York *Times*, June 27, 1857. *Missouri Republican*, April 29, 1858. 34th Cong., 1st Sess., Sen. Exec. Doc. 1, Vol. 2, Pt. II.

[13] Neff, *History of Utah*, p. 530. See also Thomas F. O'Dea, *The Mormons* (Chicago, University of Chicago Press, 1957), pp. 91 ff.

treaties with the Indians. In addition, the process of surveying Utah, tentatively begun in 1855, was suspended for ten years after 1857. Thus when anger toward the Mormons increased, opponents of the sect could threaten it with another expulsion by warning: "Not an individual in all Utah now holds a foot of land the title of which is derived from the United States, and it follows . . . that all parts of the Territory are at the present time open to pre-emption."[14] As their speeches and writings revealed, the Church's leaders were acutely aware of their tenuous possession of the New Zion and apprehensive lest the Government move to evict them.[15]

For their part, the Mormons' characteristics and activities were as conducive to strife as the temper and policies of their opponents. Some of these elements were of minor significance yet increased the accumulation of irritations during the decade. After their experiences with inflamed Gentile mobs, the Mormons were quick to look for new attacks in Utah, an attitude that at times became unjustified truculence. Furthermore, their continual insistence upon the superiority of their faith under divine sanction proved most objectionable to other Christians in Utah, as it had in Missouri and Illinois. When Heber Kimball announced, "We are the people of God . . . the foundation of which in these last days was begun by the Almighty sending an holy angel to Joseph Smith,"[16] he left no place in the divine scheme for non-Mormon denominations. With exasperating regularity the Church's spokesmen contrasted the purity of their own people, the self-styled Saints, to the wayward conditions existing elsewhere in the nation, and their references to the Mormons as "this people," in other words, the Lord's anointed, failed to win any measure of good will from nonbelievers.[17]

The political and ecclesiastical government evolved by the Mormons at the start of the 1850's inevitably became a major cause of strained relations between them and the Gentiles in later years. The Saints, believing their Church divinely instituted, yielded to their leaders an authority beyond that of merely elected officials. Their early travails had strengthened this tendency toward willing acceptance of monolithic control. While suffering persecution at the hands of tumultuous crowds in the East, traversing the plains to a little-known country, and struggling for sustenance in a desert climate, they learned that survival depended more on obedience than on the privileges of discussion and dissent. In Utah the Mormons erected a theocracy and sustained it with unanimity. It operated without friction so long as only Church members made up the area's population, but when Gentiles came to the Territory in significant numbers the system drew bitter protest. It was the same difficulty that had prevented the Mormons' permanent residence in Missouri and Illinois; the cohesive unity of the Church and the docility of its members in re-

[14] Washington *Union*, June 24, 1857.

[15] Bancroft, *History of Utah*, p. 485. Dale L. Morgan, "The Administration of Indian Affairs in Utah, 1851–1858," *Pacific Historical Review*, 17 (1948), 395.

[16] *Deseret News*, June 16, 1854.

[17] For typical remarks of this nature see Neff, *History of Utah*, p. 468; *Deseret News*, March 30, Sept. 7, 14, 1854, July 1, 1857, Feb. 3, 1858.

ligious and political matters had at best an uneasy place in the disparateness of American individuality. Enemies of the denomination soon came to view it as an undemocratic institution that had to be reformed or destroyed.[18]

Gentiles in Utah during the 1850's could discover no effort on the part of the Hierarchy to relax its strict and all-permeating control over its followers once territorial status had been attained. On the contrary, the leaders of the faith, believing theocracy "the most perfect government," held before their people as essential virtues the twin characteristics of submission and obedience. At times Heber Chase Kimball, a member of the First Presidency, was not always coherent as a public speaker: "I am almost a good mind to talk a little; that is, if you want I should, but I certainly do not want to without you want I should, and then again if I felt really like it, I should talk whether you wanted I should or not."[19] But on the subject of obedience he was clear; drawing from his experiences in former professions, he instructed the Saints to be as pliant as clay in the hands of the potter or iron under the blacksmith's hammer. "If it is necessary for me to be subject to my file leaders," he once asked, "I wish to know whether it is not equally for you, and for every high priest, elder, seventy, apostle, and all the others, to be obedient to the priesthood of those who are appointed to direct them?" On another occasion he summed up his advice to his listeners: "Our Father and our God has sent Brigham and his brethren; if you rebel against them, you rebel against the authority that sent them."[20]

Brigham Young and his colleagues heartily joined Kimball in urging dutiful obedience upon the Mormons. In elections to territorial offices they occasionally published a ticket of approved candidates to guide those who wished to cast their ballots "understandingly." To forestall any possibility that Church members might disregard the wishes of their leaders and place in political office a man unacceptable to the priesthood, the territorial legislature in 1853 established electoral procedures designed to prevent this eventuality. In the selection of denominational officials and establishment of policy there was a similar absence of democratic practice, for the Church members could do no more than approve or reject the choice of the Hierarchy. During this period the dictum of Brigham Young prevailed: "It is the right of the Twelve [Apostles] to nominate the officers and the people to sustain them."[21]

---

[18] Creer, *Utah and the Nation*, p. 92. Bancroft, *History of Utah*, p. 367. Therald Jensen, *Mormon Theory of Church and State* (Chicago, University of Chicago Press, 1940), p. 2. Dale L. Morgan, "The State of Deseret," *Utah Historical Records Survey* (Salt Lake City, Utah Historical Society, 1940), *8, 69.* "Brigham Young," *DAB.*

[19] *Deseret News*, Nov. 18, 1857.

[20] Jensen, *Mormon Theory*, p. 1. *Deseret News*, Aug. 17, Sept. 14, 1854, Sept. 12, 1855, June 17, Aug. 19, 1857.

[21] *Acts and Resolutions Passed by the Second Annual Assembly of the Territory of Utah* (1853). Morgan, "State of Deseret," p. 69. *Journal of Discourses, by Brigham Young, His Two Counsellors, and the Twelve Apostles* (Liverpool, 1857), *4,* 259 ff. *Deseret News*, Feb. 13, 1855, July 15, 1857.

The great majority of Mormons in Utah needed no lectures or regulations, for they were prepared to support willingly in secular matters the men upon whom they relied for spiritual salvation. In his first three elections as delegate to Congress, Bernhisel received unanimous support twice and only one negative vote on the third occasion. In other canvasses the Mormons endorsed the nominees with similar uniformity. The balloting for three territorial legislators in Utah County in 1852, for instance, gave Edson Whipple 245 votes, Leonard Harrington 245 votes, William Pace 243 votes, and Benjamin F. Johnson one vote. Hosea Stout, commenting on the general election in 1857, noted that "there was no opposing candidates but all went off peaceably and harmoniously as usual."[22] This tendency of the people to accept wholeheartedly the men who were officially endorsed for public office produced an interlocking of church and state that was usually complete except for the positions filled by presidential appointment. As a result, the Gentile in Utah felt that he was living in an atmosphere stifling to his liberties.

It was in the judicial rather than the political field, however, that non-Mormons felt most keenly the dictatorial authority of the Church. Lacking sufficient numbers to overcome the united vote of the Saints in the election of territorial officers, the Gentiles turned to the courts as instruments of protection from discrimination in this theocracy. The effort failed. At first the Mormons, believing that Gentile courts did not dispense justice, followed the advice of their leaders to use their own ecclesiastical tribunals in settlement of their mutual difficulties.[23] When the influx of Gentiles brought the Saints into legal entanglements that could be resolved only in territorial courts, other devices were employed to guard the interests of Church members. The legislature, for instance, by enactment in 1852 permitted anyone, with or without legal training, to serve as attorney in court; two years later a more extensive act declared that only territorial laws, and those of Congress "when applicable," could be "read, argued, cited or adopted as precedent in any trial."[24] Thus the Mormons tried to escape all laws, including English common law, that might serve to prejudice their search for autonomy.

After the federal courts were organized and upon occasion presided over by judges unsympathetic toward the Church, the Mormon priesthood attempted to control them or to reduce their effectiveness, an effort resulting in a storm of protest from Gentiles in Utah, the eastern states, and Washington. Since the juries were in most cases drawn from the predominant Mormon community, one simple expedient was for denominational officers to advise jury members concerning the decisions they should reach. Jedediah M. Grant, whose untimely death in 1856 deprived his people of a fearless, brawling, and loose-tongued fighter, described the operation of this device in a sermon:

[22] "Executive Proceedings 1850 to 1854, and Elections and Commissions" (MS, Utah Historical Society), pp. 14, 88. JH, July 26, Aug. 10, 1852. "Diary of Hosea Stout" (MS, Brigham Young University), 7, 309.

[23] Creer, *Utah and the Nation*, p. 59. Neff, *History of Utah*, pp. 186, 189. *Deseret News*, Aug. 10, 1850, Sept. 21, 1854.

[24] Neff, *History of Utah*, pp. 194–95.

Last Sunday the president chastized some of the apostles and bishops on the grand jury. Did he succeed in clearing away the fog which surrounded them, and in removing the blindness from their eyes? No, for they could go back into their room and again disagree, though to their credit it must be admitted that a brief explanation made them unanimous in their action.[25]

The case to which Grant referred was an exceptional one; in most trials the Mormon jurymen were not usually so unresponsive to their instructions. In another move to protect their customs from outside interference through the judiciary, the legislature appointed a territorial marshal whose authority infringed upon that of the United States marshal.[26]

Of all the judicial defenses raised by the Church to protect itself, none caused so much trouble as the probate courts. In February 1852 the legislature gave to these tribunals such exceptional powers that they came to have jurisdiction in criminal and civil cases. In explanation of this action, the Mormons maintained that the frequent and prolonged absences of the federal judges from the Territory had rendered the administration of justice almost impossible; the probate courts thus of necessity provided the only tribunals available to the people. In reply, many Gentiles insisted that the extravagant augmentation of the probate courts' authority was obvious proof of the Mormons' ultimate intention to establish a community effectively independent of all federal control. W. W. Drummond, a federal judge who more than any other man brought about the Mormon War of 1857–58 . . . , used this strange legal situation as one of his arguments for the need of an expedition against the Latter-day Saints. Only when Congress in 1874 passed the Poland Act, curtailing the expanded powers of these courts, did the controversy over them subside.[27]

As early as 1851, consequently, there were a number of factors capable of disrupting the relations of the Mormons' new territory with the central government. Some were trifling, others were of primary significance; but behind them all, and as a cause of many of them, stood the major irritant to the Gentiles, Brigham Young. The Saints called him President, Lion of the Lord, Prophet, Seer, and Revelator, and bowed to his authority. To many Gentiles he was the model of an oriental tyrant, a seducer of women, Anti-Christ with a Vermont accent. Only a man of his outstanding abilities could have guided the Mormons to a new home, given his people in that distant place a period of religious and temporal security, and laid the foundation for their future growth. Only a

[25] *Deseret News,* March 12, 1856.

[26] T. B. H. Stenhouse, *The Rocky Mountain Saints: A Full and Complete History* . . . (Salt Lake City, Shepard Book Co. 1904), pp. 282–83. Nels Anderson, *Deseret Saints. The Mormon Frontier in Utah* (Chicago, University of Chicago Press, 1942), p. 93.

[27] *Acts and Resolutions of the Legislature Assembly of the Territory of Utah,* 1st Sess. (1851–52). Kinney to Cushing, March 1, 1855, in Appointment Papers, Department of Justice, National Archives (NA), Washington, D.C., *Valley Tan* (newspaper), Feb. 8, 1859.

figure of his unquestionable stature could have become so intolerable to Americans of the 1850's that they demanded a military campaign to oust him from his position of political power.

Young's influence over the Mormons was nearly supreme, and he knew it. They listened with delight to his long sermons and worried about his frequent periods of bad health. Since they came to him with their problems, he could often divine their very thoughts; it was fitting that one of the sect's cherished symbols was the all-seeing eye, for Young was Big Brother to the Latter-day Saints. When in 1857, at the outbreak of the Mormon War, he called the settlers in the Church's outlying colonies back to Salt Lake, only a handful in San Bernardino and Carson Valley hesitated to leave the property they had accumulated over a number of hard years. If on rare occasions some muttered against him, he could say, "I ask no odds of them," knowing his position to be unassailable. He struck down sternly any theological innovation that might have reduced his powers, and he showed his superiority to his advisors by heaping public criticism and even biting ridicule upon such Mormon dignitaries as Orson Hyde and Orson Pratt.[28] A man of limited formal education who had no books in his home and who frequently in formal addresses gave evidence of illiteracy, even incoherence, he possessed a hard common sense and practicality that won for him the position of benevolent autocrat in his Church.[29] He could live amicably with anyone, Mormon or Gentile, who accepted his dominion, but he was quick to loose his fury upon those who opposed him.

Some Gentiles considered this Moses of the Mormons pleasant and agreeable,[30] but a great many more found him unbearable, as a man and especially as Governor of Utah, and were not hard pressed to find arguments to advance their plea for his dismissal. He had been the prime mover in the establishment of a political system that provided no place for a dissenting Gentile minority. He had urged his people to avoid non-Mormon courts, had continually instructed Mormon juries on the proper decisions to render, and had helped to establish the other devices used by the Saints to circumvent the federal courts. When he ordered the meetings of an apostate faction, the "Gladdenites," to be forceably broken up in 1853, and threatened to "unsheath my Bowie knife" against them, Young revealed that constitutional guarantees did not always protect unfavored residents of Utah.[31] His fondness for incendiary speech, disclosed in frequent references to the cutting of throats and the "shearing

[28] Wayne Stout, *Hosea Stout, Utah's Pioneer Statesman* (Salt Lake City, privately printed, 1953), p. 192. Werner, *Brigham Young*, pp. 258, 265. Neff, *History of Utah*, p. 227. Linn, *Story of the Mormons*, p. 117. *Deseret News*, Jan. 12, 1854, April 14, Nov. 28, 1858. JH, March 8, 1857.

[29] Allan Nevins, *The Emergence of Lincoln* (2 vols.; New York, Scribner's, 1950), I, 315. Werner, *Brigham Young*, p. 258. For examples of Young's speech see *Deseret News*, Dec. 10, 1856, March 25, April 15, 22, Aug. 5, 1857.

[30] Wilson to Black, Nov. 26, 1858, in Attorney General's Records, 1789–1870, NA. New York *Evening Mirror*, Feb. 20, 1855.

[31] *Deseret News*, April 2, 1853.

down" of refractory people,[32] kept the excitable Mormons in a mood prejudicial to the safety of Gentiles in the Valley.

Finally his despotism antagonized a multitude of Americans in Utah and throughout the nation. "Though I may not be Governor here," he announced in a celebrated speech in 1855, "my power will not be diminished. No man they can send here will have much influence in this community unless he is a man of their [the Mormons'] choice. Let them send whom they will, and it does not diminish my influence one particle."[33] This statement offended the Gentiles, who believed that the United States had no place for a man of such unbounded authority.

The assertion may have been un-American, but it was nothing more than plain truth. Unfortunately, few non-Mormons recognized the fact.

[32] For example, see Neff, *History of Utah*, p. 498; *Deseret News*, Aug. 1, 1855.
[33] *Deseret News*, July 18, 1855.

# Anti-Chinese Sentiment

# in

# California

## ELMER C. SANDMEYER

Too often the study of immigration in American history deals only with the Atlantic migration, overlooking the fact that there were several waves of immigration from East Asia. The first major wave of Pacific migration was a large-scale movement of Chinese into California and the West during the gold rush, beginning in 1848. The second was an influx of Japanese settlers on the West Coast around the turn of the twentieth century.

Toward the middle of the nineteenth century, political unrest in China displaced many peasants and urban poor. Many of the latter migrated to Latin America and the American tropics under a system of contract labor that was much like indentured servitude. There they sometimes replaced African slaves, whose numbers were dwindling because of the abolition or suppression of the Atlantic slave trade. These Oriental laborers were called "coolies," which in China meant merely unskilled laborers but which in the Western Hemisphere soon acquired the connotation of bound, or involuntary, laborers. In this sense of the word, very few of the Chinese immigrants to the United States were coolies, a word often used contemptuously in reference to them. Rather, most of these immigrants had belonged to the free peasantry in China and thus had roots in the same class that produced the Irish and German immigrants of the period.

If it was difficult for white European immigrants to find a place in the relatively stable Eastern society at mid-century, it was even more difficult for East Asians to move into the highly fluid, rapidly changing, rambunctious society of California. Next to the blacks, the Chinese were the immigrant group most different from the dominant whites. Their physical appearance was distinctive, and they tended to preserve their own language, religion, customs, and culture. Over half of these immigrants were married men who had left their families in China and who found it necessary to work hard and to live extremely frugally in order to send money home, to visit their families in China, or to return to China permanently. All these factors tended to set the Chinese apart from white America, though by 1852 the Chinese in California alone numbered 25,000 and made up 10 percent of the state's total population.

Although the Chinese were at first fairly well received because of a desperate shortage of unskilled labor in California, they found themselves less and less welcome as more white laborers became available. They soon came to dominate both the restaurant and the laundry businesses in San Francisco and in the northern part of the state. Furthermore, they demonstrated an ability to take over apparently worthless mining claims and make them pay by working harder and longer than the white miners. This phenomenon produced so much hostility in the mining camps that the Chinese were frequently barred from owning or working claims. The willingness of the East Asian immigrants to work long hours at low pay, which had originally worked in their favor, came to be seen by white migrants from the East and the South as unfair competition.

As early as 1852 attempts were made to bar the Chinese from admission to the West Coast. Anti-Chinese sentiment culminated in the passage of the Chinese Exclusion Act in 1882. Although this law was intended to halt immigration for only a ten-year period, it virtually put a stop to Chinese migration to the United States. Ironically, it had the effect of opening the West Coast to Japanese immigration, which was stimulated by the need to fill various jobs in the expanding economy that would earlier have been filled by the Chinese.

In the selection reprinted here, Elmer C. Sandmeyer discusses the development of antagonism toward the Chinese among white Californians and the discriminatory behavior suffered by Chinese immigrants to America during the years of the gold rush.

---

No single cause furnished the motivation of the anti-Chinese movement in California. It was only through the combination of a variety of motives, appealing to diversified groups, together with an auspicious political situation, that the movement for the exclusion of the Chinese was able to succeed.

The range of the motives which served as the bases of the anti-Chinese sentiment in California may be seen in two statements made in 1876. According to the first of these, Californians were convinced,

"Anti-Chinese Sentiment in California." From Elmer C. Sandmeyer, *The Anti-Chinese Movement in California* (Urbana, Ill.: The University of Illinois Press, 1939), pp. 25–39. Reprinted by permission.

That he is a slave, reduced to the lowest terms of beggarly economy, and is no fit competitor for an American freeman.

That he herds in scores, in small dens, where a white man and wife could hardly breathe, and has none of the wants of a civilized white man.

That he has neither wife nor child, nor expects to have any.

That his sister is a prostitute from instinct, religion, education, and interest, and degrading to all around her.

That American men, women and children cannot be what free people should be, and compete with such degraded creatures in the labor market.

That wherever they are numerous, as in San Francisco, by a secret machinery of their own, they defy the law, keep up the manners and customs of China, and utterly disregard all the laws of health, decency and morality.

That they are driving the white population from the state, reducing laboring men to despair, laboring women to prostitution, and boys and girls to hoodlums and convicts.

That the health, wealth, prosperity and happiness of our State demand their expulsion from our shores.[1]

The official spokesman of San Francisco before the Joint Special Committee of Congress expressed a similar view:

The burden of our accusation against them is that they come in conflict with our labor interests; that they can never assimilate with us; that they are a perpetual, unchanging, and unchangeable alien element that can never become homogeneous; that their civilization is demoralizing and degrading to our people; that they degrade and dishonor labor; that they can never become citizens, and that an alien, degraded labor class, without desire of citizenship, without education, and without interest in the country it inhabits, is an element both demoralizing and dangerous to the community within which it exists.

These charges were repeated in so many speeches, editorials, and other forms of expression that one can hardly escape the conviction that they represented widely prevalent belief.[2]

The contents of these charges may be considered under three heads: the economic, the moral and religious, and the social and political. Of the charges which may be designated as economic none was more frequently nor more persistently used than that of coolieism. While the evidence thus far presented indicates that the motivating influences of Chinese immigration were essentially like those operating among Europeans, Cali-

[1] *Marin Journal*, March 30, 1876.
[2] Quotation is from *Report 689*, 31. See also *ibid.*, 1001–03. *Cong. Record*, 44th Cong., 1st sess., 2850–57. *Argonaut*, Oct. 27, Nov. 3, 10, 17, Dec. 1, 29, 1877.

fornians were convinced that Chinese laborers came to this country under servile or "coolie" contracts. Senator Sargent had the support of widespread public opinion when he insisted that, in spite of laws forbidding the importation of coolies, the Chinese coming to California were not free, but were bound to service for a term of years, the faithful performance of their contracts being secured by their families at home, and that while these contracts were void under our laws, they were made effective by the superstitions of the coolies.[3]

These charges were not new to Californians. The attempt to pass the Tingley Bill in 1852 for the enforcement of contracts made in China had been defeated only after bitter debate. The following year members of the Chinese Companies admitted that they had imported men under contract but, finding it unprofitable, had discontinued the practice. Californians were inclined to accept this evidence, and the statements of Frederick F. Low to the effect that Chinese laborers were too poor to finance their passage and of Thomas H. King that practically all Chinese men came under contract for a definite period of years, rather than the report of a special committee of the legislature in 1862 or the later statement of the attorney of the Six Companies denying the existence of coolie contracts among the Chinese in California.[4] Public opinion, as represented in the press, tended to identify Chinese labor with Negro slavery in the south, a slavery not of law, but of condition and custom.

> Coolies are such pauper Chinese as are hired in bulk and by contract at Chinese ports, to be hired out by the contracting party in this or any other foreign country to which by the terms of the contract they are to be shipped. The contracting parties for California are the Six Companies, and they have imported more than nine-tenths of all the Chinese who have come to this state. . . . When the coolie arrives here he is as rigidly under the control of the contractor who brought him as ever an African slave was under his master in South Carolina or Louisiana. There is no escape from the contractor or the contract.[5]

This conviction of Californians was buttressed by the knowledge that traffic in Chinese "coolie" or contract labor was being carried on to the West Indies and South America. The term "coolie" had been applied to the Chinese by foreigners, and in the sense in which it generally was used it meant simply common laborers, with no implication whatever of involuntary servitude. But the term came to be applied to the system of

---

[3] *Cong. Record*, 44th Cong., 1st sess., 2850–54. The distinction which Sargent made between legal and customary control was probably more important than his contemporaries realized. See Roy M. Lockenour, "The Chinese Court System," *Temple Law Quarterly*, Jan., 1931, 253–59.

[4] *Report 689*, 44, 82, 93. *Senate Journal, 1852*, 67–68, 192, 217, 669–75. *Assembly Journal, 1853*, 233; Appendix, Doc. 28. *Legislative Journals, 1862*, III, Appendix No. 23.

[5] *Chronicle*, March 6, 1879. See also *Bulletin*, April 1, 1876, Feb. 10, 1879. *Call*, Oct. 24, 1880. Sacramento *Bee*, May 23, 1876.

transporting contract laborers to the mines and plantations of the Spanish and British, and was soon current in connection with the Chinese in California. The "coolie traffic" to the West Indies and South America had begun before the middle of the century, and by 1871 more than one hundred thousand had been sent to Cuba alone.[6]

Most of this traffic centered at Macao, Amoy, and Hong Kong. The recruiting, which was handled either by "coolie brokers" on a commission basis or by merchants as a speculative proposition, was permeated with fraud and graft, kidnapping, and inveigling into gambling debts. The Chinese spoke of the traffic as "the buying and selling of pigs." Conditions in transit can be compared only with the horrors of the "middle passage" of the African slave trade. Little provision was made for the comfort of the coolies, and instances were not infrequent of revolts among them, resulting often in death and destruction. The risks involved in the traffic made it difficult to procure ships.[7]

The reprehensible methods of many of those engaged in the traffic furnished many perplexing problems for the consuls in China. The Chinese government was opposed to the traffic, but did little about it, largely because of the lack of consuls in foreign countries. In 1862 Americans were prohibited from participating in it. Within the British Empire the government had exercised a certain amount of supervision over the trade from the beginning, and by 1874 had assumed full control so far as its own subjects and territories were concerned. The worst elements came to center at Macao, and the supervision of the Portuguese government was very lax. Finally, through the efforts of the British and Chinese governments and by action of Portugal, the Macao traffic was terminated, leaving only Hong Kong and the treaty ports. The Chinese government, however, barred the traffic from the treaty ports after the report of an investigating committee sent to Cuba in 1876. There is evidence, however, that the trade continued illegally for some years longer.[8]

What connection, if any, existed between this traffic and the immigration of Chinese to California? As we have seen, American ships had been rather extensively engaged in the traffic. Reports of consular officials, admissions by members of the Chinese Companies, and the attempt to pass the Tingley "Coolie Bill" are evidence that in the early years Chinese came to California under such contracts. Californians were convinced that the traffic was being continued long after it had been prohibited. As

[6] *House Exec. Doc. No. 1*, 42d Cong., 2d sess., 221–22. [Persia Crawford] Campbell [*Chinese Coolie Emigration to Countries Within the British Empire*, London, 1923], 86–160, is the best discussion of this traffic. See also *Senate Exec. Doc. No. 30*, 36th Cong., 1st sess., 64. *House Exec. Doc. No. 105*, 34th Cong., 1st sess., 152–54.

[7] Campbell, *op. cit.*, 95–105. *House Exec. Doc. No. 1*, 42d Cong., 2d sess., 194–210. *House Report No. 443*, 36th Cong., 1st sess. *Senate Exec. Doc. No. 22*, 35th Cong., 2d sess., 623. *Alta*, Oct. 4, 1870.

[8] *Call* and *Post*, April 10, 1878. Campbell, *op. cit.*, 114, 120, 135–58. Miss Campbell says of the committee which went to Cuba, "The Commission's Report is perhaps the most serious indictment ever made by responsible officials against a labor system." *Senate Exec. Doc. No. 116*, 41st Cong., 2d sess., 3. *House Exec. Doc. No. 1*, 42d Cong., 2d sess., 194–207. *House Exec. Doc. No. 1*, 43d Cong., 1st sess., 203.

proof they pointed to the apparent control exercised by the Chinese Six Companies over the immigrants, to the fact that Chinese laborers were brought into the country in large numbers for the railroads and other corporations, and to the plausible statements of men who were presumed to know the facts.[9] On the other hand, the Chinese Six Companies earnestly denied that they controlled these laborers, and the men who knew them best insisted that they were not imported under the notorious coolie system. The difference, however, seems to have been chiefly one of degree rather than of kind. The evidence is conclusive that by far the majority of the Chinese who came to California had their transportation provided by others and bound themselves to make repayment. In the words of one of the most thorough students of this problem,

> There is no doubt that the greater part of the Chinese emigration to California was financed and controlled by merchant brokers, acting either independently or through Trading Guilds. . . . Under the credit-ticket system Chinese brokers paid the expenses of the coolie emigration. Until the debt so incurred by the coolie was paid off the broker had a lien on his services—a lien that might or might not be sold to a bona fide employer of labor. . . . By the credit-ticket system . . . was made possible the large emigration of Southern Chinese to [the] U.S.A., Canada and Australia which commenced during the fifties of [the] last century and continued until it was gradually restricted or prohibited by the legislatures of these English-speaking states.[10]

Foreigners in China differed in their statements regarding this traffic. Peter Parker, S. Wells Williams, and Sir Arthur Edward Kennedy, colonial governor at Hong Kong, declared that the shipments to California were not of the notorious contract coolie order, and that they were so recognized by the Chinese. United States Consuls Denny and Bailey, however, insisted that there was no difference between those going to California and those bound for Cuba and other places in the West Indies and South America. The most evident difference was that, while the contracts of the "coolie traffic" were sold and the coolie had nothing to say as to whom he should serve, the broker retained the "credit ticket" of the California immigrant. In other words, the laborer's obligation was direct to the broker, and while the latter exercised a close supervision over him, the laborer was free to choose his employer so long as he made his monthly payments.[11]

Californians, in constantly increasing numbers, either doubted that

[9] *Report 689*, 76, 82–83, 93, 406, 674. James D. Richardson (comp.), *Messages and Papers of the Presidents, 1789–1897*, 10 volumes, Washington, 1900, VII, 288.
[10] Campbell, *Chinese Coolie Emigration*, XVII, 78.
[11] Campbell, *op. cit.*, 29. *Report 689*, 83, 1245–46. *Cong. Globe*, 37th Cong., 2d sess., 351. *House Exec. Doc. No. 105*, 34th Cong., 1st sess., 75. *House Exec. Doc. No. 1*, 43d Cong., 2d sess., 567. *Consular Reports, 1800–1881*, 175–80. *House Exec. Doc. No. 60*, 46th Cong., 2d sess. *Chronicle*, March 6, 1880. *Bulletin*, Nov. 27, 1880.

this difference existed or discounted its significance, holding that the living and working conditions of the Chinese were those of slavery, even if legal evidence were lacking. The absence of tangible evidence was accounted for on the ground that the agreements were never brought into American courts but were enforced by Chinese methods. Substantial proof of this was found in the control exercised by the Companies through an agreement with the shipping concerns, that no ticket should be sold to a Chinese unless he presented a certificate from his Company to the effect that all of his obligations had been met. When notice was posted that the legislature had prohibited this practice the Six Companies posted a counterblast: "If anyone does not pay what has been expended, the companies will get out a warrant and arrest him and deliver him over to the American courts, and then if the Chinaman loses his baggage and passage ticket it will not be any concern of the companies."[12] Whatever the actual conditions may have been, appearances convinced the average Californian that in the Chinese laborer he was meeting competition that had many of the earmarks of slavery. And the Civil War was altogether too recent to make those earmarks attractive.

No charge against the Chinese was made more frequently nor with more sympathetic hearing than that relating to their low standard of living. Practically all of the Chinese laborers in California were single men and lived in very restricted quarters. In most cases they came, not to settle permanently, but to accumulate an amount sufficient to enable them to return to China and live in comparative comfort. Accustomed to living on a few cents a day, with the higher wage scale in California the laborer hoped to be able to attain his goal in a relatively short time, even with the increased cost of supplies. Hence, ". . . they work on patiently for years, saving every cent, living cheaply and working cheaply."[13]

Those who opposed Chinese cheap labor urged that the American laborer, with his ideal of a home and family, could not compete with the Chinese because he could not live on the Chinese level of wages. Hence, American immigrants, so greatly desired in California, would not come, or if they came, would not stay. Comparisons were made with Gresham's Law of money, and with conditions in the south, where free labor was unable and unwilling to compete with slave labor. As a sample of outside opinion concerning California labor conditions the *Denver News* was quoted, "Give California a wide berth, for the laborer is not worthy of his hire in that state, even when there is work for him to do."[14] The presence of Chinese laborers was held responsible for an increasing number of "hoodlums" among the young men of California,

---

[12] *Bulletin*, Oct. 11, 13, 1883. In 1880 appeal was made to the State Board of Equalization to tax the Six Companies for their alleged assets in these contracts. *Chronicle*, July 25, 1880.

[13] Sacramento *Bee*, April 4, 1876. This is from a statement by the Chinese themselves. See also [O.] Gibson [*The Chinese in America*, Cincinnati, 1877], 36.

[14] *Chronicle*, April 2, 1876. Butte *Record*, July 1, 1876. *Bulletin*, Nov. 18, 1876. *Post*, June 14, 1878.

because the Chinese preempted the opportunities for finding work, and their wage scale degraded labor to a level so low that white boys would not engage in it. At the same time commodity prices to the consumer were not lowered.[15]

Many employers welcomed the Chinese laborer because his low wage scale enabled them to inaugurate undertakings which otherwise might not have been able to compete with the older establishments in the east. Others claimed that white labor was not available, while some insisted that the Chinese created additional labor for the whites, of a higher grade than that done by the Chinese. This was one phase of the question on which California disagreed with the east. Postmaster General Key, after a visit to California, spoke very highly of Chinese laborers. "It is wonderful to see how little a Chinaman can live on." What was, perhaps, a common view in the east was:

> If the people of California were capable of viewing their own interest without passion or prejudice, they would perceive they have a great advantage over the rest of the country in the cheapness of Chinese labor. It favors a rapid development of the resources of that wonderful state. It enables them to undersell in all markets every exportable article which their soil, climate and mineral wealth enable them to produce.[16]

Especially irritating to opponents of the Chinese were the statements of easterners, on the basis of very meager information, belittling the problem of Chinese labor. When President Anderson of Chicago University and Henry Ward Beecher, after short visits to California, gave lectures and interviews deriding the opposition to the Chinese and accusing Californians of gross exaggeration regarding the danger from Chinese immigration, the press answered with bitter denunciation. The *Post*, which was probably the most radical anti-Chinese newspaper in the state, said,

> It is difficult to preserve good temper in the face of such balderdash from such a source. This sensational word-monger [Beecher] taunts us with the theory of evolution, and twittingly declares that if least fitted to survive, then we should go to the wall. . . . But only let the general government release our people from federal obligations, and with our own state laws and local enactments we will free ourselves from the leprous evil, or, failing in that, with the same right arms that founded this western empire, will prove to the world that the imperial Saxon race, though but a million strong, can maintain its claim even against four hundred million serfs to possess and forever hold untrammeled the fair continent of Amer-

---

[15] *Call*, Aug. 29, 1877, Feb. 2, 1879. *Alta*, Jan. 23, 1874. *Report 689*, 81, 246, 322, 352, 356.

[16] *Call*, March 27, 1879. Key's statement, *Call*, Nov. 1, 2, 1878. *Report 689*, 516–58, *et passim.*

ica. . . . The silence of the grave would be all that would tell of the Chinaman's existence here.[17]

Many Californians opposed Chinese labor because it represented a standard upon which no European could live. As one writer insisted, the Chinese were denounced, not because they sold their labor cheaply, but because their civilization was such that they *could* sell cheaply. In other words, Californians objected to the Chinese because they were willing to be the mudsills of society.[18] And it was considered a turn in the tide when an eastern writer pointed out that the reason why the white laborers could not compete with the Chinese was that the standard of living of the whites made larger and more diverse requirements than the narrow range of wants of the Chinese, and that "the survival of the fittest" was not a valid argument; one might just as well argue the superiority of the Canadian thistle because it overcomes useful grasses.[19]

This phase of the working of a low standard of living was not appreciated by all Californians. Some of those who favored their employment claimed that Chinese cheap labor had an effect very much like that of machinery, apparently depriving men of work but actually providing more jobs. This argument was opposed by Henry George. He insisted that "the essential thing about Chinese laborers is that they are cheap laborers." While the principal effect of labor-saving machinery is on production, increasing and cheapening it, the effect of cheap labor is chiefly on distribution. With cheap labor production remains practically the same, but the laborer has less purchasing power. Actually, the higher labor is, the more efficient it is likely to be. Thus cheap labor may even raise the cost of production, since there may be less units produced, due both to the lower efficiency and to the lower purchasing power of cheap labor.[20] George's argument was too involved to become a popular one, but even the ordinary citizen could see the force of his statement that the cheap laborer compels other laborers to work cheaply.

This cheap labor made an insidious appeal to Californians because it offered comforts at small cost and relief from the unusually high prices of white labor. Many even of those opposed to the Chinese patronized them. William Wellock, one of Denis Kearney's lieutenants, charged that the product of the more than ten thousand Chinese cigarmakers in San Francisco was being consumed, not by Stanford, Crocker, Flood and other wealthy men, but by the workingmen. Asserting that the Chinese came and remained because Californians were profiting by their presence, editors complained:

> The Chinaman is here because his presence pays, and he will remain and continue to increase so long as there is money in him.

[17] *Post,* March 19, 1879. See also *Chronicle,* April 2, 1876. *Call,* Oct. 7, 1878. *Bulletin,* April 3, 1876. *Post,* April 3, 1876, June 29, Sept. 24, 1878.
[18] *Argonaut,* Dec. 29, 1877. See also the issues of Oct. 27, Nov. 3, 10, 17, Dec. 1, 1877.
[19] *Bulletin,* May 9, 1878, quoting from M. J. Dee, "Chinese Immigration," *North American Review,* May–June, 1878, 506–26.
[20] *Report 689,* 276–81, 541, 556, 667. *Post,* July 15, 1878.

When the time comes that he is no longer profitable *that* generation will take care of him and will send him back. We will not do
it so long as the pockets into which the profit of his labor flows
continue to be those appertaining to our pantaloons.

They do not go because the people of California, while protesting against their presence, continue to utilize their labor in a
hundred ways. In this matter private interest dominates public interest.[21]

The decades of most intensive anti-Chinese agitation were burdened
with problems of railroad, land, and other monopolies, and anything
smacking of monopoly was certain to arouse instant antagonism. Californians saw in the Chinese a developing monopoly of sinister mien. As
they entered one field of activity after another it was claimed that they
not only drove out American laborers but also tended to monopolize the
industry. This was charged particularly in regard to cigar and shoe
making and certain types of garment manufacture. They were credited
with great imitative skill, and it was claimed that the only industry into
which the Chinese had gone without monopolizing it was that of woolen
manufacture, and that this was due to the large amount of capital required. "Where little capital is required, there the Mongol is sure to
triumph."[22]

When eastern interests objected to the anti-Chinese agitation on the
ground that it would injure our trade opportunities in China, Californians
replied that this trade was very one-sided. Figures were quoted showing
that our exports to China in 1878 totaled more than $23,000,000 and our
imports over $18,000,000, but that some $16,000,000 of our exports were
in gold and silver bullion, very largely remittances by Chinese in California, covering not only about five million in savings, but also purchases
of Chinese goods. It was charged that the Chinese purchased most of
their food and clothing in China, and that factories for the duplication of
American goods were being set up in China.

We may sell them samples of goods, but in a short period they will
make goods as good as the sample. . . . It is not at all improbable
that within twenty years we shall find the East demanding protection from Chinese cheap labor in China as loudly as California
now demands protection from the same kind of labor within her
own limits. The fundamental fact of this question is that at home
or abroad the Chinese can produce cheaper than any other people
in existence.[23]

21 Sacramento *Record-Union*, Jan. 10, 1879. *News Letter*, April 1, 1876. See also
*Chronicle*, June 1, 1878. *Report 689*, 399, 424, 622.
22 *Bulletin*, March 27, 1876. See also Stockton *Independent*, April 12, 1876. *Report
689*, 80, 104, 244–47, 554, *et passim*.
23 *Call*, Oct. 18, 1879. See also *Bulletin*, Aug. 7, 1879, July 22, 1882. *Chronicle*, April
27, 1873, March 15, 1879. *Post*, July 27, 1878. [Theodore H.] Hittell [*History of
California*, 4 volumes, San Francisco, 1885–97], IV, 101.

The Chinese were charged with contributing to monopoly in connection with the great landholders and the railroads. The latter had received large grants from the government, while the former had acquired the Spanish and Mexican holdings, and were included in the general anti-monopoly agitation. Since these landed interests were among the most ardent advocates of continued Chinese immigration the charge was frequently voiced that California was in danger of having a "caste system of lords and serfs" foisted upon it, the great holders of land and the railroads being represented as "Chinese emigration bureaus" and the largest "Chinese employment offices" on the coast. The anti-Chinese element in California looked upon these "monopolists" as among the chief mainstays of the Chinese. The claim of eastern newspapers that the "better class" of Californians favored the Chinese was answered with, "Nobody is in favor of anything of the kind but the cormorants, desert-grabbers and other Judas Iscariots of their race, who would sell the whole land—people, liberties, institutions and all—for their own private aggrandizement. . . ."[24] These great landowners were regarded as worse than the plantation owners of slave days. The only way to solve the situation was to break up the large holdings into small farms. "The Mongolian will be ground out with the growth of genuine American circumstances." When J. C. G. Kennedy appeared in Washington on behalf of the Chinese Six Companies and of the "agricultural interests" of California, it was alleged that he had been connected with the slave interest before the Civil War and that President Lincoln had removed him from office because of his activities in this cause. His actions were denounced. "It is the nearest to an open declaration upon the part of the Mexican grantholders of California of a deliberate purpose to make a struggle for 'Chinese cheap labor' that has yet come to our notice. The great landowners are evidently on the warpath."[25]

From an economic viewpoint employers and those seeking employment differed widely concerning the effect of the Chinese in the state. With few exceptions employers considered them beneficial as a flexible supply of labor, cheap, submissive, and efficient; but those whose only capital was their ability to work were almost unanimous in the opinion that the Chinese were highly detrimental to the best interests of the state. Each group saw the problem through the spectacles of its own economic interests.

Of scarcely less frequent mention in the opposition to the Chinese were charges concerning their morals. Like all frontier societies, California was not distinguished for its devotion to religious and moral ideals, but this did not prevent the most severe strictures upon immoral practices of a different sort. One of the leaders against the Chinese declared, "Their moral condition is as bad and degraded as four thousand years of

[24] *Chronicle*, Jan. 2, 1877. *Alta*, July 6, 1857, Dec. 17, 1877. *Argonaut*, Dec. 29, 1877. *Call*, Jan. 21, 1878. *Cong. Record*, 44th Cong., 1st sess., 2856. *Report 689*, 767–94.
[25] *Post*, March 22, 1878. See also *Post*, Feb. 14, Dec. 1, 1877, Jan. 15, Feb. 15, 24, 1878, Aug. 18, 1879. *Bulletin*, Feb. 15, 19, 1878, July 5, 31, Aug. 3, 1879. *Chronicle*, May 31, 1877.

heathenism can make it, and . . . their physical condition is as low as the practice of all the crimes that have been known since history was written can make it."[26]

In some cases the charge against the Chinese was simply that they were dishonest and unreliable, and that the entire business life of China was permeated by the idea that every person who handled a transaction should take his share of graft. More specifically, they were accused of having no regard for the sanctity of an oath. As early as 1854 legislation was proposed forbidding Chinese testimony against whites, and while it did not pass, a decision of the state supreme court during the year accomplished the same purpose. Several later attempts to admit Chinese testimony were defeated, and this attitude was urged by Pacific coast senators with such force in 1870 as to prevent their admission to naturalization.[27] Of like character was the charge of falsifying tax records. Numerous instances were cited to show the smuggling of Chinese immigrants and the violation or evasion of internal revenue and poll tax laws.[28]

Of the other vices charged to the Chinese those of opium smoking and gambling were outstanding. Opium dens were numerous in San Francisco, but since the effect of smoking was quieting, the addicts did not come in conflict with the police as did inebriated whites. However, when white people began to frequent the opium resorts more notice was taken of them. Games of chance seem to have been the chief means of excitement and recreation for the Chinese. At one time it was claimed that there were in San Francisco Chinatown more than one hundred fan-tan games and nine organized lottery companies with three hundred agencies and two drawings daily, patronized by thousands of both whites and Chinese. This situation had been in existence for years, and the police were accused of conniving with the gambling element. The police, however, declared that since gambling was a natural passion with the Chinese, they would evade any legal restriction; that gambling was being carried on behind barred doors, and that it was almost impossible for a white man to enter.[29]

No phase of the Chinese question attracted more attention than that of prostitution. It was charged that there was not a single home, in the American sense, among all of the Chinese on the coast, and that of the four thousand Chinese women in the state all were either prostitutes or concubines. It was generally charged, also, that these women were

[26] *Report 689*, 15. Pixley usually brought the questioning around to the moral effect of the Chinese in California.
[27] *Cong. Globe*, 41st Cong., 2d sess., 5123–25, 5177. *Report 689*, 119, 1022. *Bulletin*, April 10, May 22, 1857, Jan. 17, April 9, 1862, April 27, 1882. *Alta*, March 10, 12, 26, 1854. Hittell, *California*, IV, 111–12.
[28] *Alta*, Feb. 11, 1871. *Bulletin*, Oct. 15, 16, 25, Nov. 13, 15, 19, 20, 1883, Jan. 7, 1884, May 18, 1887. *Report 689*, 996, 1129.
[29] *Report 689*, 187, 223, 403. Drunkenness was very uncommon among them. *Ibid.*, 89, 668. *Post*, June 2, Aug. 9, 16, 20, Sept. 10, 1879. *Call*, Sept. 28, 1878. *Chronicle*, July 15, 16, 1877, Sept. 15, 1878.

purchased, kidnapped, or lured by panderers in China, brought to America under contract, and sold to Chinese men, either as concubines or for professional prostitution. "They are bought and sold like slaves at the will of their masters."[30] Apparently this traffic began quite early. Frequent protests were made against the practice and against the conditions attending it, and on one occasion the heads of the Chinese Companies offered their assistance in curbing the traffic. The Page Act of 1875 was thought to have stopped it, but within a few years an extensive system of smuggling was unearthed.[31]

On first consideration one might regard the moral and religious phase of this question as insignificant, since it is hardly true that Chinese practices were "worse" than those of Californians. But the methods of the Chinese were different, and this fact alone was enough to make them an object of attack. To Californians the immoralities of the Chinese seemed to be an integral part of their way of living, ingrained through many centuries of practice, rather than an occasional excursion into a by-path. As a contemporary writer expressed it,

> They live in close quarters, not coarsely filthy like ignorant and besotted Irish, but bearing a savor of inherent and refined uncleanliness that is almost more disgusting. Their whole civilization impresses me as a low disciplined, perfected, sensuous sensualism. Everything in their life and their habits seems cut and dried like their food. There is no sign of that abandonment to an emotion, to a passion, good or bad, that marks the western races. . . . The whole matter of the Chinese religion seems very negative and inconclusive; and apparently it has little hold upon them. There is no fanaticism in it,—no appreciable degree of earnestness about it.[32]

Opposition on the basis of religion, however, was not directed primarily against the religious beliefs of the Chinese. The religious question was raised chiefly as a reaction to the attitude of the Protestant churches toward restrictive legislation. The movement against the Chinese came during a period of great missionary activity on the part of most of the American churches, and several denominations had undertaken work among the Chinese, both on the coast and in China. The church leaders feared that the anti-Chinese agitation would have an adverse effect upon this work. Their utterances, resolutions, and memorials to Congress opposing measures for the restriction of Chinese immigration elicited bitter

---

[30] *Report 689*, 405. On this subject religious leaders agreed very closely with the anti-Chinese leaders. As part of his testimony Gibson presented his translations of two bills of sale, contracts under which Chinese women were imported. See Gibson, *Chinese in America*, 139–57. [Ira M.] Condit, *The Chinaman as We See Him* [New York, 1900], 144–55.

[31] *Bulletin*, Nov. 26, 29, Dec. 6, 13, 14, 15, 16, 19, 20, 1887, Sept. 26, Oct. 3, 1889, March 13, 1890. *Alta*, April 25, 26, 1854, Sept. 14, 1867, Jan. 16, 18, 1870. *Overland Monthly*, April, 1869, 344 ff.

[32] Samuel Bowles, *Our New West*, Hartford, 1869, 407.

criticism from the California press, both for their utterances and for their missionary endeavors. When eastern Methodists sent memorials against the Fifteen Passenger Bill to President Hayes, the *Post*

> [protested] most emphatically against the criminal recklessness of religious fanaticism in the East in its bearing upon the Chinese question. . . . The Chinese, whether they profess Christianity or not, remain at heart worshipers of their ancestors. This is their religion, and none other. . . . Our opinion is that the time, money and effort wasted on Chinese missions could be turned to very much better account among our own people.[33]

The religious forces on the coast, however, were not unanimous in favoring unrestricted immigration. The first voices of dissent were those of Roman Catholic priests. Gradually disaffection made its appearance among the Protestants. A representative of one of the more liberal groups criticized an eastern religious paper for calling the agitation against the Chinese "a crazy labor reform movement, headed by Kearney and the hoodlums of San Francisco," because the evil effects of the Chinese made it a much larger question than this. However, "we must strike while the iron is hot even if Denis Kearney is blowing the bellows." Even the Methodists, who were generally regarded as the chief opponents of restriction, displayed tendencies toward a change of attitude. Some of the most prominent leaders took a decided stand against the further immigration of the Chinese. The most notable religious declaration against the Chinese, however, was that of S. V. Blakeslee before the State Association of Congregational Churches in 1877, in which he compared the conditions in California with those under slavery in the south. Thus, while eastern religious defenders of the Chinese were irritating California restrictionists, religious leaders on the coast tended more and more to oppose unrestricted immigration.[34]

No one source furnished such unfailing inspiration for criticism of the Chinese, especially from the social and political viewpoint, as the evils of Chinatown. No matter when or how often the need might arise, a short tour of Chinatown would supply ample material for any amount or degree of condemnation. Within four years of statehood a committee reported this district overcrowded, the houses filthy beyond imagination, pervaded by a "stench almost insupportable," numerous sick in every dwelling, excessive fire hazards due to inadequate cooking facilities, the

---

[33] *Post*, Feb. 22, Nov. 4, 1879. See also Sacramento *Record-Union*, Oct. 7, 1878, Feb. 24, 1879. *Chronicle*, Oct. 7, 8, Nov. 24, 1878, June 27, 1879, April 3, 6, 7, 10, 1890. Presbyterians, Baptists, Methodists, Congregationalists, and Episcopalians carried on missionary work among the Chinese in California.

[34] Blakeslee's address is in [*Chinese Immigration: Its Social, Moral, and Political Effect*, Report of the Special Committee on Chinese Immigration to the California State Senate, Sacramento, 1878], 239–49. It was excerpted by numerous newspapers. For other groups see *Alta*, Feb. 26, 1873. *Post*, Jan. 8, 1877, April 2, 1879. *Unitarian Advocate*, April, 1879.

women all prostitutes and the men inveterate gamblers. Later reports on Chinatown were elaborations of this one, as may be seen from that of the health inspectors in 1870:

> All through the dark and dingy garrets and cellars, steaming with air breathed over and over, and filled with the fumes of opium, they groped their way with candle in hand and hanging on to their official noses until they found a door or window where they could procure a fresh breath of air. Rooms, which would be considered close quarters for a single white man, were occupied by shelves a foot and a half wide, placed one above another on all sides of the room, and on these from twenty to forty Chinamen are stowed away to sleep. In many of these places there is scarcely a chance for even a breath of fresh air to creep in, and the occupants are obliged to breathe over and over again the limited allowance. How life can exist in such a place is a mystery. Besides being crowded in the manner above stated, in many of the lodging-houses filth has been allowed to accumulate to the depth of several inches, and in a number of instances the moisture, leach-like, was found dripping from rooms above. In the cellars and underground coops, which frequently extend back half a block, there is no way to obtain a circulation of air—all that does creep in being by the narrow door of the street. Here they burn oil lamps and cook their food, the smoke from which fills the air, and curls lazily up out of the door when it chances to be open.[35]

Sporadic attempts were made to remedy or remove the evil, but instead Chinatown expanded and similar conditions were reported in other cities, until it was said, "The overcrowding of Chinatown is productive of more evils than any other habit of these semi-barbarians."[36]

In addition to the stench, filth, crowding, and general dilapidation with which Chinatown was accused of afflicting the community, another serious charge was made that the Chinese were introducing foreign diseases among the whites. For instance, it was claimed by both civil and medical authorities that Chinese men and women were afflicted with venereal disease to an uncommon degree. The Chinese prostitutes were accused of luring young boys into their houses and of infecting them with the disease. A medical journal charged that the blood stream of the Anglo-Saxon population was being poisoned through the American men who, "by thousands nightly," visited these resorts.[37] A cause of rather

[35] *Alta*, May 16, 1870. The earlier report, *Alta*, Aug. 22, 1854.
[36] *Bulletin*, Sept. 2, 1885. For some of these efforts see *Bulletin*, Aug. 29, Sept. 3, 7, 1878, July 21, 1880. The Canadian Commission of 1884 reported, "There is no question that the Chinese quarters are the filthiest and most disgusting places in Victoria, overcrowded hotbeds of disease and vice." Quoted by Campbell, *Chinese Coolie Emigration*, 42.
[37] *Chronicle*, Nov. 20, and *Post*, Nov. 21, 1876, quoting the San Francisco *Medico-Literary Journal*, Nov., 1876. See *Report 689*, 117, 131, 190, 1031.

frequent concern to the officials were outbreaks of smallpox. The Chinese were suspected as the source of the disease, since cases appeared among them while they were still on shipboard. They were condemned especially for not reporting their cases of the disease. "It [Chinatown] is almost invariably the seed-bed of smallpox, whence the scourge is sent abroad into the city."[38]

The most exciting charge under this head, however, was that the Chinese were introducing leprosy into California. The very strangeness of the disease made this charge all the more ominous. It was claimed that wherever Chinese coolies had gone leprosy had developed, and that purchasers of Chinese goods were likely to contract the disease. Dr. Charles C. O'Donnell, a politically minded physician, discovered a case in a Chinese washhouse, placed him in an express wagon and drove through the streets, haranguing the crowds on the street corners concerning the dangers to which the community was being exposed. The contention of some physicians that it was not real leprosy but rather a "sporadic case of elephantiasis" did not help matters a great deal. During a period of less than ten years the Board of Supervisors of San Francisco arranged for the deportation of forty-eight cases.[39]

What many considered the most fundamental objection to the Chinese was their difference from Americans in racial characteristics and their unwillingness to adopt American customs and ideals. Some felt that the difficulty was merely superficial, and that if the Chinese would adopt western garb and mingle with Americans the most bitter prejudices against them would disappear. Others, however, were convinced that the difference was much deeper, holding that the Chinese civilization had crystallized and that they could not assimilate with the American people. Even if no natural barrier existed, the Chinese were so devoted to their native land that, in case of death in this country, their bones were to be returned to China. It was claimed that they showed no inclination to make this country their permanent home nor to become citizens; indeed, it was felt that they were not fitted to become citizens, for they were imbued with monarchistic ideals and would become the tools of bosses.[40]

Considering all of these factors it is not surprising that the leaders of the movement against the Chinese should claim to see in the situation a great struggle between Asiatic and American ideals and civilizations. It may be called race prejudice, but race prejudice is not instinctive. It generally has an economic or social basis, a fear due to a lower standard of living or to a higher standard of effort. One editor expressed it during the heat of the agitation:

> We have won this glorious land inch by inch from the red man in vain; we have beaten back the legions of George the Third for

[38] *Chronicle*, July 22, 1878. *Bulletin*, Jan. 29, 31, Feb. 5, 7, 1880, April 20, Dec. 21, 1881. *Report 689*, 127, 208.

[39] *Municipal Reports, 1884–1885*, Appendix, 234. *Post*, Nov. 19, 1877, Aug. 20, Sept. 20, 1878. See *Bulletin*, Sept. 19, 1878, April 18, 1890.

[40] *Report 689*, 16, 103, 188, 543–44, 586–87, 678–79, et al.

nothing; we have suppressed rebellion and maintained the integrity of our country for no good purpose whatsoever, if we are now to surrender it to a horde of Chinese, simply because they are so degraded that they can live on almost nothing, and underbid our own flesh and blood in the labor market. The people of California cannot endure it.[41]

It is of interest here to note that the Chinese were not the first, as they were not the last, against whom such statements were directed. Just as the American frontier has had a tendency to repeat itself across the country, so agitation against the influx of new racial groups has recurred in our history. A generation before the agitation against the Chinese it was said of the Irish that "they do more work for less money than the native workingman, and live on a lower standard, thereby decreasing wages."

The foreigners in general retained their pride for the fatherland and associated together in clannish exclusiveness, forming their own secret societies, which were sometimes political, and even their own military companies. In addition, they constituted a source of political evil with citizenship often illegally conferred upon them and as the ignorant tools of corrupt politicians in innumerable election frauds.[42]

If we place beside this California's official declaration concerning the Chinese the comparison is obvious:

During their entire settlement in California they have never adapted themselves to our habits, modes of dress, or our educational system, have never learned the sanctity of an oath, never desired to become citizens, or to perform the duties of citizenship, never discovered the difference between right and wrong, never ceased the worship of their idol gods, or advanced a step beyond the musty traditions of their native hive. Impregnable to all the influences of our Anglo-Saxon life, they remain the same stolid Asiatics that have floated on the rivers and slaved in the fields of China for thirty centuries of time.[43]

These, then, constituted California's indictment against the Chinese. Most important was economic competition, with its threat of the degrada-

[41] *Marin Journal*, April 13, 1876.
[42] Arthur C. Cole, "Nativism in the Lower Mississippi Valley," *Mississippi Valley Historical Review*, VI, 260–61. See also Stephenson, "Nativism in the Forties and Fifties," *ibid.*, IX, 185–202. The statement regarding the Irish is from Henry Pratt Fairchild [*Immigration: A World Movement and Its American Significance*, New York, 1923], 69, quoting *North American Review*, Jan., 1841.
[43] Cal. Senate, *Chinese Immigration*, 63 (Memorial to Congress).

tion of labor and the entrenchment of monopoly. Chinese moral and religious practices differed from those of Americans and seemed ingrained and unchangeable. Racial differences, the apparent unconcern for American political and social institutions, and the clannishness which produced the inevitable "Chinatown" served as constant and never-failing sources of complaint. By the frequent reiteration of these charges Californians convinced themselves and their neighbors, and finally the United States, that an effective remedy must be found.

# The Birth and Death

# of the

# Plains Indians

PETER FARB

After the appearance of the white man in the Western Hemisphere, different Indian groups went through various cultural changes as they struggled to preserve their identity and their lands. Perhaps the most impressive product of the Indians' adaptations to the white presence on the American continent was the elaborate culture that evolved among the nomadic tribes of the Great Plains once they acquired the white man's animal—the horse.

When the Indians of Latin America first saw the conquistadors astride the horses they had brought from Spain to the Western world, they thought the two were a single animal (a mistake that may also account for the mythical centaur). The Indians soon learned, how- ever, that man and horse were separate creatures and that the latter could be domesticated to great advantage. The Spaniards introduced horses in Mexico in the sixteenth century, and herds of the animals spread northward over the plains. Late in the seventeenth century, North American Indians began to breed Spanish horses. When white settlers reached the Great Plains over a century later, they met the first mounted Indians ever to be seen—the prototypes of the fierce, proud Indians encountered today in Western movies.

By the time of their first real contacts with whites, the Indians were well on their way to developing a complex culture that centered on the horse and the buffalo, the great native of the plains on which they relied for food, shelter, and clothing. The horse had literally transformed their lives by dramatically increasing their mobility and giving them greater effectiveness in waging war and in hunting the all-important buffalo. By the time of the Civil War, more than two- thirds of the Indians that remained in the United States belonged to the Great Plains civilization.

In his book **Man's Rise to Civilization as Shown by the Indians of North America from Primeval Times to the Coming of the Industrial State,** Peter Farb, an anthropologist previously on the staff of the

New York Museum of Natural History, examines the life and history of the American Indians and traces their cultural evolution. Although many scholars have quarreled with Farb's perspectives and have accused him of oversimplifying cultural and historical elements to accommodate his theory, the book stands as a valuable and beautifully written introduction to the varieties of American Indian life. The following selection, taken from this book, is a chapter in which Farb discusses the impact of the horse on the various Indian cultures that coalesced into the Plains group.

The tragic end of the Plains Indian culture at the close of the nineteenth century was marked by the massacre of Indians at Wounded Knee, South Dakota. Wovoka, the last of the great Indian messiahs, had dreamed of a resurgence of the declining Indian culture, but the greater powers of the United States government held sway.

## THE GREAT AMERICAN EPIC

To many people, the typical Indian was the Plains Indian, a painted brave in full regalia, trailing a war bonnet, astride a horse which he rode bareback, sweeping down upon a wagon train, in glorious technicolor. In actual fact, the picturesque culture of the Plains Indian was artificial, not aboriginal, and it did not last very long. The amalgam known as the Plains culture was not fully accomplished until the early 1800's—and like the spring grass of the high plains, it withered quickly.

This culture emerged almost inconspicuously in the middle of the eighteenth century as its catalytic agent, the horse, spread northward from Spanish settlements in New Mexico. Within only a few generations, the horse was found throughout the central heartland of the continent, and Indians from all directions spilled onto the plains. They originally spoke many different languages and had various customs, but they all found in the horse a new tool to kill greater numbers of bison than they had ever believed possible. They became inconceivably rich in material goods, far beyond their wildest dreams, and like a dream it all faded. By about 1850, the Plains culture was already on the wane as the "manifest destiny" of a vigorous United States to push westward shoved them aside. The fate of the Plains Indians had been sealed with the arrival of the first miners and the first prairie schooner. The battles of extermination between Plains

"The Birth and Death of the Plains Indians." From the book *Man's Rise to Civilization as Shown by the Indians of North America from Primeval Times to the Coming of the Industrial State* by Peter Farb, pp. 112–32, 299. Copyright, ©, 1968 by Peter Farb. Reprinted with permission of E. P. Dutton & Co., Inc., and Martin Secker & Warburg Ltd.

Indians and United States cavalry represent America's own great epic—its *Iliad*, its *Aeneid*, its Norse saga—but this epic was no more true than any other.

Despite the surrounded forts, the saving of the last bullet for oneself, the occasional acts of heroism, and the frequent acts of bestiality on both sides—despite this picture portrayed in the Great American Epic, there was remarkably little formal combat. Deaths and hardship there were in plenty as the Plains Indians met their catastrophic end, but most deaths were due to starvation, exposure, disease, brutality, and alcoholism, and not to bullets. In all the actual battles between White soldiers and Indian braves, only several thousand deaths on both sides were due to bullets and arrows. The wars of the plains were not epics but mopping-up operations. In the process, the millions of bison very nearly vanished without leaving any survivors, the plains were turned into a dust bowl, and the once-proud Indian horsemen were broken in body and spirit.

The famed Plains Indian culture did not exist in all its glory when Coronado first explored the plains. Lured on by tales of rich lands, where kings were supposed to be lulled to sleep by the chimes of golden bells, Coronado eventually reached Kansas in 1541. Here the Spaniards saw the beast they had been hearing so much about: the remarkable "cow," actually a bison, as large as a Spanish bull, but with an enormous mane and small curved horns. They also met some impoverished Indians who lived in conical tipis "built like pavilions," according to the chronicler of the expedition. He was particularly impressed by the way the bison seemed to provide most of the materials needed by the Indians:

> With the skins they build their houses; with the skins they clothe and show themselves; from the skins they make ropes and also obtain wool. With the sinews they make threads, with which they sew their clothes and also their tents. From the bones they shape awls. The dung they use for firewood, since there is no other fuel in that land. The bladders they use as jugs and drinking containers.[1]

Hunting bison on foot was not productive, and it certainly could not support large numbers of Indians. Such hunting was practiced largely by the wretched nomads who moved around in small groups and who lived off the occasional weakened bison they could kill or those they could stampede over bluffs. Most of the aboriginal cultures on the plains and prairies were based on the cultivation of maize, beans, and squash. Agriculture had spread westward from the eastern Woodlands, and it followed the fingerlike extensions of rivers throughout the arid Dakotas, Texas, and virtually to the foothills of the Rockies. Hunting bison, for these people, was only incidental to the primary subsistence based on agriculture. They went on a hunt about once a year to supplement their vegetable diet and to obtain hides, sinew, bone, and other raw materials.

Once the horse arrived on the plains, that way of life changed. The

---

[1] This quote and subsequent ones from the Coronado expedition are from *Eyes of Discovery* by John Bakeless, New York: Dover, 1961, pp. 92–93.

nomadic bison hunters became ascendant over the farmers, who either were driven off their lands or abandoned agriculture to become bison hunters themselves. Indians had never seen the horse until the Spaniards brought it to the New World, for sometime during the great glacial melt it had become extinct in North America. The Indians obtained the first horses after the Spaniards settled New Mexico in 1598. (Contrary to previous belief, the Indians captured no horses from de Soto, Coronado, or other early explorers, for these horses either died or were taken home again.) The Spaniards prohibited the sale of horses to Indians, but the revolt of the Pueblo Indians between 1680 and 1692 threw some of the animals on the Indian markets of North America. The Spaniards restocked their herds, which proliferated, but they were unable to prevent further horse stealing by Indians. Horses were bartered—or stolen—from Indian group to group. Soon a whole new Indian profession of horse merchant grew up, and the animals—as well as the knowledge of how to break and train them—spread northward from New Mexico. In addition, some Spanish horses had gone wild and roamed the plains in herds. The Spaniards called them *mesteños* ("wild"), from which the English word "mustangs" is derived.

By the first half of the eighteenth century, enterprising Indian merchants had already sold the horse to Indians as far north as the Northern Shoshone of Wyoming and taught them its management. The Shoshone slowly built up their herds and learned to ride as if they had been born to the saddle. No longer did they have to remain impoverished and secretive inhabitants of the Rocky Mountains, at the mercy of more powerful Indian groups. They swooped down the eastern flanks of the mountains and onto the high plains, where they found a bonanza in bison and a way to even the score with their traditional persecutors, the Blackfoot. From all over, other Indian groups converged on the plains and quickly adapted themselves to an economy based on the bison. The lands of the agriculturists were usurped, and the plains became a maelstrom of varied and often conflicting cultures.

## A LIVING EXPERIMENT IN CULTURE CHANGE

The stolen, bartered, bought, or captured horse was a new cultural element in the heartland of North America, and it changed the entire way of life there.[2] The whole of the plains, from Alberta to Texas, became peopled by groups of great diversity who had come from all directions and often from great distances. There were Athabaskans from the north (Kiowa-Apache), Algonkians (Cree, Cheyenne, Blackfoot) and Siouans (Mandan, Crow, Dakota) from the east, Uto-Aztecans (Comanche, Ute) from the west, Caddoans (Pawnee, Arikara) from the south. The plains

---

[2] An excellent summary of the effect of the horse on many Indian cultures is [F. G.] Roe [*The Indian and the Horse*, Norman: University of Oklahoma Press, 1955]. See also [J. C.] Ewers ["The Horse in Blackfoot Indian Culture," *Bureau of American Ethnology Bulletin*, 1955].

became a melting pot for more than thirty different peoples, belonging to at least five language stocks. It has given anthropologists a living laboratory of culture change. Culture change is the way in which a group alters because of new circumstances, or the way it borrows traits from other cultures and fits them into the configurations of its own.

By about 1800 the gross differences in culture among all these peoples had disappeared; the Sun Dance ceremony, for example, was eventually observed by virtually every tribe. Of course differences apparent to the trained eye of the anthropologist still existed; yet it is remarkable that a people from the eastern forests and another from the Great Basin of the West, two thousand miles away, should within only a few generations have become so nearly identical. Even more remarkable, this homogeneity was achieved with great speed, was not imposed on unwilling people by a more powerful group, and was done in the absence of a common tongue—save for "sign language," the lingua franca of the Plains tribes.

The Plains Cree demonstrate how a people originally distant from the plains in both culture and geography eventually could become so typical of it. The Cree were first recorded in the *Jesuit Relations* of 1640, but at that time they had nothing to do with the plains at all. They inhabited the forests between Hudson Bay and Lake Superior, and they were roving hunters and gatherers of wild rice. Their culture was typical of the Northern Algonkian bands, and after the Hudson's Bay Company was founded they turned to trapping. The demand by Whites for more beaver pelts led them to push westward; because they had obtained guns from White traders, they were able to dispossess the previous inhabitants. By about the middle of the eighteenth century, some of the Cree had already penetrated to the west of Lake Winnipeg. Their culture had changed considerably. It was now parasitic on the White trader for weapons, clothing, and cooking utensils—and sometimes even food, because the Cree spent his time trapping rather than hunting. Then the Cree living farthest west discovered the resource of the bison. Historical records reveal that as early as 1772 they had developed primitive ways of hunting bison, although they still did not possess the horse. Within only a generation, though, the Plains Cree had emerged—a typical equestrian Plains tribe, very different in customs and outlook from the Cree that still inhabited the forests, although both groups continued to speak the same language.

And all this was due to the horse. No longer were just stray or stampeded bison taken, but the herds were pursued on swift horses and the choicest animals killed. No longer was the whole animal utilized for raw materials, which had so impressed the chronicler of the Coronado expedition, but the Indians could now afford the luxury of waste. They stocked the tipi with supplies for the future: meat dried in the sun (jerkee), or else pounded and mixed with fat and berries to become pemmican. Even though most of the Plains Indians never saw a White close up until their swift decline, his influence was felt profoundly as his goods and trade articles flowed westward across the plains by barter from one tribe to another. Tipis almost twenty-five feet in diameter were filled to overflowing with new-found riches. An economic revolution, for which the Indians' traditions had not prepared them, took place. The women no longer toiled in the fields—for gardening was not as profitable as hunting, nor could it be practiced in the presence of nomadic horsemen —and they stopped making pottery because brass kettles were obtained from Whites. Permanent villages disappeared, and with them went the elaborate customs and crafts, rules for marriage and residence.

After the Indians discovered the effectiveness of rifles, an armaments race began on the plains. Just as Indians earlier had realized the value of horses, and those lacking them were driven to obtain them by any means, the acquisition of rifles upset the entire balance of power. As soon as one tribe acquired firepower, the competition for others to obtain equal armaments became fierce. Not only the rifles had to be acquired, but there was also a continuing need for powder and for lead. The Indians were driven to take ever greater chances in raids to steal horses which they might barter for guns and ammunition. For a period of nearly fifty years, the plains became an arena of turmoil in which the status quo changed from year to year, as successive groups became supreme in supplies of horses or guns, or in the powerful allies they could muster.

## THE MAKE-BELIEVE INDIANS

The Plains Indians in their heyday were a study in hyperbole, and as make-believe as the set for a western movie. They sprang from greatly differing traditions, from farmers and from hunters and from collectors of wild plants. Each contributed something of its own that created almost overnight a flamboyant culture whose vigor was for a time unequaled. In this world of hyperbole, many traditions that existed in non–Plains Indian societies became wildly exaggerated. Other Indians also possessed clubs and associations, but none were so extravagant in ritual and insignia as the Plains warrior societies. Indians elsewhere also believed in the reality of visions, but none so relentlessly pursued the vision quest and were so caught up in the emotional excesses of religion as the Plains tribes. Other Indians tortured captives, but none evoked pain so exquisitely in their own bodies.

A special kind of social organization developed on the plains that is known as the composite tribe. Wherever the composite tribe is found, it always signifies a breakdown in culture with a subsequent readaptation. Sometimes the breakdown is due to population loss through migration or increased warfare, as occurred to the Pueblo Indians around the Rio Grande River of New Mexico. Sometimes it is due to the disturbance of the resource base through economic exploitation by outsiders, as has been characteristic of primitive African societies. Occasionally, as happened on the North American plains, it is due to the loss of old culture traits and the borrowing of new ones. Whatever the cause, composite tribes usually arise after an alien culture appears; and almost everywhere Whites have penetrated around the world their presence has resulted in the formation of the composite tribe.

A distinguishing characteristic of the composite tribe is that descent reckoning is unspecific: It can be through either the father's or the mother's line, or both. Marital residence rules also are unspecific, and the newly married couple lives with whichever relatives expediency suggests. The composite tribe of the Plains Indians was much more a collection of bands than were the Zuni or the Iroquois lineal tribes. During most of the year the bison lived scattered in small herds, but during the late summer rutting season they came together in huge herds that blackened the plains. The Indians responded with a parallel social cycle. Most of the year a number of Plains Indian families lived together as a band, uniting only at the time of the summer encampment with other bands for tribal ceremonies and a communal hunt. Furthermore, band membership tended to change, and many Plains Indians belonged to several bands during their lifetimes. One cause of the changing membership within bands was the constant feuding, which often became so oppressive that the only way to preserve any peace at all was by fragmentation of the original band. The Plains Indians appear to have been no more complex in their social organization than the Eskimo and the Great Basin Shoshone bands, but that is not really true. They became functioning tribes at least during their summer encampments, and they managed to maintain that identity the rest of the year, even though they broke up into small bands.

The primary way in which identity was achieved was not through clans but through nonkinship sodalities. The word "sodality" is derived from the Latin *sodalis*, which means "comrade" or "associate," and in a modern society it is equivalent to fraternities and sororities, political parties, service clubs like the Rotary or the Lions, and religious organizations. It is an association that binds people together around a single interest. It may be the burial association of the Irish-American immigrants in the last century, credit associations in medieval Europe, even the crop-watching societies in Chinese villages. When the Plains tribes united in the summer, they were crosscut by a bewildering variety of sodalities with ceremonial, social, and military functions. There were dance societies and feasting societies, and even societies based on a common supernatural experience. Some societies were only for women, like the craft guilds of the Cheyenne. Others were open to both men and women, like the tobacco societies of the Crow, which revolved around the raising of special kinds of tobacco for ceremonial use.

The Cheyenne, as just one example, had six military societies that somewhat resembled the dueling societies of German students. A youth was permitted to join any one of them if he could demonstrate his courage, but he usually chose to go into the one his father belonged to. These societies served not only as the tribe's military force but as its police as well. And each of the six had a particular area of responsibility, such as protecting the movement of the encampment from one place to another, or enforcing the rules against individual hunting that might scare away the bison. Only the bravest of the brave warriors could belong to the elite military society known as the Contraries. Somewhat like the Zuni Mudheads, they were privileged clowns. They did the opposite of everything:

They said *no* when they meant *yes;* went away when called and came near when told to go away; called left *right;* and sat shivering on the hottest day.

A special development in the warrior societies was found among the Mandan, Hidatsa, Arapaho, and Blackfoot, which had a hierarchy of societies. The societies were arranged in order of the age of their members, and as the members grew older they moved up a step. In this way a warrior society existed for every male from the youngest to the oldest, with the exception of the effeminate male known as a berdache. No scorn was attached to his position; he was regarded with pity and with a degree of sacred awe for being the victim of a condition that was not of his own doing. Even the berdache found his place in Plains Indian society. He permanently adopted woman's clothing and woman's role; he became skilled in the female tasks of beadwork or skin-tanning, and he was eligible to join the women's societies.

The richness and diversity of the Plains sodalities is explained by the lack of lineal residential groups. The need for non-kin sodalities was so great on the plains because they filled the social void caused by the absence of clans. Had these non-kin sodalities failed to develop, with their complexity of rules and regulations that often seem so ridiculous to us today, the tribes would have been reduced to mere collections of bands. The sodalities brought unity to one of the most diverse collections of people on earth.

## COUPS AND SCALPING

Almost all the sodalities had religious aspects, and almost all were concerned with war in one way or another. The various cultures had engaged in warfare even before they migrated onto the plains and obtained horses, but with the emergence of the Plains Indian culture during the nineteenth century, warfare became as ritualized as medieval knighthood. Only during the very twilight of the Plains culture did large battles take place that pitted Indian against Indian or Indian against the United States Army, with each group seeking to exterminate the other. Previous to that, tactics consisted of forays and raids by small war parties; the conflicts were brief and usually indecisive.

The Plains Indians fought not to win territory or to enslave other tribes, but for a variety of different reasons. One was the capture of horses, which had a high economic value. Another reason . . . was that external strife served to unify the tribe internally. A tribe, especially one as fragile as the composite tribe unified only by non-kin sodalities, needed a common enemy as a rationale for its existence. A third reason was that war was regarded as a game in which the players might win status. In this game, exploits were graded according to the dangers involved. The exploit itself was known as the *coup*, from the French trapper's word for "blow," because originally it signified that the brave had struck the enemy's body with a special stick that was often striped like a barber pole. Later, "counting coups" referred to the recital by the brave of all his war deeds; as he immodestly proclaimed each one he gave a blow against a pole with his ax. These recitals went on endlessly. Each time a young man accumulated a new honor, he used it as an excuse to recount his old exploits. If he lied about his exploits, though, or even shaded the truth a bit, he was challenged immediately by someone who had been along on the same war party.

Each Plains tribe had its own ranking for coups. Among the Blackfoot, stealing an enemy's weapons was looked upon as the highest exploit. Among some other tribes, the bravest deed was to touch an enemy without hurting him. The least important exploit usually was killing an enemy, but even that deed was ranked according to the way it was done and the weapons that were used. The whole business of counting coups often became extremely involved. Among the Cheyenne, for example, coups could be counted by several warriors on a single enemy, but the coups were ranked in the strict order in which the enemy was touched by the participants; it was immaterial who actually killed or wounded him. Like a sort of heraldry, these deeds were recorded in picture writing on tipis and on bison robes. They gave the warrior the right to hold public office. Among many tribes, each coup earned an eagle's feather, and the achieving of many coups accounts for the elaborate headdresses of some of the Plains war leaders.

Scalps taken from dead or wounded enemies sometimes served as trophies, but they were insignificant when compared with counting coups. Many Plains tribes did not take scalps at all until the period of their swift decline, which began in the middle of the last century. Most people believe that all Indians took scalps, and that scalp-hunting was exclusively a New World custom. Neither idea is true. Herodotus, the ancient Greek historian, mentioned the taking of scalps by the Scythians, for example. In South America scalp-taking as a custom was practically unknown; in North America it *may* have existed before the arrival of Whites, but only in a few areas in the eastern Woodlands. Many historians still question whether scalp-taking was an aboriginal Indian practice or rather one learned quite early from the White settlers.

Whatever its exact origins, there is no doubt that scalp-taking quickly spread over all of North America, except in the Eskimo areas; nor is there any doubt that its spread was due to the barbarity of White men rather than to the barbarity of Red men. White settlers early offered to pay bounties on dead Indians, and scalps were actual proof of the deed. Governor Kieft of New Netherland is usually credited with originating the idea of paying for Indian scalps, as they were more convenient to handle than whole heads, and they offered the same proof than an Indian had been killed. By liberal payments for scalps, the Dutch virtually cleared southern New York and New Jersey of Indians before the English supplanted them.[3] By 1703 the colony of Massachusetts was paying the equivalent of about $60 for every Indian scalp. In the mid-eighteenth

[3] [W. T.] Hagan [*American Indians,* Chicago: University of Chicago Press, 1961], p. 15, is the source for the origin of scalping.

century, Pennsylvania fixed the bounty for a male Indian scalp at $134; a female's was worth only $50. Some White entrepreneurs simply hatcheted any old Indians that still survived in their towns. The French also used scalp-taking as an instrument of geopolitics. In the competition over the Canadian fur trade, they offered the Micmac Indians a bounty for every scalp they took from the Beothuk of Newfoundland. By 1827 an expedition to Newfoundland failed to find a single survivor of this once numerous and proud people.[4]

Among the Plains tribes, apparently only the Dakota and the Cree placed any value on scalps; both tribes were late immigrants to the Plains from the East, where they probably learned the practice from Whites. Nor was there as much torturing of captives by Plains tribes as was once believed. The tradition of the White settler's saving his last bullet for himself to avoid a horrible death was a needless precaution. Unlike the Indians of the eastern Woodlands, the Plains Indians killed swiftly. They looked upon the White custom of hanging, for example, as cruel and barbaric.

## CAUSES OF WARFARE

The Great American Epic has traditionally regarded the Plains Indians as the most "warlike" on the continent. Indeed, history does confirm that the heartland of the continent was an arena for continual strife. Yet, stating that a Blackfoot, for example, was "warlike" reveals nothing. The entire Blackfoot tribe did not habitually engage in war because individual members possessed "warlike" personalities. Individual men go to war for individual reasons: for social prestige, for economic rewards and for booty, because of religious convictions—even to escape from frustrations at home. Entire societies, though, do not go to war for such personal reasons. The fact is that the individual Blackfoot was warlike simply because his whole cultural system obliged him to be that way.

All the various theories as to why groups of people go to war fall into four general categories. The first states that it is the very physical nature of man to be pugnacious and aggressive. Such a view of man holds that a warlike urge is biologically inherent in him. This is an old theory, and it keeps popping up from time to time in new presentations, most recently in Konrad Lorenz' *On Aggression* (1966). But there is no evidence in the physical makeup of man to suggest that he has been fashioned as a warlike animal. Man, in truth, is a puny creation, lacking fangs, claws, thick skin, speed, or other adaptations for combat. The whole idea of the innate belligerency of man is laid to rest by evidence that warfare is virtually absent among the most primitive of men, those whose "true" biological nature might appear to be closest to the surface. The Great

---

[4] The extinction of the Beothuk is described in [F. W.] Hodge ["Handbook of American Indians North of Mexico," *Bureau of American Ethnology Bulletin,* 1906 (reprinted New York: Pageant Books, 1960)], p. 142.

Basin Shoshone, for example, never waged war, nor did most other very simple societies before the arrival of Whites.

The second explanation is an affront to logic: Men are warlike because they are warlike. Such an explanation is ridiculous, but even so noted an anthropologist as Ralph Linton wrote that the Plains Indians would not have been so interested in war if "they had not been warlike."[5] Similar statements exist in Ruth Benedict's *Patterns of Culture*. Obviously, such logic is akin to explaining obesity in middle-aged males by saying that many middle-aged males are obese.

The third explanation is a psychological one, and it probably boasts the most adherents—which is understandable, for these people can bolster their case by surveys, personality tests, statistical analyses, and other impressive tools of modern scholarship. Even before the widespread use of such tests and surveys, Freud, in an exchange of correspondence with Einstein in 1932 about the causes of war, agreed that "there is an instinct for hatred and destruction . . . which goes halfway to meet the efforts of the warmongers."[6] All of these psychological studies, though, can explain only the motivations behind why *individuals* go to war. The real point is that although individuals slug each other in a barroom brawl or drop napalm from airplanes over Vietnam, individuals do not go to war. Only societies do that.

That leaves the fourth explanation, which states simply that the causes for war are to be found within the cultures of the contending groups. This explanation avoids confusing the issue with related problems, such as individual motivations or the kinds of warfare practiced. The Plains Indians confirm this cultural explanation. For one thing, the composite tribes of the Plains Indians could not have survived without external enemies, real or imagined, against whom their warrior associations could unite. For another, the Plains culture was artificial, brought into being by the reverberations sent across the continent by the arrival of the Whites. The Whites upset delicate adjustments the Indians had made to each other over very long periods of time. As just one example, the French encouraged warfare between the Ojibway and surrounding groups; the Ojibway spread westward and displaced Siouan tribes, which migrated westward and southward to the plains; there the Sioux displaced Hidatsa and Mandan, who in turn stirred up the Cheyenne and others. The whole unreal situation was very much like a series of balls caroming off one another and resulting in new rebounds.

Most important, once all these groups were on the plains and had altered their cultures by acquiring horses and guns, their whole make-believe world had to be kept in motion or it would collapse. Horses had to be stolen so they could be bartered for more guns to aid in the stealing of more horses. Many White traders encouraged the strife to capitalize on it by selling guns, liquor, and kitchenware. The herds of bison, once

[5] *The Study of Man* by Ralph Linton, New York: Appleton-Century, 1936, p. 463.
[6] Freud's letter on the causes of war is in *Character and Culture*, Vol. 9 in *The Collected Papers of Sigmund Freud*, New York: Collier Books, 1963, p. 141.

thought limitless, dwindled, and as they did there was additional cause for strife over hunting territories. In any event, there were good cultural— that is, social, political, economic, and technological—reasons why the Plains Indians were warlike. They were that way not because of their biology or their psychology, but because their new White-induced culture demanded it.[7]

## THE NEW RICH

Among the Mandan, Hidatsa, Arapaho, and Blackfoot, a member of a war society purchased his way up the ladder of age-grades until he arrived at the topmost grade and was thereupon entitled to wear the famous feathered bonnet. At each step, he selected a seller from the next older brotherhood, and then purchased his rights. A buyer was free to select any seller he wanted, but he usually chose someone from his father's family. Often, as part of the payment, the purchaser had to relinquish his wife to the seller for a time; if the purchaser was unmarried, he had to borrow a wife from a relative. The whole business of joining an age-grade brotherhood was accompanied by an elaborate etiquette that was also somewhat sophomoric and not unlike the mock seriousness of today's Masonic initiation.

Membership in other kinds of societies was also often purchased, and in fact many things were for sale among the Plains tribes: sacred objects, religious songs, and even the description of a particularly good vision. The right to paint a particular design on the face during a religious ceremony might cost as much as a horse. Permission just to look inside someone's sacred bundle of fetishes and feathers was often worth the equivalent of a hundred dollars. A Crow is known to have paid two horses to his sponsor to get himself invited into a tobacco society, and the candidate's family contributed an additional twenty-three horses. A prudent Blackfoot was well advised to put his money into a sacred bundle, an investment that paid him continued dividends. The investment was as safe as today's government bond is; and it was readily negotiable at a price usually higher than the purchase price. By permitting the bundle to be used in rituals, its owner received fees that were like dividends. As the Plains tribes became richer, the price of sacred bundles continued to rise, much as the price of a stock-exchange seat goes up during prosperous times.

[7] Two excellent papers on Plains warfare are by [W. W.] Newcomb ["A Re-examination of the Causes of Plains Warfare," *American Anthropologist*, 1950, pp. 317–29; and "Toward an Understanding of War," in G. L. Dole and R. L. Carneiro, eds., *Essays in the Science of Culture in Honor of Leslie A. White*, New York: Thomas Y. Crowell, 1960, pp. 317–36]. See also [B.] Mishkin ["Rank and Warfare Among Plains Indians," *American Ethnological Society Monograph*, 1940] for the importance of economic factors. Various theories of primitive warfare in general can be found in [H. H.] Turney-High [*Primitive Warfare: Its Practices and Concepts*, Columbia: University of South Carolina Press, 1949].

Until they became horsemen, almost none of these tribes had ever known wealth. The Comanche, for example, had been an impoverished Shoshonean people from the Great Basin before the nineteenth century. Most of the other tribes only a few decades before had been marginal hunters, all of whose possessions could be dragged along by a single dog. But the Plains tribes learned the laws of the marketplace rapidly, both from each other and from the White trader. The accumulation of wealth became important, but it was not incorporated into the societies in any meaningful way. Perhaps it would have been in time, and the Plains tribes might have served economic theorists as the very models of the steps by which societies become capitalistic.

Anthropologists can do no more than guess what might have happened to the concept of wealth had the Plains culture endured for another century, or even for a few more decades. Some indication is given by tribes such as the Kiowa, who learned how to use wealth to create more wealth. A Kiowa warrior was forced by custom to give away some of his wealth, but he also learned to hoard it, not only for himself but also to keep it in his family through inheritance. Classes based on wealth arose in what had once been an egalitarian society. The wealthiest classes could afford to give their sons certain benefits. They equipped them with the best horses and guns and sent them down the road to military glory at an early age. And when the son of a wealthy Kiowa achieved an exploit, everyone heard about it, for the wealthy controlled the channels of publicity through their ability to give gifts. Such publicity paid further economic benefits: The scion of a wealthy Kiowa, with his well-publicized exploits, could increase his wealth even more because he easily obtained followers for a raiding party.

Not knowing what to do with the new-found wealth that crammed their tipis, the Plains Indians regarded it as materially unimportant, but valued it as a status symbol. It became another way to count coups, to get one up on a neighbor. And since the primary way to acquire wealth was to steal horses from someone else, wealth became a validation of bravery. The warrior also could be sure that no one forgot his prowess by the constant reminder of gifts. Gift-giving emphasized that the giver was brave enough to go out and steal more wealth anytime he felt like it.

The sudden wealth achieved by the mass slaughter of bison changed customs in other ways also. It took only a moment for a man on horseback to kill a bison with a bullet, but it still remained a long and arduous task for his wife to dress the hide for sale to the White trader. As a result, a shortage of women arose and a premium was placed on them to the extent that eventually "bride price" was paid. Men always needed the hands of extra women to dress the skins, and the parents of a healthy girl could negotiate her marriage from a position of strength. At the same time, polygyny, which probably had existed in some tribes to a limited extent, became widespread, for a good hunter needed as many wives as he could afford. There are even instances known of berdaches being taken on as second wives, not for any sexual variety they might offer, but merely because they performed women's tasks.

## VISION QUESTS

Most North American Indians greatly respected visions, but few immersed themselves so deeply in them as did the Plains tribes. Sometimes a spirit might come of its own accord in a vision, just to befriend a mortal, but usually the Plains Indian had to go in active pursuit of his vision. He did this by isolating himself, fasting and thirsting, and practicing self-torture, at the same time imploring the spirits to take pity on his suffering. The youth gashed his arms and legs, and among the Crow it was the custom to cut off a joint from a finger of the left hand. Cheyenne vision-seekers thrust skewers of wood under pinches of skin in the breast; these skewers were attached to ropes, which in turn were tied to a pole. All day the youth leaned his full weight away from the pole, pulling and tugging at his own flesh while he implored the spirits to give him a vision.

Mortification of the flesh has always held a fascination for religious fanatics everywhere, for it is the most obvious way that this too, too human flesh can break its link with the world of men and approach the threshold of the gods. Among those who have groped toward deities in this way are the Jewish Essenes around the Dead Sea, the many ascetic orders of Christian monks, the Whirling Dervishes of Islam, and the hermits of Buddhism.

The spirit might at last take pity on the Plains Indian youth—actually it was dehydration, pain, and delirium taking their effects—and give him supernatural guidance. A successful vision supported the youth for the rest of his life. He always had a guardian spirit on whom he could call for help and guidance, although from time to time he had to repeat the self-torture to renew his familiarity with the spirit. During his vision, the youth usually learned what items—such as feathers, a stone pipe, a piece of skin, maize kernels—he should collect for a sacred medicine bundle and put in a small pouch. A particularly lucky youth might also receive his own songs, which when sung served as a call to supernatural aid; that they sounded like gibberish to everyone else only reinforced the belief that he had received a unique vision. A few youths failed to receive any visions at all, even though they tried repeatedly. Those who could not obtain a vision on their own could sometimes purchase one, as well as a replica of the successful visionary's sacred medicine bundle.

What is remarkable about such visions is that they were not invariably experienced, since the entire Plains culture worked toward producing them. Every Plains youth grew up believing firmly in the reality of the vision, so no resistance to the idea had to be overcome. Secondly, the youth worked himself into an intense emotional state by starvation, thirst, self-torture, exposure to the sun, and isolation—all of which are known to produce hallucinations. Thirdly, the shape in which the vision came to him was predetermined by the structure of the myths and visions he had heard about since childhood. Finally, in retelling his vision, he unconsciously reconstructed it and filled in gaps, adapting it to the norms of behavior of his culture—much as we do in reporting an incoherent dream, no matter how sincerely we believe we are not distorting it.

Plains Indian visions were clearly recognized as differing from person to person and from tribe to tribe. Some of the individual differences were biological and psychological. An Indian with an auditory personality might hear loud calls of birds or gibberish songs, whereas a visual type would be apt to see a horse with strange markings. Probably some individual fears and anxieties went into the vision. Despite the Plains warrior's attitude of fearlessness, a common vision was the sudden transformation of rocks and trees into enemies; but the youth was made invulnerable to their arrows by his guardian spirit. Often the vision involved the visit of some animal. An eagle might fly by, the flapping of its wings sounding like crashes of thunder; and bison, elk, bears, and hawks appeared quite often among the nobler beasts. Among the Pawnee (who, alone of the Plains tribes, had worked out an orderly system of religious beliefs, including a supreme being), the stars and other heavenly bodies entered quite freely into visions.

The desire for a vision existed among most of the Indians of North America, and it seems to have developed in two different directions. Among some Indians, it led directly to shamanism, for shamans were believed to be recipients of particularly intense visions and to have the power to summon up new visions at will. The other line of development led to visions of more limited power that had to be sought after. In this second category, there was a great range of variation, from the Plains youth, who suffered ordeals, to the Great Basin Shoshone, who passively waited for the spirit to find him.

Before the contrasting attitudes of the Plains tribes and the Great Basin Shoshone can be explained, the vision must first be recognized for what it is: a resort to supernatural aid in a dangerous undertaking, in which individual skill alone is not enough to guarantee success. The Plains culture provided numerous such dangerous undertakings, such as riding among a herd of stampeding bison or stealthily entering an enemy camp. For the Plains warrior, the rewards of such undertakings were certainly great enough to compensate for the few days of self-torture and fasting required to obtain a guardian spirit. The arid country of the Great Basin Shoshone, however, provided no such rewards. There the land yielded a bare minimum, and the rewards went not to the man who showed courage and daring, but to the one who simply exerted industry in collecting seeds or grasshoppers. Any yearning for visions that existed among the Great Basin Shoshone was not for protection in the dangers of the hunt or in warfare, but for the cure of snake bites or sickness.[8]

The various responses of different cultures toward visions partly explains why some Indians took enthusiastically to the White man's alcohol and others did not. The use of firewater was particularly intense among the Plains, as well as among the nearby forest Indians, who were the ancestors of many Plains Indians. Alcohol was promptly recognized by the Plains Indians as a short-cut method of producing derangement of the senses and hallucinations. In primeval North America the Plains tribes had

[8] For a discussion of the vision quest in several cultures, see [R.] Underhill ["Ceremonial Patterns in the Greater Southwest," *American Ethnological Society Memoir*, 1948].

been remarkably free from the use of hallucinogenic plants such as peyote and mushrooms. The Plains vision-seekers were not even fortunate enough to have *Datura* or Jimsonweed, for its original range in the West was probably in only portions of the Southwest and southern California. Nor had the Plains tribes learned that tobacco, which they smoked in a few ritual puffs, could be swallowed to produce considerable discomfort and emotional upset, the way many Central and South American Indians used it.

Only when the Plains culture was disintegrating rapidly after about 1850 did a hallucinogenic cactus known as peyote take hold. Peyote is native to northern Mexico, but it spread like a grass fire from tribe to tribe as far north as the Canadian plains. Although peyote is used elsewhere in North America to a limited extent, it was most widely and promptly accepted by the Plains tribes. Peyote afforded a way to seek visions; it also provided an escape from the humiliation of the complete defeat by Whites in the latter part of the last century.

## THE END OF A CULTURE

After the Civil War, a tide of White settlers streamed westward, and they sealed the fate of the Plains tribes. Treaty after treaty was broken by Whites as the Indian lands were crisscrossed by easterners covetous of acreage and precious metals. At first the Whites tried to restrict the Plains Indians to valueless territories, but that policy soon changed to a war of extermination. Said General William Tecumseh Sherman in 1867: "The more I see of these Indians, the more convinced I am that they all have to be killed or be maintained as a species of paupers." To help clear the Indians from the plains, the Whites struck at their food base, the bison. They themselves not only destroyed the animals, but they also contrived to get the Indians to collaborate with them by offering to buy vast quantities of such delicacies as bison tongue.

Tensions between the Whites and the Plains Indians increased during the 1870's. On July 5, 1876, newspapers reporting celebrations of the young nation's Centennial reported also the news of a humiliating defeat. The elite Seventh Cavalry, a tough outfit of 260 men, which was organized specifically for killing Plains Indians—and led by Lieutenant Colonel Custer—had been annihilated on June 25 by a combined force of Sioux and Cheyenne in the battle of Little Bighorn. But for Sitting Bull and Crazy Horse, the victory over Custer had been empty, and only marked the beginning of the end for the Plains Indians. From that time on troops pursued them mercilessly from waterhole to waterhole; their women and children were slaughtered before their eyes, their encampments and their riches burned. The glory and the poetry had gone out of the Plains Indians. Mighty chiefs emerged from hiding as miserable fugitives, hungry and without bullets for their guns. The survivors, like so many cattle, were herded onto reservations, where rough handling, cheap whiskey, starvation, exposure, and disease severely depleted their numbers.

The very end of the Plains culture can be dated exactly. In 1890 the surviving Plains Indians enthusiastically listened to a native messiah who foretold the return of dead Indians and the magical disappearance of the Whites. Alarmed, the United States government sent out cavalry to suppress this Ghost Dance, as it was called. While being placed under arrest, Sitting Bull was accidentally killed; and some three hundred Sioux, mostly women and children waiting to surrender at Wounded Knee Creek, South Dakota, were massacred by trigger-happy troops. Wounded Knee marked the end of any hopes the Plains Indians still cherished. The Ghost Dance had proven as make-believe as the rest of their improbable culture.

## BIBLIOGRAPHY

The literature on the Plains Indians is unusually rich, and only highlights can be indicated here. Among general works are: [W. R.] Wedel ["Environment and Native Subsistence Economies in the Central Great Plains," *Smithsonian Miscellaneous Collections*, 1941, pp. 1–29], [R. H.] Lowie [*Indians of the Plains*, New York: McGraw-Hill, 1954 (reprinted Garden City, N.Y.: Natural History Press, 1963)], and [R.] Laubin and [G.] Laubin [*The Indian Tipi*, Norman: University of Oklahoma Press, 1957]. [E. R.] Service [*Profiles in Ethnology*, New York: Harper and Row, 1963] has a good brief discussion on pp. 112–37. Readable historical material is found in [A. M.] Josephy [ed., *The American Heritage Book of Indians*, New York: Simon and Schuster, 1961].

A pioneering work on the prehistory of the plains area is [W. D.] Strong ["From History to Prehistory in the Northern Great Plains," *Smithsonian Miscellaneous Collections*, 1940, pp. 353–94]. For more recent studies, see [W.] Mulloy ["The Northern Plains," 1952, in J. B. Griffin, ed., *Archaeology of Eastern United States*, Chicago: University of Chicago Press, 1952, pp. 124–38], [F.] Wendorf and [J. J.] Hester ["Early Man's Utilization of the Great Plains," *American Antiquity*, 1962, pp. 159–71], and [W. R.] Wedel ["The Great Plains," 1964, in J. D. Jennings and E. Norbeck, eds., *Prehistoric Man in the New World*, Chicago: University of Chicago Press, 1964, pp. 193–222].

The ethnology of particular tribes makes delightful reading, and the choice of books and papers is tremendous. For excellent brief discussions of Mandan, Teton Dakota, and Kiowa, see [R. F.] Spencer, [J. D.] Jennings, et al. [*The Native Americans*, New York: Harper and Row, 1965, pp. 337–83]. The Mandan are discussed in depth by [A. W.] Bowers [*Mandan Social and Ceremonial Organization*, Chicago: University of Chicago Press, 1950]. Three particularly good works on the Cheyenne are [G. B.] Grinnell [*The Cheyenne Indians*, New Haven: Yale University Press, 1923 (reprinted New York: Cooper Square, 1962); idem, *The Fighting Cheyennes*, Norman: University of Oklahoma Press, 1956] and [E. A.] Hoebel [*The Cheyennes: Indians of the Great Plains*, New York: Holt, Rinehart and Winston, 1960]. For the Blackfoot: [C.] Wissler ["Material Culture of the Blackfoot Indians," *American Museum of Natural History Anthropological Papers*, 1910, pp. 1–175; idem, "The Social Life of the Blackfoot Indians," ibid., 1911, pp. 1–64], [E. S.] Goldfrank ["Changing Configurations in the Social Organization of a Black-foot Tribe During the Reserve Period," *American Ethnological Society Monograph*, 1945], and [J. C.] Ewers ["The Horse in Blackfoot Indian Culture," *Bureau of American Ethnology Bulletin*, 1955; and idem, *The Blackfoot*, Norman: University of Oklahoma Press, 1958]. For the Crow, [R. H.] Lowie [*The Crow Indians*, New York: Farrar and Rinehart, 1935 (reprinted New York: Holt, Rinehart and Winston, 1956)] and [J. C.] Ewers ["Of the Crow Nation," *Bureau of American Ethnology Bulletin*, 1953, pp. 1–74]; for the Comanche, [A. F. C.] Wallace and [E. A.] Hoebel [*The Comanches*, Norman: University of Oklahoma Press, 1952]; for the Sioux, [R. B.] Hassrick [*The Sioux*, Norman: University of Oklahoma Press, 1964]. A classic on the Omaha is [A. C.] Fletcher and [F.] La Flesche ["The Omaha Tribe," *Bureau of American Ethnology Report*, 1911].

# Suggestions for Further Reading

Several available books deal in general fashion with the westward movement of settlers in North America. The standard work is Ray A. Billington, *Westward Expansion* (rev. ed.; Macmillan, 1967), but more relevant here is the same author's *The Far Western Frontier, 1830–1860*\* (Harper and Row, 1956). The basic studies of the doctrine of Manifest Destiny are A. K. Weinberg, *Manifest Destiny*\* (Johns Hopkins Press, 1935), and Frederick Merk, *Manifest Destiny and Mission in American History: A Reinterpretation*\* (Knopf, 1963).

Thomas F. O'Dea's *The Mormons*\* (University of Chicago Press, 1957) is an excellent survey of Mormon belief and practice. The migration to the Great Salt Lake is described in Wallace Stegner, *The Gathering of Zion: The Story of the Mormon Trail* (McGraw-Hill, 1964). On the development of the Mormon community in Utah, see Nels Anderson, *Desert Saints: The Mormon Frontier in Utah*\* (University of Chicago Press, 1942).

The Chinese immigration to the West Coast of the United States has received very little attention from historians. Virtually the only works on the subject are Mary Coolidge, *Chinese Immigration* (Henry Holt, 1909), which was written with the hope of reopening immigration after it was brought to a halt by the Chinese Exclusion Act of 1882, and Gunther Barth, *Bitter Strength: A History of the Chinese in the United States, 1850–1870* (Harvard University Press, 1964). A recent study of the reception met by Chinese immigrants in America is Stuart C. Miller, *The Unwelcome Immigrant: The American Image of the Chinese, 1785–1882* (University of California Press, 1969). For an account of some of the problems that the Chinese faced in the United States, see Herbert Asbury, *The Barbary Coast: An Informal History of the San Francisco Underworld*\* (Knopf, 1933).

Two basic anthropological studies of the Plains Indians are E. A. Hoebel, *The Cheyennes: Indians of the Great Plains*\* (Holt, Rinehart and Winston, 1960), and R. H. Lowie, *Indians of the Plains*\* (McGraw-Hill, 1954). For the impact of the horse on Indian culture, see F. G. Roe, *The Indian and the Horse* (University of Oklahoma Press, 1955). Mari Sandoz movingly recounts the breakup of the Plains Indian culture in *Cheyenne Autumn*\* (Hastings House, 1953). The defeat of the Sioux is described in Robert Utley, *Last Days of the Sioux Nation*\* (Yale University Press, 1963). Thomas Berger's novel *Little Big Man*\* (Dial, 1964), presents an authentic picture of elements of Plains Indian culture.

\* Available in paperback edition.

# Mindfulness

Ellen J. Langer

# Mindfulness

A MERLOYD LAWRENCE BOOK

ADDISON-WESLEY PUBLISHING COMPANY, INC.
Reading, Massachusetts   Menlo Park, California   New York
Don Mills, Ontario   Wokingham, England   Amsterdam   Bonn
Sydney   Singapore   Tokyo   Madrid   San Juan

Many of the designations used by manufacturers and sellers to distinguish their products are claimed as trademarks. Where those designations appear in this book and Addison-Wesley was aware of a trademark claim, the designations have been printed in initial capital letters (e.g., Selectric).

*Library of Congress Cataloging-in-Publication Data*

Langer, Ellen J., 1947–
  Mindfulness.

  Includes index.
  1. Attention. 2. Consciousness. I. Title.
BF321.L23   1989      153      88-33293

Jacket design by Janet Halverson
Text design by Jennie Bush, Designworks, Inc.
Set in 11-point Galliard by DEKR Corp., Woburn, MA

To the memory of my mother and grandmother

# Contents

# Contents

*

# *Acknowledgments*

Because I have written and rewritten this book many times, each time trying to make the ideas of interest to a broader audience, and each time enlisting the patient advice of friends and colleagues, I have many people to thank. Robert Abelson, Daryl Bem, Anne Bernays, Otto Brodtrick, Jerome Bruner, Marjorie Garber, Roslyn Garfield, William Goode, John Hallowell, Gerald Holton, Philip Holzman, Barbara Johnson, Jerome Kagan, Aron Katz, Phyllis Katz, Barbara Levine, Beverly London, Letty Cottin Pogrebin, Helen Rees, Eric Rofes, Howard Stevenson, Phyllis Temple, Marjorie Weiner, and Lenore Weitzman have all enriched the book with their perceptive comments. It is an understatement to say that I am grateful for their help. To Elaine Noble I am especially grateful for rich insights on the relationship between mindlessness/mindfulness theory and alcoholism. The technical aspects of preparing this manuscript were carried out with great proficiency by Julie Viens, Barbara Burg, and Andrea Marcus.

Major concepts used in this book are derived from

research conducted over the past fifteen years, at Yale, City University of New York, and, for the past twelve years, in the Department of Psychology at Harvard. I am therefore deeply indebted to all the people who collaborated with me on these investigations. Most especially I have profited from years of continued collaboration with Benzion Chanowitz.

My ideas sometimes get the better of me. Before I clearly explain one, another comes to mind and seizes my attention. For this reason, I imagine the reader shares my deep gratitude for Merloyd Lawrence's editorial skills, which have been invaluable in shaping this book.

# *Mindfulness*

# CHAPTER 1

*

# *Introduction*

I don't like the idea of a unitary subject; I prefer the
play of a kaleidoscope: you give it a tap and the little
bits of colored glass form a new pattern.
ROLAND BARTHES, *The Grain of the Voice*

*

One day, at a nursing home in Connecticut, elderly
residents were each given a choice of houseplants to
care for and were asked to make a number of small
decisions about their daily routines. A year and a half
later, not only were these people more cheerful, active,
and alert than a similar group in the same institution
who were not given these choices and responsibilities,
but many more of them were still alive. In fact, less
than half as many of the decision-making, plant-mind-
ing residents had died as had those in the other group.
This experiment, with its startling results, began over
ten years of research into the powerful effects of what
my colleagues and I came to call *mindfulness*, and of its
counterpart, the equally powerful but destructive state
of *mindlessness*.[1]

Unlike the exotic "altered states of consciousness" that we read so much about, mindfulness and mindlessness are so common that few of us appreciate their importance or make use of their power to change our lives. This book is about the psychological and physical costs we pay because of pervasive mindlessness and, more important, about the benefits of greater control, richer options, and transcended limits that mindfulness can make possible.

Although the results of this research have been published in a series of scholarly articles, I have long wanted to present their implications to a wider audience. The benefits of becoming more mindful seem to me too valuable to remain hidden in the archives of social psychology. Every time I receive a request for a reprint of a journal article from a business executive or newspaper reporter, I wish that I could run it through an instant translation machine that would expunge the jargon and statistics and reveal the underlying practical implications of the results. This book, while far from "instant" in the making, is a translation of over fifty experiments and an attempt to demonstrate their implications beyond the lab, both in literature and in daily life.

My first experience of the grave risks of mindlessness occurred while I was in graduate school. My grandmother complained to her doctors about a snake crawling around beneath her skull and giving her headaches. Her descriptions were vivid and figurative, not literal. That was just the way she talked. But the young doctors who took care of her paid little attention to what this very old lady from another culture was telling them. They diagnosed senility. Senility comes with old age, after all, and makes people talk nonsense. When she grew more confused and unhappy, they recommended electroconvulsive therapy ("shock treatment") and convinced my mother to give her approval.

Not until an autopsy was performed did anyone detect my grandmother's brain tumor. I shared my mother's agony and guilt. But who were we to question the doctors? For years afterward I kept thinking about the doctors' reactions to my grandmother's complaints, and about our reactions to the doctors. They went through the motions of diagnosis, but were not open to what they were hearing. Mindsets about senility interfered. We did not question the doctors; mindsets about experts interfered. Eventually, as I continued my work in social psychology, I saw some of the reasons for our errors and this led me further into the study of mindless behavior.

Social psychologists usually look for the ways in which behavior depends on context. When mindless, however, people treat information as though it were *context-free*—true regardless of circumstances. For example, take the statement: Heroin is dangerous. How true is this for a dying individual in intolerable pain?

Once alerted to the dangers of mindlessness and to the possibility of bringing about a more mindful attitude by such deceptively simple measures as those used in the nursing home experiment, I began to see this double-edged phenomenon at work in many different settings. For instance, consider the events that led to the 1985 crash of an Air Florida plane that killed seventy-four passengers. It was a routine flight from Washington, D.C., to Florida with an experienced flight crew. Pilot and copilot were in excellent physical health. Neither was tired, stressed, or under the influence. What went wrong? An extensive examination pointed to the crew's pre-takeoff control checks. As the copilot calls out each control on his list, the pilot makes sure the switches are where he wants them to be. One of these controls is an anti-icer. On this day, the pilot and copilot went over each of the controls as they had always done. They went through their routine and checked "off" when the anti-icer was mentioned. This time, however, the flight was different from their experience. This time they were not flying in the usual warm southern weather. It was icy outside.

As he went through the control checks, one by one as he always did, the pilot appeared to be thinking when he was not.[2] The pre-takeoff routines of pilot and copilot have a lot in common with the tiresome safety demonstrations of flight attendants to experienced, glassy-eyed passengers. When we blindly follow routines or unwittingly carry out senseless orders, we are acting like automatons, with potentially grave consequences for ourselves and others.

We do not all allow ourselves to become mindless. Some concert pianists memorize their music away from the keyboard so as to avoid the predicament in which their fingers "know" the music but they do not. In essence, these experts are keeping themselves mindful for their recitals. In the absence of the keyboard they cannot take their performance for granted.

In the chapters that follow I will demonstrate how and why mindlessness develops, and show how we can become more mindful and oriented in the present in widely differing aspects of our lives. Chapter 2 examines the nature of mindlessness and its relation to similar concepts such as habit and the unconscious. Chapter 3 explores the causes of mindlessness, including the vital role of context, and the nature of our early education. An overview of the costs of mindlessness, the limitations it sets on our skills, and expectations and potential follows in Chapter 4. In Chapter 5, I discuss the nature of mindfulness and distinguish it from related concepts found in Eastern philosophy. Chapters 6 through 10 show the applications of mindfulness research in five major areas of ordinary life: aging, creativity, work, the problem of prejudice, and health.

Those parts of my research that I've particularly enjoyed thinking about, including managing uncertainty in the workplace and the link between mindlessness and the old trap of mind/body dualism, are taken up in the appropriate chapters, in this case the work and health chapters, Chapters 8 and 10, respectively. Like so much else in this book, however, they have implications for many other fields as well. To paraphrase Ivan Illich, when he explained why he singled out education, transportation, and then the medical profession for his critique of technology and disempowerment, I might just as well have chosen to write about the post office (or politics for that matter).[3]

Because rigidly following set rules and being mindful are, by definition, incompatible, this book will not offer prescriptions. Many who have read the manuscript in earlier stages or collaborated with me on the research have found, as I have, that thinking about mindfulness and mindlessness has altered their views of the world. Some have found it easier to take risks and to welcome change, or have felt less fearful of failure; others have felt control where they once felt helpless, or freer where they once felt confined. I hope that readers will enjoy the glimpses into our research, question its conclusions mindfully, and test the implications in their own lives

# PART ONE

*

# *Mindlessness*

# CHAPTER 2

*

# *When the Light's On
and Nobody's Home*

*

Out of time we cut "days" and "nights," "summers" and "winters." We say *what* each part of the sensible continuum is, and all these abstract *whats* are concepts.

The intellectual life of man consists almost wholly in his substitution of a conceptual order for the perceptual order in which his experience originally comes.

WILLIAM JAMES, "The World We Live In"

*

Imagine that it's two o'clock in the morning. Your doorbell rings; you get up, startled, and make your way downstairs. You open the door and see a man standing before you. He wears two diamond rings and a fur coat, and there's a Rolls Royce behind him. He's sorry to wake you at this ridiculous hour, he tells you, but he's in the middle of a scavenger hunt. His ex-wife is in the same contest, which makes it very important to him that he win. He needs a piece of wood about three feet by seven feet. Can you help him? In order to make

9

it worthwhile he'll give you $10,000. You believe him. He's obviously rich. And so you say to yourself, how in the world can I get this piece of wood for him? You think of the lumber yard; you don't know who owns the lumber yard; in fact you're not even sure where the lumber yard is. It would be closed at two o'clock in the morning anyway. You struggle but you can't come up with anything. Reluctantly, you tell him, "Gee, I'm sorry."

The next day, when passing a construction site near a friend's house, you see a piece of wood that's just about the right size, three feet by seven feet—a door. You could have just taken a door off its hinges and given it to him, for $10,000.

Why on earth, you say to yourself, didn't it occur to you to do that? It didn't occur to you because yesterday your door was not a piece of wood. The seven-by-three foot piece of wood was hidden from you, stuck in the category called "door."

This kind of mindlessness, which usually takes more humdrum forms—"Why didn't I think of Susan? She can unclog sinks"—could be called "entrapment by category." It is one of three definitions that can help us understand the nature of mindlessness. The other two, which we will also explain, are automatic behavior and acting from a single perspective.

## *Trapped by Categories*

We experience the world by creating categories and making distinctions among them. "This is a Chinese, not a Japanese, vase." "No, he's only a freshman." "The white orchids are endangered." "She's his boss now." In this way, we make a picture of the world, and of ourselves. Without categories the world might seem to escape us. Tibetan Buddhists call this habit of mind "The Lord of Speech":

We adopt sets of categories which serve as ways of managing phenomena. The most fully developed products of this tendency are ideologies, the systems of ideas that rationalize, justify and sanctify our lives. Nationalism, communism, existentialism, Christianity, Buddhism—all provide us with identities, rules of action, and interpretations of how and why things happen as they do.[1]

The creation of new categories, as we will see throughout this book, is a mindful activity. Mindlessness sets in when we rely too rigidly on categories and distinctions created in the past (masculine/feminine, old/young, success/failure). Once distinctions are created, they take on a life of their own. Consider: (1) First there was earth. (2) Then there was land, sea, and sky. (3) Then there were countries. (4) Then there was Germany. (5) Now there is East Germany versus West Germany. The categories we make gather momentum and are very hard to overthrow. We build our own and our shared realities and then we become victims of them—blind to the fact that they are constructs, ideas.

If we look back at the categories of an earlier age, once firmly established, it is easier to see why new ones might become necessary. The Argentinean writer Jorge Luis Borges quotes from an ancient Chinese encyclopedia in which the animals are classified as "(a) belonging to the Emperor, (b) embalmed, (c) tame, (d) suckling pigs, (e) sirens, (g) stray dogs, (h) included in the present classification, (i) frenzied, (j) innumerable, (k) drawn with a very fine camel brush, (l) et cetera, (m) having just broken the water pitcher, (n) that from a long way off look like flies."[2] To be mindless is to be trapped in a rigid world in which certain creatures always belong to the Emperor, Christianity is always good, certain people are forever untouchable, and doors are only doors.

### *Automatic Behavior*

Have you ever said "excuse me" to a store mannequin or written a check in January with the previous year's date? When in this mode, we take in and use limited signals from the world around us (the female form, the familiar face of the check) without letting other signals (the motionless pose, a calendar) penetrate as well.

Once, in a small department store, I gave a cashier a new credit card. Noticing that I hadn't signed it, she handed it back to me to sign. Then she took my card, passed it through her machine, handed me the resulting form, and asked me to sign it. I did as I was told. The cashier then held the form next to the newly signed card to see if the signatures matched..

Modern psychology has not paid much attention to how much complicated action may be performed automatically, yet as early as 1896 Leon Solomons and Gertrude Stein looked into this question. (This was *the* Gertrude Stein who, from 1893 to 1898, was a graduate student in experimental psychology at Harvard University, working under William James.) They studied what was then called "double personalities" and which later came to be known as "split personalities," and proposed that the mindless performance of the second personality was essentially similar to that of ordinary people. Ordinary people also engage in a great deal of complex behavior without consciously paying attention to it. Solomons and Stein conducted several experiments in which they were their own subjects, demonstrating that both writing and reading could be done automatically. They succeeded in writing English words while they were otherwise caught up in reading an absorbing story. With much practice, they were even able to take dictation automatically while reading. Afterward, they were completely unable to recall the words they had written but were nevertheless quite certain they had written something. To show that reading could take place automatically, the subject read aloud from a book while a captivating story was read to him or her. Again they found that, after a lot of practice, they could read aloud unhampered while giving full attention to the story being read to them.

Solomons and Stein concluded that a vast number

of actions that we think of as intelligent, such as reading and writing, can be done quite automatically: "We have shown a general tendency on the part of normal people, to *act*, without any express desire or conscious volition, in a manner in general accord with the *previous habits* of the person."[3]

An experiment I conducted in 1978 with fellow psychologists Benzion Chanowitz and Arthur Blank explored this kind of mindlessness.[4] Our setting was the Graduate Center at the City University of New York. We approached people using a copying machine and asked whether they would let us copy something then and there. We gave reasons that were either sound or senseless. An identical response to both sound and senseless requests would show that our subjects were not thinking about what was being said. We made one of three requests: "Excuse me, may I use the Xerox machine?"; "Excuse me, may I use the Xerox machine because I want to make copies?"; "Excuse me, may I use the Xerox machine because I'm in a rush?"

The first and second requests are the same in *content*—What else would one do with a copying machine except make copies? Therefore if people were considering what was actually being said, the first two requests should be equally effective. Structurally, however, they are different. The redundant request ("Excuse me, may I use the Xerox machine because I want to make copies?") is more similar to the last one ("Excuse me, may I use the Xerox machine because I'm in a rush?") in that both state the request and give a reason. If people comply with the last two requests in equal numbers, this implies attention to structure rather than conscious attention to content. That, in fact, was just what we found. There was more compliance when a reason was given—whether the reason sounded legitimate or silly. People responded mindlessly to the familiar framework rather than mindfully attending to the content.

Of course, there are limits to this. If someone asked for a very large favor or if the excuse were unusually absurd ("because an elephant is after me"), the individual would be likely to think about what was said. It is not that people don't hear the request the rest of the time; they simply don't think about it actively.

In a similar experiment, we sent an interdepartmental memo around some university offices. The message either requested or demanded the return of the memo to a designated room—and that was all it said.[5] ("Please return this immediately to Room 247," or "This memo is to be returned to Room 247.") Anyone who read such a memo mindfully would ask, "If whoever sent the memo wanted it, why did he or she send it?" and therefore would not return the memo. Half of the memos were designed to look exactly like those usually sent between departments. The other half were made to look in some way different. When the memo looked like those they were used to, 90 percent of the recipients actually returned it. When the memo looked different, 60 percent returned it.

When I was discussing these studies at a university colloquium, a member of the audience told me about a little con game that operated along the same lines. Someone placed an ad in a Los Angeles newspaper that read, "It's not too late to send $1 to _____," and gave the person's own name and address. The reader was promised nothing in return. Many people replied, enclosing a dollar. The person who wrote the ad apparently earned a good sum.

The automatic behavior in evidence in these examples has much in common with habit.[6] Habit, or the tendency to keep on with behavior that has been repeated over time, naturally implies mindlessness. However, as we will see in the following chapter, mindless behavior can arise without a long history of repetition, almost instantaneously, in fact.

### Acting from a Single Perspective

So often in our lives, we act as though there were only one set of rules. For instance, in cooking we tend to follow recipes with dutiful precision. We add ingredients as though by official decree. If the recipe calls for a pinch of salt and four pinches fall in, panic strikes, as though the bowl might now explode. Thinking of a recipe only as a rule, we often do not consider how people's tastes vary, or what fun it might be to make up a new dish.

The first experiment I conducted in graduate school explored this problem of the single perspective. It was a pilot study to examine the effectiveness of different requests for help. A fellow investigator stood on a busy sidewalk and told people passing by that she had sprained her knee and needed help. If someone stopped she asked him or her to get an Ace bandage from the nearby drugstore. I stood inside the store and listened while the helpful person gave the request to the pharmacist, who had agreed earlier to say that he was out of Ace bandages. After being told this, not one subject, out of the twenty-five we studied, thought to ask if the pharmacist could recommend something else. People left the drugstore and returned empty-handed to the "victim" and told her the news. We speculated that had she asked for less specific help, she might have received it. But, acting on the single thought that a sprained knee needs an Ace bandage, no one tried to find other kinds of help.

As a little test of how a narrow perspective can dominate our thinking, read the following sentence:

FINAL FOLIOS SEEM TO RESULT FROM YEARS OF DUTIFUL STUDY OF TEXTS ALONG WITH YEARS OF SCIENTIFIC EXPERIENCE.

Now count how many F's there are, reading only once more through the sentence.

If you find fewer than there actually are (the answer is given in the notes[7]), your counting was probably influenced by the fact that the first two words in the sentence begin with F. In counting, your mind would tend to cling to this clue, or single perspective, and miss some of the F's hidden within and at the end of words.

Highly specific instructions such as these or the

request for an Ace bandage encourage mindlessness. Once we let them in, our minds snap shut like a clam on ice and do not let in new signals. In the next chapter we'll take a look at some of the reasons we get stuck in a rigid, closed-off state of mind.

# CHAPTER 3

*

# *The Roots of Mindlessness*

We know that the first step towards the intellectual
mastery of the world in which we live is the discovery
of general principles, rules and laws which bring order
into chaos. By such mental operations we simplify the
world of phenomena, but we cannot avoid falsifying it
in doing so, especially when we are dealing with processes of development and change.
SIGMUND FREUD, "Analysis Terminable and
Interminable"

*

As Freud points out, the rules and laws by which we
first attempt to understand the world later lead to a
falsified view. Nevertheless, we then tend to cling to
these rules and the categories we construct from them,
in a mindless manner. Among the reasons for this are
repetition, practice, and a more subtle and powerful
effect that psychologists call premature cognitive commitment. In this chapter we will examine each of these
processes in turn, as well as some of the mindsets that
tend to perpetuate them.

---

### *The Mindless "Expert"*

Anyone who is able to knit while watching TV, or listen to the radio while driving, knows how learned tasks drop out of mind. As we repeat a task over and over again and become better at it, the individual parts of the task move out of our consciousness. Eventually, we come to assume that we *can* do the task although we no longer know *how* we do it. In fact, questioning the process can have surprising results. If something or someone makes us question our competence on a task that we know moderately well but is *not* overlearned in this way, we can search our minds for the steps of the task and find them. We can then conclude that we are *not* incompetent. However, if we know a task so well that we can perform it "expertly" (mindlessly), these steps may no longer be consciously available and we may doubt our competence.

In my office there was once a very fast typist—demonically fast, in fact—who was also able to read over and retain what he was typing. He had built up these advanced skills over time. One day while he was happily typing away, I asked him if he could teach me to do what he did. As he began to take apart each skill, his quick fingers slowed way down and so did his memory for how and what he typed. Becoming conscious or mindful incapacitated him.

To learn whether this kind of mindlessness is an ingredient in other kinds of behavior, my colleague Cynthia Weinman and I conducted an experiment in extemporaneous speaking.[1] We asked people in an unemployment line in Boston to serve as our subjects for a "linguistic study of voice quality." (No one in this city is safe from our ideas.) Those who agreed were asked to talk into our tape recorder. Half were asked to speak about why it was difficult to find a job in Boston. The other half were asked to speak about finding a job in Alaska—presumably an issue to which they had not given much thought. Half of each of these two groups were asked to think about their given topic first. The results were clear-cut. Subjects were much more fluent when they were discussing a novel issue after being given time to think about it first *or* when they spoke about a familiar topic right away, with no time to think about it. Thinking about a very familiar topic disrupted their performance.

Repetition can lead to mindlessness in almost any profession. If you asked an experienced and a novice typist to type a paragraph without the usual spaces separating words, "acrossthesealives, etc.," it is likely that the person with less experience will have an edge. When any much-repeated task is slightly modified in an unusual way, the novice may do better.

A familiar structure or rhythm helps lead to mental laziness, acting as a signal that there is no need to pay attention. The rhythm of the familiar lulls us into mindlessness:

Q. What do we call the tree that grows from acorns?
A. Oak.
Q. What do we call a funny story?
A. Joke.
Q. What do we call the sound made by a frog?

A. Croak.
Q. What do we call the white of an egg?
A. Yolk. (*sic!*)[2]

Children love these word traps for mindlessness. The game called "Giant Step" or "Mother May I" is built around the pitfalls of repetition.

## *The Sacrilegious Poodle*

Another way that we become mindless is by forming a mindset when we first encounter something and then clinging to it when we reencounter that same thing. Because such mindsets form before we do much reflection, we call them *premature cognitive commitments*. When we accept an impression or a piece of information at face value, with no reason to think critically about it, perhaps because it seems irrelevant, that impression settles unobtrusively into our minds until a similar signal from the outside world—such as sight or smell or sound—calls it up again. At that next time it may no longer be irrelevant, but most of us don't reconsider what we mindlessly accepted earlier. Such mindsets, especially those formed in childhood, are premature because we cannot know in advance the possible future uses a piece of information may serve. The mindless individual is *committed* to one predetermined use of the information, and other possible uses or applications are not explored.

Moisten your mouth with your saliva—the back

of your teeth, the tip of your tongue, and so on. It should feel pleasant. Now spit some saliva into a clean glass. Finally, sip a small bit of this liquid back into your mouth. Disgusting, isn't it? Why? For a number of reasons, we learned years ago that spitting is nasty. Even when there is no sensible reason for the body to feel repelled, the old mindset prevails.

An extreme version of these early mindsets was given to me by a friend who had grown up in a small, predominantly Polish Catholic steel- and coal-mining town. Being one of the few non-Catholic members of the community she was able, indeed more or less forced, to stand on the outside and observe the ordinary peculiarities of the larger community. The priest was a familiar sight in the town, usually accompanied by his splendid gray poodle. This large dog was well trained and often could be seen carrying a newspaper or the priest's umbrella. On this particular Sunday the good Father walked along, enjoying the scenery, on his way home from Mass. His dog walked by his side, also happy and serene, carrying the priest's prayer book in his mouth just as he had carried the paper on other days of the week. The dog, a gentle creature, did no harm to the book. But the nuns who watched the priest and his poodle criticized him fiercely. In their eyes, a dog's mouth was foul, and the book of prayer was being defiled. Despite the piety and good reputation of the priest, and the gentleness of the poodle, all the nuns could see was God in the mouth of a dog.

Benzion Chanowitz and I found a way to test the effects of premature cognitive commitment.[3] For this experiment, we created a "disease," a perceptual disorder we called *chromosynthosis*. Chromosynthosis was described as a hearing problem in which the affected individuals have difficulty distinguishing between certain sounds. Our research participants were told they were going to be tested to determine whether they had this disorder. They were given booklets that described the symptoms of chromosynthosis. The disorder, the booklets said, was like color blindness in that you could have it without knowing it. The point of the study was to find out whether, if people learned about this imaginary disorder mindlessly, the impression they formed would affect their performance on a given task.

We did not give all the participants the same booklets. Some booklets said that 80 percent of the population had the disorder, the implication being that they stood a good chance of having it. For these subjects, the information in the booklet was likely to appear relevant. We asked them to think about how they could help themselves, should they be found to suffer from chromosynthosis. For another group, the booklets said that only 10 percent of the population had the disorder, the implication being that they were unlikely to have it. We did not ask them to reflect on how they would handle the problem, and there appeared to be no strong reason for them to spend time thinking about it.[4]

All the subjects were then asked to listen to two sixty-second recordings of natural conversation and to mark down the number of "a" sounds that they heard. After scoring their own performances, all the participants discovered that they had chromosynthosis. We then gave follow-up tests requiring specific abilities that the booklets said are lacking in people with the disorder.

We found that subjects who were given information about a disease that was apparently irrelevant to them became more vulnerable to the symptoms. Once they discovered that they had the disorder they performed poorly. On the follow-up tests they performed only half as well as those comparison subjects who had assumed all along that they might have the disorder and thus had reason to reflect on how to compensate for it. These results confirmed our hypothesis: The way we first take in information (that is, mindfully or mindlessly) determines how we will use it later. In later chapters we will explore this kind of premature cognitive commitment as it relates to aging and such conditions as alcoholism.

## Mindlessness and the Unconscious

Certain kinds of mindless acts, such as slips of the tongue, are attributed to the "unconscious." Because the pervasive mindlessness that we are talking about here has other origins, it is important to digress briefly and consider a few of the differences. Unconscious processes, as defined by Freud (or, centuries earlier, by Plato and Buddhist and Hindu philosophers), are considered both dynamic and inaccessible. They are dynamic in that they continuously affect our conscious lives yet, without extreme effort such as is required in psychoanalysis or various spiritual disciplines, we cannot recognize or change their influence.

It is by no means impossible for the product of unconscious activity to pierce into consciousness, but a certain amount of exertion is needed for this task. When we try to do it in ourselves, we become aware of a distinct feeling of *repulsion* which must be overcome, and when we produce it in a patient we get the most unquestionable sign of what we call *resistance* to it. So we learn that the unconscious idea is excluded from consciousness by living forces which oppose themselves to its reception, while they do not object to other ideas, the (pre)conscious ones.[5]

As Freud points out here, for unconscious thoughts there is *motivated-not-knowing*. These unacceptable thoughts and desires may sneak out sideways in dreams, giving us a clue that there is an unconscious influence in our lives, but otherwise they are unavailable to us. "In all of us," wrote Plato, "even in good men, there is a lawless wild beast nature which peers out in sleep." "Reasoning" and "shame" become suspended and the "beast within us . . . goes forth to satisfy his desires."[6]

Mindlessness is not nearly so dramatic a concept. Our motives are not involved. When we learn something mindlessly, it does not occur to us to think about it later, irrespective of whether such thoughts would be acceptable to us. Thus, while ideas in the unconscious are unavailable from the start, mindless ideas were once potentially accessible for mindful processing.

One need not work through deep-seated personal conflict to make conscious those thoughts that are mindlessly processed. However, such thoughts will not, on their own, occur to the person for reconsideration. In that way, they too are inaccessible. But if we are offered a new use for a door or a new view of old age, we can erase the old mindsets without difficulty.

## Belief in Limited Resources

One of the main reasons we may become entrapped by the absolute categories we create (or are given by someone else) rather than accept the world as dynamic and continuous is because we believe that resources are limited. If there are clear and stable categories, then we can make rules by which to dole out these resources. If resources weren't so limited, or if these limits were greatly exaggerated, the categories wouldn't need to be so rigid.

Placements in college, for example, are seen as limited. If we act as though intelligence is a single, fixed quality, then we can decide categorically who should go to college on the basis of intelligence. As soon as we realize that intelligence, like everything else, is simultaneously many things, each of which grows and fades depending on context, then we cannot use it to decide categorically who should go and who shouldn't. One could even make matters more confusing and argue that if placements were limited, perhaps the so-called less intelligent should go because they need the education more. Such reasoning would surely lead those denied college admission to recognize that, as with elementary school, there is no intrinsic reason for college education to be limited in availability.

Consider a different example: a divorcing couple with a child. Who will "get" the child? This may be the wrong question. What is actually at stake? Is it the physical presence of the child that the parents want, or is it a certain relationship with the child? Is it the child's body or the child's unlimited love they seek? Or is it a way to get back at each other for whatever hurt was experienced in their relationship? A mindful consideration of what is actually being sought might show that there is enough of the so-called limited resource to go around. A child's love is not a zero-sum commodity. Two people can love and be loved by a child. Feelings are not a limited resource, yet we often don't recognize this because we focus on elements of them that do appear limited.

As long as people cling to a narrow belief in limited resources, those who are fortunate enough to win by the arbitrary (but rigid) rules that are set up, such as SAT scores, have a stake in maintaining the status quo. Those who are not getting what they want, however, might pause to consider that they may be part of someone else's costly construction of reality.

In discussions of limited resources, someone will always bring up money. Money, in most people's experience, is limited. But even here, is money the issue? Why is rich better? Rich people have power, respect, time to play, places they can go to enjoy themselves. They can buy faster cars and finer foods. And so on.

After certain basic human needs are met, isn't what is being sought a state of mind?

If we examine what is behind our desires, we can usually get what we want without compromising: love, caring, confidence, respectability, excitement. Compromising is necessary only if what we want is in short supply. If the valuable things in life were not perceived to be limited, we might not cling so steadfastly to our rigid categories, and we would be more likely to loosen these categorical distinctions once we realize that they have been of our own making, mindlessly entrapping us.

Natural resources surely appear limited. Consider coal, for example, which is deemed a resource because of the function it serves to produce heat. While the amount of coal available may be in limited supply, other ways of serving that function are numerous. Such resources may ultimately be limited, but they are certainly less so than believed by most people.

When we think of resources being limited, we often think of our own abilities. Here, too, our notion of limits may inhibit us. We may push ourselves to what we believe are our limits, in swimming, public speaking, or mathematics. However, whether they are true limits is not determinable.[7]

It may be in our best interest to proceed as though these and other abilities might be improved upon, so that at least we will not be deterred by false limits. It was once assumed that humans could not run the mile in fewer than five minutes. In 1922 it was said to be "humanly impossible" to run the mile in less than four minutes. In 1952 that limit was broken by Roger Bannister. Each time a record is broken, the supposed limit is extended. Yet the notion of limits persists.

A curious example of apparent limits being transcended is known as the Coolidge Effect. Observers of rats, hamsters, cats, sheep, and other animals have long noted that when a male animal's sexual appetite is sated, and he has finished copulating, he needs a rest period. If a new female of the species is brought in, however, he will immediately find the energy to resume mating.[8]

Camp counselors know all about the subjective nature of limits. Every summer, a counselor friend of mine in New Hampshire takes six twelve-year-old boys for a climb up a small peak called Mount Chocorua. After many years, he knows the mountain and knows just when energy will flag. When a breathless camper asks, "How much longer?" he answers that he isn't sure. The last stretch of the climb is a ridge from which the summit can be seen, all bare rock and jagged against the sky. It was here that the Indian Chief Chocorua was chased at gunpoint by the white men who wanted his people's land.

When the sweaty campers reach this ridge, they often flop down and take off their heavy knapsacks. Just at this point, the counselor catches their attention with the story of Chief Chocorua. He also explains the particular challenge of this last stretch. Hearing this, the campers see the rest of the climb as a new task. When they reach the rocky summit of Mount Chocorua and feel the wind coming over them from the great Presidential Range of the White Mountains to the north, they are always exultant—and hardly tired. Fatigue, too, can be a premature cognitive commitment.

### Entropy and Linear Time as Limiting Mindsets

Associated with a belief in limited resources is the concept of *entropy*, the gradual dissolution or breaking down of an entity or patterns of organization within a closed system. Entropy is an idea that, on the face of it, allows people to feel control: there is more opportunity for involvement in a system that wears down over time—where things successively get worse—than in one where things stay the same or get better and better on their own. The notion of entropy gives rise to an image of the universe as a great machine that is running down. Such an image, which many of us have accepted without ever really thinking about it, may also be an unfortunate and unnecessary mindset that narrows our sense of what is possible. An alternate view of the world, for instance, one that recognizes how much of our reality is socially constructed, may actually afford more personal control.

A belief in fixed limits is not compatible with the views of many physicists. James Jeans and Sir Arthur Eddington, for example, believed the universe is best described as a great idea. It is there to be acted upon. As soon as any system seems almost complete something new, now unforeseen, will be discovered.

A related notion that may also limit us unnecessarily is the linear view of time. If we consider how
notions of time have shifted across cultures and
throughout history, it might be easier for us to question
this restrictive view.

In some cultures, time is treated as a universal
present. In the Trobriand Islands, off the coast of Papua
New Guinea, people do not think of the past as a
previous phase of present time. The Hopi Indians, like
the Trobrianders, do not hold our linear concept of
time, though they have many concepts (becoming, imaginary versus real) that fulfill similar functions. John
Edward Orme speculates that in primitive times, people
held time to be an "all at once" phenomenon.[9] Polyne-
sians are careful to deny the novelty of any adventure.
Rather, they believe that they are only repeating the
voyage of a mythical explorer.

Another view of time is one that sees it as cyclical.
Pythagoras believed that every detail of time would be
repeated. The concept of reincarnation, held by many
religions in the Far East, implies a cyclical view.
Nietzsche also argued that the universe is cyclical, that
events may be repeated. From this point of view, pre-
cognition is not so much a glimpse into the future as
seeing what happened in the past, in another cycle. In
a cyclic model of time, the future and past are indistinguishable.

Even in a one-dimensional model of time, movement may not be exclusively unidirectional. The future
may be as capable of "causing" the present as is the
past. What should I study now for the exam I'm taking

later? St. Augustine said, "The present, therefore, has several dimensions . . . the present of things past, the present of things present, and the present of things future."

Kant conceived of time as a means of organizing perception—not as something "given" by the world, nor as something "projected" on it. From this concept he developed the "synthetic a priori" in mathematics: truth we can know about the world without looking at the world.

Changing one's mindset about time may be more than an intellectual exercise. For example, in Chapter 10, which looks at mindfulness and health, we question the belief that healing always takes a fixed amount of time. Alternative views of time make such questioning seem more plausible. Actually, certainty with respect to the meaning of time seems absurd. According to an eminent physicist, Ernst Mach, "It is utterly beyond our power to measure things in time. Quite the contrary, time is an abstraction, at which we arrive by means of the change of things."[10]

### Education for Outcome

A very different, but not incompatible, explanation for why we become mindless has to do with our early education. From kindergarten on, the focus of schooling is usually on goals rather than on the process by which they are achieved. This single-minded pursuit of one outcome or another, from tying shoelaces to getting into Harvard, makes it difficult to have a mindful attitude about life.

When children start a new activity with an outcome orientation, questions of "Can I?" or "What if I can't do it?" are likely to predominate, creating an anxious preoccupation with success or failure rather than drawing on the child's natural, exuberant desire to explore. Instead of enjoying the color of the crayon, the designs on the paper, and a variety of possible shapes along the way, the child sets about writing a "correct" letter A.

Throughout our lives, an outcome orientation in social situations can induce mindlessness. If we think we know how to handle a situation, we don't feel a need to pay attention. If we respond to the situation as very familiar (a result, for example, of overlearning), we notice only the minimal cues necessary to carry out the proper scenario. If, on the other hand, the situation is strange, we might be so preoccupied with thoughts of failure ("What if I make a fool of myself?") that we miss nuances of our own and others' behavior. In this sense, we are mindless with respect to the immediate situation, although we may be thinking quite actively about outcome-related issues.

In contrast, a process orientation, which we will explore when we look at creativity in Chapter 7, asks "How do I do it?" instead of "Can I do it?" and thus directs attention toward defining the steps that are necessary on the way. This orientation can be characterized in terms of the guiding principle that *there are no failures, only ineffective solutions*.

In computer programming classes for children, a major activity is "bug fixing"—figuring out new solutions, instead of getting hung up on a particular one that didn't work. Provisional goals are subject to continual revision. The process-oriented person is less likely to be caught off-guard if circumstances change.

The style of education that concentrates on outcomes generally also presents facts unconditionally. This approach encourages mindlessness. If something is presented as an accepted truth, alternative ways of thinking do not even come up for consideration. Such a single-minded way of viewing the world can generalize to virtually everything we do. By teaching absolutes we pass our culture from one generation to the next. It brings stability. But as we will see, the cost may be high.

## The Power of Context

The way we behave in any situation has a lot to do with the context. We whisper in hospitals and become anxious in police stations, sad in cemeteries, docile in schools, and jovial at parties. Contexts control our behavior, and our mindsets determine how we interpret each context.

Many of the contexts that affect us most deeply are learned in childhood. For instance, our early visual exposure to the world may actually shape what we later see. A controversial study of Euro-Canadians brought up in urban settings where buildings surround them with right angles, and with Cree Indians raised near tents and lodges that have many shapes and angles, suggested that the effects of early visual context may be lasting. In adulthood, right angles could be seen better than other line orientations by the Euro-Canadians. At the same time, they seemed to have less visual acuity for oblique orientations than the Cree. From the beginning, the Cree have a different mental landscape which may allow them to take in a greater variety of visual cues.[11]

A classic example of the power of context is the tale of the ugly duckling. When he came out of his egg, the ugly duckling made his first premature cognitive commitment: He looked at the nearest, largest duck and "decided" that she was its mother. Then when his siblings and others tormented him, he made a second premature cognitive commitment—that he was different and, worse still, that he was ugly. So he felt ashamed and alone.

When he ran away from the bullying and teasing, the ugly duckling had a series of adventures. At one point out in a cold marsh a hunting dog came upon him, only to jump over him. For once he was glad about his appearance: "I'm so ugly that even a dog will not eat me." We all know the rest of the story. In a new context—the world of swans—the ugly duckling felt proud and beautiful. His old mindsets floated away as he saw himself next to other long necks and spreading wings.

When we talk about a context, we often make the mistake of believing that it is somehow "out there." If we take words "out of context," we think the context remains on the page. But it doesn't exist there without us. We perceive a relationship between one sentence and the next, just as the cygnet perceived a relationship between himself and the mother duck. A context is a premature cognitive commitment, a mindset.

Context depends on who we are today, who we were yesterday, and from which view we see things. Sometimes these conflict. What would you make of a "Las Vegas Night" run by nuns for the church? If someone started yelling in a hospital because his mother was being mistreated, others would look at him in alarm because yelling does not follow hospital rules. Though there are times in a hospital when it might well be appropriate to stomp and shout, we don't think to do it because of the context.

Shaw's Professor Higgins demonstrated that our perceptions of beauty shift dramatically with context. In the beginning of *Pygmalion*, Eliza Doolittle is a ragged, cockney-accented girl selling flowers in the streets of London. Professor Higgins walks into her life and decides to do her over. Realizing that context is all, he goes to work on Eliza and changes her voice, her diction, her dress, her habits. He puts her in a new setting, the way a jeweler would reset a gem. Eliza becomes a grand hit in London, hailed as a beauty and a princess. The interest of the plot is heightened because the dramatic change in context causes an equally dramatic change in Eliza's self-esteem, indeed in what we would call Eliza "herself."

The location of context in our perceptions was

vividly illustrated in an experiment conducted by psychologists David Holmes and B. Kent Houston.[12] With the permission of the subjects, they administered mild electric shocks to a group of people, half of whom were told to think of electric shocks as new "physiological sensations." Those who thought of the shock in this way were less anxious and had lower pulse rates than those who were not given the prior instructions.

The same situation or stimulus called by a different name is a different stimulus. Roller coasters are fun but bumpy plane rides are not. Imagine the following scene: A woman walking down a country road is suddenly besieged by a swarm of bees. Like most of us would be, she is afraid; her blood pressure rises, her pulse quickens. She may freeze or run in fear. On the other hand, imagine the same woman walking down the same road with a young child by her side. The sight of the bees now signals a very different behavior. In this context, she boldly protects the child instead of becoming afraid. The same bees have become a different stimulus.

Context can determine value. A postal clerk, so a report in the *Boston Globe* would have us believe, created public acceptance of the disfavored Susan B. Anthony dollar coin simply by announcing "limit two per customer."[13] For retailers, this is an old story.

Context can be an influence even when we are trying to make the most precise and specific judgments. In a study by Donald Brown, subjects were asked to lift various weights and judge them as light, medium, heavy, or very heavy.[14] In some cases Brown introduced an anchor (another weight). The hypothesis was that judged weight would vary according to how the anchor weight differed from the weight being judged. This is just what Brown found. The introduction of a heavy anchor weight made the same weight feel lighter than it had before the anchor was introduced.

Brown added an interesting variation. Some subjects were asked to make matters easier for the experimenter by picking up and moving the tray on which the weights sat. If weights were influenced by other weights, would subjects be influenced by the weight of the tray as well? Though the tray was not perceived as part of the task, one would think it existed in some absolute way independent of the perceiver's psychology. One would expect that its weight would influence the subject despite the fact that it was not officially part of the experiment. However, if context rather than so-called physical reality determines our experiences of stimuli, then the tray should have no influence.

The results of this ingenious experiment showed that judgment of weight was *not* influenced by the weight of the tray. It was as if subjects entered the context of the experiment and were influenced by the various weights and then took themselves out of that context to remove the tray. They then placed themselves back in the weight-judging situation. In a sense, for them the tray had no weight.

It has long been known that values create a context that influences sense perceptions. In 1948, Neil Postman, Jerome Bruner, and Eliot McGinnies used a machine called a tachistoscope to flash words very quickly on a screen.[15] These words were associated with various values. For example, subjects were shown political words such as *govern*, *citizen*, and *politics*; religious words such as *prayer*, *sacred*, and *worship*; and aesthetic words such as *poetry*, *artist*, and *beauty*. In all, the words represented six different values measured by the Allport-Vernon Study of Values.[16] Words were shown to subjects in random order. Despite the fact that the chosen words were equally familiar, the speed with which subjects recognized the words varied as a consequence of the subjects' values, as measured by the same Allport-Vernon Scale given earlier to subjects. The higher a subject's score on a particular value, the more quickly he or she recognized the word. Politically oriented subjects, for example, recognized political words sooner than the artistically oriented. The context created by the subjects' values appeared to affect their visual ability.

This power of context over our reactions and interpretations also makes us susceptible to what we may call *context confusion*. Here people confuse the context controlling the behavior of another person with the context determining their own behavior. Most people typically assume that other peoples' motives and intentions are the same as theirs, although the same behavior may have very different meanings. If I am out running and see someone walking briskly, I assume she is trying to exercise and would run if only she could. Yet, she might have deliberately chosen to get her exercise from walking, which she enjoys. Walking and running are mutually exclusive, as is often the case with context confused behavior: *To be accomplishing one, you are nec-essarily not accomplishing the other*. If society values run-ning, however, over time this woman may come to see herself as "not running" rather than as electing to walk. Forgetting the pleasure she felt in walking, she might come to see herself as an incompetent runner.

This context confusion often happens with "out" groups when we or they scrutinize their behavior. To their detriment, they tend to be evaluated by criteria that are irrelevant to their initial intentions and goals. They may be unaware of why they first engaged in a particular action, and thus can be persuaded by the larger, more powerful group that they are behaving incompetently. The "in" group has unwittingly rede-fined the context of the "out" group members' behavior. We will examine this further in Chapter 9 when we look at prejudice.

The various causes of mindlessness that we have just discussed—repetition, premature cognitive com-mitment, belief in limited resources, the notion of linear time, education for outcome, and the powerful influ-ence of context—influence each day of our lives. Before we discuss how to counteract them with a mindful outlook, we will take a look at just what we lose when we act mindlessly.

# CHAPTER 4

*

# *The Costs of Mindlessness*

Three older women were sitting on a park bench. One groaned. Her friend, sitting next to her, gave a sigh. The third looked at both of them and said, "I thought we weren't going to talk about the children."

*

The grooves of mindlessness run deep. We know our scripts by heart. In the routine of daily life we do not notice what we are doing unless there is a problem. Locking ourselves out of a car or throwing socks in the garbage instead of the laundry basket jolts us awake. William James tells a story of starting to get ready for a dinner party, undressing, washing, and then climbing into bed. Two routines that begin the same way got confused, and he mindlessly followed the more familiar one.

Closer to home, a friend told me a nice three-generation story of mindlessness. One day a womar was about to cook a roast. Before putting it in the pot she cut off a small slice. When asked why she did this she paused, became a little embarrassed, and said she did it because her mother had always done the same thing when she cooked a roast. Her own curiosity aroused, she telephoned her mother to ask why she always cut off a little slice before cooking her roast. The mother's answer was the same: "Because that's the way my mother did it." Finally, in need of a more helpful answer, she asked her grandmother why she always cut off a little slice before cooking a roast. Without hesitating, her grandmother replied, "Because that's the only way it would fit in my pot."

The consequences of mindlessness range from the trivial to the catastrophic. At the dire extreme is a young man who went to a party at a grand estate in the New Hampshire woods. Late in the evening he went outside to the garden with a young woman. Through the darkness he saw a big swimming pool. Feeling playful, he tore off most of his clothes, gave a Tarzan yell, banged his chest, and dove off the diving board—onto solid concrete. The young man broke his neck.

Between trivia and tragedy is a wide range of less obvious but nevertheless serious effects of mindlessness. These include an inhibiting self-image, unintended cruelty, loss of control, and stunted potential.

## A Narrow Self-Image

A single-minded self-image leaves both individuals and corporations dangerously vulnerable. Perhaps a housewife, for example, defines herself narrowly in everything she does. When meeting people, she may introduce herself as "So and so's wife." She sees herself as managing "his house," buying herself clothes "he likes," and cooking for him. Although she may very well be happy in this rigid role, what would happen if her husband decided to pack his bags and leave? Would she be able to function when the rules changed? Any "housewife" fills many other roles: daughter, sister, friend, carpenter, amateur painter, and so on. By mindfully becoming aware of these distinctions, she would be less vulnerable to the loss. If she expanded her definition of herself in terms of all these roles, or some subset of them, and something happened to her husband, there would still be great continuity in her life.

The costs of a single-minded self-image are equally severe for a corporation. Management can define a business as serving certain markets and become entrapped by its own categories. In a classic paper written for the *Harvard Business Review* in 1975, entitled "Marketing Myopia," Theodore Levitt[1] wrote:

The railroads did not stop growing because the need for passenger and freight transportation declined. That grew. The railroads are in trouble today not because the need was filled by others (cars, trucks, airplanes, even telephones), but because it was *not* filled by the railroads themselves. They let others take customers away from them because they *assumed themselves to be in the railroad business rather than in the transportation business*. [Italics added.]

The advantage of an evolving, multifaceted self- or corporate image will be seen in all the chapters that follow.

Our tendency to focus on outcome, which we discussed in the last chapter, also narrows our self-image. When we envy other people's assets, accomplishments, or characteristics, it is often because we are making a *faulty comparison*. We may be looking at the *results* of their efforts rather than at the *process* they went through on the way. For example, imagine that while talking to a professor in her office, you hear her use a word that you do not understand. You may feel intimidated and stupid. Now imagine that the same professor is sitting at her desk with an open dictionary. You would probably conclude that she knew that strange word because she spends time looking up words, finding them in books she reads, or learning them in some other straightforward way. You too could look up words, if you wanted to. Keeping an eye on process, on the steps anyone must take to become expert, keeps us from disparaging ourselves.

A self-image based on past performance may also inhibit us. Someone who has been able to diet for only two days each time he has tried in the past, or who has not been able to run more than a mile, or who has always had to bring work home on weekends, or who has never been able to figure out how to save money, may assume that this is a permanent part of his or her character. Unless the person's mindset changes, the same lack of success will probably follow these endeavors today or tomorrow. As we saw in the last chapter, however, many of the limits we accept as real are illusory. In a rather simple exercise, two of my colleagues and I instructed one group of subjects to give us as many solutions as they could to a number of ordinary problems (for example: there is no heat, yet you want to stay warm; you want a cold drink but don't have a bottle opener). After these subjects had run out of solutions, we took the largest number anyone had found and asked another group of subjects to give us that many solutions plus five more. No one in the second group had difficulty meeting this goal.[2]

Even people who have achieved a strong sense of competence can find it eroded by mindlessly accepted labels. Before getting married, Ann could balance her checkbook; once married, she let her husband take over the task; now divorced, Ann can't seem to balance her checkbook any longer. Jane is a confident lawyer; she has a baby and takes a leave of absence from her job. Now she wants to go back to work but has lost her confidence.

These rather familiar situations illustrate a phenomenon that we have called *self-induced dependence*. Former graduate student Ann Benevento and I designed a few experiments to see how it develops.[3] We decided to conduct them at the airport, on the assumption that people who travel are likely to be somewhat independent and self-assured. If they could develop self-induced dependence, it was likely to occur in others as well. In the first phase of one of these experiments, the subjects were given arithmetic problems which they could solve with ease. In phase two, we put the subjects in a position likely to lead them to question their competence. We gave some the title of "assistant" and others "boss," and had them all perform tasks in a manner appropriate to their roles. In the third phase, all the subjects returned to the same kind of easy arithmetic problems they had successfully completed in phase one. Those who had been made "assistants" now solved the problems only half as well as they had originally. Though they began participating with equal competence, the labels that they had assumed undermined their performance.

## *Unintended Cruelty*

The costs of mindlessness are not all personal. A look at the famous study on obedience to authority conducted by Stanley Milgram shows one of the ways mindlessness can hurt others.[4] Subjects of this study were asked to participate in research on the effects of punishment on learning. Each time the "learner" did not know the answer to the question, the teacher-subject was supposed to administer an electric shock. The learner didn't really receive any shocks, but the teacher-subjects did not know this. A tape recording played convincing grunts and expressions of discomfort at the apparent shocks. Subjects were asked to increase the shock intensity each time an error was made. Milgram's surprising finding was that 65 percent of these nice, normal people, under instruction from the experimenter/authority, delivered enough current to kill the learner.

This is a much condensed account of a complex and controversial experiment. What is important here is the incremental nature of the actions. Had the experimenter asked subjects to use almost maximum shock intensity from the start for each individual, it is very likely that far fewer subjects would have obeyed. What seems to happen when we take small steps is that, after the first step, we do not think to question our behavior until, by looking back, we can see how far we've unwittingly come. If we cheat somebody out of 50 cents, what's the big deal the next time of cheating him out of $1.00, then $2.00 or $5.00? And so on until something makes us realize that we've behaved poorly. If we fall into a routine rather than make decisions anew each time, we can get mindlessly seduced into activities we wouldn't engage in otherwise.

Mindlessness also allows us to compartmentalize uncomfortable thoughts. When they were little girls of four and five, I took my nieces to feed the ducks at a pond near their house in Connecticut. At first the girls were afraid but then they made friends with these appealing creatures. That evening the family went out for dinner together. I ordered duck. With a look of terror in her eyes, one of my nieces asked, "Aunt Ellie, is that the same . . .?" I quickly changed my order, unable to hold the image of live ducks in my mind while chewing on a cooked one. (Luckily we hadn't visited an entire farm before dinner.)

By locking "pets" into one category and "livestock" into another, we can eat meat without qualms. In this book we will see how much we lose by keeping thoughts in impermeable categories. At our family dinner, however, the ducks bore the cost.

In a number of nursing homes across the country, something called "reality therapy" has become popular but is often misapplied. As part of the program, a member of the staff gets on the public address system at regular times and reports a few of the relevant facts of the day: the temperature outside, the day of the week, political events that have occurred, and the like. To test their grasp of reality, residents are later asked questions such as, "What is the temperature today?" and "What day is it?" Those who cannot answer are deemed confused.

But whose reality is this? To someone indoors all day, the temperature outside is no more than a curiosity. And if every day is experienced as virtually the same, it hardly matters whether today is Tuesday or Thursday, the first or the thirty-first. Seeing "reality" from the staff's single-minded perspective may lead to misreadings of the residents' health or level of awareness and consequently to harmful labeling. The costs of mindless definitions of what is real or normal to both the elderly and the "deviant" are taken up in Chapters 6 and 9.

### Loss of Control

Mindlessness limits our control by preventing us from making intelligent choices. Advertisers cater effectively to mindlessness. Once I was walking in midtown Manhattan when my attention was drawn to a large sign in the window of a tourist shop that for the past twenty years or so has been "going out of business."

This sign announced "Candles that burn!" Thinking that special candles make nice presents, I was about to go in and take advantage of this novel offering when it occurred to me that all candles burn.

Even without advertisers conspiring to render us mindless, we often limit our own choices. One important way in which we limit our options is to attribute all our troubles to a single cause. Such mindless attributions narrowly limit the range of solutions we might seek. In research on divorce, psychologist Helen Newman and I found that people who blame the failure of their marriages on their ex-spouses suffer longer than those people who see many possible explanations for their situation.[5]

Similarly, alcoholics who see the cause of their problem as purely genetic seem to give up the control that could help their recovery. When we have a single-minded explanation, we typically don't pay attention to information that runs counter to it. This happens even if the information is given by experienced therapists. In a study of premature cognitive commitments and alcoholism, three colleagues and I found evidence of this.[6] We looked at two kinds of alcoholics: those who in their youth knew only one alcoholic and those who in their youth knew several, each of whom behaved differently from the others. We assumed that this latter group might have a less single-minded view of options. For example, if a child knew only one alcoholic who was loud and cruel, the child might grow up mindlessly assuming that this was the way alcoholics always behaved. If that child later became an alcoholic, it might not occur to him that he could behave differently. However, if the same child had met several other alcoholics with many different personalities, he might be open to a more flexible view of how he might act and of the possibility of change.

First we interviewed forty-two patients attending an alcohol clinic at a general hospital, paying particular attention to their childhood experiences. (The interviewers and therapists were unaware of our hypothesis.) We then compared the results of the interviews with the therapists' evaluations of the patients' degree of improvement. Those who had been successfully helped in therapy virtually always came from the multiple-role-model group. Those who had been exposed to only one model of alcoholism appeared to have developed mindsets so rigid that the options offered by therapy did not seem available to them.

Our tendency to persist mindlessly in using the first model presented to us can be demonstrated in a much simpler form. In a classic set of studies on the effects of *Einstellung*, or mental set, psychologists Abraham Luchins and Edith Hirsch Luchins found that after subjects could perform a mathematical task without thinking, the vast majority kept using the same solutions even when a simpler one became available.[7]

The problem in their experiment consisted of obtaining different amounts of water using three jars of different sizes. For instance, the subject was asked to get 100 quarts of water using Jar A, which holds 21 quarts, Jar B, which holds 127 quarts, and Jar C, which holds 3 quarts. One solution is to start with Jar B and subtract Jar A and then subtract Jar C twice ($127 - 21 - 3 - 3 = 100$). The solution may also be written as Jar B − Jar A − 2 Jar C. Subjects were given a series of problems that all had the same solution.

Once they presumably had this clever answer down cold, they were asked how to get 20 quarts when Jar A = 23, Jar B = 49, and Jar C = 3.

The formula used for the first problem works here also ($49 - 23 - 3 - 3 = 20$). However, there is an easier way to solve the puzzle: Subtract Jar C from Jar A ($23 - 3 = 20$). Luchins and Luchins found that 81 percent of the subjects used the more elaborate formula, apparently oblivious to the simpler alternative. Interestingly, when some subjects were specifically instructed on the answer sheet, "Don't be blind," and not to act "foolishly while solving the subsequent problems," 63 percent of them still performed mindlessly and used the more complicated solution.

### Learned Helplessness

A much more pernicious loss of choice and control is brought about by repeated failure. After a number of experiences in which our efforts are futile, many of us will give up. Well-known research by psychologist Martin Seligman and others shows that this *learned helplessness* then generalizes to situations where the person can, in fact, exercise control.[8] Even when solutions are available, a mindless sense of futility prevents a person from reconsidering the situation. The person remains passive in the face of situations that could otherwise be handled without undue difficulty. Past experience determines present reactions and robs the individual of control. If we looked for new aspects of the situations in which we find ourselves, we probably could prevent learned helplessness.

Learned helplessness was originally demonstrated in rats.[9] When placed in ice water, they have no difficulty swimming around for forty to sixty hours. However, if, instead of being put immediately into the water, the rats are held until they stop struggling, something very different happens. Instead of swimming, these rats give up immediately and drown.

Hospitals for the chronically ill often unwittingly teach a similar kind of helplessness. Particularly sad cases have been reported in psychiatric hospitals.[10] In one, the patient lived on what was affectionately called the "hopeless ward." For a time, renovations in the hospital made it necessary for the residents on this ward to be moved temporarily to another ward from which residents usually did get better and return to the community. The patient did well during this time. Once the renovations were completed, however, patients were returned to the hopeless ward. This particular patient died immediately afterward, from no apparent physical cause. The name of the ward had taught him the message written over Dante's Gates of Hell: "Abandon all hope, ye who enter here."

## Stunted Potential

William James claimed that almost all of us use only the tiniest fraction of our potential.[11] Only under certain circumstances of constructive stress or in certain states—great love, for example, or religious ardor, or the courage of battle—do we begin to tap the depth and richness of our creative resources, or the tremendous reserves of life energy that lie sleeping within us. Mindlessness, as it diminishes our self-image, narrows our choices, and weds us to single-minded attitudes, has a lot to do with this wasted potential. As I mentioned in the Introduction, this waste has become especially vivid to me because of research I have done with elderly populations. When I've worked with others in trying to make improvements for these people, the main obstacles we had to overcome, both in the older people themselves and in their caretakers, were the premature cognitive commitments about old age that people make in their youth.

Premature cognitive commitments are like photographs in which meaning rather than motion is frozen. When a child hears about stiff, testy old people, the snapshot is processed as is. The child has little stake in the issue. Later, in old age, the grown-up child may not question the image. The original picture can become the foundation for everything learned about old age. Even when corrected, so much else has been built on this foundation that a new attitude is difficult to form.

To test the effects of these early experiences, we compared elderly subjects who in their youth had lived with a grandparent before they were two years old with those who lived with a grandparent only after they were thirteen.[12] We assumed that the grandparents of two-year-olds were likely to have been younger and stronger and to have looked "bigger" than those whose grandchildren were thirteen and older. If so, the younger the subjects were during these initial contacts, the more positive would be their premature cognitive commitments about age. As a result, they might be expected to adjust more positively to their own old age.

Participants for this study were residents of nursing, convalescent, or retirement homes located in the metropolitan Boston area. Their average age was seventy-nine years. We encouraged them to reminisce, and interviewed them about the past to determine whether they had lived with a grandparent when they were growing up and, if so, how old they were when the grandparent moved in.

Later, these participants were independently evaluated by nurses unaware of our hypothesis. Those whose earliest premature cognitive commitments about aging were more youthful were rated as more alert. They also tended to be seen as more active and more independent.[13]

There may be other possible explanations for these results. Nevertheless, they suggest that we might do well to explore the ways that we have been taught to grow old.

Psychologists tend to follow where novelists have

dared to tread. One of the most harrowing pictures ever drawn of the costs of single-minded, stunted existence is Miss Havisham, in Charles Dickens's *Great Expectations*. For her, ever since the moment she was abandoned on the day of her wedding, mind and time have stopped. We see her through the eyes of the boy Pip, who does not know what misfortune and tragic mindset brought her to this state:

> In an arm-chair, with an elbow resting on the table and her head leaning on that hand, sat the strangest lady I have ever seen, or shall ever see.
>
> She was dressed in rich material—satins, and lace, and silks—all of white. Her shoes were white. And she had a long white veil dependent from her hair, and she had bridal flowers in her hair, but her hair was white. Some bright jewels sparkled on her neck and on her hands, and some other jewels lay sparkling on the table. . . .
>
> But I saw that everything within my reach . . . had lost its lustre, and was faded and yellow. I saw that the bride within the bridal dress had withered like the dress, and like the flowers, and had no brightness left but the brightness of her sunken eyes.
>
> . . . I should have cried out, if I could.[14]

PART TWO

*

*Mindfulness*

# CHAPTER 5

*

## *The Nature of Mindfulness*

Our life is what our thoughts make it.
MARCUS AURELIUS, *Meditations*

*

When Napoleon invaded Russia, he appeared to the world as a brilliant conquering hero, yet again proving his military genius by daring to march against a giant. But behind the proud banners and eagles, he carried a dangerous mindset, a determination to have Russia, to have Russia no matter what the cost in human life. As Tolstoy describes him in *War and Peace*, Napoleon had no use for alternatives; his determination was absolute.

Opposite Napoleon stood the old Russian bear of a general, Kutuzov, a mellowed veteran who liked his vodka and had a habit of falling asleep at state occasions. An uneven match, or so it would appear.

As Napoleon's army advanced, Kutuzov let his army fall back, and then fall back some more. Napoleon kept coming, deeper into Russia, farther from his supply lines. Finally, as Kutuzov knew would happen, a powerful ally intervened: the Russian winter. The French army found itself fighting the cold, the wind, the snow, and the ice.

When Napoleon at last achieved his single, obsessive goal—Moscow—there was no one there for him to conquer. Everyone had left. The Russians had set their holy city on fire to greet the invader. Once more Kutuzov played the seeming loser.

He knew that an apple should not be picked while it is green. It will fall of itself when ripe, but if plucked unripe the apple is spoilt, the tree is harmed, and your teeth are set on edge. . . . He knew that the beast was wounded as only the whole strength of Russia could have wounded it, but whether it was mortally wounded or not was still an undecided question.[1]

At that moment, when Napoleon had no choice but to retreat—from the burned city, from the winter—the mindful old general attacked. He appealed to Mother Russia, an appeal that Stalin was to use with similar success years later. He appealed to the people to save their land, and that appeal revived all of Russia. The French had everything against them, including the Cossacks, who rode down off the winter steppes. Mother Russia prevailed, just as she would when Hitler was to repeat Napoleon's mistake.

In the character of Kutuzov we can find portrayed the key qualities of a mindful state of being: (1) creation of new categories; (2) openness to new information; and (3) awareness of more than one perspective.

In each case, Napoleon's blind obsession provides a vivid mirror image, a portrait of mindlessness. First of all, Kutuzov was flexible: Evacuating a city would usually fall under the category of defeat, but for him it became the act of setting a trap. Second, his strategy was responsive to the news of Napoleon's advance, while Napoleon did not seem to be taking in information about Kutuzov's moves. Finally, while Napoleon saw his rapid advance and march on Moscow only from the point of view of conquering enemy terrain, Kutuzov could also see that an "invasion" in the context of winter and distance from supplies could be turned into a bitter rout.

## Creating New Categories

Just as mindlessness is the rigid reliance on old categories, mindfulness means the continual creation of new ones. Categorizing and recategorizing, labeling and relabeling as one masters the world are processes natural to children. They are an adaptive and inevitable part of surviving in the world.[2] Freud recognized the importance of creation and mastery in childhood:

Should we not look for the first traces of imaginative activity as early as in childhood? The child's best-loved and most intense occupation is with his play or games. Might we not say that every child at play behaves like a creative writer, in that he creates a world of his own, or rather, re-arranges the things of his world in a new way which pleases him?[3]

The child's serious *re-creation* can become the adult's playful *recreation*.

As adults, however, we become reluctant to create new categories. As we saw earlier, our outcome orientation tends to deaden a playful approach. If I asked you to make a list of what you did yesterday, what would you say? Think about it for a moment, then think of what you would say if I offered you money for each item in your answer. Did you list your day in large chunks at first—breakfast, work, lunch, phone calls? Most people will say, for example, that they "ate breakfast" rather than "bit, chewed, and swallowed a piece of toast" and so on, even when offered a reward for a longer list of activities.

Without psychotherapy or a crisis as motivation, the past is rarely recategorized. We might from time to time call upon different episodes from the past to justify a present situation or grievance, but it rarely occurs to us to change the way the events or impressions were initially stored.

For example, take a couple, Alice and Fred, whom you see quite often. Sometimes you hear them fight a bit. You don't pay any attention; don't all couples quarrel? Now you learn that they are getting a divorce. You call to mind all the evidence that explains this outcome. "I knew it, remember how they used to fight? Their fights were vicious." On the other hand, perhaps you hear that they have just celebrated their silver anniversary. "Isn't that nice," you say, "they have such a solid marriage; they hardly ever quarrel and when they do, they always make up so sweetly to each other." While we pick and choose in our store of memories, the original categorizing of what we saw remains the same. In this case, we remember certain behavior as a quarrel. It might come to mind as vicious or playful, but we identify it as a quarrel nonetheless. We don't recategorize the original behavior and say that rather than quarreling, perhaps they were engaging in foreplay or playing a game or practicing a role for a play. Initially, the behavior labeled "quarrel" may have been open to several interpretations. Once it is stored in memory as a quarrel it is not likely to be recategorized, even though it may be called up or left behind to help make some case.

When we make new categories in a mindful way, we pay attention to the situation and the context. If I need someone to help me fix a high ceiling, a tall person might be best. On the other hand, maybe someone who is 5 feet, 2 inches, would be more appropriate—if he is a mountain climber, doesn't mind ladders, and so forth. Breaking down categories of skills to more precise distinctions is a useful approach for a personnel manager. In a very noisy environment a clever programmer who is deaf might be a better job candidate than a person of equal ability but of normal hearing. If sitting for long periods of time is necessary, someone confined to a wheelchair may not mind the sedentery work as much as the next applicant. A simple list of general skills free of context would mask these and many more differentiated distinctions.

Most strong opinions rest on global categories. If we describe someone we dislike intensely, a single statement usually does it. But if, instead, we are forced to describe the person in great detail, eventually there will be some quality we appreciate. This is true of objects or situations as well, and is one way of changing an intolerable situation: We can try to have the good without the bad. Take, for example, someone who hates New England winters. If he lets his thoughts become more differentiated, he may discover that what he really dislikes is feeling restricted by heavy winter clothing. A well-insulated jacket or a better heater in his car might change his outlook. Or, consider a couple arguing over whether to get an air conditioner. She can't stand the heat but he objects violently because he gets "air-conditioner colds" all the time in the office. Perhaps the air in the office is too dry, or the attic of their house needs an exhaust fan, and so on. A mindful attitude may not avoid all need for compromise, but then again, it might. In any case, it can significantly reduce the margin of conflict. In a domestic setting and, as we will see later, in the workplace or in the realm of prejudice, mindful new distinctions and differentiated categories can smooth the way we get along.

### *Welcoming New Information*

A mindful state also implies openness to new information. Like category making, the receiving of new information is a basic function of living creatures. In fact, lack of new information can be harmful. Research on sensory deprivation shows that, if confined to an unstimulating environment for a long time, such as a submarine or a specially designed, stimulus-free chamber, we suffer a variety of psychological problems. Also, if exposed to patterns of stimulation that are perceived as repeated and unvarying, the sensory system often shuts down, since it is not "receiving" anything new.

A model of mindful receptivity is the inertial navigation system in modern aircraft. This device is constantly receiving new information, constantly letting the pilot know where the plane is at any particular moment. We have a similar mechanism operating within us as we walk or balance ourselves in other ways. Our minds, however, have a tendency to block out small, inconsistent signals.

For example, if a familiar quotation is *altered* so that it is made nonsensical (but retains sufficient structural familiarity), someone reading it out loud is likely to read the *original* quote. Even though what she was reading was not on the page in front of her, she is likely to express great confidence that the the quote was indeed read accurately.[4] (Reread the last sentence, and note the double *the*.) In contrast, mindfully engaged individuals will actively attend to changed signals. Behavior generated from mindful listening or watching, from an expanding, increasingly differentiated information base, is, of course, likely to be more effective.

Consider a relationship between two business partners, Mr. X and Mrs. Y. Perhaps they sense that although the business is growing, misunderstandings are multiplying as well. Mr. X notices that Mrs. Y is categorizing him as rigid. Attuned to subtleties, he feels a lack of approval. Realizing that he and Mrs. Y are very different, but that she may see his style as inappropriate rather than different, he explains his behavior from his own point of view, saying how hard he tries to be consistent and predictable. Mrs. Y accepts Mr. X's depiction of his behavior, now realizing the value of a business partner she can depend upon, instead of seeing these same qualities as rigid. Mrs. Y was able to make this switch because she, too, was open to cues, to another point of view. In the strongest relationships, this sets up a continuous feedback loop that keeps the partnership, marriage, or team in balance, like an aircraft.

### *More Than One View*

Openness, not only to new information, but to different points of view is also an important feature of mindfulness. For years, social psychologists have written about the differences between the perspective of an actor and that of an observer.[5] For instance, we are likely to blame circumstances for our own negative behavior: "The subway always makes me late." If the very same behavior is engaged in by someone else, however, we tend to blame that individual: "He is chronically behind schedule."

Once we become mindfully aware of views other than our own, we start to realize that there are as many different views as there are different observers. Such awareness is potentially liberating. For instance, imagine that someone has just told you that you are rude.

You thought you were being frank. If there is only one perspective, you can't both be right. But with an awareness of many perspectives, you could accept that you are both right and concentrate on whether your remarks had the effect that you actually wanted to produce. If we cling to our own point of view, we may be blind to our impact on others; if we are too vulnerable to other people's definitions of our behavior, we may feel undermined, for observers are typically less flattering of us than we are of ourselves. It is easy to see that any single gesture, remark, or act between people can have *at least* two interpretations: spontaneous versus impulsive; consistent versus rigid; softhearted versus weak; intense versus overemotional; and so on.

This list should not give the impression that for every act there are two set, polarized interpretations. As we said, there are potentially as many interpretations as there are observers. Every idea, person, or object is potentially simultaneously many things depending on the perspective from which it is viewed. A steer is steak to a rancher, a sacred object to a Hindu, and a collection of genes and proteins to a molecular biologist. Nor does being mindful mean that we can plan certain defined ways of interacting with others that will produce certain outcomes; rather, it means that we remain aware that the various possible perspectives will never be exhausted. We can see this on a grand scale or in the most ordinary circumstances. The nuclear accident at Chernobyl was portrayed in many different colors, from a "heroic sacrifice to the benefit of mankind" to "gross and destructive negligence."[6]

Closer to home, we can see how one set of circumstances gives rise to more than one view: "I go regularly to visit my mother—every week, for years now, every week—like clockwork," says a grown-up son. His elderly mother sees things differently: "He's so unpredictable, I never even know what day of the week he's coming. For years now, sometimes it's Monday, sometimes it's not until Friday. I never know."[7]

Or take the couple in Woody Allen's film *Annie Hall*, who were asked by their respective therapists how often they made love. "Hardly ever," says the man, "no more than three times a week." "Constantly," says the woman, "at least three times a week."

As observers, we judge behavior according to whether, as actors, we could or would do the same thing. If I take a basketball shot from the outer key (and make it), I am looked at as though I took a risk. What that means is that my *perceived* competence exceeded someone else's estimates of her own competence. It does not mean that I took more of a risk than someone else would have, had she felt as confident as I. I took the shot because I believed I could make it. However, since the observer would not have risked the shot and does not know my perceived level of competence, she presumes that I'm a *risk taker*. Enjoying the compliment, I do not argue. But being aware of all these elements is in the nature of mindfulness.

In trying to develop a limber state of mind, it helps to remember that people may have perfectly good reasons for behavior we consider negative. Even if their reasons are hard for us, as observers, to discern, people are rarely *intentionally* stingy, grim, choosy, inflexible, secretive, lax, indiscreet, rash, or fussy, for example. No one tries to cultivate unpleasant qualities. Take the same list and imagine yourself in a situation where the word might be applied to you. If you bought someone a present on sale, for instance, would you then see yourself as stingy or thrifty? If you took your children out of school early one Friday in spring, would you see yourself as irresponsible or fun-loving? Virtually all behavior can be cast in a negative or a more tolerable or justifiable light.[8]

The consequences of trying out different perspectives are important. First, we gain more choice in how to respond. A single-minded label produces an automatic reaction, which reduces our options. Also, to understand that other people may not be so different allows us empathy and enlarges our range of responses. We are less likely to feel locked into a polarized struggle.

Second, when we apply this open-minded attitude to our own behavior, change becomes more possible. When I used to do clinical work, it often seemed odd to me that many people in therapy not only had strong motivation to change (hence their visits to me), but the desired behavior was already in their repertoires. What was stopping them? In looking back, now I realize that, often, they were probably trying to change behavior (for example, "being impulsive") that they actively enjoyed, but from another point of view ("being spontaneous"). With this realization, changing one's behavior might be seen not as changing something negative but as making a choice between two positive alternatives (for example, "being reflective" versus "being spontaneous").

One of my students, Loralyn Thompson, and I tested the hypothesis that the reason some people have a hard time changing their behavior, no matter how hard they seem to try, is that they really value that behavior under a different name.[9] Using a list of negative traits, such as rigid, grim, gullible, and the like, we asked people to tell us whether they had tried to change this particular quality about themselves and succeeded or failed, or whether the description was irrelevant to them. Later we had people tell us how much they valued each of a number of traits such as consistency, seriousness, trust, and so on, which were the mirror opposites of the negative traits. Our hypothesis was confirmed. People valued specific qualities that, when negatively framed, were the very things they wanted most to change about themselves but had failed to change. Being aware of these dual views should increase our sense of control and our success in changing behavior (if we still feel that the behavior is undesirable). In Chapter 10 we will see the power of a flexible perspective as it applies to recovery from serious illness and also to therapy for addictions.

### Control over Context:
### The Birdman of Alcatraz

The increased control made possible by mindfulness can also help us change contexts. Irving Janis, John

Wolfer, and I investigated the influence on pain of a single-minded view of the hospital setting.[10] Patients are often certain that pain is inevitable in a hospital. Caught in such a mindset, they assume that, without the help of medication, pain cannot be controlled. In our experiment, we tried to learn whether people could control their experience of pain by putting it in a different, more optimistic context.

Patients who were about to undergo major surgery were taught to imagine themselves in one of two situations: playing football or preparing for a dinner party. In the midst of a rough skirmish on the football field, bruises are hardly noticed. Similarly, cutting oneself while rushing to prepare dinner for ten people who will be arriving any minute might also be something one would hardly notice. In contrast, a paper cut suffered while reading a dull magazine article quickly becomes the focus of attention. Through examples of this sort, participants in the study were taught that, rather than being inevitable, much of the pain we experience appears to be context-dependent.

Hospital staff, unaware of our hypothesis, monitored the use of medication and length of stay for the participating patients in this experimental group and in control groups. Those patients who were taught to reinterpret the hospital experience in nonthreatening ways took fewer pain relievers and sedatives and tended to leave the hospital sooner than the untrained patients. The same hospital experience seen through psychologically different eyes is not the same experience, and the difference could be measured in lower doses of medication and quicker recoveries. This reappraisal technique effectively loosened the hospital mindset and, by showing that pain was not a certainty, gave the participants more control over their convalescence.

Even the most apparently fixed and certain situations can become subject to control if viewed mindfully. The Birdman of Alcatraz was sentenced to life in prison with no hope of reprieve. All the world was cut off from him; one empty, grim day followed the next, as he stared at the flocks of birds flying outside his window. One morning a crippled sparrow happened into his cell, and he nursed it back to health. The bird was no longer just a bird; for him it was a particular sparrow. Other prisoners, guards, visitors started giving him birds and he learned more and more about them. Soon he had a veritable aviary in his cell. He became a distinguished authority on bird diseases, noticing more and more about these creatures and developing more and more expertise. Everything he did was self-taught and original.

Instead of living a dull, stale existence in a cell for forty-odd years, the Birdman of Alcatraz found that boredom can be just another construct of the mind, no more certain than freedom. There is always something new to notice. And he turned what might have been an absolute hell into, at the least, a fascinating, mindful purgatory.

## *Process Before Outcome*

As we saw in Chapter 3, a preoccupation with outcome can make us mindless. Turning this observation around, as we have with all our definitions of mindlessness, we can see mindfulness as a process orientation. Consider a scientist who feels stupid for not having read a journal article that is being discussed heatedly among his colleagues. A mindless hindsight makes him feel this way. He sees himself as having had the choice of either reading or not reading the important article, and having stupidly made the wrong choice. Had he been less fixated on the outcome of the choice, he might have realized that the choice had not been between reading the article and doing nothing, but rather between reading the article or working in the lab, taking a much-needed rest, or reading to his daughter. This is another example of the *faulty comparisons* described in the previous chapter. Awareness of the process of making real choices along the way makes it less likely that we will feel guilty in retrospect. After all, mindful choices are perceived to offer some benefit, or why would we intentionally make them? On occasion, after learning the consequences of a choice, we may wish we had chosen differently, but we still tend not to be quite as hard on ourselves when we know why we did what we did.

A true process orientation also means being aware that every outcome is preceded by a process. Graduate students forget this all the time. They begin their dissertations with inordinate anxiety because they have seen other people's completed and polished work and mistakenly compare it to their own first tentative steps. With their noses deep in file cards and half-baked hypotheses, they look in awe at Dr. So-and-so's published book as if it had been born without effort or false starts, directly from brain to printed page. By investigating how someone got somewhere, we are more likely to see the achievement as hard-won and our own chances as more plausible.

Our judgments about the intelligence of others can be distorted by an emphasis on outcome. In an informal inquiry, my students and I asked people to evaluate the intelligence of scientists who had achieved an "impressive" intellectual outcome (such as discovering a new planet or inventing a new drug). When the achievement was described as a series of steps (and virtually all achievements can be broken down in this way), they judged the scientist as less smart than when the discovery or invention was simply named. People can imagine themselves taking steps, while great heights seem entirely forbidding.

A process orientation not only sharpens our judgment, it makes us feel better about ourselves. A purely outcome orientation can take the joy out of life. Take playing golf. First you learn to keep your head low and not to bend your arm. You keep trying and you lower your score. But imagine that you read about clubs that would decrease your score by a third. Wouldn't you buy them? The fourth hole in four rather than six strokes—that's playing. Now to get better golf balls. Ah, down to three strokes. Finally a new ball is invented, so refined that it finds its way to the hole on one stroke. What a game, a hole in one on each stroke. What game?

In a game, we can understand that process—if not being everything—is really all that matters. But it may be the same for the rest of our lives. In business, would it be nice always to be assured of success? What if every business plan worked out, without stumbling blocks or irritations? At first it might seem appealing, like the Midas touch. What would such a life be like? A corporate nursing home? According to the Japanese, big business has a lot to learn from kindergarten children. In some Japanese firms, the thinkers and innovators are specifically encouraged to be *process-oriented*—the results can come later.[11] Bell Labs, with its focus on research, was said to be free from a drive toward products, at least until the breakup of AT&T.

### Mindfulness East and West

The definitions of mindfulness in this chapter, especially the process orientation just discussed, will remind many readers of various concepts of mindfulness found in Eastern religion. Students in my classes who are knowledgeable about such fields are continually drawing parallels. While there are many similarities, the differences in the historical and cultural background from which they are derived, and the more elaborate methods, including meditation, through which a mindful state is said to be achieved in the Eastern traditions should make us cautious about drawing comparisons that are too tidy.

My work on mindfulness has been conducted almost entirely within the Western scientific perspective. Initially, my focus was on mindlessness and its prevalence in daily life. As can be seen in the order of chapters so far in this book, the notion of mindfulness develops gradually by looking at aspects of mindlessness and then at the other side of the coin. Only after a series of experiments demonstrating the costs of rigid mindsets and single-minded perspectives do I begin to explore the enormous potential benefits of a mindful attitude in aging, health, creativity, and the workplace.

Behind Eastern teachings of mindfulness lies an elaborate system of cosmology developed and refined over time. The moral aspect of mindfulness (the idea that the mindful state achieved through meditation will lead to spontaneous right action[12]) is an essential part of these philosophies. It reaches into matters too complex for the scope of this book. Since many qualities of the Eastern concepts of mindfulness and of the one being described in this book are strikingly similar, however, we might hope that some of the moral consequences striven for by the Eastern disciplines might also result from mindfulness as understood in this Western form and context.

As an example of the semantic and philosophical tangles that arise if we try to compare Eastern and Western views of the mindful state, consider the activity of creating new categories. While this is a form of mindfulness in our definition, it appears to be in direct opposition to what one does during meditation.[13] In meditation, the mind becomes quieter and active thought is discouraged. In some forms of meditation, thoughts and images that come to mind are considered unimportant and are relinquished as soon as one discerns their presence. At the same time, in many Eastern views, the proper meditation techniques are said to result in a state that has been called *de-automatization*.[14] In this state, old categories break down and the individual is no longer trapped by stereotypes. Such freedom from rigid distinctions is very similar to the mindfulness being described in this book. This one example should show why, not being fully trained in Eastern thought, I leave it to others to tease out the similarities and differences between the two concepts of mindfulness. If a reader is familiar with a particular Eastern discipline, she or he may enjoy making comparisons, in both technique and result.

# CHAPTER 6

*

## *Mindful Aging*

When a new disability arrives I look about to see if
death has come, and I call quietly, "Death, is that you?
Are you there?" So far the disability has answered,
"Don't be silly, it's me."
FLORIDA SCOTT-MAXWELL, *The Measure of My Days*

*

Age is such a potent marker that whatever happens to
our minds and bodies in later life, we assume it to be
the result of advancing years. If older people do anything the least bit unusual, we label it eccentricity or
senility, even if they have been doing the same thing all
their lives. Within such constricting mindsets, tight as
an undersized suit of armor, growth, flexibility, and new
enterprise become impossible. Not only the quality but
the length of our lives may be affected.

---

## *Control and Survival*

The costs of mindlessness, and the potential benefits of increasing mindfulness, became particularly clear to me while conducting research with the elderly. In 1976, with Judith Rodin, a colleague from Yale, I explored the effects of decision making and responsibility on residents in a nursing home.[1] We divided the residents into an experimental and a control group. Those in the experimental group were emphatically encouraged to make more decisions for themselves. We tried to come up with decisions that mattered and at the same time would not disturb the staff. For example, these residents were asked to choose where to receive visitors: inside the home or outdoors, in their rooms, in the dining room, in the lounge, and so on. They were also told that a movie would be shown the next week on Thursday and Friday and that they should decide whether they wanted to see it and, if so, when. In addition to choices of this sort, residents in the experimental group were each given a houseplant to care for. They were to choose when and how much to water the plants, whether to put them in the window or to shield them from too much sun, and so forth.

This group was contrasted with members of a comparison group who were also given plants but were told that the nurses would take care of them. Those in the comparison group were not encouraged to make decisions for themselves but were told that the staff was there to help them in every way possible. For example, if they wanted to visit with people inside the home or outside the home, in their room, in the dining room, or in the lounge, we suggested that they tell a member of the staff, who would help them arrange it. We tried to make the issues between the two groups as similar as possible except for the distinctions about who was responsible and in control.

Before the experiment began and three weeks after it ended, we used various behavioral and emotional measures to judge the effect of this encouragement. Measures of behavior (like participation in activities of the nursing home), subjective reports (how happy residents felt), and ratings by the staff (how alert and active they judged the residents to be) all showed clear and dramatic improvement for the group that had been given more responsibility.

Eighteen months after the study, we went back to the nursing home and took the same measures. The residents who had been given more responsibility still took more initiative, and were significantly more active, vigorous, and sociable than the others. When Judith Rodin gave a lecture at the nursing home, she found that those who participated actively and asked the most questions came from the experimental group. At that time we also measured the residents' physical health. While, before our study began, the health evaluation ratings of the two groups (based on their medical records) had been the same, eighteen months later the health of the experimental group had improved while that of the comparison group had worsened. The most striking discovery, however, was that the changed attitudes we had initiated in these nursing home residents resulted in a lower mortality rate. Only seven of the forty-seven subjects in the experimental group had died during the eighteen-month period, whereas thirteen of the forty-four subjects in the comparison group had died (15 percent versus 30 percent).

Because these results were so startling, we looked for other factors that might have affected the death rates. Unfortunately, we cannot have known everything about the residents prior to our experiment. We do know that those who died did not differ significantly in the length of time that they had been in the institution or, as pointed out, in their overall health status when the study began. The actual causes of death that appeared on the medical records varied from one individual to another in both groups. Thus, the larger number of deaths in the comparison group was not the result of a certain disease being more prevalent in one group than in another. The changes brought about by the experiment in the lives of the residents did seem to lead, literally and figuratively, to more living. When we look closely at our "treatment"—encouraging choice and decision making and giving residents something *new* to look after—it seems appropriate to see it as a way of increasing mindfulness. These results have been confirmed by much research since that time.

Among other effects, increased mindfulness appears to reduce the depression associated with old age. Larry Perlmuter and I looked at whether we could decrease depression as well as increase self-knowledge and memory through a behavioral monitoring technique.[2] This technique, in which subjects take note of the choices they make in daily activities, had already been shown to be an effective way to increase mindfulness.[3] It rests on an assumption about the nature of choice: The opportunity to make choices increases our motivation. In most of our ordinary activities, however, the potential choices that once existed are long forgotten. If I have orange juice for breakfast every day, even though there are many alternatives available, chances are I am not making a meaningful choice. Meaningful choice involves some awareness of the other alternatives that have not been selected. Through this awareness we learn something about ourselves, our tastes and preferences. For instance, if I stop to ask myself why I'm not having grapefruit or tomato juice, I would know it was not just that I wanted something cold, since all of them are cold; and not that I wanted a citrus flavor, since both grapefruit and orange offer that. Perhaps I wanted something sweet and citrusy. Distinctions like this, in such minor but also in more important ways, make us aware of how we are shaping our days.

Both retirees and residents of nursing homes participated in this pilot study. They were introduced to one of four ways to monitor their daily choices over an extended period of time. The types of monitoring varied in the complexity of the thinking required, and also in the amount of control exercised by the subjects. We assumed that more complicated thinking and more control would increase mindfulness.

The first ("least mindful") group was asked simply to monitor and evaluate particular activities each day for a week (for example, the first drink they chose during the day). The second group monitored different behaviors each day. The third group was asked to focus on different activities each day, but also to list, for each one, three alternatives they could have selected but did not. The last ("most mindful") group was the same as the third group, except the subjects chose which activities to monitor. At the conclusion of the week-long experiment, the subjects were interviewed and rated by independent observers as to mood, degree of independence and confidence, and alertness.

For virtually each measure, the more decisions and control required of the subjects, the more likely they were to have become (1) less depressed; (2) more independent and confident; and (3) more alert and differentiated in their choices. These initial results make a strong case for further research into this aspect of aging. We would not expect the findings to hold if so many decisions are thrust on someone at once that, instead of making one at a time, the person might choose not to make any.

Surprisingly, we found a lot of unintentional resistance—from families and the elderly themselves—to our attempts to give them more control and make them more independent. As in many institutional settings, dependency is unwittingly but flagrantly encouraged.[4] When a nursing home resident is helped to dress for breakfast (either out of concern for the resident or to save time for the staff), he or she may feel incompetent and helpless. Ultimately such help will take more of the staff's time, since the more help people are given, the more help they will come to need.[5] Once, arriving at a nursing home before the visit scheduled for a research project, I fell into a discussion with an eighty-year-old woman who had come to visit her eighty-four-year-old sister. She told me that her sister asked her to bring her some wooden tongs so that she could put on her underwear without help, for it was hard for her to bend over. I asked her if she bought them for her sister, and she said firmly, "Heavens no; if she used them she'd probably hurt her back." Appalled at her reply I suggested jokingly that perhaps we should consider inducing a semi-comatose state. That way we could be sure she wouldn't fall and break her hip, or choke. She chuckled and quickly saw the point. Well-meant protectiveness gradually undermines any autonomy. And more coercive interference, such as tying residents into their chairs all day to keep them from "hurting themselves," defeats any shred of initiative.

Watching someone else do things that we used to do ourselves leads us to feel that we are now incapable of doing them. This is true even when the only reason for our inaction is outside ourselves (institutional policy, for example). Mindsets about old age confirm a sense of incompetence. It is unlikely that an old person will find a flattering explanation for why she isn't doing something for herself. When there is one ready explanation for something—being old—we rarely search for other possible causes. Since no one bothers to find out just what the old person can or can't do, a lowest-common-denominator level of care is administered. When the will to act is thwarted, it atrophies into a wish to be taken care of.

### Reversing Memory Loss

Perhaps the most common problem blamed on aging is loss of memory. I remember waking up one summer morning and not being able to remember what day it was. Had I been eighty, I would not have looked far for the reason. Since I was less than half that age, I puzzled over this lapse and realized that in July, with no classes to teach and no appointments to keep, every day was pretty much the same as every other. There was no reason to remember whether it was Tuesday or Wednesday, so I didn't.

The experience gave me an increased interest in the memory loss associated with age. Were there reasons for it instead of or in addition to advancing years, and was it reversible? With several colleagues, I designed some experiments to see whether giving people more reason to remember made memory loss reversible.[6] In one of these studies, residents of a nursing home were visited nine times over a three-week period. We set up one experimental and two control groups. During each visit we made increasingly difficult cognitive demands, including questions of various levels of difficulty concerning the nursing home. For instance, we asked, "How many nurses' and patients' names do you know?"; and "When will the next cocktail party (or bingo game, or concert) take place?" If the resident did not know, he or she was asked to find out by the next visit. Other questions concerned meals and daily activities. For each correct answer residents were given chips which were redeemable for a gift. One control group was questioned in the same way but given the chips only as mementos and not for motivation. A second comparison group was not given either the various challenges or the chips.

All the groups were given tests of short-term memory, as well as nurses' ratings for alertness, at the beginning and the end of the experiment. The experimental group outperformed both of the other groups on these measures. We also looked at medical records and found that at the end of the study, overall health was better for the experimental group than for the comparison group. A follow-up study[7] two-and-a-half years later showed that the benefits of this type of mindfulness training also included an effect on survival. Only 7 percent of the experimental group had died, compared with 33 percent and 27 percent of the two comparison groups. Since several other residents in the comparison groups, but only one in the experimental group, had left to go to the hospital, where many of them subsequently died, the difference in long-term benefits between the experimental group and the comparison groups is probably even greater.

## *Outgrowing Mindsets*

Many of the options and choices and opportunities to be responsible that we provide in our experiments are part of an old person's daily life in other cultures. For instance, here is how the older members of the Yadhan (a tribe now vanished) were regarded:

Their opinion is valued. If they are intelligent and upright they have great influence. Some aged widows are the heads of families, and they are strictly obeyed. The old people's experience is useful to the community: they know how to find food and carry out the household tasks. It is they who hand on the unwritten law and cause it to be respected. They give a good example, and if the occasion arises they correct and even punish those who behave badly.[8]

Despite the fact that many of us know very few elderly adults personally, we have very strong ideas about aging. Many of these ideas are premature cognitive commitments. As we saw in the study discussed at the end of Chapter 3, positive mindsets about old age may result in richer aging. Those who had been exposed to a more optimistic image of old age in their youth were more alert and more active in old age. But this is not the image most of us carry. When we are young, we hear expressions like "old bat," "doddering old fool," "poor little old lady" from people with very negative views of old age before we ever start thinking of ourselves as potentially old people.

The longer we are alive, the more opportunity there is for something that was once irrelevant, and to which we have already made a premature cognitive commitment, to become relevant.

Consider our attitudes toward nursing homes. In Cambridge, Massachusetts, I met an eighty-three-year-old woman named Mildred who has been in a nursing home for two years. The food is good, and so is the care. But Mildred had lived for many years in an old Cambridge house among neighbors who had grown old along with her and among trees older than them all. She loved her house. But Mildred got older, less able to take care of herself, and the money ran out. The house was sold and Mildred moved to the nursing home. A former teacher, she loves paperback books, though today she reads very little. They are now her sole companions, lying scattered about like stuffed animals. When I visited her I asked her about Harry Truman, who was a pupil of hers when she taught writing in Washington, D.C.: "I used to go walking with President Truman, when he was president. He was a nice man." Apparently Truman wanted to improve his English and Mildred helped him.

When I asked more about Truman, Mildred wanted to change the subject. "You hear all these reasons why people come to a place like this," she said. "Well, they're here because they have no place left to go."

Mildred's view of nursing homes reflects an accurate but unnecessary fact. Because most people share this view, nursing homes match these negative images. Not only is it painful to hold this negative view if a nursing home turns out to be our new home, which it very well might, but such negative views in younger people help create the reality of nursing homes as grim dead ends. Such is the power of mindsets.

Much of what older people experience could be the result of negative stereotypes, internalized in childhood. We do not know how many of the "infirmities of age" are actually genetically programmed into our bodies, or how many may be due to premature cognitive commitments. We do not know how many more serene or exciting options for living one's later life might be conjured up if our minds were open to them.

Cicero said, "So feeble are many old men that they cannot execute any task or duty or any function of life whatever, but that in Truth is not the peculiar fault of old age, but belongs to bad health."[9] Old age and poor health continue to be confused.[10] Illness may be more likely in old age, but it is not the same thing as old age. By unquestioningly assuming that old age means frailty and weakness, we expect little of the old people around us, and of ourselves as we grow older. The consequence of such mindsets is an interactive spiral gradually wearing us down. Self-esteem, of course, is undermined and causes more suffering because elderly people blame themselves rather than the situations they are in. An experiment is described at the end of this chapter that may give readers ideas about how to circumvent the worn mindsets and surprise themselves with a renewed old age. In it we essentially tricked the body to step back twenty years.

Florida Scott-Maxwell, a Jungian analyst who did

not begin her training until midlife, began writing a private notebook at the age of eighty-two, in which she recorded her impressions of old age. Her experiences, mindfully observed, did not fit her expectations: "Age puzzles me. I thought it was a quiet time. My seventies were interesting and fairly serene, but my eighties are passionate. . . . To my own surprise I burst out with hot conviction."[11]

## Stretching the Limits of Age

What exactly are our mindsets about old age? Ann Mulvey and I ran a study to find out what actions are most commonly cited as characteristic of older people.[12] The study implicitly asked: Is being old seen as akin to being senile? We used questionnaires to evaluate beliefs about the behavior of older people, and to determine whether information and attitudes about senile behavior vary as a function of age and/or familiarity with the elderly. Our subjects were 75 adults: 25 between the ages of 25 and 40; 25 between the ages of 45 and 60; and 25 over the age of 70.

We asked subjects to list those kinds of behavior that they thought were characteristic of people in three different age groups: 25–35, 65–75, and 76 or older. We also asked them which of these kinds of behavior, if any, indicated senility. Next, all participants read the same descriptions of various events and were asked to describe what a senile person would be likely to do in each situation. For example, "A senile person walks into

a store and picks up a loaf of bread. He or she then
_____." Finally, respondents were asked how likely it
was that they themselves would become senile.

Judges who were unaware of the experimental hypotheses rated the replies. The young and middle-aged subjects saw old people as involved primarily in nonsocial behavior and passive activities, and as possessing unpleasant personal characteristics to a much greater extent than positive ones. The elderly subjects, on the other hand, viewed older people as significantly more involved in social activities and possessing more appealing personal qualities. The younger population was more likely than the old to view the elderly as sickly.

For old, middle-aged, and young subjects alike, there appeared to be a stereotype of the elderly adult that included a fairly well-defined idea of senility. Each age group viewed senility in very negative terms and called it a condition of physical deterioration causing memory loss, mental incompetence, loss of contact with reality, and helplessness. In addition, and most interestingly, we found that over 65 percent of the younger group felt certain that *they* would *not* become senile, while only 10 percent of the elderly group expressed this certainty. To turn this around, a full *90 percent* of the elderly subjects felt that there was a good chance they would become senile, even though, according to medical accounts, only 4 percent of those over 64 suffer from a severe form of senility, and only another 10 percent suffer from a milder version.[13]

When we are young and answer questions about old age, we do so with the feeling that we will never grow old. In the meantime, we form mindsets about the relationship between debilitated performance and old age. Once we awaken to an old self, those relationships become threatening and the fears begin. Such fears are inhibiting and likely to discourage older people from trying to extend themselves in new ways.

## Growth in Age

The notion that the aging process and the physiological deterioration that accompanies it are the inevitable results of the passage of time sets us up for a self-fulfilling prophecy. It is hard to challenge. As we saw in Chapter 2, time in our culture is essentially regarded as a linear phenomenon. While many modern philosophers, as we saw, have rejected the linear model of time in favor of a variety of other concepts, it is still that model that constrains our view of human development. Within this view, most of us see aging as a process in which the body (and, consequently, the person) is inevitably worn down, after reaching peak efficiency in the earlier stages of life. Such a process, however, does not apply at the level of elementary particles or units of energy. On a macroscopic level there appears to be gradual dissolution from organization to disorganization, a "growing older" if you will, at least in a closed system. But when we look at the atoms that make up a person (old or young), a tree, or a pillow, they stay the same over time. The behavioral and social sciences, however, are still largely entrenched in a linear conception of time and an associated image of universal entropy.

Cognitive skills and psychological and physical health are presumed to be curvilinearly related to age. In this view, the individual grows to maturity and then lives out the adult years of life adjusting to diminishing capacities. Some cultures incorporate the growth of wisdom into their accounts of human aging. However, this continuing growth of wisdom is usually seen as a stream of development that is either independent of, or occurs in reaction to, a process of decline that is taking place in other areas.

In one possible alternative view of the life cycle, the path that we traverse from birth to death is a series of goal-directed mini-trajectories, relatively independent of one another. In this view, the past has less overall influence on behavior. Within any one of these separate trajectories, the mind may be more powerful in shaping development.

It is interesting to note how rarely the term *development* is used to describe changes in the later years. Despite current emphasis on a lifespan perspective, change in later years is still typically described as *aging*. In the same way, although the word *day* can refer to the twenty-four-hour span, we normally use it to refer to only the brighter hours. *Aging* has come to refer to the darker side of growing older. To make changes in later life one must fight against all sorts of popular mindsets.

When we are behaving mindlessly, that is to say,

relying on categories drawn in the past, endpoints to development seem fixed. We are then like projectiles moving along a predetermined course. When we are mindful, we see all sorts of choices and generate new endpoints. Mindful involvement in each episode of development makes us freer to map our own course.

Newly elected President Franklin D. Roosevelt came to call on Justice Oliver Wendell Holmes and asked the older man why he was learning Greek (at his age). "To improve my mind, young man," said Justice Holmes.

One of the few pieces of information about brain physiology that has caught the attention of many lay people is the loss of neurons after a certain age. Any bit of forgetfulness after age thirty is apt to be blamed on this loss. But even this scientific "fact" may not be absolute. Fernando Nottebohm studied the rebirth of neurons in the brains of canaries.[14] Knowing that only male canaries sing, he and his colleagues injected females with testosterone. They too started to sing. Nottebohm reasoned that in the presence of testosterone, new neurons would form when the birds learned songs. He and Steven Goldberg then injected the female birds with either testosterone or a neutral control treatment. They also injected them with a radioactive labeling material which is incorporated into the DNA of dividing cells. For thirty days they repeated the process. To their surprise, the researchers found a massive increase in the number of neurons in both sets of birds, even the females given the control treatment, who did not sing.

In fact, they found this rebirth of neurons occurs in adult birds annually, although testosterone and the learning of new songs were not the relevant factors.

Other research with animals demonstrates the possibility of brain development in adulthood. First, many researchers have found that the brains of animals vary as a result of rearing; those animals reared in complex environments have more dendritic material than animals in control groups.[15] (A *dendrite* is the part of a nerve cell that sends impulses to the cell body.) More exciting is the discovery that environmental complexity introduced in *adulthood* can alter the thickness of the cortex.[16] Brain physiology, chemistry, and anatomy are far more plastic than previously assumed. Despite the assumption that growing old is an irreversible process of physiological decline, some kinds of mental functioning can bring about new growth in tissues.

Most of the arbitrary limits we set on our development in later life are not based on scientific information at all. Our own mental picture of age, based on hundreds of small premature cognitive commitments, will shape the life we lead in our own late adulthood. Before examining specific strategies for changing these images, we might take a look at two more positive images of old age from an earlier century.

Lytton Strachey describes Queen Victoria in her late sixties:

Next year was the fiftieth of her reign and in June the splendid anniversary was celebrated in solemn pomp. Victoria surrounded by the highest dignitaries of her realm, escorted by a glittering galaxy of kings, and princes, drove through the crowded enthusiasm of the capital to render thanks to God in Westminster Abbey. . . . The Queen was hailed at once as the mother of her people and as the embodied symbol of their imperial greatness; and she responded to the double sentiment with all the ardour of her spirit. England and the people of England, she knew it, she felt it, were, in some wonderful and yet quite simple manner, *hers*. Exultation, affection, gratitude, a profound sense of obligation, an unbounded pride—such were her emotions; and colouring and intensifying the rest, there was something else. At last, after so long, happiness —fragmentary, perhaps, and charged with gravity, but true and unmistakable none the less—had returned to her.[17]

The feelings Strachey describes are not restricted to those who rule the British empire. A visit from one's grandchildren could evoke similar emotions.

William James's letter to his dying father conveys the same respectful, admiring view of age—an enormous contrast to the mindsets described earlier.

Meanwhile, my blessed old Father, I scribble this line (which may reach you though I should come too late), just to tell you how full of the tenderest memories and feelings about you my heart has for the last few days been filled. In that mysterious gulf of the past into which the present soon will fall and go back and back, yours is still for me the central figure. All my intellectual life I derive from you; and though we have often seemed at odds in the expression thereof, I'm sure there's a harmony somewhere, and that our strivings will combine. What my debt to you is goes beyond all my power of estimating—so early, so penetrating and so constant has been the influence. You need be in no anxiety about your literary remains. I will see them well taken care of, and that your words shall not suffer for being concealed. . . .

As for us, we shall live on in this way—feeling somewhat unprotected, old as we are for the absence of the parental bosoms as a refuge, but holding fast together in that common sacred memory. We will stand by each other and by Alice, try to transmit the torch in our offspring as you did in us, and when the time comes for being gathered in, I pray we may, if not all, some at least, be as ripe as you.[18]

We cannot be sure why some people age mindfully, nor can we know whether admiring views of older people stem from positive mindsets about aging or from mindfulness. What we do know is that models like these help all of us age a little better.

### Putting Age in Context: An Experiment

If negative premature cognitive commitments lead to unhealthy images of aging, can we reverse premature cognitive commitments and improve health? Together with a group of graduate students at Harvard, I designed a study to investigate this question.[19] We attempted to invoke in a group of elderly subjects a state of mind that they had experienced twenty years ago, and to see whether their bodies also "backtracked" to a more youthful state. The attempt could be seen as an experiment in context control. We enlisted the help of a group of elderly men who agreed to try to place themselves in a time-altered context and allow us to take physical as well as psychological measurements. These men's bodies were seventy-five to eighty years old, and we were going to encourage the state of mind they had at fifty-five. We knew this had not been done before, and *any* positive results would be meaningful since old age is taken to be a one-way street to incapacitation. Demonstrable physiological changes would confirm that psychological factors contribute to the way humans age and develop. They would also provide more evidence that the aging process is less fixed than most people think.

We tested our hypothesis by comparing the effects of two experiences: in one, participants made a psychological attempt to *be* the person they were twenty years ago; and in the other, participants merely focused on that past of twenty years ago. We designed the study so that as far as content was concerned, the two groups would be occupied with essentially similar thoughts. The major difference between the two groups that could account for any difference in results would be the context in which the two experiences took place.

The context for the experimental group was the way things were twenty years ago, while for the control group the context was the present. The challenge was to get the experimental group "into context" and then get them to go about their usual routine.

We placed an advertisement in a newspaper calling for male subjects over seventy years old. Those in reasonably good health were selected as our research participants. We arranged to take them to a country retreat for five days, where they were encouraged through props and instructions either to step back into the past or to view the past from the present. Accordingly, for the former group all conversation about the past was to be held in the *present* tense, while for the latter conversation about the past was in the *past* tense.

Several sets of measurements were made before the experimental week actually began and again on Day 5. Some were repeated throughout the week. They measured physical strength, perception, cognition, taste, hearing, and visual thresholds. The particular measures used reflected the "biological markers" recommended by geriatricians. (Interestingly, these leading physicians said there were no clear markers.[20]) Measurements included the following: hand grip, bideltoid breadth, triceps skinfold, finger length, weight, height, gait, and posture. We measured vision with and without eyeglasses, and administered a series of paper-and-pencil maze tests that would assess speed of completion and accuracy. In a test of visual memory, the participants were asked to look at a figure drawing for ten seconds and then wait ten seconds before reproducing the figure from memory with paper and pencil. Finally, each subject was also asked to fill out a self-rating form called SYMLOG that assesses values and behavior[21].

Participants chosen for the experiment had been sent an information packet in the mail containing a program for the week that mentioned testing, meals, discussions, each evening's activities, general instructions, a floor plan of the retreat including the location of their rooms, and a request for subjects not to bring any magazines, newspapers, books, or family pictures more recent than 1959. We had also previously asked for photographs of the participants from the recent past and from twenty years ago. The group that was to step into the past received the photographs of each of their fellow group members as they appeared approximately twenty years earlier, while the comparison group was given recent photographs. Information in the packet also included detailed suggestions about what clothes to bring.

On the first day of orientation the participants wrote an autobiographical sketch. The instructions read: "Specifically, the autobiography should describe you (your likes, dislikes, activities, jobs, relationships, joys, worries, etc.) as you were about 20 years ago. In fact, please focus on 1959. Please note that it is important that you be accurate. Then, begin with the day you were born and work up to the present." These directions were the same for both groups. However, the experimental group was further asked to: "Write (and talk) in the *present tense* about the past. Remember that the 'present' means 1959. So do not include any of your history past this date." We stressed the importance of this instruction before the experiment began, since speaking in the present tense about the past was to be our primary strategy.

Participants arrived at Harvard University early on the first morning. After being introduced to one another, they were asked to attend a short orientation meeting. We told the participants that one purpose of our study of reminiscence was to gather information about people in their late fifties, and we said that we believed one way to obtain new material about this age group was to question older people about their experience at that earlier time in their lives. They were told that to encourage memory of their personal histories, we wanted to bring similar people together.

While medical measurements were being made for some subjects, others were photographed. Participants, individually and at various times, were asked to go into a different room to pick up another questionnaire. Their gait and posture were videotaped as they entered the room.

After this pretesting, the men were grouped together for our final orientation comments before leaving for the retreat. The control group was told once again that they were to concentrate on the past. We asked them to help each other do this. We told them that we had reason to believe that the discussions we had planned for them, coupled with the other activities, which would all take place in a very beautiful environment, might have very positive effects on them. They might improve their physical health as well as their psychological well-being. "In fact," we said, "you may feel as well as you did in 1959."

In contrast, the orientation remarks for the experimental group stressed that the best way to learn about the past may not be through simple reminiscence. Rather, we should try to return as completely as possible in our minds to that earlier time. "Therefore, we're going together to a very beautiful retreat where we will live as if it were 1959. Obviously, that means no one can discuss anything that happened after September

1959. It is your job to help each other do this. It is a difficult task since we are not asking you to 'act as if it is 1959' but to let yourself *be* just who you were in 1959. We have good reason to believe that if you are successful at this you will feel as well as you did in 1959." They were told that *all* of their activities and conversations should reflect the "fact" that it is 1959. "It may be difficult at first but the sooner you let yourself go, the more fun you'll have." This group was also led to expect positive effects from the retreat.

All participants were also asked to use the photos they were sent in order to help them come to know each other. Thus, men in the experimental group looked for the twenty-years-younger man in each other. Then the men in the experimental group boarded the van for the retreat. As they departed we reminded them that once they left for the retreat, it would be 1959. In this spirit, a tape of music that was popular in that year, along with commercials advertising products of that time, was played on the van's "radio."

The following week the control group left for the retreat in the van and listened to the current radio programs.

The retreat center is located on approximately ten acres of tree-covered rolling hills set off from the main road—a world in and of itself. Because the men were from different ethnic backgrounds, the religious objects in the retreat buildings were all removed, and what remained was a timeless backdrop for our study. We had brought many props for the experimental group, including magazines like *Life* and *The Saturday Evening Post* for the same week in 1959, and we put them in each man's room. For the comparison group there were also old magazines available, but these were from various past years, not just that particular week in 1959.

The program consisted partly of twice-daily structured discussions, followed by lunch and then another discussion. Dinner and free time in the evening were followed by a planned activity. The discussions were about well-defined topics, led by moderators prepared in advance. Each discussion began with a three-minute audiotape about the past played through an old radio (for the experimental group) or a new radio (for the control group). Subjects had been given the questions to be discussed the night before. After the radio broadcast the moderator would engage subjects in discussion for forty-five minutes. For the experimental group discussions were held in the present tense, while the comparison group was free to discuss the issues in the past tense. Each topic had been woven into the activity the night before, which helped provide a context for remembering.

A good 1959 movie was shown the first evening, *Anatomy of a Murder*. Right after the movie, participants were given copies of the questions to be discussed the next day. The form said: "Two of the movies which were in the running for the Oscars for 1958 were *Auntie Mame* and *Cat on a Hot Tin Roof*. Which was better and why?"

The men were questioned about the movies. Then the second discussion of the day began; it had to do with sports: "From these following names, who do you think is the best player? Why? Bill Russell, Johnny Unitas, Mickey Mantle, Wilt Chamberlain, Floyd Patterson, Ted Williams, Frank Gifford, Bob Cousy, Warren Spahn, Maurice Richard."

One night the men had a game night and played a version of the old game show "The Price Is Right." We wanted to see whether they would give 1959 prices or current prices for items presented. The following day they had a conversation about financial matters. In the afternoon they heard a speech by President Eisenhower and then discussed politics. That night they were entertained by live musicians, followed the next morning by a discussion about music. Finally, that afternoon they talked about television situation comedies of the past, like "I Love Lucy," "The Honeymooners," and "Sergeant Bilko."

Late in the afternoon of the fourth day of their stay and on the last morning, all of the physical and psychological measures were taken again. A reaction time test was added, measuring the speed of recall of people who were well known in 1959. We asked the participants to look at a presentation of ten slides, one after another, each of which showed one noteworthy figure: Thomas Dewey, Phil Silvers, Jackie Gleason, Groucho Marx, Elvis Presley, Nikita Khrushchev, Milton Berle, Ethel Merman, Fidel Castro, and Douglas MacArthur. For each slide, participants were instructed to press a reaction time key as soon as they recalled the person in the slide. If, after ten seconds, the participant did not remember the person in the slide, he was given a score of ten seconds and told to prepare for the next slide. Once they pressed the key, participants were asked to identify the person. We correctly predicted that the experimental group would perform more quickly and accurately than the control group, since for the former these people seemed like more recent figures.

Also on the last day the men's gaits and postures were videotaped for comparison with the earlier tapes. Discussions were videotaped to see how active participation and ease of conversing in the present tense about the past had changed during the week. Meals were videotaped to document how much and how vigorously the men ate and also whether they took what they needed from the kitchen without waiting to be served, whether they cleaned up after themselves, and so on.

Our results fell into two classes. First, there were measures on which both the experimental and control groups showed significant improvement at the end of the experiment when compared to their at-home baseline level of performance prior to this experiment. These before/after differences are worth noting since they contrast with the psychological and physical *decrements* we usually associate with aging. The change of context in this study seems to have yielded general improvement on these measures.

The men as a whole looked younger by about three years after the experiment. Independent judges evaluated facial photographs at the beginning and end of the study. Even though lighting and printing were held constant, the participants looked younger at the end of the week. There was also a uniform tendency for hearing to improve. Improvement in psychological functioning was made evident in both groups by their steadily more efficient performance on the memory task over the course of the experiment.

The men in both groups ate heartily and, for better or worse, gained an average of three pounds over the week. Bideltoid and tricep skinfolds increased (although here we expected a decrease since people are generally less flabby when they are younger). And, finally, hand strength increased steadily over the week for both groups. By the second day the men were actively involved in serving their meals and cleaning up after they finished. This was quite a change from their evident dependence on the relatives who initially brought them to the study. They were all functioning independently almost as soon as they arrived at the retreat.

Many of these changes might take place if elderly men were simply taken on a vacation. We were not able to find a comparable "vacationing" comparison group, nor could we at the time afford to bring other groups to the retreat to find out whether various other factors might account for our results. We cannot be sure just to what to attribute these changes. Participants in both groups ate well and slept well, probably better than they were used to at home. They were treated with more respect and given more responsibility than is typical for the elderly. In fact, right from the start they were thrust into a situation unlike anything they had recently experienced. When the comparison group first arrived at the retreat, it happened that the doctoral and postdoctoral students who were helping with the experiment were off somewhere picking up equipment, so that no one was there to help with the participants' bags. I looked at all the suitcases. I looked at the participants and then back at the suitcases. Overwhelmed by the thought of carrying them myself, I told the men that they could move them toward their rooms a little at a time, or unpack them where they were and carry the items to their rooms piecemeal if necessary. Whatever they decided, they were responsible for handling their own baggage. This was a big change from the coddling and overhelping to which they had become accustomed.

Perhaps most important, these elderly men were encouraged to take a good deal of control over their lives. Other research that we have already discussed suggests that this variable is indeed powerful.[22] Making demands on the elderly, as we did here, may well have been a big factor in reversing many debilities of old age for both groups of participants.

Differences between the two groups in this study ranged from the striking to the suggestive. Our measure of joint flexibility and finger length increased to a significantly greater degree for the experimental group than for the control group. In fact, finger length increased for over a third of the experimental group and remained the same for the rest of the group, while a third of the comparison group actually worsened on this measure. There was also a greater increase in sitting height for the experimental group than for the control group. They also had gained more weight and had greater increases in tricep skinfold and bideltoid breadth. Performance on the mazes, our measure of manual dexterity, also showed a difference in the two groups. Experimental subjects showed greater manual dexterity. Their errors decreased while the average number of errors for the comparison group increased. In testing vision without glasses on, vision in the right eye improved for the experimental group and slightly worsened for the comparison group.

In addition to these physical changes, we found improvements on psychological tests. The most important of these differences occurred on the intelligence tests we administered (digit symbol, substitution test). Again, the experimental group as a whole improved while the control group's performance worsened somewhat over time. Well over half of the experimental group improved while the performance of a quarter of the control subjects declined.

All was not for the better in the experimental group, however. While the control group changed toward greater friendliness and emotional expressiveness, the experimental group rated themselves as increasingly unfriendly. (This may reflect the fact that they had to work somewhat harder to maintain the time orientation than the comparison group.)

Taken together, these results are impressive, given the way almost all of us look at aging. Change of all kinds, most of it positive, was found in these men at an age when growth and development are considered arrested or in decline.

Recently, as I thought more about these results, I

realized that the very design of the study might reflect an age bias. Why did we think that a seventy-five-year-old would like to be in his fifties again? A forty-year-old cherishes his experience and matured consciousness. We can accept that he might not voluntarily give up his current identity to return to the person he was at twenty. In the same way, the seventy-five-year-old may not be willing to return completely to the world of the fifty-year-old, even though some of the health and strength of the earlier time might be desirable.

The design of our study, however, was motivated not only by the hypothesis that the state of a person's body could be "turned back," if we could shift that person's mind back to where it was twenty years ago, but by an alternative hypothesis. This hypothesis assumed that it took a certain measure of mindfulness for men in both groups to participate in this novel experience, but that a greater degree of mindfulness was required of the experimental group since it had to comply with a set of instructions that were more elaborate than those given to the control group.

If it was this greater mindful activity that occasioned our results, then in principle, *any* intense mindful activity could have served to achieve our results (for example, composing an opera, as Verdi did in his seventies). In either case, especially in light of all of the previous research discussed, the larger point is that some of the objectively measured, "irreversible" signs of aging were altered as a result of psychological intervention.[23]

The regular and "irreversible" cycles of aging that

we witness in the later stages of human life may be a *product* of certain assumptions about how one is supposed to grow old. If we didn't feel compelled to carry out these limiting mindsets, we might have a greater chance of replacing years of decline with years of growth and purpose.

# CHAPTER 7

*

## *Creative Uncertainty*

There's an old story about two men on a train. One of them, seeing some naked-looking sheep in a field, said, "Those sheep have just been sheared." The other looked a moment longer, and then said, "They seem to be—on this side." It is in such a cautious spirit that we should say whatever we have to say about the workings of the mind.

JOHN HOLT, *How Children Learn*

*

Had the rich stranger in Chapter 2 who needed a three-by-seven-foot piece of wood simply unhinged his own front door, observers of the scavenger hunt might have thought, "What a creative solution!" Many, if not all, of the qualities that make up a mindful attitude are characteristic of creative people. Those who can free themselves of old mindsets (like the man on the train), who can open themselves to new information and surprise, play with perspective and context, and focus on process rather than outcome are likely to be creative, whether they are scientists, artists, or cooks.

---

## *Mindfulness and Intuition*

Generally, when creativity is being discussed, these mindful qualities come up under other names. Take intuition, for example. A scientist exercising intuition is very likely to be breaking loose from old mindsets and categories, or paying attention to the meaning of a surprise result.

Just as it is easier to get a grasp on mindfulness by first describing its opposite, intuition is most easily defined by comparing it to rational thought or logic. "It is by logic that we prove. It is by intuition that we discover," said the mathematician Henri Poincaré.[1] In dealing with the world rationally, we hold it constant, by means of categories formed in the past. Through intuition, on the other hand, we grasp the world as a whole, in flux.

Imagine trying to describe a brook. A running brook is never the same. New water flows past, working away, little by little, at the banks. From moment to moment it is a different brook. To talk about a brook we have to find a constant aspect of it. To perform any rational operation concerning the brook we must consider it unchanging, treat it as if it were the same. Language and rational processes both hold experience constant. To behave rationally, one uses categories formed in the past. "I'll meet you at the brook we went to yesterday." We can map its course as of today, measure its acidity at a certain point. Each time we treat it as the very same brook. An artist or writer, however, might choose not to hold it still but simply to experience the dynamic nature of the brook, to sit by it and become open to its "brookness." We call this approach mindful or intuitive; it bypasses old categories and rational thinking. The dancer Isadora Duncan, whose art is by definition motion and change, said, "If I could tell you what it meant, there would be no point in dancing it."[2]

Out of an intuitive experience of the world comes a continuous flow of novel distinctions. Purely rational understanding, on the other hand, serves to confirm old mindsets, rigid categories. Artists, who live in the same world as the rest of us, steer clear of these mindsets to make us see things anew. I recently attended a lecture by photographer Joel Meyerowitz. To my surprise his lecture was about mindfulness. He did not call it that, but to me his talk was a lesson in how to stay open to experience. When he spoke about the ocean, describing the way the light hit the undersides of the waves as they folded back into the sea, my old category of "wave" broke up into a throng of new impressions. I went back to the beach and looked for all kinds of waves, parts of waves, and patterns of waves.

Meyerowitz also described the amateur photographers who flock to the Grand Canyon. Arriving at the rim of this famous landmark, they shuffle about, searching for a sign that says "shoot here." With one pre-set image labeled GRAND CANYON in their minds, blinding them to what lies below, they search for the one and only "right" spot to stand. In advising his audience that there is no such spot and that they could search instead for whatever was "meaningful" to them,

Meyerowitz was encouraging a mindful approach applicable to far more than photography.

When our minds are set on one thing or on one way of doing things, mindlessly determined in the past, we blot out intuition and miss much of the present world around us. If Archimedes had had his mind set only on taking a bath, he probably would not have discovered the displacement of water. By keeping free of mindsets, even for a moment, we may be open to see clearly and deeply.

> While with an eye made quiet by the power
> of harmony, and the deep power of joy,
> We see into the life of things.

In these lines from *Tintern Abbey,* Wordsworth's quiet eye reflects another quality that links intuition and mindfulness. They are both relatively effortless. Both are reached by escaping the heavy, single-minded striving of most ordinary life.

Bach also spoke of the effortless flow of musical ideas. Asked how he found his melodies, he said, "The problem is not finding them, it's—when getting up in the morning and getting out of bed—not stepping on them."[3]

In an intuitive or mindful state, new information, like new melodies, is allowed into awareness. This new information can be full of surprise and does not always "make sense." If we resist, and evaluate it on rational grounds, we can silence a vital message. In the fall of 1941, during the blitz, Churchill, it is said, often went out late at night in a government car to visit anti-aircraft batteries. One night he was ready to leave a site, and an aide opened the back door on one side of his car. Churchill, however, walked around the car and let himself in the far door instead. Not long after that, a bomb exploded, nearly turning the car over. "It must have been my beef on that side that pulled it down," said Churchill. When his wife asked him why he had chosen to sit on the far side of the car, Churchill replied, "Something said to me, 'Stop,' before I reached the car door held open for me. It then appeared that I was told I was meant to open the door on the other side and get in and sit there—and that's what I did."[4]

We don't know if such episodes represent intuition—an attunement to information not perceived by most conscious minds—or merely coincidence. In any case, a respect for intuition and for the information that may come to us in unexplainable ways is an important part of any creative activity. "If man is to use his capacities to the full and with the confidence that fits his powers, he has no alternative but to recognize the importance and power of intuitive methods in all fields of inquiry—literature and mathematics, poetry and linguistics."[5]

### Creativity and Conditional Learning

In Chapter 2 we saw how the teaching of facts as absolute truth can lead to mindlessness. A good deal of my research has explored the brighter side of the picture: the encouragement of creativity by teaching facts in a conditional manner. In most educational settings, the "facts" of the world are presented as unconditional truths, when they might better be seen as probability statements that are true in some contexts but not in others. What happens when this uncertainty is allowed in? Does the uncertain information become more available to us later, when the context has changed?

Alison Piper and I conducted some experiments to explore this question.[6] We introduced a collection of different objects which we identified to one group of subjects in an ordinary, unconditional way and to another in conditional terms. For instance, to the first group we said, "This is a hair dryer," "This is an extension cord," "This is a dog's chew toy." For the conditional group we just added the phrase "could be": "This could be a hair dryer," and so on, implicitly suggesting that under some circumstances the object might be seen in different ways. After the objects had all been introduced, we gave the subjects forms to fill out. In giving the instructions we deliberately made some errors. We then announced that we could not finish the study because the original forms were filled out wrong and we had no spare forms. In effect, we created an urgent need for an eraser to correct our mistake.

Since the dog's chew toy was an unfamiliar-looking piece of clean rubber, it filled the bill very nicely. However, only those subjects introduced to the toy conditionally thought to use it in this novel way.

What happens in people's heads when they learn that "this could be . . ."? Are they really learning conditionally, or are they instead saying to themselves that "could be" means "I don't know what it *is*, but maybe it is an X." Imagine reading a newspaper and spilling hot chocolate on it so that you can't make out a letter (it could be an *r* or an *n*); the choices are not unlimited. If this is what's going on, and people still have preconceptions of the item's identity, then our experiment, while still interesting, does not necessarily tell us how to promote an enduring kind of mindfulness. The experiment showed us that uncertainty resulted in more creative solutions than did certainty, not whether people could stay somewhat uncertain. To test this possibility, we ran a similar study, but with two important additions.

First, to the subjects who were introduced to objects in a conditional way, and those introduced in an absolute way, we added a third group whom we can call a "temporarily conditional" group. We introduced each object to them by saying, "I don't know what it *is* but it could be. . . ." Second, after we created an unusual need one of the objects could fill, we created another need. If people could learn about unfamiliar things in a truly conditional way, then they might see many different uses for the object. For example, another rubber object, a float for a toilet tank, was used as a ball and then as an eraser. The group that was told, "I don't know what it *is* but it could be a toilet float," thought to use the rubber object as a ball, but once they saw it as a ball most of them did so absolutely. That is, the identity of the object was no longer conditional. They did not think to use it in another novel way. Of course, neither did the absolute ("is") group.

The results for the group that met the object in a completely conditional way supported our prediction. At least twice as many people in this group, as in either of the other groups, thought of a way to fill the second need. It is as if this conditional group came to see that people create uses for objects. A use is not inherent in an object, independent of the people using it. The successful use of an object depends on the context of its use. (As an aside, it may be interesting to note that prices are created along with uses. When a scrap of rawhide or piece of rubber becomes a "dog's chew toy," its cost rises.)

Contrast this conditional way of learning with the way we usually learn. Take an orange juice can that has been washed out so there is not a trace of juice in it. Cover it with colored paper and fill it with pencils. To some this still *is* an orange juice can being used as a pencil holder. To those trained conditionally, it would, in its current context, be more a pencil holder than a juice can, though tomorrow it could be a vase.

Uncertainty may be more natural to some of us than others. Consider a person with dyslexia, for whom perceptual information is often distorted. He may not be sure, for example, whether a *d* seen on a printed page is really a *d* or perhaps a *b*. Individuals uncertain in this way might be less likely to take the world for granted and treat it mindlessly. To assess this we performed the same conditional/absolute experiment as before but now with dyslexic students as well as a control group of nondyslexic students. For half of each group the objects described above were presented conditionally, for the other half, unconditionally.

Once again, we found a more mindful or creative response from the normal conditional group than from the unconditional group. Most interesting, however, was the finding that dyslexic people tended to be more mindful even in the explicitly unconditional learning situation.[7] Of course this experiment demonstrated only one way in which teaching can be done in a conditional manner.

Teresa Amabile studied creativity in a group of preschool children.[8] The children were asked to make collages and were randomly assigned either to a group in which they were encouraged to choose the art materials they would be using, or to a group in which they would use materials chosen for them by the experimenter. After they had finished, judges who did not know which group was which found that the collages of students who selected their own materials were made more creatively.

These results could be explained in at least two ways. First, choice makes us feel more responsible for what we are doing; the children given the choice might have cared more and tried harder. Choosing materials—making comparisons—also forces us to draw mindful distinctions. It encourages a conditional view, a sense of possibility. For example, in choosing between two colors the child might think more of what can be done with a color than if he or she were simply given one color. In this way, choice encourages mindfulness.

Teaching can be done in a much more conditional way than just offering a choice of art materials. Children are usually taught "this is a pen," "this is a rose," "this is a car." It is assumed that the pen must be recognized as a pen so that a person can get on with the business of writing. It is also considered useful for the child to form the category "pen." But consider an alternative: What happens if we instruct the child that "this *could be* a pen"? This conditional statement, simple as it seems, is a radical departure from telling the child "this *is* a pen." What if a number of ordinary household objects were introduced to a child in a conditional way: "This could be a screwdriver, a fork, a sheet, a magnifying glass"? Would that child be more fit for survival on a desert island (when the fork and screwdriver could double as tent pegs for the sheet, near a fire made by the magnifying glass)? Or imagine the impact of a divorce on a child initially taught "a family is a mother, a father, and a child" versus "a family could be. . . ."

Some may argue that to teach children about the world conditionally is to make them insecure. This belief may result from a faulty comparison. If the world were stable and we taught stability, that might indeed be better than teaching conditionally. The appropriate comparison, however, would seem to be between teaching with absolutes when the "facts" are conditional versus teaching conditionally when the "facts" are conditional. Will children taught "it depends" grow up to be insecure adults? Or will they be more confident in a world of change than those of us brought up with absolutes?

Since childhood, I have eaten tuna fish salad. Until I was in my twenties, however, it never occurred to me, a middle-class New Yorker, that "tunafish" was a type of fish like any other, labelled "tuna." It never occurred to me that one might have substituted any other fish for tuna and have, for example, bluefish salad or swordfish salad instead. Of course, had I been asked "What are all the ways you could prepare bluefish?" I might have come up with bluefish salad. But the surprise I felt when I was first served fish salad that was not tuna made me feel foolish for not having realized sooner that tuna is just one of many fish. It also made me realize the strength of these mindsets. Even in the most minor and ordinary details of our lives, we are locked in by the unconditional way we learn in childhood. (I wonder what else I would know if only it occurred to me to ask.)

We pick up rules before we have a chance to question them. Is it "feed a cold and starve a fever," or "starve a cold and feed a fever"? I've been among adults arguing vehemently over this issue, without thinking of where this saying might have originated, or what current medical knowledge might have to say on the subject. If you learn something absolutely, it must be absolutely right. (In this case, both sayings could be right if what was originally meant was "If you feed a cold, you'll starve a fever" or "If you starve a cold, you'll feed a fever.")

One intriguing, if still tentative, connection between creativity and a degree of uncertainty in early experience can be found in a well-known 1961 study of the differences between creativity and intelligence. Jacob Getzels and Philip Jackson gave a group of schoolchildren a conventional IQ test and another test designed to measure "creativity."[9] This latter test measured five kinds of ability: (1) word association—students were asked to give as many definitions as possible to common stimulus words (such as *bolt, bark*); (2) finding different possible uses for things—how many ways to use a brick, for example: as a foot warmer, a weapon, a paperweight, for building, as a step, for a bookcase, as a fulcrum, as a source of red powder; (3) finding hidden shapes in complex geometric forms; (4) fables—students were required to provide "moralistic," "humorous," and "sad" endings to each of four fables; (5) making up problems—students were required to make up as many mathematical problems as could be solved with information given in written paragraphs. Success on all these tasks was measured by the number, novelty, and variety of responses. (The advantages of a conditional education on tests of this sort may be readily apparent.)

Getzels and Jackson then compared the backgrounds of those who had scored highest on the "creativity" test with those whose IQ scores were highest. They found that parents of the high IQ group tended to have higher educational status. The mothers of this group were more stereotypic in descriptions they gave of themselves, much more class-conscious and more concerned with financial status and security. In terms of our discussion of mindfulness, these mothers appeared to have more rigid mindsets. The highly creative subjects' mothers described their families in more global/emotional terms, used more rounded descriptions, and seemed to have felt much less personally concerned with finances in their own background, whatever their situation. Particularly interesting in terms of our discussion of creativity and conditional learning is the investigators' observation that the mothers of the highly creative group showed many more uncertainties about their own child-training practices.

Getzels and Jackson's study suggests a link between intelligence as measured by IQ tests and conformity to the norms of the culture and its institutions: family, school, occupational field, and so forth. The background of the more creative students seemed to allow for more nonconformity. Some of the students deemed the most highly creative were actually described as nonconformists. This observation is borne out by our studies of mindfulness and deviance described in Chapter 8.

After we reach college, we encounter teaching done in a conditional manner. We are taught about *theories*, *models*, *hypotheses*, and not just "facts." Theories and the like are implicitly conditional and explicitly statements of uncertainty, at least by definition and at least for the moment. Later they may become laws. Nevertheless, we have found that if a theoretical model is presented absolutely, it will be thought absolute and the student may thereafter treat it rigidly.

In 1986, Jennifer Joss and I tested the effect on students of presenting a theoretical model in absolute or conditional terms.[10] Undergraduates from Harvard and Stanford were given a written lesson on urban development. The lesson concerned the way city neighborhoods evolve. For three separate, randomly chosen groups of students, the lesson was written in three different ways: (1) in absolute terms; (2) in a conditional way, using terms such as "could be," and "may be"; (3) in absolute terms but *introduced* as "one possible model" for neighborhood evolution.

All the subjects were asked to read the lesson and complete the test following it. In the test there were first some questions designed to make sure that all three groups were receiving the same information. This was important, to assure that the differences found were the result of the way the information was processed and not the content of the information. The rest of the test measured the students' ability to use the information presented. Once again, groups who received it in absolute terms were less able to put the information to creative use. They were not mindful enough to notice when a made-up case did not fit the model at all. Even Group 3 (for whom the content of the lesson was clearly identified as conditional—"one possible model"—but the presentation was still absolute) was less able to make spontaneous use of the information.[11]

The dampening of creativity in students by unconditional teaching is compounded by most textbooks. Scientific investigations yield only probability statements and not absolute facts. And yet, these probabilistic data and information that are true only under certain circumstances are presented in textbooks as though they were certain and context-free. Harvard paleontologist and writer Stephen Jay Gould has criticized what he calls the "internal cloning of text to text."[12] In an amusing article he traces the comparison of one of the early ancestors of the horse, *Eohippus*, to a fox terrier. At the turn of the century (when fox terriers were very popular) fossil evidence suggested that these horses were similar in size to the fox terrier. The comparison was made again and again and is still repeated in current textbooks. The more it appears, the more it is likely to be perceived as an unconditional fact. (After all, how can you argue with what *everyone* knows to be true?) Since these little "dawn horses" are now believed by sophisticated paleontologists to have weighed over fifty pounds, the venerable simile to a terrier less than half this weight may be mindless and outdated. (Of course, we should remember that fifty pounds is also an estimate.)

## Distinctions and Analogies

Since "creativity" and "mindfulness" may be two ways of looking at many of the same qualities of mind, there is no end to the parallels that could be made between them. One in particular may be when we look in later chapters at the implications of mindfulness research in the workplace, for an understanding of prejudice, and for healing and health.

Students of the creative process have long distinguished between two kinds of thinking: analysis and synthesis. Sometimes the Latin word *cogito*, meaning "I think" in the sense of analyzing or taking apart, is contrasted with *intelligo*, meaning "I understand" in the sense of gaining insight into the nature of something.[13] J. P. Guilford has examined the mental abilities involved in creativity, using a similar distinction.[14] On the one hand, there is the generation of new information from old information—"divergent production"—and on the other, there are abilities of "redefinition" or "transformation" of thought.

To put these contrasting kinds of thought more simply: We can look at the world and ask how things differ (make distinctions) or how they are the same (make analogies). The first approach results in the creation of new categories, the second usually involves shifting contexts, both of which we have described as mindful activities. We have discussed the mindful nature of novel distinction-making at some length. Thinking by analogy is equally important to both mindfulness and creativity.

The ability to make or spot analogies has long been of interest to people who try to judge intelligence. Candidates for graduate work in certain fields, for instance, must take an exam called the Miller Analogies Test, which contains multiple-choice questions such as the following:

> *Lion* is to *Pride* as *Horse* is to: (circle one)
> Vanity   Herd   Corral[15]

In making an analogy, we apply a concept learned in one context to another one. Such a mental operation is in itself mindful. Architects who can see how one setting, say, a hospital, resembles another, say, a hotel, can come up with designs more responsive to complex needs. Intentionally mixing metaphors with an eye toward finding similarities can spark new insights. Comparing people, businesses, and religions, across and within categories, for example, can lead to a greater understanding of both sides of the comparison. How is Pete like a library / a library like a train / a train like a restaurant?[16]

Jean Piaget wrote that his work on the child's conception of time, motion, and speed was inspired by Albert Einstein's work in the domain of physics and relativity. "Einstein," wrote Piaget, "once suggested that we study the question from the psychological viewpoint and try to discover if there existed an intuition of speed independent of time." According to the physicist Gerald Holton, one of Einstein's many contributions was to generate ideas that lent themselves to "further adaptation and transformation in the imagination of similarly exalted spirits who live on the other side of disciplinary boundaries."[17]

This ability to transcend context is the essence of mindfulness and central to creativity in any field.

# CHAPTER 8

*

## *Mindfulness on the Job*

The supreme accomplishment is to blur the line
between work and play.
**ARNOLD TOYNBEE**

*

The ability to shift contexts may be just as valuable to
a manager or on the assembly line as it is to an artist
or physicist. Fatigue, conflict, and burnout can all result
from being mired in old categories, trapped by old
mindsets. In fact, virtually all the advantages of mindfulness described in the earlier chapters can be found
in the workplace. For employer and employee alike,
mindfulness may increase flexibility, productivity, innovation, leadership ability, and satisfaction. Since most
of us, almost all day, almost all week, are either traveling
to work, working, worrying about work, or planning
the work ahead, the applications of mindfulness to the
work setting are particularly useful.

## *Welcoming the Glitch*

An old Vedic proverb admonishes, "Avert the danger not yet arisen." To catch the early warnings of trouble, we must be alert to new information, to subtle deviations from the way things typically go. In the office study described in Chapter 2, a memo was circulated that said only, "Return this memo immediately." Most of those who received it did not notice its absurdity. Because it was in most respects similar to memos they saw every day, they mindlessly returned it. From this we can see how larger problems can result from initially small, unnoticed changes. When mindful, people tend to notice such problems before they become serious and dangerously costly. Whether it is a slight shift on a dial in a nuclear energy plant, or the first hint of what Theodore Levitt of the Harvard Business School calls the "shadow of obsolescence,"[1] the early signs of change are warnings and, to the mindful, opportunities.

The workplace is full of unexpected stumbling blocks that can get in the way of productivity. To a mindful manager or employee, these become building blocks. They don't impede progress because they are seen as part of an ongoing process, rather than disastrous deviations from past procedure. Take a situation in which instead of the usual four people "required" to do a job, only three turn up, or one in which a piece of equipment routinely used in production is down for the week. If the employees in that department are locked in old mindsets, the work will come to a screeching halt. A mindful employee, oriented to the present, might reassess the job as one for three people, or for whatever equipment was at hand. Deviations from some habitual way of working are less problematic if there is tolerance for uncertainty and no rigidly set method in the first place. The "deviations" then become simply elements of the present situation.

## Second Wind

As we saw with the Coolidge Effect described in Chapter 3, fatigue and satiation do not necessarily occur at fixed points. To a large extent, mental and physical exhaustion may be determined by premature cognitive commitments; in other words, unquestioned expectations dictate when our energy will run out.

As far back as 1928, psychologist Anita Karsten studied situations that at first feel good, but with repetition become neutral or uncomfortable.[2] She put subjects in "semi-free situations" in which they were given tasks to do but were instructed that they could stop working whenever they were tired. They were told to do the work as long as they enjoyed it. Tasks were of two types: continuous activities such as drawing, and tasks that come to a quick end but are repeated, such as reading a short poem again and again. (Tasks like chess that are long but come to an end were not used.)

For each type of task, the subjects worked until they grew weary. The investigator then changed the context. For instance, after the subjects had drawn until exhausted, the investigator asked them to turn the page over and re-draw the last picture they had drawn, to show the experimenter how *fast* they could draw it. The "totally exhausted" subjects had no difficulty repeating the drawing in the new context. Another subject was given the task of writing *ababab* . . . until he had had enough. He went on until he was mentally and physically exhausted. His hand felt numb, as though it couldn't move to make even one more mark. At that moment the investigator asked him to sign his name and address for a different purpose. He did so quite easily. He was not feigning exhaustion. Rather, the change of context brought renewed energy.

When Karsten had subjects read poems aloud, after a while they became hoarse. When they complained to her how they hated the task, however, the hoarseness disappeared. Similarly, another subject, who claimed to be so fatigued that she could no longer lift her arm to make even one more hatch mark, was then seen casually lifting her arm to fix her hair.

New energy in a new context is known to most people as a "second wind." We see examples of it daily. Take a harried young scholar who has been working all day writing a book, while also taking care of his rambunctious two-year-old daughter. By the time his wife comes home to help, he is too exhausted to move. But just then a call comes from a friend asking if he would like to play basketball. He leaps up and dashes off to play for four hours.

In each of these cases, a mindset of fatigue was lifted by a shift in context initiated by someone else—

the investigator or a friend. Mindful individuals use the phenomenon of second wind to their own advantage in a more deliberate way. Staggering different kinds of paperwork, changing to a different work setting, and taking a break to jog or make a phone call are all ways to tap latent energy by shaking free of the mindset of exhaustion. (Mindfulness in itself is exhilarating, never tiring.) A self-starting, autonomous employee can do it for herself; a mindful manager can make it happen for others. The challenge for management is to introduce context changes within the required work load.

Another kind of mindset that can lead to fatigue is the way we define a task. When we begin any undertaking, we have a mental picture of its beginning, middle, and end. In the beginning we tend to be energetic and mindful. In the middle phase, we may perform the task mindlessly or mindfully. If we are performing it mindfully, we are involved in creating new distinctions while we do it. We do not have a sense of ourselves as separate from the task. The task may seem effortless as long as we are involved in process and distinctions are being created. If we do the task mindlessly, we rely on distinctions already made. As the task nears its end, we typically become focused on outcome and also expect fatigue to occur. We now notice the task as separate from ourselves as we evaluate the outcome. When we near the end of activities that we expect to be tiring, fatigue arrives. This mental picture of the end of a task is a self-imposed context and makes fatigue almost inevitable. Changing contexts *before* reaching this point may prevent fatigue. A simple change of activity will not necessarily bring this about, however. The change must be *experienced* as a new context. If a new physical exercise, for example, is still seen as exercise, the expectation of fatigue in that context may remain.

In an interesting study psychologists Janice Kelly and Joseph McGrath had subjects perform various tasks either under severe time constraints or with plenty of time. If the first task had to be completed in a hurry, there was plenty of time for the second and vice versa. Subjects apparently made a premature cognitive commitment to the requirements of the first task. When no longer under time pressure, subjects became unnecessarily fatigued, performing as though still under the clock.[3]

### Innovation

Changing of contexts, as we've seen in earlier chapters, generates imagination and creativity as well as new energy. When applied to problem solving, it is often called *reframing*. A young musician recently told me of his long-standing inability to finish the songs he composed. This had bothered him deeply, and he felt like a failure as a composer until he reframed his "problem." Rather than seeing himself as incapable of finishing a song, he realized what a great gift he had for composing new themes. He then teamed up with someone who is great with musical detail and together they are highly prolific.

---

Changing contexts is only one path to innovation. Creating new categories, exploring multiple perspectives, and focusing on process all increase the possibility that a novel approach to a problem will be discovered. A tolerance for uncertainty on the part of management is also encouraging. If a manager can risk deviation from routine ways of doing things, creative employees can thrive and contribute. If not compelled only to make a product better and better, they may find ways to make a different, better product.

The imaginative use of "outsiders" can encourage each of the types of mindfulness just mentioned.[4] A man or two in an all-female company, a teenage board member, or a blind retiree can bring in new ideas. Independent consultants can fill the same role. Creating the position of outsider in a company, regardless of the characteristics of the person hired to fill it, can keep important questions flowing. Just as a traveler to a foreign culture notices what people indigenous to that culture take for granted, an outsider in a company may notice when the corporate natives are following what may now be irrational traditions or destructive myths. When routines of work are not familiar, they cannot be taken for granted and mindfulness is stimulated.

In *Getting to Yes*, Roger Fisher and William Urey suggest ways that negotiators can generate within their own minds the kind of perspectives brought by outsiders from different disciplines: "If you are negotiating a business contract, invent options that might occur to a banker, an inventor, a labor leader, a speculator in real estate, a stockbroker, an economist, a tax expert, or a socialist."[5] This openness to multiple perspectives—an essential ingredient in mindfulness—supports a policy of workers switching responsibilities, or switching career midstream. If the switch is within a field, rather than across fields, the benefits of a fresh perspective can outweigh the problems of having to learn a new technical jargon. For example, if an art historian became a vision psychologist, or vice versa, each might have something different to bring to the question, "How is a three-dimensional object rendered in two dimensions?"

Distance from the mindsets of an industry is vital in designing products. Take a company that makes wheelchairs. Now that the elderly population is increasing, so should their business. Some people come to need wheelchairs the way others come to need eyeglasses. But unlike eyeglasses, wheelchairs have looked the same for years. There is no reason, other than habit, that wheelchairs must look so medical and ominous. Designers are now beginning to see wheelchairs as racing cars, as recreational vehicles, as colorful, comfortable, and zippy ways to get about. Eight years ago, in a nursing home where I consulted, we had residents decorate their own wheelchairs to make them more appealing and/or functional. The very word *wheelchair* seemed to take on a different flavor after this project. Just recently, I came across advertisements for the "Wildcat," the "Palmer 3," and the "Turbo"—three sleek new designs that seem to redefine what being in a wheelchair means.

As pointed out earlier, innovation can be dampened by too narrow an image of the task. People who make wheelchairs could see themselves in the transportation business or the recreation business in order to break out of the mindsets associated with handicaps and hospitals. Theodore Levitt, whose famous phrase "marketing myopia" could be translated into "mindless marketing," came up with a delightfully poignant example of obsolescent mindsets: the buggy whip industry. While one could argue that no amount of product innovation could have saved this business, a new self-definition might have: "Even if it had only defined its business as providing a stimulant or catalyst to an energy source, it might have survived by becoming a manufacturer of, say, fanbelts or air cleaners."[6]

Narrow definitions of competition go hand-in-hand with narrow mindsets about a product. Small banks, for instance, see themselves in competition with other small banks, in the role of collectors and lenders of money to and from their communities. A bank like Citibank, which saw its function as an "information-processing activity," was able to compete much more powerfully. In the same way, the maker of Royal or Remington or Smith Corona typewriters would not have found their real competition by looking at one another. Over in another corner, a division of IBM was gearing up to knock them out of the running with the Selectric typewriter. This was a totally new concept for producing words on paper, later to be supplanted by the personal computer and word processors in all their forms.

One way to escape narrow definitions is to consider the actor/observer difference. A student made me aware of a good example of this in government. At the end of every fiscal period, agencies and researchers given government monies rush to spend whatever money that remains in their budgets rather than return unspent money to the government. They've used what they needed and now waste the rest. From a taxpayer's perspective, this seems irrational. Why squander the money rather than return it to be used by others? The reason is that if the agencies do not spend the money, their budgets for the next fiscal year will be reduced— "They didn't need it last year so they probably don't need it this year either," frugal officials would say. And so agency after agency wastes money to keep future budgets healthy. The clever solution that my former student, Otto Brodtrick, suggested, based on his auditing experience for a Canadian government agency, took into account the point of view of those receiving the funds. If each year an agency's budget were guaranteed to be what it would have been had it spent all the money given, plus half of what it did not spend, both individual agency and government would prosper. For instance, if the agency were given $10,000 and spent only $8,000, it would get $10,000 the next year plus half of what it saved ($1,000), for a total of $11,000. The following year, if, of the $11,000 it spent only $10,000, it would get $11,500 the next year. Both sides would end up winning. Future budgets would be healthy and current spending would be sensible. The agency or researcher would be pleased to return rather than waste money not needed in the present because of the guarantee of more money in the future.

## The Power of
## Uncertainty for Managers

Employee behavior, mindless or innovative, is not likely to be independent of a manager's style. Of all the qualities in a manager conducive to innovation and initiative, a degree of *uncertainty* may be the most powerful. If a manager is confident but uncertain—confident that the job will get done but without being certain of exactly the best way of doing it—employees are likely to have more room to be creative, alert, and self-starting. When working for confident but uncertain leaders, we are less likely to feign knowledge or hide mistakes, practices that can be costly to a company. Instead, we are likely to think, "If he's not sure, I guess I don't have to be right 100 percent of the time," and risk taking becomes less risky. Employees are more likely to suggest process and product changes that could be beneficial. Admission of uncertainty leads to a search for more information, and with more information there may be more options.

Debra Heffernan, a doctoral student at Harvard, and I conducted research that looked at the power of uncertainty in an organizational setting.[7] We evaluated the degree of certainty of managers in the organization by asking them, among other questions, how many of the decisions they make each day have absolute correct answers. We also assessed their general level of confidence. Questionnaires were given to employees to assess their work relationships with the managers. We found that those managers who were confident but relatively uncertain were evaluated by their employees as more likely to allow independent judgment and a general freedom of action.

Because people perceived as bright and knowledgeable tend to become managers, the sense that the boss knows *the* answer is pervasive and asking questions is potentially intimidating to employees. If managers make clear that they see certainty as foolhardy, it is easier to ask questions based on one's own uncertainty. Questions provide a good deal of information for managers. Moreover, if managers seek out information from employees to answer these questions, both will probably become more mindful and innovative.

Ironically, although work may often be accomplished mindlessly, with a sense of certainty, play is almost always mindful. People take risks and involve themselves in their play. Imagine making play feel routine; it would not be playful. In play, there is no reason not to take some risks. In fact, without risk, the pleasures of mastery would disappear. Imagine mindlessly skiing or horseback riding; imagine going to the theater to see the same old play without searching for a new twist; imagine doing crossword puzzles already done, to which you remember all the answers. We tend to be more adventurous at play because it feels safe. We stop evaluating ourselves. Play may be taken seriously, but it is the play and not ourselves that we are taking seriously—or else it is not really play at all. It would seem, then, that to encourage mindfulness at work, we should make the office a place where ideas may be played with, where questions are encouraged, and where "an unlucky toss of the dice" does not mean getting fired.

Many managers, however, become anxious when faced with a question for which there are no easy answers. When challenged with a question about the rationale for a policy, they reach for the ready-made replies that we all learned in childhood: "Do it because I told you to." In organizations, a very familiar mindset is evident in the reply: "What if we let everybody do that?" Many innovative ideas have probably been squelched by that phrase. If only a few want to do something (whatever the "it" is), what difference does it make? If everyone in fact wants to do it, perhaps it should be done. At a nursing home where I consulted, an elderly woman wanted to make a peanut butter sandwich in the kitchenette instead of going to the dining room for dinner. The director said, "What if everyone wanted to do that?" If everyone did, the nursing home might save a lot of money on food. At the very least, it would have been useful information for the chef.

Should deviant procedures that occur only once in a while be tolerated? Should unanimous desires for change lead to a new policy? Such questions may be important for any organization. Answers like, "What if everyone wanted to?" or "We've never done it that way before," turn an opportunity for innovation into a dead end.

In the academic world, where certainty and scientific proof are much prized, the need to acknowledge uncertainty is valued but still often fiercely resisted. One day I arrived late for the meeting of a committee formed to award a teaching prize, only to find my colleagues upset, confronted with an "impossible" moral dilemma. The problem they faced was that there were five nominees for the prize and only three to five letters of recommendation for each. How could we make a sensible decision based on so little evidence? The question at first seemed reasonable. However, the rather unkind way the committee came down on the person in charge of gathering the nomination materials made me think twice about it. They pointed a finger at her as though she had violated some absolute unwritten rule. With three to five letters the award would be "arbitrary." There should be more information; everyone agreed. But what does "more information" mean? What would be conclusive evidence of teaching skill? Should the letters be from students who currently are taking the course, or those who just finished it? If they were taught well enough maybe the lesson should still influence them after the course is over; perhaps the letter should be from people who took the course two years ago. Or should it be five years ago? Should the letters be from the good students, the poor students, or all the students? One could make a reasonable argument for each. Or should letters be from students at all? Colleagues know what goes into teaching in the first place. What about some combination such as half of each, two faculty to every one student asked, and so on?

When I tuned back in to the meeting, I suggested that since the decision about how many and what kind of recommendations could never be based on "enough information," we should go ahead and award a prize this year and for future years make an *arbitrary* but explicit rule of thumb to follow. Instead of an endless search for certainty and mountains of paper, an arbitrary rule allows any committee, in academia or a corporation, to get on with a decision. By remembering that this rule was simply an agreement, the construction of one committee, however, one is more willing to change it when circumstances change without having to attack those who came up with it. Rules are best to guide, not to dictate.

Besides a quality of confident uncertainty, there is another quality of leadership that is well known but harder to define. Charisma in leaders has a magical aura, which may account for the belief that leaders are born and not made. In a recent investigation conducted with John Sviokla of the Harvard Business School, I tried to explore an aspect of charisma that may be linked to the power in uncertainty and mindfulness.[8]

We first looked at charisma in a theatrical setting. Actors who were performing in plays around the Harvard campus, such as *The Importance of Being Earnest*, *Miss Julie*, *The Merchant of Venice*, were randomly assigned to two groups. Those in one group were instructed to perform their parts in as novel a way as possible, varying it within the realm of the character.

Those in the other group were asked to perform their parts as consistently with the script as possible. After the play, the members of the audience, unaware of our instructions to the actors, were handed a brief questionnaire to rate the actors' charisma. Those actors instructed to perform in a novel way were rated as more charismatic.

To investigate this phenomenon further, in another setting, we gave encyclopedia salespeople instructions similar to those we gave the actors. One group was instructed to approach each new prospect as if he or she were their very first customer. Though they stuck to the "script," they subtly adapted their approach as needed. The other group was told to be as consistent in their approach as possible: "The more consistent you are, the higher your sales will be." The first group of salespeople was seen as significantly more charismatic than the second. Curiously, they were also seen by customers as more knowledgeable about their product, even though this knowledge did not vary among the salespeople. They approached each customer in a more flexible manner, and their pitch had more impact. A certain open-mindedness would seem to enhance powers of persuasion as well as charisma.

### Burnout and Control

Burnout, a problem in a wide variety of workplaces from emergency rooms to corporations, is compounded by mindlessness. Rigid mindsets, narrow perspectives, the trap of old categories, and an outcome orientation all make burnout more likely. Conversely, as we have seen, changing contexts and mindsets, or focusing on process, can be energy-begetting.

Many of us know the energizing effects of a new job. There is an excitement in learning new things, mapping out a new territory. As the job becomes familiar, however, enthusiasm and energy wane. Burnout sets in when two conditions prevail: Certainties start to characterize the workday, and demands of the job make workers lose a sense of control. If, in addition, an organization is characterized by rigid rules, problems that arise feel insurmountable because creative problem-solving seems too risky. When bureaucratic work settings are of the "we've always done it this way" mentality, burnout is no stranger.

In medical settings, where errors may cost lives, these conditions are especially characteristic. Debra Heffernan and I tried to combat burnout in Stevens Hall Nursing Home in North Andover, Massachusetts.[9] We introduced the staff to ideas of uncertainty and control so as to make them more mindful. We demonstrated that the "facts" they used to guide their caregiving were really probabilities and not certainties. We had meeting after meeting in which we questioned how they could be so sure of the rationale behind their policies. We paid particular attention to those mindsets that may induce dependency in the residents and rob them of control. For example, a blind elderly resident wanted to smoke. This was burdensome to the staff, who felt he must be accompanied to prevent him from burning down the establishment. Their solution had been to allow him to smoke only two cigarettes a day. But how could they be sure that he needed help? Another patient's disease made it hard for her to brush her hair. When a member of the staff brushed it for her, he or she was unwittingly implying that she could not do it for herself. One of the more dramatic cases was a woman who couldn't remember to go to the dining room. The staff felt they had to escort her so that she wouldn't starve. These cumulative and seemingly relentless responsibilities, seen as essential, contributed to feelings of burnout.

Once the staff understood that their justification for these solutions were much weaker than they had thought, they were able to find other ways of solving the problems. By returning some control to the residents, they made their own jobs easier. For example, they came to realize that there was no firm reason to believe that a blind man couldn't learn to smoke safely. In fact, he already knew where and how to smoke without danger. They just had to give him a chance. The woman who had trouble brushing her hair was happier doing it herself as long as she approached the task in very small, incremental steps. And no one starved. Her hunger helped the forgetful woman remember where the dining room was. Seeing that problems may be solvable without relying on old rules made the staff feel more in control; seeking solutions made them more mindful. Records comparing the period before our intervention and a similar period of time afterward showed that staff turnover was reduced by a third. Less feeling of burnout meant less reason to leave. These results, though not experimentally derived, suggest that burnout is not inevitable. In a recent experimental investigation conducted at Lewis Bay Head Injury Facility, we offered the nurses and other caregivers a similar kind of mindfulness training. With the resultant change of outlook, and a renewed sense that new solutions were possible, the staff in this demanding and potentially depressing situation showed a significant increase in morale and job satisfaction.

This kind of "care for the caregiver," restoring a feeling of control and options, may become more and more important in hospitals. Nursing shortages, pressures resulting from cost containment, legal constraints, and technical complexity all contribute to increased stress on staff. In a report from a committee at the Harvard Medical School set up to study fatigue in residency training, the reduced length of stay for hospitalized patients ("quick-in and quick-out") was seen as a cause of increased exhaustion among residents. When patients are discharged prematurely, and evaluated by other doctors before they are admitted, the resident loses a sense of control over the case, seeing his or her role as purely mechanical. A lack of mindful involvement in the patient's recovery is clearly implicated in this kind of burnout. In fact, the faculty recommendations included ways of restoring the "cognitive and intellectual function in the management of the patient," that is, mindfulness.

Since the world of work confronts us with the same puzzles that face us in the rest of our lives, these observations about the effects of mindfulness on the job could become a book in themselves. It is probably also clear to readers familiar with business and management that the more progressive thinkers in this field have long been aware of the dangers of fixed mindsets and outcome orientation and the advantages of multiple perspectives and shifting context, but under other labels. In the 1920s, Mary Parker Follett, a pioneer in management studies, anticipated certain of these ideas, emphasizing especially the value of a shift in mindsets. Follett's warnings about an obsession with outcome are pertinent for any manager today: "A system built round a purpose is dead before it is born. Purpose unfolds and reflects the means."[10]

Certainty tends to develop with continued success. There is a tendency to continue doing whatever has worked, ironically making successful businesses more vulnerable to petrified mindsets. I spent part of a recent sabbatical at the Harvard Business School, where colleagues helped me streamline some of the ideas in this chapter. Some of us even made a game out of considering desk plaques for executives:

"Mindlessness is the application of yesterday's business solutions to today's problems."

"Mindfulness is attunement to today's demands to avoid tomorrow's difficulties."

# CHAPTER 9

＊

# *Decreasing Prejudice by Increasing Discrimination*

"If I am a plaything for you giants, be gentle with me. . . ."

"Come!" said she, accepting the offer of my hand to help her over the fender, and looking wistfully up into my face, "you wouldn't mistrust me if I was a full-sized woman."

I felt that there was much truth in this; and I felt rather ashamed of myself.

"You are a fine young man," she said, nodding. "Take a word of advice, even from a three foot nothing. Try not to associate bodily defects with mental, my good friend, except for a solid reason."
CHARLES DICKENS, *David Copperfield*

＊

David Copperfield is having a lesson in discrimination. By distinguishing between mental and physical defects, he will avoid discriminating against people of short stature. Distinctions that are specific rather than global can be very useful in breaking down the mindsets of prejudice.

Most attempts to combat prejudice have been aimed at reducing our tendency to categorize other people. These efforts are based on the view that, in an ideal world, everyone should be considered equal, falling under the single category of "human being." Yet categorizing is a fundamental and natural human activity.[1] It is the way we come to know the world. Any attempt to eliminate bias by attempting to eliminate the perception of differences may be doomed to fail. We will not surrender our categories easily. When we cease (for whatever reason) to make any particular distinction among people, we will probably make another.

An understanding of the nature of mindfulness suggests a different approach to combating prejudice—one in which we learn to make more, rather than fewer, distinctions among people. If we keep in mind the importance of context and the existence of multiple perspectives, we see that the perception of skills and handicaps changes constantly, depending on the situation and the vantage point of the observer. Such awareness prevents us from regarding a handicap as a person's identity. Instead of a "cripple" or a "diabetic" or an "epileptic," we would see a man with a lame leg, a woman with diabetes, or an adolescent with seizures. These distinctions become more useful when further refined, for example: a person with 70 percent hearing instead of a deaf person, someone with non-insulin-dependent diabetes instead of diabetes.

## A Patient by Any Other Name

Most of our labels for people tend to be global: genius, midget, homosexual, giant. Such labels tend to influence every other judgment of, or reaction to, the person who bears them. I first came to notice this effect when I was a clinical intern in the psychology department at Yale. When people walked in the door of the clinic, they labeled themselves "patients," and at the time I saw them this way as well. When we discussed certain behaviors or feelings that they saw as a problem, I also tended to see whatever they reported as abnormal. I saw their behavior as consistent with the label of patient. Later, outside of the therapy context, when I encountered exactly the same behavior (for example, difficulty in making a decision or in making a commitment) or feelings (like guilt or the fear of failure) in people whom I know, it appeared to be perfectly common or to make sense given the circumstances. To test the impact of labels, Yale psychologist Robert Abelson and I designed an experiment using a videotape of a rather ordinary-looking man being interviewed.[2] He and the interviewer sat in armchairs facing each other and talked about work. We showed this videotape to psychotherapists. For half of the therapists, we called the man being interviewed a "job applicant." For the remaining half, we called him a "patient." The therapists to whom we showed the tape were of two different backgrounds. Half had been trained in various traditional ways; the training of the other half had specifically emphasized the avoidance of labels.

We found that when we called the man on the tape a job applicant, he was perceived by both groups of therapists to be well adjusted. When he was labeled a patient, therapists trained to avoid the use of labels still saw him as well adjusted. Many of the other therapists, on the other hand, saw him as having serious psychological problems.

Because most of us grow up and spend our time with people like ourselves, we tend to assume uniformities and commonalities. When confronted with someone who is clearly different in one specific way, we drop that assumption and instead look for more differences. Often these perceived differences bear no logical relation to the observable difference. For instance, because of the unusual gestures of a person with cerebral palsy, we might assume a difference in intelligence. Such faulty assumptions tend to exaggerate the perceived gap between "deviants" and "normal people." In the following passage from *Gulliver's Travels*, we can see this process taking place as Gulliver watches some "strange creatures."

Their shape was very singular, and deformed, which a little discomposed me, so that I lay down behind a thicket to observe them better. Some of them coming forward near the place where I lay, gave me an opportunity of distinctively making out form. Their heads and breasts were covered with thick hair, some frizzled and other lank; they had beards like goats, and a long ridge of hair down their backs, and the fore parts of their legs and feet; but the rest of their bodies were bare, so that I might see their skins, which were of a brown buff color. They had no tails, nor nay hair at all on their buttocks, except about the *anus*; which, I presume, nature had placed there to defend them as they sat on the ground, for this posture they used as well as lying down, and often stood on their hind feet.[3]

When we observe the people around us as we go about each day, so many details escape us: slight tics, gestures, features such as moles, spaces between the teeth, and the like. When face to face with someone who is different, however, we tend to notice these details or quirks. Because we do not typically notice them, the various traits we notice in someone perceived as "deviant" will be seen as extreme or unusual.

In another study, conducted at Harvard, a videotape was shown to three groups of students.[4] For the first group, the person on the tape was given one of several labels: a millionaire, a homosexual, an ex-mental patient, a divorcé, or a cancer victim. The second group of students watched the video without being given a label for the person on the tape. This group was composed of students who were instructed to attend to and think about the tape that they would see. The third group just watched the video monitor without instructions, as if watching TV. The viewers in the first and second groups, whether or not they had been given a label for the man they were watching, saw him more accurately than did the third group. When tested, they recalled more of his physical characteristics correctly. In fact, when we later showed slides of several different people, including the person on the tape either as he was or "doctored up" (with glasses and a mustache), the first two groups recognized him. Both the deviant label and the instructions to pay attention made them more mindful. The third group did not recognize him.

Despite this accuracy in recognition, the two mindful groups (label and no label) evaluated the characteristics of the person on the tape as extreme. They judged him to be different from most people they know. The third group simply "saw" the person on the tape as normal and ordinary. From the results of this study, we can see that the presence of a person labeled as deviant makes us more mindful (that is, we notice specific details) but also reveals how mindless we generally are. The traits and details that we pick up when mindful are taken to be unusual or extreme. If we use these mindfully collected observations to justify biased mindsets, prejudice is reinforced.

### The Painted Cast

The mindful curiosity generated by an encounter with someone who is different, which can lead to exaggerated perceptions of strangeness, can also bring us closer to that person if channeled differently. A most undramatic little incident that happened many years ago in New Haven made this effect clear to me. I was walking to the supermarket and noticed a young woman approaching from the opposite direction. She had a heavy cast on her leg, which I looked at as we passed. We exchanged friendly smiles and I paused to wonder why our interaction left me with pleasant feelings. I had not felt any awkwardness when I looked at her large cast. The cast had been colorfully decorated, inviting me or anyone else to stare at it and thus to think about it. My curiosity had been made legitimate.

When I discussed this little incident with colleagues, we came up with a hypothesis to explain why we avoid encounters with people who are physically different and also how this effect can be overcome. People stare at novel stimuli. When the novel stimulus is a person, however, it is culturally unacceptable to stare. Therefore, we reasoned, people may avoid those who are different in an effort to avoid the conflict between wanting to stare and feeling it inappropriate to do so. The painted cast resolved this conflict; people were invited to stare. With no conflict, there was no avoidance. (As I now understand it, novel stimuli provoke mindfulness. When the context of that mindfulness is not taboo, interactions may proceed smoothly.)

To test this hypothesis we designed an experiment.[5] Subjects were asked to sit in a waiting room where they would later meet a partner pre-selected by us. This woman, whom the subject had never met, either wore a leg brace, was pregnant, or had no striking characteristic. A glass partition in the room looked out into another waiting room. We casually explained to subjects that this was an experimental room and that from the other side of this partition was a one-way mirror. The partner entered the other waiting room and the subject could see the partner without being witnessed in return. The subject, thus, could stare without embarrassment until the novel stimulus was familiar. For half of the subjects the curtain on the mirror was drawn so that they could not look at their partners surreptitiously. All subjects waited in the first room under the assumption that the experiment had not yet begun.

After a certain time, we introduced the subjects to their partners and observed their reactions. Those who did not view the partner before meeting her acted more distant when she was either in a leg brace or pregnant. For example, they chose to sit farther away from her than from the "normal" partner. Thus far, of course, this was not an unusual finding. People tend to avoid people who are "deviant." In contrast, however, when subjects viewed the person ahead of time and sated their curiosity, they did not sit away from the pregnant or disabled person or show other signs of avoidance. This rather straightforward experiment suggests many ways in which encounters with people seen as different (for instance, in schools where handicapped children are "mainstreamed") can be enhanced by providing an outlet for mindful curiosity.

### Mindfully Different

As we saw in the last chapter, being an outsider in a company or other situation can increase mindfulness. A disability or deviant label of any kind can have the same effect, leading a person to question the shared mindsets of the group.

Dyslexia, as we saw in Chapter 7, can have the effect of maintaining in the afflicted person a certain level of mindfulness. Because people with dyslexia often do not see letters and numbers in the same way that others do, they may not take other "accepted facts" for granted. In carrying out schoolwork, dyslexic children may not trust themselves to process information mindlessly, because they are not sure they have it right in the first place. Learning for these children thus becomes more conditional, a mode that, as we pointed out earlier, is potentially conducive to greater creativity.[6]

Sensory as well as physical handicaps create a series of hurdles that require mindful solutions. The deaf, blind, or wheelchair-bound person must approach simple activities, that others pursue mindlessly, in a more problem-solving frame of mind. Hadi Madjid, a blind, Harvard-trained economist, tells of wanting to go skiing with his friends. He figured that by attaching bells to the poles of the skier just ahead, he could learn to weave his way down a trail.[7] Stephen Hawking, the very distinguished British physicist, has learned to master one complex communication device after another (such as a keyboard that produces artificial speech) as he keeps one step ahead of the neurological disease that has paralyzed most of his muscles and left him unable to speak.

Ironically, the greater mindfulness generated by a handicap, or other difference, can create yet one more way in which the person differs from the majority. Greater mindfulness may lead to original perceptions that others may view as bizarre. These perceptions often may be more informed (that is, may result from noticing more distinctions about the world). In combating prejudice, then, the issue is not simply how we might teach the majority to be less judgmental, but also how we might all learn to value a "disabled" or "deviant" person's more creative perceptions.

When those who are considered deviant find no support for their original views of the world, they often join others who are similar, to affirm their perceptions. Paradoxically, this may not foster continued mindfulness. Consciousness-raising efforts that lead to shared mindsets rather than to continued questioning may actually promote mindlessness. When taught that it is okay to be old, black, gay, disabled, divorced, a recovering alcoholic, and so on, people may become less likely to question their perceptions, including those in areas unrelated to their different status or level of ability.

While a mindful view of the world may come more naturally to a disabled person, this may not extend to his or her own handicap. A mindless assumption of limitations associated with particular handicaps may in itself be disabling. This kind of mindlessness, which lowers the expectations of a handicapped person, can arise as a protection for that person's self-esteem. The disability is used as a justification for failure or poor performance. Such excuses are useful to all of us. Individuals without disabilities frequently employ "self-handicapping" strategies, building in explanations for possible failures.[8] For example, people might drink or avoid studying much before an exam so as to feel that if they hadn't been drinking or had studied, they would have done well. These fabricated explanations are more apt to have the flavor of a rationalization than the more compelling, "real" handicap of the deviant.

Consider, for instance, two teenage girls who both love to ride horses and are learning to jump. One of the girls has inherited a condition called albinism, which can cause poor eyesight. The two girls ride equally well, and one day they ride out to practice jumping. The riding teacher keeps raising the jump. Finally, it becomes so high that neither girl can get over it; their horses refuse.

As they ride back, the "normal" girl is berating herself endlessly, whereas the albino girl is not so hard on herself. Because of her condition, for better or worse, she did not have the same rigid expectations. People with disabilities may be protected from the negative effects of failure by lower expectations of success. If someone with a disability and someone without it confront a new task and fail (and that failure is perceived by both performers to reflect low ability), the person with a disability may be better protected from a drop in self-esteem. That same protection, however, may hold a disabled person back, insofar as low expectations undermine performance.[9]

In a society for which outcome rather than process is of primary value[10] (by our definition, a more mindless society), deviance and disability are much more apt to lower self-esteem. For instance, a deaf student who is constantly comparing his comprehension of the lectures against that of his classmates who are not hearing-impaired might feel demoralized. The same student concentrating instead on mastering the subtleties of lipreading might feel highly encouraged. In fact, in a society concerned primarily with process, the notion of deviance might have much less, if any, significance.

## Disabling Mindsets

Unless we grow up with a handicapped person in the family, most of us first learn about handicaps as something not relevant to our lives. Mindless stereotypes (premature cognitive commitments) may be un-critically accepted. If the issue later becomes relevant, these mindsets may be hard to shake. For instance, what happens to people who become handicapped through an accident? They may become victims of their own mindsets. If, for example, they had mindlessly accepted a relationship between physical and mental handicaps, they may worry unnecessarily that their mental faculties have been impaired as well. If a handicap becomes relevant to us not through personal injury but rather through injury to a close relative, a child, for example, the old stereotypes may affect that relationship. A parent who had once picked up an antiquated image of a "village idiot" might respond to a deaf-mute child as if he or she were mentally deficient.

These global stereotypes also prevent us from taking advantage of the talents around us. If the school football team needed to plan better strategies against a competitor, for instance, and the best person to help was a certain superb football strategist, she might not be asked because she sits in a wheelchair. If you with-hold your vote from a politician because he is gay, overlook a surgeon because she is a woman, a psychi-atrist because he is blind, or a potential consultant because she has only one arm, you may miss out on the most qualified person.

The very definition of *deviance* may of course be misleading in the first place. Earlier we mentioned that any categorical distinction can be broken down into further distinctions. Once we are aware of these dis-tinctions and make enough of them, it may no longer be possible to view the world in terms of large polarized categories such as black and white, normal and disabled, gay and straight. With skin color, this difficulty is pretty obvious. But take the distinction between homosexuals and heterosexuals. These categories do not seem to overlap; there are people who prefer sexual behavior with their own sex and they are called homosexuals, and there are people who engage in sexual behavior with members of the opposite sex and they are called heterosexuals. Surely this is clear.

The bisexual who enjoys sex with both genders is the first obvious exception to this distinction. Next, where do we put a man who prefers to fantasize about men while making love to women? Then, what about a completely celibate person; or the married transves-tite; or the person who makes love with a transsexual presently of the opposite sex; or the person who was heterosexual, had one homosexual experience, and is now without a partner? To continue this just a bit longer, where do we put the so-called heterosexual couple, or for that matter homosexual couple, who no longer makes love? This is not a small group of people.

If the categories "heterosexual" and "homosexual" apply exclusively to sexual activity, then during the time people are not making love, they might be classified either way. We could call them heterosexual if their last encounter was heterosexual; homosexual, if their last encounter was homosexual. If the majority of their sexual experience was heterosexual, however, perhaps we should consider them heterosexual. But what if the best of these experiences were homosexual? And so on. Moreover, if one's definition of sexuality were based on the nature of the behavior, rather than with whom it took place, what sense would it make to label couples "gay" or "straight" if they engaged in all the same behavior? Consider where we would put a man who is impotent but still tries to satisfy his wife or a woman who enjoys foreplay but not intercourse.

For even more obvious reasons it makes no sense to speak of physically handicapped people as a category. Describing particular activities for which a person with a particular disability might be less competent reduces the global quality of the handicap label and thus, as we said before, makes it only an aspect of that person instead of a whole identity. This mindful perspective should reduce the importance of deviance for both actor and observer, for we would soon see that we are all "handicapped." Deviance as a category relies for its definition on another category, "normal," with which it is mutually exclusive. To define "normal" necessitates evaluative judgments. To be a "paraplegic" or a "diabetic," or to be "too fat" or "too thin," suggests that there is one ideal way to be a human being. To be "deviant" means that one does not belong to this so-called "normal" group. In itself, the notion of deviance has no meaning.

## Discrimination Without Prejudice

A mindful outlook recognizes that we are all deviant from the majority with respect to some of our attributes, and also that each attribute or skill lies on a continuum. Such an awareness leads to *more* categorizing and consequently fewer global stereotypes, or, as we said earlier, increasing discrimination can reduce prejudice.

To test the effect of increasing mindful distinctions on the perception of deviance, Richard Bashner, Benzion Chanowitz, and I conducted an experiment in a local elementary school.[11] We tried to find out whether encouraging children to make distinctions actively would teach them that handicaps are task- and context-specific. Children were shown slides of people and then given a questionnaire relating the people shown with different kinds of skills. For the experimental group, we asked for several answers to each question on the questionnaire. For the control group, we asked for only one answer to each question.

Most of us are brought up to find *the* answer rather than *an* answer to questions. We do not easily come up with several alternatives. By requiring that the children in the first group give several different answers to each question, we were also requiring them to draw mindful new distinctions. The group that gave one answer (albeit a different one for each slide) was not exercising this capacity. Our general hypothesis was that training in mindfulness would result in less *indiscriminate* discrimination.

One of the slides, for example, pictured a woman who was a cook. She was identified as deaf. The experimental group was asked to write down four reasons why she might be good at her profession and four reasons why she might be bad. The control group was asked to list one good and one bad reason. This group was asked six additional questions requiring only one answer in order to keep the number of answers constant. Several questions were asked of this kind about different professions.

A second part of this training in discrimination presented problem situations and asked the children "how" they might be solved. They were to list as many ways as they could think of (experimental group), or they were simply asked whether they could be solved (control group). For instance, when viewing a woman in a wheelchair they were either asked in detail *how* this person could drive a car or simply asked, *Can* this person drive a car?

A third exercise in making distinctions involved finding explanations for events. We gave the children a slide and a short written description of what was happening (for instance, a girl spilling coffee in a lunchroom). The experimental group was told to think up several different explanations for the situation while the control group again considered only one explanation. The number of explanations required for each set of questions increased throughout the training for the experimental group. The same number of slides was presented to every child.

After all this "training" the children were given several tests to assess prejudice. One was a measure of general disability discrimination. They were shown slides of children with and without various handicaps and were asked to indicate whom they wanted on their team for activities such as checkers, soccer, a singalong, a tug of war, a wheelchair race, a game of Frisbee, seesawing, and pinning the tail on the donkey. We chose handicaps and activities so that nonhandicapped children would be more suited for some activities, handicapped children for others, and for some activities it would not matter. For example, experience in a wheelchair would be helpful for the wheelchair race just as blindness would not hinder performance on pin the tail on the donkey. However, neither would be especially helpful in a game of soccer, and for a singalong these handicaps would be irrelevant.

Our results showed that children can be taught that handicaps are function-specific and not person-specific. Those given training in making mindful distinctions learned to be discriminating without prejudice. This group was also less likely than the control group to avoid a handicapped person. In essence, the children were taught that attributes are relative and not absolute, that whether or not something is a disability depends on the context. Such a mindful view of disabilities may be a valuable asset as these children grow up and move into that large category of people that our society sees as disabled, the elderly—or, on the way, join the category of "patient."

# CHAPTER 10

\*

# *Minding Matters: Mindfulness and Health*

Is there a split between mind and body, and if so, which
is it better to have?
WOODY ALLEN, *Getting Even*

\*

From earliest childhood we learn to see mind and body
as separate and unquestioningly to regard the body as
more important. We learn that "sticks and stones may
break your bones, but words can never hurt you." If
something is wrong with our bodies we go to one kind
of doctor, while with a "mental problem" we go to
another. Long before we have any reason to question
it, the split is ingrained into us in endless ways. It is
one of our strongest mindsets, a dangerous premature
cognitive commitment.

Mind and body have not always been seen as separate, however. There have been periods of history and
cultures in which this dualism was not an assumption.
Sir Charles Sherrington, speaking of Aristotle's concept
of mind, points out that the "impression left by *De*

*Anima* is Aristotle's complete assurance that the body and its thinking are just one existence . . . the oneness of the living body and its mind together seems to underlie the whole description."[1] Today among the !Kung, a people of the Kalahari Desert of southern Africa, healing practices for physical and psychological disturbances are the same. Their all-night healing dances are performed to treat problems ranging from marital troubles to coughs to insufficient breast milk. The healing energy of the community is focused on the whole person, not just on a disease or body part.[2]

As we saw in the discussion of entropy in Chapter 3, many scientists, such as James Jeans and Arthur Eddington, have questioned the view of the universe as a great machine, a purely physical reality. "Throughout the physical universe runs that unknown continent which surely must be the stuff of our consciousness,"[3] wrote Eddington. In psychology, however, a dualistic view has been persistent. Since, until the end of the last century, psychology as a discipline was considered a branch of philosophy, psychologists' notions of mind were derived from those held by philosophers. The separation of mind and body is traced by many historians to Descartes, who saw the mind as nonmaterial and the body as material. Only the body was subject to mechanical laws. Though many later thinkers have quarreled with this view, it persisted for a long time in psychology and still persists in the way most of us look at ourselves.

Behaviorists such as Watson and Skinner challenged this view earlier in this century and argued that behavior could be understood by focusing only on that which can be observed, including the antecedents to and the consequences of behavior. Early behaviorism held that behavior had environmental or situational, but not mental, causes. In this school of thought, life can be described without reference to mental events; there are only physical stimuli and physical responses. Mind is viewed as an empty construct, an epiphenomenon.

Until the 1950s the choice for psychologists lay between dualism or behaviorism. The language of dualism prevailed. Even among those who were studying only behavior, there remained, in life away from the lab at least, an implicit acknowledgment of the mind/ body distinction. Today, much of the focus in psychology has shifted to the study of cognition. While the word *cognition* is synonymous with mental activity, research in this field is designed so that tests of cognition and cognitive processes are behavioral. In the newer field of neuroscience, dualism seems to have resurfaced as a mind/brain distinction.

### Dualism:
### A Dangerous Mindset

All this would be a matter of semantics or academic philosophy were it not for the fact that a rigid view of mind as separate from body has serious consequences. Among the most extreme of these consequences is the phenomenon of "psychological death." The patient mentioned in Chapter 4, who improved when moved to a more hopeful ward and died when moved back to the "hopeless" ward, shows that distinctions between physical and mental illness are questionable. The "failure to thrive" syndrome, seen in institutions where babies are given adequate physical care but not enough cuddling and stimulation, is another consequence of ignoring the interdependence of physical and mental health.

A related kind of dualism, also with potential to harm, is the distinction between thought and feeling (cognition and affect). Although cognition is generally seen as necessary in order to experience emotion,[4] some psychologists, including William James[5], have viewed emotion as a purely bodily state. Visceral change, in this view, *is* the emotion.[6] Robert Zajonc, at the University of Michigan, has argued that one does not need cognition in order to experience affect.[7] He has shown that when subjects are presented with tones that they had, albeit unwittingly, heard before and others they had never heard, subjects preferred the familiar tone sequences even though they couldn't discriminate between the two on the basis of familiarity. Here feeling seems to precede thought. Though they did not know they had heard them before, they liked them more.

Neither separating these two functions, nor trying to reduce one to the other, seems to me to make sense. Nor is it enough to see them as simply related. Viewing them instead as part of one total simultaneous reaction, a reaction that may be measured in many different ways, may be more clarifying. For instance, an intelligence

context. The response of our bodies does not reflect a one-to-one correspondence to stimuli in the external world because there is no one-to-one correspondence between the external world and how we perceive it. Any stimulus can be seen as simultaneously many stimuli. Our perceptions and interpretations influence the way our bodies respond. *When the "mind" is in a context, the "body" is necessarily also in that context.* To achieve a different physiological state, sometimes what we need to do is to place the mind in another context.

The power of context to affect the body may be considerable, even to the point of influencing basic needs. In an experiment on hunger, subjects who chose to fast for a prolonged time for personal reasons tended to be less hungry than subjects who fasted for extrinsic reasons (in this case, because of the scientific value of the experiment and a payment of $25).[8] A fee or other extrinsic reason to undertake a difficult task may not change the way we feel about the task. Freely choosing to perform that task, however, means that one has adopted a certain attitude toward it. In the experiment, those who had made a personal psychological commitment to fasting reported less hunger. They also showed less of an increase in free fatty acid levels, a physiological indicator of hunger. Thus, the different state of mind meant a different state for the body.

The effect of context on pain has been known for a long time. In *The Principles of Psychology*, William James describes a Dr. Carpenter who suffered severe neuralgia:

He has frequently begun a lecture while suffering neuralgic pain so severe as to make him apprehend that he would find it impossible to proceed; yet no sooner has he by a determined effort fairly launched himself into the stream of thought, than he has found himself continuously borne along without the least distraction, until the end had come, and the attention has been released; then the pain has recurred with a force that has overmastered all resistance making him wonder how he could have ceased to feel it.[9]

When one can take one's mind off pain, it seems to go away. Conversely, when the mind returns to pain, so does the body. If one can reinterpret a painful stimulus, it may cease to be painful. The results of this strategy may be more lasting than simply distracting the mind since, once the stimulus is reinterpreted, the mind is unlikely to return to the original interpretation. In Chapter 5 we saw how patients can learn to tolerate pain by seeing it in a different context (thinking of bruises incurred during a football game, or cutting oneself while rushing to prepare for a dinner party). This mindful exercise helped them use fewer pain relievers and sedatives and leave the hospital earlier than other patients matched for comparison.

Henry Knowles Beecher compared the frequency of pain severe enough to require medication in soldiers wounded in World War II and in a matched group of civilians.[10] Although the soldiers had extensive wounds, only 32 percent required medication, compared to 83 percent of the civilians. Robert Ulrich reported that gall-bladder-surgery patients who had been assigned to hospital rooms with windows facing brilliantly colored fall trees had shorter postoperative stays and took fewer pain relievers than those assigned to rooms that faced a brick wall.[11]

Part of the hospital context is its strangeness. But seen in a different way, this unfamiliarity may disappear. Hospital staff, after all, are people, windows are windows, and beds are beds. And yet we let this perceived strangeness have a great impact on us. In a dramatic investigation, K. Järvinen studied patients who had suffered severe heart attacks and found that they were five times as likely to experience sudden death when unfamiliar staff made the rounds than would be expected in any comparable time period. However, the strangeness did not reside in the staff. Novelties and familiarity are qualities we impart to the environment.[12] Had patients been helped to see the way these staff members were like people they already knew and cared for—thereby making them less unfamiliar—the consequences might have been different.[13]

Context can influence even the acuity of our senses. This may be seen in a study of vision, which I undertook together with several student colleagues at Harvard.[14] We made use of the belief held by many people that pilots have excellent vision. Our subjects were students in R.O.T.C. They were asked to imagine themselves as air force pilots—that is, they were told to try to *be* pilots, rather than thinking of acting a part. Our hypothesis was that their eyes would match what their minds believed pilots' vision to be. One of the investigators, Mark Dillon, was in R.O.T.C. and was able to arrange use of a flight simulator. Our subjects got into uniforms and, with instructions, "flew" the simulator, an activity that very closely mimics actual flying. A comparison group also got into uniform, but for them the simulator was broken so that they had to simulate the simulation.

No mention of vision was made. At the start of the study, before the pilot context was introduced, subjects were given a short general physical in which a test of vision was included. While flying (or pretending to fly, depending on the group), subjects were asked to read the markings on the wing of a plane that could be seen out the cockpit window. These "markings" were actually letters from an eye chart. Although the findings need further replication, vision improved for approximately 40 percent of the subjects when they were in the pilot context, while no one improved in the comparison group. When other groups were added, designed to control for arousal and motivation, the results remained basically unchanged.

Context affects the physiology of animals as well as people. Chronic overcrowding of rats, especially during growth and development, may result in heavier adrenal and pituitary glands.[15] Another study suggests that the difference found in cortical weight and thickness between rats reared in enriched environments versus those in isolated environments persists for as long as the rats live in these different social settings.[16] Many other studies by neuroscientists have shown similar anatomical changes resulting from psychological influences.

A wide body of recent research has been devoted

to investigating the influence of attitudes on the immune system. The immune system is thought to be the intermediary between psychological states and physical illness. The emotional context, that is to say, our interpretation of the events around us, would thus be the first link in a chain leading to serious illness. Richard Totman, a British clinical psychologist, describes one of the possible "psychosomatic" chains of events:

Psychological states, through their impact on the higher centre of the brain and the limbic-hypothalamic-pituitary-adrenal pathway, could tip some of the sensitive balances which govern the body's response to a vast number of diseases in which the immune system is involved. These range from infections and allergies to arthritis, auto-immune diseases and cancer, and include numerous other degenerative complaints associated with ageing. There would thus seem to be no shortage of potential "ways in" for psychological influences in the causation of such conditions.[17]

Since context is something over which we have control, the continuing clarification of these links between psychological states and illness is good news. Diseases thought to be purely physiological and incurable may be more amenable to individual control than we have believed in the past.

Even when the course of a disease may appear to progress inexorably, our reactions to it can be mindful or mindless and change its impact on us. A very common mindset, for example, is the conviction that cancer means death. Even if the tumor has not yet had an effect on any body function, rarely will one think of oneself as healthy after having a malignancy diagnosed. At the same time, there are almost certainly people walking around with undiagnosed cancer who consider themselves healthy. Many doctors have observed that after a diagnosis of cancer, patients seem to go into a decline that has little to do with the actual course of the disease. They appear, in a sense, to "turn their faces to the wall," and begin to die.

## *Addiction in Context*

While alcoholism and drug addiction are often seen as intractable problems, very difficult to treat, the importance of context in both conditions leaves room for optimism. For instance, even the degree of intoxication can be changed by changing the drinker's expectations. In one experiment, researchers divided a group of subjects according to whether they *expected* to receive an alcoholic (vodka and tonic) or a nonalcoholic (tonic) drink. Subjects were told that they were taking part in a taste-testing contest and were instructed to sample the liquids ad-lib and rate them. Despite the presumed physiological effects of the drug on behavior, expectations were the major influence. What the subjects expected determined how much they drank, how aggressively they behaved, and in general how intoxicated they seemed.[18] In a similar study, investigators found that the groups of men who believed they had been given alcohol, whether or not the belief was true, showed a tendency for reduced heart rate.[19]

These are just a few of the many investigations showing that thoughts may be a more potent determinant of the physiological reactions believed to be alcohol-related than the actual chemical properties of alcohol. The antics of high school kids at parties, generation after generation, are probably also influenced by context just as much as by the quantity of beer consumed. As we've seen in Chapter 3, we all grow up with firm premature cognitive commitments regarding how alcohol affects behavior. These mindsets are potent influences on the role alcohol plays in our later lives.

Drug counselors have observed that heroin addicts are less likely to report withdrawal if they don't consider themselves addicts. Those who take the same amount of heroin and call themselves addicts often suffer much greater withdrawal symptoms. Informal reports from people who work with heroin addicts show that those addicts who are sent to prisons having the reputation of being "clean" (that is, where they believe there is absolutely no chance they will be able to get drugs) do not seem to suffer intense withdrawal symptoms, while addicts in other facilities who are denied the drug but believe they might be able to get their hands on it do experience the pain of withdrawal. Out of mind, out of body.

The strong effect of context on addiction can also be seen in work with Vietnam veterans. In a study carried out by Lee Robbins and colleagues, soldiers who had a drug problem while serving in Vietnam were compared with a similar group of addicts who had picked up the habit nearer to home. The veterans may have taken up drugs to handle the acute stress of war. Since this external justification was left behind in Vietnam, so was their perceived need for the drugs.[20]

An even more dramatic effect of context has been reported in relation to drug overdose.[21] As experience with drugs such as opiates increases, a tolerance builds up. Users progress to doses that would have been fatal earlier. Many users die, however, from a dose that should *not* be fatal to them. Shepard Siegel and some fellow researchers have suggested that the failure of tolerance on the day of the overdose is a function of context. In an experiment with rats they found that if a large dose of a drug is given in the presence of cues that are associated with sublethal doses, the rats were more likely to survive than those given the same dose in a situation not associated with the drug at an earlier time. The tolerance of both groups of rats was lowered when the drug was given in an unfamiliar environment. Siegel and his colleagues conclude: "Identical pretest pharmacological histories do not necessarily result in the display of equivalent tolerance to the lethal effect of heroin." In each study they ran, those in the strange testing situations were more likely to die of an "overdose than those in the familiar situation."

If context can change not only the severity of withdrawal symptoms but even the effect of a drug overdose, addiction may be more controllable than is commonly believed. For, unlike rats, human beings can change both the situational context (for example, putting ourselves in a familiar or drug-free environment or seeing the familiar in the seemingly unfamiliar environment) and, more important, the emotional context (the meaning of the addiction).

We all know people who have stopped smoking "cold turkey." Are they successful because their commitment to stop puts withdrawal symptoms into a new context? For many years I stopped smoking from time to time, found it too difficult, and began again, as so many people do. When I stopped the last time, almost ten years ago, I felt no withdrawal symptoms. There was no will power involved; I simply did not have an urge to smoke. Where did it go?

Jonathan Margolis and I explored this question in two stages. First we tried to find out whether smokers in a nonsmoking context experienced strong cravings.[22] We questioned smokers in three situations: in a movie theater, at work, and on a religious holiday. In the lobby of a movie theater that prohibits smoking while inside the theater, we approached people who were smoking and asked if we could question them briefly during the film and again on their way out but before lighting up their cigarettes. In the work setting we tested subjects in situations where smoking was prohibited, and also before or after a break, when it was allowed. Finally, Orthodox Jews, prohibited from smoking on the Sabbath by their religion, were questioned during and immediately after the holy day. The results in each setting were very similar. People did not suffer withdrawal symptoms when in any of the nonsmoking contexts. Returning to a context where smoking was allowed, however, their cravings resurfaced.

All these subjects escaped the urge to smoke in a

mindless manner. Could they have achieved the same thing deliberately? "I can resist everything except temptation," says a character in Oscar Wilde's *Lady Windermere's Fan*. Our question here is: Can people control the experience of temptation?

In designing the second experiment to answer this question, Jonathan and I assumed that a mindful addict would look at the addiction from more than one perspective.[23] From an open-minded position, it is clear that there are advantages as well as disadvantages to addictions. Though perhaps obvious, this is not the usual point of view for someone trying to break a habit or addiction. People who want to stop smoking, for example, generally examine only the negative consequences of smoking. They remind themselves of the health risks, the bad smell, other people's reactions to the smoke, and so on. But when they smoke, people are not thinking of the health risks or the smell, so trying to stop because of these reasons often results in failure. Part of the reason they fail is that all the *positive* aspects of the addiction still have a strong appeal. The relaxation, the taste, the sociable quality of stopping for a cigarette remain tempting. A more mindful approach would be to look carefully at all these pleasures and to find other ways of obtaining them. If the needs served by an addiction can be served in other ways, it should be easier to shake.

To test whether this dual perspective was at work when people quit smoking, Jonathan and I tried an indirect tactic. We picked a group of subjects who had already quit and complimented each one for having succeeded. We then paid careful attention to whether they accepted the compliments. To understand our strategy, imagine being complimented for being able to spell three-letter words. A compliment does not mean much when the task is very easy. If you solve a horrendously difficult problem, on the other hand, a compliment is probably most welcome. We then asked the same subjects what factors they considered when they decided to stop smoking. Those who gave single-minded answers, citing only the negative consequences, were more likely to be the ones who had accepted the compliment. Those who saw both sides usually shrugged it off. Months later we got in touch with people in the study to see if they were still nonsmokers. Of those we could reach, the subjects who had considered positive aspects of smoking and fended off the compliments were more likely to have been successful in quitting.

This work opens up some interesting questions for addiction research and therapy. While recognizing the positive reasons for the addiction and finding substitutes is not easy, the attempt to do so may help us find more mindful ways of breaking destructive habits.

### The Traditional Placebo: Fooling the Mind

A well-known technique for helping us control those functions of the body not previously thought to be under conscious control is biofeedback. In the 1960s it became clear that intentional control of one's "involuntary" internal systems such as heart rate, blood flow, and brain waves was possible with the aid of biofeedback equipment. This equipment monitors the internal processes and makes them visible to patients on various kinds of dials and measuring devices. In this way it provides feedback for patients as they try to affect the working of their own bodies. Through trial and error, "involuntary" responses seem to come under a person's control. In the years since biofeedback was first demonstrated, researchers like myself have asked why these external devices are necessary. Why must people look to biofeedback machines for feedback rather than to internal cues? In other words, can we train ourselves to become mindful of processes within our own bodies?

Another method of harnessing the healing powers of the body in an indirect or passive way is the use of placebos. As commonly used a placebo is an inert substance, prepared to resemble an active drug and given to patients in experiments so as to have a basis of comparison for the results of that drug. Most such experiments are "double-blind," meaning that neither the investigator nor the patient knows who is receiving the drug and who is receiving the placebo. Usually the placebos have an effect as well, and the difference in degree between this effect and that of the drug is taken as a measure of the drug's effectiveness. For a drug to be marketed, it must outperform the placebo. If the investigators find no difference between real pills and placebos, they are led to believe that the physical medication was ineffective. There is room for question here, however, because placebos can have powerful effects. In fact, a considerable part of the effect of most prescriptions is considered to be a placebo effect. A well-known quip about new drugs warns doctors to use them as soon and as often as possible, while they still have the power to heal.

When patients are given a placebo and then get well, the illness is considered to be "only psychological." (Here we see the old mind/body dualism, alive and well.) It is interesting that no one tests the effectiveness of active drugs by telling patients that "this is only a placebo." (Is this implicit recognition of the power of the mind to change the effect of the drug?)

Despite great interest in placebos, no one yet knows exactly how they work. In an effort to explore this, investigators have used "placebo" treatments to change the immune system of rats. One remarkable study asked how long the lives of rats genetically predisposed to a disease called *systemic lupus erythematosus* could be extended with a placebo treatment.[24] In this "autoimmune" disease, the immune system turns on the body itself. One group of rats received a weekly injection of a drug that suppressed the immune reaction, immediately after being given a new liquid to drink. A second group received the same treatment, the drug and the new liquid, but an inert injection was substituted for the drug half the time. Thus, this second group received only half the total amount of the drug received by the first. The third group was identical to the second, except that the injections and new liquid to drink were not paired, but given on different days.

Finally, a control group of rats was given the new drink once a week, together with an inert injection. This group never received the immunosuppressive drug.

The critical comparison, for our purposes, is between the second and third groups. If the disease developed more slowly in the second group than the third, the rats were somehow suppressing their own immune systems in a way that could not be attributed to the drug. This is precisely what was found. The mortality rate of the second group was significantly lower. The mortality rate of the third group, in fact, was the same as that of the control group. Also striking was the fact that the mortality rates for the first and second groups were almost the same, even though the first group received twice the amount of the active drug. The power of the placebo to produce a strong effect on the immune system was dramatically confirmed.

Placebo effects are real and powerful. Who is doing the healing when one takes a placebo? Why can't we just say to our minds, "repair this ailing body"? Why must we fool our minds in order to enlist our own powers of self-healing? Placebos, hypnosis, autosuggestion, faith healing, visualization, positive thinking, biofeedback are among the many ways we have learned to invoke these powers. Each can be seen as a device for changing mindsets, enabling us to move from an unhealthy to a healthy context. The more we can learn about how to accomplish this mindfully and deliberately, rather than having to rely on these elaborate, indirect strategies, the more control we will gain over our own health.

### *The Active Placebo:*
### *Enlisting the Mind*

In several of the healing practices just mentioned, the role of the individual in bringing about change is by no means passive. An intentional effort to change an unhealthy mindset or a premature cognitive commitment is evident. Take hypnosis, for instance. Most contemporary writers on the subject agree that hypnosis cannot take place without the compliance of the subject. Some go so far as to say that all hypnosis is self-hypnosis.[25]

The treatment of warts makes a graphic illustration of this self-healing power. Believed to be caused by viral invasion, warts qualify as a "real" physical condition: they are visible, touchable, and lasting. Yet they respond to hypnosis. As the biologist Lewis Thomas wrote in *The Medusa and the Snail*, "warts can be made to go away by something that can only be called thinking or something like thinking. . . . It is one of the great mystifications of Science: warts can be ordered off the skin by hypnotic suggestion."[26]

Thomas goes on to describe one of several experiments where a group of subjects was given a hypnotic suggestion to be rid of warts and another group, control subjects, was not given these instructions. Of the experimental group, nine out of fourteen successfully got rid of the warts compared to none in the control group. Thomas points out how difficult it would be to accomplish this without the wisdom of the body. One would have to be a "cell biologist of world class" to know what orders to send out to eliminate the wart. Yet the experimental subjects who removed their warts were average educated individuals.

Another dramatic experiment with warts reveals how very specific our orders to the body can be. Fourteen subjects under hypnosis were asked to rid themselves of warts, but only on one side of their bodies. Nine of these subjects were able to bring about this result, becoming completely free of warts on that side.[27]

Despite the part we play in the healing that takes place under hypnosis, the process still feels somewhat passive. What are the ways we can work on our health more actively? First of all, we have to regain the control taken away by the experience of consulting an "expert" in a mindless fashion. Ever since we relied on our mothers to make a bruised knee better with a Band-Aid and a kiss, we have held on to the assumption that someone out there, somewhere, can make us better. If we go to a specialist and are given the Latin name for our problem, and a prescription, this old mindset is reconfirmed. But what if we get the Latin name without the prescription? Imagine going to the doctor for some aches and pains and being told that you have *Zapalitis* and that little can be done for this condition. Before you were told it was Zapalitis you paid attention to each symptom in a mindful way and did what you could to feel better. Now, however, you have been told that nothing can be done. So you do nothing. Your motivation to do something about the aches, to listen to your body, is thwarted by a label.

In the past decade or so, a new brand of empowered patient/consumer has tried to restore our control over our own health. Many of the alternative therapies sought out by these patients have as their active ingredient increased mindfulness. For instance, Carl Simonton has worked for years to erase the mindset of cancer as a death sentence. He believes that cancer is often a symptom of difficulties in a person's life. "The cancer patient has typically responded to these problems and stresses with a deep sense of hopelessness, or 'giving up.'"[28] This emotional response, Simonton believes, begins to set off physiological responses that suppress the body's natural defenses, which in turn make the body susceptible to producing abnormal cells. The Simonton technique for helping cancer patients involves active imagination on the part of the patient. The patient is to visualize the cancer and visualize the "good" cells in the body, or the chemotherapy or radiation, destroying the cancer. In order to participate in this process, the patient must exchange the mindset of cancer as a killer for that of the tumor being killed.

Norman Cousins's approach to his own serious illness (one of the earliest of the "alternative" therapies) involved a clear-cut change of context. He took himself out of the hospital and into a hotel, where he exchanged intravenous tubes and sterile conditions for old Marx Brothers films. In *Anatomy of an Illness*, he describes the shift that took place in his mind as swift and complete.[29]

There are many other alternative healing methods than those described here. The point is simply to show the similarity between these methods and the definitions of mindfulness described earlier. Whenever we try to heal ourselves, and not abdicate this responsibility completely to doctors, each step is mindful. For example, we question destructive categories of disease (such as the image of cancer as a death sentence). We welcome new information, whether from our bodies or from books. We look at our illness from more than a single perspective (the medical one). We work on changing contexts, whether it is a stressful workplace or a depressing rather than a positive view of the hospital. Finally, the attempt to stay healthy rather than to be "made well" necessarily involves us with process rather than outcome.

In applying mindfulness theory to health, I have so far worked mostly with elderly people. Success in increasing longevity by making more cognitive demands on nursing home residents (as mentioned earlier) or by teaching meditation or techniques of flexible, novel thinking gives us strong reason to believe that the same techniques could be used to improve health and shorten illness earlier in life.[30] In one recent experiment we gave arthritis sufferers various interesting word problems to increase their mental activity. For example, subjects in this group were given slightly doctored sayings such as "a bird in the bush is worth two in the hand," and were asked to explain them. Comparison subjects were given the old familiar versions. In the mindful group, not only did subjective measures of comfort and enjoyment change, but some of the chemistry of the disease (sedimentation rates of the blood in this case) was affected as well.[31] There were no significant changes in the comparison group.

In this chapter I've implicitly described two ways in which we have learned to influence health: exchanging unhealthy mindsets for healthy ones and increasing a generally mindful state. The latter is more lasting and results in more personal control. The real value of "active placebos" will come when people put them to work for themselves. Consider how you learned to ride a bike. Someone older and taller held on to the seat to keep you from falling, until you found your balance. Then, without your knowledge, that strong hand let go and you were on your own. You controlled the bicycle even without knowing it. The same is true for all of us most of our lives. We control our health, or the course of our diseases, without really knowing that we do. On the bike, however, at some point you realized that you were in control. Now may be the time to learn how to recognize and use our control over illness.

In a sense, we should be able to "take" a placebo instead of a pill. Conceiving of the mind and body as one means that wherever we put the mind, we may be able to put our bodies. For most of us, at present at least, the mind may have to be fooled to reach a healthy place. Once we learn how to put it there consciously, the evidence suggests that the body may well follow. In a book aptly called *New Bottles for New Wine*, Julian Huxley quotes his grandfather, the great nineteenth-century scientist Thomas Huxley, on the subject of belief: "Everyone should be able to give a reason for the faith that is in him. My faith is in human possibilities."[32]

# EPILOGUE

*

# *Beyond Mindfulness*

*Corin*: And how like you this shepherd's life, Master
Touchstone?
*Touchstone*: Truly, shepherd, in respect of itself, it is a
good life; but in respect that it is a shepherd's life, it is
naught. In respect that it is solitary, I like it very well;
but in respect that it is private, it is a very vile life. Now
in respect it is in the fields, it pleaseth me well; but in
respect it is not in the court, it is tedious. As it is a
spare life, look you, it fits my humour well; but as there
is no more plenty in it, it goes much against my stom-
ach. Hast any philosophy in thee shepherd?
**WILLIAM SHAKESPEARE**
*As You Like It*, act 3, scene 2

*

Whenever I give a talk about mindfulness, I'm inevitably asked certain questions: How can people possibly
be mindful all the time? Doesn't it take too much effort?

---

If we keep making mindful new distinctions, how would we ever make a decision?

When examples of mindfulness such as those in the second half of this book do not seem to answer the questions, I try various metaphors. For instance, to understand why it is not necessary to be mindful about everything all of the time, think of the brain as a large corporation, with a Chief Executive Officer. This CEO is charged with monitoring the overall functioning of the corporation and its transactions with the outside world—but does not, cannot, and should not actively monitor everything. The job of maintaining the heating system at corporate headquarters, for example, is routinely delegated to the custodial staff. The CEO need not attend to it unless and until it requires a major investment for replacement. Similarly most of us can routinely delegate the responsibility for our breathing. We need not become "mindful" of it until a cold, a passionate kiss, or preparation for a marathon makes breathing a problem. Many complex activities, such as driving a car, require keen attention in the early learning stages but don't require mindfulness later on. The effective person—like the effective CEO—allocates attention wisely, choosing where and when to be mindful.

The effective CEO must also be mindful about his or her own job. In a crisis, the CEO who mindlessly applies routine solutions learned in an MBA program or used on previous occasions may fail to meet the challenge. A mindful CEO can be mindful on two levels: by simply resolving the crisis in a mindful manner, or by using it as an opportunity for innovation.

For example, when employee productivity declines, the mindful CEO would notice and might increase management supervision over the workers while a mindfully mindful CEO might rethink the whole employment situation and consider stock option plans or a corporate day-care center.

This second-order mindfulness, choosing what to be mindful about, is something that we can be doing all the time. Though we cannot and would not want to be mindful of everything simultaneously, we can always be mindful of something. The most important function task for any CEO, and for the rest of us, is choosing what to be mindful about. Rather than spending all day inspecting every expense account or widget in the factory, the mindfully mindful executive chooses where to pay attention.

And yet, I'm also asked, isn't it necessary to be mindless about some things in order to come to a decision? Take the choice of a restaurant: Should I go to a Chinese or a French restaurant for dinner? If I decide on Chinese food, should I go to Joyce Lee's, Peking Delight, Lucky Eden, or Ming's Hunan? Joyce Lee's has the best mooshi chicken but Peking Delight has better spare ribs—sometimes. Lucky Eden is more convenient, but Ming's has more privacy. Peking Delight is less expensive. If I go to Joyce Lee's, maybe I'll run into Norm, Carol, Carrie, and Andrea there—it would be nice to see them tonight. But what about that new Thai restaurant that just opened down the block?

The problem here is not the need to survey all the

alternatives mindfully; the problem is the belief that if you construct more and more arguments and ask yourself even more questions, then you will eventually know *the* answer. Typically, we believe that there are purely rational ways to make choices and that if we can't come to a decision it is because there are insufficient data. Second-order mindfulness recognizes that there is no right answer. Decision making is independent of data gathering. Data don't make decisions, people do—either with ease or with difficulty. Ambivalence about a decision, or about an individual—friend, lover, spouse—becomes a problem if we are convinced that more information can resolve the ambivalence in one direction or another. Generating more questions will not help because there is no logical stopping point. We might just as well pick a moment to stop asking questions, recognize that it is an arbitrary moment, and then make a "gut" decision. We can then work on making the decision right rather than obsess about making the right decision.

To understand this presumed pitfall of mindfulness, and ways around it, we can look at more serious examples. Take the case of a physician or judge interested in the question of whether to prolong life in the face of intolerable pain. Tom Schelling, a colleague in the John F. Kennedy School of Government at Harvard, suggested that providing a person, for example, someone suffering from a wretched disease, with the means to bring about his or her own death might have two quite different consequences. On the one hand, shorter lives may result if people take swift advantage of this opportunity. On the other hand, the increase in control over one's own destiny might lead people to want to live longer than they would without such control.[1]

The conflicting information brought by these mindful reflections might seem to make the decision more difficult. It actually throws the discussion back to where it belongs: on individual values. The doctor, judge, and patient must decide between the principle of prolonging life at all costs and the "right" to determine the quality of life. Making more distinctions will not result in absolute right answers.

Living in a mindful state may be likened to living in a transparent house. In the houses in which most of us now live, if we were in the living room and needed an object (idea) that was in the basement, we might not be aware of its presence. But in our transparent house, objects would be ever available. When in the living room, we could still see the object in the basement even if we chose not to think about it or use it at the moment. If we were taught mindfully, conditionally, we could be in this ever-ready state of mind. Thus, while it is true that we cannot think of everything at once, everything can be kept available. To be alert in this fashion, open to new perspectives and new information, is not effortful. What may take effort is the *switch* from a mindless to a mindful mode, just as in physics effort is required to change the course of a moving body and energy is required to put a still body into motion.

Mindful awareness of different options gives us

greater control. This feeling of greater control, in turn, encourages us to be more mindful. Rather than being a chore, mindfulness engages us in a continuing momentum.

One reason mindfulness may seem effortful is because of the pain of negative thoughts. When thoughts are uncomfortable, people often struggle to erase them. The pain, however, does not come from mindful awareness of these thoughts, but from a single-minded understanding of the painful event. A mindful new perspective would erase the pain more effectively.

Anxious thinking has similarly given mindfulness a bad name. Imagine you are in a car that makes an ominous grinding noise. Surely, you say, mindfully considering all the things that could be wrong is not something we would want to do. However, being mindlessly certain that the noise has an alarming cause is neither pleasant nor helpful. At the least, if there is a solution, the more mindful person is more likely to find it. Anxiety is not mindful, and mindlessness is not relaxing. Indeed, stressful events are probably less stressful when considered from multiple perspectives.

While some people think that mindfulness takes a lot of work, the research discussed in this book shows that mindfulness leads to feelings of control, greater freedom of action, and less burnout.

Even with the best definitions, the finest research designs, and the most careful answers to each question, mindfulness, like the brook we compared it to earlier, cannot be captured, cannot be analyzed once and for all. The experiments my colleagues and I have done, and the anecdotes from ordinary life told in this book, only hint at the enormous potential of the mindful state. In trying to quantify it, or reduce it to a formula, we risk losing sight of the whole. C. M. Gillmore tells a splendid fable, a cautionary tale for those who insist on tidy, definitive results:

Once upon a time, a highly respected and revered psychometrician of a great university was sailing about from sea to sea enjoying a well-deserved vacation. On a fine sunny day, his ship put in at a very small harbor of a very small atoll where, the crew informed him, they occasionally stopped to leave food for three hermits who were the only inhabitants. Sure enough, there they were standing on the sand to greet the Professor, their long white beards and their white lab coats blowing in the breeze, looking exactly as hermits should look, and their delight in seeing him was gratifying. For, they explained, they had come out to this solitary archipelago long, long ago, in order to enter into pure animal behavior research, and not be interrupted by the cares of the world, such as teaching, faculty meetings, and the myriad of other distractions. But, during these many years, they had forgotten a good deal of the proper statistical methods taught them at the University and were most eager to refresh themselves at the fount of the professor's wisdom.

So the wise doctor spoke with them for many hours, reviving their memories of simple and complex designs, of methods and techniques necessary for publications, and instructed them so they could recognize the proper statistical test for their data once more. Feeling that he had done a fine day's work, the psychometrician returned to his ship and sailed away.

At dawn—for he was ever an early riser—he was sitting in his deck chair in the clear light and against the bright horizon he saw a strange—an unbelievable—sight. After trying for some time to identify a boat, or a canoe, or a kayak, or even a raft, the Professor sent for the captain, and they stared through the binoculars and soon had to admit the impossible, for a rhesus monkey was riding on the back of a large porpoise. So there seemed nothing to do but lean over the rail as the monkey and fish guided to below it. The monkey cried out,

"Dear and wise Professor, we have been trained in the laboratory of the hermits, and they crave your forgiveness for sending us to trouble you with their difficulty, but none of them can remember how you said to determine the denominator degrees of freedom, and since they must know this in order to get their results published . . ."[2]

In the laboratory of the hermits, no one noticed that the monkeys could talk.

# *Notes*

## Chapter 1

1. E. Langer and J. Rodin, "The Effects of Enhanced Personal Responsibility for the Aged: A Field Experiment in an Institutional Setting," *Journal of Personality and Social Psychology* 34 (1976): 191–198; J. Rodin and E. Langer, "Long-term Effects of a Control-Relevant Intervention Among the Institutionalized Aged," *Journal of Personality and Social Psychology* 35 (1977): 897–902.

2. C. Gersick and J. R. Hackman, "Habitual Routines in Task-Performing Groups," *Organizational Behavior and Human Decision Processes*, in press.

3. I. Illich, *Medical Nemesis* (New York: Pantheon, 1976).

## Chapter 2

1. C. Trungpa, *Cutting Through Spiritual Materialism* (Boulder and London: Shambhala, 1973).

2. T'ai P'ing, *Kuang Chi* [Extensive Records Made in the Period of Peace and Prosperity] (978 A.D.), as cited in

Jorge Luis Borges, *Libro de Los Seres Imaginarios* (Buenos Aires: Editorial Kiersa S.A., Fauna China, 1967), p. 88.

3. L. Solomons and G. Stein, "Normal Motor Automation," *Psychological Review* 36 (1896): 492–572.

4. E. Langer, A. Blank, and B. Chanowitz, "The Mindlessness of Ostensibly Thoughtful Action: The Role of Placebic Information in Interpersonal Interaction, *Journal of Personality and Social Psychology* 36 (1978): 635–642.

5. Ibid.

6. To understand the more complex relationship between automatic information processing and mindlessness, compare E. Langer, "Minding Matters," in L. Berkowitz, ed., *Advances in Experimental Social Psychology* (New York: Academic Press, in press) and W. Schneider and R. M. Schiffrin, "Controlled and Automatic Human Information Processing: I. Detection, Search, and Attention," *Psychological Review* 84 (1977): 1–66.

7. The correct answer is 8. A similar quiz was printed on the business card of the Copy Service of Miami, Inc.

## Chapter 3

1. E. Langer and C. Weinman, "When Thinking Disrupts Intellectual Performance: Mindlessness on an Overlearned Task," *Personality and Social Psychology Bulletin* 7 (1981): 240–243.

2. G. A. Kimble and L. Perlmuter, "The Problem of Volition," *Psychological Review* 77 (1970): 212–218.

3. B. Chanowitz and E. Langer, "Premature Cognitive

Commitment," *Journal of Personality and Social Psychology* 41 (1981): 1051–1063.

4. The study actually employed a 2 x 2 factorial design in which the variables of interest were relevance (i.e., likelihood of having the disorder, 10% vs. 80%) and instructions to think about the problem (yes vs. no).

5. S. Freud (1912), "A Note on the Unconscious in Psychoanalysis," in *The Standard Edition of the Complete Psychological Works of Sigmund Freud*, ed. J. Strachey, vol. 12 (London: Hogarth Press, 1959), p. 265.

6. Plato, *Republic,* Book IX (Oxford: Clarendon Press, 1888), p. 281, as cited in M. Erdelyr, *Psychoanalysis* (New York: Freeman, 1985).

7. Scientists know that while one can fail to find evidence *for* a hypothesis—the hypothesis in this case being that some particular ability is unlimited—that is not the same thing as finding evidence *against* a hypothesis. One cannot prove that there are no limits. One may just keep surpassing past limits.

8. D. Dewsbury, "Effects of Novelty on Copulatory Behavior. The Coolidge Effect and Related Phenomenon," *Psychological Bulletin* 89 (1981): 464–482.

9. J. E. Orme, *Time, Experience and Behavior* (London: Illif Books, 1969).

10. E. Mach, *Science of Mechanics* (Chicago: Open Court Publishing, 1983).

11. R. Arnis and B. Frost, "Human Visual Ecology and Orientation Anestropies in Acuity," *Science* 182 (1973): 729–731.

12. D. Holmes and B. K. Houston, "Effectiveness of Situation Redefinition and Affective Isolation in Coping

with Stress," *Journal of Personality and Social Psychology* 29 (1974): 212–218.

13. *The Boston Globe*, March 11, 1980.

14. D. Brown, "Stimulus-Similarity and the Anchoring of Subjective Scales," *American Journal of Psychology* 66 (1953): 199–214.

15. L. Postman, J. Bruner, and E. McGinnies, "Personal Values as Selective Factors in Perception," *Journal of Abnormal Psychology* 48 (1948): 142–154.

16. Allport-Vernon Study of Values (Boston: Houghton Mifflin, 1931.)

## Chapter 4

1. T. Levitt, "Marketing Myopia," *Harvard Business Review* 38, no. 4 (1960): 45–56, reprinted in 53, no. 5 (1975): 26–174.

2. E. Langer, J. Johnson, and H. Botwinick, "Nothing Succeeds Like Success, Except . . . ," in E. Langer, *The Psychology of Control* (Los Angeles: Sage Publications, 1983).

3. E. Langer and A. Benevento, "Self-Induced Dependence," *Journal of Personality and Social Psychology* 36 (1978): 886–893.

4. S. Milgram, *Obedience to Authority* (New York: Harper & Row, 1974).

5. E. Langer and H. Newman, "Post-divorce Adaptation and the Attribution of Responsibility," *Sex Roles* 7 (1981): 223–232.

6. E. Langer, L. Perlmuter, B. Chanowitz, and R. Rubin,

"Two New Applications of Mindlessness Theory: Alcoholism and Aging," *Journal of Aging Studies*, Vol. 2:3 (1988) 289–299.

7. A. Luchins and E. Luchins, "Mechanization in Problem-Solving: The Effect of Einstellung," *Psychological Monographs* 54, no. 6 (1942).

8. M. Seligman, *Helplessness: On Depression, Development and Death* (San Francisco: Freeman, 1975).

9. C. P. Richter, "The Phenomenon of Sudden Death in Animals and Man," *Psychosomatic Medicine* 19 (1957): 191–198.

10. H. Lefcourt, as cited in Seligman, *Helplessness*.

11. W. James, "The World We Live In," *The Philosophy of William James* (New York: Modern Library, 1953).

12. Langer, Perlmuter, Chanowitz, and Rubin, "Two New Applications of Mindlessness Theory."

13. Happiness is not stereotypically related to age in the same way that lack of alertness and independence are. Accordingly, participants did not evaluate themselves as happier people, nor did independent raters do so. This indicates that the ratings were not indiscriminate.

14. C. Dickens, *Great Expectations* (1860–1861). (Cambridge, MA: Riverside Press, 1877), p. 51.

## Chapter 5

1. L. Tolstoy, *War and Peace*, 1869 trans. Louise and Aylmer Maude (Oxford: Oxford University Press, 1983).

2. J. Bruner, J. Goodnow, and G. Austin, *A Study of Think-*

*ing* (New York: Wiley, 1956); R. Brown, *Words and Things* (New York: Free Press, 1958).

3. S. Freud (1907). "Creative Writers and Daydreaming," in *The Standard Edition of the Complete Psychological Works of Sigmund Freud*, ed. J. Strachey, vol. 9 (London: Hogarth Press, 1959), 143–144.

4. E. Langer and C. Weinman, "Mindlessness, Confidence and Accuracy" (1976), as described in B. Chanowitz and E. Langer, "Knowing More (or Less) Than You Can Show: Understanding Control Through the Mindlessness/Mindfulness Distinction," in *Human Helplessness*, ed. M. E. P. Seligman and J. Garber. (New York: Academic Press, 1980).

5. E. Jones and R. Nisbett, "The Actor and the Observer: Divergent Perceptions of the Causes of Behavior," in *Attributions: Perceiving the Causes of Behavior*, ed. E. Jones et al. (Morristown, NJ: General Learning Press, 1972).

6. I. Lindahl, "Chernobyl: The Geopolitical Dimensions," *American Scandinavian Review* 75, no. 3 (1987): 29–40.

7. These points of view are different in another way that is important in the study of psychology. The more specific the level of analysis, the greater the likelihood of unpredictability. The study of personality does not generally pay attention to the individual's prototypical level of analysis. As in the example cited, differences on this dimension, whether stemming from trait or even state, may give rise to interpersonal difficulty.

8. If one makes a *conscious decision* to consider alternative frames for complex negative information in this way, one cannot sensibly be accused of "rationalizing."

9. E. Langer and L. Thompson, "Mindlessness and Self-

Esteem: The Observer's Perspective," Harvard University (1987).

10. E. Langer, I. Janis, and J. Wolfer, "Reduction of Psychological Stress in Surgical Patients," *Journal of Experimental Social Psychology* 11 (1975): 155–165.

11. R. Pascale and N. Athos, *The Art of Japanese Management* (New York: Simon & Schuster, 1981).

12. S. Druker, "Unified Field Based Ethics: Vedic Psychology's Description of the Highest Stage of Moral Reasoning," *Modern Science and Vedic Science*, in press.

13. See E. Langer, *Minding Matters* (chapter 2, note 6) for a discussion of the latent vs. expressed modes of mindfulness. Only the expressed mode is being considered in this book.

14. A. Deikman, "De-automatization and the Mystic Experience," *Psychiatry* 29 (1966): 329–343.

## Chapter 6

1. E. Langer and J. Rodin, "The Effects of Enhanced Personal Responsibility for the Aged: A Field Experiment in an Institutional Setting," *Journal of Personality and Social Psychology* 34 (1976): 191–198; J. Rodin and E. Langer, "Long-Term Effects of a Control-Relevant Intervention Among the Institutionalized Aged," *Journal of Personality and Social Psychology* 35 (1977): 275–282.

2. E. Langer and L. Perlmuter, "Behavioral Monitoring as a Technique to Influence Depression and Self-Knowledge for Elderly Adults," Harvard University. (1988).

3. L. Perlmuter and E. Langer, "The Effects of Behavioral

Monitoring on the Perception of Control," *The Clinical Gerontologist* 1 (1979): 37–43.

4. M. M. Baltes and E. M. Barton, "Behavioral Analysis of Aging: A Review of the Operant Model and Research," *International Journal of Behavior Development* 2 (1979): 297–320.

5. J. Avorn and E. Langer, "Induced Disability in Nursing Home Patients: A Controlled Trial," *Journal of American Geriatric Society* 30 (1982): 397–400; E. Langer and J. Avorn, "The Psychosocial Environment of the Elderly: Some Behavioral and Health Implications," in *Congregate Housing for Older People*, ed. J. Seagle and R. Chellis (Lexington, MA: Lexington Books, 1981).

6. E. Langer, J. Rodin, P. Beck, C. Weinman, and L. Spitzer, "Environmental Determinants of Memory Improvement in Late Adulthood," *Journal of Personality and Social Psychology* 37 (1979): 2003–2013.

7. E. Langer, P. Beck, R. Janoff-Bulman and C. Timko, "The Relationship Between Cognitive Deprivation and Longevity in Senile and Nonsenile Elderly Populations," *Academic Psychology Bulletin* 6 (1984): 211–226.

8. S. de Beauvoir, *Old Age* (London: Andre Deutsch Ltd., 1972).

9. Cicero, *Two Essays on Old Age and Friendship*, trans. E. S. Shuckburg (London: Macmillan & Co., 1900).

10. J. Rowe and R. Kahn, "Human Aging: Usual and Successful," *Science* 273 (1987): 143–149.

11. F. Scott-Maxwell, *The Measure of My Days* (New York: Knopf, 1972).

12. A. Mulvey and E. Langer, as discussed in J. Rodin and E. Langer, "Aging Labels: The Decline of Control and

the Fall of Self-Esteem," *Journal of Social Issues* 36 (1980): 12–29.

13. P. Katzman and T. Carasu (1975). "Differential Diagnosis of Dementia," in *Neurological and Sensory Disorders in the Elderly*, ed. W. S. Fields (Miami, FL: Symposia Specialist Medical Books), 103–104.

14. G. Kolata, "New Neurons Form in Adulthood," *Science* 224 (1984): 1325–1326.

15. B. A. Fiala, J. N. Joyce, and W. T. Greenough, "Environmental Complexity Modulates Growth of Granule Cell Dendrites in Developing but not Adult Hippocampus of Rats," *Experimental Neurology* 59 (1978): 372–383; W. Greenough and F. Volkmar, "Patterns of Dendritic Branching in Occipital Cortex of Rats Reared in Complex Environments," *Experimental Neurology* 40 (1973): 491–508; D. Krech, M. R. Rosenzweig, and E. L. Bennet, "Relations Between Brain Chemistry and Problem Solving Among Rats Raised in Enriched and Impoverished Environments," *Journal of Comparative and Physiological Psychology* 55 (1962): 801–807; F. Volkmar and W. Greenough, "Rearing Complexity Affects Branching of Dendrites in the Visual Cortex of the Rat," *Science* 176 (1972): 1445–1447; R. A. Cummins and R. N. Walsh, "Synaptic Changes in Differentially Reared Mice," *Australian Psychologist* 2, no. 229 (1976).

16. M. Rosenzweig, E. L. Bennett, and M. Diamond, "Brain Changes in Response to Experience," *Scientific American* 226, no. 2 (1972): 22–29.

17. L. Strachey, *Queen Victoria* (New York and London: Harcourt Brace Jovanovich, 1921).

18. W. James, *Letters of William James*, Vol. 1, ed. H. James (Boston: Atlantic Monthly Press, 1920).

19. E. Langer, B. Chanowitz, M. Palmerino, S. Jacobs, M. Rhodes, and P. Thayer (1988). "Nonsequential Development and Aging," in *Higher Stages of Human Development: Perspectives on Adult Growth*, ed. C. Alexander and E. Langer (New York: Oxford University Press, in press).

20. We contacted twenty of the country's leading research physicians who have specialties in geriatric medicine, heart disease, and endocrinology. Each pointed out that there do not seem to be any reliable measures of aging. "If we put a fifty-year-old in one room and a seventy-year-old in another," we asked, "how would you tell them apart?" Virtually each physician said, "It would be extremely difficult. The best guess would be outward appearance. The only possible exception would be X rays of the skeleton. The age-related changes of osteoarthritis, particularly on the spine, are quite distinctive. . . . However these changes are in no way uniform with age and sometimes begin to develop quite early in middle age and sometimes not until very advanced age." Another physician said, "One needs baseline measures for each individual." One of the most sophisticated researchers in the area said, "In studies of the variables that change most dramatically with age (cardiac function, pulmonary function, renal function) there are always old individuals (over eighty) who perform as well as the average thirty-year-old, and there are usually young individuals who perform at the same level as the average old individual." This lack of agreed-upon measures made it rather difficult to design our study. We settled on measures of body function that are at least somewhat correlated with aging. There are common changes in appearance that occur during old age. The nose elongates, the eyes seem to dull and become lusterless and often watery. The skin becomes wrinkled and dry, and

dark spots, moles, or warts may appear. The hair turns gray or white or is lost. The shoulders droop. The upper arms become flabby and the lower arms smaller. The hands become thin and the veins become quite visible. In the same way, visual acuity decreases and people tend to become more farsighted. The ability to hear high tones diminishes and taste buds atrophy. On the psychological side are decrements in the capacity to learn and remember newly learned information. Gait slows, as does reaction time. With these in mind we developed a battery of measures to assess improvements in the domain of physical and psychological competence as a function of our "treatment."

21. R. Bales and S. Cohen, *SYMLOG: A System for Multiple Level Observation of Groups* (New York: Free Press, 1979).

22. E. Langer and J. Rodin, "Effects of Enhanced Personal Responsibility for the Aged"; J. Rodin and E. Langer, "Long-Term Effects of Control-Relevant Intervention."

23. Limited funds precluded a follow-up invetigation. One might expect a return to lower levels of competence, however, with a return to living in low-expectation contexts.

## Chapter 7

1. H. Poincaré, "Intuition and Logic Mathematics," *Mathematics Teacher* 62, no. 3 (1969): 205-212.

2. I. Duncan, as quoted in G. Bateson, *Steps to an Ecology of Mind* (San Francisco: Chandler Publications, 1972), p. 137.

3. As quoted in P. Goldberg, *The Intuitive Edge* (Los Angeles: J.P. Tarcher, 1983).

4. W. Churchill, as cited in P. Goldberg, *The Intuitive Edge* (Los Angeles: J.P. Tarcher, 1983).

5. J. Bruner and B. Clinchy, "Towards a Disciplined Intuition, in *Learning about Learning*, no. 15, ed. J. Bruner (Bureau of Research Co-operative Research Monograph).

6. E. Langer and A. Piper, "The Prevention of Mindlessness," *Journal of Personality and Social Psychology* 53 (1987): 280-287.

7. E. Langer, A. Piper, and J. Friedus, "Preventing Mindlessness: A Positive Side of Dyslexia," Harvard University (1986).

8. T. Amabile, *The Social Psychology of Creativity* (New York: Springer-Verlag, 1983).

9. J. W. Getzels and P. Jackson, "Family Environment and Cognitive Style: A Study of the Sources of Highly Intelligent and Highly Creative Adolescents," *American Sociological Review* 26: 351-359.

10. E. Langer and J. Joss, as described in E. Langer, M. Hatem, J. Joss, and M. Howell, "The Mindful Consequences of Teaching Uncertainty for Elementary School and College Students," Harvard University (1988).

11. Further confirmation of the value of conditional learning can be found in G. Salomon and T. Globerson, "Skill May Not Be Enough: The Role of Mindfulness in Learning and Transfer," *International Journal of Educational Research* (1987) 11:623–627, and G. Solomon and D. Perkins, "Rocky Roads to Transfer: Rethinking

Mechanisms of a Neglected Phenomenon," *Educational Researcher*, in press (April 1989).

12. S. J. Gould, "The Case of the Creeping Fox Terrier Clone," *Natural History* 97, no. 1: 16-24.

13. J. Barchillon, "Creativity and Its Inhibition in Child Prodigies," in *Personality Dimensions of Creativity* (New York: Lincoln Institute for Psychotherapy, 1961).

14. J. P. Guilford, *The Nature of Human Intelligence* (New York: McGraw-Hill, 1967).

15. The more educated one is, the harder it may be to find absolute right answers. Lions in a group are called a *pride* of lions, making *herd* an appropriate answer. A comparison of an animal to an emotion would make *vanity* appropriate. The "correct" answer on a test may be unclear if it is written as if it were context-free. The most mindful mind, free of context, can see much more than is intended.

16. Watching television is another pursuit in which the use of novel perspectives may be beneficial. Even television may be watched mindfully. In a study conducted with Alison Piper, I had subjects watch "Dynasty" from different perspectives. The results—which are described in E. Langer and A. Piper, "Television from a Mindful/Mindless Perspective," *Applied Social Psychology Annual*, Vol. 8, Los Angeles: Sage Publications, 1988—included increased control for the viewer and other positive consequences.

17. J. Piaget, "Psychology and Epistemology" (New York: Grossman, 1971), p. vii, quoted in G. Holton, *The Advancement of Science, and Its Burdens* (Cambridge: Cambridge University Press, 1986).

# Chapter 8

1. T. Levitt, "Marketing Myopia," *The Harvard Business Review* 38, no. 4 (1960): 45–56, reprinted in 53, no. 5 (1975): 26–174.

2. A. Karsten (1928), "Mental Satiation," in *Field Theory as Human Science*, ed. J. de Rivera (New York: Gardner Press, 1976).

3. J. R. Kelly and J. E. McGrath, "Effects of Time Limits of Task Types on Task Performance and Interaction of Four-Person Groups," *Journal of Personality and Social Psychology* 49 (1985): 395–407.

4. Rosabeth Moss Kanter and Howard Stevenson, both of Harvard Business School, write about a version of this idea in business: R. Kanter, *The Change Masters: Innovation for Productivity in the American Corporation* (New York: Simon & Schuster, 1983); H. Stevenson and W. Sahlman, "How Small Companies Should Handle Advisers," *Harvard Business Review* 88, no. 2 (1988): 28–34. Also, Irving Janis describes a version of this idea in the political arena: I. Janis, *Victims of Groupthink* (Boston: Houghton Mifflin, 1972).

5. R. Fisher and W. Urey, *Getting to Yes* (Boston: Houghton Mifflin, 1981).

6. T. Levitt, "Marketing Myopia."

7. E. Langer and D. Heffernan, "Mindful Managing: Confident but Uncertain Managers," Harvard University. (1988).

8. E. Langer and J. Sviokla, "Charisma from a Mindfulness Perspective," Harvard University. (1988).

9. E. Langer, D. Heffernan, and M. Kiester, "Reducing

Burnout in an Institutional Setting: An Experimental Investigation," Harvard University. (1988).

10. M. P. Follet, *Dynamic Administration: The Collected Papers of Mary Parker Follett* (Bath, England: Bath Management, 1941), quoted in P. Graham, *Dynamic Management: The Follett Way* (London: Professional Publishing, 1987).

## Chapter 9

1. R. Brown, *Words and Things* (New York: The Free Press, 1956); J. Bruner, "Personality Dynamics and the Process of Perceiving," in *Perception: An Approach to Personality*, ed. R. R. Blake and G. V. Ramsey (New York: Ronald Press, 1951), pp. 121–147.

2. E. Langer, and R. Abelson, "A Patient by Any Other Name . . . : Clinician Group Differences in Labelling Bias," *Journal of Consulting and Clinical Psychology* 42 (1974): 4–9.

3. J. Swift (1726), *Gulliver's Travels* (New York: Dell, 1961).

4. E. Langer and L. Imber, "The Role of Mindlessness in the Perception of Deviance," *Journal of Personality and Social Psychology* 39 (1980): 360–367.

5. E. Langer, S. Taylor, S. Fiske, and B. Chanowitz, "Stigma, Staring and Discomfort: A Novel Stimulus Hypothesis," *Journal of Experimental Social Psychology* 12 (1976): 451–463.

6. A. Piper, E. Langer, and J. Friedus, "Preventing Mindlessness: A Positive Side of Dyslexia," Harvard University (1987).

7. H. Madjid, "The Handicapped Person as a Scientific Puzzle in Search of a Solution," Paper presented at the annual meeting of the American Academy for the Advancement of Science, Boston, 1988.

8. E. E. Jones and S. Berglas, "Control of Attributions About the Self Through Self-Handicapping Strategies: The Appeal of Alcohol and the Role of Underachievement," *Personality and Social Psychology Bulletin* 4 (1978): 200–206.

9. E. Langer and B. Chanowitz, "A New Perspective for the Study of Disability," in *Attitudes Towards Persons with Disabilities*, ed. H. E. Yuker (New York: Springer Press, 1987). The best solution, however, might be to have high expectations and, as seen in Chapter 5, see failures simply as ineffective solutions rather than indications of lack of self-worth.

10. D. McClelland, *The Achieving Society* (New York: The Free Press, 1961).

11. E. Langer, R. Bashner, and B. Chanowitz, "Decreasing Prejudice by Increasing Discrimination," *Journal of Personality and Social Psychology* 49 (1985): 113–120. The study, simplified here, actually used a 2 × 2 factorial design in which the variables of interest were mindfulness training (high versus low) × target person (disabled versus nondisabled). The advanced student of psychology is encouraged to read the original work for more subtle details.

### Chapter 10

1. Sir Charles Sherrington, *Man on His Nature*, 2nd ed. (New York: Doubleday Anchor Books, 1953), p. 194.

2. R. Katz, *Boiling Energy* (Cambridge, MA: Harvard University Press, 1982).

3. A. Eddington, *The Nature of the Physical World* (Ann Arbor, MI: University of Michigan Press, 1958).

4. S. Schacter and J. Singer, "Cognitive, Social, and Physiological Determinants of Emotional State," *Psychological Review* 69 (1962): 379–399.

5. W. James, "What Is Emotion?" *Mind* 9 (1883): 188–204.

6. C. Lange, *The Emotions* (Baltimore: Williams & Wilkens, 1922); W. Cannon, "The James Lange Theory of Emotion: A Critical Examination and Alternative Theory," *American Journal of Psychology* 39 (1927): 106–124.

7. R. Zajonc, "Attitudinal Effects of Mere Exposure," *Journal of Personality and Social Psychology Monograph Supplement* 9 (no. 2, part 2) (1968): 1–27.

8. P. Brickman, *Commitment, Conflict and Caring* (Englewood Cliffs, NJ: Prentice-Hall, 1987).

9. W. James (1890), *The Principles of Psychology* (Cambridge, MA: Harvard University Press, 1981).

10. H. K. Beecher, "Relationship of Significance of Wound to Pain Experience," *Journal of American Medical Association* 161 (1956): 1609–1613.

11. R. S. Ulrich, "View from a Window May Influence Recovery from Surgery," *Science* 224 (1984): 420–421.

12. Awareness of the fact that novelty/familiarity is a social construction makes possible a good deal of personal control. For example, to decrease anxiety one can look for the familiar elements in a situation while, if one is bored, searching out novel features would be an advantageous strategy.

13. K. Järvinen, "Can Ward Rounds Be a Danger to Patients with Myocardial Infarction?" *British Medical Journal* 1 (4909) (1955): 318–320.

14. E. Langer, M. Dillon, R. Kurtz, and M. Katz, "Believing is Seeing," Harvard University (1988).

15. R. W. Bell, C. E. Miller, J. M. Ordy, and C. Rolsten, "Effects of Population Density and Living Space Upon Neuroanatomy, Neurochemistry and Behavior in the C57B1-10 Mouse," *Journal of Comparative and Physiological Psychology* 75 (1971): 258–263.

16. M. Rosenzweig, E. L. Bennett, and M. Diamond, "Brain Changes in Response to Experience," *Scientific American* 226, no. 2 (1972): 22–29.

17. R. Totman, *Social Causes of Illness* (New York: Pantheon Books, 1979), p. 96.

18. G. A. Marlatt and D. J. Rohsenow, "Cognitive Processes in Alcohol Use: Expectancy and the Balanced Placebo Design," in *Advances in Substance Abuse: Behavioral and Biological Research,* Vol. 1, ed. N. K. Mello (1980), p. 199.

19. G. Wilson and D. Abrams, "Effects of Alcohol on Social Anxiety and Physiological Arousal: Cognitive versus Pharmacological Procedures," *Cognitive Therapy and Research* 1 (1977): 195–210.

20. L. Robbins, D. David, and D. Nurco, "How Permanent was Vietnam Drug Addiction?" *American Journal of Public Health* 64 (1974): 38–43.

21. S. Siegel, R. Hirsan, M. Krank, and Y. McGully, "Heroin Overdose Death: Contribution of Drugs as Actual Environmental Cues," *Science* 216 (1982): 436–437.

22. J. Margolis and E. Langer, "An Analysis of Addiction from a Mindlessness/Mindfulness Perspective," in press.

23. Ibid.

24. R. Ader and C. Cohen, "Behaviorally Conditioned Immunosuppression and Nurive Systemic Lupus Eurythemastosus," *Science* 215 (1982): 1534–1536.

25. S. F. Kelly and R. J. Kelly, *Hypnosis* (Reading, MA: Addison-Wesley, 1985), p. 21.

26. L. Thomas, *The Medusa and the Snail* (New York: Harper & Row, 1957).

27. A. H. C. Sinclair-Gieben and D. Chalmers, "Evaluation of Treatment of Warts by Hypnosis," *Lancet* (October 3, 1959): 480–482.

28. O. C. Simonton, S. Matthews-Simonton, and J. L. Creighton, *Getting Well Again* (Los Angeles: J. P. Tarcher, 1978).

29. N. Cousins, *Anatomy of an Illness as Perceived by the Patient* (New York: W. W. Norton, 1979).

30. E. Langer, J. Rodin, P. Beck, C. Weinman, and L. Spitzer, "Environmental Determinants of Memory Improvement in Late Adulthood," *Journal of Personality and Social Psychology* 37 (1979): 2003–2013; E. Langer, P. Beck, R. Janoff-Bulman, and C. Timko, "The Relationship Between Cognitive Deprivation and Longevity in Senile and Nonsenile Elderly Populations," *Academic Psychology Bulletin* 6 (1984): 211–226; C. Alexander, E. Langer, R. Newman, H. Chandler, and J. Davies, "Transcendental Meditation, Mindfulness and Longevity: An Experimental Study with the Elderly," *Journal of Personality and Social Psychology*, in press.

31. E. Langer, S. Field, W. Paches, and E. Abrams,

"A Mindful Treatment for Arthritis," Harvard University (1988).

32. Thomas Huxley, as quoted in J. Huxley, *New Bottles for New Wine* (London: Chatto & Windus, 1957).


## Epilogue

1. T. Schelling, personal communication. For a general discussion of death and decision making, see T. Schelling, "Strategic Relationships and Dying," in *Death and Decision*, ed. E. McMullin (Boulder, CO: Westview Press, 1978), 63–73.

2. C. M. Gillmore, "A Modern-Day Parable," *The American Psychologist* 26 (1971): 314.

# Index

\*

# *About the Author*

Ellen J. Langer is Professor of Psychology at Harvard University. She is Chair of the Social Psychology Program and a member of the Division on Aging of the Faculty of Medicine at Harvard. The recipient of a Guggenheim Fellowship, Professor Langer is the author of over seventy-five journal articles and chapters in scholarly works. Her two previous books are *Personal Politics* (with Carol Dweck) and *The Psychology of Control*. In 1988, she received the Award for Distinguished Contributions to Psychology in the Public Interest of the American Psychological Association.